Residential Development Handbook

Third Edition

ULI Development Handbook Series

Urban Land Institute

About ULI–the Urban Land Institute

ULI–the Urban Land Institute is a nonprofit education and research institute that is supported by its members. Its mission is to provide responsible leadership in the use of land in order to enhance the total environment.

ULI sponsors education programs and forums to encourage an open international exchange of ideas and sharing of experiences; initiates research that anticipates emerging land use trends and issues and proposes creative solutions based on that research; provides advisory services; and publishes a wide variety of materials to disseminate information on land use and development. Established in 1936, the Institute today has more than 23,000 members and associates from some 80 countries representing the entire spectrum of the land use and development disciplines.

Richard M. Rosan
President

Project Staff

Rachelle L. Levitt
Executive Vice President, Policy and Practice
Publisher

Gayle Berens
Vice President, Real Estate Development Practice

Adrienne Schmitz
Director, Residential Community Development
Project Director

Nancy H. Stewart
Director, Book Program

Barbara M. Fishel/Editech
Manuscript Editor

Helene Y. Redmond/HYR Graphics
Book Design/Layout

Anne Morgan
Cover Design

Diann Stanley-Austin
Director, Publishing Operations

Karrie Underwood
Photo Technician

Recommended bibliographic listing:

Schmitz, Adrienne, et al. *Residential Development Handbook*. Third Edition. Washington, D.C.: ULI–the Urban Land Institute, 2004.

ULI Catalog Number: R41
International Standard Book Number: 0-87420-918-8
Library of Congress Control Number: 2004110831

Books in the ULI Development Handbook Series
Mixed-Use Development Handbook, Second Edition, 2003
Business and Industrial Park Development Handbook,
    Second Edition, 2001
Multifamily Housing Development Handbook, 2000
Shopping Center Development Handbook, Third Edition, 1999
Office Development Handbook, Second Edition, 1998
Resort Development Handbook, 1997

For more information about ULI and the resources that it offers related to residential development and a variety of other real estate and urban development issues, visit ULI's Web site at www.uli.org.

Cover photo: Photodisc.

Authors

Principal Author and Project Director

Adrienne Schmitz
ULI–the Urban Land Institute
Washington, D.C.

Primary Contributing Authors

R. Bird Anderson, Jr.
Wachovia
Charlotte, North Carolina

Leslie Holst
ULI–the Urban Land Institute
Washington, D.C.

Wayne Hyatt
Hyatt & Stubblefield
Atlanta, Georgia

Frederick Jarvis
EDSA
Columbia, Maryland

Jennifer LeFurgy
Metropolitan Institute at Virginia Tech
Alexandria, Virginia

Ehud Mouchly
READI, LLC
Los Angeles, California

Sam Newberg
Dahlgren, Shardlow, and Uban, Inc.
Minneapolis, Minnesota

Peter Smirniotopoulos
petersgroup companies, LLC
Falls Church, Virginia

Meghan Welsch
Consultant
Washington, D.C.

Contributing Authors

Kenneth Braverman
The Braverman Company
Stowe, Vermont

Adam Ducker
Robert Charles Lesser & Company
Bethesda, Maryland

Clair Enlow
Consultant
Seattle, Washington

Steven Fader
Steven Fader Architect
Los Angeles, California

Anne Frej
ULI–the Urban Land Institute
Washington, D.C.

Richard Haughey
ULI–the Urban Land Institute
Washington, D.C.

Charlie Jacoby
Consultant
London, England

Charles Lockwood
Writer
Topanga, California

Laura Million
Consultant
Franklin, Wisconsin

Jason Scully
ULI–the Urban Land Institute
Washington, D.C.

Julie Stern
Consultant
McLean, Virginia

Clifford Treese
Association Information Services, Inc.
Honolulu, Hawaii

Acknowledgments

The ULI Foundation, as part of its commitment to support ULI's core research program, provides major funding for the new and revised editions of the ULI Development Handbook Series. The *Residential Development Handbook, Third Edition,* was funded in part by grants from the Foundation. The Urban Land Institute gratefully acknowledges these contributions.

This third edition of *Residential Development Handbook* is the collective effort of many professionals who contributed their expertise and hard work. Although it is impossible to mention everyone who participated in this project, a number of individuals deserve special acknowledgment and thanks.

First, special recognition goes to the individuals who drafted major portions of the book. Clifford Treese provided the historical section of Chapter 1. Ehud Mouchly and Rick Haughey contributed the financial section of Chapter 2. Chapter 3 was the work of Peter Smirniotopoulos and Bird Anderson. Fred Jarvis wrote an entire book's worth of material for Chapter 4, and some of his material was used in other chapters as well. Meghan Welsch wrote Chapter 5, Sam Newberg wrote Chapter 6 as well as a case study, Wayne Hyatt wrote Chapter 7, and Jennifer LeFurgy wrote Chapter 8 and a case study. Leslie Holst wrote Chapter 10, with Julie Stern adding finishing touches.

The authors of the case studies—Ken Braverman, Adam Ducker, Clair Enlow, Steve Fader, Anne Frej, Charlie Jacoby, Jennifer LeFurgy, Charles Lockwood, Laura Million, Sam Newberg, and Jason Scully—deserve recognition for their thorough research. We also thank the developers, architects, designers, and photographers who cooperated with the case study authors, providing the written materials, data, and photographs needed for each case study.

The book incorporates articles that were previously published in *Urban Land* and other sources; these authors and sources are cited with the articles in the text. It also draws on material developed by Lloyd Bookout for the second edition of *Residential Development Handbook,* published in 1990.

We would like to thank the Urban Land Institute staff for its skill and dedication in bringing this book together. A book of this size and scope requires the talents of many individuals, and they all deserve thanks. First, much credit goes to Gayle Berens, who expertly guides every ULI book, including this one, from conception through completion.

We thank the editorial staff for ensuring that the information was clearly written and presented, making it most useful to our audience. We would like to thank Barbara

Fishel for editing the entire text, Helene Redmond for her excellent job of designing and laying out the entire book, Nancy Stewart for managing the editorial process, Diann Stanley-Austin for handling the printing schedule, and Anne Morgan for designing the cover. Special thanks go to Karrie Underwood, who developed a system for coordinating the electronic images and provided constant follow-up support.

And to all the others who had a hand in this book, we offer our appreciation.

Adrienne Schmitz
Principal Author and Project Director

Contents

Foreword

This third edition of *Residential Development Handbook* is part of the ULI Development Handbook Series, a set of volumes on real estate development that traces its roots to 1947, when ULI published the first edition of the *Community Builders Handbook*. That edition was revised and updated several times over the following 25 years, and a replica of the original edition was reissued in 2000. In 1975, ULI initiated the Community Builders Handbook Series, which expanded on each development type. The first of the series was *Industrial Development Handbook*. A number of titles were published in this series over a period of years, covering industrial, residential, shopping center, office, mixed-use, downtown, recreational, and multifamily housing development, which, for the first time in 2000, was considered a topic distinct from for-sale housing. Because developing, marketing, and managing multifamily rental housing is so different from developing and selling owner-occupied housing, ULI decided that multifamily rental housing merits its own text. Thus, this volume marks the first time that the *Residential Development Handbook* is being published without including rental housing.

The objective of this handbook, like all the handbooks in the series, is to provide a broad overview of the land use and real estate sector under discussion as well as a guide to the development process. This book therefore presents a comprehensive discussion of for-sale residential development, covering such topics as types of residential properties, market analysis, feasibility analysis, legal and regulatory issues, project financing, site planning, project design, community associations, marketing, and trends.

Among the strengths of the book are its reliance on a variety of examples and real-world situations. The case studies in Chapter 9 document 15 residential projects, ranging from large master-planned communities to small infill projects occupying less than an acre. Other examples are discussed in the text and in accompanying feature boxes. The overarching theme of the case studies is "best practices," with an emphasis on smarter growth and increasing density.

Meeting the challenge of residential development requires expertise in all the disciplines that make up the development profession. A well-planned residential community should offer a pleasant and satisfying dwelling place that enhances the overall environment and the community. Creating such a property requires hard work and imagination; succeeding can provide both financial and professional rewards. It is hoped that this book will help the reader to better understand the residential development business, achieve success on applying its principles and best practices, and reap the rewards of that success.

Adrienne Schmitz
Project Director

Residential Development Handbook

1. Introduction

We shape our dwellings, and afterwards our dwellings shape us.
—Winston Churchill, October 28, 1944

How people live defines the kind of communities they choose and the kind of homes they purchase. A home is typically the largest financial investment a household makes. But it is also a major investment in other ways. A home demonstrates its owner's tastes, values, status, and self-worth. In turn, a home and its surroundings determine to a large degree how its owners live: what social associations they will make, what transportation options will be available, what schools their children will attend, what job opportunities are nearby, what government services are available, and what taxes they will pay for those services.

Residential development is a highly competitive business. The key to successfully developing new homes and communities is to understand buyers' lifestyles and to develop communities that accommodate those lifestyles. In addition to understanding the market and its needs, developers must work within a framework of many challenges and constraints. Costs and risks are high, regulations determine what must be done and what cannot be done, and public opinion is a growing force that must be dealt with. Some major factors that affect residential developers today include:

Harrison Square, Washington, D.C.

- Regulations—Concerns about the environment, growth, and development have led federal, state, and local governments to create the regulatory framework within which developers must work. In many communities, increased regulations have resulted in an approval process that takes several years to navigate, compounding the expense and the risks of development. Regulations are discussed in depth in Chapter 5.
- Shortages of Infrastructure—As a result of shrinking public coffers, the nation's basic infrastructure—transportation systems and public services—has not kept pace with growth and development. Residential developers are required to make up these shortfalls by funding new roads, schools, parks, and other public facilities through increased development fees and proffers. These issues are discussed in Chapters 4 and 5.
- Labor Shortages—Low unemployment has brought the challenge of labor shortages. Finding skilled labor and the cost of that labor are considered major obstacles for developers and builders. A survey of the largest homebuilders conducted by *Professional Builder* magazine in 2001 reveals that 42 percent of those surveyed consider labor shortages a major obstacle to growth.[1] Among management, recruiting has been hurt by competition from the more exciting and profitable technology sector.
- NIMBY—Although NIMBY (not in my back yard) factions used to protest only such land uses as hazardous

Adrienne Schmitz

waste dumps and high-security prisons, citizens groups today band together in opposition to any and all development, including residential. Such protests have become a major impediment to new development, and learning how to deal with NIMBY groups is crucial for today's developers.

• Shrinking Affordability—Increased development costs have driven the cost of market-rate housing beyond the reach of most low-income and even many middle-income households. Chapters 3, 8, and 10 include discussions of affordable housing strategies.

• Changing Demographics—This country's demographics changed markedly during the 20th century, with a profound effect on lifestyle and in turn the shape of communities. The generally aging population means that fewer young families (the staple of many residential developers) enter the market. Changing household characteristics—delayed marriage, two-worker families, single-parent households, nonfamily households and other nontraditional household types—are leading to an interest in new kinds of residential communities. Appealing to evolving market segments through new kinds of communities, homes, and marketing strategies is among the major themes of this book.

• Increased Land Costs—The high cost of land is pushing housing prices ever higher, making affordability a problem for increasing numbers of buyers. Rising land costs and changing locational preferences and lifestyles are driving suburban residential densities higher and adding to pressures to redevelop inner-ring suburbs. Urban infill has become a profitable niche market for some developers. Yet despite all obstacles, the overwhelming choice of today's home-buyer remains the traditional single-family house. A major portion of Chapter 4 discusses higher-density designs, and many of the case studies depict solutions for higher densities as well.

• Growth Management—Under the banner of smart growth, many municipalities and states have responded to concerns about sprawl with ordinances designed to control growth. Developers must work with communities to ensure that such initiatives accomplish what they intend to without prohibiting growth.

• Financing—Chapter 3 covers the major types of financing, how to structure ownership, and how to go about obtaining financing for the different stages of development. Developers who take the time to investigate the options can tap an increasing array of financial products and sources of funding.

Developers of residential property should be aware of the major impact they have on the type of community that results. And in turn, how they build communities that serve the intended residents has a long-term effect on developers' financial success. As creators of residential communities, developers must be sensitive to long-range needs and expectations, in a sense bearing responsibility for the judicious long-term management of land.

Continuum Partners LLC

Average house size has increased nearly every year since 1975.

Residential Development Today

A defining element of modern life is a shortage of time. More than money, many of today's households value their time and do what they can to maximize the quality and quantity of free time they have. But the ideal home can mean different things to different households. To some, it means a country home with sprawling acreage, where time spent is quiet and relaxing. To others, it means a compact home within walking distance of the workplace so that precious hours are not lost commuting and home maintenance is minimized. Developing communities for today's consumers is not a one-size-fits-all proposition.

For most households, their home is their most significant asset. Because of shrinking household size, many experts long predicted that homes would also shrink, but in fact, new homes have grown larger nearly every year since 1975 (see Figure 1-1). A home is considered an expression of wealth and status, and many homebuyers continue to purchase the largest and most luxurious home they can afford.

Along with larger homes has come increased homeownership, particularly during the latter part of the 1990s, after remaining fairly stagnant in the 1970s and 1980s (see Figure 1-2). Although larger homes and greater ownership imply increasing wealth, not all households have shared in this prosperity; many households face a crisis in housing affordability. In some parts of the United States, high land and development costs, shortages of developable land, and opposition to new development have created a serious shortage of affordable shelter for lower- and even middle-income residents.

Changing Demographics Means New Housing Types

In the 1950s, the typical homebuyer was assumed to be a family comprising children, a working father, and a stay-at-home mother. Today, that prototype homebuyer is a minority. In 1950, 43.2 percent of all households were married couples with children. By 2000, married couples with children represented only 24.1 percent of all households. During the same time, household size declined from 3.37 in 1950 to 2.62 in 2000. Married couples in 1950 represented 78.2 percent of households; in 2000, the share declined to 51.7 percent (see Figure 1-3).

The number of women in the labor force doubled between 1960 and 1997. In 2000, one in ten Americans was an immigrant, and nearly one-third of the total population was a minority. In 1940, just under 7 percent of the population was 65 years or older; by 2000, 12.4 percent was 65 or older. These changes, together with rising incomes, significantly expanded what might constitute underserved housing market niches.

Homebuyers include single people, couples without children, retirees, divorced parents with children, unrelated individuals, and others. The ethnic mix has

figure 1-1

Median Size of New Single-Family Homes in the United States

Year Built	Median Square Feet/ Square Meters
1975	1,535/143
1980	1,595/148
1985	1,605/149
1990	1,905/177
1995	1,920/178
2000	2,057/191
2002	2,114/196

Source: U.S. Census Bureau, Characteristics of New Housing, http://www.census.gov/const/C25Ann/sftotalmedavgsqft.pdf.

figure 1-2

Homeownership Rates, 1965 to 2004

Year	Percent Owner Households
1965	63.4
1970	64.0
1975	64.5
1980	65.5
1985	63.5
1990	64.1
1995	65.1
2000	67.5
2004, 1Q	68.6

Source: U.S. Census Bureau, Housing Vacancy Survey, http://www.census.gov/hhes/www/housing/hvs/q104tab5.html.

figure 1-3

Households by Type, 1950 to 2010

	1950	1975	2000	2010
All Households	100.0%	100.0%	100.0%	100.0%
Family Households	89.2%	78.1%	68.8%	67.8%
Married Couple Households	78.2%	66.0%	52.8%	51.7%
Married Couples w/Children	43.2%	35.4%	24.1%	20.1%
Average Household Size	3.37	2.94	2.62	2.53

Source: U.S. Census of Population; ULI–the Urban Land Institute.

STH Architectural Group

expanded too, with various ethnic groups having specific housing and community preferences. And homebuying preferences vary by region as well. Because today's homebuyers cover such a broad spectrum of household types, ages, ethnicities, and economic conditions, developers must understand their markets and design communities and homes to suit specific needs and demands.

Historical Perspective

At one time, residential development involved simply acquiring a tract of land, filing a plat of its division into blocks and lots, then selling lots to buyers. New subdivisions were usually extensions of existing communities. But over time, a series of social, economic, and physical factors brought about significant changes and increasing complexity to the process. In the early 20th century, zoning ordinances and subdivision regulations were instituted as land use controls to protect public health and safety. The Great Depression brought housing construction to a halt, and the New Deal, which followed, responded with various housing initiatives, including the Federal Housing Administration (FHA) and Federal National Mortgage Association (FNMA, or Fannie Mae). These and other programs, together with the standardization of information and construction methods, were designed to stabilize the housing market, encourage mortgage lending, stimulate private construction, foster homeownership, and eliminate slums.

Housing in the 1940s and 1950s
In 1940, the U.S. Census produced the first comprehensive examination of housing, documenting the dramatic difference in the quality of housing between urban and rural areas. Although more than 80 percent of urban homes had running water, private baths, and flush toilets, only about half of rural homes had those facilities.

In urban areas, 96 percent of homes had electricity, compared with only 78 percent in rural areas.

During World War II, housing production fell from 706,000 units in 1941 to 142,000 units in 1944. By the end of World War II, the housing shortage was estimated at nearly 3 million units. Homebuilders began adapting wartime production techniques to the mass production of homes, and housing policy advocates envisioned a future that would rectify all the urban ills that the New Deal had failed to eliminate. By war's end, FHA insured 19 percent of residential mortgage debt. In 1944, Congress supplemented FHA insurance by passing the Serviceman's Readjustment Act—the GI Bill—which provided low-interest mortgages for veterans and boosted new housing development, ultimately creating one of the largest housing booms in history. Land was available and cheap on the urban fringe, and public investment in infrastructure made development in outlying areas possible. Thus, the suburbs became a major focus for homebuilding.

Adrienne Schmitz

Urban neighborhoods developed during the early 20th century are being revitalized today as urban lifestyles gain favor once again.

Many of today's developments emulate pre–World War II neighborhoods, such as Cherry Hill Village in Canton Township, Michigan.

Looney Ricks Kiss

The Housing Act of 1949 is often cited as a reminder of an unfulfilled commitment that every American deserves "a decent home and a suitable living environment." According to the act, by 1955 there were to be 810,000 new public housing units built, a number finally reached by 1969. Although public and affordable housing posted a problematic record, market-rate housing set production records. In the decade following the enactment of the GI Bill, housing starts averaged nearly 1.5 million units per year. Homeownership rates increased from 40 percent in 1940 to nearly 59 percent by 1956.

Housing through the 1970s
The mid-20th century was an era of rapid suburbanization. Americans generally have not favored high-density living, so new housing was added through outward expansion of urban areas, the creation of new towns, and expansion into new regions of the country. Suburbanization always has been a part of housing growth. In the 19th century, development moved readily along streetcar and rail lines, canals, and country highways. After World War II, suburbanization increased momentum, driven by a significant housing shortage. Although the Highway Act of 1956 contributed to this trend, Americans, whether native born or immigrants, have always been movers and speculators. The sheer physical size of the country, combined with its immense natural resources and boosterism at all levels of government, encouraged housing and housing speculation.

As New Deal reforms allowed Americans to more readily finance their housing, substantial improvements in housing production and construction after World War II made housing more affordable. The mass production of housing, begun by William Levitt in Levittown, brought affordable housing to middle- and working-class Americans. Critics complained of tract housing, of its unimaginative architecture and site design, but the country continued to grow and spread west and south, buying as much housing as VA (Veterans Administration, now the

Department of Veterans Affairs), FHA, and, eventually, private mortgage insurers could support.

In the decade after World War II, starts of single-family homes amounted to 84 percent of total production, while the role of noninstitutional lenders in providing mortgages had shrunk from 31 percent to 15 percent of total debt, reflecting FHA's and VA's preference to deal with savings and loan institutions (S&Ls). FHA insured 14 percent of the mortgage debt, VA guaranteed 13 percent, and public housing provided 2 percent of the housing during this decade.

From the mid-1950s to the mid-1960s, more than half of all housing starts shifted to the West (24 percent) and the South (36 percent). During this period, manufactured housing began to appear as an important element, accounting for nearly 9 percent of housing production. Also during this period, multifamily housing increased from 13 percent of housing starts in the 1950s to 35 percent by the mid-1960s.

By the end of the 1960s, S&Ls were in full stride, accounting for nearly 45 percent of outstanding nonfarm residential mortgage debt. FNMA still accounted for only 2 percent of mortgage debt. The Department of Housing and Urban Development (HUD) was created in 1965, elevating housing to cabinet-level status. Private mortgage insurers emerged during this period, beginning in 1957 with MGIC in Milwaukee. By the early 1970s, the FHA and VA's combined share of the market had declined by more than 10 percent from the beginning of the decade.

Housing to the 20th Century's End
By 1954, the federal programs were recast as "urban renewal" to emphasize conservation rather than demolition; numerous neighborhoods and their housing stock were improved. The concept of using a "federal bulldozer" to create urban housing and foster urban development, however, came under increasing attack from critics on both the right and the left at the same time that public

HOPE VI funding helped the city of Portsmouth, Virginia, redevelop a failed public housing project to a desirable mixed-income community called Westbury.

Urban Design Associates

housing was becoming racially and economically stigmatized. By the 1970s, the federal government began to move away from public housing and direct initiatives toward those that encouraged private sector creation of ownership and rental housing.

Various FHA programs were developed in the 1960s to stimulate private sector activities. The Kennedy New Frontier and Johnson Great Society initiatives contained wide-ranging programs to deal with the need for low-income housing and the continued existence of a racially divided society. The Housing and Community Development Act of 1968 contained several housing-related initiatives, including Section 8 housing vouchers. Lax underwriting as well as abuses and scandals in FHA insurance programs during this time further eroded public support for government programs for low- and moderate-income housing. By the end of the 1970s, active and sustained federal involvement in public housing, urban redevel-

opment, and housing—legacies of World War II and the New Deal—began to run out of advocates, commitment, and money.

In 1999, the Fannie Mae Foundation convened a group of urban specialists to reflect on the top ten influences on the American metropolis over the previous 50 years and to speculate on the top ten for the next 50 years (see figure 1-4). Keeping in mind that the focus was the American metropolis and not housing per se, one is struck with the placement of the Interstate Highway Act of 1956 as number one for the prior 50 years. The interstate highway system was the infrastructure, but Americans also needed cars. In 1960, nearly 22 percent of all households did not have a car, but by 2000, this percentage was down to 10 percent. Moreover, by 2000 nearly 20 percent of all households had at least three cars.

In the early 1970s, housing production reached its highest sustained levels to date: 2.6 million units in 1971

figure 1-4

Top Ten Influences on the American Metropolis

Last 50 Years	Next 50 Years
1. 1956 Interstate Highway Act	1. Growing disparity in wealth
2. FHA mortgage financing and subdivision regulation	2. Suburban political majority
3. Deindustrialization of central cities	3. Aging of baby boomers
4. Urban renewal, downtown redevelopment, and public housing	4. Perpetual underclass in central cities and inner-ring suburbs
5. Levittowns (mass-produced suburban tract houses)	5. Smart Growth: environmental and planning initiatives to limit sprawl
6. Racial segregation and job discrimination in cities and suburbs	6. The Internet
7. Enclosed shopping malls	7. Deterioration of first ring of post-1945 suburbs
8. Sunbelt-style sprawl	8. Shrinking household size
9. Air conditioning	9. Expanded superhighway system of outer beltways to serve new edge cities
10. Urban riots of the 1960s	10. Racial integration as part of the increasing diversity in cities and suburbs

Source: Robert Fishman, *Housing Facts & Findngs* (Fannie Mae Foundation), Vol. 1, No. 4, Winter 1999.

and 1973 and 2.9 million in 1972. These huge production increases were the result of subsidized housing, manufactured housing, and unsubsidized multifamily construction—especially condominiums and cooperatives. By the mid-1970s, however, the impact of the global oil crisis and inflation at home set in motion the first of a series of S&L crises that would eventually cause these institutions to collapse during the 1980s.

By 1990, several pieces of federal legislation had essentially dismantled key aspects of the housing finance apparatus put in place during the New Deal. The federal government salvaged the S&L industry through a bailout of more than $140 billion. Before this legislation was enacted, FNMA had been split in two and eventually re-created, along with FHLMC (Federal Home Loan Mortgage Corporation, or Freddie Mac), as a government-sponsored enterprise (GSE). Although mortgage debt passed the trillion dollar mark in 1980, GSEs accounted for only about 10 percent of such debt. With the collapse of the S&Ls, the GSEs' share of conventional single-family mortgage debt grew to 33 percent by 1990 and to 45 percent by 1999. Mortgage pools that accounted for 12 percent of housing debt in 1970 now made up 37 percent of that debt. The GSEs, together with collateralized mortgage obligations facilitated by computerized origination and servicing, became the main players in housing finance for both underserved and market-rate homebuyers.

Along with the shift in financing and decreased direct involvement of the federal government came new issues facing housing development. The most important of them involved fair housing, environmental concerns, and local government impact fees. In 1983, the New Jersey Supreme Court established that municipalities in the state must build their *fair share* of affordable housing. Since the first Earth Day in April 1970 and creation of the Environmental Protection Agency later that year, concern for the environment has been increasingly inserted into the planning process and has even become a marketing consideration.

Underserved Markets. By the time the federal government's role in public housing and urban renewal collapsed in the 1970s, the thinking had already changed about how best to meet the housing needs of low- and moderate-income households and other underserved markets such as singles, single parents, immigrants, and minorities. The Home Mortgage Disclosure Act (1975), the Community Reinvestment Act (1977), and the Equal Credit Opportunity Act (1977) became the important vehicles driving the financial services industry into underserved markets. In 1988, the Fair Housing Act Amendments further expanded the scope of the Civil Rights Act of 1968, helping to loosen the constraints of bias in mortgage underwriting. By the 1990s with the application of computer technology to processing and credit scoring, mortgage underwriting began to improve in terms of fairness and efficiency.

Federal housing efforts were restructured again in the late 1980s and early 1990s, with greater emphasis

Corcoran Jennison Companies

Originally built in 1943, Pittsburgh's largest public housing development was redeveloped by Corcoran Jennison Companies. Now called Oak Hill, it provides attractive homes for mixed-income residents.

placed on housing and neighborhood rehabilitation. The Section 8 project-based housing voucher program was supplemented with an individual or tenant-based program. Fears about the financial burdens imposed on the federal budget by the project-based vouchers led to the development of other programs such as low-income housing tax credits (LIHTCs) in 1986 to facilitate the creation of affordable housing. The tax credit approach in turn led to the rise of community development corporations as homebuilders for low- and moderate-income households. In 1990, the National Affordable Housing Act was passed to provide funds for state and local affordable housing programs and for the preservation of existing subsidized housing. The role of the FHA and VA continued to decline so that by the 1990s, they contributed to around 12 percent of housing starts, a long slide from more than 40 percent just before the end of World War II.

Community Design. Architecture and planning for housing, like other development types, experienced a renaissance during the latter part of the 20th century. Urban centers began to bounce back after decades of decline, and civic and commercial architecture gained a richness that had been lacking. In residential architecture, new ideas began to surface. With *The Not So Big House*, architect Sarah Susanka led a movement favoring high-quality design and materials over large size.[2] Production housing followed, with an emphasis on regional architecture and the use of new man-made materials that closely simulate traditional materials like stone, wood, and slate but afford greater ease of construction than the real thing. Small builders and developers have created niches based on a particular style of housing, such as cottages targeted to single women.

Dissatisfaction with the degraded quality of life offered by disconnected pods of uniform beige boxes led to the movement known as neotraditional development, or the new urbanism. The new urbanism focuses on the neighborhood rather than the individual house, with consid-

The Cottage Company of Seattle has built communities of finely crafted cottages targeted to single women, empty nesters, and young households.

eration for how people will live and interact among each other and the built and natural environment. An emphasis on convenience for pedestrians encourages mixing uses. Shops and services, schools, parks, and other public facilities are integrated into the community near residences. Streets are connected, typically in a traditional grid pattern, so that vehicles and pedestrians have multiple choices rather than being channeled onto collector roads. Higher densities are encouraged for efficiency and to allow for preservation of meaningful open space. Goals of new urbanism include improved aesthetics, convenience, social integration, and a more sustainable way of developing communities.

The new urbanism borrows much from traditional planning and traditional architecture. The built environment is scaled for people rather than stepped up for vehicles driving through at highway speeds. Buildings use traditional materials and are designed to emulate and blend with the regional vernacular. Neighborhoods take cues from the best pre–World War II neighborhoods, where houses and apartment buildings face the street, wide, shaded sidewalks provide a pleasant pedestrian environment, and the messy necessities—parking, garbage, and utilities—are hidden behind the houses in alleys.

New urbanism has become a major force affecting new development. Although "pure" new urbanist communities make up a small—but growing—percentage of all new development, increasing numbers of communities show the influence of the new urbanism. In many cases, streets are narrower and interconnected, lots are narrower, and development is denser. Land uses are more mixed, with a broader range of housing types within communities. And nearly every large development is trying to incorporate some kind of town center into its fabric.

The Development Process and the Development Team

The transition of a parcel of raw land to a residential community is a complex multistage process that involves many participants and many steps: conducting preliminary studies, negotiating sale or other ownership agreements, securing financing, undertaking the approval process, initiating planning and design, and starting site work—followed by construction, sales, and governance of the completed project. Development of a residential community is not straightforward or linear. The developer and other participants in the process must constantly reposition and renegotiate. Public approvals and the evolving market often necessitate changes. Development is more art than science. It is creative, multidisciplinary, and often very complex. It requires the skills, talents, and intuition of many players. It is the job of developers to assemble the needed talents to accomplish their objectives, and then to manage the development team effectively.

The new urbanism, with its emphasis on the public realm, has influenced how residential communities are designed. Seaside, Florida, is often cited as the first such community.

Throughout the process, a developer relies on the skills of a wide range of experts. It is important to assemble key members of the development team during preliminary stages, because much of the conceptualization that will be carried into project design is generated during the initial evaluation of the project's feasibility. The increased front-end costs attributable to specialists in land planning, geology, marketing, civil and traffic engineering, and the social and biological sciences represent a protective investment, or "insurance" for the developer. The value of this investment is most evident when alternative land purchases are screened. Without the advice of specialists, developers might well purchase a site with physical, market, or regulatory constraints that will prove fatal to the development. More positively put, these expenses for physical, economic, and environmental evaluations can significantly shorten the project's design time.

The development team may include any number of specialists from a variety of disciplines. The following discussion includes some professionals whose responsibilities may overlap with others, and certain team members may serve multiple functions. For example, the project engineering firm may be able to provide planners, surveyors, architects, environmental engineers, traffic consultants, and other experts.

Developer

The developer's role is to orchestrate the development process to bring the project to completion. Developers are the central actors in the development process, because their actions determine what land will be considered for development, when improvements will begin, and for whom the project will be developed. In most development companies, an individual in the company is designated as the project manager and assigned the responsibility for day-to-day decision making. Throughout the development process, however, owners and investors retain the ultimate responsibility for determining how to proceed. Their decisions should be based on the realities of the marketplace and input from all members of the development team.

Developers might install streets, utilities, and other infrastructure and some or all of the amenities necessary for the development, and they must initiate a phasing schedule consistent with their cash flow and development objectives. If the project involves lot sales, developers sell parcels to homebuilders; otherwise, they begin to construct the units themselves. As the first units near completion, sales and marketing and the establishment of some entity for maintaining the development (such as a community association) begin. And an evaluation upon completion of development is vital if developers wish to learn from their mistakes. Questions developers ask themselves and residents of the project help to program future projects or subsequent phases of the same project.

Most developers, even large diversified development companies, do not retain a staff with all the technical talents needed by the development team. Instead, they hire consultants. One advantage of relying on consultants is that the developer has to pay for expertise only when it is needed. Moreover, the consultant usually has built a depth of expertise in a particular area. In evaluating prospective consultants, developers should inspect other projects in which the consultants have participated. They should ask other developers about their qualifications and experience. Developers must also make certain that the most competent members of the consultant's staff are assigned to their projects.

Depending on a particular project's complexity, the team might include attorneys, planners, market researchers, engineers, geologists, environmental specialists, architects, landscape architects, financiers, contractors, and sales managers. The preparation and execution of a business plan includes all these functional pieces—the expertise to determine demand, response, and profitability.

Florida-based St. Joe Company developed WaterColor, a coastal resort community on the Florida panhandle.

St. Joe Company

Developer/Builder

Some developers sell lots to homebuilders, while others act as both developer and builder. Typically, land developers are responsible for acquiring development permits, rough grading of the site, and bringing major components of infrastructure (roads, water and sewer, utilities) to the site. They might also implement an overall marketing program to promote the community. Builders purchase the site from a land developer, build the houses, complete on-site infrastructure (local streets and utilities, for example), and are responsible for marketing the units and providing certain follow-up repairs and warranties. Some builders contract with lenders to provide mortgages to homebuyers.

A builder might be a local or regional concern or a large national firm. Often a builder specializes in a particular market niche—starter homes or high-end homes, for example. A builder's reputation is an important consideration for a developer selling lots.

Market Analysts

Developers retain market analysts to provide professional assessments of the feasibility of proposed developments. The go/no go decision made by developers is largely based on a market study, which typically is prepared by a market analyst with input from other key team members. Market studies delineate the demand for the proposed project, assess the current and projected competition, and estimate the sales pace and price points. All of these data become the basis for the pro forma.

Market analysts often participate in the dynamic decision-making process that characterizes most residential development projects. During all phases—from site selection to design, financing, construction, and marketing—market analysts can help define the needs and preferences of the target market and provide guidance in positioning the product to meet those preferences. An independent assessment from a well-regarded market analyst adds considerable credibility to a project

What Makes a High-Quality Planned Community?

Greater than the sum of its parts, a high-quality planned community is the product of plans and components effectively organized to create the intangibles of community and place. Regardless of their size, good planned communities incorporate a variety of housing types, sizes, and prices; they include a complementary mix of land uses and provide ample common space and a vital public realm. Developers and professional planners agree on other critical characteristics: a form of community governance to maintain resources and character, a comprehensive approach to planning and delivery, and a long-term vision zealously adhered to by a single entity.

Finally and not least is the critical ingredient of connectivity, of playing a complementary part in a planned regional network of preserved open space and balanced greenfield development. But what are the important characteristics of a proposed site, what uses need to be included in the community, and how should they be spatially organized to create a lively, high-quality environment for residents, employees, and visitors?

The best of today's planned communities encompass several principles:

- Systems-Based Structure—One of the most enduring and fundamental benefits of comprehensive planning, a systems-based structure is a hallmark of planned community development. Thorough understanding of a site and its carrying capacity is critical to sustainable development. Today, the power of geographic information systems and improved scientific analysis allow much more intelligent analysis and modeling of development alternatives.
- Contextual and Locational Responsiveness—When a project's location is a greenfield, planning or studying land outside the parcel boundary to identify affected systems, linkages, and potential synergies within an appropriate development shed will result in a more responsive and appropriate development plan.
- Efficient Use of Resources—A contribution of the green development movement, resource efficiency is a simple term with diverse implementation strategies. It starts with reducing dependence on vehicles and progresses to the efficient use of energy in habitable spaces and the analysis and recognition of the energy embedded in materials used in construction. It also includes water, wastewater, and stormwater management, their impacts on energy consumption, and viewing them as a resource rather than a nuisance. Finally, recycling and waste stream management programs all impact the use of resources.
- Streets as the Public Realm—What had been banished to the infrastructure column in land development pro formas has reemerged as the cornerstone of the public realm. Attentive and detailed understanding of the complex interplay of width and scale, pedestrian character, texture, light and shadow, architectural and landscape edge conditions has allowed us to convert asphalt to agora, a higher plane of public connection and place making.
- Infrastructure as Asset—With streets removed from the category of infrastructure, one can focus on the capital-intensive and entitlement-critical issues of stormwater and wastewater management. Designers now recognize that what were once considered nuisances to be piped away as quickly as possible can be significant resources. Today's solutions are scientifically possible, biologically beneficial, and aesthetically appealing. In arid climates, the simple act of reusing effluent on the landscape reduces the requirement

in the eyes of lenders and investors. It provides evidence of the marketability of the proposed development.

In choosing a market analyst, the developer should consider technical proficiency and familiarity with the local market and with the type of development being considered. Good analysts are able to understand subtle distinctions of the local market that are not readily apparent to the average observer.

Although market analysis used to be a number-crunching exercise, it increasingly involves qualitative analysis as well. Focus groups, surveys, and psychographic reports are used to determine the kinds of people in the market area and how a development might address their lifestyles.

Sales and Marketing Staff

Under the sales and marketing umbrella are advertising, public relations, merchandising, lot sales, and sale and rental of homes and other buildings. The marketing team prepares and implements a marketing plan with the goal of maximizing the project's sales potential. Marketing consultants should be brought into the process in the early planning stages so that the team can be involved in major decisions and so that the staff becomes familiar with all aspects of the project and a comprehensive long-term strategy can be established. A qualified marketing staff can help to ensure that all aspects of the project—unit sizes, pricing, design, amenities, and so on—are appropriate for the target market.

Under the heading of marketing are advertising and public relations efforts such as promoting media coverage; producing news releases, press kits, newsletters, and mailings; and staging events that expose the project in a positive light. Developing brochures, newspaper ads, signage, and other print material are part of the marketing function as well.

The sales team may be in-house staff or a team of outside consultants. Real estate agents most often work on

for potable water and piping for disposal while also recharging the aquifer. The role of stormwater retention, detention, and first-flush treatment has generated the opportunity for new landscape and habitat environments while reducing infrastructure costs.

- Places, Not Projects—Place making, however difficult to define, is an ingredient without which there can be no smart growth. Program mix and synergy; material color, light, and transparency; landscape and pedestrian space; the type and spatial organization of furnishings, signage, and art; and soft programming are all carefully woven into environments that make places out of projects.

- Fine Grained Mixed Uses—Although many new developments of the 1970s and 1980s sought to create the vitality and energy evocative of small villages and towns, their application and execution reflected a naivete about market dynamics and a lack of sophistication in physical design. The "build it and they will come" approach to village centers created programmatically correct but locationally deficient struggling retail centers. But the concept of re-creating the small town main street was given a considerable boost with the advent of Celebration, Florida. A visit to Celebration today suggests that it is hard to deny the vitality and exciting vibrancy the town center brings the community. Less ambitious but equally important examples at Haile Plantation, Florida, and even Hidden Springs, Idaho, show that both place making and mixing land uses are critical to differentiating a community and making it sustainable. Much more than a utilitarian gathering point for goods and services, they provide a focal point, marketing icon, and family gathering place for residents and visitors alike.

- Connecting People and Culture—One of the most compelling ideas to emerge from recent land development success stories is that buyers will pay a premium to be part of something authentic. A site properly selected and analyzed yields a wealth of information that affords not only land use and spatial organization cues but also the essence of the community or its roots. A carefully developed understanding of the site and the region's history (genuinely incorporated into the development program, not a trite marketing ploy) forms the soul of the community that connects buyers with shared values. After a community's essence is captured, individuals should be included in its evolution, not through a set of dogmatic and aesthetically driven codes but through a shared set of goals and values that allow new residents and guests to develop authorship of their community, taking it to an even higher level of connection to each other, the community, and the region at large. ∎

The marketing team helps to establish the character of a development.

a straight commission, but some developers hire salaried sales staff. Finding the right sales and marketing staff can make or break a project. If the developer is to hire an outside firm, he or she should select one that is experienced with the type of project being developed. Local experience can be particularly desirable, for every local market has its own nuances and preferences. The marketing team should believe in the project and should be willing to commit the time and effort required to ensure

its success. If sales agents do not actively market the project or do not understand its niche, sales will not reach their potential.

Engineers

Engineers test the soil, establish the precise location of streets and infrastructure, and determine lot and building lines. They furnish topographic maps, detailed data, and working drawings needed to establish grades, earthwork, street improvements, stormwater drainage systems, sanitary sewers, water supply mains, and other public utilities, and they specify the types of materials that can be used. Engineers can be a resource for preparing cost estimates. They are also responsible for preparing final subdivision maps and other working maps and drawings.

Some projects may require specialists in various engineering fields. A project located in an earthquake-prone location, for example, might require a seismic geologist to determine the precise location of the faults on the site and to recommend appropriate setbacks or construction standards. Some projects may require specialists in soils, hydrology, flood protection, environmental mitigation, or transportation engineering. Not every civil engineering company has all these technical specialists on its in-house staff, so it may be necessary to subcontract with an expert in a particular field. Normally, the project engineer can recommend qualified subcontractors.

Planners

Also known as site planners or land planners, these professionals must be generalists capable of working with a variety of technical specialists. They are responsible for site evaluation and for determination, allocation, and location of specific land uses. They should be familiar with local zoning regulations and codes. Planning involves topography, access and circulation, vehicular and pedestrian traffic, open spaces, and areas for residential, commercial, and industrial uses—all coor-

Environmental consultants are an important component of the development team.

As sprawl takes over more and more of the countryside, the costs are multiple. Sprawl creates increased traffic and environmental problems, stresses the interstate highway system, fragments communities, and diminishes quality of life. Financially, taxpayers must foot the bill to create additional infrastructure and services for each new far-flung suburb.

According to a Brookings Institution study of 281 U.S. metropolitan areas, land development on greenfield sites actually is outstripping population growth to such an extent that population densities are declining in all but 17 of the areas examined.

In the near future, urban sprawl will worsen as the population continues to grow and employees move farther from their jobs and are forced to use their cars for transportation. Though the march away from city centers cannot be halted immediately, it can be slowed by encouraging more infill in urban areas, better planning in existing suburban areas, and giving transit priority.

The Natural Resources Defense Council reports that in addition to destroying the natural landscape and threatening bodies of water with runoff, the increased use of motor vehicles will contribute:

- 32 percent of total U.S. carbon dioxide emissions;
- 62 percent of total U.S. carbon monoxide emissions;
- 26 percent of total U.S. volatile organic compounds;
- 32 percent of total U.S. nitrogen oxides; and
- 50 percent of total U.S. carcinogenic and toxic air pollutants.

Researchers studying the effects of sprawl find increasing evidence that indicates a link between the suburban lifestyle and the country's rapidly rising rate of obesity, which in turn leads to a variety of health problems. A study coauthored by Lawrence D. Frank, associate professor of urban planning at the University of British Columbia, determined that people who live in areas of low building density—where they cannot walk to their destinations and therefore spend many hours in their cars—tend to weigh more than people in higher-density mixed-use areas. Similar results were documented by the University of Maryland's Reid Ewing: in older cities like New York and Chicago, people walk to destinations. In contrast, the typical cul-de-sac suburbs have no sidewalks, only vast parking lots and busy highways cutting off access for pedestrians.

The key to making the suburbs better revolves around creating effective ways for people to move around by foot, on bicycles, and on local public transportation systems. Americans cherish the freedom and luxury that their automobiles promise, but they may not fully understand the negative impact of their cars on pollution, traffic, and the family budget. American families reportedly spend more than 19 cents of every dollar earned on transportation, an expense second only to housing. Low-income families are especially hard hit by the enormous cost of owning and operating vehicles. But this financial burden can be eased by creating prominent community nodes linked by transit. ∎

Source: Bill Valentine, president, HOK Inc.

---

dinated to produce a unified development that can be built economically, operated efficiently, and maintained with normal expense. Planners also have the primary role of relating the proposed project to the overall comprehensive plan for the area. Engineers should be consulted to verify and refine the planner's concept but not to drive the concept.

Although planners have traditionally been associated with physical design, they also play a key role in policy, having gained importance in that area with the increasing complexity of regulations, environmental concerns, and permitting requirements. Many planning firms retain staff members who are experts in writing development regulations, processing plans through the permitting maze, and negotiating with public agencies and citizen groups. Such planners work closely with physical designers to ensure that the physical plan responds to the municipality's comprehensive plan and other relevant public and private planning programs.

Planners are often responsible for processing projects through local, state, and federal agencies and for obtaining development permits. They may coordinate preparation of the environmental impact assessment and are therefore key players in developing mitigation programs to lessen impacts, many of which are eventually built into the physical land plan.

Environmental Consultants

Environmental consultants ensure that the project complies with current environmental regulations. They are responsible for environmental inventories, site assessments, wetland and stream delineation, and environmental permitting, Most residential development projects require some level of environmental assessment. Some states mandate an environmental review, while in other states it is a municipal requirement. Generally, the larger the project, the greater the degree of environmental analysis required. Brownfield developments may require extensive reviews and mitigation plans, no matter what size they are. Specialists in various environmental sciences will likely be required if a full environmental impact report is necessary. Wetlands, another critical issue that has come under scrutiny from federal agencies, have caused the emergence of new specialists in developing wetland mitigation programs and obtaining permits. Residential developers need to understand which environmental issues are relevant and be prepared to bring in the appropriate experts. Various environmental specialists might become part of the developer's team of experts: historians, archaeologists, biologists, air-quality experts, acoustical engineers, and others.

Archeologists and Historians

In some cases, initial work includes identifying any archeological conditions on the site. It is also useful to understand the cultural history of a property, both to preserve any existing buildings or remains and to create a community that respects its context.

Financiers

Almost all real estate developments rely to a large degree on the proper supply of equity and borrowed funds for the risks of development. Financing is one element in the process that is subject to a great amount of fluctuation, yet adequate financing can in large measure determine whether a project ultimately is profitable. Developers must tap into this supply of funds at just the right time to secure the amount needed under the right terms.

Developers should shop thoroughly and be prepared to wait until better terms can be secured if possible. A good working relationship with lenders and investors is indispensable to developers. In all cases, the source of money, whether an investor or a financial institution, must be convinced of the project's feasibility. That real estate developers must understand the techniques of financing cannot be overstressed, but if developers do not understand the techniques of financing, they should surround themselves with those who do.

Public Officials

Private sector real estate developers have a public sector partner in every deal. Government—federal, state, and local—permeates the U.S. system under which developers operate. Real estate development is a highly regulated process. Taxes, labor law, property law, public infrastructure, financial market operations, zoning, building permits, and impact fees all issue from legislation, regulations, and public policy. If developers do not work hand in hand with local governments, giving them the same attention and cooperation they give private sector partners, costly delays may occur and approvals denied.

Duany Plater-Zyberk & Company

Architects might be involved in any or all aspects of community design, from master planning to designing individual homes. Amelia Park was master planned by Duany Plater-Zyberk & Company.

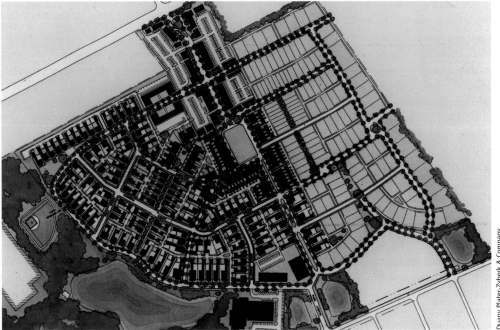

Duany Plater-Zyberk & Company

Attorneys

Attorneys who are experienced in land development can save developers many times their own fees. Attorneys can be responsible for preparing and reviewing the documents for the project's legal structure and the documents for project financing, consultants' services, land purchase, leases, and rezoning. The extent of the attorney's role in zoning and processing permits tends to vary by region. For example, in the East, attorneys often play a major role in permitting and are directly involved in negotiations between developers and local governments. In most western states, however, attorneys have a less visible role in permitting, and developers or professional consultants (the planner, for example) take the lead. Attorneys have two other important tasks: 1) to draft lease and sales contracts, especially those with subdevelopers and builders, and 2) to draft the declaration of covenants, conditions, and restrictions and other legal documents necessary to establish a community association.

If developers operate within their own local market, attorneys are probably already a member of the team. Attorneys become identified with a developer, and if the developer's track record is clean, negotiating with local public officials and lending institutions becomes increasingly easier. Developers working outside their own markets, however, must create a sympathetic climate for their actions. They therefore must acquire a local image, and well-respected local attorneys can be key avenues of communication.

Architects

Architecture involves planning, designing, and constructing buildings and other improvements, and most developers find architects to be essential members of the team. In residential development, builders must offer purchasers more than just a well-built structure on a good lot. They must produce an architecturally pleasing home well adapted to the topographic features of the site, with a good relationship to other buildings, and a good, livable floor plan. But developers are finding that talented architects also provide them with much more, including site planning and community design, selection of building materials and colors, professional supervision, and suggestions on merchandising the finished product. These extra services can pay for themselves by helping to produce superior communities that sell faster for higher prices. In addition, architects can be an essential part of the team during the approval process. Their ability to convey design concepts to public officials and neighborhood groups can be instrumental in obtaining approvals.

Architects should be involved in the process early because of the decisions that must be based on architectural and planning concepts. Decisions about programming and budgeting made during concept planning without architects' participation can strip them of effective control over design. Excluding an architect at this early stage may lock the design into a preconceived solution, severely limiting the architect's future options. This concern is especially important when the development

Marina Gardens in Palm Beach Gardens, Florida, was designed by Quincy Johnson Architects for Mutual Land Development Corp.

program calls for a higher-density residential product where the size, shape, and grade of development parcels can substantially determine which products will work and which will not.

Landscape Architects

Landscape architects deal with planning, design, management, preservation, and rehabilitation of the land. The scope of the profession includes site planning, garden design, environmental restoration, urban and regional planning, park and recreation planning, and historic preservation.

Landscape architects understand how to integrate buildings and other site improvements with a site's natural features—topography, vegetation, drainage, water, wildlife, and climate. They might design parks and open spaces or entire communities. Landscape architects are usually well versed in environmental regulations as well as local zoning codes.

Like other design consultants, landscape architects should be brought in early, before roads and buildings are built, for their trained eyes may perceive possibilities that planners, architects, and civil engineers miss. They help to determine the image a residential project will convey to prospective residents. Landscape architects design the project's entrances, and they are largely responsible for creating the streetscape—the features that often form one's first impression of a residential neighborhood. The landscape architect's contributions can add both perceived and real value to a residential project, which ultimately translates into quicker sales and higher prices.

Building Contractors

Usually much of a development's quality rests with the actual builders of houses, the products eventually marketed to consumers. Contractors, licensed professionals who construct a project in accordance with plans and specifications, perform the task of building. Typically, *general* contractors assume the lead role in residential construction, and they may retain the services of numerous subcontractors for specialized aspects of construction: roofing, drywall, windows, masonry, cabinetry, and so forth. General contractors are often referred to as *builders,* but they may be just a contractor to the homebuilder as defined earlier. Most residential builders retain the full-time services of a general contractor within their organizations, however.

Residential developers also require the services of contractors for a variety of construction projects that occur before houses are built. Under the general term *site preparation* are included grading, installing utilities and stormwater systems, and paving streets. Most residential developers do not retain such contractors in house, but larger organizations frequently employ an experienced individual to manage contractors.

Contractors are skilled in assembling and organizing materials and labor, supervising construction in the field, and hiring and managing subcontractors. They are responsible for quality control, managing construction schedules, and controlling construction costs. Their input to a development plan during preconstruction helps developers generate reasonable estimates of construction costs and schedules.

Types of Ownership

Ultimately, the homes in a residential development are sold to residents or investors. Housing ownership is of three primary types: fee simple, condominium, and cooperative. A fourth type, "interval ownership," describes a variety of options for ownership that allow the owner's use of real property on an occasional basis.

Fee Simple

Most housing sold in this country is fee simple; that is, the owner is invested with the right to dispose of the property in any way he or she wishes. The owner can use the property so far as it will not interfere with the rights of others as typically controlled by zoning ordinances. The purchase of the property can be financed outright or, more commonly, through a mortgage arrangement.

Fee simple ownership is used for most single-family detached projects; the property owner owns the house in its entirety, the land the house sits on, and generally the property around the periphery of the house—the front and rear yards and two side yards. Most townhouse projects are also sold on a fee simple basis, with the homeowner owning the structure, the land under the house, and the front and rear yards.

The design of the lot and the house is largely a function of the sale price the developer hopes to receive as determined by the market analysis. As a rule, the larger the lot, the more expensive the house, although luxury homes on small lots or expensively finished attached houses are becoming more prevalent as available land becomes more scarce. And with aging populations and today's lifestyles, homeowners may actually prefer smaller lots to reduce maintenance chores and costs.

Condominium

A condominium is a form of ownership, not a housing type. Each dwelling unit is owned outright by its occupant, not in common with other tenants like a cooperative. Each condominium may carry an individual mortgage, while a co-op has a common mortgage. A mortgage for a condominium might be reduced as the individual's financial position permits, while the owners of a co-op are bound by a set schedule of payments on the cooperative corporation's mortgage.

The condominium form of ownership first acquired legal status in the United States and its possessions in 1951 with the passage of a law in Puerto Rico. It was followed by another Puerto Rican law in 1958, the Horizontal Property Act, which governed the ownership of property categorized as condominiums. Congress amended the National Housing Act in 1961 to extend government insurance of mortgages to condominiums, and by 1968, all 50 states had enacted their own enabling legislation for condominiums.

Condominiums may be structured so that a unit is defined as an airspace or as a portion of real property, such as walls and land. All parts of the condominium development not specifically owned by an individual (as described on the deed) are owned in common by all the development's owners. Ownership of common elements is typically defined as a percentage proportionate to the square footage of each unit; the percentage interest in common elements is granted to owners by deed.

Owners of condominiums have a choice of owning their units free and clear of any mortgages or financing them through regular mortgage channels. Typically, a condominium is financed in two phases: the developer finances the entire project through a blanket mortgage, and owners finance individual units through individual mortgage or government-insured loans. Owners may sell,

Evergrene is a sustainable community in Palm Beach Gardens, Florida, that was developed in partnershp with Audubon International.

will, or give away the property. Each deed is recorded separately, and taxes are levied individually. These advantages of actual ownership appeal to many—especially those who may not be able to afford a fee simple lot and those who may not want the responsibilities of maintenance associated with more conventional homeownership.

Because the condominium form of ownership is not tied to a particular design, it may appear in mid-rise or high-rise buildings, garden-density units, attached townhouses, or even single-family detached houses. It might also exist as a combination of two or more of these types of houses as part of a single condominium association. The condominium form of ownership is so versatile that it exists in commercial and industrial buildings as well as in residential housing; condominium associations can also include combinations of residential and commercial uses.

Management of a condominium is controlled by a condominium association.[3] The developer who has constructed the units and established the condominium association usually assumes responsibility for managing the association initially, before passing it on to homeowners. Common responsibilities typically shared by the association may include maintenance of the building(s), landscaping, private streets and parking areas, recreational facilities like swimming pools and tennis courts, and any common interior elements like lobbies, elevators, heating and air-conditioning equipment, and hallways.

The association is also responsible for acquiring insurance coverage for the building; owners of individual units carry separate coverage for their personal belongings. Owners are charged a monthly fee to cover costs of maintenance, insurance, and a reserve account according to the value of their units. Often, fees are based on square footage so that those with larger units pay a proportionately greater share of the costs. Without agreement of the owners in accordance with the condominium's legal documents, neither the assessment nor the maintenance liability can change.

Cooperative

In the cooperative form of ownership, a single property is divided into units, or *use portions,* with each user or "buyer" owning shares of stock in the corporation that owns the building. Typically, cooperative ownership is employed in a multiunit building—garden density, mid-rise, or high rise—where all the customary services are offered but where ownership and cost of operation are shared by the occupants in proportion to the value of the space they occupy. Co-op buyers are entitled to a proprietary lease of their space.

The predetermined rental rate for each unit is reached by prorating the costs of operation among tenants. The lease requires the co-op owner to make a monthly maintenance payment to the corporation to cover its operating expenses, mortgage interest, and real property taxes. Because interest and property taxes

Condominiums are an ownership form in which each dwelling unit is separately owned. Co-ops are owned in common with other occupants.

are obligations of the corporation, deductible only for calculating its taxable income, the proprietary tenant must be an individual, who is under strict requirements by the Internal Revenue Service to receive tax deductions.

To qualify as cooperative housing under IRS regulations, at least 80 percent of the corporation's gross income must come from tenant shareholders (defined as individuals entitled to occupy dwelling space in the building by virtue of ownership of stock in the corporation). Thus, not more than 20 percent of the corporation's income may come from tenants who are not individuals (that is, income from commercial space, offices, garages, concessions, and restaurants).

The cooperative form of ownership has existed for some time, notably in major urban markets like New York City. The form of ownership appeals to confirmed city dwellers and those who seek the tax advantages of a corporation. The cooperative has not caught on in this country as a popular form of ownership, although it is suitable for many suburban locations and offers advantages to investors who might otherwise be merely tenants. A primary disadvantage lies in the prorating of the building's operating costs among owners. Further, responsibility for mortgage payments is shared with other owners, each according to its own portion of ownership. Only that amount of the mortgage interest for which an individual owner is responsible can be deducted from his or her income tax.

Perhaps the most significant reason that cooperative housing has not been more popular is that ownership rests with the corporation, not in the individual units. Thus, owners cannot pass their shares in the corporation on through their estates or by any other means. The shares instead are sold back to the cooperative's board of trustees, which has ultimate authority over their disposition. Further, the co-op can incur liabilities, and stockholders may find themselves obligated for the liabilities of other stockholders.[4]

Interval Ownership

The most commonly known form of interval ownership is vacation timesharing. Most timeshare units are located in popular resort settings; owners of the units are guaranteed a period each year (usually a week) when they can use the unit. Ownership in vacation timeshare units is usually in fee simple title, with each owner holding a deed. Alternatively, owners may purchase a "right to use" the unit for some period (usually 30 years) without a deed.

Alban Towers in Washington, D.C., combines rental apartments and ownership townhouses.

Most vacation timesharing developments are structured as condominiums, with all owners belonging to the condominium association and paying fees.

Another form of interval ownership is "fractional ownership." Rather than purchasing one week, owners purchase up to 13 weeks, or a quarter year. Thirteen-week purchases are often called "quarter shares." Fractional ownership is most often purchased with a deed that gives the owners the right to use the unit in a solid block of time or in "floating" blocks that may be reserved in advance.

Vacation timeshare and fractional ownership programs have historically been most popular with active retirees, but as baby boomers age, there may be wider market opportunities for this type of homeownership.[5]

Summary

This book explains the residential development process, beginning with site selection and feasibility analysis (Chapter 2), financing (Chapter 3), planning and design (Chapter 4), regulatory approvals (Chapter 5), marketing (Chapter 6), and postdevelopment community governance (Chapter 7). Chapter 8 covers a variety of specialized opportunities, and Chapter 9 presents case studies that illustrate real examples of the development process. The final chapter (Chapter 10) identifies emerging trends that will shape the residential development industry in the coming years.

Notes

1. Heather McCune, "A New Order," *Professional Builder,* April 2001, pp. 48–53.

2. Sarah Susanka, *The Not So Big House: A Blueprint for the Way We Really Live* (Newtown, Connecticut: Taunton Press, 1998).

3. See Chapter 7 for additional information about condominium associations and their management structures.

4. For additional information, contact the National Association of Housing Cooperatives, 1707 H Street, N.W., Suite 201, Washington, D.C. 20006 (202-737-0397); www.coophousing.org.

5. For additional information on interval ownership, see Dean Schwanke et al., *Resort Development Handbook* (Washington, D.C.: ULI–the Urban Land Institute, 1997).

2. Project Feasibility

Project feasibility begins even before the formal due diligence process and continues throughout the life of a project. It is the analytical evaluation that precedes major real estate decisions, including buying a land parcel or beginning a development. It includes evaluating the environmental, financial, legal, and other aspects that relate to developing and marketing the property. The analyses that typically are part of the feasibility study can be divided into four primary components: 1) site selection and engineering, 2) market analysis, 3) financial feasibility or cash flow analysis, and 4) regulatory analysis. This chapter covers site selection and engineering, market analysis, and financial feasibility. Chapter 5 covers regulatory issues.

Site Selection

Locating and securing raw developable land in attractive locations has become increasingly difficult, as the most desirable and economically viable sites have often already been developed. Because of increasing land costs and the scarcity of prime sites, properties that previously were once considered unbuildable have become candidates for development. Thus, careful analysis is more important than ever for determining a site's potential for development.

Westridge, Valencia, California.

John Connell

Selecting a parcel of land depends on a number of factors, including the type of development planned, the anticipated size of the development, general location of the site, costs (including costs for unusual grading, environmental mitigation, or removal of existing structures), and the market potential. Usually, the worst reason for developing a parcel is that "I already own it." In an ideal world, a developer would always determine a development concept based on thorough market analysis and then set out to find a site with the necessary characteristics for that concept.

Given the scarcity of buildable land, however, developers frequently do have to conceive a project around a site they already own. More often, a site becomes available to a developer and a concept must be tailored to that site. At other times, a developer purchases a site for a specific project, but because of outside forces such as a change in market conditions or the inability to obtain jurisdictional approvals, the original concept is no longer viable. In such situations, the developer must sell the property or create a new concept for it. In any situation, it is absolutely necessary that the site and development concept be appropriate for each other.

With suitable raw land at such a premium, some developers are turning to other options. Infill and redevelopment sites have become increasingly appealing. Such sites are available in many areas. They often come with public services and amenities in place, suitable zoning, and sometimes even financial incentives to develop

Residential development can fit in many locations, depending on its scale, character, and density.

the property. In many cases, the surrounding population provides a ready-made market for the new housing as well. But such properties have their drawbacks, too. They may be difficult configurations or may require complex land assembly. Expensive environmental mitigation may be required. Or they may require a certain kind of vision to see beyond existing circumstances and develop a concept that will be a catalyst for neighborhood revitalization. Like exurban greenfield sites, the ones that are easiest to develop have already been taken in many areas.

Factors Affecting Location

Developers often say that site selection involves three factors: location, location, location. Certainly, a residential development's success has a great deal to do with its location within a metropolitan area, access to roadways and other transportation facilities, and the character of existing and prospective development in the surrounding area. Some entrepreneurial developers have been able to overcome the location factor and create demand in areas perceived as poor locations. Such locations are risky, however, and usually the development must be large enough or unusual enough to create its own locational identity. Moreover, such developments require significant vision and creativity to ensure success. Although location is very important in site selection, balancing factors are the cost of the land, its suitability for development, and the developer's vision.

Foreseeing changes in the urban fabric before others do is one of the hallmarks of the most successful developers. Whether their predictions are based on careful research, intuition, or a combination of both, successful developers understand the locational dynamics well enough to survive over the long term.

Residential development can be suitable for a wide range of locations. Higher-density forms are particularly suited to urban areas where land is too expensive for less dense housing. A downtown urban core could not support single-family houses on quarter-acre lots, but it could be an ideal site for a high-rise condominium project. Midrise or townhouse developments can work nicely in a neighborhood business district or a fairly dense, largely residential area. Single-family units tend to fit best in lower-density neighborhoods where land is less expensive and development patterns are more compatible with that type of development.

Often, master-planned communities are designed to include a range of housing types of varying densities. A community might concentrate mid-rise residential buildings in a town center, including residential units above first-level shops and offices. Townhouse development might be clustered around the town center, with single-family homes in the more outlying areas. Or the plan might call for higher densities at the edges of the community, along major roadways, while the lower-density housing fills in areas with quieter streets. Some new urbanist communities have mixed small multifamily

At Baxter Village in South Carolina, a town center serves as a desirable amenity for residents.

Urban Design Associates

Palace Lofts is an infill development in Denver's LoDo district that takes advantage of an urban site with many amenities.

buildings, townhouses, and single-family homes on the same block.

Fighting tradition or creating demand in traditionally nonresidential areas or declining areas may carry more risks for the developer than a site in a solid, well-established residential community. But such areas may also offer greater rewards to offset the risk. And because of the dynamic nature of cities and their economies, perceptions of a location constantly change.

Convenience is an increasingly important factor in selecting a location. In most metropolitan areas, residents pay a premium for a location that is convenient to employment, schools, shopping, and other destinations so that driving time is minimized. Access to good public transportation and walkability are assets for a residential development.

Economists speak of macro- and microeconomic factors. Locational considerations can be broken into macrolocational (or regional) and microlocational (or site-specific) considerations.

Macrolocational Factors. Past city growth trends should be carefully studied to determine the direction in which high-, medium-, and low-value development has moved. Higher-priced residential areas, sometimes called "the favored quarter," usually show the same general direction of movement over years, outward from the urban center. If high-end residential development began northwest from the center, for example, successive outward extensions of higher-cost units usually continue in the same direction, and the lion's share of employment growth occurs in the same area. Some experts consider it unwise to ignore established trends in land development, especially when the project is a conventional one. Although it is much easier to satisfy demand than to create it, creative developers often break the rules. Mixed-income developments have been successful in many locations, despite the conventional wisdom.

Access is one of a site's major attributes. If access to the site is available only on congested routes or through unattractive areas, it may be difficult to market the project. Congestion, however, is relative, and an unattractive area could offer unique potential for redevelopment if the project's economic parameters are favorable. In some instances, it may be possible to acquire additional land or obtain rights-of-way that will permit a new or improved approach, thereby avoiding the negative image of undesirable existing land uses. In advertising the project, developers sometimes select the most attractive route to the project rather than the shortest.

Accessibility takes several forms: regional, local, site specific, vehicular, public transit, and pedestrian. In its broadest context, a site should be evaluated for its accessibility to major employment and commercial centers in the metropolitan area. In urban areas, it might mean access to the downtown, while in suburban regions, edge cities or town centers are often the focus of jobs and commercial activity. A site with easy access to an existing or emerging suburban core is easier to market than a more remote site that lacks such access. Developers should evaluate the growth dynamics of the metropolitan area and then determine whether a proposed site offers good regional accessibility, taking account of planned prices or rents.

Residential developments near commercial, recreational, and cultural services are easier to market than those located in areas where such services do not exist. The location and quality of public schools might be considerations for families with children. The quality of the school district can prove an effective marketing tool in some market niches. But schools may not be a factor at all if the project is geared toward nonfamily households. Developers will benefit by asking themselves the same questions a prospective homebuyer would ask: "How far must I travel to shop, go to school, and be entertained? How long must I sit in traffic?"

The availability of utilities and public services must be evaluated carefully. In many parts of the country, permission to develop a site depends on the availability of water and sewer lines, with the jurisdiction deciding the location and timing of installation of utility systems. In other areas, lack of capacity has resulted in moratoriums on residential construction until additional capacity can or will be provided. When a residential development has several phases, the *future* availability of utilities must be carefully assessed, even when hookups for *current* phases are available.

Every prospective residential site is located within the regulatory jurisdiction of a county or municipality that will be responsible for considering the eventual development proposal. Developers must therefore consider the local government's position on growth and development. Governments often resist higher-density development, and a developer would be wise to meet with staff and otherwise evaluate how amenable the government is likely to be to the proposed uses before committing to a site.

These regional location considerations do not form an exhaustive list, but they point to some of the most frequent issues that developers should consider before committing to a site. Each site, locale, and intended housing product requires its own set of considerations. Prudent developers know what is important in their intended market and examine the site with respect to its locational advantages and disadvantages.

Microlocational Factors. For site-specific, or microlocational, access, a property being considered for residential use must be accessible to streets and major roadways. The actual nature of the streets connecting the project with the larger community depends on the size and character of development planned. A downtown development, for example, does not need highway access so much as it requires good access to local streets, sidewalks, and public transit. Suburban projects usually generate significant amounts of traffic; thus, locations adjacent to collector streets and highways are advantageous. A site's visibility is a marketing factor. A certain amount of visibility is essential, but a property without much road frontage

has a quieter, more secluded feel. Secluded sites often require additional budget for advertising and promotion. The developer should be aware of any off-site road construction scheduled to take place during the project's marketing phase. Such construction could make it difficult for potential residents to visit the project or could aesthetically deter prospects and damage marketing efforts.

If a property has poor access, a developer must be prepared to invest in roadway improvements. A difficult left turn across traffic into the project may require a traffic light. Any evaluation of a site must include a cost and feasibility analysis of providing access and a determination of who will pay for it. If the project's access points conform to the jurisdiction's future land use and transportation plans, the local government might aid the developer in funding certain improvements. More often, the jurisdiction looks for funding from the developer to advance its planned improvements. Alternatively, an improvement district can sometimes be created to fund improvements for one or a group of developments in which all properties in the "benefit area" are assessed their share of costs and the jurisdiction may pick up the public's share.

Although reliance on private automobiles for all transportation has been the norm for suburban areas since the 1950s, worsening traffic and longer commuting times contribute to the increased use of transit in many metropolitan areas, especially for commuting to work. Development sites near rail transit stops and bus routes offer a good opportunity for higher-density development and for lower-income residents, who normally have lower rates of vehicle ownership. Unfortunately, the population most in need of convenient transit is the least able to afford the well-located housing that can provide it.

Convenience for pedestrians is an increasingly important consideration. Urban communities generally have a well-developed sidewalk system, but suburban communities have not consistently provided access for pedestrians.

Emery Station in Emeryville, California, is a transit-oriented development that includes an affordable housing component. The project is located at an Amtrak transit station.

Heller.Manus Architects

Summerset at Frick Park in Pittsburgh was built on a reclaimed brownfield, a former slag heap.

Sometimes suburban sidewalks are more ornamental than functional, with no links to adjacent properties. Master-planned communities usually provide an internal pedestrian system of trails or sidewalks linking residential, commercial, recreational, and public uses, but they may not be adequate for walking to schools, shopping, parks, and other facilities, especially when those destinations are located outside the development.

Land Use

Existing, proposed, and historical land use patterns on and adjacent to a potential development site should be studied carefully to determine whether a potential conflict exists. Well-documented land use studies can reduce a developer's liability in potential lawsuits filed by future residents and can eliminate difficulties in marketing caused by incompatible adjacent uses. A complete land use analysis includes several subjects: historical uses, current uses, surrounding uses, and possible conflicting uses.

Historical Uses. As infill and redevelopment sites attract increasing interest from developers, environmental issues must be addressed. Often the most desirable sites are those that have had previous lives. A property's past, particularly if that past included any industrial uses, could significantly affect its potential for development. Federal legislation regarding cleanup and reuse of contaminated sites has opened new possibilities for land that was once abandoned as useless. Such sites, called "brownfields," are "real property, the expansion, redevelopment, or reuse of which may be complicated by the presence or potential presence of a hazardous substance, pollutant, or contaminant."[1]

Brownfields in the core of larger cities, along waterfronts, and near major transportation routes often were the sites of heavy industrial use. Those in first-ring suburban locations were more often used for light industry or even retail-related uses such as dry cleaners or gas stations, and now are contaminated from spills and leaks.

Many such sites are ripe for redevelopment, but the issues surrounding brownfield sites must be thoroughly understood before proceeding. It is important that the cost of remediation be carefully estimated and built into the economics of the project. The majority of states have instituted cleanup programs that make it easier for owners of contaminated properties to develop, receive approvals, and implement remedial actions. Many programs include grants, loans, or tax incentives to offset the costs of site analysis and remediation. Environmental insurance has been established to protect property owners from liability after cleanup has been completed.

The costs associated with surveys of historical use must be in proportion to the level of risk. A site that has been used only for agriculture may require only a cursory examination, while a site with a history of industrial activities may require both research and field tests to determine the likelihood of contamination. Prudent developers undertake the appropriate levels of analysis and then document their findings as protection against future legal action.

Some developers have begun to realize the potential of brownfields with only minor contamination. Many such sites are in excellent locations with ready access to transportation and infrastructure. Because environmental laws are constantly being revised, it is essential that the developer of a potentially contaminated site be thoroughly educated on the most current federal, state, and local legislation. Potential funding sources and tax incentives for brownfield redevelopment should also be fully investigated. The Environmental Protection Agency's (EPA's) Comprehensive Environmental Response, Compensation, and Liability Inventory System (CERCLIS) is the federal data repository for brownfields, including information on site assessment and remediation and an up-to-date list of identified sites eligible for federal assistance with cleanup.

Even land that appears pristine may have environmental issues that need to be addressed. Undeveloped, or "greenfield," sites have been covered with forest, field, or farmland. Farmland can bring its own set of problems caused by historic use of pesticides that are now banned but remain in the soils. In some cases, such contaminated soil must be removed, capped, or treated. Some states require developers of all properties to test soils for pesticides. Others have variable regulations based on location and site history. Some lenders also require soils testing as part of due diligence.

Typical Treatments for Soil Contaminants

- Excavation—Often viewed as the simplest but probably the most expensive way to deal with contaminants. Typically, the contaminated soil is excavated, transported by specially fitted vehicles to a federally approved landfill, and disposed of there. This treatment is particularly advantageous in removing wastes from sites close to people or in regularly flooded sites.
- Capping—A quick and relatively inexpensive method that seals the surface of waste sites with a layer of soil (usually clay), asphalt, concrete, or a synthetic membrane. This approach, which is most effective for contaminants that do not migrate, may require additional technologies such as slurry walls and groundwater pumping if leakage is a possibility.
- Slurry Walls—Barriers constructed below ground to redirect groundwater away from a contaminated area and to contain leachate within a site. Normally, bentonite clay, alone or in combination with soil and cement, is used to fill a narrow trench. Although construction companies are familiar with slurry walls, which are often used in conventional construction, these barriers are expensive and take time to install, and they often leak.
- Subsurface Drains—Gravel-filled trenches intended to intercept and collect leachate and contaminated groundwater. They are quite effective in draining groundwater but may become clogged with silt and soil over time.
- Groundwater Treatment—Involves the use of several technologies such as subsurface drains or wells that collect water that is then treated on site to remove contaminants.
- New Technologies—Include mobile incinerators, bioremediation (use of microorganisms to destroy toxic organic chemicals), and solvents to extract contaminants. ∎

David Salvesen, "Contamination and the Reuse of Land," *Urban Land,* December 1993, p. 35.

Not all historical uses pose development obstacles; some can be assets. Many times developers have capitalized on existing historical structures on a property by incorporating them into the development plan. The jurisdiction may require the developer to preserve and/or rehabilitate any historically significant properties on a site. Historic houses, barns, and other buildings have been successfully adapted for use as community centers or other focal points. Properly treated, such structures can lend a theme to the design and help to set the development apart from its competition. But incorporating historical features into a new development adds costs that must be weighed against probable benefits.

Current Use. Developers also need to be aware of a site's current use. Nonconflicting uses that generate income, such as farming or grazing or even certain recreational uses can help carry the land economically during predevelopment and development phases. Other uses—those that generate waste or damage the site's aesthetic quality—are less advantageous. The concept and purpose of a proposed project influence a developer's willingness to accept the difficulty of site assembly, removal of existing structures and physical constraints, and other limitations.

In valuable urban locations and in some more desirable suburban locations, it is often economically justifiable to assemble multiple parcels with existing structures, clear the site, and develop a different, more intensive use, such as higher-density or more upscale homes. This economic reality has led to the loss of housing for low- and moderate-income households in many inner cities. Many municipalities offer incentives for developers to include affordable housing in new developments and often require them to do so. When a site includes occupied housing, displacement becomes a major issue. Most often, the new project is higher priced than the one it will replace, so residents of the existing development will not be able to afford to move into the newer housing.

Costs incurred in purchasing and improving a site derive from several factors:

- Carrying Costs—When property is acquired, expenses begin to accrue for site acquisition, taxes, and interest. During the time it takes to gain approvals, clear the site, and develop and market the project, the developer incurs substantial costs without any return.
- Demolition—Better methods of demolition—heavy equipment to bulldoze small frame buildings and dynamite to remove large masonry buildings—have greatly reduced the expense of site clearance; sometimes, the expense is reduced further by the sale of salvaged materials. A small or awkwardly configured site, however, can necessitate more expensive and time-consuming demolition methods.
- Assembly—Site assembly is most complex in urban locations where property has been subdivided many times. Some local governments offer assistance programs that can aid in the complex task of land assembly by acquiring blighted properties through con-

Fifth Avenue Lofts is a rehabilitation of an old office building to condominium housing in San Diego, California. It is located adjacent to Balboa Park and close to other urban amenities.

demning and clearing them and making the sites available for use at less than cost.

Surrounding Uses. The character of adjacent areas in large measure determines the use for an undeveloped parcel. If adjoining areas are compatible, they can enhance the desirability of a proposed residential project. When they are deleterious or conflicting, developers should proceed very cautiously. Most desirable for a residential development are sites adjacent to open space and community facilities like parks or libraries. Such facilities provide an attractive setting and frequently impart prestige. Because most sites are not blessed with these kinds of neighbors, however, on-site recreational facilities have become an important part of projects large enough to include them. These amenities can include improved open space, tennis courts, pools, trails, and greenbelts. In very large developments, the recreational facilities and design features that can be included are limited only by cost and the developer's requirements for return.

Existing residential areas or mixed-use areas that already include a residential component are a desirable setting for new residential development. A site may be a previously undeveloped parcel or an underdeveloped tract in the path of suburban expansion or a bypassed parcel in the midst of a built-up residential neighborhood. If a shift to a higher density is proposed for an infill site, problems may arise with regard to site planning, access and other physical factors, and the local government's and residents' perceptions of what the changes in density will mean to the neighborhood. Generally, the proposed development should be of a character and density that is compatible with neighboring uses.

The municipality's comprehensive plan and zoning regulations provide an excellent perspective of the public's position about appropriate uses for any property under consideration. An appealing new concept should not necessarily be rejected because it does not fit the

locality's current notions of appropriate uses. Sometimes the jurisdiction may be enticed to rework its regulations to accommodate an innovative new approach to land use.

For many years, it has been common practice to place higher-density residential areas closest to commercial and industrial districts. Doing so serves to buffer single-family areas and to allow the high-density residential areas to benefit from proximity to the higher-capacity street system and more extensive commercial and employment districts required for heavier population densities. In turn, cluster and attached housing is often located as a buffer between multifamily and lower-density, single-family development.

More recently, however, these planning practices have come into question. Local governments increasingly are willing to view development proposals in terms of integrating rather than separating different uses, a point illustrated by the increasing flexibility of land use controls through the widespread acceptance of mixed-use

Vickery in suburban Atlanta is a mixed-use project designed by Duany Plater-Zyberk and developed by Hedgewood Properties.

zoning, new urbanist concepts, and new towns. These kinds of development plans permit the mixed development of uses previously separated into exclusive districts, provided they are properly designed. The result is often a more livable, efficient, and attractive development.

Another concept of new urbanism is transect zoning, which classifies land in an urban-to-rural continuum of six zones. Within each zone, detailed guidelines describe the appropriate densities, street and block dimensions, buildings, public spaces, and land uses. Transect zoning is an attempt to coordinate planning on a regional scale and to provide for all intensities and types of development in a logical form.

The concept of synergy—that the whole is greater than the sum of its parts—is usually applied to commercial or mixed-use projects but is also applicable to residential sites. A good site for residential development is one that has positive synergy with surrounding land uses. For example, a high-density residential site in an established or emerging suburban business core offers residents the convenience of employment and commercial services within easy driving or possibly even walking distance. A site in an area with several other successful multifamily projects also has a kind of synergy and is more desirable than one that lacks such neighboring development. The best locations are naturally more costly than those with detrimental surroundings but are usually worth the expense, particularly for a high-end development.

Conflicting Uses. When an area's preconceived image has been created by uses incompatible with residential development, the probability of establishing a successful new development diminishes. Primary among the uses likely to pose problems for new residential development are power lines, railroad tracks, rundown commercial development, noxious industrial uses, shoddy and poorly planned existing residential development, and noise generators such as airports or congested highways.

Sites that are suitable for development can range in size from less than an acre to several thousand acres. Ladera Ranch in Orange County, California, is a 4,000-acre (1,620-hectare) master-planned community.

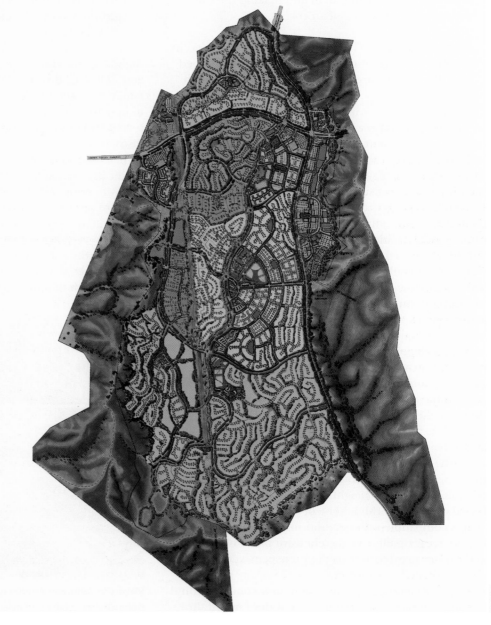

EDAW, Inc.

Kicking Horse Lodges in Silver Creek, Colorado, occupies fewer than five acres (2 hectares) and includes 120 units.

In considering compatibility, developers should be aware of potential liabilities that could be incurred from building residential units too close to conflicting uses. Proximity to large storage tanks of gas, oil, and other flammable materials should be avoided. Fire protection must be considered in heavily wooded or fire-prone areas, and flood damage could be an issue in flood-prone areas. Generally, protecting the public from such hazards rests with the municipality through its police powers (including zoning), but developers also need to protect themselves against possible liability by examining the potential conflicting uses near a given site.

Minimizing the adverse effects of through traffic is important. Whenever possible, neighborhoods split by existing or potential major thoroughfares should be avoided. If it is impossible to plan around a proposed highway, the developer should work with the local planning and highway departments to have the proposed road alignments as compatible as possible with the planned project. Any land that a developer might be required to dedicate to the highway department can pay big dividends in terms of better marketability for the project. To avoid interference with daily life in the residential project, noise abatement measures, including sound walls, earth berms, landscaping, building setbacks, and increased window and wall soundproofing, might be required in buildings abutting heavily traveled thoroughfares.

Airports present a special case of potential adverse impacts. The possible adverse effects noise has on a res-idential neighborhood make it imperative for a developer to investigate fully a site within 15 miles (24 kilometers) of an airport to determine whether the site falls within a designated or proposed flight path. Because airports generate business and have become important employment centers, nearby residential development has been spurred despite the noise. If a residential development is under consideration for a site near an airport, noise attenuation measures must be factored into the project's design and costs.

The Site

A tract of land has numerous characteristics that affect its suitability for development. Some characteristics are related to the natural geography of the land such as slope, drainage, vegetation, and soil types, while others are manmade, including boundaries, legal restrictions, and utilities.

Size and Shape. The best size for a development depends on local market conditions such as absorption rates, acceptable densities, and preferred amenities. For example, a developer seeking to sell out a new project within 12 months of its completion needs to estimate the number of sales expected per month. If four homes can be sold per month, then the developer can plan a project of about 48 homes. If zoning permits an average density of four units per acre (10 per hectare), then the ideal site for this project would be 12 acres (4.8 hectares) of buildable land. A larger site would accommodate more

Development costs increase as a result of slopes or other difficult terrain. Shown here is Steiner Ranch, a 4,600-acre (1,860-hectare) development in Austin, Texas.

RVI Planning

units and would require a longer sales period under this scenario. Because of taxes and carrying costs, the developer should not carry more land than is financially manageable. Many developers have gone bankrupt doing just that. Whenever possible, a developer should make future expansion possible through long-term options rather than outright purchase.

Design options increase as the site's size increases. The larger the site, the greater the amount of unusable land that might be incorporated into the development. For small parcels, under ten acres (4 hectares), alternative designs tend to be somewhat limited, although this fact is less true for higher-density products such as townhouses and other attached products and multifamily configurations. When selecting small sites, developers should avoid those with a high percentage of unusable land and carefully consider the tract's dwelling unit yield before purchase. A developer should always have a preliminary site plan drawn before proceeding with a contract to anticipate any development difficulties caused by physical site constraints.

A project's amenities, such as pools, tennis courts, tot lots, community centers, and especially golf courses, take additional land and require a certain number of housing units to be economically justified. A project with extensive amenities needs to be large enough to spread the costs of constructing and operating the facilities over enough units.

The process of land assembly is a business in itself, offering its own risks and rewards. Beginning developers should look for individual tracts that are large enough to accommodate the product they really want to build rather than trying to assemble several parcels under different ownership. Assembling tracts could involve numerous problems: multiple closings with corresponding legal fees, multiple lenders, and the possibility that key parcels cannot be acquired. Incomplete assembly carries costly penalties for developers who may have to pay exorbitant prices for outparcels or have

to redesign a project to fit an inadequate site or give up the project altogether because of a single reluctant seller.

A skilled land planner can quickly prepare conceptual land plans showing alternative layouts for the desired development that emerged from the market analysis. Successful developers always take a market-based approach to land planning and product selection. Environmental and regulatory constraints also play a role in land planning. Although zoning determines the project's maximum densities, this maximum may not be attainable. Only after deducting acreage for streets, parks, proffered sites, environmental features, buffers, and other unbuildable areas can a planner determine a site's yield in dwelling units.

Natural Characteristics. The parcel's natural features have a considerable impact on its suitability for development and its value. Slope, soil conditions, geology, and hydrology all must be considered. Climate is sometimes viewed as part of the site's natural character, and solar orientation, wind, and shadows from adjacent development should be considered. Investigation of a site's development potential includes a study of natural features, usually by a civil engineer specializing in such studies.

Topography, Geology, and Soil. A site's topography influences the nature of the project and development costs. Moderately sloping sites, between 1 and 10 percent slope, are preferable to either steep or flat land. Gentle slopes create opportunities for more interesting site planning and allow for better drainage. Flat land can present drainage problems that raise development costs. A site with steep slopes, greater than 15 percent, presents challenges that increase development costs. Some jurisdictions prohibit development or decrease allowed densities on steep slopes. On any site, however, a certain amount of grading will be necessary.

A site's geology must be considered, particularly if it lies in an earthquake-prone region. Unstable land is likely to be unsuitable for development. An understanding of the site's soil conditions is also important. Soil acts as an engineering variable not only in construction but also in waste disposal systems and water supply maintenance. The best soils are deep and moderately pervious. Heavy clay soils tend to expand and contract with water, causing foundations to crack. Impervious soils saturate quickly and cause problems with runoff. If rock is located close to the surface, excavation costs may escalate dramatically.

Radon, a radioactive gas found mainly in rocks and soil in certain geological areas of the northern United States, can exist in localized pockets anywhere. Radon gas enters buildings through foundations and moves through the building as air circulates. The greatest danger from radon exists immediately after it is released into the air. It has therefore been thought that taller buildings provide some protection. Some ongoing studies, however, indicate that air circulating through a building might transfer radon quickly enough to pose a potential hazard throughout the building. The EPA has issued a series of recommendations on reducing the risk of exposure to radon. Developers should be aware of current standards and potential liability regarding radon.

Hydrology. Water is another consideration in the selection of a site. Surface water is exposed in lakes or streams; subsurface water occupies cracks and rifts in the soil or bedrock. Both surface and subsurface water

can affect a development's feasibility. Surface water can be both a resource and a nuisance. Although people enjoy living in sight of water features and will pay a premium for views or for the privilege of direct access to water, the existence of water on or near a site can complicate the development process and add to costs. If a site contains or borders on a stream or other body of water, a floodplain study must be conducted. Some portion of the site will almost certainly be unbuildable. A developer should obtain a rough approximation of how much land lies within the floodplain before going ahead with a contract. Inland and coastal wetlands play a role in natural stormwater management and are vital for certain vegetation, fish, and wildlife. Because of these important ecological functions, development in wetlands is strictly regulated.

Subsurface water must also be protected from development-related pollution. Groundwater can become tainted from sewer lines, which can leak, and from polluted storm runoff.

Flood Control. A developer needs to be aware of any floodplains that affect the property. The potential for floods increases when development reduces the natural floodplain or adds to runoff. Federal and state policy on flood damage control has shifted from an emphasis on structured controls such as dams and levees, which often just relocate flooding, to regulatory controls, including floodplain zoning codes, building codes, and open-space programs that prohibit encroaching on the

Wooded sites are highly prized by homebuyers and are often worth the extra site work they entail. Shown here is the Ledges in Huntsville, Alabama.

Urban Design Associates

floodplain. If the site includes a flood hazard area, this land area will likely be removed from the tabulation of buildable acreage but can be used for open space and certain recreational amenities.

Vegetation and Wildlife. Selective clearing enables efficient building while maintaining some natural areas. Special efforts should be made to preserve mature trees, especially around sensitive environmental features such as streams or slopes, despite the temporary inconvenience during construction. Preservation efforts are rewarded with increased value and marketability for the project. Mature trees provide more than aesthetic appeal; they also help with erosion control, sound control, and energy efficiency and consistently rank high among consumers as a desirable amenity.

Large trees face considerable stress during construction. Heavy foot or vehicular traffic around the roots packs the soil hard and may kill trees. Trees often die as a result of exposure to chemicals. Even if trees survive construction, they often die later because their root systems have been disturbed or because the amount of water or sunlight they receive has changed. All of these factors

can be avoided through use of a careful tree saving plan that should be an integral part of the early design process; in fact, the jurisdiction may require such a plan. Mature trees are a valuable asset to any development and often cost no more to preserve than replacement with new saplings would. Developers who do make the effort to save mature trees are typically rewarded with higher sale prices that more than compensate for the cost of saving the trees.

Although trees are the most obvious form of vegetation to consider, other forms of vegetation may require special handling. Grasslands, particularly in coastal areas, are a crucial component of erosion control. Many kinds of grasses, vines, shrubs, and wildflowers provide wildlife habitats or are included on endangered species lists, and their preservation becomes a legal issue.

Some jurisdictions require an environmental impact study as part of the approval process to assess the impact of a project on an area's natural features—including water quality, wildlife habitat, and ambient noise level—and on the built environment, including public services, traffic conditions, and historic sites.

figure 2-1

Players and Their Influence in Planned Community Development

	Policy Makers/Reviewers	Developers	Citizens
Open Space	Create regional priorities and establish standards based on scientific data.	Shape plans to support regional systems. Fund long-term endowments to maintain and operate through REIT (real estate investment trust) or percentage of sale prices.	Embrace competing imperatives of growth and conservation and define areas of critical sensitivity.
Transportation	Establish funding and long-range plans for transit.	Accommodate future transit with "transit-ready" corridor planning. Assure density support for future transit concepts.	Be realistic about cost and timing of transit systems. Be willing to fund for the long term through tax programs that support regional transit.
Affordable Housing	Establish realistic targets based on econometrics of region. Reduce or remove development and impact fees that increase cost of housing for affordable components. Enact zoning changes and codes to accommodate nonaggregated forms of affordable housing.	Do not rely on just impact fees or other fees in lieu of solutions. Look for innovative answers, including housing above retail, granny flats, and mixed-size lot products.	Recognize the importance of diversity in communities and avoid NIMBY reactions. Support higher-density products and mixed-rate developments.
Balance of Jobs and Housing	Look at location and opportunities for job creation on a contextual basis. Be realistic about number of jobs and retail that can be supported by corresponding number of rooftops.	Broaden planning context to look at regional influences. If your project has limited employment potential, how can you support nearby employment centers—that is, financial marketing support, rubber tire transit program, joint marketing approach?	Remember "a rising tide lifts all boats." Think about best places for employment to be created and support clusters of employment in key areas that will allow transit and amenities to work.

Drought-tolerant landscaping, like that used at Santaluz in San Diego, California, is a way to reduce water use in dry climates.

SWA Group

Easements and Covenants. An easement is the right of one party to use another's property for a specific purpose, such as running a utility line or gaining access to a landlocked parcel. Unless an easement is created with a specific termination date, it survives indefinitely, regardless of the property's ownership. Only the beneficiary, or the party benefiting from the easement, can terminate it, typically at some cost to the property owner. Utility easements usually grant access for making repairs, and new development cannot interfere with that access. For example, if pavement or a building is constructed over an easement, the utility company has the right to make utility repairs with no obligation to restore any damage done to the property owner's improvements. Utility easements commonly prohibit any placement of structures, surface improvements, or large landscape materials within the easement right-of-way.

Easements have other purposes. Scenic easements have been developed as a mechanism to preserve undeveloped rural areas with great aesthetic value. Such easements are used to protect important views in the natural landscape. Conservation easements are applied to preserve areas of ecological, historic, or scientific significance. Air rights grant permission to develop in the air space over a property, as, for example, when a railroad allows construction of an office building over a railroad station.

Covenants, also called deed restrictions, are private restrictions that remain in force for all future property owners, usually restricting the activities or uses permitted on the property. Covenants typically extend beyond regulations enforceable by public authority, but they cannot supersede public regulations or be illegal under any existing laws. A property owner may create deed restrictions at any time. Once created, however, they remain in force unless all parties subject to the covenants agree to remove them. A title survey is the only reliable document for investigating easements and covenants; they do not show up on plats. Developers must carefully review any easements and deed restrictions to ensure that none exist that will affect development.

Utilities and Public Services. Water, sanitary and storm sewers, electricity, gas, and telephone are critical factors in site selection. Before purchasing a site, a developer should always confirm the proximity of services and whether they are available to the site. For example, a water line adjacent to the site may be unavailable to that property because the line's capacity is already committed or because the jurisdiction restricts development by limiting access to utilities. A developer should never simply take the word of the property seller but should verify availability with each utility company. Developers should ask the following questions before putting an option on the site:

- How long will it take to obtain service?
- How much will it cost?
- When is payment due?
- When must application for service be made?
- Are public hearings involved? (Public hearings may cause delays and increase political risk.)
- Is the provision of service subject to any potential moratoriums?
- Are easements needed from any other property owners before service can be obtained?
- Is the service capacity adequate?

Water and Sewerage. Ideally, developers want to tap into an existing suitably sized public water main on or near the site because it costs less. Thus, a developer should determine whether it is possible to connect the proposed project with an existing system and where that connection can be made. This connection could affect the planning and staging of development. If such a connection is possible, available capacity should be ascertained.

Whether an existing water main will be sufficient to serve a proposed project depends on the development's size and nature and the main's size and water pressure. The developer may be required to provide funds for upgrading the water distribution system if the existing water main proves inadequate.

The availability of water has become a critical issue in the arid western states. For decades, development has been possible in those areas largely because water was imported from northern California and the Colorado River. In recent years, however, limitations have been imposed on importing water supplies because of economic and ecological concerns. In some cases, long-term water rights agreements can be purchased from a nearby locality or an Indian reservation.

Municipalities with scarce water have responded by imposing high water hookup fees on residential building permits. Others have imposed strict requirements for conserving water, such as requiring the installation of drought-tolerant landscaping and, in extreme circumstances, partial or total moratoriums on development until new water supplies are available. Developers should check the availability of water at a site and, if it appears that supplies are limited, understand fully what will be required before a supply can be hooked up to the site.

If connection to a municipal sewer system is not immediately available, a developer should investigate the possibility of extending lines from the sewer main. Some localities maintain a policy against such expansion as a means of controlling development. Others, eager to see urban growth, may assist developers in financing and negotiating sewer consortiums with other property owners to develop new sewer lines.

Stormwater. In the past, stormwater runoff has been handled by the most convenient method possible: the rapid disposal of surface water through closed manmade systems. Stormwater runoff has often been mismanaged under this philosophy, aggravating the velocity and volume of new runoff problems downstream and increasing pollution of local streams. Potential legal issues concerning the effects of stormwater management on adjacent properties during and after construction have led many jurisdictions to adopt stormwater management standards restricting the runoff's quantity and velocity after development to no more than predevelopment levels. Many areas also require filtration of stormwater before its release.

The preparation of a functional and aesthetic stormwater runoff plan requires coordination among the project's engineers, planners, and landscape architects. Much runoff can be handled through passive design elements, including proper grading and landscaping materials, rather than engineering systems. Such considerations need to be part of the early design plan. Recent trends in stormwater management encourage eliminating large stormwater ponds in favor of smaller "rain gardens" located throughout the development. Rain gardens are low areas that are planted with water-tolerant plants. During rainstorms, these areas contain and filter water that would otherwise become runoff.

Iron Horse Lofts in Walnut Creek, California, provides housing near jobs, shopping, and transit for residents of mixed incomes.

Energy and Communication Utilities. Utility companies design, install, and maintain gas, electric, telephone, and cable TV lines according to their own specifications. Developers should ascertain each utility's capacity to serve the proposed development and its policies about extending and financing the services. Utilities may be provided at no expense to the developer, or the developer may be charged the costs of extending service to the property. Relocating existing utilities may be the developer's responsibility or the utility company's obligation.

Solid Waste. The developer should determine what agency or private company is responsible for picking up solid waste, what fees are involved, and the magnitude of any potential problems with solid waste disposal to ensure that building permits are not delayed. Generally, trash pickup will not impose a constraint on development, but it will entail a tax or assessment that will be passed on to future residents.

Emergency Services. Emergency services include primarily police and fire protection, which the local jurisdiction almost always provides. Many municipalities have found it difficult to maintain emergency services during cutbacks in funding and rapid growth, however, and developers of large projects may be required to provide funds or land for new facilities in exchange for certain development rights. When evaluating a site's suitability for development, developers should consider the potential for such unexpected costs. When examining fire protection services, developers should consider the site's distance from the nearest fire station and the expected response time. Adequate access to public water supplies and adequate water pressure for fire protection should be available to the site. If the property will be gated, arrangements must be made with the relevant agencies to permit emergency access to the site.

Schools. For some residential developments, particularly those higher-density projects targeted toward non-family households, schools are not a major concern. But if the market analysis indicates that a project's residents will be families with school-age children, the developer must be especially concerned about the location, quality, and capacity of nearby schools. In some areas, schools are the single most important element in determining where a family decides to locate.

In an effort to create buffers for single-family areas, multifamily sites are often located adjacent to schools, making those multifamily developments more appealing to families with school-age children. Developers of large projects, especially those targeted toward families with school-age children that would increase enrollments in schools, may be required to contribute fees or dedicate land for new schools.

Parks and Recreation. Facilities and open space for recreation are of great importance in site selection. A site adjacent to a park or recreation center comes with amenities already established, saving the developer the considerable costs of land, development, and operations. The amount and type of recreation needed vary with residents' anticipated lifestyles. Young families require play areas, young adults look for active recreational facilities, and retirees often want community centers and golf courses.

The developer's obligation to provide parks and recreation increases with the project's size. A small, ten-unit subdivision may require nothing of the developer, but a 1,000-unit community demands considerable recreational facilities, on site or off site. The municipality or county may require that the developer provide public recreational facilities in exchange for development rights. The extent of recreational facilities a developer must provide depends on the size and number of units proposed, availability of existing parks and recreation near the proposed site, and the local government's regulatory requirements. Further, with government resources on the decline, it is increasingly up to developers to provide the recreational facilities that residents demand.

Fiscal Impact. Local governments increasingly require developers to submit fiscal impact analyses prepared by independent consultants. These studies evaluate the various tax revenues that will be generated by a project and compare them with the operating and capital costs that the project will generate.

Market Analysis

A well-conceived residential project begins with a thorough understanding of the marketplace where the proposed development will compete. Market feasibility is fundamental to a development's financial success. Careful analysis is particularly important when the product type and geographical area are not very familiar to the developer, as it serves as a tool to educate the developer.

Understanding the market involves defining classic factors of demand and supply. Analysis of demand includes demographic and economic characteristics of households in the determined market area. Analysis of supply examines trends in prices and absorption and—most important—surveys the potentially competitive projects that will likely be marketed during the same time as the proposed subject property. A market analysis should first answer the most basic question: is there a real demand for a residential project at this location? It should then move on to seek answers to the following basic questions:

1. What is the appropriate target market and market position for this project?
2. What is the size and rate of growth of the target market, and what percentage of that market can be attracted to the subject project?
3. What are the opportunities, gaps, or specialized niches where a need exists in the marketplace?
4. What is the appropriate price or rent range for the market?
5. What types and sizes of homes are suitable for the market?
6. What amenities and features should be provided to appeal to this market?[2]

Bradburn outside Denver, Colorado, offers a range of housing types to meet market demand.

Continuum Partners

Real estate market analysis requires statistics and calculations but is not an exact science. Much of the analysis must rely on a qualitative understanding of the market and its dynamics. Both the product and the consumer must be understood in terms of choices people make, evolving lifestyles, personal tastes, and many other considerations that are difficult to quantify. Further, housing does not act like other consumer goods, because it is limited to a very local market. Thus, the universe of potential consumers is relatively small compared with that for most consumer products.

Market studies serve two main purposes. The studies facilitate internal decision making, providing necessary data for developing the concept and for preparing a realistic cash flow analysis. Lenders and investors also use the documentation in their decision making. A thoroughly researched report with rigorous methodology becomes an invaluable aid for gaining financing. Analytical lenders and equity sources scrutinize the market data in a good report.

A well-documented market analysis can help a developer obtain the necessary public approvals. More innovative projects in particular might need the political support that can be fostered by a clearly presented market rationale. And market studies provide invaluable guidance for planners, architects, and engineers in their design process, answering several questions: Who is this project for? How will the project affect the overall community? Further, investing in a detailed market analysis saves time and money in the long run because it provides most of the information required for constructing a development or fiscal impact analysis. Localities increasingly require development impact studies in making decisions on requested rezonings and determining impact fees.

A market analysis can address a broad spectrum of concerns. Developers of residential communities use general market studies to survey local or regional markets when gathering information about available land

Clarksburg, Maryland, is a 270-acre (110-hectare) new town based on a traditional main street plan. Homes are priced to appeal to a wide range of buyers.

Newland Communities

Rancho Viejo near Santa Fe, New Mexico, takes advantage of the southwestern desert setting and architectural heritage.

Design Workshop

The town center at WaterColor in Florida is a gathering place for residents as well as visitors from the surrounding area.

and determining feasible locations from the standpoint of costs and regulatory constraints. Market analyses also point to where the dynamics of supply and demand match the characteristics of the proposed development.

Many observers disagree about whether a local firm's real estate market analysis is better than one conducted by a well-known national firm based elsewhere. Some market analysts argue that the methods are identical no matter who conducts the analysis. Others point out that a local firm is more likely to have its finger on the pulse of the local development community and to have ready-made contacts, existing databases of local development activity, and a better understanding of the local market's nuances. Conversely, national firms can draw on experience with development concepts that may be new to the market being studied and may view an area with a fresh viewpoint that facilitates identification of new opportunities.

Regional Context

Market analysts generally begin by looking at the regional setting where the proposed development will occur, including population and household trends, recent or anticipated changes in the economic base, and employment patterns, and then narrow the focus to a smaller area such as a county or city for more specific information. They collect data about population, households, employment, housing needs and activity, regulatory issues, transportation patterns, and local schools and other services. From there, the subject property undergoes more detailed analysis about the market areas that will specifically affect the project's development program and ultimately its success in the market.

Identifying the Primary Market Area

The primary market area is the geographic area from which the majority of homebuyers will be drawn and the region that contains most of the competitive projects. Because of housing's local nature, the primary market

area usually centers on a major employment node, a transportation corridor, or a desirable locational amenity. Physical barriers, either natural or manmade, or political considerations, such as a county line, usually determine the borders. Market analysis should target identifiable regions where the infrastructure creates market sectors of geographic, demographic, and socioeconomic interdependence.

The size of the primary market area varies, depending on the size and type of project proposed and the community. For example, in a densely populated city, a market area for a typical medium-priced condominium development might encompass only a few blocks. In a sparsely populated semirural community with few competitive projects, the market area most likely comprises the entire county or even several adjacent counties. Further, a distinctive project with little or no competition will draw from a larger market area than a more standard project with a large pool of similar competitive projects.

Housing consumers usually prefer certain geographic locales but not precise locations within those broad areas. Consumers select a geographic area based on such factors as areawide prices, short commutes to work, cultural amenities, neighborhood quality, and the reputation of schools or other services. For developments that target families, the quality of local schools is often a primary consideration. For projects of smaller homes or homes targeted to empty nesters, young singles, or others unlikely to include children, schools may not be a major factor. Nevertheless, the quality of a school district may affect the overall quality of a neighborhood and its demographics.

Some questions are key in defining the primary market area: Where will most residents come from? What properties surrounding the subject project would a typical homebuyer consider a suitable home? The housing search for employed consumers often centers on where the unit is relative to the place of work. But increasingly, other lifestyle amenities are important, such as the nearness of an attractive town center or desirable recreational amenities.

The market analysis defines two market areas: the demand side of the economic equation (or target market area) and the supply side (or competitive market area). In most cases, these market areas are identical, although competitive projects can exist outside the target market area. In some instances, the two market areas are regions apart, as in the case of second-home resort developments. Most market areas for primary shelter, however, are within a one-hour commute of major employment centers or other key destinations.

Target Market Area. Target market areas define the location where the majority of demand for a proposed residential project exists. Various factors are considered in delineating the target market area for a proposed development:

- Travel Time from Major Employment Centers—By identifying major employment centers and making assumptions regarding acceptable commuting time, market analysts can define a target market area. A new wrinkle in weighting this factor is the growing number of telecommuters and other home-based workers, creating new opportunities for housing for those who can live anywhere.
- Mass Transportation Facilities and Highway Links—Commuting patterns and times are based largely on

ease of access; thus, the target market's geographic size is influenced by the availability of mass transit, the location of transportation corridors, and the speed at which they operate during peak travel times. Convenience of transportation is an especially important consideration for residential development.
- Existing and Anticipated Patterns of Development—Most urban settings contain areas of both growth and decline. Growth areas might be distinguished by certain desirable attributes, such as proximity to employment, housing affordability, physical attractiveness, and/or outstanding community facilities. Sometimes building a desirable attribute can improve an area's desirability. Examples include new on-site amenities or services such as concierges or retail stores.
- Socioeconomic Composition—An area's income, age, household characteristics, and other demographic characteristics influence housing choice and location and thus target market areas (but note that it is illegal in the United States to target market segments based on race, religion, or ethnicity).
- Physical Barriers—Natural features like rivers, bluffs, and parkland and manmade features like highways or intensive development can sometimes form a wall through which a market's boundaries do not penetrate.
- Political Subdivisions—Local government boundaries can be especially important when adjoining jurisdictions differ markedly in political climate, tax policies,

The developer of Maple Trace in Fairfax, Virginia, had to create two kinds of neighborhoods because the project straddles two jurisdictions with different zoning regulations.

or status, or when different attitudes about growth exist. School district boundaries are important if households with school-age children represent a major market segment. For easier data collection, a target market area sometimes must be manipulated somewhat to conform to a political jurisdiction, such as a county or planning district within a county or city.

With these and potentially more local factors in mind, analysts should define the target market area with the objective of gathering meaningful data about market characteristics and the existence of core consumers willing and able to purchase the proposed housing product. That core comprises not only households already existing in the market area but also those willing to relocate to the area. The existing location of this core group varies with the type and location of the proposed property.

Identifying the demand-based target market area brings the analyst halfway to fully understanding the project's market potential. Often, the more significant area of market potential is the supply side of the equation—the competitive market area.

Competitive Market Area. Unmet demand or residual demand is a key element that a market study seeks to identify, though in some cases a new project can capture demand that would otherwise go to an existing project. *Residual Demand* equals *Total Demand* minus *Net Absorption by Competitive Products.* To distinguish these parts of

Doe Mill in Chico, California, is a 48-acre (19.5-hectare) development of more than 300 homes, including single-family houses, courtyard homes, and flats, to appeal to a broad market.

the equation, the supply of competitive projects must be understood in terms of both quantity and quality.

The competitive market area encompasses projects that potential consumers would consider comparable to the proposed development. Usually, the competitive market area's boundaries are loosely drawn to include projects that might not quite fall within the geographic market area but might be comparable for other reasons such as similar house types, amenities, or neighborhood

LeMoyne Gardens is a public housing community that is being remade with a HOPE VI grant. The resulting mixed-income community takes on the character of the surrounding neighborhoods.

A good location can make a project work. Developers of the Residences at Alban Row in northwest Washington, D.C., capitalized on a desirable location, adding luxury duplexes to a historic apartment building. Average sale prices exceeded $1.3 million.

quality. An analyst usually excludes projects within the designated geographic market area that do not compete in terms of price, quality, or product type.

The projects identified as competitive provide the data the analyst uses to measure the competition and ultimately estimate absorption and capture rates and prices for the proposed project. Competitive analyses usually include only recent construction and proposed developments that will be marketed during the same period as the subject, because such projects are most suitable for assessing absorption trends. In locales with little or no recent competitive development, however, resales may have to be used as comparables.

Ideally, the market area consists of sufficient comparable properties to allow the survey to exclude any others. If the proposed project is, for example, a luxury townhouse project, only other luxury townhouse projects are included in the inventory. Similarly, a proposed mid-priced single-family project relies only on this type of project for its competitive survey. Projects that include multiple product types and a range of price points should find comparables for each product type being planned.

Demand Factors

Demographic trends and projections form the basis for determining the demand for housing. Four demographic factors are of primary importance in analyzing the market potential for a project: employment, popula-

tion, households, and income. Other demographic statistics also may be relevant for evaluating the project's potential. An area that appeals to families but contains few small households may not generate the appropriate number of households for condominium units. A neighborhood with an aging population might be a good area for a retirement development.

Employment. Employment usually drives population growth, other than for retirees and second-home buyers. If an area has an increasing employment base, new workers will likely take up residence in the local area. Demographers use projections of employment growth as one of the bases for determining population growth. For the residential market analyst, however, employment data serve as background, providing supporting evidence of market potential.

Because employment throughout a region determines population growth, the statistics gathered should be regional. Some of the employment statistics to examine include historical growth trends, wages, total employment projections, and comparisons of local unemployment figures with regional, state, and national unemployment rates. These figures give some indication of the area's general economic health. A survey of major employers in the area, including expansion plans, reductions in force, relocations, and any new employers entering the region, should be part of the employment background data. A major new industry moving into an area will most likely affect housing demand.

Population. Population and household projections provide the number and characteristics of current and future households and thus the forecast of demand for new housing in the market area. An analysis of in-migration and out-migration also offers insight into present and future demand for housing in the market area. Resale activity is also an indication of demand.

Increases in population estimates typically rely on two factors: more births than deaths in the market area, and more in-migrants than out-migrants in the market area. Although population growth has slowed nationally, many regions of the country are experiencing significant surges of population growth as a result of shifts in population from other parts of the United States and immigration. Population may also shift because of changes in lifestyle and cohort- or age-related reasons, such as retirement or changes in household structure from marriage or divorce.

A population trends analysis should begin with the population count from at least the last decennial census. Next, the analyst looks at the population for the current year, or sometimes the mid-point between the last census and the next, depending on the availability of data. More important are the population projections for the next ten to 20 years. Some larger city, county, or regional planning agencies release reliable demographic projections, or they may be ordered from a private data provider.

Households. Of greater significance in determining housing demand and market potential is an analysis of the number and type of households that contain a given population. Growing populations signal a corresponding, but not proportional, increase in the number of households. In many areas of the country in recent years, increases in the number of households have been more a function of decreasing household size and immigration than of natural population growth.

Since the 1950s, national trends have pointed to smaller households. In 1950, the average household contained 3.37 persons. By 2000, the average household contained only 2.62 persons.[3] Today's household mix includes a broad array of nontraditional family and nonfamily household formations: unmarried couples, single or divorced parents, childless couples, singles at all stages of life, unrelated roommates, and others. Each household type has specific housing needs, and all these nontraditional segments make for increased opportunities in niche housing markets. Studying specific local trends in household size and type can help determine the overall design and amenities of the project.

Income. An analysis of household incomes in the target market area indicates the region's economic vitality and provides valuable insight into the scope and magnitude of the available consuming power (not counting a household's equity and appreciation). This part of the analysis involves tracking historic changes and projections in median or average household income for the target market area, secondary market area, and region, including the rate at which incomes rise and the number of households in each income bracket. Such information is invaluable in determining price or rent ranges that a significant portion of the population can afford. Income alone, however, cannot be used as an indicator of housing affordability. Because the affordability of housing is tied to a household's wealth (that is, the household's income and assets), not just its income, it is not possible to construct precise predictors of affordability, but these estimates can be refined by considering the value of owner-occupied homes and the likely equity associated with those homes.

Data on employment, population, households, and income can be obtained from a local planning agency, office of economic development, or a firm that prepares customized demographic reports on specified study areas. The U.S. Census Bureau maintains a Web site[4] with the most recent census data, including details on population and housing characteristics. Data service companies offer computer-modeled demographic statistics, usually based on the most recent census figures. Local building permit data (with allowances for noncompletion and vacancy) can be a source for estimating recent household growth, because a dwelling unit represents a household. Margin of error for any of these data increases when market area boundaries differ from census tracts, particularly when market areas are small and, more important, when the census data are several years old. An area's demographics can change dramatically during the ten-year period between census years.

Real estate is different from other consumer products in that it cannot be moved to the consumer: the consumer must move to the product. Location is real estate's primary characteristic. Most projects must be custom tailored to the local market and cannot be mass produced for all markets. Because housing markets are so localized, the demographic data must be for the local area. National and even statewide trends are of minimal value in determining the market potential for a specific project.

Market Segmentation. In today's competitive environment, understanding the local market and targeting

Consumer research can help identify demand for new product types, like loft-style condominium units.

specific segments can help to set a development apart from the competition. After defining the market segment, the analyst must be careful not to overgeneralize with regard to the target customers' needs. Within age or income groups, markets can be quite diverse, and to reach potential consumers, their preferences must be understood. Techniques for learning about preferences include focus groups, surveys of local residents, and surveys of current home shoppers. Consumer research can yield a wealth of information on the potential residents of a new project.

Psychographics are an increasingly important part of market research. Trade area lifestyle profiles are available from private data vendors that compile characteristics such as education, occupation, the presence or absence of young children, hobbies, recreational pursuits, and community involvement—all factors that influence housing preferences. Analyzing lifestyle clusters can help determine consumer preferences for lot sizes, interior amenities, community rooms, exercise facilities, privacy, open space, and other aspects of the development.

Survey research can also play a vital role in real estate market analysis, providing direct information on homebuyers' perspectives. Using surveys and/or focus groups improves the accuracy of real estate market studies. Survey research can:

- Identify the strengths and weaknesses of individual project features or of the entire property.

Playa Vista successfully met pent-up housing demand in Los Angeles, California.

- Help to determine how a property is positioned in the marketplace and what its advantages or disadvantages are when compared with its competition.
- Gauge customers' interest in new concepts or features not previously seen in the market.
- Reveal which factors (location, price, amenities) are most important in customers' decision making.
- Suggest how much buyers will be willing to pay for a home in a proposed project.

Supply Factors

The current and projected new housing stock in the competitive market area forms the supply side of the market analysis equation. Supply factors include the total number of units by unit type, price level, and absorption. These factors enable analysts to translate data about employment, population, households, and income into estimates of potential demand for a specific new development. The present housing stock is determined through an extensive survey of comparable, currently selling projects in the competitive market area. The future housing market must be estimated by an analysis of the proposed projects, which can be identified through preliminary and final plan approvals and relevant rezonings.

Analyzing the Competition. In most housing market studies, the analysis of existing competitive projects is the study's most detailed portion. The existing project inventory provides a wealth of information about successful and not so successful projects at the current time in the specific market area. To identify competitive projects, there is no substitute for getting out and visiting each project in the competitive area and talking with a sales broker or other representative from each project. It is the only way to determine whether a project will be truly competitive with the planned development. Discussions with those already operating in the market are the most effective way to learn where buyers come from, who they are, what they like (or do not like) about current offerings, and what the most desirable products are for this specific group of consumers.

Market area averages and totals indicate how specific projects compare with the average and show overall pace of sales, absorption, units remaining on the market, average sale prices, and average square footage. Data also show which projects are selling better than the market average and allow analysis in terms of size and price per square foot. The market area's average prices and average absorption rate can help gauge how quickly competitive products are selling. A data table or a regression can reveal the gaps in the market that offer development opportunities and show where the market is saturated. Communities with the lowest average prices or the lowest average price per square foot should report the highest absorption rates, assuming all other factors are equal. If consumers are not responding consistently to value, then all things are *not* equal and other factors must be examined.

Historical sales data for projects selling over a three- to five-year period provide insights into the relative

Belle Creek in Denver, Colorado, provides a range of housing types, including affordable housing for first-time buyers.

strength of the area's market and short-term trends. To be most useful, trend data must be put into a larger context. Analysts must determine plausible reasons for abrupt rises or falls in absorption. For example, restrictive zoning could keep absorption levels low despite strong demand. Changes in the infrastructure or land uses can affect average sale prices and pace. Completion of a new highway opens up a region, making it more accessible and causing prices to rise. A regional or national economic recession triggers a decline in absorption and prices in most housing markets.

Nonquantifiable characteristics of competitive projects should be evaluated. Factors such as location, design, and marketing program must be considered. The quality of amenities or site advantages sometimes makes the difference between a top performer and a less successful project. These intangible factors can often be ascertained only through discussions with sales agents or surveys of potential homebuyers.

Gauging the Development Pipeline. Because it can take several years for a project to finally enter the market, the competitive analysis includes not only existing projects but also those in the development pipeline that will be in the marketing phase at the same time as the proposed property. They include projects requesting rezoning for residential use and those requesting site plan approval or other governmental approvals. They also include projects that did not require approvals or that have approvals but were put on hold. Such projects can be more daunting to track through local government agencies, often requiring that an analyst maintain contacts with local lenders, architects, developers, and others involved in the development process.

Once the proposed projects have been identified, relevant data, similar to those for existing projects where possible, should be provided: the project name, the developer or builder, location, number of units planned, and, if known, the type of units planned, estimates of prices, and completion dates. Some data may be un-

available for projects in the early planning stages. Occasionally, a developer may be unwilling to reveal plans for a proposed development. Some planned projects may never actually get off the ground. Although the inventory of proposed projects usually fails to identify some developments and includes others that never become reality, it does provide a good overall indication of future plans for local building activity.

Identifying Product Types and Niche Markets. Location, site, and market potential are the factors that determine the appropriate product to be developed. An urban locale demands a different type of residential development from a suburban one. The typically higher price of urban land requires higher densities. An infill site might have compatibility issues or architectural controls that dictate product type or style. If the site is part of a master-planned community, any number of specific limitations could determine the type of project to be developed.

The identified market segment should suggest a special type of development. If the target market is young, first-time buyers, a moderately priced community with few amenities and maximum square footage for the dollar might fit the bill. A growing population of empty nesters might suggest demand for luxury townhouses or condominiums. Amenities, features, and unit design and size should be determined through the market research.

Although it may be easy to continue developing and marketing housing products that have sold well in the past, it can be rewarding, both financially and in terms of serving a public need, to develop a new type of product. Comparable residential projects might not currently exist in the immediate market area, but if the demand analysis shows a need for something different, the developer should explore the possibilities. In an overbuilt market, thinking in terms of less standard types of development may lead to better opportunities but will require looking beyond the immediate market area for examples of successful comparable projects.

Island Cohousing at Martha's Vineyard, Massachusetts, includes 16 houses plus communal facilities. The residents developed the project, and eight of the units were subsidized, making possible a mixed-income community.

Any successful project results from a combination of careful analysis and instinct. But the more unconventional the concept, the less one can rely on hard data analysis to justify it. It becomes necessary to examine successful projects relevant to the proposed concept and to determine what their attraction is. What are the project's specifics that make it better than its competitors—development configurations, deluxe recreational facilities, or exceptional value? Community amenities are an important tool in marketing a project. Many residential developers are racing to come up with newer and better amenities than last year's model. In addition to the usual recreational facilities, some developments feature town centers, urban-style plans, concierge services, and planned social events for residents. Housing units compete with ever more lavish kitchens and baths, media centers, and high-end materials. In markets where prices are high, consumers expect deluxe features and amenities.

Sometimes a new product type can be appealing to a narrow but profitable market niche. A well-conceived infill development, mixed uses in a single structure (living above a store), or a co-housing community might find enough of a market niche to succeed.

Determining Capture and Absorption Rates. The market analysis provides a wealth of information for sound decision making. The most valuable product of market analysis is the number of units of a particular type that a submarket can absorb over a given period (which can be thought of as demand minus supply or

as the likely share of demand, taking into account anticipated competition).

Housing demand includes newly formed households, households moving into the market, and households moving within the market. Housing supply includes new and existing units. Analysts must estimate shares of total demand that major housing types will attract—single family versus multifamily and for-sale units versus rental units. These allocations should be based on historic trends in the local market and projected based on economic and demographic changes. As an area becomes more urbanized, a larger percentage of its households tend to reside in higher-density housing types.

Once these data are refined, analysts can identify all components of the basic equation for demand (total demand minus likely total absorption by competitive products equals residual demand). Total absorption is projected based on the absorption performance of existing communities as well as projections of the expected performance of proposed competitive communities, taking into account the potential impacts of the planned development. The residual demand yields the number of units that can be absorbed by additional projects, including the subject property.

Once residual demand is known, the analyst must determine what share of that demand the subject project is likely to capture. Determining this capture rate is highly subjective and must take into account all the project's advantages and disadvantages in relation to all other projects that will be on the market. Factors to consider include location, site, features, amenities, design appeal, and value. The capture rate should not be overestimated. Projects currently being marketed provide a reasonable model for the potential capture rate.

Developers frequently confuse current supply with demand, interpreting a product's strong sales pace as indicative of more demand for that same product—which often leads to overbuilding. It is more useful to examine current and future holes in the market than to concentrate on what has been selling well. The analyst should consider some specific issues:

- What geographic submarkets have the greatest need for new housing?
- What product type is needed most?
- What are the characteristics of households that have the greatest housing need?
- What types of features, amenities, and services do residents expect?

- What product types attract local consumers and why?

Although a market study is one of the first elements in the development process, market research does not end with a project's completion; it continues throughout the marketing phase, allowing the developer to fine-tune prices and products to fit the evolving market. None of the project feasibility components end with the beginning of construction or at the end of the project; they should be continually reviewed and updated to ensure the best outcome for current and future development activity.

Financial Feasibility

Formal or semiformal financial projections are at the core of the feasibility analysis and are the most commonly used tool for making the go/no-go decision and analyzing all the how, what, who, and where issues once

On the site of a former elementary school, St. Hugh Oaks is a 23-unit development of affordable homes designed by Duany Plater-Zyberk and developed by the city of Miami to perserve moderate-income neighborhoods with infill housing.

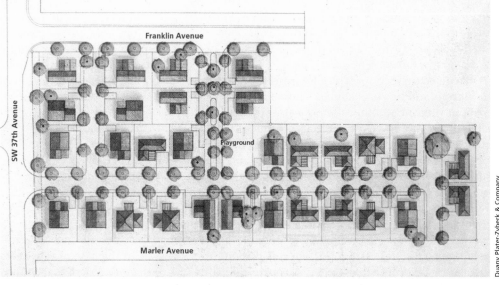

Duany Plater-Zyberk & Company

Keene's Pointe in Windermere, Florida, is a master-planned community developed by Castle & Cooke.

Castle & Cooke

the decision to go ahead has been made. The financial projection is crucial for lenders, who want assurances that the project will live up to its expectations. Financial projections are sometimes referred to as *pro forma* (from the Latin for "for the sake of form") projections or, colloquially, *pro formas*.

Financial projections typically consist of cash flow and profit and loss projections. These financial projections indicate whether the project is financially feasible, that is, whether the project's revenues will cover its costs, including financing, while also producing a profit and return on the equity for builders and other investors. The builder or developer can use the data generated to help decide whether the projected return is acceptable, given the risks inherent in the project, including market, physical, legal, political, design, implementation, and financial risks. The builder or developer can also use data to help decide whether the return on the proposed project is adequate compared with the expected returns from other projects planned or under development or from investments in other asset classes.

The financial projections are based on data from the following sources:

- Detailed market studies that document and quantify the demand for the residential units to be developed and the revenues that the units will generate;
- Estimates of the predevelopment, development, and marketing costs to produce the project and bring it to a successful conclusion and sellout; and
- An estimate of the time that will be required to develop and sell out the project; these estimates of absorption are also derived from the detailed market study.

No set industry standard exists for formatting or displaying cash flow or other projections. As long as it accounts for all projected revenues and costs, the format usually is dictated by the financing sources (debt and/or equity) for the project. As a general rule, experienced builders segregate the economics of their projects ("all equity" or "unleveraged" cash flow) from projected financial performance of the project after leveraging the equity with borrowed funds ("leveraged" cash flow).

The cash flow section of the financial projections shows the periodic and cumulative project cash flows over its life cycle. Stages in the life cycle of for-sale projects include:

- due diligence
- land acquisition
- predevelopment
- development
- unit sales.

In the case of rental apartment projects, another stage is added, that of the "holding" of the income-producing project, eventually followed by a sale of the project at the conclusion of the desired holding period. The projections must also include quantification and timing of how the project will be financed—whether by equity and/or debt—and quantification and timing of how debt will be repaid and equity will be paid back ("return of") and receive "returns on" the investment.

This approach is demonstrated in the sample financial analysis of a proposed project, "Vista del Oro," by Buildmore Homes. The builder has made the following key assumptions:

- Economic: No inflation or appreciation factors will be used in the analysis.
- Property: A 25-acre vacant suburban infill site
- Yield: 71 single-family detached houses on 7,000-square-foot lots
- Product: Four house plans:
  - Size: 1,200–2,100 square feet, with a weighted average of 1,694 square feet

- Sale price: $160,000–215,000, with a weighted average of $191,690, or $113.13 per square foot. In addition to the revenue from the base prices of homes, revenue will include:
  - Average lot premiums of $4,000 per house
  - Average (net) revenue of $1,000 per house for options
- Model site: Four models will be built.
- Direct construction ("brick and mortar") cost: $41.00–45.00 per square foot, with a weighted average of $42.51 per square foot
- Other direct construction costs:
  - Permits and fees, architectural fees, and school fees averaging $5,589 per house
  - Lot fencing and landscaping averaging $3,000 per house
  - Warranty and repair budget at 0.5 percent of sale price, or an average of $958 per house
- House construction cycle: 4 months
- Absorption rate: six houses per month
- Land cost: $1,400,000
  - Applicable three-month option payments of $15,000
  - The balance of $1,355,000 all due and payable at close of escrow with the seller. The builder will receive a "free and clear" title to the property at that time.
- Legal, planning, and predevelopment fees: $250,000
- Property taxes: 1.1 percent of land value plus improvements, increasing at a rate of 2 percent per year, applied against unsold inventory, payable twice a year
- Engineering and other consultant fees: $200,000 at the front end plus $1,000 per unit for field supervision and so on during construction
- Bonds, permits, and fees for the total project: $300,000 at the front end
- Off-site construction and infrastructure improvements:
  - Phase I: $500,000 plus 15 percent contingency at start of project
  - Phase II: $1,600,000 plus 15 percent contingency starting two months before the first foundation is poured
- Utility rebates: $1,000 per house following eight months from house closings as houses connect to public utilities
- Major landscaping: $250,000 spread over three months concurrent with first starts
- Park and recreation amenity: $200,000 over four months concurrent with construction of models
- Project overhead: 1 percent of revenues plus $100,000 per year
- Contingencies: 10 percent on costs other than land and land development
- Marketing and sales:
  - $100,000 of incremental model site costs for furnishings, of which $20,000 will be recovered upon last sale
  - Period marketing: $85,000 at the front end plus $12,000 per months for the duration of the sales period

- Commissions and closing costs at 3 percent of revenues
- Homeowners' association subsidy: $75 per house per month, charged to started houses until they close
- Project capital:
  - Debt: Acquisition, development, and construction debt:
    - The loan will fund eligible costs at a loan-to-cost ratio of 85 percent.
    - Interest rate: Prime (assumed at 4 percent) plus 2 percent
    - Loan fees: 1 percent at commitment plus 1 percent at loan draws plus 0.5 percent loan release fee at house closings
    - Loan repayment: 80 percent of sales proceeds
  - Equity: Co-investment joint venture[5]
    - Investors:
      - Contributing 85 percent of required equity beginning with land acquisition
      - Receiving
        - Accrued preferred and compounded return of 12 percent
        - 70 percent of distributable cash after repayment of debt, return of equity, and return on equity
    - Builder:
      - Ratios corresponding with those of the investors

The cash flow projections illustrate the outcome of these assumptions, detailing the timing and quantities of revenues and costs. The taxable income projections illustrate the same information timed to the recognition of costs and revenues based on generally accepted accounting principles.

Figure 2-2 illustrates the absorption and inventory projections and the sources and uses of funds. The absorption and inventory projections clearly lay out the sale, foundation starts, completions, and closings of all 71 homes. Note that the first homes are sold in September 2002 and followed by closing on these homes three months later in December 2002, when the project begins generating cash flow. Note that all 71 homes are shown to be absorbed in a one-year period, reflecting the absorption level estimated by the market analysis of six units per month, or 72 per year.

Figure 2-2 also illustrates the sources and uses of funds along with unleveraged cash flow. Note that prefinancing sources in this example are made up entirely of cash flow from home closings, including lot premium charges and options income. Cash flow begins in December with the first closings. The quantities and timing of the uses of the funds are illustrated per the key assumptions listed above. Unleveraged cash flow is illustrated on a monthly and cumulative basis.

Figure 2-3 illustrates the financed, or leveraged, cash flow for the Vista del Oro project. Note that the quantities and timing of the draws and the repayments for debt financing are all illustrated here. This figure also includes

figure 2-2

Absorption and Inventory Projections

	Life-of-Project Total	Jan/02	Feb/02	Mar/02	Apr/02	May/02	Jun/02	Jul/02	Aug/02	Sep/02	Oct/02
Absorption and Inventory Projections (Number of Units)											
Sales	71	–	–	–	–	–	–	–	–	5	4
Cumulative Sales		–	–	–	–	–	–	–	–	5	9
Foundation Starts	71	–	–	–	–	–	4	–	–	5	4
Cumulative Foundation Starts		–	–	–	–	–	4	4	4	9	13
Completions	71	–	–	–	–	–	–	4	–	–	–
Cumulative Completions		–	–	–	–	–	–	4	4	4	4
Closings	71	–	–	–	–	–	–	–	–	–	–
Cumulative Closings		–	–	–	–	–	–	–	–	–	–
Projected End-of-Period Backlog and Work in Process											
Backlog											
Sold and Started		–	–	–	–	–	–	–	–	5	9
Sold and Not Started		–	–	–	–	–	–	–	–	–	–
Total Backlog		–	–	–	–	–	–	–	–	5	9
Work in Process											
Under Construction		–	–	–	–	–	4	–	–	5	9
Complete and Unclosed		–	–	–	–	–	–	4	4	4	4
Total Work in Process		–	–	–	–	–	4	4	4	9	13
Sources of Funds ($000)											
Home Closings—Base Price	13,610	–	–	–	–	–	–	–	–	–	–
Lot Premiums	284	–	–	–	–	–	–	–	–	–	–
Options Income (Net)	71	–	–	–	–	–	–	–	–	–	–
Total Prefinancing Sources	13,965	–	–	–	–	–	–	–	–	–	–
Uses of Funds ($000)											
Land Costs											
Land Option Payments	45	15	15	15	–	–	–	–	–	–	–
Land Acquisition Cost	1,355	–	–	1,355	–	–	–	–	–	–	–
Legal, Planning, and Predevelopment	250	–	63	63	63	63	–	–	–	–	–
Property and Special District Taxes	46	–	–	–	12	–	–	–	–	–	–
Land Development Costs											
Engineering and Consultants	271	–	–	50	50	54	50	–	5	4	4
Bonds, Permits, and Fees	300	–	–	300	–	–	–	–	–	–	–
Off–site and On-site Infrastructure, Phase I	575	–	–	192	192	192	–	–	–	–	–
Off–site and On-site Infrastructure, Phase II	1,840	–	–	–	368	368	368	368	368	–	–
(–) Utility Rebates	(71)	–	–	–	–	–	–	–	–	–	–
Common Area Costs ($000)											
Landscaping	250	–	–	–	–	–	–	–	–	83	83
Park/Recreation Area Facilities	200	–	–	–	–	–	50	50	50	50	–
Construction Costs	5,086	–	–	–	–	–	143	143	–	90	161
Other Construction Costs	610	–	–	–	–	–	22	12	–	28	22
Warranty/Repair Costs	68	–	–	–	–	–	–	–	–	–	–

Nov/02	Dec/02	Jan/03	Feb/03	Mar/03	Apr/03	May/03	Jun/03	Jul/03	Aug/03	Sep/03	Oct/03	Nov/03	Dec/03
4	4	5	7	7	9	9	7	6	4	–	–	–	–
13	17	22	29	36	45	54	61	67	71	71	71	71	71
4	4	5	7	7	9	9	7	6	–	–	–	–	–
17	21	26	33	40	49	58	65	71	71	71	71	71	71
–	5	4	4	4	5	7	7	9	9	7	6	–	–
4	9	13	17	21	26	33	40	49	58	65	71	71	71
–	5	4	4	4	5	7	7	9	9	7	6	4	–
–	5	9	13	17	22	29	36	45	54	61	67	71	71
13	12	13	16	19	23	25	25	22	17	10	4	–	–
–	–	–	–	–	–	–	–	–	–	–	–	–	–
13	12	13	16	19	23	25	25	22	17	10	4	–	–
13	12	13	16	19	23	25	25	22	13	6	–	–	–
4	4	4	4	4	4	4	4	4	4	4	4	–	–
17	16	17	20	23	27	29	29	26	17	10	4	–	–
–	958	767	767	767	958	1,342	1,342	1,725	1,725	1,342	1,150	767	–
–	20	16	16	16	20	28	28	36	36	28	24	16	–
–	5	4	4	4	5	7	7	9	9	7	6	4	–
–	983	787	787	787	983	1,377	1,377	1,770	1,770	1,377	1,180	787	–
–	–	–	–	–	–	–	–	–	–	–	–	–	–
–	–	–	–	–	–	–	–	–	–	–	–	–	–
–	–	–	–	–	–	–	–	–	–	–	–	–	–
–	20	–	–	–	15	–	–	–	–	–	–	–	–
4	5	7	7	9	9	7	6	–	–	–	–	–	–
–	–	–	–	–	–	–	–	–	–	–	–	–	–
–	–	–	–	–	–	–	–	–	–	–	–	–	–
–	–	–	–	–	–	–	–	–	(5)	(4)	(4)	(4)	(5)
83	–	–	–	–	–	–	–	–	–	–	–	–	–
–	–	–	–	–	–	–	–	–	–	–	–	–	–
233	304	304	358	412	501	573	573	555	394	233	107	–	–
22	37	40	51	51	65	71	60	61	27	21	18	–	–
–	5	4	4	4	5	7	7	9	9	7	6	4	–

continued

figure 2-2

Absorption and Inventory Projections *continued*

	Life-of-Project Total	Jan/02	Feb/02	Mar/02	Apr/02	May/02	Jun/02	Jul/02	Aug/02	Sep/02	Oct/02
Overhead											
G&A Overhead	323	–	15	15	15	15	15	15	15	15	15
Marketing and Sales											
Model Site Cost	100	–	–	–	–	–	–	100	–	–	–
(–) Recoverable Model Site Costs	(20)	–	–	–	–	–	–	–	–	–	–
Period Marketing	229	–	–	–	–	–	–	–	–	97	12
Sales Commissions, Closing Costs, and Buyer's Incentives	419	–	–	–	–	–	–	–	–	–	–
Homeowners Association Subsidy	20	–	–	–	–	–	0	0	0	1	1
Contingencies	696	–	–	–	–	–	22	31	5	35	28
Total Prefinancing Uses	12,592	15	92	1,989	699	691	670	719	443	402	327
Prefinancing (Unleveraged) Cash Flow ($000)	1,373	(15)	(92)	(1,989)	(699)	(691)	(670)	(719)	(443)	(402)	(327)
Cumulative Prefinancing Cash Flow ($000)		(15)	(107)	(2,096)	(2,795)	(3,486)	(4,156)	(4,875)	(5,318)	(5,720)	(6,046)
Peak Negative Cash Flow	(6,452)										
Payback (Months)	21										
Net Present Value @ 20% (from First Spending Period)	($48)										
Internal Rate of Return	19%										
Nominal Unleveraged Profit Margin	10%										

Nov/02	Dec/02	Jan/03	Feb/03	Mar/03	Apr/03	May/03	Jun/03	Jul/03	Aug/03	Sep/03	Oct/03	Nov/03	Dec/03
15	15	15	15	15	15	15	15	15	15	15	15	15	–
–	–	–	–	–	–	–	–	–	–	–	–	–	–
–	–	–	–	–	–	–	–	–	(20)	–	–	–	–
12	12	12	12	12	12	12	12	12	12	–	–	–	–
–	30	24	24	24	30	41	41	53	53	41	35	24	–
1	1	1	2	2	2	2	2	2	1	1	0	–	–
35	39	39	45	50	62	71	70	69	48	30	17	3	–
406	467	445	517	578	715	799	786	775	533	344	194	41	(5)
(406)	516	341	270	208	268	578	591	995	1,237	1,033	986	746	5
(6,452)	(5,936)	(5,594)	(5,324)	(5,116)	(4,847)	(4,269)	(3,678)	(2,683)	(1,446)	(413)	573	1,319	1,324

figure 2-3

Cash Flow and Taxable Income Projections

	Life-of-Project Total	Jan/02	Feb/02	Mar/02	Apr/02	May/02	Jun/02	Jul/02	Aug/02	Sep/02	Oct/02
Financed (Leveraged) Cash Flow											
Recap: Absorption											
Home Closings (Units)	71	–	–	–	–	–	–	–	–	–	–
Lot Closings	–	–	–	–	–	–	–	–	–	–	–
Recap: Prefinancing Cash Flow ($000)	1,373	(15)	(92)	(1,989)	(699)	(691)	(670)	(719)	(443)	(402)	(327)
(+) Draws (Excluding Interest Reserve and Fees)	9,843	–	–	165	699	691	670	719	443	402	327
(–) Cash Interest	(4)	–	–	–	–	–	–	–	–	–	–
(–) Loan Release Fees	–	–	–	–	–	–	–	–	–	–	–
(–) Repayments	(10,335)	–	–	–	–	–	–	–	–	–	–
Cash Flow after Construction Financing	878	(15)	(92)	(1,824)	–	–	–	–	–	–	–
Cumulative		(15)	(107)	(1,931)	(1,931)	(1,931)	(1,931)	(1,931)	(1,931)	(1,931)	(1,931)
Financed (Leveraged) Cash Flow	878	(15)	(92)	(1,824)	–	–	–	–	–	–	–
Cumulative Pretax Equity Cash Flow ($000)		(15)	(107)	(1,931)	(1,931)	(1,931)	(1,931)	(1,931)	(1,931)	(1,931)	(1,931)
Peak Negative Cash Flow	(1,931)										
Payback (Months)	21										
Net Present Value @ 30% (from First Spending Period)	$54										
Internal Rate of Return	34%										
Investment Multiplier	1.5 : 1										
Debt Financing Memos: Loan Balances ($000)											
Acquisition, Development, and Construction Debt Financing											
Beginning Loan Balance		–	–	–	271	978	1,681	2,366	3,104	3,567	3,991
(+) Loan Draws	9,843	–	–	165	699	691	670	719	443	402	327
(+) Loan Fees—Front End	104	–	–	104	–	–	–	–	–	–	–
(+) Loan Fees—At Loan Draws	98	–	–	2	7	7	7	7	4	4	3
(+) Funded Interest Reserve	289	–	–	–	1	5	8	12	16	18	20
(–) Loan Repayments	(10,335)	–	–	–	–	–	–	–	–	–	–
Ending Loan Balance	–	–	–	271	978	1,681	2,366	3,104	3,567	3,991	4,341
Pretax Profit and Loss (Project) ($000)											
Memo											
Home Closings	71	–	–	–	–	–	–	–	–	–	–
Revenues											
Home Closings—Base Price	13,610	–	–	–	–	–	–	–	–	–	–
Lot Premiums	284	–	–	–	–	–	–	–	–	–	–
Options Income (Net)	71	–	–	–	–	–	–	–	–	–	–
Gross Revenues	13,965	–	–	–	–	–	–	–	–	–	–

Nov/02	Dec/02	Jan/03	Feb/03	Mar/03	Apr/03	May/03	Jun/03	Jul/03	Aug/03	Sep/03	Oct/03	Nov/03	Dec/03
–	5	4	4	4	5	7	7	9	9	7	6	4	–
–	–	–	–	–	–	–	–	–	–	–	–	–	–
(406)	516	341	270	208	268	578	591	995	1,237	1,033	986	746	5
406	438	422	493	555	686	758	744	722	505	–	–	–	–
–	–	–	–	–	–	–	–	–	–	–	(4)	–	–
–	–	–	–	–	–	–	–	–	–	–	–	–	–
–	(787)	(629)	(629)	(629)	(787)	(1,101)	(1,101)	(1,416)	(1,416)	(1,101)	(736)	–	–
–	167	134	134	134	167	234	234	301	326	(68)	246	746	5
(1,931)	(1,764)	(1,630)	(1,496)	(1,362)	(1,195)	(961)	(727)	(426)	(100)	(168)	78	824	829
–	167	134	134	134	167	234	234	301	326	(68)	246	746	5
(1,931)	(1,764)	(1,630)	(1,496)	(1,362)	(1,195)	(961)	(727)	(426)	(100)	(168)	78	824	829
4,341	4,772	4,451	4,270	4,160	4,112	4,038	3,722	3,391	2,721	1,829	736	–	–
406	438	422	493	555	686	758	744	722	505	–	–	–	–
–	–	–	–	–	–	–	–	–	–	–	–	–	–
4	4	4	5	6	7	8	7	7	5	–	–	–	–
22	24	22	21	21	21	20	19	17	14	9	–	–	–
–	(787)	(629)	(629)	(629)	(787)	(1,101)	(1,101)	(1,416)	(1,416)	(1,101)	(736)	–	–
4,772	4,451	4,270	4,160	4,112	4,038	3,722	3,391	2,721	1,829	736	–	–	–
–	5	4	4	4	5	7	7	9	9	7	6	4	–
–	958	767	767	767	958	1,342	1,342	1,725	1,725	1,342	1,150	767	–
–	20	16	16	16	20	28	28	36	36	28	24	16	–
–	5	4	4	4	5	7	7	9	9	7	6	4	–
–	983	787	787	787	983	1,377	1,377	1,770	1,770	1,377	1,180	787	–

continued

figure 2-3
Cash Flow and Taxable Income Projections *continued*

	Life-of-Project Total	Jan/02	Feb/02	Mar/02	Apr/02	May/02	Jun/02	Jul/02	Aug/02	Sep/02	Oct/02
Costs and Expenses ($000)											
Capitalized Costs (by RSV)											
Land Costs	1,400	–	–	–	–	–	–	–	–	–	–
Land Carry and Predevelopment	296	–	–	–	–	–	–	–	–	–	–
Land Development Costs, Permits, and Fees	2,915	–	–	–	–	–	–	–	–	–	–
Common Area Costs	450		–	–	–	–	–	–	–	–	–
Finished Lot Cost	5,061	–	–	–	–	–	–	–	–	–	–
Construction Costs	5,764	–	–	–	–	–	–	–	–	–	–
Finance Costs	495	–	–	–	–	–	–	–	–	–	–
Marketing and Sales	519	–	–	–	–	–	–	–	–	–	–
Contingencies	696	–	–	–	–	–	22	31	5	35	28
Contribution to Profit and Overhead	1,429	–	–	–	–	–	(22)	(31)	(5)	(35)	(28)
Period Expenses											
Expensed Overhead and Marketing	552	–	15	15	15	15	15	15	15	112	27
Net Profit (Loss) before Taxes	878	–	(15)	(15)	(15)	(15)	(36)	(45)	(20)	(147)	(55)
Profit Margin	6%										

Nov/02	Dec/02	Jan/03	Feb/03	Mar/03	Apr/03	May/03	Jun/03	Jul/03	Aug/03	Sep/03	Oct/03	Nov/03	Dec/03
–	99	79	79	79	99	138	138	177	177	138	118	79	–
–	21	17	17	17	21	29	29	38	38	29	25	17	–
–	205	164	164	164	205	287	287	370	370	287	246	164	–
–	32	25	25	25	32	44	44	57	57	44	38	25	–
–	356	285	285	285	356	499	499	642	642	499	428	285	–
–	406	325	325	325	406	568	568	731	731	568	487	325	–
–	35	28	28	28	35	49	49	63	63	49	42	28	–
–	37	29	29	29	37	51	51	66	66	51	44	29	–
35	39	39	45	50	62	71	70	69	48	30	17	3	–
(35)	111	81	75	69	88	139	140	200	222	179	163	117	–
27	27	27	27	27	27	27	27	27	27	15	15	15	–
(62)	84	55	48	43	62	112	113	174	195	165	148	102	–

figure 2-4
Investment Cash Flows

	Life-of-Project Total	Jan/02	Feb/02	Mar/02	Apr/02	May/02	Jun/02	Jul/02	Aug/02	Sep/02	Oct/02
Recap: Leveraged Pretax Equity Cash Flow ($000)	878	(15)	(92)	(1,824)	–	–	–	–	–	–	–
Investor(s) Cash Flow Summary											
(+) Equity Co-Investment @ 85%	(1,699)	–	–	(1,641)	–	–	–	–	–	–	–
(+) Priority Return on Equity @ 12%	261	–	–	–	–	–	–	–	–	–	–
(+) Priority Return of Equity	1,699	–	–	–	–	–	–	–	–	–	–
(+) Profit Distribution @ 70%	399	–	–	–	–	–	–	–	–	–	–
Investor(s) Cash Flow	659	–	–	(1,641)	–	–	–	–	–	–	–
Cumulative Investor(s) Cash Flow ($000)		–	–	(1,641)	(1,641)	(1,641)	(1,641)	(1,641)	(1,641)	(1,641)	(1,641)
Cumulative Cash-on-Cash Return	39%	0%	0%	0%	0%	0%	0%	0%	0%	0%	0%
Annualized Cash-on-Cash Return	21%	0%	0%	0%	0%	0%	0%	0%	0%	0%	0%
Peak Negative Cash Flow ($000)	(1,641)										
Payback (Months)	19										
Net Present Value @ 30% (from First Spending Period)	($7)										
Investor Internal Rate of Return	29%										
Investment Multiplier	1.4 : 1										
Development Company Cash Flow Summary											
(+) Equity Co-Investment @ 15%	(300)	(15)	(92)	(182)	–	–	–	–	–	–	–
(+) Priority Return on Equity @ 12%	47	–	–	–	–	–	–	–	–	–	–
(+) Priority Return of Equity	300	–	–	–	–	–	–	–	–	–	–
(+) Profit Distribution @ 30%	171	–	–	–	–	–	–	–	–	–	–
Development Company Cash Flow ($000)	218	(15)	(92)	(182)	–	–	–	–	–	–	–
Cumulative Development Company Cash Flow ($000)		(15)	(107)	(290)	(290)	(290)	(290)	(290)	(290)	(290)	(290)
Cumulative Cash-on-Cash Return	73%	0%	0%	0%	0%	0%	0%	0%	0%	0%	0%
Annualized Cash-on-Cash Return	67%	0%	0%	0%	0%	0%	0%	0%	0%	0%	0%
Peak Negative Cash Flow ($000)	(290)										

Nov/02	Dec/02	Jan/03	Feb/03	Mar/03	Apr/03	May/03	Jun/03	Jul/03	Aug/03	Sep/03	Oct/03	Nov/03	Dec/03
–	167	134	134	134	167	234	234	301	326	(68)	246	746	5
–	–	–	–	–	–	–	–	–	–	(58)	–	–	–
–	142	28	16	15	14	12	10	9	6	–	7	2	–
–	–	86	98	99	129	187	189	247	271	–	202	193	–
–	–	–	–	–	–	–	–	–	–	–	–	361	4
–	142	114	114	114	142	199	199	256	277	(58)	209	555	4
(1,641)	(1,499)	(1,385)	(1,272)	(1,158)	(1,016)	(817)	(618)	(362)	(85)	(143)	66	621	625
0%	0%	0%	0%	0%	0%	0%	0%	0%	0%	0%	4%	37%	37%
0%	0%	0%	0%	0%	0%	0%	0%	0%	0%	0%	2%	20%	20%

Nov/02	Dec/02	Jan/03	Feb/03	Mar/03	Apr/03	May/03	Jun/03	Jul/03	Aug/03	Sep/03	Oct/03	Nov/03	Dec/03
–	–	–	–	–	–	–	–	–	–	(10)	–	–	–
–	25	6	3	3	2	2	2	2	1	–	1	0	–
–	–	14	17	17	23	33	33	44	48	–	36	35	–
–	–	–	–	–	–	–	–	–	–	–	–	155	2
–	25	20	20	20	25	35	35	45	49	(10)	37	190	2
(290)	(265)	(244)	(224)	(204)	(179)	(144)	(109)	(64)	(15)	(25)	12	202	204
0%	0%	0%	0%	0%	0%	0%	0%	0%	0%	0%	4%	67%	68%
0%	0%	0%	0%	0%	0%	0%	0%	0%	0%	0%	57%	87%	84%

figure 2-5
Project Summary

Project Data		Debt Financing		LTV	LTC
Total Homes	71				
Absorption Rate (Units)	1.4/week, 6/month, 72/year				
Project Life	1 year, 10 months				
Average Home Base Sale Price	$191,700				
Average Home Size	1,694 square feet				
Average Production Tract Size (Lots)	6				
Projected Revenues ($000)					
Home Sales	13,610	**AD&C Debt ($000)**			
Lot Premiums and Option Revenues	355	Funds Advanced	9,843		
		Funded Fees and Interest Reserve	492		
Total Revenues	13,965	Total Construction Debt Facility	10,335	74%	83%
		Peak Loan Balance	4,772		
Projected Accounting Returns ($000)					
Profit Margin	878				
Profit Margin	6%				
Payback/Breakeven	1 year, 9 months				
Economic Feasibility of Project ($000)					
Projected Unleveraged Cash Flow					
Net Cash Flow	1,373				
Net Present Value @ 20%	(48)				
Internal Rate of Return	19%	**Investor(s) Pretax Summary ($000)**			
Peak Cash Out	6,452	Equity Investment	(1,699)		
		Peak Equity Requirement	(1,641)		
		Priority Return on Equity @ 12%	261		
Projected Leveraged Cash Flow ($000)		Profit Participation @ 70%	399		
Net Cash Flow	878	Net Cash Flow	659		
Net Present Value @ 30%	54				
Internal Rate of Return	34%	Payback/Breakeven	1 year, 7 months		
Peak Cash Out	1,931	Annualized Cash-on-Cash Return	21%		
		Net Present Value @ 30%	(7)		
		Internal Rate of Return	29%		

Summary for Total Project	Total	2002	2003	2004	2005	2006	2007	2008	2009	2010
Units Closed	71	5	66	–	–	–	–	–	–	–
Lots Sold	–									–
Unleveraged Cash Flow ($000)	1,373	(5,936)	7,260	49	–	–	–	–	–	–
Leveraged Cash Flow ($000)	878	(1,764)	2,592	49	–	–	–	–	–	–
Income ($000)	1,574	(145)	1,718	–	–	–	–	–	–	–
Debt Balances ($000)										
Purchase Money Debt		–	–	–	–	–	–	–	–	–
Acquisition and Development Debt		–	–	–	–	–	–	–	–	–
Construction Debt		4,451	–	–	–	–	–	–	–	–
Line–of–Credit Debt		–	–	–	–	–	–	–	–	–
Total Debt Balances		$4,451	–	–	–	–	–	–	–	–

pretax profit and loss projections. The profit and loss section shows the project's total revenues, costs, and profits. Together with the cash flow projections, it helps the builder to decide whether the project's potential profits meet minimum criteria.

Figure 2-4 illustrates the investment cash flows, highlighting the quantities and timing of the return on equity and the return of equity for the investors and the development company. It also illustrates the cash-on-cash return, which is the rate of return on an investment measured by the cash returned to the investor based on the investor's cash investment without regard to income tax savings or the use of borrowed funds.

Figure 2-5 is the project summary, which projects the financial performance of the Vista del Oro project. The projected performance in this case study as measured by the several indices used in the summary is within a normative range. As a practical matter, no consensus exists among builders and financing sources as to what constitutes an "acceptable return" or an "acceptable profit." Individuals and entities tend to establish their own rules by using their own scales of perceived risk-adjusted returns and profits.

Although tax considerations may play a role in the financial analysis, they should not be a major factor. Since the 1980s, the decline in tax rates, smaller deductions for depreciation, and restricted ability to shelter income with real estate losses in large measure have made it more practical to base business decisions on underlying economic factors than on tax considerations. If a project makes sense only after consideration of tax consequences, in most cases it should be viewed as too risky and should not be undertaken.

Further, tax laws and regulations change frequently, and the results of these changes are anything but predictable. Tax consequences to the participants depend to a large degree on their own or their organization's tax circumstances, and it is not reasonable to provide generic tax consequences of a project.

Notes

1. http://www.epa.gov/swerosps/bf/glossary.htm#brow.
2. G. Vincent Barrett and John P. Blair, *How to Conduct and Analyze Real Estate Market Feasibility Studies* (New York: Van Nostrand Reinhold, 1982), pp. 28–30.
3. www.census.gov.
4. Ibid.
5. This deal illustrates one possible equity structure out of an infinite number of possibilities.

3. Financing Acquisition, Development, and Construction

The viability, profitability, and ultimate success of a residential development project come down to a matter of money. And—depending on the scope and nature of the project—it may require a substantial sum of money. A critical component of any residential project, as well as an important factor in the long-term prospects of a residential development entity, is the identification and cultivation of the necessary financial resources. Where do developers get the capital for each new development project? Although a very broad range of equity and debt financing is available to the residential development industry, the best sources of financing vary from project to project.

Risk and Reward

The balance between risk and reward plays a pivotal role in any investment analysis, regardless of asset class, but nowhere is the impact of this balance felt more acutely than in residential development. Any number of variables contribute to a project's risk profile:

- the project's type, size, and location;
- regulatory, environmental, and political obstacles that must be overcome during the predevelopment phase;

Acqua Vista, San Diego, California.

- the accuracy with which competitive supply and future demand for the product have been forecast;
- the amount of financial risk assumed by the developer, as well as its relative financial strength and development experience.

That risk profile in turn dictates the terms on which financing for the project will be made available. The greater the risk that the investment will not provide a competitive return or, worse yet, may result in the loss of all or part of the funds invested, the greater the return on investment necessary to justify that assumption of risk, benchmarked against returns available from less risky investment opportunities.

Although some variables may be within the developer's direct or indirect control, others are inherent in the real estate cycle and the process of real estate development. A successful search for financing for a particular project depends on the developer's ability to identify and assess the magnitude of each risk associated with the project and to project accurately the potential rewards. Tolerance for risk and expectations for returns vary widely among financing sources. In the end, financing a residential development project is a matter of matching the risks and rewards with the investment expectations of each potential financing source.

This chapter provides a framework for understanding the financing process, serving as a guide to the sources and means of obtaining funds. Throughout the chapter,

Tuxedo Park in Chicago is an urban infill development of 56 townhouses and stacked flats.

the focus is on the effects of risk and reward on the financing process. The chapter starts with a discussion of the various types and sources of financing available and then addresses the variables that may affect the availability and cost of financing. It concludes with a discussion of the process and analysis required to procure financing for residential development.

Types of Financing

Project financing comes in two forms—equity and debt. Equity is money invested in a project, while debt is money loaned to a project or to an entity undertaking the project. Financing may also be a hybrid form that combines debt and equity.

Equity versus Debt

Equity represents and carries with it all the attributes of ownership, including sharing in the project's profits and losses. An equity investor generally shares in all the risks and rewards of a project, not just those risks and rewards associated with the contribution of funds to help make the project happen. The legal rights of an equity investor to any return on invested capital and distributions of assets, up to and including the return of that capital investment in the event of dissolution of the enterprise, are inferior to those of the project's lenders.

Senior debt lenders typically are legally entitled to receive all accrued but unpaid interest plus the return, in full, of the principal amount of the loan; whatever remains after accounting for the project's expenses, debts, and liabilities is shared among the equity investors in accordance with their agreement regarding such distributions. As a consequence of the relative priorities among debt and equity, however (and wholly consistent with the concept of risk-based rewards), equity investors have the potential to reap substantial rewards if the project meets or exceeds expectations. In other words, equity

investors assume the greatest risk of loss but also enjoy the greatest potential for reward. For example, an equity investor may be legally liable (if guarantees are involved) for amounts that well exceed the initial investment in the project, subjecting that investor's unrelated assets to the claims of others, whereas a debtor's exposure to liability is generally limited to the amount of the financing commitment (that is, the initial cash investment plus any legal obligation—such as in the form of a promissory note—to make additional loans).

These rules are not immutable, however; a seemingly infinite array of hybrid arrangements blurs and transforms the distinction between debt and equity. Unconventional forms of financing available from the federal and some state governments, made available for "qualifying" residential development projects, behave like neither equity nor debt; some are in the form of grants, for which no return or even repayment is expected. Others are low- or no-interest loans repayable on very favorable terms.

Other forms of junior capital that blur clear distinctions between debt and equity include mezzanine debt and preferred equity. These alternatives generally fit, behave, and are structured to provide a higher return (but greater risk) than senior debt but a lower return than pure equity.

Even with conventional sources of project financing, numerous examples of investment types reflect some characteristics of equity and other characteristics of debt. For example, a limited partnership involves an equity investor whose exposure to loss is limited to cash invested in the limited partnership plus any legal commitments to make additional contributions to capital. Although the limited partner's priority to either a return on that equity investment or the return of amounts invested is still *inferior* to that of all debtors of the limited partnership, the limited partner, unlike a general partner, does not suffer exposure to liabilities beyond invested capital (subject to some legally recognized exceptions that generally go to whether the "limited partner" was a limited partner in fact and not merely in name).

Similarly, a limited partner may be promised a prioritized return on invested capital, with the amount of that return agreed to in advance (for example, 10 percent) rather than expressed simply as a "proportionate share" of the distributable cash available to all equity investors. Such a guaranteed return may, however, have to be accrued and carried forward for the future benefit of a "preferred limited partner" to the extent that other priorities for the allocation of cash from operations favor current expenses and debt service. In other words, although the priorities among equity investors may be structured in a particular way, they cannot be elevated above the priorities of the project's lenders, absent an express agreement by a debtor to subordinate its priority to the interests of an equity investor.

In sum, the key characteristic of equity is that no promise exists that equity investors will receive a return on their investment or that they will even recoup that investment. Because of this risk, equity investors generally expect higher returns than lenders.

The need to secure an equity investment may be more a function of the nature of the development or the structure of the transaction than a matter of preference. Often, the developer does not have the cash available to make up any difference between the total development cost of the project and the aggregate amount of debt the project is able to support. It is important to distinguish, in this regard, between a developer's net worth (which would include the current value of equity interests in other ventures) and liquid assets that can be converted quickly to cash or pledged to borrowed funds that will not also require a security interest in the underlying development project being financed. Alternatively, the decision to seek equity investors may reflect a strategic business decision to share the risk of each development project with others, which may have the benefit of allowing the developer to pursue more than one project at a time (the goal of diversification, itself, being a potentially effective strategy to minimize development risk).

Whatever the reason, the absence of equity investors means that the developer alone bears all the risk associated with the project and that the total amount of and terms for debt that may be placed on the project could be constrained. Naturally, the downside of bringing equity investors into the project is that it limits the total potential return to be realized by the developer, because returns must be shared among all equity investors. If the developer is unable to bring any equity to the transaction then, the question will inevitably arise as to what the developer *is* bringing to the table (and what it is *worth*).

If the developer's equity investment is simply "bringing the deal" to the table, then the developer needs to quantify the value of the opportunity being presented before inviting other investors to the project. The developer needs to balance the need for outside capital—in terms of both limiting the developer's risk *and* presenting potential lenders with an amount of project equity critical to the project's feasibility—with the consequences of sharing the potential profits with equity investors on terms sufficient to attract the investors' interest in the project. Moreover, depending on the amount and importance of the outside equity to the feasibility of the project, the introduction of outside capital may complicate the decision-making process unless equity investors are willing to rely exclusively on the unfettered judgment of the developer on the security and return potential of their investment. The participation of a truly "silent partner," unlike a general partner, however, is rare. Consequently, *participation* and *control* are also key issues to be worked out when inviting the involvement of equity investors.

Debt

Debt is money loaned directly to the project, to an entity created to undertake the project, or to the developer, whether a sole proprietorship or a legal entity such as a corporation or a limited liability company. Debt is evi-

Park West in Charlotte, North Carolina, is a 30-unit town-house project developed by the Boulevard Company.

The Boulevard Company

Orenco Station in suburban Portland, Oregon, takes advantage of a location along a commuter rail line.

PacTrust

Since 1981, the Macauley Companies has developed dozens of new home communities throughout the Atlanta region. Shown here is the Reserve in Marietta, Georgia.

Macauley Companies/Bill Massey

HarBer Meadows in Springdale, Arkansas, is a 425-acre (170-hectare) master-planned community that includes a mix of housing types and significant open space.

SWA Group

denced by the borrower's legal promise to pay the lender (a promissory note, for example), which promise may be secured by the underlying real estate assets (land and improvements), by other assets of the borrower, or both, and may be guaranteed by one or more individuals or legal entities.

Absent an express relinquishment by the lender of its superior right to a return and repayment, debt has a priority claim over equity investments. Thus, a lender is entitled to receive payment of both the stated annual yield and the return of the full amount borrowed, in accordance with the terms of the debt instrument, before any payments or distributions are made to equity investors. This hierarchy of priorities also extends to debtors. For example, the lender under a *first deed of trust* has a superior right to yield and repayment over a subsequent lender, to whom a *second deed of trust* is granted—hence the terms "senior" and "junior" or mezzanine debt capital. It simply refers to the priority of repayment generated from the project's cash flows.

In contrast to an equity investment, the lender's exposure to liability is limited to the amount of the loaned funds plus the expected return, as directed by the interest rate or coupon. Accordingly, the risks assumed by a debtor are limited to when, and whether, principal and interest required under the debt instrument will be received and, in the event of a default by the borrower in its obligations, the extent to which the borrower will be made whole upon the exercise of its express remedies as well as those recognized under law. Essentially, the lender's risks are mitigated by the right to proceed against the debtor, any guarantors of the obligation, and/or the collateral pledged by the debtor to secure repayment (the "security"). Because the risks associated with debt financing of a residential project are both finite and easily quantifiable, the return on a loan is generally a function of 1) the priority of the loan relative to any other debts incurred in connection with the project, 2) the likelihood that interest and principal will be paid on time and in accordance with the terms of the debt instrument, and 3) the creditworthiness of the borrower and any guarantors of the obligation to pay the lender.

Types of Debt. Debt can be full recourse, limited recourse, or nonrecourse; it can also be secured or unsecured. A secured loan such as a mortgage is backed by a specific pledge of assets. The assets securing a loan may be the entire project or a specified group of assets. A secured loan may also be full recourse, limited recourse, or nonrecourse. Secured debt has a claim against the pledged assets that is superior to those of the equity investors as well as to the claims of unsecured creditors. An unsecured loan does not have specified assets pledged as collateral to secure repayment. Because the likelihood of repayment is greater with a secured loan than an unsecured loan, the former represents a lower risk to the lender and, as a consequence, should also reflect more favorable terms for the borrower.

A full-recourse obligation is one the borrower is legally obligated to pay, regardless of whether the value of the security is sufficient to satisfy the obligation. In the event of default on a full-recourse loan, the lender can look to the project's assets for repayment as well as to the borrower's personal assets. Depending on the terms and conditions of the debt instrument, the lender may not need to proceed first against the collateral pledge for repayment (the security) and may instead proceed first against the borrower. It is generally accepted within the lending community that one of the principal benefits of a full-recourse loan is that it keeps the borrower motivated to avoid any defaults under the debt instrument.

A full-recourse loan also provides the lender with a means of recovering the entire outstanding amount of the loan plus accrued but unpaid interest and all costs of collection, regardless of whether the value of the security is sufficient, in and of itself. This benefit is particularly important to lenders of projects to be constructed —whether that lender provided a construction loan or an acquisition and development loan secured by the land to facilitate the purchase of land and completion of the predevelopment activities—because, at the time an "event of default" occurs as defined under the debt instrument, substantial additional funds may need to be expended before the value of the collateral is sufficient to make the lender whole. Although such risks can be mitigated through other means dictated under the debt instrument, such as the requirement that the borrower provide some sort of completion guaranty backed by a bond or letter of credit, it may not be in the best interests of the lender to have to pursue the completion of the improvements to have the debt instrument paid in accordance with its terms. The ability to proceed directly and immediately against a full-recourse borrower for the full amount of the obligation may expedite the resolution of the event of default. Moreover, the mere possibility that the lender will not hesitate to exercise its right to proceed against the borrower on a full-recourse debt is generally sufficient to prevent an event of default from occurring. Like most aspects of the relationship between lender and borrower, what is in the lender's best interest is often not in the borrower's best interest. Borrowers therefore prefer nonrecourse debt for their projects.

In a nonrecourse loan, the lender agrees to look exclusively to specifically identified assets to secure repayment of all obligations, including the outstanding principal balance of the loan plus any accrued but unpaid interest and any costs of collection. Depending on the type, amount, and timing of the loan, the assets pledged to secure the debt instrument may not represent a priority claim on all of the assets of the real estate development project. Upon the occurrence of an event of default on a nonrecourse loan, the lender's sole legal remedy is to proceed against such of the project's assets as have been pledged as security for the obligation. The lender's recovery is limited to the value it is able to secure in the disposition of the pledged assets, after netting out the costs of its collection and enforcement efforts. If the net amount realized by the nonrecourse lender is less that the aggregate amount of the borrower's outstanding obligation, the borrower is *not* responsible for the difference.

This does not necessarily mean that the nonrecourse lender does not have any influence over the borrower's efforts to prevent the lender from proceeding against the collateral in the case of default. For example, if the borrower has a substantial equity investment in the pledged collateral, preserving that equity investment may provide sufficient motivation to the borrower to prevent an event of default or to cure those that occur. Alternatively, if by proceeding against pledged collateral a nonrecourse lender causes an inferior, recourse lender to automatically suffer an event of default under its debt instrument with the borrower, the borrower's liability to the second lender is determined by whether any value remains, after disposition of the pledged collateral, to satisfy the second lender. Consequently, the borrower needs to be aware of the status of each of the project's lenders and their respective rights and priorities.

Under a limited-recourse loan, the lender agrees to cap the borrower's exposure to liability to a specified dollar amount or percentage. A limited-recourse lender may also agree to look to the assets of the borrower only *after* the lender has enforced its rights against, and realized the net value of, the pledged assets securing the loan, and then only to the extent of the difference between the outstanding obligation and the net value of the security realized by the lender. Under certain scenarios, a lender may view a limited-recourse loan as sufficient to adequately protect its interest in timely debt service and full repayment at loan maturity. More important, the lender should consider carefully the practical effect of recourse financing in appropriately securing the lender's position as a creditor and refrain from imposing requirements that ultimately may constrain the developer's ability to make adjustments necessary to ensure timely performance of all obligations attendant to the transaction. For example, an individual developer or general partner in a development entity who is personally liable

on a full-recourse loan, regardless of whether the value of the pledged development assets exceed by a substantial margin the principal amount of the outstanding loan, may nonetheless be unable to secure additional funds to contribute to the transaction, because the amount of the full-recourse liability does not conform with other lenders' underwriting criteria, precluding a personal unsecured loan.

Interest Rates. The terms of most loans used to finance residential development projects are determined by the cost of funds to the lender and the lender's evaluation of its risk of nonpayment, based on the credit quality of the debt (determined largely by the extent to which the debt is secured and the creditworthiness of the borrower and all guarantors, if any). Certain terms, however—in particular the annual rate of interest or annual percentage rate (APR) and the amount of any upfront fees or points—are determined by the risk that the economic value of the loan in the lender's hands will decline if prevailing interest rates on similar loans rise during the term of the loan.

Because of the construction component of residential finance (shorter terms, variable funding depending on the progress of completion), interest rates typically "float." In a variable-rate loan, the amount of interest payable on the outstanding balance is determined by reference to a published index tied to short-term interest rates, plus a number of basis points representing the lender's margin (100 basis points equals 1 percent), the amount of which typically remains fixed over the life of the loan. Fluctuations in the indexed interest rate result in changes in the rate of interest payable on the variable-rate instrument at any given point in time; the terms of the variable-rate instrument determine the timing and amount of rate resets. A variety of short-term interest rate indices are used to set the rates of variable-rate debt, varying by lender, for example, *The Wall Street Journal Prime Rate* (a consensus established by *The Wall Street Journal* among large banks of the interest rate at which

The Meadows in Castle Rock, Colorado, emphasizes neighborhood scale and promotes water conservation.

they lend money to their most favored customers); the one-month LIBOR (London interbank offered rate), a wholesale lending rate among international banking institutions; and the one-year Treasury constant maturity (the average yield, adjusted to a one-year equivalent term, of a variety of Treasury securities as determined by the Federal Reserve Board, which is used as an index for approximately half of all adjustable-rate home mortgages).

Like that for a variable-rate loan, the interest rate charged on a fixed-rate loan is established by adding the lender's margin to a specified index or base rate used by that lender. The index often used is the rate of U.S. Treasury notes having a term the same length as that of the loan. Or a specified corporate bond index such as Moody's AAA bond index might be used. Unlike a variable-rate loan, the rate charged on a fixed-rate loan does not change during the term of the loan, absent an event of default.

Loan Terms. The term of a loan also depends on the nature of the funds being borrowed and the types of financing contemplated to take the project from conception to completion. For example, development financing, including acquisition and development loans, is intended to be fully paid when the project is completed and lot, unit, or housing sales (closings or settlements) typically are 60 to 85 percent complete. Such financing is often accomplished through the mechanism of an "accelerated release price" at a rate greater than 100 percent, which is the rate at which the full principal gets repaid when all the lots are sold. An average release price is 125 percent or more. These loans generally have a term of 18 to 36 months, depending on the scope and nature of the project. Similarly, a construction loan is, by definition, intended to be outstanding for a finite period of time, that is, the amount of time required to begin and complete construction, secure the necessary occupancy approvals, and sell (and close) the completed units. Not all lenders are in the business of making all the types of loans that may be necessary to provide the debt financing component of a residential development project. The number of lenders in the market to make predevelopment loans is a fraction of the number of lenders in the business of providing construction financing.

Although the amount of the loan, the amortization schedule determining debt service requirements, the type (fixed rate versus variable rate) and amount of interest, and the security (recourse versus nonrecourse and secured versus unsecured) are critical considerations, myriad other more technical terms and conditions in every loan instrument merit careful review and negotiation with the lender—for example, what constitutes an event of default, the lender's obligation to provide the borrower with a formal notice of default and an opportunity to cure defaults, the borrower's obligation to maintain certain financial covenants during the term of the loan (for example, preserving the loan-to-value ratio required at the time the loan was made and maintaining a specified debt service coverage ratio), and preserving the lender's legal priority to proceed against pledged

Budget-Saving Housing in Ohio

The Mills of Carthage is a development of manufactured and modular homes built on a reclaimed brownfield in Cincinnati, Ohio. It incorporates single-story and two-story bungalow and craftsman-style houses that are compatible with the surrounding neighborhood.

When Cincinnati decided to revitalize a reclaimed industrial area with new housing, city leaders called in local homebuilders. The homebuilders told the city, however, that they could not construct homes that would meet the affordable housing guidelines the city had imposed for the inner-city project. The solution was manufactured and modular homes, 50 of which make up the Mills of Carthage, the first new housing development in the Carthage area of Cincinnati in 40 years. The homes are mostly one- and two-story bungalow-style structures that include front porches and back-alley garages on 40-foot-wide (12-meter-wide) lots.

The project is the result of five years of activism by Carthage residents, who convinced city leaders to spend more than $6 million to relocate industrial businesses out of the working-class neighborhood and to move in new homeowners. Rising costs prompted the Cincinnati city council to defer the project in 2000; in January 2001, the council killed a proposal to spend another $6 million to build traditional site-built homes. Instead, the council wanted to hire a private developer to pay costs or consider turning the site into a park. In April 2002, the council unanimously approved the sale of the Mills of Carthage property for $1.00 to local residential developer Potterhill Homes, which has agreed to take on the project at its own expense. ■

Source: Bruce A. Savage, vice president, public affairs, the Manufactured Housing Institute, Arlington, Virginia.

Parque Vina Cousino in Santiago, Chile, was developed following enactment of a law that required all projects to go through an environmental approval process. All infrastructure is privately financed.

collateral. Under the loan agreement, the violation of any term or condition may constitute an event of default, triggering a variety of remedies from the lender up to and including "calling the loan" (requiring immediate payment in full of all accrued, unpaid interest plus the full outstanding balance).

Some terms and conditions benefit the borrower, such as the borrower's right to prepay the outstanding balance of the loan without penalty, providing the developer with greater flexibility in addressing—and possibly benefiting from—refinancing opportunities during the life of the project. Variable-rate debt instruments generally can be prepaid at any time without restriction or penalties, because the lender does not suffer any adverse economic consequences from such prepayment.

Hybrid Financing

Some financing components may possess some attributes of both equity and debt and may be referred to as *hybrid financing*. For example, an equity investment may provide for a guaranteed return (a defining characteristic of debt) yet still be in an inferior position to all debt on the project and subject to the current payment of all operating expenses, the funding of any required reserves, and current payment of debt service on all outstanding loans. Such a preferred or priority return may be offered to an equity investor in exchange for a lesser return on that equity investment than would otherwise be expected in the absence of a guaranteed return. An *equity participation loan* is another example of hybrid financing. It has all the traditional features of conventional debt; however, in exchange for more favorable loan terms, the lender receives a specified interest in distributions of profits generated from the project, which otherwise would be reserved exclusively for equity investors. The existence and variety of hybrid financing demonstrates the need to match up the return requirements and security expectations of a broad range of potential investors (of both equity and debt) with the financing needs of the project and the financing capacity of the developer.

The use of debt as part of the financing structure for a development project is commonly referred to as *leverage*. The greater the percentage of debt to the total development costs, the greater the leverage. The amount of leverage available to a project depends, at least in part, on the underwriting criteria of the prospective lenders. For example, if a lender is not willing to lend more than 80 percent of the total value of the project (referred to as an 80 percent loan-to-value ratio) and the terms of the loan prohibit the developer from adding any subordinate debt on the project, then the amount of leverage available to the project is controlled by the lender's terms, not the developer's preferences. For planning purposes, however, the developer should endeavor to determine, at the outset, how much leverage would be most beneficial to the project and to the developer's investment objectives. In general, the greater the percentage of equity invested in a project, the lower the risk and the lower the potential return, because equity generally demands a greater overall return on investment than does debt. Conversely, as the amount of debt as a percentage of the overall financing for a project increases, the greater the risk to the project and the greater the potential return to the developers. The issue of how much leverage to use cannot be taken up in a vacuum, however, as it depends on a number of factors, many of which are addressed above.

Positive leverage occurs when the use of borrowed money results in an enhanced return to the equity investors. Figure 3-1 illustrates the effect of positive leverage when the property is sold. In this example, the return to the developers increases dramatically as the level of leverage increases. In fact, assuming all other parameters of the project are the same, the more debt used, the greater the return. The problem is that although greater leverage increases the potential return, it also increases the risk of failure.

The example in Figure 3-2 illustrates the negative effects that leverage can have. In this example, leverage combined with a modest reduction in sale prices results in what would have been a profitable project's becoming a money-losing proposition. This scenario is generally referred to as *negative leverage.* In addition to a reduction in sale price, negative leverage can result from cost overruns, delays that result in increased interest costs, and increasing interest rates. Any item that results in more expenses, a reduction in gross profits, or a longer period to achieve revenues or sales (thereby lowering the net present value of the gross profits) can lead to negative leverage. Using leverage makes a project much more sensitive to any failure to achieve its time schedule or projections.

Leverage can have a similar effect, positive and negative, during the operation of the property. In these examples, it is easy to see that appropriate leverage can greatly enhance the return on the equity invested in the property. When the property fails to meet its cash flow projections, however, leverage can greatly reduce the return on the investor's equity. Leverage makes a project much more sensitive to the risk of failure, for if the property's cash flow is insufficient to pay the mandatory debt service, the property may be lost through foreclosure.

No simple answer exists as to how much leverage to use in any particular project. It is a matter of balancing the availability and cost of equity with the availability and cost of debt. Frequently, the answer is more a matter of necessity than of preference. Because leverage increases the risk to both the equity investor and the lender, both frequently impose limits on the amount of debt they will allow to be used to finance a development project.

Home Mortgage Financing

Some developers arrange financing for individual buyers through a takeout commitment from the permanent lender, usually a commercial bank or savings bank.[1] Some large development or home building companies have mortgage financing subsidiaries that provide financing directly to buyers. Alternatively, buyers can arrange financing on their own, which they would do if they could obtain financing on more favorable terms than through the developer or builder.

During periods when interest rates are high, developers may offer "buydown" programs as a means of qualifying borrowers for mortgage loans. The developer pays a lender a fee to buy down the interest rate, that is, to charge a below-market interest rate in the initial years of a loan. The buyer's monthly interest payments are lower

figure 3-1

Example of Positive Leverage in Financing a Development

Developer's Equity	$5,000,000	
Loan	5,000,000	at 10% interest
Total Investment	$10,000,000	
Gross Profit	$1,500,000	15% return on $10 million investment
Interest Expense	−500,000	
Net Profit	$1,000,000	10% return on $10 million investment
Developer's Return	$1,000,000	20% return on $5 million investment

figure 3-2

Example of Negative Leverage in Financing a Development

Developer's Equity	$5,000,000	
Loan	5,000,000	at 10% interest
Total Investment	$10,000,000	
Gross Profit	$250,000	2.5% return on $10 million investment
Interest Expense	−500,000	
Net Loss	($250,000)	2.5% loss on $10 million investment
Developer's Loss	($250,000)	5% loss on $5 million investment

The Bluffs at Pinehurst consists of 54 luxury townhouses. The development overlooks Pinehurst Country Club in Denver, Colorado.

at first, step up over the initial three to five years of the loan, then level off for the remainder of the loan term. The buydown enables the buyer to qualify for a larger loan and a higher-priced home than with conventional financing. Some or all of the developer's cost of buying down the loan may be added to the price of the home, or the cost may come out of the developer's profit. As the secondary market for home mortgages has become more liquid and efficient, such buydown programs have become less commonplace, because mortgage companies and banks now offer a sweeping array of mortgage programs.

Ownership Structures

A number of different ownership structures can be used for residential development: direct ownership (sole proprietorship), a general or limited partnership, a C corporation or subchapter S corporation, or a limited liability company (LLC).

Direct Ownership
Direct ownership is the simplest ownership structure. In fact, it is not really an ownership structure at all, because no separate legal ownership entity is created. In direct ownership, an individual developer owns the project in her or his name, owns 100 percent of the total equity, and controls the entire project outright. If the project is successful, the individual realizes the full benefit of 100 percent of the return. The individual developer also assumes 100 percent of the responsibility for any and all losses or liabilities arising out of the project, which may exceed not only the value of the developer's equity investment in the project but also the entire value of the project itself. Even if debt incurred against the project is all nonrecourse to the individual developer, the developer still is exposed to personal liability for any other claims that may arise out of or in connection with the

project. All tax characteristics and attributes of the development project must be reported on the developer's personal income tax returns and may shelter or add to the developer's personal tax liability.

Unless the developer has sufficient equity to commit to the project and/or a substantial net worth sufficient to satisfy the underwriting requirements of prospective lenders on the project, securing debt financing may be problematic or impossible. The need for additional equity and the desire to share the project's risk with others generally lead an individual developer to seek equity investors. In that case, alternative forms of ownership need to be determined or the arrangement may be treated as a de facto general partnership under state law and federal income tax law. The developer has to carefully consider the ownership strategy most beneficial to all parties. Moreover, even if an individual developer has the asset liquidity and net worth sufficient to permit direct ownership of real estate assets, other considerations—including the desirability of protecting other nonproject assets from the claims of creditors and others arising out of the subject project—should play a role in the decision about the best ownership structure for the project.

Partnerships
A partnership is a creature of state law—an unincorporated legal entity formed by two or more persons or entities to pursue a common business undertaking. No limits are placed on the number of partners in a partnership; the partners may be individuals, corporations, or other partnerships. The existence of a general partnership may be implied under law or by the actions of individuals acting as partners. A limited partnership, on the other hand, is a statutory convention that is expressly created through an agreement of limited partnership. A written legal agreement among general partners is not a prerequisite to demonstrating the existence of a de facto partnership. In the absence of an agreement governing their partnership, however, state statutes and common

law govern the rights and responsibilities of general partners. The rights and obligations of general partners, their activities on behalf of the partnership, and the partnership's relationships with other individuals and entities are generally governed by a formal partnership agreement, which is preferable to relying on after-the-fact determinations under common law or state statutes of the relationships of general partners based on interpretations of their conduct.

A principal reason for adopting a partnership structure is that losses, as well as profits, are distributed to all partners. A partnership, although a legal entity for business purposes, is not a taxable entity and does not pay taxes. A partnership is a conduit, a "pass-through" entity. All tax characteristics and attributes, including but not limited to profits, losses, and depreciation, are distributed among all the partners, who are responsible for reporting all such tax attributes on their individual tax returns. In the absence of a written partnership agreement to the contrary, general partners in a de facto partnership are presumed to be equal partners, receiving their ratable share of all tax attributes. Legally, a partner who "participates materially" in the business of the partnership may apply the distributed tax attributes, including losses and tax credits, to offset other income and income tax liability. Although partners are free to arrange the affairs of the partnership as well as their respective rights and obligations vis-à-vis each other as they see fit through the creation of the partnership agreement, the Internal

Revenue Code, Treasury regulations, and IRS administrative rulings interpreting the tax code and federal cases interpreting the law address what is allowable in terms of partnership allocations of income, gain, losses, and tax credits.

Structuring a real estate partnership to maximize the tax benefits and minimize the tax consequences for each partner can be a complex undertaking. Such determinations are best left to experienced tax attorneys and certified public accountants well versed with the myriad IRS regulations. Despite these complexities, the partnership's status as a pass-through entity for tax purposes and the ability, within the constraints of federal tax law, to make special allocations among partners make the partnership structure one of the most flexible forms of ownership.

Partnerships can be structured as general partnerships or limited partnerships. The distinguishing characteristics of the two include the formality (or lack thereof) required to create each partnership, the number of classes of partners, who is responsible for decision making (and who is proscribed from decision making), and the extent of personal liability assumed by each partner. In the absence of a formal written partnership agreement, general partners share equally in the partnership's management and in all profits and losses. Most important, general partners are fully liable for the partnership's debts, obligations, and liabilities. By contrast, a limited partnership must be formally created through the filing of

The design for Champs Elysees Terrace in Shenzhen, China, was inspired by the tree-lined boulevards of Paris.

RTKL/Tim Griffith

Mixed-use projects with residential components require extra care.

Well-positioned mixed-use developments that respond to demographics and create a sense of place and synergy among uses usually succeed, but with the higher development costs associated with mixed-use development, avoiding some common pitfalls is critical.

Unclear Business Plan
- Pitfall—Escalating capital costs driven by architecture, structure, and mechanical and electrical systems.
- How to Avoid—Design according to the project's business priorities. Understanding the cost tradeoffs among different components and where to allocate them helps the development team establish clear priorities and make reasoned, timely decisions. A project business plan—articulated early and to the entire design and delivery team so it can design and build within the plan's parameters—can save thousands, if not millions, in design fees and much more in construction costs.

Poor Timing and Inflexibility
- Pitfall—Missed market opportunities as a result of bad timing and/or a lack of flexibility. Mixed-use developments are long-lead-time projects by nature. As such, plans should include flexibility. These projects can take five years to complete, and the world will change a lot over that time.
- How to Avoid—Plan for flexibility during design and construction phasing. A phasing plan that lets each component be introduced according to market demand and/or whose buildings can be built differently depending on market opportunities allows projects to be built out at a steady rate, with strong occupancy at each milestone.

The Fortress Effect
- Pitfall—A lack of street presence fails to draw people into a project. Some developers have focused too much on creating synergy among the various uses at the expense of street identity, resulting in formidable, uninviting, and unfriendly facades. As a result, many mixed-use projects from the past 20 to 30 years are undergoing renovations at the street level.
- How to Avoid—Pedestrians and drivers need to see and access the various uses as they walk or drive by. When a project has the right tenant mix, the tenants themselves are the draw, so they need to be given the street visibility and access necessary to succeed. Residential and office components demand access that is more private and secure. Having distinct entrances for these components is more effective and attractive to residents and office tenants in the long run.

A team of three developers, Crosland Development, Pappas Properties, and Forest City, brought the required expertise to Birkdale Village in Huntersville, North Carolina. The project mixes single-family houses, apartments, offices, and specialty retail space in a town center configuration.

Developers need to plan a tenant mix that creates synergy among the uses rather than rely solely on architecture to do it. Individual uses need to work individually; the street—or the entire neighborhood—can be the connection.

Missing the Market
- Pitfall—A surprising number of projects are built with little more than a best guess of what end users need and want. This lack of understanding compromises the ability to draw the best traffic, attract the best tenants, and negotiate the best deals.
- How to Avoid—Do market research, and do it early. Spending tens of thousands of dollars to find out the needs and aspirations of a project's end users is a drop in the bucket compared with what will be lost if the market is missed.

Focus groups of prospective users and retail/entertainment tenants, and surveys of office brokers regarding a six-acre (2.4-hectare) development in Bellevue, Washington, for example, uncovered concerns about parking access and street visibility. Preferences included additional restaurants, extended-hour establishments, and fewer fashion retailers. User groups also suggested paradoxical qualities such as an iconic sense of place with convenient access to retailers, interaction and refuge, civic formality with a casual style, and European timelessness with a woodsy northwestern sensibility.

Ownership Tangles

- Pitfall—Mixed-use development often involves multiple owners whose priorities regarding design, governance, and changes in use or ownership can conflict both during development and after the project is complete. Reactive resolutions are time-consuming, costly, and potentially fatal to the project.
- How to Avoid—Be proactive; get early counsel. A project may have only one owner, but it needs to be structured for many. Organize project and legal documentation for future changes based on each land use. It may require extra effort upfront, but it is ultimately the most cost-effective strategy. Shared physical boundaries and various common building systems and amenities make different components dependent on one another for completion. In the long run, it usually is better to create distinct systems wherever possible to avoid reliance on another owner.

  If owners choose to act as individuals rather than forming a joint venture, it is critical to establish strong agreements with creditors that allow continued funds disbursement if any party defaults.

Incomplete Capital Plan

- Pitfall—Interim financing runs out, stalling or killing the project because there is no bridge to long-term financing.
- How to Avoid—Be careful not to get so wrapped up in the front end of a project that no one is dealing with the long-term capital plan. Each project component needs to have a viable business plan—one that should connect to the capital plan. Assemble the project to respond to the financial market. Be conservative.

Untapped Available Public/Private Benefits

- Pitfall—Not using all funding sources available from the city or county.
- How to Avoid—Mixed-use projects are difficult, and the margins are tight. They are also very attractive to cities. Seeing the social and economic value of good mixed-use projects, most jurisdictions are getting more aggressive about finding ways to make them happen. Do the homework and take advantage of available land deals, funding sources, and other incentive programs offered by local governments.

Following the Letter of the Law

- Pitfall—Missed opportunities and higher costs as a result of land use restrictions, height limits, and other jurisdictional requirements.
- How to Avoid—Understand the intent of the law and find out the special agendas of the county or city to negotiate what the project needs. Early identification of municipal and county needs (transit center parking, open space, housing, government offices, assembly space, and so on) can lead to fruitful negotiations and concessions when there is a way to accommodate needs through the project. Also consider performance-based design, which, by allowing building systems to meet the intent rather than the letter of the law, can result in significant cost savings. Initiating discussion early in the development process can make allies out of potential opponents to achieving one's vision.

Parking

- Pitfall—Insufficient or inappropriate parking allocations (separate versus shared, location, security, sight lines) can severely compromise a project and one's ability to attract tenants and customers. Projects with major residential components need to pay even more attention to parking, security, and appropriate access.
- How to Avoid—Realize that parking is not an area to neglect or to try to get away with less. Even if parking floors are the last to be painted, they should be among the first to be thoroughly thought out. Know when parking can be shared and when it needs to be secured. Having direct access to each parking zone is ideal. Some developers look to maximize the early cash influx that parking can achieve.

No Exit Strategy

- Pitfall—Getting saddled with property one no longer wants or is not equipped to manage. The owner may not have the expertise or funding necessary to make the most of each use, resulting in dark buildings and diminishing revenue streams.
- How to Avoid—As part of the business plan, establish an exit strategy. Many mixed-use developments begin as a single-owner proposition. Although upfront capital costs can be gained by letting uses share systems, owners need to consider the likelihood of selling off individual uses early on to help finance the project or later on to raise capital. Organize this complicated network of uses in a way that can be physically, financially, and legally unraveled and unloaded. ∎

Source: Tracy Funderburk, Insight Alliance, Bellevue, Washington.

a limited partnership agreement creating two classes of partners: general partners and limited partners. General partners have decision-making authority and are responsible for the partnership's day-to-day operations; they also assume legal liability for the partnership's debts, obligations, and liabilities. Limited partners do not participate actively in the endeavors of the limited partnership, and they are not liable for the partnership's debts or liabilities beyond the amount of their investment (which may comprise both contributed cash and legally binding promises to make additional but finite contributions to capital). Limited partners enjoy a limited level of control over the limited partnership, including the right to remove and replace the general partner(s) and to liquidate the limited partnership under specific circumstances.

Joint Ventures

A development project may be structured as a joint venture between two or more existing entities. Although similar in several respects to a partnership, a joint venture is not an ownership entity. In a joint venture, two or more entities agree to combine their expertise and resources to carry out a common business activity. The joint venture participants, who may be individuals, partnerships, corporations, or other legal entities, enter into a joint venture agreement that defines their respective roles in the joint venture as well as their rights and obligations. A joint venture is frequently used for development activities when the project is beyond the scope of

resources, capabilities, and/or risk tolerance of a single participant. For example, a landowner may be interested in developing a property but lacks the expertise or the cash necessary to hire the expertise to accomplish it. By seeking out a developer with the expertise and resources necessary to develop the property, the developer and the landowner might jointly undertake the development project through a joint venture; the landowner contributes the land, and the developer provides the expertise and possibly whatever additional equity and/or financial guarantees are necessary to secure the financing for the project. Both the landowner and the developer in this example need to agree at the outset about the relative worth of their respective contributions to the joint venture as a means for determining how they will share in the profits once the project is completed.

Many urban mixed-use projects are undertaken through joint ventures among developers with the requisite expertise to develop and market each specialized use in the larger project. Similarly, a suburban residential land developer may acquire a large tract of land, take it through master planning, sell developable residential lots to various merchant homebuilders and multifamily rental developers, but enter into a joint venture with a shopping center developer to provide the community retail amenity that makes the entire project work and improves the marketability of the residential component. Or a fee developer may enter into a joint venture with an institutional investor such as a large insurance com-

Orenco Station, developed by PacTrust, includes 1,800 housing units plus office, retail, and other commercial uses.

Developed by Taylor Woodrow, Steiner Ranch encompasses 4,600 acres (1,860 hectares) near Austin, Texas.

pany to take raw land through development, construction, and lease-up, with the developer's compensation under the joint venture agreement determined by the operating value of the property after rent stabilization. The common theme in each of these examples is that the parties do not intend to enter into the kind of long-term legal relationship that warrants the creation of a partnership, limited liability company, or other entity; the parties join together for a discrete period of time to achieve specific goals. Once the period is completed, there is no ongoing relationship related to the specific project.

Corporations

A corporation is a legal entity organized and maintained under state law. Corporations are recognized as taxable entities under the Internal Revenue Code. The specific federal tax treatment of a corporation depends on whether it is organized as a C corporation or a Subchapter S corporation under the federal tax code. Corporations are owned by their shareholders, governed by a board of directors (whose fiduciary duty is to maximize the corporation's value for the benefit of shareholders), and managed by its officers, commonly referred to as "management." In a closely held corporation, the shareholders, the board of directors, and officers may all be the same people, while in FORTUNE 500 corporations, there may be a policy imperative favoring an independent board of directors with very little management overlap. In those situations where millions of shares of stock are widely held by tens of thousands of shareholders, management's percentage of stock ownership is an important factor.

C Corporations. The C corporation—what most people think of when they hear the word "corporation"—is a creature of the Internal Revenue Code and not a function of state corporation statutes. Virtually all public companies (that is, corporations that trade stock on a public exchange) are C corporations, regardless of the state in which they are incorporated.

Shareholders in a C corporation are passive investors. Their control and influence over the day-to-day operations of the company are limited to electing the board of directors and voting on matters that require a vote of the shareholders. The day-to-day operations of all publicly traded corporations and many large privately held corporations are controlled by the company's management, which in turn reports to the board of directors.

A shareholder of a C corporation is not liable for any of the corporation's debts or liabilities; the shareholder's exposure to liability and risk of loss is limited to the value of the investment in the shares owned. A shareholder does not pay taxes based on her or his ratable share of the corporation's annual taxable income. Rather, shareholders are taxed on the aggregate value of any dividend distributions received as a result of the shares owned and must pay capital gains, if any, on the disposition of shares owned. Because C corporations are taxable entities under the Internal Revenue Code and for state tax purposes, and because a shareholder is separately taxed on the distribution of dividends paid out of the corporation's after-tax revenues, it is commonly stated that C corporations are subject to "double taxation." As a consequence of this aspect of C corporations and the fact that losses and credits are not passed through to shareholders, the use of C corporations for residential development is limited and is generally not suitable for single-purpose development entities. In fact, C corporations are perhaps best suited to those residential development activities that are capital intensive because of the opportunities that exchanges create for capital formation through the sale of publicly traded securities.

Subchapter S Corporations. A Subchapter S corporation combines features of a corporation and a partnership. The shareholders of a Subchapter S corporation are not individually liable for the corporation's liabilities or subject to double taxation. A Subchapter S corporation, limited to 75 shareholders, is not a taxable entity. It does not pay taxes on its earnings like a C corporation but instead passes its income and losses through to its shareholders. A Subchapter S corporation cannot make special allocations of income or losses like those made by a partnership, but it can pass through certain tax preference items to its shareholders. In many respects, the limited partnership and the more recently created limited liability company have replaced the Subchapter S corporation as the preferred pass-through entity for real estate transactions.

Limited Liability Company. An LLC is a legal entity very similar to a Subchapter S corporation. It is, however, a creature of state statute. An LLC offers investors limited liability, single taxation (at the "shareholder" level only), and the ability to be actively involved in management (thereby avoiding the negative impact of the passive activity loss rules under the Internal Revenue Code for investors seeking to shelter other income through real estate–related losses). Unlike a Subchapter S corporation, however, no limits are placed on the number of investors in an LLC.

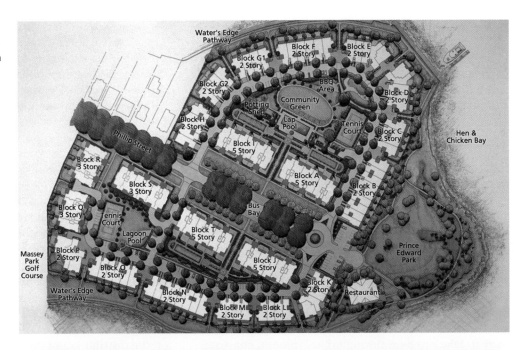

Cape Cabarita in Sydney, Australia, is a lifestyle resort community that was developed on an industrial brownfield.

Investors in an LLC are referred to as "members." Managers, who may be members, control the operations of the LLC. An LLC has no restrictions on a member's involvement in management. Generally, the members and managers of an LLC are not personally liable for the LLC's debts and obligations; their liability is limited to the amount of their investment. For tax purposes, an LLC is a pass-through entity. It passes all income and loss on to its members and thus avoids double taxation. Unlike a Subchapter S corporation, an LLC can make special allocations of income and loss. The LLC has generally taken the place of the Subchapter S corporation and to some extent has also supplanted the limited partnership as a pass-through ownership structure for residential development projects.

Choosing an Ownership Structure

Because the ownership structure defines the rights and relationships of the equity owners, choosing an ownership structure for a particular development project is determined by the nature and frequency of the underlying development activity and by the expected sources of equity. Anticipating the overall investment expectations of potential equity investors also helps to determine the appropriate ownership structure for the development project, because the ownership structure affects the manner and tax treatment of distributions from the entity and whether or not tax losses and credits may be passed along to equity investors.

Each ownership structure has characteristics that may or may not make it suitable for a particular residential development project. In selecting an ownership structure, the developer must consider:

- the amount and type of equity needed;
- the complexity and cost of creating and maintaining the status of the entity;

- the extent and frequency of the equity holders' involvement in the management of the project;
- the amount of the project's liabilities that equity holders are willing to assume;
- the equity holders' willingness and ability to increase or decrease their investment in the project;
- the tax ramifications to the entity and to equity investors; and
- the relative value and importance to equity investors of tax benefits generated by the project.

Selecting the most appropriate ownership structure should seek to balance the attributes of the various ownership structures with the project's needs and the equity investors' expectations and requirements. By offering a combination of relatively low formation and maintenance costs, pass-through tax benefits, and flexibility, the limited partnership, Subchapter S corporation, and limited liability company are well suited to single-purpose, residential development projects, particularly those requiring a limited number of equity investors. The complexities inherent in electing Subchapter S status under the Internal Revenue Code, however, make it a less desirable alternative to the LLC or limited partnership. Direct ownership, while certainly the easiest to form, does not provide any mechanism for raising equity, requires the individual developer to assume 100 percent of the project risk, and generally limits the prospects for debt financing. Publicly traded C corporations and real estate investment trusts (REITs), on the other hand, offer the best opportunities for large-scale capital formation, involve high-cost barriers to entry, and are expensive to maintain, limiting their applicability to only the most substantial development enterprises. Because of the nature of capital formation through exchanges, these ownership structures require a substantial amount of management experience and success to attract the amount of capital necessary to amortize the transaction costs attendant to the ownership structures.

Financial Analysis

Matching the risks and rewards of a residential development project with the expectations for returns and other investment criteria of a potential funding source is critical to securing the necessary project financing. Expecting equity investors and lenders to invest in a project with which they are neither familiar nor comfortable with the expectation that the developer will be able to educate these potential funding sources about the benefits of the project is an exercise in futility. Securing the necessary equity and debt investments is most likely when following the path of least resistance; an investment opportunity or type of ownership or investment structure with which the prospective investor or lender is not comfortable merely creates resistance. So long as other, more familiar investment opportunities are available to which that capital is allowed to flow, the nonconforming invest-

ment opportunity may never overcome the resistance it creates.

Once the developer has matched the project's financing needs with the investment objectives of prospective investors and underwriting criteria of potential lenders, the developer still must persuade all funding sources that the project is financially feasible. The developer demonstrates financial feasibility by quantifying the project's risks and rewards through a feasibility analysis.

Each prospective investor and lender will likely undertake its own analysis of the project, called *due diligence.* Due diligence consists of an evaluation of the developer and the project, including the financial information provided in the developer's feasibility analysis. Because of the preliminary nature of the developer's feasibility analysis, however, it must rely on a set of assumptions about the anticipated cost of the equity and debt financing components, predevelopment and hard and soft construction costs, the duration and cost of the entitlement pro-

High Desert is a 1,048-acre (425-hectare) master-planned community encompassing 1,650 residential units at the base of the Sandia Mountains in Albuquerque, New Mexico.

Croasdaile Farm in Durham, North Carolina, is a 1,050-acre (425-hectare) community comprising 2,030 homes, a village center, and a 6.5-acre (2.6-hectare) lake.

cess, the market demand for the residential units being developed, the rate of absorption for that demand, and the prices the units will command. In their examination of the developer's feasibility analysis, prospective equity investors and lenders assess the reasonableness of all assumptions underlying the developer's analysis and evaluate whether the financing structure as a whole is sound.

Ultimately, the decision to invest or lend money for a project is a subjective judgment based on a review of the feasibility study and the financial analysis. It is important to provide accurate and detailed information in the feasibility study and financial analysis so that potential investors or lenders can become as comfortable with the project as possible. The developer should anticipate the concerns of prospective investors and lenders and address them in advance as part of the feasibility analysis. The thoroughness and accuracy with which the financial information is presented and the integrity of the assumptions and supporting data on which the analysis is based should reflect well on the developer and the project. The developer should view this process as an opportunity to test the viability of the proposed project by allowing independent, objective financial experts to evaluate it; full disclosure yields the most productive results.

The assumptions underpinning the feasibility analysis have a dramatic impact on the projected returns from the project. If the assumptions are overly conservative, an accurate picture of the project's true potential is not portrayed. If the assumptions are too aggressive or not well grounded, the credibility of the developer may be jeopardized, or, worse yet, all parties may be misled into undertaking a financially disastrous project. Every effort should be made to develop reasonable assumptions, and the feasibility analysis should be constructed in a manner that allows each assumption to be tested and changed as necessary.

Equity Investors' Analyses

In addition to the feasibility analysis prepared by the developer, potential equity investors prepare their own analyses. These analyses focus on the investment's potential return and the foreseeable risks. The two most important studies for a potential equity investor are a *discounted cash flow analysis,* which measures the potential return, and a *sensitivity analysis,* which attempts to measure the risk of each variable (see Chapter 2 for an example of discounted cash flow).

Lenders' Analyses

In addition to the general feasibility analysis, all potential lenders conduct their own financial analyses. This analysis focuses on two key leverage calculations: the *loan-to-cost ratio* and the *loan-to-value ratio.* In making these calculations, the lender relies on the pro forma financial statements provided in the developer's feasibility analysis. Additionally, the lender focuses on the performance-related criteria of a project—the more subjectively measured evaluations such as the owner/developer's expe-

Living above the store has never been more popular. At Pier Village along the oceanfront at Long Branch, New Jersey, 420 residential units occupy upper floors, with shops and restaurants on the main level, all in a pedestrian-friendly village setting.

Applied Development Co.

China's explosive growth and strong economy are spurring much new development. Shown here is Chang Ying, a new community in Beijing.

The HOK Planning Group © 2004

rience developing comparable projects successfully; the ability to withstand cost overruns, slower absorption than expected, or other surprises; the surety of entitlement efforts (permitting, zoning, environmental issues, and so on); and the owner/developer's relationships and history with the vast array of stakeholders (equity investors, municipal officials, realtors, subcontractors, marketing firms, other builders/developers as potential lot purchasers).

Marketability must also be analyzed extensively. Some of this analysis is covered in the feasibility study, some is covered during appraisal, and some must be analyzed more subjectively. This evaluation is broad in range and scope. It includes lot sizes and prices relative to comparable projects, anticipated housing sizes, prices, and styles, neighborhood amenities, schools, accessibility to employment centers, buyers' anticipated sensitivities, and so on.

Loan to Value. The loan-to-value ratio is a baseline measure used by the lender to determine the maximum loan amount it is willing to extend to the proposed project. The loan-to-value ratio is calculated by dividing the loan amount by the property value:

Loan-to-Value Ratio = Loan Amount/Property Value.

The loan-to-value ratio is an expression of the amount of equity the lender needs to see in the project to be comfortable extending credit. All lenders have specified maximum loan-to-value ratios for various project types. The loan-to-value ratio is a measurement of default risk, both the likelihood of default and the expected loss in the event of default. The more equity invested in the project, the less likely that a failure to achieve pro forma financial results will lead to default under the loan agreement. And the more equity invested in the project, the less likely that a drop in value will result in the lender's failure to recoup its principal in the disposition of the property. To estimate the property value used in the cal-

The HOK Planning Group © 2004

culation of the loan-to-value ratio, the lender examines the cost of construction and the completed project's estimated market value.

In calculating market value, lenders tend to focus on three primary measurements. The first is loan to cost:

Loan Amount/Total Cost of Acquisition and Development.

For residential properties financed at the asset level (as opposed to the enterprise level) of the borrower, financing is generally arranged for land acquisition and development (horizontal construction) separately from home construction (vertical construction). Although not always the case, it is the typical case, as many subdivisions are financed phase by phase and several different homebuilders often take down the lots. The loan-to-cost ratio gives the lender a quick and relatively simple way to determine total project equity, which, as noted above, is a good proxy for determining risk.

The lender also evaluates the loan-to-value ratio from the perspective of "retail value." For a subdivision acquisition and development loan, it is determined as follows:

Loan Amount/(Average Anticipated Lot Price × Total Number of Lots).

This calculation gives the lender a sense of the loan risk versus the total gross value of lots financed, but it excludes considerations of absorption rate and the resulting net present value (or discounted value). Because it excludes the discounted valuation, loan to retail value is a more relevant tool when evaluating risk for smaller, shorter-term projects or those with complete lot takedowns (bulk lot purchases) contracted to occur immediately at the completion of horizontal development.

Loan to Discounted Value. The third and perhaps most important valuation tool is loan to discounted value. This formula essentially evaluates the loan amount in relation to the net present value of the completed project. Thus, it *discounts* the total gross revenue to current value based on the longevity or timing of receipt of those revenues over the anticipated life of the project. This value is after project costs (again, including the timing of the input of those costs), reasonable or historical developer profit, and a *discount rate* are applied to the revenue receipts. The discount rate is determined by evaluating blended costs of capital, alternative investment opportunities, and comparable projects. Local appraisers and active residential subdivision developers and lenders are good sources to help determine current market discount rates.

Lenders must evaluate their risk based on the loan-to-value and loan-to-cost analyses. It is important to know that all require assumptions and estimates (total costs, absorption rates, prices, and so on). Therefore, the intangible strengths of the developer's experience, market knowledge, and confidence in assumptions and estimates used by appraisers, engineers, developers, municipalities, and others are critically important.

Types of Debt Financing

Loans are generally characterized by their length of maturity and are commonly referred to as *short-term* or *long-term* debt (the latter also is known as *permanent financing*). By definition, most financing associated with the development of for-sale residential product is short term, as the long-term or permanent financing is provided by individual homebuyers in the form of home mortgages.

Interim loans are short-term loans used to fund the project's development up to completion. Generally, interim loans are structured as variable-rate debt, are full recourse to the borrower (because of the higher level of risk combined with the limited value of the underlying security at the time the interim loan is made), and are due in full, including all accrued but unpaid interest, at maturity (that is, there are no scheduled interest or principal payments until maturity because, at this stage in the development process, no revenue is being generated). Interim loans generally include those used to fund predevelopment activities, land acquisition and development, interest, and project construction. Interim financing also includes any "bridge" or "gap" financing during the period following the completion of construction but before the sale of the property to its ultimate owner(s) or the developer's closing on the permanent financing. The interim loan generally is repaid with proceeds from sale of the property or with funds from a permanent loan placed on the completed property.

Permanent loans are long-term loans that fund property ownership and operation after construction is completed. These loans may have a variable- or fixed-interest rate.

As the project moves sequentially through each stage of development, the total amount of money invested in the project increases. Although some of the risks—in particular, those associated with the intended use of the property and the likelihood of securing all necessary regulatory approvals for that use—may be eliminated entirely in the early phases of the development process, other project risks with much greater monetary implications arise, particularly those risks associated with construction. Once the project is completed, many of the development risks are eliminated or reduced substantially, replaced by market demand and operational risks. The risk-weighting of interest rates is reflected in the varying terms and conditions for different types of loans made throughout the development process; construction loans, for example, are generally riskier than permanent loans, and the interest rate and other loan terms reflect this increased risk. Any number of events, such as construction delays and cost overruns, can adversely affect the repayment of a construction loan.

Financing the Various Stages of Development

The developer must assemble an array of short- and long-term financing to cover the various stages of development, usually beginning with land acquisition. In some cases, these forms of financing are combined, and in others, they are separate. Some projects involve more than one developing partner, and so each may get financing for its particular component.

Land Acquisition and Development

A number of options are available to developers seeking financing for land acquisition and development. Only well-capitalized, well-established developers will be able to obtain a loan from an institutional lender for land acquisition because of the perceived risk to the lender. Lenders look to the cash flow generated by the project and underlying value of the project's assets for repayment. At this early stage, no cash flow exists and the land value may even be reduced once development begins. Thus,

Elizabeth Lofts, occupying a one-acre (0.4-hectare) site in downtown Charlotte, North Carolina, consists of 43 condominium units.

loans for land acquisition are typically made only as full-recourse loans and only when the developer has significant equity or assets at risk. Because they are considered so risky, land acquisition and development loans are usually expensive, compared with interest rates and fees for construction loans.

To proceed with a project, the developer must have control of the land. But if a loan from an institutional investor is not a viable alternative, how does the developer gain control of the land? Fortunately, a number of ways can be used to acquire control of land that require little or no money from the developer.

Seller Financing. The selling landowner can provide financing by taking back what is commonly referred to as a *purchase-money mortgage*. In this situation, the seller transfers landownership to the developer in exchange for a loan secured by the property. Although the seller frequently requires some downpayment, it is not uncommon for the loan to be for the full purchase price of the land. The loan is generally due in full upon sale of the completed project or, in cases when the developer intends to hold and operate the property, when the developer receives permanent financing. Depending on the loan agreement, interest payments may be required during the term of the loan, or the interest may accrue and be included in the payoff amount. When the seller finances the loan, the seller must agree to subordinate its loan to any future development loan, as all development lenders will require that the development loan be a first lien.

Seller Contribution. Seller contribution is similar to seller financing except that instead of taking back a loan, the seller takes an equity interest in the project. The contribution may be structured as a joint venture, a partnership, or a limited liability company. A seller contribution offers several advantages to the developer. First, it does not require the developer's capital. Second, because it is considered equity invested in the project, it increases the developer's ability to obtain development and permanent financing. Third, it does not raise the subordination issue created by seller financing.

Land Option. Another method for gaining control of the property without using much cash is to obtain an option to acquire the land. In this approach, the developer pays the landowner for the exclusive right to buy the property for a predetermined price during a specified period of time. Although no standard amount is attached to a land option, it represents a modest amount—often 1 to 10 percent of the specified purchase price. The option payment may be made in one lump sum or in a series of takedown payments over the life of the option. The option may include additional payments for extensions or the occurrence of certain events, such as the successful rezoning of the property. Once an option payment has been made, it is usually nonrefundable.

Planning/Predevelopment

A developer generally bears the cost of planning and predevelopment. Well-capitalized developers may be

Usable open space is a valuable asset for a community. Shown here is Grand Cascades in Suwanee, Georgia.

able to find a lender willing to make a full-recourse loan backed by the developer's assets to fund planning and predevelopment. Because the project has limited value at the predevelopment stage, however, the value of the underlying asset (most likely raw land without any development entitlements or approvals) is insufficient or too speculative to adequately secure the lender's interest in repayment. Consequently, predevelopment loans, when available at all, are almost always made with full recourse. Once land acquisition and development are completed, some lenders allow relevant predevelopment costs to be counted toward full development costs and therefore leveraged to some extent.

A developer may be able to find equity investors willing to help fund planning and predevelopment, but this equity is generally very expensive, because such an early stage equity investment is very risky. Many events can prevent the project from proceeding, and because the assets have limited value at this stage, the failure to proceed usually means a total loss of the invested equity. During the planning/predevelopment, or due diligence, phase, the developer typically places the property under contract to protect his or her investment.

Horizontal Development
Development loans are short-term loans used to finance development; most have terms of fewer than three years. The loans are almost always full recourse and carry a variable interest rate. Generally, interest is payable on loan amounts outstanding on a monthly or quarterly basis. This interest is often paid through an interest reserve in the loan, provided that sufficient upfront equity was obtained to warrant it. Principal curtailments are sometimes required on acquisition and development loans (before loan maturity) and are generally matched up to coincide with anticipated lot sales and the cash flows generated from them. Development loans are funded in a series of draws or payments made as the construction reaches certain specified levels of completion. Interest

is charged only on the outstanding balance at any point in time.

Any number of factors can lead to a financial default: cost overruns, construction delays, changing market conditions, rising interest rates. Because of the perceived risk, construction loans are more expensive than the permanent financing available after completion. Generally, the interest rate charged for a construction loan is a variable rate tied to a specified index of short-term interest rates plus some specified amount. The amount added to the base rate to determine the interest rate on the loan is referred to as the *spread*. Although spreads vary with market conditions at the time the loan is made, spreads of 0 to 2 percentage points above the prime rate are typical. The spread could be considerably higher, however, depending on general economic conditions and the lender's perception of risk. LIBOR and prime are the two most common indexes.

In addition to the interest charged during the term of the loan, the lender usually charges a fee upfront, sometimes referred to as an *application* or *commitment fee*. This fee is generally expressed in units called *points*. One point represents an amount equal to 1 percentage point of the loan amount. The number of points a lender charges depends on market conditions and the lender's assessment of loan risk, but a 0.5- to 2-point charge is typical for an acquisition and development loan. The lender also holds the developer responsible for any costs associated with making the loan, such as the cost of a survey, an appraisal, an environmental report, and the lender's legal fees. If a loan is extended, the lender generally charges the developer additional fees and expenses.

Commercial banks have been the primary source of acquisition and development loans, but the loans may also be available from credit companies and certain government agencies; loans may even be available from lenders normally associated with permanent loans, such as pension funds and life insurance companies, but to secure a construction loan from these sources generally requires the developer to commit to placing the permanent loan on the property with the lender making the construction loan.

Construction Loans
Construction loans for homebuilders are originated in many different forms and structures. They range from a "pooled collateral" borrowing base in which the availability of a revolving credit line is driven by the cost and market values of a wide array of housing inventories in various stages of completion to an individual construction loan to a builder for the purpose of building one house. Most homebuilding financing vehicles are structured somewhere in the middle of this range of complexity, usually in the form of a commercial bank offering a guidance line of credit in which terms are structured that identify how many homes, in what location, in what completion period, and in what sold status (model, under contract, or speculatively built to sell) the bank will finance for a particular building enterprise.

Like land acquisition and development loans, construction loans and lines are typically variable rate. Spread and fees (pricing) are also similar, although typically discounted a bit, as construction loans do not carry the same land risk. Terms are typically one to two years with the principal due at maturity or as individual homes under the line sell and close. Because the purpose and result are still performance related (construction completion risks still apply), structures usually include personal or corporate guarantees strong enough to provide the lender confidence that the builder will assure completion and repayment.

Summary

All land, land acquisition and development, lot acquisition, and construction loans typically depend on a sale for repayment or, at a minimum, are the primary repayment source expected. Therefore, assurance of completion, deep market understanding, and developer equity are critical components for determining risk. Structures and pricing for the various residential lending types generally follow the liquidity of the asset financed. Land assets are the least liquid (fewest buyers, longest sales cycle), and completed homes are the most liquid. The liquidity chain identifies the depth of buyers and financing alternatives for a particular asset class (see Figure 3-3).

Postconstruction

Several alternatives are available for financing the postconstruction phase of a development project.

Takeout Commitment. The construction or land acquisition and development loan is generally repaid using the proceeds from the sale of the development or from closing on the permanent financing. The lender issuing the construction loan may require the developer to

have a commitment from a buyer or permanent lender, demonstrating that the necessary takeout financing will be available to pay off the construction loan when due. It is generally referred to as a *takeout commitment.*

In some cases, the construction lender may be willing to accept an investor's or another lender's promise to issue a bridge loan or gap financing as a takeout commitment upon the project's completion. Virtually all sales contracts and commitments for permanent financing contain contingencies that, if not met, relieve the purchaser or new lender from its obligation to buy or finance the property. At the very least, the takeout lender is not obligated to fully fund the takeout loan until the property has met the occupancy and revenue standards specified in the takeout commitment. Construction lenders are very concerned about any such contingencies. From the construction lender's point of view, the fewer such contingencies, the stronger the commitment.

Bridge Financing. Sometimes the construction loan matures before the property can be sold or long-term permanent financing can be obtained. In such cases, the developer needs a loan to bridge the period from maturity of the construction loan to sale or permanent financing. *Bridge loans* are usually one- to three-year recourse loans at a variable interest rate. A bridge loan is generally repaid with proceeds from sale of the property.

Gap Financing. Occasionally, a developer is unable to obtain sufficient permanent financing to repay the construction loan in full when it matures. Perhaps the property has not yet achieved the performance standards required for full funding of the takeout commitment or perhaps the property's performance does not yet support a new permanent loan in an amount sufficient to pay off the construction loan. In such cases, the developer needs a gap loan—usually a short-term full-

figure 3-3

Comparison of Loan Terms and Risk

Residential Asset Class	Structure (Term, Equity)	Pricing Relative to Other Residential Assets
Raw Land to Be Developed Soon (not many buyers, specialty financing needed)	Short term, highest equity requirement (35–50%)	Highest
Land under Development (completion/ performance market and term risk; not many buyers for partially developed land except other developers)	2- to 4-year term, high equity requirement (20–30%)	High
Lot Acquisition (lots already developed and permitted with builders and developers available as buyers)	1- to 3-year term, medium equity	Moderately High
Home Construction Loan (model or spec, many potential homebuyers and liquid mortgage market)	1- to 2-year term, moderate equity requirement (15–25%)	Moderate/Lower
Home Construction (presold, buyer already identified and has qualified for financing)	1-year term, moderate equity requirement (15–20%)	Lowest

recourse loan with a variable interest rate. Repayment of the loan comes from additional releases from the takeout loan as the property achieves the specified performance standards or as the property's performance improves to the level that allows for a permanent loan of sufficient size.

Sources of Financing

A number of variables influence the sources of both equity and debt financing for residential development projects: a project's size and complexity; the tenure of the residential units being developed (rental, for sale, lease to own, or mixed tenure); the residential building types being developed (single-family detached, attached, or multifamily); the income ranges the units are intended to attract; prevailing market conditions, including the existing and anticipated supply of comparable units; the current development phase; and the track record and financial position of the development entity.

Sources of Equity Financing
Equity financing can come from the developer, the landowner, individuals, and/or groups of investors and joint venture partners.

Developer. The starting point for the equity required to develop a property is the developer's own resources, which may include cash or other assets that can be bor-

rowed against or pledged as additional collateral to help secure the loans required. By relying totally on his or her own resources for the project's equity, the developer retains ownership and control of the project and is in the best position to maximize profits. But few developers have sufficient assets to provide the equity capital except for the smallest projects. The developer's available equity may be in the form of cash or cash equivalents or may already be invested in the purchase price of the land.

Landowner. The landowner from whom the developer is acquiring the land can contribute the land in exchange for an equity interest (see "Joint Ventures" and "Land Acquisition and Development" above). The value of the contributed land is considered equity invested in the project; it increases the developer's ability to obtain the balance of the financing required for the project. The contribution may be structured as a subordinated purchase money mortgage, a joint venture, a partnership, a limited liability company, or, under certain circumstances, a contribution to a REIT's operating partnership.

Individuals. Virtually every developer, early in his or her career, has approached relatives, friends, or business associates seeking funds for a development project. Although the average developer, particularly one just starting out, is not going to be well acquainted with investors large enough to provide equity financing for any but the smallest projects, some individual investors in

At the 423-acre (170-hectare) Frenchman's Reserve in Palm Beach Gardens, Florida, Toll Brothers is developing 443 single-family houses, a golf course, and other resort-style amenities.

Toll Brothers, Inc.

Sun City Texas is an age-restricted community for adults age 55 and older. The community is located in Georgetown, Texas.

RVI Planning

the marketplace are actively invested in residential development projects. The difficulty is finding them and then negotiating prudently the terms of their equity investment. In addition to the variety of real estate and related professionals—attorneys, accountants, bankers, real estate brokers, business and investment advisers—who serve such individual real estate investors and thus may serve as points of contact, individual investors can be found through national, regional, and local professional organizations, real estate investment clubs, and the classified advertising section of metropolitan area newspapers.

Investor Groups. Groups of investors can be formed to invest equity capital in a development project. The process of forming the group and finding investors is referred to as *syndication*. Syndications are generally organized as partnerships or limited liability companies. They may be private, with a limited number of investors, or public, with hundreds of investors. In the early 1980s, syndications attracted tens of thousands of potential investors to real estate and other somewhat speculative investment transactions, offering very attractive and often highly leveraged tax losses against which other income could be sheltered from taxation. The principal advantage of these investment syndications was that they greatly increased the number of prospective investors and the aggregate capital that potentially could be raised at a much lower cost than raising capital through a public offering of securities. These tax-advantaged syndications were expensive to undertake, however, and the developer generally relinquished a majority ownership interest in the project. The Tax Reform Act of 1986 ended the syndication era of private capital formation by proscribing a passive investor from using the tax losses to shelter earned income for federal income tax purposes. As an alternative to syndication, developers now seek out joint venture partners or large institutional investors to put up to 100 percent of the capital required for each project. Possible joint venture partners include REITs, pension

plans, insurance companies, and boutique investment firms focused specifically on residential equity and joint capital opportunities. Typically, these investors need a profit participation percentage that will produce a target internal rate of return (IRR) of 20 to 30 percent for a single-family development. Required IRRs for apartment projects tend to be much lower.

Sources of Debt Financing
The best source for a loan depends on a number of factors, including the type of project, stage of development, size of the loan required, and the experience and financial strength of the borrower. Potential borrowers must understand that lenders enter and leave the market continuously. A lender who may be willing to make a particular loan today may not make any development loans tomorrow. Some key factors influence a lender's willingness to lend funds for multifamily development: the general state of the nation's and the region's economies, their future economic health, the outlook for the multifamily housing industry, and the lender's financial and business strategy. Even if a lender is in the market to make loans on multifamily projects, the terms and conditions of loans that are available at any particular time vary greatly. Thus, in planning a development, the developer should survey the market, determine which lenders are making which types of loans under what terms and conditions, and then decide the best source of debt financing for a particular project. Debt financing comes from commercial banks, savings and loan institutions, REITs, pension funds, insurance companies, credit companies, securitized lenders, government and quasi-government agencies such as FHA, Fannie Mae, and Freddie Mac, and tax credits such as those for low-income housing and historic properties.

Commercial Banks. Commercial banks are the principal source of construction loans and may be a funding source for planning, predevelopment, land acquisition, and development, but loans for these purposes are available only to financially strong, experienced developers. When making loans for planning or predevelopment, the bank must totally rely on the developer's financial strength and experience. Loans for this purpose are in the form of personal loans to smaller developers or lines of credit. When making loans for land acquisition and development, the bank not only evaluates the developer's financial strength and experience but also requires the developer or the investors to make a substantial equity investment in the project. In addition, commercial banks can, for a fee, provide letters of credit for a developer who needs to enhance its creditworthiness to obtain financing from another source.

Savings Institutions. Savings and loan associations and other savings institutions provide a full range of real estate loans, from construction loans to permanent financing. In recent years, savings institutions have become more focused on loans for smaller projects in their local markets.

Pension Funds. Although pension funds generally make equity investments in existing properties, they also occasionally provide debt for construction loans. Pension fund loans may be structured as pure debt or as hybrid-type loans such as participating or convertible loans. As a rule, pension funds prefer investment-grade or institutional-quality properties.

Insurance Companies. Some insurance companies provide construction loans but generally do not provide other types of interim financing. Insurance companies do not make loans generally for planning and predevelopment or for land acquisition and development. As a rule, insurance companies are interested only in larger projects, and they are not generally a good source for small projects.

Credit Companies. Many credit companies provide short-term real estate loans, including construction, bridge, and gap loans. They may even provide short-term loans for the acquisition of existing properties. As a rule, credit companies are much more flexible than banks and insurance companies and often make loans that could not be obtained from those sources. In exchange for flexibility, credit companies generally charge higher interest rates than banks or insurance companies. Loans from credit companies are often hybrid, with both a base interest rate and a participation interest rate. Such loans also frequently have a look-back provision; that is, the lender is entitled to receive a minimum rate of return over the life of the loan that is more than would be provided by the base interest rate. At maturity, the lender compares the total amount of base and participation interest paid over the life of the loan with the interest required for the lender to receive its minimum return. If both base and participation interest paid to date is more than the amount required for the lender to receive its minimum return, no additional interest is due. If the amount paid is not sufficient to provide the lender with its minimum return, the lender is entitled to a deficiency payment sufficient to bring the return up to the specified minimum.

Design Workshop

The Rocks at Pinnacle Peak in Scottsdale, Arizona, is a 22-acre (9-hectare) development of 40 villas, each with a private courtyard and connection to a trail system.

Government Finance Programs. In addition to the myriad sources for different types of equity and debt, a potential layer of financing may be available for qualifying residential projects through federal, state, and local subsidy programs. Although such financing is reserved for very specific types of projects (for example, housing that is affordable to households earning not more than 80 percent of the area median income), it is often made available on very favorable terms. These sources of project financing—which run the gamut from tax-exempt, private activity bonds to locally administered allocations of Community Development Block Grant monies to state-administered housing trust funds—are collectively referred to as *gap financing*, because they provide the last dollars for project financing that enable a qualifying project to go forward that otherwise lacks all the necessary financing.

Because of the number and complexity of these programs, a developer would not likely venture into this area without hiring the necessary expertise to maneuver through the vast regulatory frameworks and bureaucracies attached to them. Moreover, it cannot be overemphasized that securing the necessary gap financing under these programs—complying with all the application requirements and overcoming all the administrative and regulatory hurdles—is not the end but the beginning of the developer's and the project's relationship with the administering agency or agencies. All these programs have monitoring and compliance requirements with which the developer must conform.

Because these programs make taxpayer-generated funds available to fund public policy goals (such as providing affordable housing for low- and very-low-income families), many of the terms may be dictated by governmental regulation. For example, developer and general contractor fees are often capped under these programs, limiting the return to be realized by the developer and potentially constraining the number and quality of available general contractors. Other programs require the provision of employment opportunities for the households to be served; still others impose obligations to provide opportunities for minority and/or local contractors and subcontractors to work on the project.

The details of such government subsidy programs supporting specific types of residential development and their attendant rules and regulations are well beyond the scope of this chapter. Residential developers need to know, however, that such programs exist, that their applicability is limited to providing housing intended to serve specific groups of people, generally those with limited annual incomes, and that these program are highly prescriptive, both for purposes of initially qualifying for the funding and for maintaining that qualified status throughout the life of the financing.

The federal HOPE VI program encourages local public housing authorities to involve private developers in efforts to transform public housing to full-service mixed-income communities of both owner- and renter-occupied housing. HOPE VI allows public housing funds to be combined with other public and private development funds to attract greater resources to projects. The program has been instrumental in revitalizing severely blighted neighborhoods in numerous cities. At this writing, the program is at risk of losing its federal funding.

The Financing Process

Once the development plan has been finalized and the project's total development cost has been projected, the developer arranges financing. The goal is to find the proper blend of equity and debt from the available sources to raise sufficient funds to finance the project.

Developers must undertake a detailed survey of the financing market at the initiation of the planning stage to determine possible sources of financing and likely terms and conditions. A mortgage broker can be helpful, especially for less experienced developers. A good mortgage broker has detailed knowledge of the market, the types of loans available, and the likely terms and conditions of available loans. Knowing which lenders are most likely to respond to a loan request can greatly reduce the time and expense required to obtain the required financing. A mortgage broker can also help with the loan application. Preparing the application is no small task; many lenders have very specific requirements for its format and content.

Note
1. A takeout commitment is a lender's promise to provide permanent financing after the completion of construction.

4. Planning and Design

Site planning and design is the process of designing a real estate project and obtaining the necessary governmental approvals to begin construction. It often begins at the conceptual level with the study of alternative sites and grows more formalized and specific when a site has been selected. When used as a tool in decision making, the site planning process minimizes the developer's risk and maximizes the project's long-term benefits. The terms *land planning* and *site planning* are used interchangeably.

Planning and Design Process

Site planning proceeds through three general stages: 1) concept planning, 2) preliminary planning, and 3) final planning. Each stage involves the collection and analysis of information about the site, the identification and evaluation of alternatives, and public review. The activities are highly interdependent and are normally undertaken in several cycles during each stage. Developers typically go through preliminary and final planning for each phase of a multiphase project.

Concept planning deals with site-specific issues at the broadest possible level and is often conducted before committing to a site to explore its opportunities for and constraints on development. During this stage, the developer evaluates alternative arrangements of generalized land uses (neighborhoods of housing, sites for commu-

nity facilities, corridors of open space, and so on) and alternative alignments for major roads as well as conducts site research and evaluation. The site's natural constraints (wetlands, soil conditions, topography, or adjacent uses) are important considerations, as they affect the site's effective use. It is important to begin with an understanding of the marketability of different land uses. The professionals drafting the conceptual plan weigh these variables and then produce a plan tailored to the site's natural and market conditions. The product of concept planning is a diagram of the site where generalized land use areas and major road alignments are depicted schematically—the concept plan. During this stage, developers should attempt to obtain a clear understanding from local authorities of the amount of their contributions for roads, infrastructure, and other public services, information that is integral to evaluating a project's economics.

During preliminary planning, the concept plan is refined through the identification and evaluation of alternative locations for buildings, streets, parking areas, major elements of the pedestrian circulation network, and new landscape features. One of the most informative products that can be prepared during preliminary planning is an illustrative site plan that schematically depicts how the site might appear after development. (An illustrative plan is essentially an artistic rendition of the plan.) By the end of preliminary planning, the local government and the developer often make commitments concerning such issues as the total number and type of housing

Celebration, Florida.

units, the alignment and width of major roads, and the amount of land to be provided for other land uses, such as open space and community facilities.

During final planning, the preliminary plan is refined, detailed construction drawings are prepared, economic projections are confirmed, and final approvals are granted. After final approval is granted, minor changes can normally be made to the final plans through amendments.

Developers and the project planning team undertake site planning in consultation with representatives of public agencies and interested citizens. Preparation of a realistic work program and schedule to guide site planning is essential. The work program and the schedule must reflect specific requirements for submitting materials and review periods that are necessary for the project's approval. Once the required approvals have been identified, a realistic schedule for completing the approval process can be prepared. As new requirements are identified during planning, the work program and schedule will need to be revised. The length of time required for a project to receive all of the approvals necessary for construction to begin varies widely among jurisdictions. It can take from a few months to several years.

The planning and design process follows a general sequence of events:

- Phase I—Baseline information gathering
  - Regulatory analysis and evaluation of site's potential
  - Systematic summary of findings
  - Market research and evaluation
  - Summary site analysis
- Phase II—Preparation of alternative concepts
  - Financial analysis of alternatives
  - Selection of the preferred concept
- Phase III—Preparation and submission of the concept plan
  - Securing project zoning
  - Preparation and submission of the preliminary plan
  - Preparation and submission of final development plans.

Baseline Information

To initiate the planning and design process, certain baseline information must be obtained. Research includes collecting base data about the property and surrounding community, conducting a literature review, and performing an environmental audit or environmental site assessment (ESA).

Preparation of the Base Maps. Base maps of the site must show the site location, boundaries, and site features. Several base maps should be prepared for any residential development: 1) a regional context or location map, 2) a community context or surrounding neighborhood map, and 3) a site or property base map. Regional context involves growth management policies, the condition and capacity of regional infrastructure such as roads, transit, and open space, the balance between housing and employment locations, and the natural, geographic, and cultural resources specific to the region. Commu-

nity context pertains to community-wide infrastructure, public facilities and services, development patterns, and local controls such as land use plans or master plans and development policies and regulations.

Base maps should be accurate, easy to read, and sized so that they are easy to handle and reproduce. Base maps may initially be prepared from the U.S. Geological Survey's 7.5-minute quadrangle maps but should be updated as aerial photographs, site surveys, and other sources of information are gathered.

The base map of the site should cover an area extending slightly beyond the boundaries of the site to provide a physical context and to allow for consideration of adjacent features and uses. The scale and size of the site map should conform to any local requirements for submitting site plans. Most local requirements specify a scale of one inch equals 100 feet or one inch equals 200 feet. The boundaries of the site, topographic contour lines at regular intervals, and existing roads and utilities to the site should be included on the base map.

The context maps should be prepared at smaller scales, for example, one inch equals 500 feet or one inch equals 1,000 feet. The principal uses for these maps are to orient the site in terms of location and configuration and to record relevant off-site information. The boundaries of the site, existing roads, and local boundaries and landmarks should be included on the context maps.

Topographic Survey. A careful field or aerial topographic survey should be undertaken to show contour

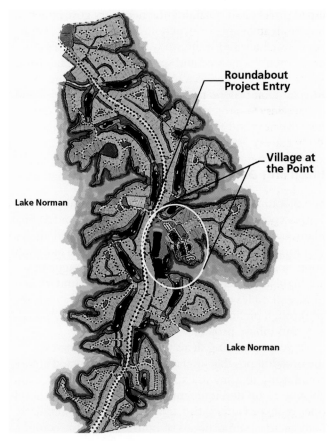

The illustrative site plan for the Point Lake and Golf Club in Mooresville, North Carolina.

elevations of the property. It should indicate topographic features; rock outcroppings; springs, marshes, or wet areas; soil types; and the vegetative cover, including the location, size, and species of trees. Many municipalities, townships, and counties have completed comprehensive topographic maps that are available to the public. The topographic map for a typical site should clearly show:

- Contours at an interval of one foot, two feet, or five feet, depending on the slope conditions (one foot for slopes averaging 3 percent or less, two feet for slopes between 3 and 10 percent, and five feet for slopes greater than 10 percent).
- All existing buildings and other structures, such as walls, fence lines, culverts, bridges, and roadways, with spot elevations indicated.
- The location and elevation of rock outcroppings, high points, watercourses, depressions, ponds, and marshes, with any previous flood elevations determined by survey.
- Boundaries of any floodplains or areas subject to periodic inundation.
- The size, variety, circumference, and accurate location of all significant trees and an outline of all wooded areas.
- Boundary lines of the property.

An aerial survey is a commonly used method to obtain topographic maps. It has the advantages of economy and speed, and the resultant topographic map will be current, accurate, and completely indicative of the site's physical features. Aerial topographic mapping ("flown topo") is commonly used for large or remote sites and where a site's topographic features change frequently as the result of natural actions like landslides, rockslides, soil creep, and sedimentation.

Boundary Survey. A boundary map should be at a scale of one inch equals 100 feet for parcels 100 acres (40 hectares) or smaller and at a scale of one inch equals 200 feet for larger parcels. The boundary survey should provide as much of the following information as pertinent:

- Bearings, distances, curves, and angles of all outside boundaries, and boundaries of all blocks and individual parcels.
- The location of any existing connecting streets along the boundary of the property and the intersection lines of any adjoining tracts.
- Any encroachments on outside boundaries as determined by survey.
- Existing easements of record.
- All streets within or contiguous to the property with reference to deeds or dedications; all existing and proposed street elevations.
- Names of owners of record or reference to recorded subdivision of adjoining property.
- Any cornerstones, pipes, or other physical boundary markers as determined by survey.

With careful planning, utilities can be screened from view.

- All U.S., county, or other official benchmarks, monuments, or triangulation stations within or adjacent to the property, with precise position and description.
- Computed area of all parcels making up the property in square feet or acres, gross and net.
- True and magnetic meridian on the date of survey.

Permanent steel pipes or stone or concrete monuments should be set at each corner or angle on the outside boundary if markers are not already established.

Utility Survey. The amount of site data sometimes makes combined maps confusing; therefore, it is often desirable to provide a separate map of utilities showing the following information, all of which the surveyor should verify:

- All utility easements or rights-of-way.
- Location and size of existing water, gas, electric, and steam mains and underground conduits.
- Location, size, and invert elevations of existing sanitary sewers, storm drains or open drainage channels, catch basins, and manholes.
- Location of existing underground or overhead telephone and electric service and trunk lines, and street lighting with locations of poles.
- Location of any rail lines and rights-of-way.
- Location of police and fire alarm call boxes and similar appurtenances.

Regulatory Analysis

Regulatory analysis involves identifying applicable local, state, and federal regulations and their particular requirements for submissions and reviews. These regulations directly affect the project's viability and schedule and can often be an important consideration in evaluating alternatives.

Local requirements for approving similar projects can vary from jurisdiction to jurisdiction, and requirements for different types of projects can vary within the same jurisdiction. Local land use regulations for residential

Riverbend in Bluffton, South Carolina, takes advantage of its lush natural setting and water views.

EDSA

projects traditionally are contained in zoning and sub-division ordinances. Most states have some type of enabling legislation for local regulations, which often provides the best foundation for interpreting the intent and validity of a particular municipality's regulations. Depending on the nature of the project and applicable regulations, a proposed development can be processed under conventional, planned unit development, or flexible zoning standards. (Additional information on regulatory analyses can be found in Chapter 5.)

Systematic Summary of Findings

Once collected, basic information must be organized to permit an easy evaluation of the possible development options. The evaluation can be performed manually, through the creation of exhibits or overlays, or by using computer applications. Computer technology for land development has advanced considerably in recent years. Computer-aided design and drafting (CADD) tools are the most visible extension of this technology.

The newest technology permits rapid and inexpensive evaluation of such factors as market potential, environmental constraints, and engineering limitations. Data from the U.S. Census Bureau are incorporated into a geographic information system (GIS) and used for the rapid determination of demographic and socioeconomic trends. The use of GIS permits the analysis of many complex, interrelated items such as environmental constraints, severe slopes, and stormwater runoff. Computer technology can also be used to create a highly realistic representation of the proposed community. Whether modeled through the use of a three-dimensional CADD system or created with video simulation, the results provide a valuable communication tool for the review process.[1]

Market Evaluation

The market evaluation should be prepared before or concurrently with the site evaluations. (The role of the market consultant and the need for a market analysis are discussed in Chapters 1 and 2.) A full market analysis investigates historical and current market activity, projects probable trends, and creates a development program to be tested. The investigation should include economic factors, demographics and psychographics, competitive projects, demand analysis, and site programming.

Site Analysis

Useful data about the site may have already been collected during the feasibility study and site selection. At this stage, however, the development team should add to the preliminary database, collecting more detailed information from both public and private sources.

The project team should first check to see what data are available from local sources, much of which can be obtained free of charge or at a modest cost. A check with municipal agencies, planning staffs, public works and building departments, utility companies, state highway departments, county offices, public libraries, and local engineering firms will identify existing data, for example, topographic maps, soil surveys, soil borings, percolation tests, and environmental assessments for other projects in the area. Tax assessment offices and recorded deeds are sources of information about existing easements, rights-of-way, and covenants that may be placed on the property. Site analysis is most effective when information is collected and mapped systematically.

One method for determining the suitability for development on the site is to overlay maps to identify where various characteristics of the site coincide. After slopes, geologic features, floodplains, and other environmental considerations are located on the map, land parcels can be classified according to suitability for various types and intensities of land use, graduating from those requiring protection and maintenance to those that can accommodate more intensive development. The final map or maps that result from this synthesis provide an ecological description of the site and its natural processes that will enable the development team to understand and test the consequences of various alternatives for planning and design.

Another method for analyzing information about the site is to identify opportunities for and constraints on development. Opportunities are features that make the site attractive for development (views, well-drained soils, gently sloping terrain), whereas constraints are features that may need to be avoided or preserved (floodplains, steep terrain, biologically sensitive areas, utility corridors). Most sites contain both such areas, and creative design can often turn constraints into opportunities. The map showing opportunities and constraints also identifies potential design strategies for further consideration, such as planting buffer strips to screen unsightly areas, creating water features to contain stormwater runoff, and orienting development around scenic natural features.

A complete and well-substantiated site analysis map is an indispensable component of the planning and design process. A site analysis should be prepared even for a small, uncomplicated site, lending clarity and rationale to the process. The site analysis should be used continuously throughout the planning and design study and can be helpful in obtaining jurisdictional approvals and in the eventual marketing of the community.

Preparing Alternative Concepts

The results of the regulatory analysis, site analysis, and definition of the program provide the basis for the study of alternative concept plans. From the regulatory analysis, it is possible to determine what type of development local authorities may be willing to permit on the site. The site analysis indicates which portions of the site are developable and what opportunities and constraints exist for developable parcels. The development program identifies the developer's objectives and expectations.

Concept planning is the first opportunity to test a specific development program for the site under consideration. During concept planning, the development team should articulate the optimum development program for the site based on the developer's understanding of the local market, regulatory constraints, determination of the project's feasibility, and the site's character. In particular, the program should specify a minimum number of dwelling units by type. Information about the type and use of amenities, the character of the project, nonresidential land uses to be accommodated, and functional relationships among the various land uses envisioned for the site should also be specified as part of the development program.

Identification and evaluation of alternative concepts is an iterative process. Alternatives can be based on any one or more of several variables: program mix (number of residential units by type, price range, acreage, or square footage of other land uses, for example), intensity of development, physical form (location of uses, patterns of

access), development "themes," and amenity packages. Evaluation of the initial set of alternatives may suggest several new alternatives to evaluate. After several review cycles, the project planning team normally is able to identify an alternative that conforms to regulatory guidelines, responds to the site, and fulfills the developer's objectives. Alternative concept plans can be developed using several strategies:

- Do not be satisfied with the first solution.
- Do not assume that there is only one way to make a proposed project work.
- Ask questions that elicit multiple answers.
- Recognize that a lot of ideas create better solutions.
- Look for the second right answer.
- Ask "what if" questions.
- Challenge the rules.[2]

Preapplication Conference. Once the developer and the project team agree on a preferred alternative, it is useful to schedule a preapplication conference with the municipality, even when one is not formally required. Such a meeting is a good way to learn whether local officials are hostile to a particular development proposal. Rather than presenting a specific plan of action, developers may find it useful to review the range of options during the meeting to get a sense of the municipality's receptivity to various alternatives. In turn, the planning staff can inform the developer about requirements to

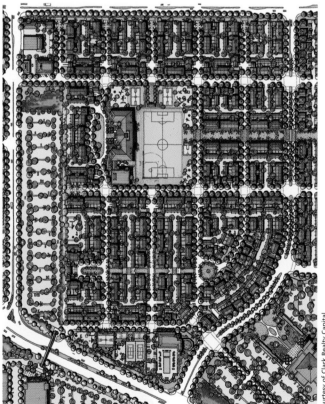

The Village at NTC, in San Diego, California, was developed by a public/private venture to provide 500 townhouses for military families.

be met and, in general, what factors should be considered during the planning process.

Planning staff and representatives from related departments (engineering, public works, traffic, parks, police, and fire) usually attend the preapplication conference. The developer should bring key members of the project planning team and the preliminary base maps, both site and context, as discussion exhibits. Of special importance to local authorities is what portions of the site will be public and what portions will remain private. The more knowledgeable the project planning team about applicable regulations, the site, and the potential range of alternatives, the more productive the meeting will be.

Preferred Concept Plan. A concept plan is a schematic diagram that identifies the organization of the major components of a proposed development. A well-prepared concept plan responds to the site's opportunities and constraints, to the development program, and to the applicable local, state, and federal requirements. Following the preapplication conference, the preferred concept alternative can be fine-tuned and documented into a preferred concept plan. The concept plan should be one that best satisfies the developer's goals and best fits the site. It should be one that can be implemented. It may not necessarily be the easiest one to implement, as rezoning or an amendment to local regulations may be required. The preferred concept plan should, however, be one that will afford benefits at reasonable costs to the developer and the jurisdiction.

The Design Charrette. A process that has become increasingly popular is the *design charrette*. A design charrette is normally a two-day to week-long intensive and interactive approach to problem solving. The length of the charrette usually depends on the complexity of the design problem. The design charrette is a coordinated approach that focuses participants' energy and creativity on solving site and land planning problems.[3]

The charrette process can be applied successfully to distressed properties, project workouts, or infill development as well as to the design of new neighborhoods. This innovative and interactive approach can save developers and community leaders much time, effort, and money through consensus building early in the planning process. As an approach for evaluating a site, the design charrette can lead to plans that are supportable by and acceptable to all affected parties.[4]

Securing Project Zoning

If the appropriate zoning is not in place, the developer needs to request a rezoning of the property. It may be necessary, however, to first demonstrate consistency with an approved comprehensive plan by amending the plan before the formal rezoning process can be initiated. Another process that is sometimes required is to seek a *special exception* to allow the property to contain a specific land use or type of use not allowed by right. The following tips will help in preparing a request for rezoning or for a special exception:

The Ledges in Huntsville, Alabama, began with a charrette, which helped build community support.

Urban Design Associates

Heritage at Miami Bluffs is an active adult community in Hamilton Township, Ohio.

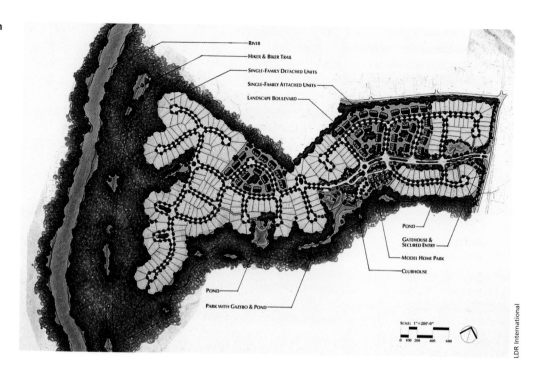

RIVER
HIKER & BIKER TRAIL
SINGLE-FAMILY DETACHED UNITS
SINGLE-FAMILY ATTACHED UNITS
LANDSCAPE BOULEVARD
POND
GATEHOUSE & SECURED ENTRY
MODEL HOME PARK
CLUBHOUSE
POND
PARK WITH GAZEBO & POND

SCALE: 1"=200'-0"
0 100 200   400   600

LDR International

- Work with community groups and neighbors to develop consensus before initiating the formal rezoning or special exception process.
- Have small group meetings with community groups, meeting on their turf.
- Present a conventional development plan or "by right" development plan to illustrate the advantages of your creative development concept.
- Use graphics and three-dimensional images such as perspective sketches, bird's-eye views, house elevations, and cross-sectional views to help others visualize your design concept.
- Look for ideas and successful examples in resource materials such as the Urban Land Institute's Development Case Studies and model ordinances; use them to show local planning and zoning officials innovative and creative approaches to land planning.

Preliminary Plan

Preparation of the Preliminary Plan. The preliminary plan is more detailed than the concept plan. Once the concept plan has been established, the project planning team will be in a position to identify additional information that must be collected and analyzed. At a minimum, topographic, boundary, and utility surveys of the site will need to be completed. The developer normally initiates preparation of the preliminary plan by submitting a formal application. Requirements for submission vary, but they often include written documents as well as site plans and other graphic information. The list of required documents may include, but is not limited to:

- A legal description of the site, including ownership;
- A statement of planning objectives for the project;
- A construction schedule;
- Quantitative information, including the number of units proposed, lot sizes, lot coverage, densities,

and amount of nonresidential construction proposed; and
- Any market, feasibility, or other studies required by the review body.

Required graphic information may include the following items:

- Site plans showing existing site conditions;
- Proposed lot lines and plot designs;
- Maps showing the location and size of all existing and proposed structures and improvements;
- Maps showing the location and size of all areas to be reserved as common open space, developed as recreational facilities, or conveyed as public parks, school sites, or other uses;
- Existing and proposed utility systems;
- A general landscape plan, which may include the proposed treatment of the development's perimeter; and
- Any additional information regarding adjacent areas that might assist in the evaluation of the proposed project's impact.

Information about the design and construction of residential units and buildings, including typical floor plans and building elevations, may be required. In most instances, however, specific building information is not required until final site plans are submitted to obtain building permits.

Processing the Preliminary Plan. The planning staff normally reviews the preliminary plan, often under a time limit imposed by the ordinance. During this period, staff members may confer with the developer to clarify information or to request additional material. The staff might also suggest minor changes that could contribute to a favorable review. Some planning departments distribute copies of the plan to appropriate local agencies

SWA Group

for review and comment. The planning staff then incorporates any comments received into its report of findings and recommendations, which is then transmitted to the planning commission.

The developer may have an opportunity to make a formal presentation before the planning commission. As part of this hearing, public comment may be invited. The commission may pose detailed questions about the proposal during the hearing and usually renders its decision immediately after the hearing or within some specified period of time. The commission may approve or deny the application, or grant conditional approval and require the applicant to modify some aspects of the proposal before approval is granted. All conditions should be put in writing, in language acceptable to both the commission and the applicant. If an application is denied, the applicant normally has the right to appeal the decision.

After the preliminary development plan is approved, the applicant usually has a set time period to submit a final development plan. If a final plan is not submitted within this stipulated period, preliminary approval is often revoked.

If a development is to be phased, as most large-scale projects are, a preliminary development plan should be submitted for the first phase. The developer should work in increments that can be geared to actual market absorption. It is good policy, however, to submit the essentials of the remaining phases, even though the review authority may not approve them at this stage.

Final Development Plans

Preparing and Filing Final Development Plans. Most ordinances require the planning staff or commission to certify that the final plan substantially complies with the approved preliminary plan. Whether or not the municipality required certain changes to the plan during preliminary approval, the final plan typically varies slightly from the preliminary plan submitted. The appropriate regulations and the reviewing authority usually take into

account the need for minor variations, perhaps specifying the parameters for such changes.

The major difference between the preliminary and final plans is the level of detail required. Drawings that might have been presented in schematic form in the preliminary submission must be engineered for the final development submissions. Site plans must be sufficiently detailed for legal recording, and any other graphic information, such as landscape plans, must also be submitted in final form. Where subdivision is involved, most ordinances require the submission of a tentative plat ("map") for final approval. Legal documents for establishing a community association or dedication of public land may also be required.

The final development plan is normally submitted to the planning staff, which may issue another staff report documenting compliance with the preliminary plan and with any conditions of preliminary approval. This process is normally administrative and does not require a public hearing or review. Following approval of the final plan, other necessary administrative approvals can be obtained, building permits issued, and construction begun. Failure to begin construction within an allotted period normally results in revocation of the approval.

Developers should keep in mind that the total planning and development process can take a long time (from several months to several years), so it is necessary that the first phase be scaled to meet market demand at the time construction can proceed. Usually, the larger the project and more complex it is, the longer the approval time frame.

Amendments. Often, changes in final development plans become necessary. Minor changes will not affect the overall integrity of the development and are sometimes easily administered. Major changes, however, may force developers back through the preliminary plan approval process. Sometimes the limits of permitted deviations from the plan are specified; other times they are left to the discretion of staff or public officials.

Changes to the final plan most often involve changing the product type or mix to better respond to the market. For example, after opening the first phase, a developer may find that one product sells much better than another. Changing building footprints is usually not a problem for the municipality, but more drastic changes in the product line (from single-family homes to townhouse, for example) may send the developer back for new discretionary approvals. Developers need to be aware of the local agency's "limits" for allowing final plan amendments.

Alternative Forms of Land Development

The most basic decision about planning and design that developers face is how the land will be divided and used for the residential community. Many factors influence this decision and affect the design of the project:

- The physical conditions of the site, the surrounding patterns of development, and infrastructure capacity.
- Market factors, including residential product types, and density and types of ownership of the residential units.
- Land use controls, and zoning and regulatory requirements.
- The size of the site (large parcels can offer many opportunities for creative and diverse land plans, while small sites offer a more limited array of possibilities).

Residential Product Types and Density

The three general categories of residential product types are single-family detached, single-family attached, and multifamily. In most parts of the United States, homebuyers have a strong preference for single-family detached homes. Growing market segments, particularly in more urban areas, however, are choosing attached housing, for reasons of affordability or lifestyle. The following paragraphs discuss the range of housing types available.

Single-Family Detached. A single-family detached house is a freestanding structure that occupies its own lot. Conventional subdivisions rigidly prescribe setbacks for frontyards, side yards, and rear yards, but some localities have instituted more creative regulations that allow flexibility.

In developing single-family detached housing, it is important to ensure that the placement of houses responds to the site's natural features. Net savings in site development costs and a better neighborhood result from close attention to the relationships between houses and sites and to privacy and good orientation for each house.

The identity of each single-family home can be enhanced by providing some variety in building style and configuration. The front entrance to each house should generally be visible from the street, and garage doors should be placed or treated so as to minimize their street presence. On linear streets, blocks should be short to minimize long views of house fronts and driveways and to improve pedestrian connections. Setbacks should reinforce

In most parts of the United States, homebuyers exhibit a strong preference for single-family houses.

the hierarchy of the street system—deeper on collector streets and shallower on minor residential streets.

It is often appropriate to vary the size of lots within a project to accommodate a site's natural features and to provide some variety in site planning and unit design. Price range, the intended character of the development, house design, and local custom are all important factors in determining the size of lots.

The high cost of land and infrastructure has brought major changes to the design of single-family houses. In the most active markets, lots have become smaller and more complicated in their configuration. And with smaller lots, designers need to consider issues related to privacy, usable outdoor space, entries, and streetscapes. Developers must understand these issues and the potential pitfalls. The decision about which concept to build will be determined after carefully considering the target market, the economics of the project, and the capacity of the land.

Single-Family Detached Lot Configurations. The typical residential lot in a conventional subdivision is square or rectangular. A quarter-acre (0.1 hectare) used to be considered a standard size, but today lots can range from about 3,000 square feet (280 square meters) in very-high-priced regions to more than an acre (0.4 hectare).

Sometimes it is impossible to maintain a uniform shape and size of lots, especially when designing curvilinear streets and culs-de-sac. Two common variations are pie-shaped lots and flag lots. Pie-shaped lots are common around culs-de-sac and sharp street turns; they are narrower at the street and wider at the rear of the lot. Flag lots or pipe-stem lots are created to provide a building site and access to what would otherwise be a landlocked parcel; only the access drive of a flag lot actually fronts the street.

For conventional single-family subdivisions, zoning codes have been used to establish minimum lot sizes and minimum setback distances from each of the four property lines. Typically, codes require the front of the house to be at least 20 to 25 feet (6 to 7.6 meters) from the street to allow space for cars to be parked in the driveway. Minimum setbacks can range from five to 15 feet (1.5 to 4.5 meters) from side property lines and from 25 to 30 feet (7.6 to 9 meters) or more from rear property lines.

To provide greater flexibility, some municipalities allow lot sizes to be averaged so that some lots can be smaller and others larger. In such cases, the zoning code typically specifies a permitted percentage of variation from the average size. For example, if the average lot size is set at 10,000 square feet (930 square meters) but a 25 percent variation is permitted, lots may actually range from 7,500 to 12,500 square feet (700 to 1,160 square meters). Thus, developers have the flexibility to accommodate physical constraints such as topography and environmental resources.

Zero-Lot-Line Houses. Zero-lot-line houses, long common in cities, have been a response to the rising cost of land in suburban areas in almost every region of the country. Zero-lot-line houses are a type of detached house generally characterized by narrow but deep lots. Instead of locating the house between two side yards that might each be only five feet (1.5 meters) wide, the house is located along a side property line, thereby creating a more usable ten- to 15-foot-wide (3- to 4.5-meter-wide) side yard on the other side of the house. The homeowner is granted an easement (usually five feet [1.5 meters]) across the neighbor's lot to provide for periodic maintenance of the exterior of the house and to provide for drainage from the roof. Lot sizes typically range from 3,000 to 5,000 square feet (280 to 465 square meters) at densities of about five to seven units per acre (12 to 17 per hectare). The lots typically range from 40 to 50 feet wide and 80 to 100 feet deep (12 to 15 meters wide and 24 to 30 meters deep). Because lots are narrow, garages are usually located near the front of the lot facing the street or at the rear accessed by an alleyway. Another characteristic of zero-lot-line houses is the

Garden Court at Stapleton in Denver, Colorado, is a community of zero-lot-line homes built around a green space.

lack of windows and doors in the wall located on the property line.

Although zero-lot-line houses offer many planning advantages, some design issues must be addressed. The long, windowless wall located on the property line ensures privacy but reduces natural light and air in the interior of the house. If garages are placed toward the street, streetscapes can be dominated by visually unattractive parallel garage doors, and sidewalks are broken up by curb cuts and driveways, greatly inhibiting pedestrian safety and aesthetic appeal. Increasingly, garages are located at the rear for these reasons.

Further, with narrower lots, the amount of street parking available to each house is often limited to one car. Parking limitations become even more significant if driveways are short. Some ordinances require that the garage be set back at least 18 to 20 feet (5.5 to 6 meters) from the sidewalk to ensure adequate space for a car to park or no more than five feet (1.5 meters) from the sidewalk to make parking on the short driveway apron infeasible. Placing the garage between five and 18 feet (1.5 and 5.5 meters) from the sidewalk only tempts residents to park on the apron, letting the car hang over the sidewalk or into the street. Despite the challenges of design, the concept of zero-lot-line housing has been successfully implemented for many years.

Wide-Shallow Lots. The concept of wide-shallow lots gained popularity in the 1980s as an alternative to the various options for narrow lots. By keeping lots at a more conventional width of 55 to 70 feet (16.8 to 21.3 meters) but reducing the depth to only 55 to 70 feet (16.8 to 21.3 meters), developers can achieve a density of about six to eight units per acre (15 to 20 per hectare). A wide-shallow lot offers the image from the street of a traditional single-family neighborhood by exposing more of the houses' fronts and by orienting front doors directly on the street. The wider lots add proportionately to development costs for streets, utilities, and landscaping, but some buyers will pay more for this kind of streetscape.

Wide-shallow lots also raise several design considerations. Floor plans tend to be less flexible because of the wide and shallow dimensions of the house. Standard requirements for front, side, and rear yards reduce the size of the house's footprint, usually dictating a two-story design, which might be unacceptable in some markets. If lots are very shallow, the distance between the backs of houses may be too short to afford privacy.

Alternate-Width Lots. Alternate-width lots (sometimes called "odd lots") combine narrow and wide lots to offer a more varied streetscape. A wide variety of combinations of unit plans and lot shapes and sizes can be created. Besides offering the advantage of a highly varied streetscape, the mixture of unit plans and lot sizes can help to diversify target markets. Generally, alternate-width layouts do not achieve densities as high as those using one type of narrow lot, and matching specific floor plans to specific lots in particular must be considered. The alternate-width approach is versatile, however, and can

Townhouses (rowhouses) can run from affordable to very high prices. Shown here is Courthouse Hill, a luxury infill project in Arlington, Virginia.

be applied successfully in markets where other nontraditional lot layouts might fail.

Single-Family Attached. An increasing array of configurations has emerged under the category of single-family attached housing. Typically, such housing is attached by sharing one or more walls with adjacent units. Units might be one, two, or more stories in height. Fee simple ownership predominates, but when configurations become complex, condominium ownership may be necessary because of shared lot areas, roofs, or other property.

Townhouses. Townhouses, sometimes known as "row houses," are single-family attached units sharing common walls with adjacent units. Narrow lots are the rule in townhouse developments; widths generally range from 18 to 32 feet (5.5 to 10 meters). Each unit has its own entrance from the outdoors, usually facing the street. Each house is a complete entity with its own utility connections. Although townhouses have no side yards, they can have front and rear yards. In most instances, the land on which the townhouse is built—and any front and rear yard—is owned in fee by the resident; however, townhouses can also be structured as condominiums. Townhouses have been popular housing options for urban dwellers for centuries and have been adapted to suburban sites as a more affordable alternative to detached housing. Since the 1970s, townhouses have become popular at higher prices as well, because they offer less maintenance for busy households.

At Marina Gardens in Palm Beach Gardens, Florida, townhouses with two-car garages back up to a lake.

Quincy Johnson Architects/Chuck Wilkins

Townhouses may be offered for sale (straight sale, cooperative, or condominium) or may be rental units. Townhouses offer several advantages over detached houses: lower costs for construction and land development, conservation of land and open space, lower long-term maintenance costs, greater energy efficiency, and—because of the closeness of neighbors—increased security for both the house and the neighborhood.

Townhouses are usually constructed in buildings of four to ten units laid out in a linear configuration. Only the end units have side yards. A unit may have one, two, or three stories above grade and may or may not include a basement. Garages increasingly are included, either attached at the rear, tucked under the unit at the front or rear, or detached at the rear (adding to the privacy of the rear yard). Although rigid linear configurations with minimal unit offsets can create an attractive streetscape, staggering the units can be a way to handle rolling or undulating topography.

The density that can be achieved with a townhouse project varies with site conditions, size of the units, and size of the building clusters. The number of parking spaces required also greatly affects the density. Generally, eight to 12 units per acre (20 to 30 per hectare) is normal, but densities can be as high as 25 units per acre (62 per hectare) with tight building clusters and structured parking, as found in some townhouse mews projects.

Two adaptations of townhouses are the cluster and mews configurations. In a cluster, the units are arranged around a central courtyard that provides access to each townhouse. The clusters usually contain four to ten units and can be sited to protect natural landforms and sensitive site features. In a mews configuration, rows of townhouses are organized in pairs and are placed either facing each other or back to back. Front-to-front arrangements create a linear, landscaped courtyard that provides access to each unit's front door; back-to-back arrangements allow for a shared driveway between the buildings to garages or carports.

Besides varying the layout of the units, designers sometimes mix townhouses with other unit types, which can diversify the market appeal of the project and provide for more varied architecture and design. For example, a row of townhouses can be anchored on each end by stacked flats; the flats add a more affordable unit type to the mix, help to increase the overall density, and provide exposure to open space for four units at the ends of the building instead of the standard two units. Another technique is to place a single-level flat above or below a two-level townhouse or a two-level townhouse over another two-level townhouse. Stacking units in this fashion can be particularly effective on sloping sites where the natural grade permits both upper and lower units to have an entrance at grade.

Privacy is a paramount consideration when designing townhouse communities. Visual and auditory privacy can be enhanced through proper site design. Distances between buildings and the physical relation of one unit to another should be studied carefully. The proper location of entrances, bedroom windows, and patios and decks is particularly important for visual privacy. Privacy screens and landscaping can be used, but it is important for security that entrance doors be visible from other units and, if possible, from the street.

For acoustical privacy, party walls must be adequately soundproofed. The density, stiffness, and thickness of material used in party walls determine their efficiency. The only completely soundproof party wall comprises two separately constructed walls with at least two inches (5 centimeters) of air space between the walls, drywall on both sides of each wall, and insulation in each wall. This separation must begin at the footing and continue all the way to the roof sheeting with no penetrations through the interior drywall barriers.

Patio or Atrium Homes. The patio home is derived from the atrium home, which was popular in California during the 1950s. Atrium homes are characterized by an open court with rooms oriented around it. Although internally focused, atrium homes were most often placed on conventional lots with conventional side yards; thus, they were single-family detached designs.

A patio home usually retains a central atrium but uses the entire area of the lot by building up to at least two, and sometimes three, property lines. The side yards (and sometimes rear yard) are consolidated into one or more garden courts, either partially or completely bordered by rooms or walls. The outdoor and indoor areas become one secluded space for living, with no openings on two or more exterior side walls. This inward-directed house provides privacy yet allows increased density.

Patio lots are usually square and range from about 2,000 to 3,500 square feet (185 to 325 square meters), providing for a density of about seven units per acre (17 per hectare). Usually the houses are single level and are built without basements, but in the East, they may have two stories and basements. Each patio home is attached to one or more other houses.

Patio homes have been used throughout the country but frequently have been modified to meet regional housing preferences. Today, the term is often used to describe any housing type characterized by a strong orientation to the outdoors, even houses that are clearly detached.

Duplex, Triplex, or Quadruplex. A duplex is two units attached by a common wall, a triplex is three attached units, and a quadruplex is four attached units. Generally, duplex and triplex units are attached in somewhat linear rows similar to townhouses. Quadruplex units can be attached in a row as four units or as two units side by side and located back to back with two other units. This configuration creates a generally square building with a unit at each corner. The challenge in site planning for a quadruplex building configured in this manner is that there is no front or back. Circulation and access must be provided to at least two opposing sides, making the creation of privacy and private outdoor living space for each unit somewhat difficult. Fences and walls may be used in this configuration to create outdoor living areas.

Multifamily Housing. The third primary type of housing design is generally known as *multifamily*. A multifamily unit is one contained within a single building that includes five or more units. In most instances, units are stacked atop each other and therefore are physically attached to three or more other units. Multifamily buildings might be garden-style, walk-up buildings of two or three stories, mid-rise (four to eight stories), or high-rise (more than eight stories) buildings with elevators. Garden apartments are usually about 30 units per acre (75 per hectare), while high-rise construction can yield densities of 100 or more units per acre (245 or more per hectare).

The word *multifamily* is sometimes used to refer generally to all forms of rental housing. Although most rental units are in fact contained in multifamily buildings, the ownership of the units is not necessarily related to the size or design of the buildings. During the 1980s, a myriad of multifamily building types emerged specifically designed to contain for-sale units.

Garden Density. The historical form for this type of housing was the "garden apartment," which was built widely in suburban areas during the post–World War II housing boom. Today, garden apartments may be rental or owner-occupied units. Typical garden apartment buildings are two or three stories, do not contain an elevator, and usually have ten or more units in a single building. Buildings are placed on a site to allow areas for landscaping and surface parking lots. Densities of 12 to 20 units per acre (30 to 50 per hectare) can be expected for these types of buildings. The design appeals to several markets: singles, young couples, and empty nesters. Because they lack elevators and structured parking and can be of inexpensive wood frame construction, they tend to be less costly to build than mid-rise or high-rise buildings.

In some markets, garden apartments have been built with carports, internal garages, and even individual garages instead of surface parking lots.

At Evergrene in Palm Beach Gardens, Florida, a "mansion neighborhood" is made up of buildings of three multifamily units designed to look like one large house.

Mid-Rise and High-Rise Buildings. Mid-rise buildings are generally from four to eight stories, although in some markets, such as New York City, buildings up to 12 stories may still be considered mid-rise. Mid- and high-rise buildings are always equipped with elevators; the number of elevators is a function of the building's height, the level of sales or rent the developer has targeted, and local building codes. Luxury buildings are often equipped with more than the minimum number of elevators.

Although garden density units are typically wood frame, taller buildings are required to meet higher building and fire protection standards. As a rule, buildings with more than six floors are constructed of steel frame or reinforced concrete, and buildings with more than three floors are typically required by state and local building codes to install a sprinkler system throughout the building. Developers contemplating a mid- or high-rise project must weigh the higher costs against the potential income.

Mid- and high-rise buildings vary in form as well as height. The most common forms include:

- Rectangular slab, which is derived from an internal single- or double-loaded corridor;
- Tower, which consists of a centralized service and elevator core opening to a limited number of apartments; and
- Multiwing building, a combination of the rectangular slab and the tower or two or more adjoining slab buildings.

With the high cost of land, contemporary mid-rise buildings often incorporate structured or underground parking.

A trend in the design of mid-rise and high-rise structures has been to more articulated building forms. Modern mid-rise and high-rise buildings often incorporate residential elements like roof gables, varied roof slopes and

The Dunes in Naples, Florida, includes 641 luxury condominium units in high-rise buildings.

STH Architectural Group

A row of single-family houses at Baxter Village in South Carolina.

heights, chimneys, and balconies to help reduce the perceived scale of the building and to make the buildings generally more appealing to middle- and upper-income homebuyers.

Products for Niche Markets. A trend that developed during the 1980s and is expected to continue is the specialization of housing products designed for very specific markets, often referred to as *niche markets*. Such niches include houses for first-time buyers, move-up products for second- or third-home buyers, housing for the elderly, housing for low- and moderate-income households, and second-home or resort-oriented housing. Even within these segments is further segmentation, such as housing for first-time young urban singles or for high-income, move-down suburban retirees. Each market segment implies special considerations in product design.

In the years ahead, designing for particular market niches is likely to become much more complex. The aging population, for example, means strong demand for housing suitable for the elderly. Older people will be a highly segmented group demanding different types of residential products and environments. Active retirees will likely seek detached or attached houses requiring low maintenance and offering access to amenities; those more advanced in age will need housing that offers convenient access to health care professionals and, for some, congregate care housing. As markets become more highly specialized, successful developers will tailor products, amenities, and residential environments to these opportunities. Niche housing products are discussed further in Chapter 8.

Development Forms

Conventional Subdivisions. Since the suburban explosion of the 1950s, the subdivision has been the most common mode of land development for residential uses. Subdivision is the division of a parcel of land into two or more lots, and it can take the form of a simple split or the creation of hundreds of residential lots. The practice of sub-dividing land is regulated by state laws enforced primarily by local (municipal or county) governments. Within the framework of a subdivision, residential developers can choose from numerous possibilities. The most common examples of subdivisions are those that grew in suburbs around central cities during the postwar era. Seemingly overnight, large tracts of land were subdivided for single-family houses, roads, schools, shopping centers, and other uses. Residential developers constructed tract houses on the lots created; typically, three to five floor plans were used per subdivision, with minor variations made to exteriors to suggest individuality.

During the 1960s and continuing through the 1990s, subdivisions became more varied in terms of patterns and lot sizes, street alignments, open-space networks, and mix of residential products. A set formula for residential sub-divisions no longer exists. Today, developers must be more creative, crafting land patterns that work within physical and social contexts. These land patterns must create a greater sense of community, incorporating a mix of uses and innovative transportation alternatives.

Cluster Development. Cluster development is a land pattern in which houses are arranged in proximity, with the remaining land reserved for open space. Rather than spreading houses uniformly over the entire site, developers of cluster communities build units at higher densities on portions of the site while preserving natural features such as stream beds or wooded areas in others. Structures are usually placed on the most suitable terrain that minimizes site development costs associated with grading and installing infrastructure.

Cluster planning requires attention to details to ensure that privacy is maintained. The approach can be adapted to any market in the country and has a proven track record as a viable alternative for land development. It is especially applicable for sites with physical constraints (wetlands, wooded areas, steep terrain). Cluster development offers an economic return on the land and still preserves important features of the site.

Evergreen in San Jose, California, is an 865-acre (350-hectare) planned community.

Planned Unit Development. A planned unit development (PUD) is a land development pattern that 1) is planned as an entity, 2) groups dwelling units into clusters or neighborhoods, 3) allows an appreciable amount of land for open space, 4) mixes housing types and land uses, and 5) preserves useful natural resources. A key benefit of PUDs is flexibility in terms of lot sizes, densities, street layout, and product selection. The PUD's flexibility sometimes allows the developer to respond to changing market conditions by switching products as demand changes over time. These changes must be consistent with the PUD's original intent and ceiling on dwelling units.

A simple PUD may contain a number of dwellings of the same type clustered with common open space. A complex PUD may include a variety of housing types—single-family houses, townhouses, and multifamily units—along with open space and common areas containing recreational and community facilities. Some PUDs include retail and commercial components as well. The amount and types of nonresidential land use included in a primarily residential PUD vary with the size of the parcel.

PUDs can range from a few acres to thousands of acres. Residential density averaged over the entire area being planned, not specifications of minimum size and setback for individual lots, dictates the regulatory control. Contrary to most conventional zoning ordinances, which rely on a separation of uses, a PUD ordinance frequently allows (even encourages) mixed uses. The flexible nature of the PUD provides an opportunity for creative land planning and residential design and requires sophistication on the part of designers and developers. Approval authorities also must understand, evaluate, and endorse the concept.

Fundamental to the process of planning a PUD is consensus among the principals involved—the developer, a public review authority (typically a professional planning staff and a lay planning commission), a public approval authority (town council or board of supervisors), and the public at large. Because a PUD ordinance usually sets out parameters in very general terms, the local government has a certain amount of discretionary control. Consequently, a PUD works best when all the parties understand the process and conduct their negotiations in a well-disciplined governmental framework.

General rules and standards are prescribed for the submission of a PUD application and plans, which local staff and officials then review and approve. In most jurisdictions allowing PUDs, the process for approval consists of three stages: 1) the preapplication process, 2) submission of a preliminary development plan, and 3) submission of final development plans.

During the preapplication conference (which may not be mandatory), the planning agency helps to familiarize developers with the review process that lies ahead. It is also an opportunity for the agency's staff to convey to developers any parameters of design they hold for the land at issue. Developers in turn inform the staff of their ideas. Nothing during the preapplication stage is legally binding; it is an opportunity to share ideas and preconceptions about the project.

The second stage, submission of a preliminary development plan, concept plan, or sketch plan, is the most critical, because a major portion of project review takes place at this time. The developer formally applies for a PUD to the local planning commission by submitting the required documentation—usually schematic drawings showing the site's character and how people will use it, a site plan, written design guidelines, and other supporting documents. The planning staff reviews the documentation and forwards its recommendation to the planning commission: approval, approval with conditions, or denial.

Following review and approval of the preliminary plan, developers usually have a set period of time before they are required to submit a final development plan. The final development plan is a refinement of the preliminary plan and allows participants to discuss any items that remain unsettled, especially how the developer has responded to any conditions of approval imposed during the preliminary plan approval. Usually, the final development plan does not vary substantially from the approved preliminary plan. Following formal acceptance of the final plan, the PUD is recorded and the zoning approval phase is complete. Subsequent steps are typically administrative ones: a detailed site plan and architectural approvals for each phase of development, issuance of grading and building permits, and construction inspections. Often, subdivision review and approvals are processed concurrently with the PUD; recording maps usually occurs in phases after review of the detailed site plan and before issuance of grading permits.

Master-Planned Community. Government involvement in large-scale community development began in the 1930s with the development of three new towns—Greenbelt, Maryland; Greendale, Wisconsin; and Greenhills, Ohio—under Franklin Roosevelt's New Deal. A brief resurgence of the government's interest in the development of new towns occurred with Title VII of the Federal Housing Act of 1970, but since the demise of that program, it has been up to the private sector to plan and develop new communities. Although many have used the term *new town* to describe a large planned development, these projects are generally not freestanding, self-contained towns. Instead, they tend to relate closely with an existing urban area and may not in fact be an incorporated city or town. Although a number of terms have been used to describe this type of large-scale development, the one most universally applied today is *master-planned community*. Such communities are often developed under PUD, mixed-use, or other similar regulatory procedures.

A master-planned community is a very specialized form of development because of its large size. Whereas a planned unit development can range from a few to a few hundred acres, master-planned communities can be as large as several thousand acres and are long-term, multiphase development projects. Because of the communities' size, developers can incorporate comprehensive design elements that might not otherwise be possible under multiple ownerships. Master-planned communities allow an emphasis on neighborhood and community identities, a variety of housing types, a mixture of land uses (including centers of employment), coordination between land planning and architecture, and emphases on amenities and lifestyles.

A master-planned community provides an opportunity for a large tract of land to be planned comprehensively from the outset and implemented (usually) by a single landowner or development company. Typically, a master developer assumes responsibility for coordinating the construction of infrastructure and community services and makes building sites available to developers or builders for the actual construction of houses. Sometimes the master developer also serves as homebuilder. In either case, as building sites become available, houses are constructed in accordance with the original master plan's specifications for type and density.

The master developer is responsible for implementing the master plan, although the municipality normally reviews specific development plans along the way. Because most large master-planned communities require 20 years or more to complete, the original plan must often be modified; thus, the flexibility to make periodic reviews and changes must be provided in the original master plan.

Large-scale, master-planned communities are most prevalent in Sunbelt states like California, Arizona, Texas, and Florida, where large tracts of developable land still exist. For the right parcels of land, master-planned communities can hold several advantages over smaller, more fragmented development types. Because of the emphasis on coordinated planning and design, homebuyers have generally responded favorably to the concept.

In addition to potentially greater market acceptance, planned communities can be easier for municipalities

First Colony in Fort Bend County, Texas, is a 9,000-acre (3,645-hectare) master-planned community developed by Sugarland Properties, Inc.

SWA Group

to regulate than smaller projects. Instead of dealing with perhaps hundreds of landowners or developers, each trying to maximize its development potential, planned communities usually reduce the municipality's negotiations to a single master developer, making negotiations and permitting easier to manage and making it easier to balance new residential growth with needed infrastructure and community services like roads, schools, and parks.

Neighborhoods. A neighborhood is the geographic area within which residents conveniently share the common services and facilities needed in the vicinity of their dwellings. Neighborhoods are often set by physical boundaries: 1) natural features such as topography or watercourses; 2) streets or highways; 3) manmade features such as power lines, railroads, or other obstructions to development; and 4) planning elements such as parks, open-space corridors, and community facilities. Neighborhoods can also be set by social boundaries within which most residents share a common lifestyle or ethnic or socioeconomic characteristic; the neighborhoods that have characterized many of our larger cities are examples.

For contemporary planners, neighborhood boundaries are often defined as the service area of an elementary school and convenience shopping center. To promote the concept of neighborhood, major roadways should be designed around the periphery of the neighborhood, and only local streets serving the needs of residents should be built within the neighborhood.

New neighborhoods in planned unit developments or master-planned communities often contain various types of residential products at different densities. The trend has been to provide for a variety of households and lifestyles and a range in prices or rents within what might be considered the same neighborhood. This concept permits developers to expand the market considerably by offering products that will appeal to a larger and more diverse segment of the population. Some localities, however, discourage such diversity by regulatory controls that prohibit higher-density housing. Existing residents of a neighborhood may also resist the introduction of substantially different types of housing or densities in an effort to preserve the status quo.

The concept of neighborhood is not limited to the development of raw land. Planning commissions use the concept as a basis for studies of new growth areas in cities or in replanning older sections. The size, type, boundaries, and community facilities of a neighborhood are often determined on the basis of existing physical barriers and a land use survey, modified in accordance with plans for major thoroughfares, transportation, parks and playgrounds, and other physical, social, and economic factors.

Although the concept of neighborhood is valid for developers as an overall planning tool, perhaps more important is the creation of subneighborhoods that, more than anything else, lend a sense of place to the residents of a development. Residents sometimes perceive their

Park DuValle is a mixed-income neighborhood that mixes a variety of residential types with schools and commercial facilities.

immediate environment more vividly than the larger context called a neighborhood.

Infill Development. Every city and its suburbs contain vacant parcels of land in otherwise built-up areas. These "infill" sites can result from a lack of public services, physical or environmental limitations, or general unattractiveness to the market. Encouraging development of such parcels has become an objective for federal, state, and local governments faced with rising land costs, decreasing capability to expand infrastructure at the urban fringe, and pressures to preserve environmentally sensitive or agricultural land. Infill development is a key component of smart growth strategies. Successful infill development can strengthen older neighborhoods through preservation and rehabilitation, and it helps improve access to transportation and address a growing concern about the distance between jobs and housing.

Urban infill projects make sense for several reasons. They meet emerging demand from people moving back to the city and can spark neighborhood revitalization. They can usually be higher density than suburban housing, thus making better use of increasingly limited urban land. Because they are in developed areas, they are often less destructive to the natural environment than is suburban development. And because of their locations and densities, they can help support mass transit.

Infill projects can also yield great financial reward and have therefore gained favor among many developers. Building on infill sites near existing infrastructure can be less costly than building on land at the urban fringe, where developers are often required to donate land or contribute fees for such public services as schools, parks, roads, and utility extensions.

Context-sensitive design is a fundamental concept that underlies the planning and design of infill development. The existing urban context must be fully understood in all dimensions: physical, social, economic, and regulatory. Infill projects hold a particular potential for controversy from existing residents of surrounding parcels, but developers can reduce the opportunity for controversy by designing a project that blends with the surrounding community. Developers must balance what is economically feasible for the site with what is perceived to be compatible with the existing urban fabric.

The New Urbanism. The new urbanism (or traditional neighborhood development [TND]) seeks to integrate the components of daily life—housing, workplace, shopping, recreation, and worship—into compact, pedestrian-friendly, mixed-use communities. Although the terms *neotraditional* and *new urbanism* were coined in the 1980s, the principles relate to preautomobile 19th-century towns and early 20th-century suburbs. The compact, neighborhood-focused development patterns of those older models are viewed as an antidote to the sprawling anonymity of standard suburban subdivisions.

The new urbanism borrows many elements from these older communities, with a focus on creating pedestrian-friendly neighborhoods with a mix of uses that encourage social interaction. The ideal neotraditional town plan

A small infill development brings new luxury housing to a neighborhood in Cleveland, Ohio.

contains a full mix of uses—homes of varying sizes and types, shops, offices, schools, recreation facilities—all within walking distance of one another. "Walking distance" usually means an area that can be covered in a ten-minute walk or within a radius of one-quarter mile (0.4 kilometer). Sidewalks, well-defined public spaces, and human-scale buildings that face the streets are intended to encourage residents to walk rather than drive to their destinations. Every effort is made to deemphasize the automobile both visually and functionally; residential garages and commercial parking facilities are placed behind buildings, and streets are narrower.

A particularly distinctive feature of new urbanist town plans is the street system. New urbanism planners reject the meandering, hierarchical street networks of the standard suburb, favoring an urban-style connected grid, with homes set close to the street. Service alleys provide parking areas, access to garages, and space for trash cans and mailboxes. The resulting streetscapes are more attractive, intimate, and pedestrian oriented. In 1991, the Local Government Commission, a Sacramento-based nonprofit, brought together a group of new urbanists to develop a set of community and regional principles. Called the Ahwahnee Principles, they provide a framework for community development.

Transit-Oriented Development. Transit-oriented development (TOD) is a specific type of development that focuses on reducing areawide automobile dependence by locating residential units and other supporting uses

Preamble

Existing patterns of urban and suburban development seriously impair our quality of life. The symptoms are more congestion and air pollution resulting from our increased dependence on automobiles, the loss of precious open space, the need for costly improvements to roads and public services, the inequitable distribution of economic resources, and the loss of a sense of community. By drawing upon the best from the past and the present, we can plan communities that will more successfully serve the needs of those who live and work within them. Such planning should adhere to certain fundamental principles.

Community Principles

1. All planning should be in the form of complete and integrated communities containing housing, shops, workplaces, schools, parks, and civic facilities essential to the daily life of the residents.
2. Community size should be designed so that housing, jobs, daily needs, and other activities are within easy walking distance of each other.
3. As many activities as possible should be located within easy walking distance of transit stops.
4. A community should contain a diversity of housing types to enable citizens from a wide range of economic levels and age groups to live within its boundaries.
5. Businesses within the community should provide a range of job types for the community's residents.
6. The location and character of the community should be consistent with a larger transit network.
7. The community should have a center focus that combines commercial, civic, cultural, and recreational uses.
8. The community should contain an ample supply of specialized open space in the form of squares, greens, and parks whose frequent use is encouraged through placement and design.
9. Public spaces should be designed to encourage the attention and presence of people at all hours of the day and night.
10. Each community or cluster of communities should have a well-defined edge, such as agricultural greenbelts or wildlife corridors, permanently protected from development.
11. Streets, pedestrian paths, and bike paths should contribute to a system of fully connected and interesting routes to all destinations. Their design should encourage pedestrian and bicycle use by being small and spatially defined by buildings, trees, and lighting and by discouraging high-speed traffic.
12. Wherever possible, the natural terrain, drainage, and vegetation of the community should be preserved with superior examples contained within parks or greenbelts.

13. The community design should help conserve resources and minimize waste.
14. Communities should provide for the efficient use of water through the use of natural drainage, drought-tolerant landscaping, and recycling.
15. The street orientation, the placement of buildings, and the use of shading should contribute to the energy efficiency of the community.

Regional Principles

1. The regional land use planning structure should be integrated within a larger transportation network built around transit rather than freeways.
2. Regions should be bounded by and provide a continuous system of greenbelt/wildlife corridors to be determined by natural conditions.
3. Regional institutions and services (government, stadiums, museums, et cetera) should be located in the urban core.
4. Materials and methods of construction should be specific to the region, exhibiting a continuity of history and culture and compatibility with the climate to encourage the development of local character and community identity.

Implementation Principles

1. The general plan should be updated to incorporate the above principles.
2. Rather than allowing developer-initiated, piecemeal development, local governments should take charge of the planning process. General plans should designate where new growth, infill, or redevelopment will be allowed to occur.
3. Prior to any development, a specific plan should be prepared based on these planning principles.
4. Plans should be developed through an open process, and participants in the process should be provided visual models of all planning proposals. ∎

within walking distance of a transit node. The primary emphasis of TOD is to encourage development at a density that supports transit and to provide a full range of pedestrian-accessible community facilities, including schools, shops, daycare centers, and recreation areas.

Rural Village and Hamlet. A rural village may be the planned extension of an existing community or a new settlement built on previously undeveloped land. In either case, rural villages involve more concentrated residential development than is typically allowed by rural zoning.

Designed as an alternative to scattered large-lot development, rural villages minimize disruption of the rural landscape and help preserve agricultural land. In some locations, nonprofit preservation groups have worked cooperatively with the planners of rural villages, using techniques such as land trusts to further ensure that the land surrounding the villages remains undeveloped. The rural village is intended to serve as a physical, social, and economic focal point in the rural landscape, reinforcing traditional settlement patterns. Although rural villages are seen mainly as residential settlements, they are also appropriate locations for schools, government offices, churches, and stores. Small villages may be no more than a few homes located at a crossroads, perhaps grouped around a single commercial building such as a general store. Larger rural villages may contain a small "downtown" surrounded by homes. Hamlets are essentially smaller versions of rural villages.[5]

Land Plan Elements

Land Use

Local governments employ many standards of land use to regulate development. Most of these standards were created to regulate conventional lot-by-lot development and have been modified and adapted for newer forms of development like PUDs. Conventional standards for residential development seek to control the number, type, and placement of housing units that can be constructed on a parcel of land by regulating such variables as size, lot coverage, street frontage, width and depth of lots, building setbacks from lot lines, and building height. Codified in zoning and subdivision ordinances, these standards are responsible for the land use patterns and character of most communities developed in the United States between 1920 and 1980.

As clustering, PUDs, and other forms became more prevalent and desirable, density replaced lot size as the most commonly used regulatory standard. Other variables normally regulated in conjunction with density include lot coverage, open-space ratios, building setbacks, building height, width, and depth, unit size, and the amount of parking per unit.

The trend in regulations seems to be away from lists of permitted and prohibited uses and accompanying standards and toward the use of criteria and standards that measure the performance of a development. The goal of more flexible regulations is to encourage greater

Esplanade Place brings very high density to Phoenix, Arizona, a city not normally known for this kind of development. The units sold out in eight months.

sensitively toward specific site conditions and to create neighborhoods containing a mix of housing choices as well as complementary land uses. Performance standards are being incorporated into zoning and subdivision ordinances, and developers will encounter them more frequently in the years to come. Other trends in assigning land uses include greater mixing of land uses, both vertical (within the same building) and horizontal, achieving a balance between housing and jobs, providing on-site services and amenities to reduce off-site traffic trips, and linking land use to innovative transportation solutions.

The process of determining the appropriate land uses for a property starts with the locality, dictated by its comprehensive plan or land use plan. The plan is further defined by zoning ordinances and other land use controls. When the jurisdiction has flexible and innovative ordinances that will allow mixing of land uses, the developer can assign the most appropriate land uses to the property. This parcelization is reflected in the concept

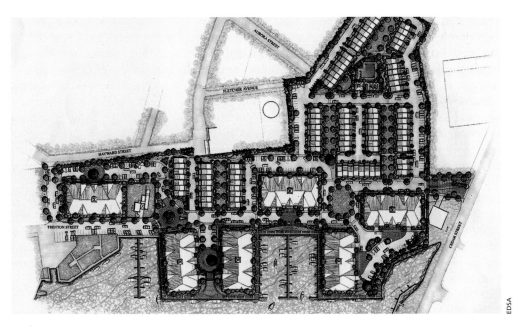

Higher densities are increasingly acceptable. Deep Harbor in Cambridge, Maryland, is an infill waterfront community that combines townhouses and mid-rise condominiums.

EDSA

plan and establishes the framework for parcel-by-parcel site planning and subdivision. In addition to the land for residential development, land use parcelization needs to account for rights-of-way for major arterials and collector streets, areas to be reserved as open space, and sites for commercial facilities and public purposes. The plan identifies the approximate acreage of each parcel and its intended use. In large, multiphase residential developments, planners and developers should maintain some flexibility in assigning specific land uses to individual parcels.

Plan Organization. Two primary organizing elements —the roadway or street system (along with its resultant spaces) and the open-space network—determine how a plan will be structured. Structure in land planning or site planning refers to the way the plan is organized and how the various elements relate to each other. The streets and the open space are the organizing elements that link the various land uses. They can also separate land uses from each other. It is through the street and open-space networks that the whole plan is created by the joining together of all its parts. The streets and open-space network must be designed in tandem to create a cohesive whole for the residential community.

Residential Land Parcels. Density is the method of expressing the number of dwelling units in a particular area, normally per acre (per hectare). *Gross density* is based on a site's total land area, including streets, nonresidential uses, and open space. *Net density* represents the number of dwelling units per net acre of land devoted to residential and accessory uses, excluding land for streets, public parking, playgrounds, nonresidential uses, and open space.

Density has always been a matter of interpretation. Historically, lower density was often interpreted as synonymous with higher quality. But today, it is widely recognized that density in and of itself does not guarantee quality and that high-quality, livable neighborhoods can be developed at high densities.

Municipalities often establish maximum gross and net densities for residential projects. Other common regulatory techniques for controlling density include specifying minimum lot size and maximum lot coverage, building height, and front, rear, and side yard setbacks. Another technique is to specify open space ratios that mandate requirements for usable open space. Most zoning and subdivision ordinances use some combination of these techniques.

In localities where an urban character is desired, the minimums and maximums are essentially reversed. Maximum lot sizes are proscribed, along with minimum lot coverage, minimum building heights, and maximum setbacks. Such regulations are often part of codes that encourage the new urbanism.

Clearly, density is a major factor affecting a developer's return on investment, because the fewer the number of units, the higher the cost of land and improvements per unit. Although low density may keep a project from being feasible, a high density does not guarantee its success. For a project to be viable, the market's expectations must also be met. A project's success depends on many factors: the price of the homes, the number of units, development costs, and sales pace (and thus the length of time interest charges must be carried).

The trend in residential development today is toward higher densities, in part because of increased acceptance of cluster subdivisions, which permit higher densities on some portions of the site to provide open space on others. It also relates to a decreasing supply of land. When developing at higher densities, environmental impacts like increased runoff, traffic, and demand for services become important considerations during planning. Higher densities also require more attention to the design of streetscapes and public spaces. Sensitivity to these considerations can make the critical difference in the project's approval, market acceptance, and ultimate livability.

During much of the 20th century, it was common practice to physically segregate housing types, thus creating separate, uniform sections of homes. Although many local development controls still encourage this practice, it is often criticized for producing homogeneous and sterile residential landscapes. A better recent trend that creates more livable neighborhoods and communities blends different housing types and densities in proximity to each other.

School Sites. Public uses include schools, libraries, and facilities for public services like police and fire protection. The need for such sites in a residential development depends on the availability of such services off site and plans for their provision in the future. Developers should consult with appropriate public agencies to determine whether it is necessary to reserve land for public uses. Appropriate locations for public uses in a residential development should be determined as part of the site planning and design process.

The availability of good elementary schools is an important consideration for developments where family households will form a substantial market segment. Often, the quality of the schools that serve an area significantly affects the potential price range of housing. The presence of nearby high-quality private or religiously affiliated schools may also positively affect the market. Like elementary schools, preschool or daycare centers may be an important consideration for family-oriented markets.

Providing schools is usually a responsibility of the public sector, but providing the land for schools is another matter. Subdivision ordinances often require dedication of land or fees for schools. Courts have generally held this practice to be reasonable if the requirement is based on the need created by the new development.

Ideally, an elementary school site should be accessible to all sections of the project through a good, safe pedestrian network. Sites for elementary schools should not front on a major thoroughfare, exposed to heavy traffic and noise. Each school district has its own criteria for locating schools, and developers should meet with officials before proceeding.

Schools are a desirable amenity for young families, so the developer's objective should be to site a school near the maximum number of units that will probably house the maximum number of school-age children. Placing a school near the highest-priced housing planned for the community is not recommended, because the number of school-age children tends to decline as housing prices rise. Junior and senior high schools usually serve larger areas than elementary schools, and their sites require greater accessibility by both vehicles and pedestrians.

Institutional Uses. Developers should not overlook the value that institutional land uses, such as churches and synagogues, can bring to a development, particularly if the project is larger than 1,000 units. Such facilities require parking, and sites should either be large enough for on-site parking or located where a logical shared parking strategy can be established. Parking requirements relate to the size of the congregation and to the building's seating capacity.

It is generally beneficial to site institutional uses near commercial areas, schools, and other public facilities. Parking can often be shared and trips combined, thus reducing the land required for parking. Further, institutional sites can provide a buffer between neighborhood shopping centers and residential areas, provided that parking does not overflow onto residential streets.

Streets

Residential streets should be safe, efficient, convenient, and economical. They should be designed for the particular purpose, traffic volume, and development density they serve. Historically, standards for and advances in street design have been largely confined to highways and major thoroughfares, and standards for residential streets were usually adapted from highway designs. Requirements for residential streets were often established in anticipation that a street might eventually be converted to a higher classification. These practices have been insensitive to the needs of residential communi-

A residential street must do more than just move traffic. It must provide a safe place for pedestrians and fit in with the neighborhood's character.

Heritage Partners

EDSA

Narrow streets slow the traffic naturally, without speed bumps or other measures.

ties and have often resulted in needlessly wide and expensive streets.

Residential streets should be designed to be in scale with the neighborhood they serve. People live on them. It is desirable, therefore, to move traffic safely and efficiently but also to see that the needs of people are met. Streets must provide for movement of automobiles, places to park, and access for service and emergency vehicles. But certain qualities must be given a higher priority to develop "smarter" residential streets.

Smarter residential streets are ones that achieve:

- Low traffic volumes
- Slow speeds
- Minimal noise
- Easy access
- Multiple routes
- Security and safety
- Facilitated pedestrian and bicycle use
- Visual attractiveness.

Many municipalities have antiquated street design standards that result in higher than necessary costs for infrastructure. But many developments have reduced costs significantly while at the same time improving the character of the development by using innovative street design standards. The Urban Land Institute, the American Society of Civil Engineers, and the National Association of Home Builders have cooperatively prepared a book, *Residential Streets*, which provides information for residential developers about innovative street design.[6]

The street plan of a neighborhood should build up the circulation element of a community's comprehensive plan, which normally identifies future alignments for collector and arterial roads. New residential areas need to be accessible from existing streets and roads, which might mean that a major road must be extended through a development and that the road must be wider than those that serve just the residential development

alone. Residential streets, however, should generally be planned to discourage use by through traffic. A recent trend has placed great emphasis on "traffic calming" (discussed later in this chapter).

The street plan should relate to the natural contours of the site, and existing features of the landscape should be preserved. The street system should respond to the site's soil and geologic conditions, potential drainage and runoff, existing or abutting land uses, and the purpose, length, and intended character of the streets themselves. The street pattern can be curvilinear, straight, or a hybrid of the two, depending on site conditions and the intended character of the development.

The new urbanist movement has placed great emphasis on the desirability of traditional grid street patterns. Traditional grid streets do achieve many desirable results, including dispersing traffic, providing more direct routes, encouraging more pedestrian use, and better enabling transit. Curvilinear street alignments with culs-de-sac also have advantages—keeping through traffic out of neighborhoods, creating safer and quieter local streets, responding to natural site features and rolling topography, and generally working better in golf course communities. No single solution exists, but each site and community layout should be evaluated to determine the best possible approach.

Classification. The two main types of residential streets are collector streets and local streets. Collector streets convey traffic between local streets and arterial streets or highways. Local streets, which include both subcollectors and access streets, convey traffic between collector streets and dwelling units or off-street parking areas.

Collector streets are intended to carry a relatively high volume of traffic. Collectors typically carry an average daily traffic (ADT) volume of more than 1,000 vehicles. Collector streets have one or more moving lanes in either direction, depending on the anticipated traffic load, and are intended to carry major public transportation, such as buses. On-street parking and direct access to individual dwelling units are not considered appropriate for collector streets.

Subcollector streets are intended to carry traffic between collectors and access streets. Subcollectors typically carry an ADT volume of 250 to 1,000 vehicles. They can provide frontage for and access to individual dwelling units and can accommodate on-street parking; they generally require one traffic lane in each direction.

Access streets, sometimes called places or lanes, are the lowest-order streets in the hierarchy and are not intended to carry through traffic. Examples of access streets include culs-de-sac, private drives, lanes, courts, and short streets serving a few houses. Access streets typically carry an ADT volume of fewer than 250 vehicles. They usually can accommodate on-street parking and may require only one traffic lane.

Alignment and Width. Wide residential streets are not better streets. Oversized streets require more clearing and grading, destroy natural landscape, increase runoff, and add to storm drainage requirements. They are more expensive to maintain and increase the potential hazard for pedestrians by encouraging drivers to speed. And overly wide streets detract from the aesthetics of a neighborhood. It is in the interest of the developer, the locality, and the residents of the proposed development to minimize roadway widths and rights-of-way wherever possible.

Horizontal alignment of residential streets should be based on terrain, sight distances, and appropriate roadway speeds. Vertical alignments should be sensitive to adverse weather conditions and limited visibility. Local customs and such factors as energy conservation, aesthetics, and drainage dictate vertical alignment. Good drainage is of the utmost importance in street design, especially in areas subject to periodic freezing and thawing. The project engineer should recommend a street cross section that ensures adequate drainage.

Widths of street rights-of-way should be considered carefully. Unnecessarily wide rights-of-way may reduce final lot yields where maximum allowable densities are calculated as a percentage of the net land area. Providing additional rights-of-way (for future widening of local streets) is usually not necessary. The right-of-way width must accommodate the required street pavement. Additional width usually accommodates sidewalks, utilities, plant materials, and grading, but these features can also be located within easements on land owned in common by a community association or on other private property.

Traffic Calming. With traffic issues plaguing so many communities, "traffic calming" has become an important factor in the planning of residential communities. Existing residential neighborhoods are being retrofitted to slow down or divert traffic. Traffic calming is the combination of mainly physical measures that reduce the negative effects of motor vehicle use, alter drivers' behavior, and improve conditions for nonmotorized street users.[7]

Traffic calming can involve changes in street alignment and the installation of barriers and other measures to reduce traffic speed and/or cut through traffic volumes.

Traffic calming is increasingly common in residential neighborhoods. By narrowing a street at the intersection, traffic is slowed to a safer speed.

Two categories of devices are used: those that control speed and those that control traffic volume. Speed control measures include speed humps, speed tables, raised intersections, traffic circles or roundabouts, narrower center islands, neckdowns, and bulb-outs. Volume control measures typically involve diverting traffic to other areas by closing or partially closing streets.

Culs-de-Sac. Culs-de-sac are dead-end streets with a turnaround at the end for cars. They are popular in single-family developments because of the privacy and freedom from traffic noise they offer. Culs-de-sac up to 1,200 feet long (365 meters) are satisfactory, but 500 feet (150 meters) is considered a more reasonable length for dead-end streets. The design of the turnaround at the end of a cul-de-sac should depend on the street's anticipated traffic volume and the type of vehicles that will use the street. Circular turnarounds are most common, but T- or Y-shaped turnarounds can also work and can be more cost-effective.

The recommended minimum radius for the paved area of a circular turnaround is 30 feet (9 meters), the outside turning radius for large passenger cars. Larger vehicles need to back up once to negotiate the turnaround, but this minor inconvenience is considered acceptable in a residential area. In any case, a paved turnaround with a radius greater than 40 or 45 feet (12 or 14 meters) should be discouraged because it is more expensive to install and maintain, it results in increased stormwater runoff, and the large expanse of pavement is generally considered unattractive.

A center island can be used to break up the expanse of pavement in a circular turnaround. If used, the road around the island should be 20 feet (6 meters) wide, and low-maintenance landscaping materials should be used. The recommended right-of-way for circular turnarounds is usually a radius ten feet (3 meters) greater than the paved area.

Driveways and Curbs. Driveways provide access to off-street parking or garages. The greater the number of driveways intersecting a street, the greater the number of points of conflict that lower the street's capacity. The resulting decrease in traffic speed is desirable, however, on local residential streets. On the other hand, driveways diminish pedestrian safety and comfort on sidewalks. A minimum width of ten feet (3 meters) is recommended for a single-lane driveway. For parking lot entrances and other high-volume driveways, both a wider lane and a transition radius of ten to 15 feet (3 to 4.5 meters) are recommended.

Curbs may not be necessary on local streets in low-density residential neighborhoods unless they are required for stormwater control or road stabilization. Curbs serve three purposes: to provide lateral support for the edge of the pavement, to prevent water from seeping under the pavement, and to contain pavement base materials and provide rigid channels for stormwater runoff. Aesthetically, curbing also provides a hard edge to the street that clearly defines the street from the adjacent lot and open space.

The two basic types of curbing are *vertical* (or barrier) curbs and *mountable* (or rolled) curbs. Neither type of curb acts as a safety barrier to protect those on sidewalks, as an out-of-control car can generally mount both types. Curbs are much more a psychological than a physical barrier and are really effective only for preventing encroachment. Railings, posts, and shrubbery achieve the same effect.

Vertical curbs create a greater capacity to channel stormwater runoff than do mountable curbs. On steep grades of 8 percent or more, mountable curbs are impractical and are not generally recommended. Installation costs of both types of curb are similar, with mountable curbs being slightly less expensive than vertical curbs. Mountable curbs also make it possible to dispense with the installation of curb depressions for driveways. This feature increases design flexibility during construction in that the locations of driveways do not have to be determined before curbs are installed.

Alleys. Alleys are again becoming popular in residential plans. Alleys can be a beneficial part of certain patterns of development at higher densities. They are frequently used in the new urbanist form of development. Alleys provide a second means of auto access to lots between 20 and 40 feet (6 and 12 meters) wide, allowing the number of curb cuts, driveways, and garage doors on the front street to be reduced. This arrangement can improve the streetscape and pedestrian safety and increase availability of on-street parking for guests.

Ten to 12 feet (3 to 4 meters) wide is generally adequate for an alley to accommodate cars. If alleys are to accommodate service vehicles, however, they should be 12 to 16 feet (4 to 5 meters) wide. This width will also provide just enough clearance for two cars to pass. Alleys can be private or public, depending on the requirements of the local jurisdiction. If they are public, the rights-of-way should be coincident with the width of the pavement. Garages and parking spaces should be set back from the alley adequately to provide enough turning space for vehicles.

Private Streets. Regardless of whether a street is public or private, it should be designed in response to the situation and specific needs. Municipalities are sometimes concerned that private streets are designed to lesser standards than those required by the municipality. Developers should be afforded the opportunity for innovation, and in keeping with the flexibility and discretion inherent in PUDs, private streets should be considered.

Many developers propose that all streets or certain streets within a development be designed and built as private streets to allow innovative design or for more cost-efficient street standards. For example, some municipalities do not allow medians, signs, lights, or certain types of landscaping in rights-of-way for public streets because of responsibilities for maintenance and the liabilities they incur. Most jurisdictions do not permit a guardhouse or security gate if streets are to be public. Developers must therefore consider how the streets will be used and how they can best be designed and maintained from the perspective of future residents before deciding whether streets should be public or private. One of the major drawbacks of private streets is that the cost of ongoing maintenance and repairs must be borne by the residents in the community homeowners' association.

Parking. Preparation of a parking plan for a residential neighborhood is affected by code requirements, costs, and topography. Parking is also a function of households' size, composition, and income; housing density; proximity to services like schools and shopping centers; and access to public transportation.

The parking plan should take into account trends in the size of automobiles and ownership patterns. Multicar households are increasingly common. According to the 2000 Census, more than 16 percent of households had three or more vehicles.[8] Changes in demographics and energy costs will certainly continue to affect these trends.

Minimum parking requirements for residential developments differ from one municipality to another, and needs vary according to type of dwelling, locality, and

At One Ford Road in Newport Beach, California, rear alleys are used to keep garages, curb cuts, and utilities off the main streets.

Adrienne Schmitz

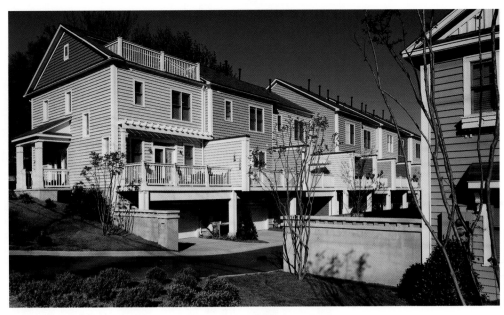

At Latta Heights in Charlotte, North Carolina, parking is provided in rear garages tucked under the houses and camouflaged by decks on the main level.

The Boulevard Company

household composition. For example, 2.5 spaces or more per dwelling unit are likely to be needed for developments with households including teenage children or for apartments shared by unrelated adults. One space per unit or less is more likely in housing for the elderly, especially in locations with good access to public transit. Yet many ordinances stipulate the same parking ratio for the elderly as for family-oriented projects.

At least two off-street parking spaces per dwelling unit should usually be provided for residents and guests in single-family detached projects. When zoning or subdivision regulations stipulate two parking spaces per dwelling unit, the developer must clarify whether the requirement can be satisfied by a two-car garage or whether that space must be provided for outside the garage. If the garage or carport is to be counted as required off-street parking space, this allowance should be clarified in the covenants, conditions, and restrictions (CCRs) so that future conversion of the garage to living space does not cause parking shortages.

Two parking spaces per unit should also generally be provided for residents and guests in new single-family attached projects. Traditionally, 1.5 parking spaces per unit have been provided for multifamily projects, regardless of the number of bedrooms, with additional space for guest parking also advisable. Generally, 1.75 to two spaces per unit is a better measure unless the project is convenient to public transit. The recommended minimum requirement for off-street parking for multifamily housing projects is usually 1.25 spaces per unit for studio apartments, 1.5 spaces for each one-bedroom unit, 1.75 spaces per unit for two-bedroom units, and two spaces per unit for units with three or more bedrooms. Providing too much parking can be just as bad as not providing enough. Zoning ordinances that require an unreasonable amount of parking in effect dictate the ultimate design of the project, affecting density and the visual appearance of the community and contributing to additional stormwater runoff and sprawl.

On-Street Parking. Parking for residents in planned communities is normally off street, although guest parking may be provided on the street. In particular, many new urbanist communities have encouraged a return to providing more on-street parking. Two options are available for on-street parking: parallel parking lanes and diagonal or angled parking spaces. Parallel parking is generally considered safer and requires less street width, making it less expensive. Parallel parking lanes should generally be eight feet (2.4 meters) wide and can be provided on one or both sides of a street. In some situations, parking bays may be the best solution on local residential streets, such as in the center of turnarounds for culs-de-sac. Diagonal or 90-degree parking in recessed bays along access streets and interior service drives can be used successfully for single-family attached and multifamily housing.

Off-Street Parking. Locations for off-street parking include driveways, carports, garages, surface lots, and above-ground, below-ground, or integral parking structures. The choice depends on such variables as density, type of dwelling unit, the market, and site conditions, especially the cost of land. In determining the area required for surface parking, a good rule of thumb is to reserve approximately 225 square feet (21 square meters) for each automobile, including the parking space and a proportional share of moving lanes. Cars parked in surface lots can never be completely screened from view, but large surface parking areas should be subdivided by landscaping. Surface parking should also be screened from adjacent structures and streets with hedges, dense vegetation, earth berms, changes in grade, or walls. The selection of plants for hedges or screening should consider the plants' size at maturity, differences in seasonal foliage, and maintenance, including feeding, pruning, spraying, watering, and eventual replacement.

Off-street parking facilities vary greatly in price. A single uncovered surface parking space in a parking lot may cost $1,000 to $2,500, depending on the total size of the lot and other variables. The average cost of a sin-

The Bristol in Charleston, South Carolina, includes two levels of structured parking with condominium units above.

gle space in an above-grade parking structure is about $8,500—$15,000 if the parking structure supports a building above it. The typical cost of a single space in a below-grade or integral parking structure can be as high as $20,000, with integral parking slightly less expensive. The use of structured parking can therefore be justified only if the market is willing to bear the higher cost. It is desirable to locate parking spaces close to the entrance to residences. An indirect or inconvenient route that offers no protection from the elements is not a satisfactory solution.

Sometimes simple but well-designed carports in a parking compound are a suitable solution for off-street parking. Garages built under multifamily units save land on hilly sites, but they may raise construction costs because they must be fireproofed. Enclosed garages are usually not used for multifamily construction except where land costs or the project's density dictate it. Increasingly, particularly at higher price levels, multifamily dwellers consider garages important and are willing to pay for them.

Early marketing studies should establish the sale value of garages, the number required, and the importance of attaching them to individual units. In almost all markets, a two-car garage is essential for single-family detached housing. In some markets, even three-car garages are considered standard. Providing garages, however, means additional land coverage, greater setbacks, additional costs, and potentially negative impacts on the appearance of the streetscape. Especially in townhouse and small-lot detached neighborhoods, accommodating garages aesthetically is an increasingly important challenge in design. It can often be solved, however, with the use of alleys and garages in the rear.

In most cases, residents prefer a garage that is attached to the house. Carrying in groceries during inclement weather must be considered, and security is a growing influence on design. The convenience, privacy, and individuality afforded owners of a house with an attached garage are strong reasons for their inclusion.

If the walk to the house is pleasant, the market might accept separate garage clusters rather than attached garages. Clustered garages can work well for townhouses and garden-density multifamily units. For flexibility, a combination of both attached and detached garages as close as possible to individual houses is often desirable. Using small garage clusters reduces the scale of the buildings, permits parking areas to be closer to the homes they serve, and adds another architectural form to accent and vary the development's visual image.

Strategies to deal with parked recreational vehicles, boats, and trailers are increasingly important in residential communities. In general, oversized vehicles should not be permitted on residential streets, in front yards, or between dwellings because of their visual impact and potential fire hazard. The problem is particularly difficult in townhouse and multifamily developments. Special garages and remote screened storage yards have been used successfully in many large-scale planned communities.

Bikeways. Accommodating bicycle use should be an integral part of the transportation planning for a residential community.[9] Bikeways should be designed with regard to users' ability, specific corridor conditions, and facility cost. Several types of provisions for bicycles are possible: shared roadways (no bikeway designation), signed shared roadways, bicycle lanes, and shared-use paths.

When they are provided, bicycle lanes and shared roadways are generally located on collector streets and arterials. Such bikeways should be four feet (1.2 meters) wide if located at the edge of the pavement and five feet (1.5 meters) wide if parallel to on-street parked cars. For a shared-use path, an eight- to ten-foot (2.4- to 3-meter) paved area is desirable. Pavement striping helps separate different uses. Hiker/biker trails or regional bikeways are usually paths that are completely separated rights-of-way for the primary use of bicyclists, roller bladers, joggers, and hikers. In general, the trail should be at least ten feet (3 meters) wide, permitting two-way traffic.

Pedestrian Circulation. A well-planned system of sidewalks and paths is an important element for a residential community. Walking continues to be the number one recreational activity for most people. A number of objectives should be met when developing the pedestrian element of a site plan:

- A continuous pedestrian network should connect origins and destinations by means of direct, barrier-free paths and/or sidewalks.
- Recreational pathways should be continuous but not necessarily direct.
- The number of conflict points between pedestrians and motor vehicles should be minimized, particularly where traffic flow is heavy.
- Clear delineation of pedestrian paths should ensure that effective walking routes can be selected. Signing may be needed, particularly in large developments.
- Pedestrian facilities should be designed for easy maintenance.
- Pedestrian amenities (greenery, shade trees, benches, and so forth) to enhance walking and socializing should be provided.
- Pedestrians' special needs must be accommodated; meeting requirements of the Americans with Disabilities Act (ADA) should be part of the plan.
- Facilities should be designed to maximize pedestrians' security and safety. Visibility and surveillance from streets, parking lots, and buildings should be considered in designing the walkway system.

Access for pedestrians from each home or cluster of homes to a variety of destinations—open space, recreational facilities, schools, daycare facilities, commercial centers—is an important consideration in site planning. Such access can be from the front or the rear of a home. Traditionally, access has been provided from the front, and a sidewalk is used to link the house to the community's street-oriented pedestrian system. Access can also

Shared paths for biking, walking, and jogging are among the most popular and cost-effective amenities in residential communities.

SWA Group

be provided between houses or clusters of houses to an off-street pedestrian system built in open-space areas.

At-grade street crossings should be located where sight distance along the road is good, and curb cuts should always be provided for users of wheelchairs, bicycles, wagons, tricycles, and strollers. At-grade street crossings on major streets require safety devices such as appropriate signs, signals, and crosswalks. When paths or sidewalks intersect arterial streets, special signal controls, underpasses, or overpasses may be necessary. Underpasses can be a security problem, however, unless they are designed for visual surveillance, and pedestrian overpasses are often expensive and often not used unless they are very direct and readily accessible routes.

Public streets, private trails, park areas, and abandoned rights-of-way should all be considered opportunities to accommodate pedestrians, but public access must be balanced with residents' privacy. Accommodating handicapped residents also is necessary. Wheelchair accessibil-

ity must be provided for any pedestrian byways in accordance with the Americans with Disabilities Act of 1990.

Sidewalks. Sidewalks provide meeting areas for neighbors and play areas for children as well as direct circulation routes. Providing sidewalks along both sides of all residential streets is one way to meet pedestrian needs. The location and width of sidewalks are important considerations and should be determined by the size and scale of the street, traffic volumes, pedestrian/automobile conflict points, destinations, and community focal points. For example, in a low-density neighborhood on a short cul-de-sac with only a few homes, a sidewalk may be needed along only one side of the street. In such cases, sidewalks are often supplemented with off-street walkways that create an interconnected pedestrian system. But in neighborhoods with grid streets and continuous block frontages, sidewalks are always warranted on both sides.

Sidewalks are usually located within the public right-of-way or within a public easement immediately adjacent

At Baxter Village, South Carolina, sidewalks are separated from the street by a planting strip that accommodates a row of shade trees.

Urban Design Associates

At Rivermark in Santa Clara, California, mews with walkways connect the public and private realms.

Adrienne Schmitz

to the right-of-way. Current thinking on minimum side-walk widths is divided. Many experts believe that five feet (1.5 meters) is an appropriate width, while others, citing cost, believe four feet (1.2 meters) is more reasonable. A width of five feet (1.5 meters) is enough space for two people to walk side by side. It also allows a wheelchair to turn around or two wheelchairs to pass each other. Advocates of a four-foot-wide (1.2-meter-wide) sidewalk point out that providing five-foot-wide (1.5-meter-wide) passing spaces at regular intervals can mitigate the need for a sidewalk with a continuous width of five feet (1.5 meters). Regardless of which minimum width is a better choice, experts agree that the width of a sidewalk should relate to its environment. For example, high-density areas, those with more attractions, and roadways with high traffic volumes should be served by wider sidewalks.

A planting strip between the edge of the street and the sidewalk is desirable to provide a space for shade trees, enhance safety for pedestrians, and provide a storage area for plowed snow. The more generous the width of the planting strip, the more easily large shade trees can be accommodated. In arid climates where water conservation is encouraged, the planting strip should be land-scaped with drought-tolerant ground covers, gravel, or other low-maintenance, water-conserving treatments. Where water is not a critical issue, planting strips are usually covered with grass. Although these border areas enhance pedestrians' comfort and safety and usually enhance aesthetics, they can become eyesores if they are not properly designed and maintained.

Paths

Paths should supplement sidewalks, connecting points of origin and destination within and adjacent to the res-idential community. For example, paths should be pro-vided between residences and parking areas, recreational areas, schools, clubhouses, and bus stops. The pedestrian circulation plan should be functional and contain pri-mary, secondary, and even tertiary routes of desirable widths and appropriate materials in appropriate locations. Walks should be laid out to generally follow the natural path of circulation, but more formal designs and layouts may also be incorporated. In addition to paths that di-rectly connect points of origin and destination, recrea-tional paths should take advantage of the site's natural amenities, following features like streams or shorelines. If a development includes woodlands or conservation areas, paths can run through them for hiking and biking.

Paths should be stabilized, surfaced, or paved as ap-propriate for the amount and character of their pro-posed use. An occasionally used footpath may work with minimal improvement such as mulch or stabilized soil pavement. Heavy pedestrian use or bicycle traffic usually requires a hard surface such as asphalt or concrete.

Streetscape

The scale of residential streets should be consistent with the density and type of housing. As density increases and lot size decreases, the importance of good design increases.

A wide range of ground covers can be used instead of lawns for a more natural, low-maintenance landscape.

The character of a residential streetscape is influenced by the relationships between such factors as building heights and setbacks, street widths and lengths, tree locations and heights, street furniture, and signs.

Trees and Landscaping. Probably no other site feature is more widely appreciated by homebuyers than mature trees. Trees improve the quality of a residential neigh-borhood by:

- Defining and organizing space,
- Providing unity and scale,
- Creating a sense of enclosure and privacy,
- Providing shade and cooling,
- Serving as windbreaks,
- Softening the visual impact of undesirable elements,
- Providing erosion and pollution control,
- Adding seasonal interest, and
- Creating habitats for wildlife.

Preserving existing trees wherever possible is the first step in planning the landscape. Planting new trees should be considered a part of every residential plan. Plantings may be formal, informal, or a combination of both. Formal planting incorporates the ordering of trees and landscape elements to provide a sense of importance and grandeur to a particular setting. Both native and ornamental plant materials may be used. The most effective formal treat-ments are those that are bold yet simple in design.

Informal planting incorporates trees and landscape elements as an extension of the natural landscape. Groves of native evergreens and deciduous trees can be planted to extend and relate to natural forests, wetlands, and marshes. In public areas and private yards, informal groupings of trees, shrubs, and ground covers can create a pleasing natural effect. Informal plantings usually are easier to maintain than formal plantings.[10]

The types of trees to be planted along the street de-pend on climate, aesthetics, and maintenance. When choosing plants for yards and common areas, it is impor-

Picket fences define property lines and give a sense of privacy, even when houses are close to the street.

Frederick Jarvis

tant to consider their mature height and the function that they serve. Species that will maintain an acceptable appearance and height without constant trimming and pruning are always preferred. Low-lying plants do well as ground covers and borders, and they can also be effective at controlling foot traffic. Hedges can increase privacy and screen objectionable features such as utility boxes.

Water conservation is a major concern in many parts of the country. During dry periods when conservation measures are imposed, watering lawns and plants is often one of the first uses to be restricted. In areas where such a possibility is likely, drought-tolerant plant materials should be selected.

Lawns require a high level of maintenance and have been overused as a landscape treatment. Lawns are best suited for fairly level outdoor living and play areas. Low-maintenance ground covers should be considered as an alternative to manicured lawns, particularly on steeper slopes where erosion control is necessary. Wherever possible, open areas should be retained in their natural condition to minimize maintenance costs and disturbance of the site.

It is in the developer's interest to provide homeowners a set of design guidelines or controls. These guidelines set forth certain design principles and may control placement, quantity, and quality of plant materials. The guidelines may also contain a series of typical landscape plans, serving as a basic landscaping design manual. Maintenance techniques and specifications can be included. Homeowners should also be made aware of any state, county, or local requirements for landscaping, particularly along the street rights-of-way.

Regardless of size, most healthy trees are worth saving. The first step during land planning for a project is to note the areas of trees to be preserved and identify them accordingly on the plans. It is generally easier to preserve larger groups of trees than individual or isolated trees, as saving isolated trees requires more care. In site planning for individual homes or buildings, careful siting

of buildings also can help to save trees. Several procedures can help ensure the survival of retained trees:

- Carefully inventory, identify, and assess trees to be preserved.
- Install durable protective fences around trees to be saved.
- Protect root zones of trees from compaction and construction debris during site construction.
- Monitor construction and maintain field control.
- Follow up with postconstruction cleanup and maintenance such as pruning, watering, and fertilizing.

Mature trees add significant value to a residential project, and the locations of roads and buildings can often be adjusted slightly to preserve mature trees. Root zones of these trees must be protected from compaction during site construction. In general, soil should be left undisturbed in a ten-foot (3-meter) radius around any tree to be preserved, and fences or walls should be constructed to prevent encroachment. Some trees, such as dogwoods, beeches, and most conifers, do not tolerate fill because they root near the surface. Other varieties may survive with some fill, but a layer of coarse gravel or broken stone six to eight inches (15 to 20 centimeters) deep should be spread over the feeder roots before filling to ensure air circulation. A tree well built at least two feet (0.6 meter) from the tree trunk and extending to the old ground level should keep the trunk from rotting. Vertical tiles are sometimes set at intervals above the feeder roots down to the level of the gravel or broken stone to permit additional air circulation. A tree can also be killed by changes in the soil's moisture conditions, increased exposure resulting from removal of its neighbors, or root damage during the installation of underground utilities.

Walls and Fences. The use of walls and fences should be considered in the context of the homes they serve, including overall lot sizes, housing types, style of architecture, topography, and landscaping. In large-lot subdivisions, fencing may not be necessary, but in higher-density communities, fences and walls can be selectively placed to provide privacy and protection.

Fences are often located to increase residents' use and enjoyment of the outdoors by defining property lines and creating outdoor "living rooms." Beyond screening other houses, fences or walls can mitigate many undesirable elements: adjacent highways, shopping centers, trash collection areas, and mechanical equipment. Noise from neighbors can be filtered, wind lessened or redirected, and snow accumulation controlled. Off-site lighting and automobile headlights can be blocked from view. Fencing helps segregate private from public spaces and can help increase a neighborhood's security. As a landscape detail, fencing can have a major impact on the visual environment:

- Fencing adds three-dimensional form, color, line, and texture to the landscape.
- Fencing can effectively divide space into two or more spaces, providing privacy for each.
- Fencing can establish a theme for a landscape; for example, a split-rail fence sets a rural character, while a white picket fence signals a traditional touch.
- Existing architectural concepts can be extended into the landscape or enhanced by an appropriate fence. For example, classic brick architecture is complemented by a wrought iron fence, while a contemporary, cedar-clad house may be extended into the landscape with a low fence constructed out of similar wood material.

The type of fencing must be carefully considered to keep ongoing maintenance and repairs to a minimum. Image and identity are also important concerns where the perimeter of the site is perceived as a community or neighborhood boundary. Fences and walls should be used selectively and only where they are needed to protect privacy and neighborhood quality. Fences or walls should not block views to open spaces or create the look of a fortress around a neighborhood.

Noise from traffic is a common problem when residential areas are adjacent to heavily traveled roads. Acoustical barriers can be used to reduce noise to acceptable levels. Noise is generally reduced more as the height of the barrier increases. Noise traveling around the ends of a barrier can compromise the effectiveness of the barrier, however. As a general rule, acoustical barriers must break the line of sight to the entire roadway corridor to be effective. Performance of a noise barrier is also affected by terrain, ground cover, and the heights of sources of noise. The feasibility of noise attenuation and optimum height of barriers can be determined by an acoustical engineer. Other methods of mitigating noise can be used during building construction, such as the use of double-glazed windows, and site planning, such as orienting buildings so that opening windows and doors face away from the primary source of noise.

If noise mitigation and security control are not necessary, vegetation can provide an effective visual screen along the perimeter of a residential area. Plants requiring minimal care are best. Security control on the perimeter of a site can be provided by walls or fencing and sometimes lighting. Where walls or fences are installed, plantings should be used to soften the effect of large expanses of hard surfaces. Vines and evergreens are particularly effective in this regard.

Retaining Walls. Retaining walls provide many practical benefits beyond their primary function of retaining soil. Steeply sloped areas that are difficult to maintain can be developed and maintained more easily by the installation of retaining walls. The cost of retaining walls is usually high, but conditions corrected by the construction of the walls often become more cost-efficient to maintain. Installation costs must be weighed against the benefits and project economics. The methods used to design and construct retaining walls are critical, for the walls must bear soil weights and must

Low stone retaining walls are an attractive landscape element.

accommodate natural water flow and drainage of the retained area.

The use of retaining walls on steep slopes can permit development that otherwise would not be feasible. Retaining walls can generate more usable level space on a small lot. Depending on their height, retaining walls can be used to define exterior spaces; they can be used to control access between levels. Retaining walls in combination with fencing provide privacy. They may be used to segregate automobile from pedestrian circulation.

The most commonly used materials for retaining walls are large rocks or boulders, wood timbers, brick, concrete blocks, and precast or poured-in-place concrete. Gabions, another form of retaining wall, are created by placing rocks in wire baskets or bundles. The design of the retaining wall can often complement the architecture or become an extension of the architectural statement.

Entrance Features. Entrance features can be very important for establishing the image and identity of the community or neighborhood. Gateways can also provide security and privacy. Landscape materials requiring a higher degree of maintenance may be appropriate for the entrance gateway, provided that the effect is compatible with the character of the project. Typically, maintenance of entrance landscaping and hardscaping is the responsibility of the homeowners' association.

A clear system of signage should begin at the entrance to direct visitors to the sales office, the model units, and special features of the community. The marketing sign

Lighting provides security and enhances aesthetics.

system can be integrated with an overall signage system for the project that includes entry and identification signs, directional signs to provide orientation at major decision points, and street and regulatory signs. Signs should be well designed and compatible with the design of the project.

A rapidly growing, often controversial, trend in many areas is the completely gated and secured community. The community entrance may include a guardhouse and have round-the-clock security, or it may have a gate that is activated by a card or transmitter. Initially, gated communities were upscale and built around an exclusive golf course, or they were retirement or age-restricted communities. Today, they occur in all price levels and product types.

To be gated, the community usually must be built with private streets, because access on public streets cannot be closed off. Requirements of local jurisdictions must be considered in the planning and design of a gated community and should include street standards, access and connectivity requirements, and fire, police, emergency, and safety concerns. Proponents of gated communities believe that they are a market response to safety and security issues. Opponents believe that they increase isolation and fragmentation of communities. Developers should consider all the social implications, as well as the economic factors, of gating a community.

Lighting. Lighting provides character, security, and a distinctive aesthetic look to a community, and it can extend the use time of outdoor activity spaces. Decorative lighting at community or public facilities can accent public spaces. Lighting fixtures can be concealed or decorative. For example, lighting for vehicular or pedestrian circulation can effectively illuminate the ground plane while the source of light is concealed. Or period lamp posts can be used to establish a theme while lighting the way. Several areas in residential communities generally warrant lighting:

- Entrance gateways or features
- Streets (particularly intersections)
- Courtyards, mews, or clusters
- High-use open-space areas
- Entry walks to units
- Entrances to units.

Outdoor lighting is expensive to install and can consume a significant amount of energy. Therefore, unnecessary lighting should be avoided. Further, too much lighting can disrupt the residential character of a community. In some cases, particularly single-family and townhouse developments, adequate lighting can be achieved with lampposts near the street owned and controlled from each house. The local utility company can help developers and landscape architects select lighting that offers sufficient illumination but consumes low levels of energy.

Because of their higher traffic volume, collector streets should have adequate street lighting. Normally, the util-

Lighting is an important design component. At Esplanade Place in Phoenix, Arizona, indirect lighting helps to create an elegant entrance.

ity company installs standards for street lights. Developers should establish a close working relationship with the utility company to ensure that light standards are of an appropriate design and are placed on the right-of-way to best serve open space and to enhance safety and security while minimizing glare into houses.

Mercury vapor, metal halide, and high-pressure sodium lamps are generally used for outdoor lighting instead of incandescent lamps. Several attractively designed and energy-efficient low standards are now available. Such lamps should be mounted at a height of 20 to 50 feet (6 to 15 meters) along residential streets and in parking areas and a height of ten to 15 feet (3 to 4.5 meters) along paths and walks.

Structure and orientation within a residential development can be enhanced by providing a hierarchy of lighting that corresponds to the different areas or uses of the site. For example, major and minor roads can be subtly distinguished by varying the distribution and brightness of lights and by varying their height, spacing, and color of the lamps.

Residential developers should provide selective lighting for open spaces to gain the maximum benefit from them. Even marginal illumination of the pedestrian walkway system will improve the investment in amenities because of the added hours the areas can be used. Lighting should emphasize natural features or accent points of a pathway or open space. Unless very large areas must be illuminated, fixtures no higher than ten to 12 feet (3 to 3.6 meters) may be placed on center at intervals of 50 or 60 feet (15 or 18 meters).

Fixtures mounted at doorways are necessary for most types of housing. With proper architectural detail, low-cost incandescent fixtures can often lend a customized appearance. The decision about the type of fixture to use at entries should be based not only on appearance but also on light quality and maintenance costs.

If the budget for lighting is limited, lighting might be located only at the walkways that lead from houses to garages, parking bays, or lots. In some situations, walkways can be illuminated adequately and with surprising visual impact by using ground-mounted spotlights. They are particularly effective for lighting trees from the ground or illuminating architectural features.

It is generally desirable to use special fixtures with sharp cut-off illumination patterns. This type of fixture is designed to somewhat hide the light source; through the use of lenses, mirrors, or refractors, it directs the light onto the surface to be illuminated, such as a street or parking lot. Such fixtures avoid glare into residential units and private outdoor spaces. Areas requiring intense lighting, such as recreation centers, parks, tennis courts, or model home complexes, should also use sharp cut-off fixtures when adjacent to residential units.

Benches and Gathering Areas. Benches and gathering areas, while relatively easy additions to landscaping, are intangible elements that add to the way residents perceive a community. Benches and gathering areas should be located throughout the neighborhood, especially in locations visible from the model home center and entrance to the community.

Certain areas in a community may warrant a more elaborately designed sitting and gathering area. Such an area could incorporate a special landscape feature, a spectacular view, a rock outcropping, a stand of mature trees, or a water feature. In some climates, it may be appropriate to provide cover for protection from the sun or rain. Small, well-designed bus shelters located throughout the community for school bus pickup or community transit can also be a desirable feature.

Fountains and Sculpture. Fountains can serve as a marketing tool, particularly for higher-density neighborhoods in urban areas. They can set the theme and be used as a logo on marketing materials. Several functional and aesthetic principles are important for their design:

• A fountain should be self-draining to avoid breakage in winter.

- An automatic water level valve and feeder line should be used, even if the development will have a full-time maintenance staff.
- The fountain should serve as both a visible and audible feature; thus, it should be located where people can hear it as well as see it.

Sculptural elements are another feature for open space or along main roads. The selection of an appropriate piece of sculpture should be guided by the architectural theme of the community and the profile of the intended market. Like fountains, sculpture should be located in a visually prominent area—perhaps along an entry road or in a courtyard.

Mailboxes. Many areas of the country require the use of cluster mailboxes (termed *neighborhood delivery and collection box units* by the U.S. Postal Service). The postal service often helps to determine the location of NDCBUs and installs the unit on a concrete pad provided by the developer. This approach works for both single-family and multifamily neighborhoods. In neighborhoods with the lowest residential densities, curbside mailboxes are generally more appropriate; if used, they should be consistent in design, color, and locational criteria. For security reasons, neighborhood mailboxes should be visible from homes and may need to be lighted at night. They should be located near a street or parking lot so that postal carriers can reach them from their vehicles. Because centralized mailboxes often function as community gathering areas, residents appreciate their location in gazebos or other shelters.

It is sometimes appropriate to provide a mail delivery center or postal center at entrance gateways to larger communities. A delivery center is typically a freestanding shelter with 30 to several hundred boxes for mail delivery clustered together. A postal center is similar to a delivery center but may be a more elaborate structure. Customers can also purchase stamps and mail parcels as well as pick up their mail.

Trash Collection Facilities. Provisions for trash collection and storage vary, depending on project density and housing type. At lower densities, curbside collection may be the most practical method. At higher densities, neighborhood trash storage areas are usually a better solution if the areas are appropriately screened and conveniently located. Such areas also provide an opportunity to store presorted, nonbiodegradable recyclables, which may need to be collected at different frequencies from other trash. During the 1980s, many localities adopted laws requiring recyclable glass, aluminum, metal, and paper products to be separated. Developers can assist homeowners in complying with these laws by providing convenient containers for each house or building, or for the neighborhood.

Signs and Graphics. Signs and graphics are among the many details that create the character of a community. Well-executed and -placed signs can create an attractive image and give a sense of order to the plan. A well-designed signage system organizes the community visu-

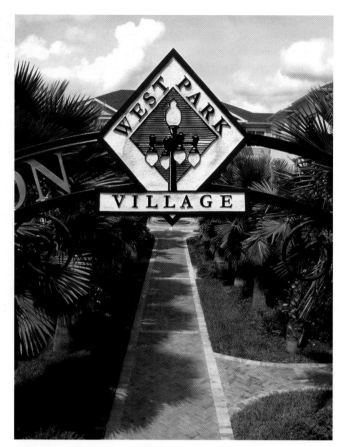

Signage should be clear and should direct visitors to the sales office.

ally, enabling residents and guests to know where they are. It can also enhance the identity of housing clusters or subneighborhoods.

During preliminary design, requirements for signage and graphics should be analyzed and included in the budget. At this stage, it is not necessary to develop specific designs or standards, but collector and subcollector routes within the development often must be named at this time. Street names on the preliminary site development plan aid in communications among members of the design team, government agencies, utility companies, and others involved in the development. The selection of street names should not be overlooked for its value in enhancing the project's image.

Graphics for the signage system should be located and identified on preliminary site plans—especially for neighborhoods with townhouses and other attached housing. Most successful projects pay close attention to the design and placement of informational signs, including entry markers, groups of house numbers, special amenity features, and designation of guest parking areas. Signs at the entrance provide the first impression of a new community. While the details of the design should not be selected until final contract documents are prepared, establishing locations early during site planning is beneficial. Discussions with local street departments or county and state highway agencies may be necessary to secure certain locations. Safe sight distances must also be considered in sign placement. A location close to the arterial roadway within the public right-of-way may be approved only after review and determination that the sign will have a low profile and will be far enough from the pavement so as not to interfere with sight lines.

Informational and directional signs are usually differentiated from traffic control signs. Informational signs should not detract from or interfere with the visibility and prominence of traffic signs. Standard shapes and colors should be used for traffic control signs (octagonal for stop, triangular for yield, for example). They can often be framed in a standardized framing system, which will help provide project unity. Informational signs need not be governed by the standard sign regulations, but they should use standardized materials and perhaps the same framing system and should complement other materials used in the development.

On-site signage and other graphic materials prepared for the development (community logo, marketing brochures, and letterhead, for example) should be consistent. Consumers are constantly presented with high-quality graphic materials in every medium, and developers can enhance a community's image by incorporating quality graphics and signs. Once a lettering style and logo have been prepared, they should be used consistently on printed materials, signs, and graphics.

Utilities

New residential development creates a demand for many types of facilities and services, both on and off site. This demand needs to be addressed during project planning to ensure that the required utilities and services will be provided efficiently and in a timely manner. The entities that provide these facilities and services may include the developer, private utility companies, and public agencies at many different governmental levels. In obtaining approval for the project, it is often the developer's role to identify the project's requirements and to seek the necessary commitments from the responsible entities.

Developers must plan ahead to ensure that installation of the required facilities goes smoothly. Coordination with the local municipality is imperative to ensure that utilities and utility connections can be delivered in a timely manner. Negotiation and continual communication among the developer, the municipality, and the various utility companies are essential. A preconstruction meeting on the site between the developer's construction manager and the utility company's installation supervisor is a good idea. Such a meeting can keep each party advised from the outset, rather than solving problems after they occur. A coordinated installation schedule with specific commitments is also a good idea.

Developers often are required to make improvements and install utilities in excess of those needed to serve a specific project. For example, a developer may be required to install a larger sanitary sewer main to serve future development than the particular project needs. The problem can be resolved in a number of ways. The municipality can pick up the costs for oversizing the improvement, or the developer can be reimbursed for such costs when new development is added. Developers should attempt to install only that infrastructure necessary to serve each phase of development. Advance installation greatly increases the financing costs of the project and reduces future flexibility in site planning.

Water. Water supply is typically the responsibility of a municipality or a special district. Particularly in the West, where long-term availability of water is a politically charged issue, it is often necessary for developers of new residential areas to assist the municipality or special water district in determining where the required quantity of water can be obtained. Only rarely are suitable sources of groundwater or surface water available on site. Once a source has been identified, a developer might have to subsidize the construction of infrastructure required to tap the source and transport the water to the site. This infrastructure may include wells, reservoirs, storage tanks, aqueducts, and treatment facilities. With the availability

The community's entrance creates a first impression.

of adequate water supplies a growing concern in many parts of the country, it is in developers' best interests to incorporate water conservation measures in the development plans.

A central water supply is always preferable to individual wells, just as a central sewage disposal system is usually preferable to separate septic systems. As areas are developed, water supply from wells may become undependable and water quality suffer. Wells placed near each other can interfere with one another, and saltwater intrusion is a common problem in coastal areas. Many types of wells are available for different situations—drilled, jetted, bored, and dug—but the initial construction and subsequent maintenance costs of a central supply are often less and the results far more satisfactory. Small, private water companies can render satisfactory service when larger municipal water services are not available.

When discussing extensions of water mains, developers must be aware of not only who pays the costs involved but also the legality of the extensions. Generally, the obligation of a private water company to extend its lines within its franchised territory is undeniable. With nonfranchised companies or those operating outside their franchised territory, the obligation is based on the extent of their profession of service. Denial of application for extension can be appealed to the state public utilities commission and ultimately the courts.

With municipally owned water systems comes more discretion in whether to extend service within municipal boundaries. Generally, the utility has a duty to supply water to all residents of a community. Extending its obligation beyond corporate limits is another question. A municipal utility must generally have made some profession of service in the area to service it, and in this regard it comes under the purview of the public utilities commission. The issue of financing water main extensions is sometimes unclear. In some cases, developers bear the costs, either with or without reimbursement. In other cases, the utility does.

In outlying areas where the nearest public water supply may be several miles away, a last resort might be to create a private water company to serve the new development. Under most state laws, it is necessary to obtain incorporation papers for the proposed utility company, a franchise from the local jurisdiction to lay mains in the projected streets, permission from a water control board to drill a test well after offering proof of need, and the submission of evidence of proper and safe construction and the safeguarding of other water supplies. The state board of health must approve plans for wells and the distribution system, and the public utility commission must approve rules, regulations, and rates. Usually, public hearings are also required.

Once a source of water and the means of getting it to the site have been ensured, the next step is to plan the on-site water distribution system. The on-site water distribution system is often the most expensive utility to provide. Its primary purpose is to convey potable water to dwelling units; secondarily, it is to provide water for fire protection. Water mains should be located in street rights-of-way or in utility easements. Water mains vary in size, depending on demand from users; typically, residential mains are six or eight inches (15 or 20 centimeters) in diameter. Water mains are constructed in a loop system wherever possible to maintain sufficient water pressure. A civil engineer should determine the appropriate size for water mains.

Fire hydrants should be readily accessible without creating a hazard either to pedestrians or to automobile traffic. Like water mains, water lines for fire hydrants often must be constructed in a loop system.

Wastewater. Two basic alternatives are available for disposing of domestic waterborne wastes: piping the wastes off site to a municipal sewage treatment system or treating and disposing of the wastes on site. The use of on-site systems is expected to increase as areas beyond existing sewage collection systems are developed and as existing public treatment plants reach capacity.

At Anthem outside Phoenix, Arizona, the availability of water was a major concern. To resolve the issue, the developer purchased water rights from a group of Native Americans and installed a pipeline.

Adrienne Schmitz

Desert communities like High Desert, New Mexico, raise concerns about water.

Since passage of the Clean Water Act in 1972, the federal government through the EPA has given construction grants to municipalities to help build sewage treatment facilities. Federal funding, however, is decreasing, and state and local governments are searching for alternative means of financing these projects. Localities are likely to continue to insist that new development pay its own way through fees and exactions for off-site improvements in public facilities. Further, small-scale wastewater treatment systems will likely be an increasingly attractive alternative to capital-intensive centralized plants. A variety of small-scale systems are available, often combining small-diameter collection systems with common on-site disposal systems, package plants, or alternative treatment systems, such as lagoons. For conventional subdivisions and PUDs of up to eight units per acre (20 per hectare), these systems can be ideal if a conventional system is not accessible. Small-scale technologies have not been used widely in the past, partly because they are perceived as land intensive, environmentally unsound, or only a

temporary solution. In the future, demand will grow for development of new technologies and alternatives to the costly extension of public sewer service.

In general, sanitary sewer lines should be located in utility easements or street rights-of-way. In many new communities, the sewers are located in the areas of lower-lying topography behind the units and within the open-space network. When located in street rights-of-way, sewers should generally not be located under roadway paving unless laterals are extended to front property lines at the time of installation. If sewer lines are constructed only on one side of the street, laterals are necessary, and the roads cannot be completed until laterals are installed. Requirements for laterals can be reduced by placing multiple units on each lateral.

The system should be coordinated with other utilities and located to avoid trees. As a rule, lateral sewers are not laid in the same trench with water supply lines. When permitted by local authorities, however, it is sometimes possible to combine the lines in a double-shelf trench, with the sanitary sewer on the bottom and the water lines on the shelf. Preventing improper or illegal connections between surface water systems and sanitary sewer systems is extremely important.

Municipal Systems. When planning a sewer system, developers should investigate several questions:

- Is the existing system to which connections are to be made adequately sized? Is it a separate or combined sanitary and stormwater system? What is the present capacity?
- How many hookups are under contract but not installed? Normally, more potential users are eligible than the system can handle.
- How does the municipality charge for installation of sewers? Is it charged entirely to the developer? Is total or partial recovery of the initial cost possible?
- Can a special sewer improvement district be set up to cover the new development? How are costs allocated

Plans must include stormwater and wastewater systems.

SWA Group

SWA Group

if mains and trunk lines must be constructed through the development to serve property beyond its borders? A municipality that charges fees for sewage disposal should also pay for the installation costs of sewage mains from the revenues produced by those user fees.

• Is a permit to discharge surface drainage into natural watercourses required by local or state government? And in what condition may it enter those waters? Developers should be sure to check this point, as it will save trouble, litigation, and expense later.

Community Systems. If extending public sewers is impossible, a small central community system may be used. A state permit for any discharge of sewage effluents into streams and rivers is required, and effluents must meet the standards set for the receiving body of water. In many cases, secondary treatment is required. Often a discharge permit can be denied if the community system does not comply with the local areawide wastewater treatment plan.

Community systems include large septic tanks with subsurface leaching systems, large aerobic digesters (often called *package plants)* with surface infiltration beds, large aerobic digesters with evapotranspiration disposal of effluent, unaerated lagoons with overflow disposal to surface infiltration beds, and aerated lagoons with overflow disposal to surface infiltration beds.

Individual Systems. Individual on-site systems include septic tanks combined with any of a variety of subsurface leaching systems (leaching trenches, leaching beds, and leaching pits, for example), aerobic digesters combined with the same variety of subsurface leaching systems, aerobic digesters combined with surface infiltration beds, or aerobic digesters combined with evapotranspiration disposal systems. Determination of effectiveness and feasibility of any of these disposal systems depends on site conditions, costs, and the local government's regulations and policies.

Sewage disposal by septic tanks and tile fields for each dwelling should be used only when absolutely necessary,

and then only after state and local departments of health have cleared their use. Individual on-lot disposal requires a parcel of land considerably larger than the usual suburban lot for an adequate disposal field. The disposal field must also slope away from the house and be kept free of trees and shrubbery to ensure the action of sunlight. The type of soil and subsoil affects both the amount of area needed and the possibility of polluting nearby surface water or wells. The wide variation in the use of water by individual households (ranging from 30 to 150 gallons [115 to 570 liters] per person per day) causes the design of individual septic tanks to be difficult. The addition of garbage disposal units to a septic tank system means doubling the capacity of the tank and more frequent attention to maintenance. These and other considerations often negate the use of septic tank systems.

Energy, Communications, and Technology Infrastructure. Investor-owned utility companies typically provide infrastructure for telephone, natural gas, and electric service, and private companies typically provide infrastructure for cable and satellite TV service. Typically, the companies finance this infrastructure, known as *commercial* or *specialized infrastructure,* and it is in the developer's interest to assist the companies with planning and installing any on-site facilities.

Underground lines for electric, telephone, and cable service are now typical. Advances in trenching equipment, protective coating for wiring, and the elimination of tree maintenance costs associated with overhead lines have contributed to greater use of underground utilities. Cost-reducing equipment is now available to power companies for quickly locating any interruptions in service, further lowering maintenance costs. Telephone companies find that underground wiring also eliminates paying rent on utility poles. Electric, telephone, and cable companies routinely cooperate in common trenching, because it is more cost-effective and facilitates subsequent location of these utilities. Most gas companies, however, prefer to install gas lines in a separate trench, which may or may not be located in a common public utility easement.

Underground utilities are aesthetically superior to poles running along easements or street rights-of-way. Electrical transformers mounted on pads and utility junction boxes can be unsightly, however, if they are not properly planned for and located. If surface appurtenances like pad-mounted transformers are used, developers should work with utility companies to obtain a favorable location that will provide utility companies with adequate maintenance access yet not be prominently displayed. Transformers can also be screened with earth berms and landscaping to minimize visibility from public spaces. Current practice dictates the location of underground utility lines within street rights-of-way or adjacent to them in separate utility easements.

The concept of "bundled" communication systems for new residential communities is an evolving trend. Such systems may include telephone, internal connectivity, community intranet, home intelligence, and home, business, and community security. They promote the use of state-of-the-art technology and communications that connect community residents, schools, and businesses with each other and to the rest of the world. They also offer developers the possibility of providing such services to their communities for a fee.

Consumer demand is growing for sophisticated communications services, including voice, video, and data transmission. Development of broadband is driven by the Internet, which has grown exponentially in accessibility and importance since its introduction to consumers in the mid-1990s. Several technologies have emerged as feasible options for delivery of broadband: fiber optics, fixed wireless, digital subscriber line (DSL), and cable (hybrid fiber/coaxial). High-tech communications services are increasingly important in homes, particularly as the distinction between home and work is blurred and more people work at home, full time or part time.

It takes years for new saplings to grow to maturity, so preserving existing trees improves a community's aesthetics and marketability.

Site Work

Before a single home can be built, the site must be prepared for development. Site preparation includes grading and other measures to accommodate drainage and to control stormwater and erosion. Site preparation also includes any necessary environmental remediation, such as removing contaminated soils. If a project is large, the site work is likely to be performed in phases.

Grading. Grading is more than just leveling a site for a building or moving earth to solve drainage problems. Grading is an important design technique to enhance a site's distinctive and attractive qualities. Preparation of a grading plan is an integral part of site planning and design. In residential development, grading can accomplish a number of functional and aesthetic purposes:

• Create building sites for individual houses or groups of housing units;
• Create acceptable sites for community facilities, such as playgrounds and playfields;
• Provide for proper drainage;
• Create berms as noise or wind barriers;
• Capture views or hide undesirable views;
• Increase soil depth for planting or increase topsoil over unfavorable subgrade conditions, such as groundwater;
• Create circulation routes, such as paths and roads;
• Emphasize the site's topography or provide interest for a naturally flat site;
• Relate the site to the surrounding area and structures to the site;
• Create illusions about the size or shape of spaces;
• Relate landforms to bodies of water.

With some imagination, a relatively flat site can be transformed into one with visual variety. If foundations and basements must be excavated, the material can be sculpted to create berms, saving the cost of trucking earth off site. Berms can be integrated into the open-space system, providing good sites for pathways. Berms can be used as visual and physical screens, eliminating the need for walls and fencing.

Moderate terrain is characterized as land with slopes ranging up to about 10 percent. In developing areas of moderate terrain, economic considerations require that a balance be struck between the amount of grading and the resulting number of units that can be constructed. An advantage of cluster development over conventional lot-by-lot development is that grading can be minimized by constructing houses on the more suitable portions of the site and reserving the remaining areas as permanent open space.

Steep terrain has average slopes exceeding 10 percent. Because of the challenges associated with the development of hillsides, such areas warrant special consideration by developers and planning departments. Imposing traditional subdivision regulations on hillside developments is rarely successful and often leads to improper or needlessly expensive development. Engineering studies generally must be undertaken if development of a steep slope is contemplated. Such studies should focus on geological, soil, and drainage conditions and identify measures that will be required to ensure safe, stable, and functional building sites.

Flexible standards for lot size and shape, frontage, rights-of-way, street width, easements, and setbacks can permit sensitive and appropriate development of steep sites. In particular, steep topography frequently necessitates unusually shaped lots to use the land efficiently without excessive grading. With regard to the design and placement of units, it is important to consider the view of the project from the surrounding area. Building profiles should be kept low, preferably below the skyline. The preservation of natural terrain, vegetative cover, rock outcroppings, and other special features should also be encouraged.

Massive cut-and-fill operations are obviously expensive. The cost of grading for development of a given site is determined by several factors:

- Composition of the material being moved,
- Geological and soil conditions (blasting rock might be required on some sites and compacted clays are difficult to move),
- Site location and access and distances required to haul dirt,
- The achievement of balanced cut and fill on the site,
- The extent of stabilized slopes specified in the grading plan, and

- Weather conditions (for example, grading is prohibited in parts of California during the winter rainy season unless extensive measures to control erosion are implemented).

To minimize requirements for cut and fill, roads in steeply sloping areas should generally be located on ridgelines or parallel to the contours of a slope. Roads in hillside and mountain areas should usually take on rural characteristics. Where feasible and appropriate, retention walls or special bank treatments should be considered as an alternative to extensive grading.

Drainage. Land development activities alter the natural drainage patterns of a site and sometimes off-site locations as well. Historically, many land development projects have adversely affected waters and land uses downstream. It is now generally accepted that development should have no significant impact on off-site drainage and that on-site drainage should respect or emulate natural drainage patterns whenever possible.

The planning and design of a drainage system must be an integral part of project planning and design rather than just an aspect of site engineering. Major functions of site drainage systems include preventing flooding and erosion, minimizing soil swelling and frost heave, maintaining high water quality, recharging the groundwater, protecting wildlife habitat, and creating on-site amenities. Alternative strategies for site drainage must be evaluated in conjunction with the review of alterna-

Drainage is a major factor in site planning.

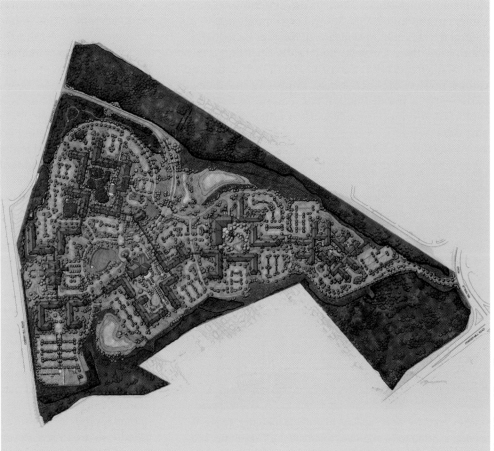

Every site comes with its own challenges and constraints.

tives for other planning elements and other aspects of the overall site design.

Site drainage can be handled in a variety of ways. Recent trends have focused on minimizing the use of "hard" engineering techniques and devices (such as pipes and paved channels) to control runoff in favor of "soft" or bioengineering approaches, such as natural drainage swales and bioretention areas. This type of approach is not only more environmentally sensitive but also can afford significant savings in both short- and long-term costs. When designed in conjunction with natural drainage techniques, conventional storm drainage systems can be designed to carry smaller amounts of stormwater, thereby reducing infrastructure requirements.

Stormwater Management. In the past, stormwater runoff from residential development sites was essentially handled by underground storm sewers. The storm sewers collected runoff from the street system during and immediately following a rainfall and discharged the flow directly into local streams. This approach was very efficient for the rapid elimination of runoff from a site. Over time, however, it became increasingly clear that the cumulative effects of this approach often caused increased flooding downstream and reduction of local groundwater reserves. It also changed the temperature of the waters, causing disruptions in natural ecological systems.

Current stormwater management practices recognize that every parcel of ground is part of a larger drainage area and that alterations such as regrading the land,

increasing the impervious cover, or modifying natural drainage systems can lead to a series of environmental changes downstream—flooding, erosion of stream profiles, undermining of stream banks, sedimentation, turbidity, and loss of water quality in water bodies downstream—and loss or adverse alteration of the habitat of aquatic biota.

The design of any stormwater system should strike a balance among capital, operating, and maintenance costs, public convenience, risk of significant water-related damage, and environmental and other community objectives. Engineering techniques that protect natural resources and processes should be implemented whenever possible. Examples of sound stormwater management include use of on-site detention storage, increased use of on-site storage to balance peak flows, and use of land treatment systems for the handling and disposal of stormwater. An overall tenet to follow is that water falling on a given site should be absorbed or retained on site to the extent that the quantity and rate of water leaving the site would not be significantly different from the site's undeveloped state.

On-site stormwater storage facilities, including detention and retention basins, should be located in common open space whenever possible. Design of such facilities should consider safety, appearance, recreational use, and effective, economical maintenance. Stormwater management systems, street layout, lot patterns, and the horizontal and vertical locations of curbs, inlets, and site

Wetlands can be part of a
natural stormwater drainage
system.

EDSA

drainage should be designed concurrently. Streets play
an important role in collecting and conveying stormwater runoff. Typically, runoff collected in the roadway is
conveyed to the main drainage system through basins or
inlets in the curb. The number and spacing of such
inlets should be carefully calculated, and their design
should consider the safety of pedestrians and bicyclists
as well as efficiency in transporting water.

Stormwater management systems should be designed
to facilitate recharging the aquifer, especially when it may
be advantageous to compensate for groundwater with-
drawn. In certain situations, perforated storm sewers can
be used to distribute water to the subsoil. If perforated
storm sewers are to be used in highly permeable soil, care
must be taken to maintain them properly and to remove
debris from the inlets periodically. Conversely, designs
should avoid recharge where effects on the groundwater
might be harmful.

Natural overland flow and routing through open vegetated channels and swales are the preferred methods
for carrying runoff from the street to storage basins.
When large natural drainage swales exist, site planning
and engineering design should respect and even enhance
them as landscape features. Constructed drainage swales
should reflect a natural design and not look like artifi-
cially trenched ditches. For practical construction, the
minimum slope for a sodded drainage swale is 2 percent.
Under exacting standards of construction, a 2 percent
drainage swale permits flow, yet the slightest variation
during or after construction may result in ponding and
possible damage. These specifications for slope should
be shown on preliminary and final grading plans.

Like drainage swales, stormwater retention ponds
should be treated as elements of design and varied in
shape, size, treatment of slopes, and plantings. Carefully
designed stormwater flumes may be transformed into
landscape features containing trickling water or even
waterfalls. In some cases, it might be desirable to augment
the flow of stormwater with an artificial recirculating water

supply. A permanent water level should be maintained
within a waterproof lower section of the basin, with the
remainder taking up the necessary volume of storm
retention.

Underground outfall pipes may be necessary to convey runoff when the surface method is not practical. Outfall pipes should be located in the community's open
space where possible or in drainage easements that follow lot lines. The amount of runoff can be decreased by
reducing the amount of street paving through careful
planning and by lessening driveway surface areas by
reducing frontyard setbacks.

Stormwater runoff from streets, parking lots, and
roof drains is normally heavily laden with a variety of
contaminants—phosphates, nitrates, putrescible organics
—that can have severe adverse effects on waters downstream. The sources of contaminants are complex; they
may include airborne fallout from industrial pollution,
organic detritus, motor oil, detergents, and pesticides.
Soil effectively absorbs most contaminants, so the use
of overland flow, vegetated open channels, and swales
can be very effective in avoiding potential adverse impacts on downstream waters. Additional measures of
control, if they are necessary, might include the use
of sand filters or degreasers as part of the stormwater
retention system.

Erosion and Sedimentation Control. Problems with
erosion and sedimentation are primarily the result of
improper grading and poor design and maintenance
of erosion and sediment control measures. Careful site
planning that respects and responds to natural site conditions can reduce or prevent most erosion and sedimentation. Development of portions of the site that are the
most highly erodible should be avoided. Natural vegetation should be preserved to the maximum extent possible,
and clearing and grading should be kept to a minimum,
reducing the percentage of the site exposed to erosion.
Grading should also be done in phases so that only a
small area is disturbed at any given time.

Measures to control erosion and sedimentation can be temporary or permanent, and often both types of measures need to be employed. Although their functions are similar, temporary and permanent measures differ in design and construction materials. Temporary measures like putting sand bags around catch basins of storm drains or laying plastic sheeting over newly graded slopes are inexpensive and are designed to last only for the duration of the construction period. Permanent measures, such as desilting basins or landscaping exposed soil, are designed to remain in place for many years beyond the end of construction and generally cost more to construct but require less frequent maintenance. To be most effective, permanent measures to control erosion and sedimentation should be integrated with stormwater management systems and should suit the aesthetic character of the development.

Measures to stabilize the soil protect exposed soil from the impact of rain and subsequent erosion. Temporary measures protect soil during construction delays and until permanent vegetative covers are established. Temporary measures include mulches, nettings, and chemical binders. Mulches not only protect the soil from erosion and prevent seeds, fertilizer, and other soil additives from washing away but also improve the soil's capacity for infiltrating rainfall, reduce variations in the soil's temperature, reduce surface evaporation, and shield delicate young plants. The most common mulch materials are hay, small-grain straw, wood chips, jute matting, glass fiber netting, plastic and asphalt emulsions, and various paper products. Most fibrous mulches must be anchored to prevent their dispersal. Seeding can be used to stabilize the soil temporarily and permanently. When further grading is deferred, a temporary plant cover that can subsequently form the mulch for permanent vegetation is often appropriate.

Permanent vegetative cover to stabilize the soil should be long-lived and require minimal care or maintenance. Grasses and legumes are generally superior to shrubs and ground covers because of their more complex root systems, which encourage formation of a water-stable soil structure. In addition, their leaves and stems protect the ground against erosion from wind and water. The selection of plants should be based on what can be expected to grow at the site, the purpose of the planting, and foreseeable ensured maintenance.

Permanent nonvegetative measures of stabilization are used where conditions preclude the use of vegetation, such as steep slopes, areas of groundwater seepage, soils that do not absorb or retain moisture well, or waterways subject to high flow velocities. Coarse crushed rock and gravel are commonly used for gentle slopes. Except in unusual circumstances, rock and gravel should not be used for temporary stabilization, as they will interfere with the establishment of permanent vegetative cover.

Structural measures for controlling runoff intercept surface runoff and convey it to a safe disposal area, keeping it away from erodible soil and preventing the erosion of gullies. Diversion structures, including dikes, channels, and terraces, collect water and direct it to an outfall, where it can be released without causing excessive erosion. Structural measures for controlling runoff can also include berms, waterways, down drains, flumes, and level spreaders. To provide proper protection at all times at the most reasonable cost, temporary measures of controlling runoff must be relocated or removed as construction progresses. Regular preventive maintenance is needed for continued effectiveness of permanent control measures.

Measures to control sediment generally act to slow the flow of surface runoff by filtering or trapping it, enabling sediments in the runoff to settle out. Measures based on filtering can be divided into two general categories: vegetative and structural. The choice depends primarily on economics and space available. Vegetative buffers are often economical and when properly used require little maintenance, but they require a relatively large land area. The more expensive structural filters, such as

Stormwater can be handled structurally by using terraces and manmade ponds.

Canin Associates

gravel inlet barriers, loose rock berms, and straw bale barriers, use less space by concentrating filtering in localized structures but require regular maintenance, particularly after storms.

Two methods for trapping sediment are sediment basins and sediment traps. Sediment basins are the more effective approach in terms of the percentage of sediment removed from runoff. Dry sediment basins are constructed on waterways that flow only during storms; wet basins are constructed on intermittent or perennial streams and may impound a permanent pond. Because trapped sediments must periodically be removed from permanent basins, a permanent disposal site for waste material must be provided. Sediment traps are small, temporary detention structures used to intercept runoff and trap sediment. They are rarely practical for drainage areas larger than about five acres (2 hectares). Traps can be constructed with earth, pipe, or stone outlets, or they can be installed at storm drain inlets. Selection of outlets is based on construction costs.

Lake Management. In addition to their value as visual and recreational amenities, natural and manmade lakes or ponds can be used for controlling flooding and sedimentation, storing water, managing wildlife, treating water, and recharging the aquifer. Creating a lake is a highly complex undertaking that requires a thorough knowledge of the natural processes at work on the site. A geohydrologist or lake ecologist should be consulted to determine whether a lake is feasible on a given site.

Creating a lake involves upfront development costs, and the cost of maintaining one is an ongoing responsibility that affects the long-term value of the lake as an amenity. Other major concerns are liability and insurance. It is therefore important to consider who will maintain the lake in the future. Local governments may be reluctant to accept responsibility for managing a lake, particularly if public access is restricted, and a community or homeowners' association may have difficulty funding the necessary maintenance unless it has been adequately financially planned and budgeted.

Lakes can be major amenities for residential communities. People enjoy living where they have an extended view of water, and if they have direct access to the water, they are even more willing to pay a premium for the privilege. An important consideration is the structure of ownership and property rights along the shoreline. A cluster arrangement for lots away from the shoreline with access to the water through common property is one solution to providing limited public access while maximizing returns from the value created. Public access to the shoreline can reduce property values for adjacent landowners, although the reduction may be compensated for by the views afforded to those houses.

The size of the lake or pond is affected by the nature of the source of water, the purpose of the water body, and the characteristics of the site. Adequate depth is necessary to promote good water quality without a high degree of maintenance. A depth of at least ten feet (3 meters) in some

Homesites with lake frontage can command significant premiums.

Common space and amenities typically are conveyed to a community association.

portion of the water body, possibly near the dam, allows thermal stratification of the water and seasonal turnovers. In cold climates, 15 feet (4.5 meters) is desirable to prevent killing fish when the lake is covered with ice.

Standards for water quality for lakes and ponds vary, depending on how the body of water is to be used, with the highest standards applying to water for swimming. A program to monitor water quality is necessary to determine whether standards are being maintained and to provide a reliable baseline of information to diagnose future problems. Restrictions on use of the lake by power boats may be necessary to protect water quality as well as to avoid increased wave action, which can aggravate erosion of the shoreline. The North American Lake Management Society provides advice on constructing and managing lakes.[11]

Open Space

Open space describes those portions of the property that are not included in the salable lots, houses, commercial properties, and so forth. The open space may contain stormwater management systems, lakes, creeks, ponds, landscape buffers, natural topographical features, entry (monument) areas, pedestrian pathways, and parks. Some community plans may incorporate a golf course within the open-space areas.

Including open space gives the developer greater flexibility in site planning by providing a use for undevelopable land and reducing the expense of grading

and landscaping a difficult portion of a site. Open space can be used to preserve natural features, vegetation, or ecosystems, and to create a social focus for a community. It can also increase the project's image, salability, and value and provide leverage for rezoning.

Three types of open space are generally described as private, public, or common. Private open space is usually land that is improved for use in a recreational capacity, for example, a golf course or tennis club. Its use, however, is reserved for members of the recreational facility. Public open space is land that has been purchased or dedicated for public use. Traditionally, these areas are to be used by the public and are dedicated to the local municipality for ownership and perpetual maintenance. Common open space is land that is deeded to a community property owners' (or homeowners') association that the developer creates and operates for the benefit of property owners in the development. Common open space may contain improved and unimproved property, including the entrance to the community, parks, pedestrian pathways, recreational facilities, and possibly private streets. Open space can be used as a buffer between separate neighborhoods or between the community and surrounding land uses.

Common open space is conveyed to a community association that is responsible for its maintenance; the association is established by recording the declaration of CCRs. All property owners, including the developer, pay prorated assessments for all the costs relating to com-

Walking paths like this one at Croasdaile Farm in Durham, North Carolina, are among the most cost-effective amenities. They are inexpensive and rank high among amenities sought by homebuyers.

Frederick Jarvis

mon open space, and payment of assessments is enforced through a lien against an owner's property. (This topic is discussed in more detail in Chapter 7.)

In public requirements for open space in a PUD or in exchange for density bonuses, developers must recognize the value of the land as open space versus its value as developed land. No standard ratio exists for how much open space should be reserved in a development project. Some zoning ordinances have minimum requirements, which may range from 20 percent to as high as 60 percent.

The basis for defining open space is critical to understanding what will qualify to meet minimum requirements. In some cases, open space might be defined as any land not covered by buildings or paving. This standard might translate into ratios as high as 70 percent open space to total site acreage. In other cases, open space might be defined as land not covered by buildings or paving but not including land that is privately owned or land that is smaller than a certain area and not contiguous with other open space. A project that might have 60 percent open space under the first definition might have only 10 or 15 percent under the second.

Some standards of quality must be maintained for open space. The physical characteristics, dimensions, location, slope, and improvements are important factors in determining whether open space will be of value. Quality standards and maintenance provisions for open space should be considered an integral part of overall site planning and design. When planning open space, developers should be aware of short- and long-term maintenance costs. It is possible to set aside too much open space that requires maintenance, overburdening members of the community association or the responsible public agency.

The type of open space provided should be tailored to meet the profile of prospective residents. For most markets, it is desirable to provide both maintained areas and natural open space. Some markets, such as empty nesters and retirees, may place a higher value on open

space left in its natural state. The perceived amount of open space in a project is increased if adjacent areas like forests, hillsides, or lakes are maintained or managed as permanent open space.

Special Features and Amenities

The definition of an amenity as applied to real estate development is a rather broad concept and can encompass virtually any feature that is attractive to a given market and thus adds value to the community. An amenity may be a recreational feature such as a trail or a swim center, or it may be a social or activity amenity such as a daycare facility or town center shopping area. For any community to be successful, selecting the right type, quality, and number of amenities is important. If not properly planned, amenities may be of little use to the residents, who must ultimately bear the cost of maintaining them. Changes in lifestyles are causing residential developers to reconsider what amenities will be of value to residents. Developers should conduct market research before formulating the amenity package for a project; what is right for one community may not be right for another. The availability of existing amenities in the area is an important consideration. If public amenities are available nearby, fewer amenities may have to be provided on site.

A developer's decision to include or exclude certain amenities is largely based on the following factors:

- What is being offered in similar local projects,
- Who the future residents are for whom these amenities are planned,
- How much money is available to install and maintain the amenities,
- What the climate will allow, and
- What the marketing benefits will be.

A project's amenity package can provide an important edge over nearby resale homes that are competing directly with new houses. Although a bad location for a development will hardly ever be overcome by a superior amenity package, a good amenity package might make the marketing difference in a marginal location.

Amenities should be phased in increments suitable to the phasing of housing construction. This approach keeps financing and maintenance costs to a minimum and avoids a situation in which facilities are built and require maintenance but go largely unused for several years. Opening memberships to nonresidents may make it possible to reduce the initial cost of amenities like golf courses and swimming pools and decrease their carrying costs to the developer or the community association.

Because of marketing objectives or municipal requirements, a developer might be required to build the entire package of amenities during the first phase of construction. In most cases, residential developers should try to avoid this costly and often unnecessary expense, especially in large, long-term projects. Residential developers should construct a phased schedule for delivery of amenities, if possible tying the delivery of certain amenities to a specific number of units sold. And developers should never promise amenities they are not sure of building.

The amount per unit spent on amenities is determined by dividing the total number of units into the entire cost of the amenity package. Always included in the cost per unit is the developer's share of maintenance and operating expenses until the succeeding phases are completed.

Certain amenities may require a daily management structure to be useful to residents. Such costs must be factored into the developer's budget for amenities as well as into the community association's long-term operational budget. For example, if the development is a tennis community, a full-time manager/tennis professional may be needed. The feasibility of daily management depends largely on the size of the community, the household income of residents, and the emphasis placed on amenities. Customer profiles can help determine the need for ongoing professional management and whether the cost will be considered acceptable.

Some recreational amenities (golf courses, marinas, ski slopes, equestrian facilities, for example) are so large or costly that they cannot be provided in a typical residential development. The sense of identifying with a group offered by these kinds of specialized recreational developments, however, is increasingly important to many residential developers. Developments that feature these major amenities are discussed in Chapter 8.

Developers must carefully consider long-term operating and maintenance and possible replacement costs of an amenity, not just initial installation expenses. Charges for maintenance and operations that escalate above the developer's estimate damage his reputation. If the cost of a facility exceeds residents' willingness to pay, they can close it, but dissatisfaction will remain. Developers must make tradeoffs so that operating costs are kept as low as possible.

At Terrabrook's Vista Lakes, an extensive recreational complex includes access to a lake.

Adrienne Schmitz

Play Areas. Play areas include tot lots, playgrounds, play fields, parks, and other open spaces used for a combination of active and passive recreation. Play areas are needed in most new residential developments. Which facilities will be provided and maintained by the municipality and which will be constructed by the developer and maintained by the community association must be decided.

The type and size of play areas to be provided depend on the type of community being created. Higher-density developments may need more space for children's active play than a single-family development where private yard space is available. But even single-family projects require play areas and tot lots for common use by neighborhood children.

As a general guideline, a minimum of 5 percent of the gross area of a project should be reserved for active parks and recreational purposes. But need is further determined by the project's density, character, and zoning requirements. If the municipality desires more parkland than is necessary to serve the project, the municipality usually negotiates with the developer to determine whether or not the land is to be dedicated or purchased by the municipality. Under ideal conditions, play areas should be located within one-quarter mile (0.4 kilometer) of all dwelling units where children might live and should be linked to residential enclaves with pedestrian paths. Children's play areas should be visible from public areas and easily reached by emergency vehicles. A playground requires a level, well-drained site, but to maintain adequate drainage, the site should not fall below a 0.5 percent slope.

A full-service neighborhood recreation area or playground of about five acres (2 hectares) can accommodate the following features:

• A section for preschool children,
• Apparatus for older children,
• Open space for informal play,

• A surfaced area for court games like handball, basketball, shuffleboard, and volleyball,
• A field for softball and group games,
• An area for storytelling and quiet games,
• A shelter house with water and toilets,
• A corner for table games for older people, and
• Landscaping.

Sturdy equipment is necessary, but it does not have to be expensive. Studies show that children, when given the choice between designed play sculptures or conventional play equipment like swings or slides, often prefer the latter. Safety should be carefully considered in the selection of playground equipment for children. In hot climates, for example, reflective metal slides can burn a child. Accessories like trash cans, drinking fountains, and benches should be located appropriately on the playground.

Basketball courts or multiplay courts should be provided for older children and teens. Depending on the size of the development and its projected demographics, several half courts for practice may be better than one full court. Some goals can be less than standard height to ensure a court for younger children. If the area is to be lighted for use at night, it should be located away from houses to reduce noise and the effect of lighting glare.

A good location for playgrounds is on or near an elementary school site, where the municipality or community association can ensure adequate supervision. Sharing space and facilities between schools and playgrounds is efficient for both parties.

Tot lots can be quite small—usually 2,400 to 5,000 square feet (225 to 465 square meters) is sufficient—but they require special considerations in design.[12] They require a sheltered but sunny location, smaller play equipment, grassy areas, and benches. As a general rule, tot lots should be designed for children aged four and younger.

Market data usually indicate the expected population of children by various age groups. These data help planners to size and locate appropriate play areas through-out the development and help to determine the specific design and facilities for each. Materials that go into a play area should complement those used in the rest of the project. Play areas can be integrated with natural land-forms, making the architectural construction blend with the landscape.

A casual observation of children's play demonstrates that if an area does not present a certain degree of chal-lenge, children will soon grow disinterested and seek more exciting territory. A balance must therefore be achieved between safety and challenge, much as the developer must also balance maintenance, budget, and aesthetics.

Recreation Centers. A large centralized clubhouse or recreation center offering facilities such as a swimming pool, tennis courts, indoor game rooms, social space, and so on has been a common sales tool for residential developers since the 1960s. Maintenance and operating expenses for such facilities typically come out of home-owners' monthly dues to the community association, and the association often uses the facilities as its headquarters. These facilities rarely pay for themselves, however, so developers must assess their value. Smaller clubhouses or recreation centers can often be built, maintained, and operated less expensively and may prove to be of more value to residents.

The size of the residential development often deter-mines the need for a recreation center. Generally, it is not feasible to support a recreation center with fewer than 150

residences. In fact, in most price categories, a minimum of 250 to 300 homes is needed to support the cost of main-tenance and operation for a reasonable annual fee.

If a pool is planned for the community, it is sometimes easier to enlarge the pool building and turn it into a small recreation center than to build a separate club-house. Amenities that could be installed in this type of building include a sauna, a spa, an exercise room, kitchen facilities, an arts and crafts room, and meeting rooms.

Swimming Pools. A swimming pool can be the key fea-ture of an association's recreation facilities and a main-stay of association vitality, to say nothing of the sales ap-peal generated during the marketing phase. Developers must evaluate a pool's long-term usefulness to residents and the costs, however, before deciding to install one.

In addition to the cost of the pool itself, developers must consider items like lighting for night use, heating, any enclosures, and pool furniture, which increase costs dramatically. The market's demographics should be care-fully checked to determine whether a pool is needed in the development. The developer should investigate the number, location, and attendance figures for municipal and private open-membership pools in the area; if ade-quate facilities already exist in the immediate area, the capital and operating costs of constructing a community pool may not be warranted.

In townhouse, condominium, and multifamily com-munities, however, a swimming pool is often one of the most desired amenities. Even in areas with a short

The pool complex at Playa Vista in Los Angeles, California, is a desirable amenity and gathering place.

summer season, a swimming pool helps to establish an image for the community of a maintenance-free, leisure-oriented lifestyle and a certain prestige. It can also be a place to socialize with neighbors, a focus for open space, and a meeting ground for the entire community. After a project is completed and the community association takes authority, the swimming pool takes on another important function, becoming the key feature of the community association's recreation facilities and a mainstay of the association's vitality. All of these reasons are central to a developer's decision to install this rather costly amenity.

If research indicates that a pool would be a useful amenity, developers have some options. They can provide the land, build the pool and its fixtures, and then operate the facility as a private commercial club or turn it over to the community association. Alternatively, they can donate the site and subsidize construction costs, helping residents to organize a community association and contract for the construction. The community swim club, through its charter and bylaws, stipulates the assessment and dues to cover amortization, maintenance, and operation. In most cases, developers construct the pool and its accessory facilities and turn them over to the community association along with other common open space and amenities.

The physical layout of a pool requires careful planning, because pools generate noise and activity. Adequate buffering between a pool and nearby residential units is essential. Some families with children prefer to live close to a pool, but others—particularly those without children—prefer to be separated from this activity center.

Unless targeting specialized markets such as retirees, the swimming pool complex should serve the full range of age groups, with shallow areas for young children, lanes for lap swimming, and areas for leisurely swimming and relaxing. Some consideration should also be given to the construction of spas in addition to the pool.

The pool and its paved apron must be completely fenced for safety. Local building and zoning codes dictate minimum fencing requirements. In addition to the pool itself, the pool area should include some sort of structure containing showers, toilets, a small office, and a storage room. This building may be part of a larger clubhouse, if one is needed for other purposes. The size of the swimming pool varies with the number of residents it is intended to serve. The National Spa and Pool Institute recommends about 40 square feet (4 square meters) of surface area for each swimmer. Thus, a basic 16-foot by 32-foot (5- by 10-meter) pool accommodates about 12 or 13 persons.

In large developments, a series of smaller pools relating to individual housing groups is an option instead of one large, centrally located pool. The depth of pools depends on the type of use intended: casual playing areas need be only three feet (0.9 meter), while swimming areas should be about four feet (1.2 meters) deep to allow for turning.

If competitive swimming is anticipated, a regulation 25-meter pool should be considered. If buyer profiles indicate few families with children, the wading pool can be omitted. In all cases, users' enjoyment will be enhanced if the deck or patio area is three to four times the pool area. Part of the area may be well-drained lawn. The main deck area should be located along the long axis of the pool.

The pool's filter-bathhouse structure, fencing, benches, and lighting provide an opportunity to complement the architecture of the community. Structures in the pool area can be constructed of similar materials and styles as homes in the community but in a more playful way. In most situations, a well-placed pool complex provides good general views of open space and screens out undesirable views.

Tennis Courts. Tennis courts require little land (one acre [0.4 hectare] is enough for four to six courts), are easy to maintain, and can be constructed relatively quickly. The popularity of tennis peaked in the late 1970s and early 1980s, however, and since then, tennis

Courts for basketball might be more practical than tennis courts.

Open space can be passive or active, like this recreation facility at Natomas Park in Sacramento, California.

has somewhat diminished in popularity. Developers therefore must assess the cost and benefit of providing tennis courts. Construction of tennis courts can be planned for and phased in response to actual demand in the community.

It is difficult to quantify the number of outdoor tennis courts required in residential areas, because demand is related to such variables as the number of times per week people wish to play, climate, the availability of courts for night use, the availability of indoor courts, and whether they are operated using reservations or on a first come, first served basis.

Two courts are generally adequate for a 300-unit residential community with a minimum recreation package. More tennis courts may be required in some types of projects. If the tennis facility is the primary amenity, it may be necessary to build more courts than if it is an ancillary amenity. A higher ratio of courts to units is often appropriate in second-home developments, where they could attract more tennis-playing buyers. Demand may also be higher in developments catering to empty nesters and upper-income families. In markets with a particularly high demand for tennis courts, developers might consider building a large facility and initially opening it to outside membership. This concept, however, entails some risk and requires an expert operational staff as well as an operating budget.

Scattered courts create problems with maintenance and operation. Generally, tennis courts should be clustered in the community. Once a tennis facility's general location has been chosen, it should be oriented properly relative to the sun's movement.

Development Phasing

As residential projects grow in size from a few lots to large master-planned communities of several thousand acres and a mix of housing and amenities, the phasing

of development and the timing and sequence of construction become more critical. Developers desire flexibility, but it must be balanced against practical assurances that the public interest will be safeguarded. Local requirements for phasing vary, based on existing ordinances and state enabling legislation. Regardless of legal requirements, however, developers of large, complex projects almost always find it necessary to phase the development.

Development staging in conventional lot-by-lot projects generally refers to the developer's movement toward final plat approval of the project, which usually occurs after the preliminary plat is approved. In conventional development, then, approval of the final plat (usually within a specified period) is the assurance to the municipality that the final plat is in accordance with the preliminary plans approved earlier and that construction will take place according to those plans. The sale of houses cannot begin until this final plat has been recorded. Moreover, most local subdivision ordinances require that all public improvements be assured by the posting of an appropriate bond or money deposited in escrow. And in some cases the tax-assessed valuation of land is increased as soon as it is platted rather than when construction is completed.

With the outcome hinging on approval of the final plat, developers are discouraged and in many cases financially prohibited from seeking final platting of a whole project at one time. Final platting all at once gives the developer more control over unforeseen hurdles, such as a locality's reluctance to grant further plat approval, but normally developers plat only that portion of a project they are certain of completing and marketing in a short time. It is good business practice for developers to obtain final plat approval in stages.

A system that rests entirely on a single approval of development has some disadvantages. For example, a PUD cannot function within a framework that relates all commitments to a single filing, for the emphasis in a planned unit development is on continually upgrading site plan-

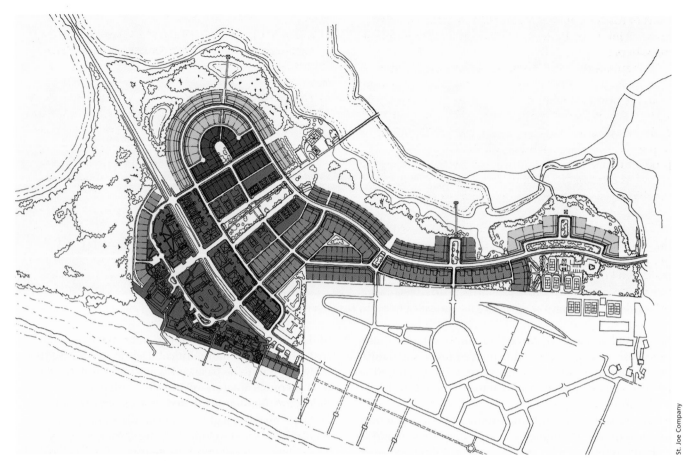

Large projects are usually completed in phases.

ning and architectural design. These innovative techniques do not come without a higher outlay of capital by the developer, but they may not be justified if the developer is uncertain about a municipality's changing the ground rules. The courts have recognized this fact yet have generally afforded developers protection only on that part of the project where they can demonstrate that they have already undertaken substantial construction.

Densities and the general type of housing in a PUD may vary from phase to phase, with the densities of all phases averaged to arrive at an overall density for the project. Some jurisdictions require simultaneous development of different elements of a project in proportion to one another. Others require that individual stages of the project stand on their own and meet the requirements of the entire development. It is important that the requirements and conditions of the jurisdiction be achieved while at the same time allowing a certain amount of flexibility for the developer. The developer needs assurance that financial and marketing calculations for the project will not be changed in the future by zoning amendments, the composition of the planning and zoning commission, or the local climate for growth, even if the project is proceeding on schedule and the developer is acting in good faith.

The size of the phases is based on several factors, with utilities, storm drainage, and topography obvious considerations. Confining phases to small drainage areas is a commonly used option because doing so

minimizes siltation and erosion and provides a natural boundary within which to undertake construction. Developers must also consider cut-and-fill operations needed and phase the project accordingly. Grading is an expensive part of development, and developers should strive to limit grading to only the area needed for each phase to reduce carrying costs on the land (interest on construction money borrowed to carry out grading and development) and to save the costs associated with protecting graded areas from erosion while awaiting construction.

Above all, the size of the first phase must be geared to what the market can absorb in a reasonable period of time. Absorption is based on anticipated demand and the existing supply of competitive dwelling units. It is of prime importance to complete a section large enough in absolute numbers to offer a broad housing mix and a sufficient number of unit types to get a good idea of the market's preferences.

Access to public services and utilities must be considered when selecting which portion of the development should be the first phase. If the project is relatively inaccessible by existing roads, roads must be extended to the first phase before development begins. It might be necessary to increase the price of the lots in the first phase to offset these initial costs; it is more typical, however, for developers to spread the costs of extending infrastructure over the entire project, which requires a carefully planned cash flow analysis. If long extensions of roads or utilities are needed to service the first phase, it might be better to decide on a different phasing scheme.

Sometimes the location of the first phase is governed by marketing considerations, such as visibility or proximity to the primary amenity. The sequence of construction and the separation of construction traffic from potential and new residents' traffic are also factors. The order of importance varies, depending on the particular type of product being marketed. Moreover, because many land contracts contain land purchase releases, developing a feasible phasing schedule to minimize carrying costs is vital.

The planning agency's approval for staged or phased development should afford developers reasonable flexibility. It is best to get the public agency to approve a general overall plan with a firm overall density. The specifics of the first phase should be set and approved, with parcels in the remaining phases zoned for an overall density by phase and an indication of the general type of housing. Market conditions change over time, and, especially in long-term projects, it might become necessary to adjust the type of product offered in the original plan. Residential developers need to work with the municipality to devise a phasing program and procedure for amendments that allow for change without compromising the integrity of the original plan.

Perhaps the issue of greatest concern to municipalities when considering long-term developments is amenities. Consumers are not often willing to buy a developer's promises; they want to see the amenities proposed. But the carrying costs of some major amenities may well increase the prices of lots in subsequent development phases to the extent they are no longer competitive.

The balance between marketing, which may require all amenities in place before a project is completed, and the cash flow cycle, which would suggest deferring amenities until later phases, relates to the product's salability. If developers cannot market the product for lack of amenities, cash flow will suffer. Again, developers must consider this tradeoff early and devise a phasing plan for amenities that will appeal to homebuyers without resulting in a negative cash flow.

In large communities whose construction extends over a period of years, amenities should be phased as units are constructed. Initial amenities should be representative of future amenities in terms of quality and type so that no question exists of misrepresentation by the developer. A general rule of thumb is to measure costs of amenities in terms of dollars spent per unit; each phase should include appropriate amenities to maintain a roughly equal expenditure per unit. Developers must include in the cost per unit of amenities the cost of carrying part of the maintenance and operating expenses, pending completion of other phases. With all types of development, a developer's reputation hinges on the quality of the community he or she delivers, which includes the amount and timing of the community's amenities.

Notes

1. Frederick D. Jarvis, *Site Planning and Community Design for Great Neighborhoods* (Washington, D.C.: NAHB Home Builder Press, 1993), p. 38.
2. Ibid., p. 42.
3. The word *charrette* comes from the French word for "little cart." In previous centuries, French artists hired someone to push a cart containing their paintings to the art auction so that they could apply the finishing touches to their work on the way to the auction. Over the years, the word has come to mean an intensive, often last-minute work effort by architectural, planning, and design professionals to refine their designs.
4. Jarvis, *Site Planning and Community Design,* pp. 44–45.
5. Ibid., p. 28.
6. Walter M. Kulash, *Residential Streets,* 3d ed. (Washington, D.C.: National Association of Home Builders, American Society of Civil Engineers, Institute of Transportation Engineers, and ULI–the Urban Land Institute, 2001).
7. Reid Ewing, *Traffic Calming: State of the Practice* (Washington, D.C.: Institute of Transportation Engineers, 1999).
8. www.census.gov/apsd/www/statbrief/sb95-23.pdf.
9. A good reference document is "Guide for the Development of Bicycle Facilities," published by the American Association of State Highway and Transportation Officials, 1999.
10. Jarvis, *Site Planning and Community Design,* p. 54.
11. http://www.nalms.org/.
12. Charles W. Harris and Nicholas T. Dines, *Time-Saver Standards for Landscape Architecture* (New York: McGraw-Hill, 1997), pp. 520–521.

5. The Legal and Regulatory Context for Residential Development

Early in the life of any project, perhaps before site acquisition, a regulatory and land use entitlement analysis should be performed to determine how federal, state, and local laws apply to a project. Federal, state, and local environmental, land use, and infrastructure requirements applicable to residential projects have become more prevalent as a result of increased concerns about urban and suburban growth. The public sector has strived not only to keep growth under control but also to make sure that the natural environment is protected. Local requirements can vary from jurisdiction to jurisdiction, and requirements for different project types may vary within a jurisdiction.

This chapter discusses federal regulations, state and local land planning controls, and relevant litigation that affect residential development. When selecting a site for residential development, developers must study their project in light of these regulations to project the overall feasibility, cost, and success of the development.

Federal Regulations

Federal regulation of land use proliferated from the 1960s through the 1980s; it encompasses a range of interests, from housing discrimination to environmental protection.

Summerset at Frick Park, Pittsburgh, Pennsylvania.

Fair Housing

Historically, discrimination and segregation have been woven throughout the residential real estate landscape. Up until 1950, the code of ethics for Realtors® prohibited Realtors® from being "instrumental in introducing into a neighborhood . . . members of any race, nationality, or any individual whose presence will clearly be detrimental to property values in that neighborhood.[1] A 1970 Prentice Hall textbook went so far as to note to real estate appraisers that "the mixing of residents with diverse historical backgrounds within a neighborhood has immediate and depressing influence on value."[2]

Title VIII of the Civil Rights Act of 1968, more commonly known as the Fair Housing Act, addressed this discriminatory practice, making it illegal to discriminate on the basis of race, color, religion, sex, familial status, or national origin in the sale or rental of housing. The act's strength was that it identified discriminatory practices in financing, selling, and renting housing; its weakness was that it did not provide for an effective means of enforcing the resulting violations. Twenty years later, after countless efforts to bolster the act's enforcement powers, the Fair Housing Amendments Act of 1988 was passed, expanding the scope of the original Fair Housing Act and strengthening its enforcement procedures. Today, the Secretary of the U.S. Department of Housing and Urban Development (HUD) is the chief enforcer of the Fair Housing Act, registering all complaints and taking action to achieve conciliation and to investigate all claims.[3]

In its amended form, the Fair Housing Act makes it unlawful for someone to turn down or refuse to negotiate a valid offer to purchase or rent a dwelling because of race, color, religion, sex, familial status, or national origin. It is also unlawful to discriminate against a person when negotiating terms, conditions, and privileges of sale or rental or in the use of related services and facilities.[4]

Discrimination against handicapped individuals is also detailed in the Fair Housing Act. Section 804(c) of the act states that handicapped individuals may not be denied housing or be discriminated against in the terms, conditions, or privileges of sale because of their handicap. Furthermore, handicapped individuals must be given the opportunity to make reasonable modifications to their dwelling to get full enjoyment of their premises. When renting, the handicapped individual must not be denied the opportunity to modify the unit so long as the lessee restores the unit to its original condition once vacated.[5]

Multifamily dwellings built after March 13, 1991, must be built to accommodate residents in wheelchairs. Common areas must be accessible by wheelchairs, and units must be available on the premises that can accommodate a person in a wheelchair. Doors in such units must be wide enough to allow for passage of wheelchairs, kitchens and bathrooms must allow for use by someone in a wheelchair, and light switches, outlets, and thermostats must be of proper height and location for use by someone in a wheelchair.[6] The Americans with Disabilities Act also states that sales offices, rental offices, and model units must be accessible to those in wheelchairs when it is not too costly to make them accessible.[7]

The Fair Housing Act extends beyond negotiation for the sale and rental of housing, addressing the financing and advertising of available housing and the housing's location. Lenders may not discriminate when negotiating terms, conditions, or the final approval of a mortgage or home equity loan. Developers, real estate agents, and others also must be very careful when advertising their developments or homes. One cannot advertise residential real estate in a way that indicates preference or limitation of a class of people.

This law is most commonly violated when advertisements contain human models who depict a certain race, familial status, or socioeconomic class. If the choice is made to use human models in advertising a residential community or individual home, careful steps must be taken to ensure that the development or home is marketed as a community open to all people equally. The same holds true for the language of advertisements. Real estate advertising cannot indicate, for example, that the lessor is looking for a white man to rent the apartment or that families with children are not welcome. Advertisements are safe, however, if they indicate that the particular unit for rent is above a garage. Although such a unit is obviously not wheelchair accessible, the language is not discriminatory in nature.

Real estate agents and lessors have also been found to violate the Fair Housing Act through what is called "steering." Steering in sales occurs when an agent tries to direct a client to or away from a particular neighborhood to keep the community segregated. In St. Louis, a real estate company was brought to court after the Metropolitan St. Louis Equal Housing Opportunity Council conducted research that showed agents were not giving African American clients all available listings in the clients' price range and size requirements to keep them out of certain neighborhoods.[8] Steering in renting takes place just as easily. In Baltimore, a rental apartment company was found guilty of steering by having its employees place African American residents in the back of an apartment complex, even when there were units available for rent in the front of the building. The company ended up settling out of court for $900,000.[9] Although steering is most commonly associated with independent realtors, developers should train their staffs against inadvertent behaviors that could result in violations of the Fair Housing Act.

Briar Chapel is a 1,500-acre, (600-hectare) development in Chapel Hill, North Carolina, that will include a range of townhouses and single-family houses with supporting retail and community facilities.

The Village at NTC in San Diego, California, is a carefully conceived development that integrates military housing with the surrounding community.

The Fair Housing Act, like most laws, has its exceptions. In two circumstances, a seller or lessor may discriminate in the sale or rental of housing. The first is when the seller, who must not own more than three single-family homes at one time, sells or rents his home without the assistance of a real estate agent. This seller, however, must abide by the Fair Housing Act's advertising requirements, which make it illegal to print or publish an advertisement that indicates a preference or limitation or to discriminate based on race, color, religion, sex, handicap, familial status, or national origin.

The second instance is when the dwelling allows for the independent living of up to four families and the seller or lessor maintains and lives in one of the living quarters as his home.

Environmental Controls

The impacts of federal environmental laws on residential development can come into play during many stages of a project's time line. It is important for developers and their consultants to be informed of such laws and their implications.

National Environmental Policy Act. The National Environmental Policy Act (NEPA), the country's national policy for environmental responsibility, was signed into law in 1970. Congress recognized the mounting impact that society was having on the natural environment, specifically in the areas of population growth, high-density urbanization, industrial expansion, resource exploitation, and new and expanding technological advances. To maintain a balance between society and the natural environment, Congress codified its national commitment to protecting and promoting environmental quality through NEPA. The act requires that all federally funded, permitted, or licensed projects assess, before development, whether the project will have any negative impacts on the environment.[10]

Although the application of NEPA is associated with federal projects and the assessment process is run by federal agencies, private developers can become involved when their projects require a federal permit or license or receive federal funding. Such was the case in Loudon County, Tennessee, where a private developer had to be party to the NEPA process because of his intention to acquire federal land for a residential, resort, and golf course community.[11]

The NEPA process has three phases. The first phase is to determine whether the act applies. If the project involves a federal action, then NEPA applies. If the project is privately funded and is being developed on privately owned land, NEPA does not apply. If state or local government actions are involved, however, it is important to determine whether the state has its own environmental policy act, which may be applicable.

If a federal action is involved, an environmental assessment is completed to determine whether or not the project would significantly affect the environment (the second phase). The assessment must include sufficient evidence and analysis to enable the government to determine whether further review of the environmental impact is necessary. If it is not necessary, a Finding of No Significant Impact is prepared, and the project may move forward. If further analysis is necessary, Phase III occurs, preparation of an *environmental impact statement* (EIS).[12]

The EIS provides a full discussion of all significant impacts that project development may have on the environment. The statement also provides reasonable development alternatives that would avoid or minimize adverse environmental impacts. Once a draft of the EIS is published and comments are received from all necessary parties, a final EIS is published, and the development of the project is then able to continue, taking into consideration any necessary alternatives discovered through the process.

Hazardous Waste. Commonly known as "Superfund," the Comprehensive Environmental Response, Compensation, and Liability Act (CERCLA) of 1980,[13] as amended

The risk of flooding can be mitigated with appropriate treatment of floodplains.

Dahlin Group

by the 1986 Superfund Amendments and Reauthorization Act, empowered federal officers, employees, and representatives to respond directly to releases or threatened releases of hazardous substances that may endanger public health or the environment.[14] Superfund sites are discovered in a variety of ways, including citizen petitions to clean up land and informal or community observation or notification to the EPA, which oversees the Superfund cleanup process. Such petitions, observations, and notifications are made when ignitable, corrosive, or reactive agents are found on the land or when there is a high level of toxic chemicals on the site. Once hazardous substances are discovered on a site, site assessments, inspections, ranking, and removal begin. Parties deemed liable for the pollution, regardless of intent, must pay for the cleanup. The process, depending on the degree of pollution, can be time-consuming and costly, so residential developers should conduct an environmental assessment on property they wish to develop to ensure that prior use of the land did not result in toxic chemical spills.

The EPA has recognized that this liability has kept prospective purchasers and lenders from acquiring and redeveloping contaminated land for fear of a huge liability bill. In response to this fear, the EPA has initiated prospective purchaser agreements (PPAs). These agreements, between the EPA, the Department of Justice, and the prospective purchaser, ensure that the purchaser will not incur Superfund liability so long as certain conditions are met. Although these agreements are more common for commercial development, one result is that these brownfield areas are being redeveloped for commercial and industrial purposes, leaving the greenfields to remain as open space or for residential use. PPAs have helped to reduce sprawl by keeping commercial and industrial activity centralized on redeveloped land.[15]

Flood Insurance. The National Flood Insurance Act, enacted in 1968, provided a federally instituted national flood insurance program at a time when private sector insurance providers found such insurance too costly. The 1968 act provided the opportunity for property owners who have improved their land to purchase flood insurance if their community participates in the National Flood Insurance Program (NFIP). Participating communities are those communities that enforce floodplain management measures to regulate new construction and to make sure that new construction located within a *special flood hazard area* (SFHA)[16] is constructed to eliminate or minimize damages that may occur by future floods.[17]

After the floods in the Midwest in summer 1993, which resulted in billions of dollars in flood damage, Congress revisited the 1968 act and determined that current participation in the NFIP was only one-fifth of what it should be. In 1994, Congress enacted the National Flood Insurance Reform Act, significantly increasing the obligation of lenders to require flood insurance.[18]

The 1994 act mandates that any building located within a SFHA of participating communities must have and maintain flood insurance to receive a loan from a regulated lender. The requirement of flood insurance is a prerequisite to closing on a property located within the SFHA. For those improved properties located within an SFHA that had loans before the enactment date (September 23, 1994), flood insurance will be required if and when the owner wants to refinance, increase, renew, or extend his current loan. Although the law applies to those buildings located within the SFHA, property owners within a participating community who live outside the SFHA are permitted but not required to obtain insurance coverage.

Before building, developers should determine whether their property falls within the parameters of this act. The Federal Emergency Management Agency (FEMA) has extensive maps, readily available to developers, that outline flood zones. Developers should also be aware of local floodplain regulations. Although federal regulations make it possible to develop within an SFHA if the structure's elevation or other restrictive measures are met, local regulations are often more restrictive, limiting development in floodplains to nonstructural development such as golf courses, open space, parks, and parking.[19]

Cross-Cutter Laws

A number of additional environmental laws address the protection and conservation of special resources. The EPA refers to these laws as "cross-cutters," because the requirements cut across all federal programs and agencies. The evaluation conducted under cross-cutters is usually integrated into other statutory reviews, such as the environmental review carried out under NEPA. The following cross-cutter laws are most likely to affect the development business.

Endangered Species Act. Endangered and threatened wildlife, fish, plants, and their habitats are protected under the 1973 Endangered Species Act. An endangered species is one that is "in danger of extinction through all or a significant portion of its range," while a threatened species is one that is "likely to become an endangered species within the foreseeable future throughout all or a significant portion of its range."[20] The process of listing a species as endangered or threatened may begin with the petition of a federal agency or a private party. Private party petitions are often in response to a proposed development project in the area of the species. Once a petition is received, the Secretary of the Interior has 90 days to conduct a review of scientific and commercial data to determine whether the petition is appropriate. Once the review is complete, the Secretary determines either that no alteration to the species's status is necessary or that the proposed listing is warranted and the review process will continue for the next 12 months until a final determination is made. Within that 12-month period, the public is given the opportunity to comment on the intent to list the species.

When conducting an environmental assessment, developers must look for species that may be threatened or endangered before going ahead with their project.

If a developer fails to do so, begins development, and then later finds a species, the delay before a final determination is made could be two years or even longer.

Although endangered and threatened species are listed per the federal Endangered Species Act, individual states also have their own wildlife preservation statutes that are equally effective in preserving the land that houses animals or species that fall under the parameters of the state regulation. Vermont offers an example of such a regulation. Vermont's preservation statute states that "permits will be granted only if the subdivision or development will not have an undue adverse effect on the scenic or natural beauty of the area, aesthetics, historic sites or rare and irreplaceable natural areas." It continues, "a permit will not be granted if it is demonstrated . . . that a development or any subdivision will destroy or significantly imperil necessary wildlife habitat. . . ."[21]

National Historic Preservation Act. Growth and development, particularly in existing urbanized areas, have resulted in the razing and altering of historic structures and lands, sometimes obliterating the landmarks and places of our nation's past. The National Historic Preservation Act (NHPA), which became law in 1966, was created to protect land, buildings, homes, and objects that have contributed to the nation's historical makeup to ensure that future generations can experience them. NHPA, although a very important regulation, is usually addressed by developers only when they find themselves in the middle of litigation. NHPA gives individuals the ability to nominate land or property for placement on the National Register of Historic Places to halt development on historic land or prevent the razing of a structure of historic significance. Each state has a slightly different process, but nominating a property typically entails a submission to the state historic preservation officer (SHPO). Once the application is submitted, the SHPO contacts the owners of the property to give them a chance to object to or allow the nomination. If objected to, the nomination then is turned over to the National

Vermillion Village is being developed in south central Utah with sensitivity for the environment in a unique resort destination.

The HOK Planning Group © 2004

Wetlands are an important part of the ecosystem and must be protected. Keene's Pointe in Windermere, Florida, uses lake frontage without destroying the natural plant life.

Park Service to determine its eligibility. If allowed, it goes to the National Park Service to be considered for inclusion on the National Register of Historic Places.[22] NHPA prohibits development on land or structures that are on the National Register of Historic Places.

Developers should also be aware of local regulations that take the form of easements that run with the land. These agreements, often initiated by private historic preservation foundations, can be as restrictive as NHPA. For example, the Foundation for the Preservation of Historic Georgetown has been granted deeds of scenic, open space, and architectural facade easement from former and current homeowners in the Georgetown neighborhood of Washington, D.C. These deeds of easement are between the foundation and the land itself and therefore cannot be altered by current and future landowners. Although foundations are often willing to work with developers and owners, special attention must be paid to these potential roadblocks before beginning to invest in a project.[23]

Clean Water Act. The Federal Water Pollution Control Act Amendments of 1972, commonly referred to as the Clean Water Act and later amended in 1977, were enacted in response to public concern over increasing surface water pollution. The act requires the EPA to establish guidelines, referred to as the "208 planning process," to guide the planning and implementation of water pollution control programs nationwide. The 208 planning process is implemented by local government agencies

that enforce land use regulations intended to control nonpoint sources of water pollution. "Non-point-source water pollution comprises all sorts of contamination that enters surface water by means other than ditches, drains, and pipes, such as street runoff, dumps and septic system leachate, mining, forestry, agricultural runoff, and construction erosion."[24] Developers should check with their local 208 planning agency to determine what needs to be done to keep their construction project within the 208 planning process. If the construction project would produce a high amount of water pollution resulting from sediment, mitigation measures may need to be taken throughout construction.

Wetland Preservation. Wetlands are defined as "those areas that are inundated or saturated by surface or groundwater at a frequency and duration sufficient to support, and that under normal circumstances do support, a prevalence of vegetation typically adapted for life in saturated soil conditions. Wetlands generally include swamps, marshes, bogs, and similar areas."[25] Since European settlement began in the 1780s, more than 50 percent of the wetland acreage in the lower 48 states has been lost.[26] Although the environmental significance of wetlands is well known today, wetlands used to be viewed as a breeding ground for disease, and developers were encouraged to fill in the wetland for a more productive use of the land. In 1990, Congress adopted the Water Resources Development Act, which set the twofold goal of not losing any of the remaining wetlands and improving the quality and quantity of those wetlands that exist.

Section 404 of the Clean Water Act speaks directly to the preservation of wetlands. It prohibits the discharge of dredged or fill material into navigable waters (which include wetlands) without a permit issued by the Environmental Protection Agency or an authorized state agency. The rationale for the law is to protect the quality of water. Wetlands trap pollutants in their soil, keeping toxins from entering water sources. Eventually these pollutants break down and are absorbed into the vegetation. Disturbing or filling the wetlands releases pollutants into the water source. In *United States* v. *Deaton*,[27] the deposit of excavated material from a wetland into that same wetland was shown to increase the amount of pollution that reaches the water, even though no additional materials were added to the fill. Deaton purchased a 12-acre (5-hectare) parcel to develop a subdivision but could not get a permit for sewage disposal, given the high groundwater elevations on the site. Knowing that the property was considered wetlands but ignoring that a permit was needed from the U.S. Army Corps of Engineers, Deaton corrected his sewage disposal problem by digging a ditch through the middle of the property. The Corps filed a complaint seeking a ruling that Deaton violated the Clean Water Act through "sidecasting"[28] and was therefore liable for the restoration of the property and subject to civil penalties. The court held that sidecasting constitutes a discharge of a pollutant, therefore violating the act and holding Deaton liable for restoration. This case reiterates the importance of determining

Coastal development must comply with numerous regulations.

what federal legislation is applicable to a developer's property before the start of development. Failure to properly research the nature of the property could prove costly.

Coastal Zone Management Act. The Coastal Zone Management Act of 1972, as amended by the Coastal Zone Protection Act of 1996, recognizes that coastal areas in the United States hold a wealth of resources yet are under constant stress from population growth and development. To preserve, protect, and restore the resources of the U.S. coastal zone, Congress, through the Coastal Zone Management Program, encourages states to develop management programs for development within their coastal zones. The Coastal Programs Division of the National Oceanic and Atmospheric Administration's Office of Ocean and Coastal Resource Management administers the program at the federal level. To date, 34 states have approved management programs covering nearly all of the nation's shorelines.

Marine Protection, Research, and Sanctuaries Act. This act enables the Secretary of Commerce to designate as marine sanctuaries any ocean waters, coastal waters, or the Great Lakes and connecting waters and to control activities within them.[29]

Fish and Wildlife Coordination Act. This act states that for any federal action that modifies a watercourse or any public or private action under a federal permit, one must first consult with the Department of Interior's Fish and Wildlife Service and with the head of wildlife resources

of the particular state. This provision could have a broad impact on wetlands.

Qualified land planners and real estate attorneys are aware of most federal regulations. Processing applications through many federal agencies takes time, but the job can be less onerous if handled by qualified and experienced professionals. Often it is possible to combine the requirements of two or more agencies, saving both time and money. To ignore these federal agencies and their requirements or to postpone contacting them can jeopardize an entire development.

State and Local Planning Controls

Development is most closely regulated at the state and local levels, whereas federal enabling legislation, supported by judicial review, supports the local planning process in states, regions, counties, and municipalities.

The Comprehensive Plan
The comprehensive plan provides a statement of goals and objectives for the future development of the community. These goals and policies are then translated into land use designations for the jurisdiction. While not always required, every state's enabling legislation permits each jurisdiction to create a comprehensive plan.

A comprehensive plan consists of maps, charts, and text outlining the policies and objectives of the municipal-

ity. Typically, the plan's objectives address issues relating to the municipality's future development, including but not limited to the location, character, and timing of future development. The comprehensive plan may also dictate the amount, density, and character of development proposed for each land use. The housing needs of present and future residents are often addressed by including within the plan where residential development will occur. The comprehensive plan also addresses infrastructure, designating where expressways, highways, local streets, parking facilities, and bike trails will be placed in the jurisdiction. In addition to where each use will be placed in the jurisdiction, comprehensive plans discuss the interrelationships among all the components of the plan and the implementation and staging strategies for the plan.[30]

Regardless of whether or not state enabling legislation requires a comprehensive plan for local jurisdictions, states must determine whether zoning has to conform to the comprehensive plan. The Standard Zoning Enabling Act of 1926, one of the original land planning acts set forth by the Department of Commerce and adopted in part by most states, asserts that zoning must be in compliance with the comprehensive plan. Most states' enabling legislation follows the 1926 act, holding that zoning must be in accordance with a comprehensive plan.

It is important for developers to understand that the staging and implementation element of the comprehensive plan is just as important as the land use. In the 1983 case *Phillipi* v. *City of Sublimity*,[31] a residential developer sought subdivision approval on agricultural land that the comprehensive plan had zoned for residential development. The city denied the subdivision permit, however, because although the land was zoned for residential development, the comprehensive plan indicated that the land was to be used for agricultural purposes until it was needed for urban development. The location of the property was not under development pressure at the

time subdivision approval was sought, and therefore the city was able to legally deny the approvals.

Zoning

Land use laws, including zoning, were formed in the United States largely in reaction to human health problems. In urban areas, densely developed, overpopulated tenement housing with few or no sanitary facilities created deplorable sanitary conditions. Nearby factories that emitted waste into both the air and water only added to the appalling situation. Although cities such as Boston and Los Angeles used forms of zoning in the early 1900s, it was New York City that established the first comprehensive zoning ordinance with the New York City Building Zone Resolution of 1916. Led by Edward M. Bassett, the "father of zoning," a committee spent three years researching and planning a comprehensive system of building and land use for New York's five boroughs. After surviving constitutional attack in the New York court in 1920, zoning began to spread and by 1926, 43 of the then 48 states had adopted zoning enabling acts.[32]

Zoning came to the forefront of land use law, however, in Euclid, Ohio, with Euclid's comprehensive zoning ordinance. Euclidian zoning, as it has become known, regulates and restricts the location of trades, industries, apartments, single-family residences, dual-family residences, and other uses as well as lot size and height of the buildings. The zoning ordinance established six classes of use districts, three classes of height districts, and four classes of area districts. The zoning ordinance became well known and widely followed after the U.S. Supreme Court confirmed its constitutionality in the 1926 case *Village of Euclid* v. *Ambler Realty Co.*[33]

Although Euclidian zoning served its purpose and separated the industrial from the residential from the retail, it was inflexible, and in the 1970s, more flexible zoning regulations began to surface.

Incentive Zoning. Usually located in urban areas, incentive or bonus zoning is a tradeoff between the developer and the municipality whereby the municipality may allow the developer to exceed the allowed height or density limitations in return for various public amenities. Often these amenities take the form of public parks, open space, or affordable housing.

Performance Zoning. While traditional zoning determines whether a project may be developed based on use, performance zoning makes that determination based on the performance of the project—how it will impact the surrounding environment and public facilities. Performance zoning is more flexible than traditional zoning because it allows for project approvals to be determined project by project by considering both capacities and demands on such things as water, traffic, and sewer.

Infill Zoning. Most often seen in urban areas, infill zoning is applicable in developed areas where vacant parcels remain, scattered and too small to meet current zoning standards for new construction. Municipalities allow for zoning changes to promote development of compatible but different uses. From a policy standpoint, infill development is viewed favorably, as it promotes development and redevelopment in urban areas rather than moving development out to undeveloped suburban areas.

Planned Unit Development. Planned unit developments came into wide use beginning in the 1960s and gained strength through the 1980s. A PUD is a deviation from a jurisdiction's traditional zoning ordinance and is granted as the result of a developer's submission to the municipality of a detailed development plan that does not comply with traditional zoning but provides elements that traditional zoning is not able to offer. Developed as a single plan, a PUD includes a specified number of residential units and often commercial, service, and other uses as well. The purpose of the PUD is to give the developer the flexibility to create a development that uses the land more efficiently than traditional zoning would allow, potentially creating a better community for the occupants and neighbors.

Cluster Zoning. Cluster zoning, often referred to as "open-space" or "density" zoning and most applicable to residential development, is designed to meet the need for community development while providing specific plans for retaining open spaces and preserving the natural environment. Cluster zoning allows the developer to group buildings closer together, thereby increasing the density in some portions of the development and so create a larger contiguous open space for recreation and other purposes. Although this method allows for more open space than is feasible under traditional zoning, cluster zoning not only preserves more of the natural environment but also creates lower development costs by reducing the linear footage of street and sewer necessary for development.[34]

Floating Zone. A floating zone is similar to conventional zoning. It carries with it the same requirements, stating a use, setbacks, and other necessary regulations. The difference is that it is not affixed to the zoning map in any specific location. It requires further action by the zoning board in essence to bring the zone down to earth. This zoning technique is considered flexible because the petition to bring the zone down to earth comes from a landowner who wishes to develop his or her land in accordance with the zone's requirements. The zoning, once approved, replaces the prior zoning that was applicable to the land and allows the community to meet the changing needs of development.[35]

Transfer of Development Rights. Transfer of development rights (TDR) is another flexible zoning technique that was first suggested in the early 1960s by David Lloyd, a New York developer. Lloyd contended that if a community did not want development in a certain area, the community should allow landowners to sell their development rights to someone who owns land in the area where development is encouraged. The idea was largely ignored until the early 1970s, when John Costonis, a law professor, championed it as a way to preserve Chicago landmarks where no public funds were available.[36]

Rancho Viejo is a large master-planned community near Santa Fe, New Mexico.

Spring Island is a purist's recreational community that focuses on protecting its environmental heritage. Its no- and low-impact land and habitat management philosophy emphasizes economic viability, community livability, and environmental sensitivity in preserving an authentic piece of South Carolina's Lowcountry for future generations.

The concept of private communities as environmentally sensitive developments has branched out, in evolutionary fashion, from the pioneering efforts at Hilton Head Island to permutations thriving along the barrier islands of North Carolina, down the Atlantic Coast, and up the Gulf Coast. One of the purest examples is Spring Island, southwest of Beaufort, South Carolina, halfway to Hilton Head.

The principals of Chaffin/Light Associates, Spring Island's owner/developer, learned their development craft at Sea Pines Plantation and applied it with increasing refinement at adjacent Callawassie Island, at Amelia Island, and then at western outposts in Washington State and Colorado. By the time they purchased Spring Island in 1991, they had distilled the essence of environmentally sensitive development to its pure-play concept: that the highest and best use for the land was its preservation.

This approach is a new twist on an attitude that once abounded in rural, agricultural America, an attitude held by its indigenous peoples: that land—and its flora and fauna—is an heirloom to be preserved, enhanced, and passed on. Even when settlers came to own the land, they used it without degrading it. A single family had owned the Spring Island parcel for the previous 189 years, from the cotton plantation days to the aftermath of the Civil War, when the land was used for subsistence farming and hunting by rich northern industrialists. During the hunt club era, for almost a century, Spring Island and most of the Lowcountry tidewater lands remained in their natural state.

A previous developer had obtained permission from the county to build 5,500 dwelling units and two golf courses on Spring Island's 3,000 acres (1,215 hectares). Chaffin/Light downzoned it to 500 units (later 410) and one golf course and established Spring Island Trust to conserve and manage the 1,200 acres (485 hectares) that were set aside as a nature preserve. This private nature park of fragile ecosystems consists of a 100-acre (40-hectare) live oak forest, marsh lands, and ponds, habitat for a wide number and variety of animals—wild turkeys, bobcats, deer, and residential and migratory birds. Here, too, are preserved the human traces of Spring Island's history: aboriginal shell mounds, camps, villages, and ruins of plantation houses, outbuildings, and gardens.

Homeowners at Spring Island are required to maintain natural vegetation at the periphery of their lots.

Chaffin/Light wrote design guidelines for residential construction that support the understated, hand-crafted lifestyle at Spring Island. The 285 "estate" homesites are two to ten acres (0.8 to 4 hectares); 125 "cottage" homesites are one-quarter to 1½ acres (0.1 to 0.6 hectare). Building setbacks are twice the county minimum. Homeowners are allowed a small envelope of residential landscaping around houses but are required to maintain natural vegetation at the periphery of their lots to screen all houses from view and to provide additional wildlife habitat.

The project took on very little debt, and undercapitalization was a constant. Except for the Arnold Palmer/Ed Seay–designed golf course, amenities could not be provided upfront, so early purchasers had to buy into a dream. The primary amenity was nature—and the developer's philosophy of nature stewardship.

At first, the market of homeowners who desired a simple lifestyle based on harmony with nature was unknown; Spring Island was the first high-end coastal development that had no beachfront. Only by word-of-mouth referrals from owners and by recognition from environmental, recreational, and cultural agencies did absorption finally reach critical mass in the mid-1990s. Despite the slow start, most amenities were paid for by equity capital and cash flow. To date, product sales have totaled more than $160 million, and land and infrastructure costs have totaled $53 million, for a net profit of $65 million on a capital investment of $17.4 million—a 27 percent rate of return.

Spring Island today includes a full-service golf house; River House, a community gathering and dining place; and tennis, equestrian, and art facilities. Spring Island Trust also sponsors, and maintains its headquarters in the Mobley Nature Center. The nature center is staffed by full-time naturalists, who manage the trust's wildlife conservation program. All amenities and features reflect the focus of Spring Island on preservation of the natural environment for the continuing enjoyment of its residents. ∎

TDRs offer a landowner, whose potential to develop land is limited, the opportunity to sell development rights to a landowner in an area where development is encouraged. They can be used to preserve open space, prime agricultural land, and sensitive ecological areas. TDRs can be cumbersome to administer, however, and they raise several constitutional issues.[37] When a site is subject to TDRs, it is best to contact a qualified land use attorney early in the process. In areas using TDRs, local attorneys, planning consultants, and public agency staffers have developed expertise in arranging such transfers and can provide developers with valuable guidance.

Extraterritorial Zoning. Rapid development of some suburban areas has forced governments to plan for balanced and systematic growth within their jurisdictions. Municipalities are often forced to expand their boundaries and annex, or limit development of, adjacent land. But often by the time a municipality is forced to take such action, its jurisdiction is already overdeveloped, and an attempt to establish a rational land planning scheme is too late. It is at this point that a municipality enacts extraterritorial zoning. Extraterritorial zoning implicitly or explicitly empowers local units of government to zone land outside their borders to conform development of adjacent land to their own zoning. Although this technique is often applied to land that will more than likely be annexed to the jurisdiction, municipalities use this form of zoning to prevent chaotic, dangerous, unaesthetic development around their borders. Although the constitutionality of extraterritorial zoning has been affirmed in most jurisdictions, state legislature has the ability to take this power away from municipalities.[38]

Exclusionary Zoning. Exclusionary zoning is the term applied when municipalities require minimum lot and house sizes and other restrictions that exclude multifamily or other high-density development and in effect exclude low- to moderate-income members of society.[39] As most notably publicized through the 1975 New Jersey Supreme Court case, *South Burlington NAACP* v. *Township of Mount Laurel*,[40] exclusionary zoning occurs when land is zoned in a manner that excludes certain members of society. Mount Laurel's zoning ordinance required minimum lots of 0.5 acre (0.2 hectare) and disallowed apartments, duplexes, and mobile homes in the township. As a result, low- to moderate-income households were priced out of the market and could not afford to live in the township, resulting in both class- and race-based segregation. The court ruled in favor of the NAACP and ordered the township to take affirmative steps to assure the development of low- and moderate-income housing. Today, jurisdictions must provide for all types of uses within their borders. Proactive programs in Virginia, Maryland, California, New Jersey, and other states have turned to inclusionary zoning to help reverse exclusionary zoning and the inevitable accompaniment of race- and class-based segregation.[41]

Inclusionary Zoning. As housing prices and rents rise, low- to moderate-income households are increasingly priced out of the real estate market and must live in hous-

The Village at NTC in San Diego, California, provides high-quality housing for military families, who typically have a difficult time finding affordable housing.

ing beyond their means. According to the Joint Center for Housing Studies of Harvard University, 14.3 million households, or one in seven, spend more than half their incomes on housing, while it is advised that less than 30 percent of one's income be allocated to housing.[42] High prices have also forced families to look for more affordable housing farther from the cities where they work, squeeze their families into overcrowded dwellings, or reside in dwellings that are not in compliance with health and safety codes. These statistics have led a number of state and local jurisdictions to address the growing housing affordability crisis through inclusionary zoning.

The goal of inclusionary zoning is twofold: to create more homes that are affordable to low- and moderate-income households,[43] and to integrate those units into a diverse development fabric throughout the jurisdiction. Whether voluntary or mandatory, a common way for zoning ordinances to achieve this goal is to require or allow for height or density bonuses in return for the inclusion of affordable or moderately priced units in the development. One of the most successful programs in the country is the Moderately Priced Dwelling Unit (MPDU) Law in Montgomery County, Maryland, passed in 1974.

Montgomery County, a suburb of Washington, D.C., had experienced a rapid increase in senior citizens on fixed incomes, young adults, government employees in moderate-income ranges, and service personnel. Given the inadequate supply of affordable housing, the county also realized that people who worked within its boundaries were forced to live elsewhere, making the long commute to and from work daily. These factors not only led to a shortage of employees and high turnover but also overtaxed roads and transportation facilities. Although the county wanted to take charge of this situation, it realized that the private sector was better equipped and possessed the necessary resources and expertise to provide the type of moderately priced housing needed in Montgomery County.[44]

The county therefore established a mandatory program whereby all developers, in exchange for a density bonus of up to 22 percent, would have to include MPDUs in all developments of 50 or more units. To receive the density bonus, 12.5 to 15 percent of the total number of units in the development would have to be MPDUs. At least 15 percent of the development must include MPDUs to receive the maximum density bonus of 22 percent. The program also provides an alternative whereby developers can apply to have the required MPDUs built on a nearby property or instead contribute to the County Housing Initiative Fund for the production of MPDUs. Although this approval is difficult to obtain, it may be necessary, for example, when the development is for a high-rise luxury building that has associated high monthly condominium fees.[45]

The density bonus was created to ensure that private developers would not incur a financial loss but would have the prospect of financially profiting from the inclusion of MPDUs. Between 1976 and 2003, more than 11,000 affordable units were built in Montgomery County under this policy. The Montgomery County program is just one example of a successful inclusionary zoning program. State and local governments across the country have created mandatory and voluntary programs to bring more affordable housing to their communities.

Moratoriums. Although zoning and land use laws exist to promote the health, welfare, and safety of the community by regulating land development, these controls can serve their purpose only if they are supported by a planning process that is responsive to the community's needs and objectives. When land development proceeds in an uncontrolled, rapid fashion, short-term development controls are necessary to manage development. Interim or stop-gap zoning freezes existing zoning and prevents new growth while areas are studied for initial zoning or the revision of current zoning. This measure is often taken to relieve overburdened public services or to protect newly annexed land perceived as environmentally sensitive. Although the development that would have taken place but for the moratoriums would have been legal, it may have been inconsistent with the community's needs as determined by the planning study done during the moratorium.[46]

Subdivision Regulations. Subdivision regulations are a long-accepted method of municipal and county control over the development of land. Originally enacted by states in the late 19th century, subdivision regulations allow a public authority to control the platting and conversion of raw land into building sites, and, as such, they have a much greater impact over a longer period of time on all development than does zoning. Once a residential development is created and sold to individual property owners, for example, it is very difficult to reassemble the land for another use.

Subdivision regulations are concerned mainly with the layout and standards for lot-by-lot development, normally accomplished through plat approval, whereby a developer is not permitted to make any improvements

Subdivision regulations are one way that localities control development. Shown here is Orenco Station in suburban Portland, Oregon.

on the land or divide and sell the land until the planning commission (and/or city council) has approved the map or plat of the proposed subdivision. Approval or denial is based on conformance with the development standards set forth in the ordinance.

Planners' coordination of the unrelated plans of individual developers is one obvious benefit of subdivision regulations; for example, subdivision regulations ensure the alignment of streets and infrastructure between adjacent developments. For developers, they are a safeguard against competitors who would drive down the value of a well-planned subdivision with an adjacent substandard development. Subdivisions can be judged communitywide against a comprehensive general plan. Like zoning regulations, however, most cities had subdivision regulations long before they had comprehensive plans, and, in fact, much subdivision regulation takes place without reference to the comprehensive plan.

But the practical need for conformity between planning and subdivision control is greater than between planning and zoning. Although zoning regulates uses, bulk, and height, it does so on developed and undeveloped land and can be changed. Subdivision regulations affect undeveloped lands, and whatever is permitted initially—street, sewer, and water main location, widths and standards for these improvements, park and school site locations, and lot size—will be present for a long time.[47] Once streets and utilities are laid, changing the subdivision layout is very difficult.

Generally, subdivision regulations require following a set of steps before an approved final plat is recorded. Many jurisdictions suggest that developers submit thumbnail sketches of proposed subdivisions showing locations and special features but do not actually require them. Most planning agencies believe that a consultation before the application is submitted is helpful, because it gives them information that is useful later when they must review the formal plat. Likewise, developers can secure guidance from planners to smooth out the processing of the application before they incur great expense preparing detailed plans.

The first formal action required of developers is an application for approval of a preliminary plat. The local subdivision regulations specify in considerable detail what information is to be shown on the plat. Usually the plat must be submitted with multiple copies and in enough time for all affected agencies to review it and make recommendations. After interested agencies have considered the plat, the approval agency either approves (usually with conditions) or denies it. During review, considerable negotiations between the developer and the approval agency can be expected, often resulting in modifications to the proposed plat.

When a final plat is submitted, the approval agency has its last chance to do anything about a subdivision. The purpose of approval of the final plat is to ensure that the recorded plat is in accordance with the approved plans and that construction will proceed according to those plans.

The final step before the development and sale of lots is the recordation of the approved plat. When the required improvements have actually been completed, the public agency inspects them; a formal action is required to accept them for public dedication and maintenance. Many lending institutions require the filing of an approved plat before committing money to homebuyers in a subdivision.

Although subdivision regulations are clearly necessary, developers sometimes complain that municipalities have adopted unreasonable requirements as a prerequisite to subdivision approval. For example, requirements might include excessively wide street rights-of-way, overly generous parkland or open space, and oversized utilities at the developer's expense to serve property (either developed or undeveloped) beyond the proposed development. Moreover, many conventional subdivision regulations have become obsolete in light of contemporary forms of design and development. Many PUDs, for example, do not lend themselves well to traditional subdivision codes; such projects require greater flexibility if they are to respond to varying site conditions. Likewise, applying rigid standards to a sloping site can result in excessive grading and removing too many trees.

Another frequently encountered constraint relates to minimum lot sizes. Usually sizes of lots are regulated by zoning and subdivision codes that specify a minimum, for example, of 10,000 square feet (930 square meters). Developers may find it very difficult to satisfy the requirement for minimum size when trying to preserve sensitive site features (such as a stand of trees or a stream) or developing a steep site. To provide greater flexibility, some jurisdictions call for an average (instead of a minimum) standard, which allows developers to plat the lots more sensitively without compromising the jurisdiction's overall objectives for density. An average standard is also less cumbersome than requiring developers to file for a series of variances.

Chatham Club is an urban infill development in a middle-income Chicago neighborhood. It includes 143 single-family houses on small lots.

Garrison Partners Consulting

Residential developers should not take subdivision regulations as a given when standards are excessive for the development being proposed. Like zoning ordinances and most other local regulatory devices, periodic amendments to the subdivision code are necessary to keep pace with development practices.

Typological Coding. The new urbanism is an increasingly mainstream development pattern. To accommodate this type of planning, many communities are supplementing traditional zoning, or even abandoning it altogether, in favor of typographical coding. Introduced to the planning profession in the early 1980s by architects Andrés Duany and Elizabeth Plater-Zyberk, typological coding contrasts markedly with zoning in that land uses are not prescribed. Instead, coding defines a set of building, street, and open-space "types" to be used as building blocks to design the community. A detailed regulating plan maps all the streets, blocks, and lots and assigns a building type or types to each lot. Other diagrams show how the building should sit on its lot.

Unlike zoning's diagrams, which dictate density and land use with little design control, the first priority of typological coding is to shape a community's public realm —its streets, squares, and parks—through the configuration of surrounding buildings. Drawings of proposed designs are fairly detailed, because critical elements are pinned down at the planning stage rather than hashed out during design review. Because the approach establishes so specific a plan initially, it enables the jurisdiction to eliminate the often contentious and arbitrary design review process and offers developers the assurance that if the project is in compliance with the code, it will be approved. Many regulating plans and codes are extremely short and to the point, with the full document as few as two or three poster-sized sheets.

Exactions, Impact Fees, and Negotiations

Increasingly, local governments have found it difficult to fund the public improvements and services that are necessary for new subdivisions and their residents. Although traditionally these improvements would be financed through property taxes, from a policy standpoint it is seen as unfair to have existing homes bear the burden through higher taxes or lower-quality services. Through state enabling legislation that allows for local municipalities to use their police power to control growth through zoning and planning, local jurisdictions have been given the authority to impose exactions and impact fees on new development.[48]

Exactions started as a simple tradeoff; to receive approvals, a developer would dedicate land or provide for streets and other interdevelopment improvements such as water and sewer lines. Exaction requirements, however, have expanded. To receive subdivision approvals, developers often must comply with park and school dedications. In the face of explosive growth affecting more than the facilities in the new subdivisions, dedicating land has been at times an inadequate approach to compensating for the burden of new development on the public infrastructure. As such, local municipalities have turned to *in lieu fees* when land dedication is no longer practical. These fees go to off-site improvements such as widening adjacent streets and expanding off-site public facilities like sewage and drainage facilities.[49]

Impact fees are another form of exactions; they are imposed by municipalities through their police power to regulate for the health, safety, and welfare of its citizens. Impact fees are usually imposed on the developer at the time building permits are issued and are allocated to off-site public facilities. Impact fees have been challenged when they are imposed on developers as a form of tax rather than a regulation. Unless a municipality receives express taxing authority from the state, which is uncommon, municipalities are not allowed to use their police power to establish a tax for new development. Impact fees must be established as a land use regulation; they will be struck down as invalid if they are established as a tax.

Typological coding defines building, street, and open space "types" that become the building blocks of a community.

Duany Plater-Zyberk & Company

Riverwalk at Port Imperial in New Jersey is located across the river from midtown Manhattan, making it appeal to condominium buyers who thrive on urban living.

When determining whether an impact fee is valid, developers should look at a number of things. First, it is important to realize that impact fees are charged only to provide new developments with needed public facilities. Collected fees may not go to rehabilitate or replace existing facilities or deficiencies. Second, the *rational nexus test* applies to impact fees; that is, there must be a logical connection between the public facility that the impact fees fund and the needs of those who will live in the new development. In other words, the new facilities must benefit those who live in the new development. If no direct link exists, then the fee is invalid. Finally, impact fees collected must be spent within a reasonable time period. It is generally agreed that six years is a reasonable time frame, although ten years has also been found to be acceptable.[50]

When applying the rational nexus test, developers in the past have taken issue with the allocation of impact fees to schools, given that future residents may not have school-age children and therefore will not directly benefit from the public improvement. Many, but not all, states have included impact fees for schools in their enabling laws, and where enabling laws have not specifically included school impact fees, many courts have found the fee allocation to be legitimate. What is important to look at when reviewing a school impact fee is its relationship to each specific housing unit. Miami–Dade County, Florida, took this relationship into consideration when adopting its ordinance for school impact fees.[51]

Miami–Dade County, Florida, which has the fourth largest public school system in the nation, experienced an increase in its enrollment of elementary and high school children by 40 percent between 1984 and 1995. Its school district's construction budget rose 360 percent between 1992 and 1995. Although the county had an impact fee ordinance for roads and parks, it was not until 1995, at the request of the county school board, that legislation was passed for school impact fees. A sliding scale to determine school impact fees was adopted after local, state, and national research showed that the larger the housing unit, the greater the number of school-age children.[52] Taking into consideration the fact that the greater the square footage, the more likely the more school-age children the unit will house, the sliding-scale formula ensures that the fee increases as size of the unit increases. Although this fee is applied to all projects, developers of atypical developments are given the opportunity to request an independent analysis of the appropriate school impact fee. Even though the sliding-scale formula is one method of coming up with a fair impact fee, set fees are equally as viable so long as they are proportionate to the share of burden that the unit is placing on the public school system.[53]

Negotiations

Despite the plethora of ordinances regulating development actions, private developers still initiate most of the changes in the landscape, and municipalities are the accommodators. At some point in the development process, the public and private sectors must meet. It may be over a single variance from the zoning ordinance, or it may be over a complicated proposal for a planned unit development involving protracted negotiations and communication. Whatever the project's size, negotiation is important in building a rapport between the public and private sectors; it prevents the parties from becoming adversaries.

The development process is in the center of the political arena. Developers, builders, and other private real estate interests have large roles to play. The developer's role has diminished to a degree, however, because public involvement in land development decisions has increased; the arena is crowded with special-interest groups—citizens, local, state, and federal governments, and local planning agencies and commissions. Most recently, this trend has been manifested in initiatives or ballot measures that seek direct control over major land use decisions. In short, communities are becoming more entrepreneurial and responsive to the needs of the entire community rather than strictly letting the marketplace dictate land use patterns as they have in the past.

Municipal negotiations typically involve tradeoffs and compromises, but not all those offered by a municipality will be useful to a developer. For example, a community might offer developers a density bonus because it has satisfied certain municipal requirements. But the density bonus will be useless to developers whose initial proposal for density represented the share of the market the project was capable of capturing. Developers need to be aware of what tradeoffs and compromises are likely to be offered and then pursue those that will be of greatest benefit to the proposed project.

For developers, the best way to influence the development process is to begin long before they need a particular type of zoning for a particular parcel of land. Developers should actively support good local planning by pushing for a good planning staff and planning commission. They should also make sure that the community

Cherry Hill Village in Wayne County, Michigan, includes single-family houses, townhouses, and condominiums in a village setting.

has up-to-date regulatory tools such as zoning and subdivision ordinances or, even better, a combined development ordinance to complement its comprehensive plan. Developers should also participate in formulating and updating the municipal capital improvement plan, because it is important to the ultimate provision of infrastructure. And developers can make it easy for themselves by improving their image with the public by building quality developments and living up to their word. Working from a basis of trust rather than hostility greatly aids developers when they seek approval for a project. Involving public officials early in the planning process gives them a certain sense of ownership in the proposal.

Almost always when dissension arises between planners and developers, it is because each fails to understand or appreciate the other's viewpoint. Developers should analyze the public interest and evaluate their proposals in light of the community's comprehensive plan and applicable ordinances. If developers find that their proposals do not fit in, then they should drop or modify them, for in the end it will save all parties a good deal of time and money. But if they find that the comprehensive plan and ordinance do not respect a community's present and future general welfare and must be amended to be responsive, then they should indicate the necessary changes and, if necessary, offer assistance in preparing the revised documents.

It is advantageous for developers to establish contact with a public agency at the project's conceptual stages. A project's feasibility and acceptance can be discussed openly before substantial amounts of time and money are committed. Problems that might result from redesign can often be avoided through early and continuous contact. Before assuming financial commitments, developers can go informally to the planning agency when they need an indication of the receptiveness to the proposal.

A local community's political climate can change over time. A practice once accepted can become unacceptable, and developers caught in the middle may find that

a project underway cannot be completed. Written agreements and statements of intent that address major issues can prove extremely beneficial to developers. They are the best and perhaps the only assurance that the community will follow through in good faith, but they are not always easy to get. Following California's lead in 1976, several states have provided enabling legislation authorizing local governments to enter into binding development agreements.[54] Although originally intended to better establish a developer's vested rights, development agreements have proved beneficial to both the public and private sectors by offering a forum for negotiating large-scale and long-term development projects.[55]

After meeting initially with planners and after developing preliminary concepts, developers should meet with local interest groups as a good way to get the community's advance reaction to a project. People seem to fear most what they do not understand, and they oppose most of what they fear. It is essential, however, not to overwhelm local citizens in an effort to get them involved. Their concerns must be heard, and they must believe that the developer is hearing them. A developer's worst enemy is a rampant neighborhood rumor. Real estate councils, community groups, the local League of Women Voters, the school board, and various environmental groups all have sound opinions and good advice that developers should solicit and heed.[56]

All indications are that negotiation will become even more difficult in the future, because a greater number of agencies with many more requirements will be involved. Private and public awareness of the rights of consumers will make the process lengthier. Successful residential developers will need to master the art of negotiation, but they will also need to establish a positive public image through actions, not just words.[57]

Litigation

In residential development cases as in other land use cases, litigation generally results when a private property owner challenges the validity of a local or state government regulation because the owner's property rights have been infringed upon. Other types of litigation may occur during the course of development because of breaches of contractual relationships between the lender and the developer or between the developer and the contractor. These types of litigation raise issues on contract law rather than land use law and are addressed only briefly in this section.

Land use cases are usually litigated in state courts rather than federal courts. Conflicts over impact fees, zoning, growth moratoriums, and other issues of growth control generally arise out of local or state laws rather than federal law and thus come under the jurisdiction of state courts. Cases involving a potential infringement on constitutional rights, however, such as violations of takings, due process, and equal protection clauses of the Constitution or violations of the protections in the Civil Rights Act raise federal issues that may be tried in federal court. Any conflicts arising over federal wetlands or other environmental laws may also be brought in federal court.

Often when land use regulations are involved, developers must exhaust all administrative remedies before they can seek trial through the court system. Thus, only after they have attempted unsuccessfully to resolve the problem through local or state hearings and appeals can developers turn to the courts.

Traditionally, the courts have presumed that zoning and other land use regulations are valid as a constitu-

tionally permitted exercise of the police power, unless they are shown to be clearly in violation of the constitutional rights of the landowners. In recent years, however, the courts have been increasingly sympathetic to the perspectives of landowners, resulting in less latitude for municipalities to regulate land use as they desire. Basically, if the right to be protected falls under the category of "civil liberties," then any restriction of these activities by the government will be justified only by a strong regulation.[58] In fact, some would argue that all zoning decisions must further the public welfare rather than hinder it. The change in judicial attitudes toward land use restrictions, away from the absolute immunity and broad discretion previously accorded to local governments, has increased the risk of liability for governmental entities.

The Takings Clause of the Fifth Amendment

Federal, state, and local jurisdictions are empowered to manage land use and development for the health, safety, and welfare of their citizens through the use of police power. Although the police power is broad, both the Fifth and Fourteenth Amendments to the U.S. Constitution limit its applicability. The Fifth Amendment limits the federal government's reach when it says, "No person shall be deprived of life, liberty, or property, without due process of law; nor shall property be taken for public use without just compensation." The Fourteenth Amendment similarly applies to states, providing that "no state . . . shall deprive any person of life, liberty, or property

Ridenour in Cobb County, Georgia, is an 88-acre (35-hectare) community with a variety of housing types and a town center. The project was developed by the Macauley Companies.

Built in the 1930s, Laurel Homes, in Cincinnati, Ohio, was the second largest Public Works project in the United States. Today, it has been revitalized with a HOPE VI grant to accommodate 500 families in a mixed-income setting.

Torti Gallas and Partners/Steve Hall © Hedrich Blessing

without due process of law; nor deny to any person within its jurisdiction the equal protection of the laws." Although the Fourteenth Amendment does not specifically indicate that states may not take private property for public use without just compensation, 47 of the 50 state constitutions expressly prohibit this action, and in the three states whose constitutions do not address the takings issue, courts have held that this action is also prohibited.

Litigation involving takings has covered a number of scenarios, ranging from the physical condemnation, where property is taken for public improvements such as highways, to regulatory takings, whereby a landowner's use of the property is limited as a result of zoning requirements or environmental regulations.

When fighting a regulator's taking, the landowner's case often hinges on what uses of the land are left after the taking. This issue came before the U.S. Supreme Court in the 1992 case *Lucas* v. *South Carolina Coastal Council*.[59] In 1986, Lucas, a residential developer, purchased two oceanfront residential lots on a South Carolina barrier island, Isle of Palms, for $975,000, with the intention of building single-family homes. Two years later, South Carolina enacted the Beachfront Management Act,[60] which, by taking into account beach erosion, established a baseline within which future development and construction would not be allowed; Lucas's properties were within the baseline. Lucas quickly filed suit claiming that the Beachfront Management Act affected a taking of his property without just compensation. Lucas did not argue the validity of the act but rather contended that by not allowing him to develop his land as he intended and was authorized to do when he purchased the property, the act extinguished all of the property value and he was therefore entitled to compensation.

Lucas went through the courts until the U.S. Supreme Court heard it in 1992. The court held in Lucas's favor, saying, "When the owner of real property has been called upon to sacrifice *all* economically beneficial use in the name of the common good, that is, to leave his property economically idle, he has suffered a taking."[61] The distinction in this case, compared with similar cases in which the courts have ruled that there was not a taking warranting compensation, is that Lucas lost all economically viable use of his land, not just a preferred, more financially lucrative use of the land.

Notes

1. Jonathon Brown, "Opening the Book on Lending Discrimination," *Multinational Monitor,* November 1992, p. 8.
2. Ibid.
3. Michael H. Schill and Samantha Friedman, "The Fair Housing Amendments Act of 1988: The First Decade," *Cityscape: A Journal of Policy Development and Research,* Vol. 4, No. 3 (1999). To register a complaint, go to www.hud.gov/complaints/housediscrim.cfm or call 1-800-669-9777.
4. The Fair Housing Act, 42 USC §§3601 et seq.
5. 42 USC §3604(f).
6. Ibid.
7. 42 USC 26 §§12101 et seq.
8. National Fair Housing Advocate Online, May 1998, Press Release, www.fairhousing.com/news-archive/releases/ehoc_2.htm; *Metropolitan St. Louis Equal Housing Opportunity* v. *Gundaker Real Estate Co.* (2001).
9. National Fair Housing Advocate Online, October 1997, www.fairhousing.com/news_archives.advocate/October97.
10. NEPA §101; 42 USCA §4331.
11. *Federal Register,* June 17, 2002 (Vol. 67, No. 116).
12. Ronald E. Bass, Albert I. Herson, and Kenneth M. Bogdan, *The NEPA Book: A Step-by-Step Guide on How to Comply with the National Environmental Policy Act* (Point Arena, California: Solano Press Books, 2001).
13. 42 USCA §§9601 et seq.
14. CERCLA overview: www.epa.gov/superfund/action/law/cercla.htm.
15. www.epa.gov/brownfields.

16. Property is considered to be within a special flood hazard area when it has a 1 percent or greater chance of a flood in any given year.

17. FEMA guidelines for the mandatory purchase of flood insurance are found at www.fema.gov/nfip/mpurfi.htm.

18. Ibid.

19. Daniel R. Mandelker, Roger A. Cunningham, and John M. Payne, *Planning and Control of Land Development: Cases and Materials,* 5th ed. (New York: Matthew Bender, 2001), pp. 796–798.

20. Endangered Species Act, Section 3, subsections 6 and 20.

21. Vermont Statute, 10 V.X. A. §6086(a)(8).

22. See National Park Service, www.cr.nps.gov; for further information, see the Web site for the Advisory Council on Historic Preservation, www.achp.gov.

23. See *Sagalyn* v. *Foundation for Preservation of Historic Georgetown,* 691 A.2d 107 (1997); and *Bagley* v. *Foundation for the Preservation of Historic Georgetown,* 647 A.2d 1110 (1994).

24. Nicholas A. Robinson, *Environmental Regulation of Real Property* (New York: Law Journal Press, 1983), p. 16.

25. Code of Federal Regulations, 33 CFR §328.3(b), Navigation and Navigable Waters.

26. Cyril A. Fox, *Cases and Materials on Real Estate, Regulation, and the Environment,* Chapter 7 (Pittsburgh: University of Pittsburgh School of Law, 2000). See also Thomas E. Dahl, "Wetlands Losses in the United States, 1780s to 1980s," (St. Petersburg, Florida: U.S. Fish and Wildlife Service, National Wetlands Inventory, 1990).

27. 209 F.3d 331 (4th Cir. 2000).

28. *Sidecasting* is the deposit of dredged or excavated wetland back into that same wetland.

29. 16 USC 1401.

30. Mandelker, Cunningham, and Payne, *Planning and Control of Land Development.*

31. 662 P.2d 325 (Or. 1983).

32. Mandelker, Cunningham, and Payne, *Planning and Control of Land Development.*

33. 272 U.S. 365 (1926).

34. Patrick J. Rohan, *Zoning and Land Use Controls,* Volume 2, Chapter 8 (New York: Matthew Bender, 1997).

35. Brian W. Ohm, *Guide to Community Planning in Wisconsin* (Madison: Board of Regents of the University of Wisconsin System, 1999).

36. Charles J. Hoch, Linda C. Dalton, and Frank S. So, eds., *The Practice of Local Government Planning,* 3rd ed. (Washington, D.C.: International City Management Association, 2000).

37. Daniel R. Mandelker, *Land Use Law,* 3d ed. (Charlottesville, Virginia: Michie Co., 1993).

38. Patrick Rohan, *Zoning and Land Use Controls,* Volume 3, Chapter 20 (New York: Matthew Bender, 1997).

39. Mandelker, *Land Use Law.*

40. 336 A.2d 713, 719 (N.J. 1975).

41. Robert W. Burchell and Catherine C. Galley, "Inclusionary Zoning: A Viable Solution to the Affordable Housing Crisis? Inclusionary Zoning Pros and Cons." *New Century Housing Newsletter,* October 2000.

42. Joint Center for Housing Studies of Harvard University, "The State of the Nation's Housing," 2003.

43. Those who qualify for affordable or low-income housing earn up to 60 percent of the area median income (AMI), and those who qualify for workforce or moderate-income housing earn between 60 and 120 percent of AMI.

44. Montgomery County Maryland Inclusionary Zoning Code, Section 25A-1, Legislative Findings.

45. Joyce Siegal, *Inclusionary Zoning around the Country,* March 2000, Innovative Housing Institute, www.inhousing.org.

46. Rohan, *Zoning and Land Use.*

47. Donald Hagman, *Urban Planning and Development Control Law* (St. Paul, Minnesota: West Publishing Co., 1971), p. 249.

48. Susan M. Denbo, "Development Exactions: A New Way to Fund State and Local Government Infrastructure Improvements and Affordable Housing," *Real Estate Law Journal,* Summer 1994, pp.7–38.

49. Mandelker, Cunningham, and Payne, *Planning and Control of Land Development.*

50. Paul S. Tischler, "Impact Fees: Understand Them or Be Sorry," *Land Development,* Spring/Summer 1994.

51. Emil Malizia and Richard Norton, "Reading, Writing, and Impact Fees," *Planning,* September 1997.

52. The public use microdata from the 1990 Census support this research, showing that there are more children in single-family housing than multifamily housing.

53. Malizia and Norton, "Reading, Writing, and Impact Fees."

54. California Government Code, §65864 et seq.

55. For additional information, see Douglas R. Porter and Lindell L. Marsh, eds., *Development Agreements: Practices, Policy, and Prospects* (Washington, D.C.: ULI–the Urban Land Institute, 1989).

56. See Douglas R. Porter, Patrick L. Phillips, and Colleen Grogan Moore, *Working with the Community: A Developer's Guide* (Washington, D.C.: ULI–the Urban Land Institute, 1985).

57. For additional information on project approval and the negotiation process, see Albert Solnit, *Project Approval: A Developer's Guide to Successful Local Government Review* (Belmont, California: Wadsworth, 1983).

58. Norman Williams, Jr., *American Planning Law: Land Use and Police Power,* Volume 1 (Chicago: Callaghan, 1974), p. 91.

59. *Lucas* v. *South Carolina Coastal Council,* 112 S.Ct. 2886 (1992).

60. S.C. Code §48-39-250 et seq. (Supp. 1990).

61. *Lucas.*

6. Marketing

Marketing residential communities is about more than just getting prospects to buy or lease units. It is about communicating with people—on an emotional level—about one of the most important decisions in their lives. It is about alleviating fears, tapping into dreams, and realizing the potential to create an exciting new way to live.

The best residential marketers create a buzz throughout the community about their development and succeed at selling a lifestyle experience to prospects. They complete a wide range of planning activities behind the scenes and put on a well-orchestrated, clear, compelling communication campaign in front of the full community.

A well-done marketing effort establishes the vision for a development through market research, then drives prospects to the development site through efficient, targeted communications. Marketing also directs the sales and leasing process, culminating in closed sales or signed leases. Finally, marketing provides structured feedback to the developer about the success of various marketing tactics, helping to ensure a stronger effort next time.

This chapter discusses the full process of marketing residential communities. The process is essentially the same for for-sale or leased products; however, this book focuses mainly on for-sale products.[1]

Marketers must recognize that homebuyers are increasingly sophisticated. They know what they want and demand that products address their needs. Residential marketing programs vary according to residential product type and the size and characteristics of the target market. Products designed to appeal to special niches or those that are pioneers in a market may require a more detailed marketing program, unusually creative approaches, and higher budgets than a more typical project. Marketing housing for seniors, for example, requires the marketer to understand that the product is marketed to both the senior and his or her grown children, who may guide the decision. The marketer must approach the senior prospect differently from the grown children, because their interest in the product and their needs are different. Marketing to baby boomers may require a carefully tailored merchandising and promotional plan, as this market segment is independent, opinionated, and interested in remaining hip in their older years. And many marketers report that marketing to the children of baby boomers—sometimes referred to as Generation X and Generation Y—is even more difficult.

Developers often retain marketing specialists to identify the psychographic profile (that is, family structure, lifestyle, personal tastes) of the target market and then help design programs to attract these members to the project. Marketing to reach the target audience involves advertising and promotions, on-site merchandising, and sales team training. Developers must constantly monitor sales, prospective buyers who visit the sales complex or view model homes, and buyer profiles to gauge accep-

WaterColor, Florida.

figure 6-1
The Real Estate Marketing Process

Step 1: Market Research
Confirming and Fine-Tuning the Vision of the Product

↓

Step 2: Developing the Marketing Strategy
Deciding How to Communicate the Vision to Prospective Buyers

↓

Step 3: Establishing the Marketing Budget
Setting Aside Enough Resources to Pursue a Strong Effort

↓

Step 4: Choosing the Marketing Tactics
Delivering the Product Message within Budget

↓

Step 5: Monitoring and Measuring the Effort
Minimizing Ineffective Effort and Pursuing Timely Course Correction

RTKL/David Whitcomb

Identifying target markets helps designers to tailor the project to the expected buyers. Acqua Vista in San Diego, California, is targeted to sophisticated urban dwellers.

tance of the product and the effectiveness of the marketing strategy.

Clearly, successful marketing depends largely on developers' ability to convey a sense of quality and workmanship; a willingness to offer reasonable warranties against structural problems alleviates buyers' concerns and contributes to the marketing team's ability to sell homes.

Market Research

The first step in marketing is the completion of market research (see Chapter 2). Market research helps shape the community's overall concept, providing information to fine-tune the site plan, product mix, unit types, and package of amenities for the proposed community. Effective market research examines in detail the competitive supply of units and the likely preferences of consumers. This latter bit of information comes from focus groups, questionnaires, and interviews with buyers and real estate agents, and from the analysis of key demographic characteristics of the market, such as income, lifestyle patterns, age, and family status. And by identifying target markets, research helps to focus the marketing campaign, including what market areas should be targeted and what types of promotions would be most effective.

The 2000 Census revealed several key changes in population and households that affect how homes are marketed. For example, the aging of America's population means greater demand for specialized seniors' housing in the future. Moreover, the decline of the proportion of traditional nuclear families to less than 25 percent of American households means that the demand for housing other than the traditional single-family house has undoubtedly increased. More and more, greater numbers of people—young and old—are looking to urban centers for entertainment, convenience, and maintenance-free living.

Competent market research can reveal these and other trends, leading to the introduction of products to serve a new market niche, such as communities for active older adults who no longer want the hassle of maintaining a single-family home and homes for childless households who want a more urban lifestyle.

Market research helps the developer and the marketing team outline the full product that they will deliver to the market and helps to shape that product's identity. Market research ensures that the proposed community occupies a unique position in the market, ideally one that satisfies a demand that no other development in the competitive market area fills. Market research helps the developer accomplish two important tasks early on: determining market positioning, and projecting absorption.

Determining Market Positioning
Developers must understand how their development fits in the market relative to the competition. Making meaningful distinctions between a developer's product and that of the competition is the art of positioning. The

Solavita in Florida was targeted to a market of retirees who seek an active lifestyle.

goal of positioning is to discover those product distinctions that the market desires and will place significant value on. Communicating these distinctions through the marketing program helps buyers distinguish between products, leading to their loyalty and their purchase of a home. Strong positioning is based on detailed market research regarding the competitive supply of units and the demographic characteristics and lifestyle preferences of the target market.

Cost is the most common element used to position residential product. Developers may construct units that are essentially similar to other units in the marketplace but position them based on price. Low-cost positioning can be tenuous because it does not necessarily create a high amount of customer loyalty. Further, most buyers want more than just the best price per square foot. In all but the most price-sensitive markets, buyers are making lifestyle choices and want their homes to reflect who they are, how they live, and what kind of image they want to project.

Location often produces a strong competitive position for a residential development; for example, marketing for those located near parks, in attractive urban settings, or in close-in commuting areas often stresses the advantage of the location. This approach often appeals to the emotional or experiential quality of a development. Statements such as "downtown living at your doorstep" and "escape to nature" evoke strong positive imagery and resonate strongly with certain target markets.

Amenities can make a project more competitive. Many large master-planned communities have based their reputations and sales success on the wealth of recreational amenities they offer. At Anthem, Del Webb's family-oriented community north of Phoenix, Arizona, the developer built all the major amenities before a single homesite was developed. The developer wanted buyers to have the complete picture of the project and to be confident that the promised lifestyle would actually be there from day one. Anthem's amenities include two golf courses, a 43,000-square-foot (4,000-square-meter) recreation center, an outdoor water park, and playing fields.

The design of units is another positioning point for residential product. "Loft living," "maintenance free," and other similar marketing statements reflect market positioning based on the design of individual residences. This method speaks more to the practical aspects of living in a residential community and less directly to the emotional aspects. The developer's or homebuilder's reputation can also help to position residential product, although the value of this reputation is unclear unless prospects are already familiar with the firm.

Most developers, particularly those marketing large projects, are likely to attract prospects from several different target audiences. For example, a project might contain condominiums geared to first-time buyers, townhouses targeted to young families, and larger single-family houses that appeal to move-up buyers. Large master-planned communities often include a full range of hous-

In some markets, amenities make the sale. At Bellaggio in Lake Worth, Florida, a well-appointed clubhouse features numerous facilities.

ing types—from starter homes to housing for seniors—that appeal to every market segment in the local area.

Projecting Absorption

Absorption, the second key piece of information produced by market research, is simply an inventory of sales or leasing rates at projects similar to the one being proposed. Market researchers generally call or visit competitive sites and interview leasing personnel to gather this information, rely on published data from market data providers, or use a combination of the two sources.

The market researcher applies typical rates of absorption for the proposed product type to the number of units proposed by the developer, taking into consideration the geographic area covered by the marketing effort, the percentage of qualified prospects that need to be captured, and the number of prospects lost to other developments being marketed at the same time.

The absorption figure is crucial because it provides the timetable that can be expected for sales and therefore the pace of development. The developer may choose to reduce the total development size or divide the project into phases or market niches based on a longer-than-expected absorption figure.

Absorption projections also determine how quickly lots are released to builders or to the public. If too many lots flood the market, prices will languish. If lots are released too slowly, sales pace suffers and buyers' interest may decline as well.

Developing the Marketing Strategy

Armed with market research and analysis, developers and marketing teams turn to the creation of the marketing strategy, an outline of how best to communicate to the target prospects. The marketing strategy should clarify the overall community concept; identify the ap-

Harrison Square in Washington, D.C., brought new construction to a deteriorating urban neighborhood and achieved a sales pace of 6.1 per month.

A community's image is reinforced in each element. The sales center at Santaluz in San Diego, California, reflects a luxurious yet casual lifestyle.

Style Interiors

propriate target markets and the best ways to reach them; determine unit types, sizes, and price ranges; determine the marketing timetable and budget; and choose the marketing tactics, including the on-site merchandising plan, advertising and promotional efforts, and sales team.

In clarifying the overall concept, developers and their marketing teams must ensure that the project has a distinct identity. Ideally, the proposed community should establish a special niche for itself in the market, one that satisfies a demand that other developments in the competitive market area do not meet. The project's distinct identity is based on a combination of target markets, location, prices, housing types, amenities, and themes.

Defining the Concept and Target Markets

Perhaps the most difficult aspect of marketing is defining target markets. Many developers create a generic product and generic marketing messages and react to the prospects that show interest. The strongest marketers, however, choose the market segments that they can effectively serve, develop knowledge about the lifestyle and housing preferences of those segments, clarify the full residential concept that fits the segment, and devise a messaging plan to reach target prospects.

A residential community is the bundle of benefits that the target market receives by living there: the unit and its features, on-site and neighborhood amenities, a specific lifestyle pattern, and perhaps even a new or reinforced self-image. Understanding the full concept of the development helps marketers define specific target segments, usually defined by income, geographic location, age, occupation, lifestyle, interests, and preferences for specific housing styles and amenities. Many marketers suggest that narrowing the target market and fine-tuning the product to fit the specific niche can give a development a competitive edge—as long as the target market is large enough.

Although a good marketing plan tries to identify target markets, those markets identified are not the only market segments that will be interested in the product. In fact, even the most well-researched marketing program can underestimate or misinterpret demand, especially for a new or unusual type of development. For example, when loft apartments were first marketed in some cities, marketers were surprised that a large segment of buyers were empty nesters, not just the young professionals who had been identified as the target market.

Discrimination against certain age groups or ethnic minorities is not only illegal but also bad business, shutting out a significant portion of potential buyers of any project. According to census estimates, about one-third of all Americans are minorities. Some marketers in regions with large immigrant populations make a concerted effort to reach out to specific ethnic minorities, realizing that they can represent an untapped opportunity. Sales representatives who speak a second language and are trained to be sensitive to various cultural differences can make a big difference in the bottom line.

Determining the Timetable and Strategy for the Marketing Campaign

The marketing team should be an integral part of the development process, involved in early decision making. A marketing viewpoint is important to ensure that every aspect of the development is appropriate for the target market. The project's location, design, theme, unit types and sizes, and amenities all relate to marketing issues. The marketing plan should begin as soon as the site is secured. Marketing functions include analysis (see Chapter 2 for details about the market analysis), strategic planning, and creating and running the advertising and public relations campaigns.

Marketing starts well before construction. Ideally, a significant portion of units are sold even before groundbreaking, giving clues as to the strength of the product and marketing strategy. The marketing timetable will affect such decisions as the timing of model construction and the opening of the sales center, both of which are costly items. The marketing timetable also determines when sales staff are hired, the purchase of on-site merchandising elements, the retention of various consultants, and more. The marketing timetable should also drive project phasing so that the right amount of product and the right product mix and location are available throughout the sales period. For example, the best locations in the development should not be the first ones released for sale. Because prices typically escalate during the project's sale period, prices are maximized by saving some of the best product for the end. On the other hand, it may be necessary to sell some of the most desirable sites early if the project needs a jumpstart. Project phasing may require a series of smaller marketing campaigns that periodically renew interest in the full development.

Marketers must weigh the various means of advertising, promotion, and other means of customer contact against the budget, keeping in mind that the main goal

Gardens, Not Golf

The nation's aging baby boomers are not interested in buying retirement homes that look just like the one next door. Golf is not their favorite hobby, and they do not want to go through their golden years living like their parents did.

They want houses laden with state-of-the-art technology and surrounded by walking and hiking trails; a growing number of boomers would even forgo the golf course for gardens.

The 78 million Americans born between 1946 and 1964 will redefine retirement living just as they have redefined every other era they have been a part of, predicts Barbara Caplan, a consumer analyst with New York–based Yankelovich Partners.

Speaking at NAHB's 2001 "Building for Boomers" conference in Phoenix, she told homebuilders that they need to offer a lot more choices if they expect to cater to their biggest group of customers ever. "Boomers are defining what they want, and 'one size fits all' will not work for them," Caplan insists. "Anything that reeks of the cookie-cutter approach will turn them off."

Traditional retirement communities and other age-restricted developments built mainly around golf courses and large activity centers are being revamped to prepare for the affluent baby boomers, the first of whom are now edging toward retirement.

Data from a magazine aimed at boomers, *55 and Better*, report that a quarter of all Americans 50 and older are active gardeners, slightly more than the number who are golfers. "Gardens can replace a 70,000-square-foot [6,500-square-meter] clubhouse for some up-and-coming retirees," maintains Peter Studl of Evanston, Illinois–based Villas of America and publisher of the magazine.

Because of baby boomers' different preferences, builders are pouring money into research and planning for this significant group of potential homebuyers. The Meyers Group, a national housing research firm, estimates that the retirement housing market will grow by at least 140,000 units annually for the next several years and predicts that the big markets for future retirees will be anywhere in Arizona and Florida, the Las Vegas area, and Ocean County, New Jersey. Areas also growing in popularity include Chicago, Sacramento, Denver, Charlotte, North Carolina, and cities in Texas.

Yankelovich Partners estimates that boomers will spend an average of $255,000 on a retirement home, almost $100,000 more than the U.S. median for home prices. Boomers have considerable money to spend. Significant appreciation in the housing market is giving them the extra cash needed to buy their retirement homes. Further, their frugal parents, whose spending habits were shaped by the Great Depression, are expected to leave them trillions of dollars in inheritances. ∎

Source: Adapted from Catherine Reagor, "Gardens, Not Golf," *Urban Land*, August 2001, p. 40.

Many homebuilders create model home "parks" with "trapped" models that require visitors to go through the sales office before going through the model home.

for the marketer is to use those tactics that communicate with the most targeted prospects over the life of the marketing campaign. In advertising, it is often referred to as "cost per impression."

In selecting on-site merchandising tactics, the marketer should choose those devices that best communicate the product. Marketers may decide that an extra model home is worth the added cost, for example.

Establishing the Marketing Budget

A vital step in developing the overall marketing plan is to determine the marketing budget, which should occur before the marketer considers the various merchandising, promotional, and other marketing tactics. The marketing budget should cover all aspects of marketing: the sales office and staff, model homes, landscaping, signage, design center, promotional activities and events, brochures, advertising campaigns, Web sites, and so on. The marketing budget contains two important sections: projections and the pro forma budget.

The budget begins with projections of the number of sales over time. Projections must allow for fluctuations in consumer activity as the result of changing seasons. In most markets, sales peak during spring and summer and dip during winter.

Projections of sales should be detailed. Ideally, the marketing staff or consultant sets up a spreadsheet indicating how many units of each type will be closed in each month along with the projected sale price for each unit. This spreadsheet can also be used during the absorption period to see how closely actual sales track against projections, thus allowing the developer to alter marketing tactics to speed up sales, if necessary.

After projecting the timing and amount of income expected, the residential marketer then builds the pro forma budget. The pro forma budget spreads out all marketing costs over time, by line item, comparing them with the sales pace. The budget estimates marketing costs as a percentage of total sales as well as per unit.

Typically, a marketing budget for a small for-sale housing development runs between 5 and 8 percent of gross sales. Projects of 100 units or more, however, may have a lower budget-to-sales percentage as a result of economies of scale. One midwestern developer devoted a hefty $1.1 million to the marketing budget for its 147-unit project, which translated to just 1.3 percent of expected gross sales, or $7,400 per unit.

Spending for different marketing items depends on which tactics the marketers believe will best reach the target market. Advertising, including radio, television, and newspaper coverage, usually amounts to 1 to 2 percent of sales, although costs in major metropolitan areas may rise to 3 percent of sales because such advertising is more expensive. Brochures and other print materials, displays, decorating for model homes, landscaping, and on-site signs usually run from 3 to 3.5 percent of gross sales. Sales commissions run from 0.75 to 1.5 percent of sales but depend greatly on the compensation arrangement for the sales staff.

The pro forma gives developers specific information on how funds will be allocated over time. It is common for one-third of the budget to be spent early in the process to get the development moving. As with other real estate pro formas, the marketing budget should be subject to periodic review and updated when new information warrants it.

Choosing the Marketing Tactics

Once residential marketers define the marketing strategy that best communicates to the target market, they turn to implementation of the plan. This section analyzes the various marketing efforts, from on-site merchandising to Web sites. Marketers usually choose marketing activities based on the budget and target markets.

In projects with multiple homebuilders, the marketing costs and responsibilities may be divided among the developer and the builders. The developer might build a visitors center that later becomes a clubhouse, while

Model homes at Baxter Village in South Carolina greet prospects with inviting porches and other details.

Adrienne Schmitz

The sales office at Covenant Hills in Orange County, California, is elegant yet includes all the practical necessities for providing information and closing deals.

Style Interiors

The iGallery at Ladera Ranch in southern California is a 6,000-square-foot (560-square-meter) freestanding information pavilion that features state-of-the-art technology.

Style Interiors

the builders are responsible for model homes. The developer usually makes decisions regarding whether all models are located in a single model home "park" or each builder has its own section of models near its own lots. Typically, the developer runs one ad campaign, and each builder runs a separate one to sell its brand and its homes. Also to be decided are how builders pay for model home lots and how presales trailers are handled.

Once the marketing strategy has been refined, developers should address ways to implement the plan. One of the first steps is the on-site merchandising of the community, which can be one of the most important elements in the marketing budget and among the most effective marketing tools. Model units, the sales office, print materials and graphics, and scale models help establish a tone or theme for the development and, when professionally executed, present a strong first impression to prospects.

Model Homes. Model homes are perhaps the most important single item in the marketing mix. Models give prospects the clearest idea of the final product, and they can draw the most interest and excitement from potential buyers. Everything about the model home—furnishings, color schemes, brochures on the table—should speak directly to the target market, with consideration given to the target buyer's age, income, and family status. All elements of model homes should also convey the consistent marketing themes or positioning statements that override the complete marketing effort. If the development targets professional couples, for instance, a comfortable, beautifully furnished home office sends a clear signal to prospects that people like themselves could live and work here. Setting up a "life scenario" or a story about the family who "lives" in the model home is a common practice. The model home targeted to a growing family might be the scene for a birthday party, complete with party clothes laid out in the bedroom, table settings in the dining room, trays of artificial food in the kitchen, and presents waiting in the living room. Such scenarios tell prospects that a happy family lives there and that the development could be an ideal place to raise their children.

For budget and practical purposes, the model home is more than just the home itself. The program also includes furnishings, outdoor landscaping and lighting, entry and interior signs, and possibly maintenance and cleaning. These costs may be considerable, although a well-done model can lead to a faster pace of sales and even higher prices and therefore may pay for itself. Many developers leave the coordination of the model unit to their marketing consultant or even a specialist whose business is model homes.

The cost to produce a model unit depends on the level of finishing and decorating and the time the unit remains unsold as a model. Some of the unit finishing costs can be recaptured when the unit is sold, but designer fees, furniture and decorations, and utilities represent sunk costs, which can add up very quickly. Costs can be far higher with top-notch resources and an ex-

tended absorption period. Skimping on the quality of furnishings is a bad idea. Often, the model is the first contact the prospect has with the development, so it should make the best possible first impression. The model is the best way to show off options, so it usually features the items the builder wants to promote—marble flooring, deluxe appliances, built-in bookcases, sunroom addition, and so on.

The developer should consider reserving one or two lots in the model area to allow for the construction of new models in case house types change over the sales period. Such lots can serve as visitor parking until they are needed. Parking should be geared to peak sales periods, typically weekends.

Sales Office. The sales office is a necessary on-site component. Most projects establish sales centers, if not also a model home, before the start of construction. This approach allows presales to begin, which often puts the developer ahead in the pro forma budget. The sales office is often the prospect's first exposure to the development, so it must make a good impression. It should be located so that it is quickly surrounded by an attractive part of the community. It should be well landscaped and designed to project the image of the community.

The sales center should be located so that it is easy for prospects to find, out of the way of construction activity, and very close to model homes, preferably connected directly to them. In most cases, the sales office is located adjacent to the project's entrance. In a large or multiphase community, the office may be strategically located well into the site, forcing prospects to drive past completed houses and landscaped areas. In single-family developments, the sales office and model homes are often located on a cul-de-sac or short street, presenting a finished look and clear image of the streetscape. In multifamily projects, the sales office might be on the main level and later converted to a management office.

With all sales centers, the developer should provide enough parking to handle peak prospect traffic, which occurs on weekends. Many sales centers open in the late morning during the workweek but are open from roughly 9 a.m. to early evening on weekend days. Because traffic is typically slow during the middle of the week, Tuesday or Wednesday is often chosen as the day to close the office.

Depending on the size of the development, the marketing budget, and the sophistication of the competition in the market area, the sales office can be structured and located accordingly:

- Garage—A sales office in a double garage is the most popular option for single-family home sales. It allows for a separate area without impairing the presentation of the model home or floor plan. Further, the initial expense and the cost of subsequent remodeling are fairly minimal. For the sales office, glass French doors replace standard garage doors, and the interior is finished with carpeting, display space, and private offices. Once the home is sold, it is converted back to a garage.

- Model Home—A sales office in the model home can be economical, especially for small developments. This arrangement impacts the presentation of the model, however, as some space—usually a den, library, or secondary bedroom—is not truly marketing space but is the sales office. In some cases, developers put a sales office in a partially completed model, keeping some of the interior walls uninstalled and postponing the installation of the kitchen until the model is sold. This choice is not the best solution, however, because kitchens are the most important feature for selling homes.

- Detached—A detached sales center, the most expensive option, is often used in large projects with several phases and/or several builders. Often, this type of sales office is located in a building that later serves as the community clubhouse. Developers may also choose temporary structures such as trailers for the sales center. Such trailers can have added architectural detailing and landscaping so that they appear almost like permanent buildings. Often, even when a permanent model or sales office is planned, a trailer is used to capture early interest until those buildings are ready. Very large long-term projects might have a sales center built exclusively to serve as a sales center and then torn down when the sales period is over. At Stapleton in Denver, Forest City built an energy-efficient green building for its sales center. The building, which features interactive displays telling the story of Stapleton will eventually be removed.

- Design Centers—Homebuilders increasingly use design centers where customers go to select the options and finishes for their new home, including flooring, hardware, moldings, fireplaces, appliances, roofing and siding materials, and paint colors. A design center might be on site, or it might be centrally located in a shopping mall or business district to serve all the builder's projects. The center contains displays of all the options for buyers to examine and compare. Design

center staff are trained to help buyers make their selections. In some cases, the staff includes professional interior designers. Builders who use design centers say that they increase customer satisfaction and can increase the options that buyers choose.

Another option is available for builders who do not have the capacity to manage their own design center. Several firms provide a service that includes setting up and running a design center at a central location that can be shared by several builders. The companies also offers consulting services for builders who want their own separate design center.

Print Materials and Graphics. Brochures are essential to any residential marketing campaign. They tell the compelling story of a development using a combination of graphics, color, paper, and text to present a clear image of the benefits of living in a given community. The best brochures are designed by professional designers, written by professional copywriters, and produced on high-quality paper in printed, not photocopied, color. Each marketer must consider the tradeoff between quality and price.

Graphics should present a coordinated image. They should have a logo or distinguishing symbol that serves to identify the project. The logo should be repeated on all promotional materials for the project, including signage, advertising, brochures, letterheads, and any giveaways such as baseball caps, T-shirts, and coffee mugs.

Brochures often come in the form of a portfolio with pockets where the sales team can place individual sheets that discuss community amenities, floor plans, pricing schedules, finishing materials, optional upgrades, and information about the developer and/or homebuilder. A cutout for a business card also helps. The project's Web site address should be printed on all marketing materials.

Residential marketers often decorate the walls of the sales center with building renderings or other graphics that tout the community's lifestyle. They further estab-

Some communities are marketed from a sales center that later becomes a community clubhouse. Others prefer to keep those functions separate.

Print materials should present a uniform image.

Communique Group

lish the product positioning and marketing themes outlined in the marketing plan.

Scale Models. Developers of large-scale communities may find it worthwhile to contract with a professional model builder to construct a three-dimensional scale model of the full site and the immediate neighborhood. Scale models generate great interest and can help prospects visualize the finished development in the context of the neighborhood, which may be important for urban infill sites that are changing dramatically.

Scale models are relatively costly, especially when they depict a large, multiphase development or present detailed building facades. It is not unusual to spend $50,000 or more on a professional, detailed model for a large development. A scale model can be the focal point of a sales center, giving the sales staff a powerful tool to talk with prospects about neighborhood features, common area amenities, traffic patterns, and more. They also help buyers visualize and select their lots.

Virtual Tours. Increasingly, virtual tours are becoming part of the marketing package. Either online or at a visitors center, prospective buyers can view the community, homes, and amenities in a virtual three-dimensional presentation. Virtual tours can be less expensive than scale models and can provide a more realistic experience.

Advertising and Promotion

Developing advertising and promotional programs constitutes a significant portion of marketing. This entire effort is undertaken to create awareness of the development among target prospects and to drive them to the sales office, where the developers' or homebuilders' representatives close the deal.

Even the best advertising and promotional programs do not sell houses; they can only deliver qualified prospects to the development site. But strong advertising and promotion establish or reinforce the image of the develop-

ment in prospects' minds and therefore are vitally important. An effective program communicates unmistakable market positioning and key consumer benefits. Consumers visit the site with clear expectations about the product, thus helping the sales staff easily step in.

Developing effective advertising and promotional messages that can be used in newspapers, magazines, and perhaps television and radio requires a level of expertise that developers normally do not have in house. Developers often hire an advertising agency to manage this process.

An advertising agency typically develops a long-range advertising and promotion strategy, completes plans for individual tactics, selects appropriate media, prepares copy and design layouts, and monitors results of the campaign. The budget varies depending on project size, the amount of "noise" in the market from competitive builders, media used, and other factors. The goals of advertising and promotion are usually to reach the highest number of prospects as often as possible (reach and frequency) and to ensure that those contacted understand the product positioning and its benefits. Good ads also include a call to action, which asks prospects to visit a sales office or Web site or to contact a representative.

The advertising budget usually includes costs for production of an ad concept, placement of newspaper and outdoor media ads, direct-mail programs to target prospects, and agency fees. Promotional tactics such as move-in gifts, referral fees, and a grand opening party are also included in larger budgets. Many marketers maintain a reserve fund so that they can respond with more advertising during unusually slow periods or take advantage of an opportunity not covered in the original budget. Advertising and promotion budgets typically account for 15 to 30 percent of the full marketing budget. Print media often account for one of the single highest budget items.

Selecting the appropriate advertising media depends on the target market. Local and regional newspapers are

Selecting the appropriate marketing image and advertising media depends on the target market.

Lesnik Himmelsbach Wilson Hearl Advertising/Public Relations

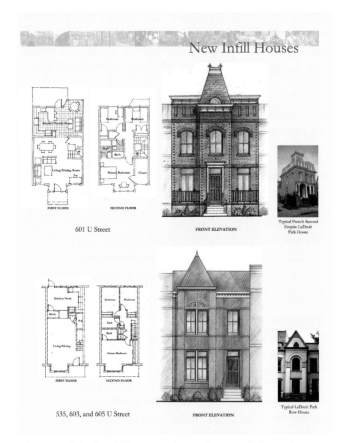

New Infill Houses

601 U Street   FRONT ELEVATION   Typical French Second Empire LeDroit Park House

FIRST FLOOR   SECOND FLOOR

535, 603, and 605 U Street   FRONT ELEVATION   Typical LeDroit Park Row House

FIRST FLOOR   SECOND FLOOR

Print materials should be attractive and convey information clearly.

a good way to reach a broad audience, while magazines, radio, and television can be more effective for specific target markets. Virtually every medium conducts its own surveys of the demographics of its audience, the results of which are made available to prospective advertisers.

The following sections discuss the key tactics that make up typical residential advertising and promotional campaigns:

- public relations
- local and regional newspapers
- real estate guides and magazines
- the Internet
- radio and television
- signs and billboards
- direct mail.

Public Relations

A good public relations image does not happen overnight; it takes time and a concerted effort to establish a variety of positive connections with the community. Developers with a history of construction in an area can build good will with past performance. A well-respected developer can use this good will to gain more referrals faster, thereby making the selling task that much easier. Less-well-known developers, however, need to work to establish positive public relations. In some cases, the in-house marketing director may assume the role of public relations director; in other instances, such as high-profile,

controversial projects using public money, the hiring of a public relations firm makes more sense.

The main goal of public relations is to develop and maintain a positive relationship with the press, which means concentrating the effort on television, radio, local newspapers, specifically those covering real estate and business, and city desk editors. Marketers often develop press kits containing a variety of materials and information specifically targeted to the press in the hope that the press will create a news story based on the information. Among the news items an editor might consider are the unveiling of the development concept, a discussion of positive changes in the neighborhood, an innovative plan or housing type, detailed project plans, ground breaking, grand opening, or residents' initial moving in.

Outside firms typically establish their fees in one of three ways: a fixed monthly retainer, a fixed retainer with monthly billing for staff time, or a base fee billed monthly. To ensure strong performance by an outside public relations firm, a developer might link a portion of fees to the sales pace, the number of prospects drawn to the site by articles, or some other measure of performance. Bonus fees might be appropriate when sales exceed estimates and the developer is confident that public relations was the cause.

The public relations budget also covers that portion of print materials used to work with the press: stationery, envelopes, thank-you cards, brochures, floor plans, site plans, price lists, and so on. It also includes costs for special photography used in articles and any mailing costs. The budget should allow for entertaining the media and perhaps a VIP party held before the official grand opening. A reserve fund is also important, as all public relations opportunities cannot be identified in the initial marketing strategy.

A public relations campaign typically begins during the presale period and continues through a project's grand opening.

Marketing materials help to create awareness and reinforce the image of the development.

John Connell

Newspaper Advertising

Newspapers provide the best return on investment for real estate marketing. Most consumers turn to the local newspaper first in their search for property. Newspapers can be used several ways to reach prospects.

Newspapers offer expanded real estate sections in the Saturday or Sunday paper, allowing the placement of numerous sizes of display ads. Large builders often purchase multipage ads or inserts that cover numerous development sites. The classified section also offers a promotional opportunity, although the sheer number of listings makes it difficult to present a distinguished market position in this portion of the paper.

As mentioned, a savvy residential marketer can use a story angle—ground breaking or neighborhood redevelopment, for example—to gain the attention of editors, real estate specialists, or community development writers. This approach can lead to virtually free advertising.

Real Estate Guides and Magazines

All major markets have sales and leasing guides that, like newspapers, are among the first places prospects look. New home guides offer display ads in a variety of sizes in color or black and white. In this medium, professional design and copywriting are essential, as the competition from other developments can be substantial.

Developers can reach a targeted market by advertising in specific regional or city publications such as *New York, Los Angeles, Washingtonian,* and *Southern Living* or business magazines, real estate journals, or small, neighborhood newspapers. The demographic profile of the readership indicates the effectiveness of reaching likely prospects. Some marketers find that advertising in local editions of national publications, such as home design magazines, is also an effective means of reaching target groups.

The Internet

The Internet has quickly become an essential component of a company's marketing strategy. It is the pre-ferred method of initial shopping for many residential buyers, especially those moving from out of town. Some developers and homebuilders create stand-alone sites; others simply tap into newspapers' existing classified sites or into real estate clearinghouse sites, some of which are run by the larger real estate brokerage firms.

Most developers rely on the help of outside consultants to design and manage their Web sites. Increasingly, ad agencies include this element in their overall advertising and promotional package; all the developer needs to do is communicate the larger product vision and fund the effort.

A Web site should be viewed as an investment. Costs can run from about $10,000 for a simple site to as much as $1 million for a sophisticated, highly interactive site. The best Web sites are easy to navigate, quick to load, and packed with useful information, yet uncluttered. Information should include maps, site plans, information about the neighborhood, schools, links to the homebuilders, if they are not the same company as the developer, and contact information. Increasingly, Web sites are the preferred research tool for homebuyers; in response, marketers are providing an ever-expanding and more sophisticated array of research tools. Interactive house plans and elevations allow shoppers to see how a home will look with selected options. They can print out their choices to take with them to the sales center. Having done their research, they are more ready—and likely—to purchase a home.

Elaborate Web sites can make economic sense for marketing large-scale developments that have an absorption period of one or more years. Clearinghouse site listings are fast, inexpensive avenues that make sense for smaller developments seeking to lease or sell quickly. Like other marketing tools, Web sites drive prospects to a development site, where the sales agent gains control of the transaction. Web sites also serve as great reference tools for prospects long after they have left the sales office or model home.

Radio and Television

Radio and televison have become less common media for residential marketers, mainly because they are not cost-effective. Although they reach large audiences, they provide few opportunities to target highly specific market segments, and they are relatively expensive. Grand openings and ground breakings, however, are opportunities for a clever marketer to capture news coverage free of charge. Some major builders or developers run radio ads that promote their image as a way to build brand recognition.

Signs, Billboards, and Banners

Signs are an important aspect of the marketing program. A sign on a major thoroughfare exposes the development to thousands of potential households per day and can be an effective marketing tool. Signs represent a small portion of the budget unless the marketing effort includes few other marketing tactics.

Billboards, like signs, reach a broad range of prospects, but the cost of billboards is typically too expensive to use for the long term and may be cost-effective only for larger developments. Billboards may be appropriate for the introduction of a niche product that needs to draw prospects from a large area, such as downtown urban lofts in a market that has no lofts. Billboards require the assistance of a marketing or advertising consultant. Billboards have a negative image in some parts of the country and may not relate the appropriate impression for a development.

Banners on buses and other forms of transit advertising (posters on benches at bus stops and commuter stations) can also be effective in making the public aware of a development.

Direct Mail

Some developers consider direct mail the best way of reaching prospective buyers. They rely on direct mail campaigns to promote unusual product to a highly tar-

geted group. For example, assisted living and dementia-care housing for seniors typically attracts many prospects scattered over a large market area; in this case, the developer might find that direct mail to all prospects of a given age or above would be the most cost-efficient means of reaching the largest potential market. Direct mail to high-income zip codes is an effective tool for marketing luxury-level developments. Direct mail can also be excellent for exclusive showings or previews.

Management of Sales

No matter how effective the marketing program, it can go only so far. The sales staff is arguably the most important part of the marketing campaign, because they actually make the sales. A developer could forgo all other tactics—simply open a sales office—and theoretically do just fine. Without a staff to work with prospects and close sales, however, the development would surely fail. All marketing efforts attempt to drive prospects to the sales and leasing team. Thus, the marketing plan and budget must devote ample resources to compensating and training a strong staff.

A key decision for most developers is whether to employ an on-site sales staff or to contract with a local realty firm. In smaller market areas or for smaller projects, developers often find that employing an outside real estate firm is the more cost-effective option. For larger developments with long absorption periods, an internal staff is the better option, providing continuity over time, stronger loyalty to the development, and better control of the sales process for the developer.

Marketing directors often run larger sales or leasing efforts. Marketing directors motivate the sales or leasing staff and manage changes in the selling strategy. Other valuable assets to the sales or leasing team include architects and marketing consultants, each of whom can provide valuable information to help sell the project.

Most developers structure compensation for the sales team on the basis of salary plus commission, typically a minimum salary plus a commission per unit. Developers often pay higher commission rates for speculative houses, and sales personnel may receive bonuses if they exceed monthly or yearly quotas. Commissions typically range from 0.75 to 1.5 percent of the sale price, depending on unit prices, sales rate, and the difficulty of the marketing task; this arrangement includes projects in highly competitive markets or those with less than perfect locations. Sales commissions are sometimes based on a sliding percentage that increases with the volume sold and length of service in the organization.

Upfront training of the sales staff allows agents to learn the developer's vision, understand the full range of marketing efforts, and become excited to meet with prospects. The process of sales is the transfer of enthusiasm from the seller to the buyer, and the sales staff is the conduit through which customers become excited. The sales staff must be able to respond to objections,

Detailed scale models can help prospects to see what the new development will look like and increase their confidence in deciding to buy a home.

Well-appointed model units let prospective buyers see themselves living comfortably in a home.

deal with the intricacies of sales contracts, and understand the whole range of issues about the development, the neighborhood, the competition, and the developer.

A good sales staff does more than simply wait for prospects to show up at the office. Effective salespeople follow up with prospects after they have visited the site and with customers after they have signed the purchase agreement. Word-of-mouth referrals from satisfied customers and impressed prospects often yield new visitors to the site.

Monitoring and Measuring Acceptance

Marketing does not end with the grand opening. Marketers continue to execute advertising and promotional tactics to produce a steady stream of prospects, and they use on-site merchandising resources to help close deals. Marketers also complete the important tasks of monitoring the marketing effort and measuring the success of the various marketing tactics.

Marketers can easily gauge consumers' opinions on site through exit polls and telephone follow-up calls. Exit polls ask prospects as they leave the sales office about their opinion of various on-site elements—styles and features of units, pricing, and sales staff, for example—to determine the impact of marketing elements and the desirability of different units. A follow-up telephone call leverages the information prospects provide on the entry card to gather additional information about the site visit, learn how they heard of the development, and determine whether the prospect would like additional information. Both tactics can yield valuable information that allows the marketer to adjust the marketing campaign as it proceeds.

Other methods to gauge the performance of the marketing effort include measuring on-site traffic volume and hits on the Internet Web site. Simply asking prospects how they heard about the development, however, is

perhaps the most direct measure of the success of different tactics.

Tracking changes in traffic volume against the timing of particular tactics—a newspaper ad placement, for example—can give the marketer an indication of the level of awareness spurred by specific efforts. Tracking Internet hits several days after a direct mail piece has been mailed (with a call to action to visit the Web site) is another example of measuring a specific effort. In-

Special promotional events can help to publicize a community. At Baldwin Park in Orlando, Florida, a decorated show house benefited a local charity and was featured in a national magazine.

Scaletta Photography

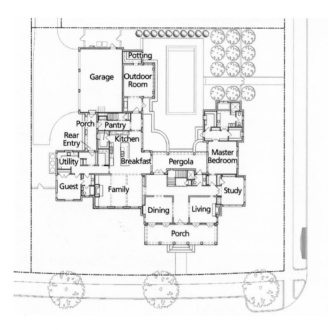

Looney Ricks Kiss

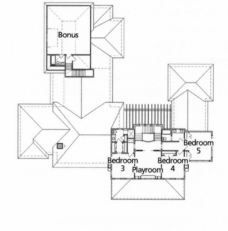

Looney Ricks Kiss

formation about the cause and effect of specfic efforts can lead the marketer to shift resources from those approaches that do not seem to be working to those that are.

The best marketers hold a postmortem after the marketing program has run its full course. This meeting convenes all the key players involved in the marketing effort, including consultants, to discuss what worked and what did not. Ending a marketing campaign in this fashion ensures that the organization learns from its mistakes and takes advantage of the lessons learned to do a superior job on the next campaign.

Marketing Large Communities

Not all residential developments can be built and sold over one or two years. Large-scale communities, comprising multiple housing products built by several builders,

are a major part of the mix in many regions of the country. In such cases, the master developer assumes responsibility for developing and implementing the community-wide marketing strategy, leaving individual builders to implement their own (but compatible) strategies for selling specific products.

In some markets, particularly those in the Sunbelt, it is not uncommon for planned communities to encompass 1,000 or more acres (400 or more hectares) and require more than 20 years to complete. Because long-term projects require substantial upfront costs and carry potentially large financial risks, it is essential for developers to execute a well-planned and aggressive marketing campaign, integrating all the different housing components.

Marketing budgets for large-scale communities vary considerably among regions. As a guideline, a master developer should plan to spend about 6 percent of total income from lot sales on marketing. About half of this

Resort communities require special marketing efforts because they typically draw a nonlocal market. Lake Town is a resort community in the Mose Valley, India.

amount represents the contribution of individual builders for media and promotional materials. The master developer contributes the remaining half to cover the costs of the community sales office and on-site merchandising.

Because of the long-term nature of large projects, the master developer must continually monitor and refine the marketing strategy to meet evolving market niches and economic conditions. It is common for the market at the beginning of the project to be substantially different from that at the end. Developers track market changes through surveys of buyers, focus groups, telephone surveys, and other techniques, then continually refocus marketing efforts.

Marketing Second-Home Communities

Resort communities are all about lifestyle and location, and marketing these communities requires a different strategy from that for primary-home developments. Buyers might come from great distances, so marketing must be targeted to a regional or even national audience. Market research should determine what locales and specific demographics to target.

The Internet and national or regional magazines on golf, skiing, boating, or the sport or activity the community features can be the ideal advertising media for such a market. Some magazines include supplements or pages that appear only in certain markets that can be effective for advertising a resort community. Referrals and word of mouth play a very important role in marketing second-home communities. In fact, some projects rely almost entirely on referrals. Another strategy is to offer free weekend getaways at or near the resort to introduce targeted prospects to the project.

Decisions to purchase second homes are based even more on lifestyle than decisions to purchase primary homes. The location, amenities, and activities offered are all likely to be more important than the homes them-

Large-scale communities may require as many as two or three decades to complete. They require significant marketing budgets over a long period of time.

selves. The developer must be sure to promote all of those elements and to ensure that they are of a quality and character that appeal to the target market.

Note

1. For marketing residential rental properties, see Adrienne Schmitz et al., *Multifamily Housing Development Handbook* (Washington, D.C.: ULI–the Urban Land Institute, 2000).

7. Community Governance

Setting the Stage

What Is Community Governance and Why Do It?

Governance is frequently the last thing a developer wants to consider or spend time addressing; in many ways, however, governance is one of the most important parts of project planning and execution. To accomplish all that the developer envisions for a community, the internal governance and regulatory system must combine a sense of stewardship with enforcement techniques that truly work. In addition, that governance must work not only during the period of developer control but also after the developer passes these powers to the property owners. The entire structure must be one that engenders a sense of the genuine value to be realized from its effective and ongoing operations. This chapter discusses one of three vital community association strategies: governance. The other two, amenities and exit strategies, are very important but left for other publications.

Governance is both a power and a process. The process is the dynamic fulfillment of the provisions of the founding documents that vest in the community association the powers to govern the community and the obligations for the care, upkeep, and maintenance of some or all of the various lands and facilities within the community. The powers are those legal ways and means of exercising authority over the community and its members

Marina Gardens, Palm Beach Gardens, Florida.

to ensure that the community's purposes and visions are achieved. The powers must be exercised in such a way that they do not diminish the sense of community itself or give rise to the feeling that the members are controlled.

Just as governance is both a power and a process, any master-planned community combines a product and a process. The product is the component of the shelter industry that the developer and homebuilders produce. It could be a condominium unit, a townhouse, a single-family home, or any of a multitude of varieties of residential product. The process that is such an integral part of the overall development is the community governance itself, the way the community's values and qualities are created and protected. A successful planned community is one that combines standards of excellence for both the product and the process.

Governance rests on a foundation of covenants and restrictions that are recorded in the land records and bind all present and future owners. In addition to establishing the standards and guidelines for development, operation, use, and maintenance of the community, these covenants create the governance entities that administer and enforce the process. That governance process is the subject of this chapter.

The key to successful community governance is the creation of systems—structures—that balance multiple interests, foster a culture of excellence, preserve the functions of the community, provide the flexibility to make the community and its governance dynamic, and

Quincy Johnson Architects/Chuck Wilkins

John Connell

reasonably protect owners' expectations while preserving developmental rights and flexibility. To work, the system must be flexible, tailored, realistic, reasonable, and understandable. This chapter explores how to make governance work.

Implicit and frequently explicit in a discussion of governance is reference to a *common interest community*. For purposes of this book, the common interest community is a development in which owners have a common interest, which normally involves sharing. The things shared can be both tangibles and intangibles; for example, privately owned property is managed and enjoyed by numerous people. A common interest community involves mandatory membership in some governing entity combined with an obligation to pay assessments for services rendered or benefits provided and an obligation to comply with a set of standards or guidelines.

Any common interest community shares other essential components as well, and they can be created under various developmental formats (discussed and defined later). It is first appropriate, however, to ask, Why use governance?

The development of a successful community involves more than just a good master plan, an attractive amenity package, and desirable real estate products. The developer must recognize the need for and the synergy that can be created by a unifying management structure. That structure may include one or more governmental bodies, tax-exempt organizations, community associations, or some combination specifically designed to meet the needs and goals of the particular community. In selecting the most appropriate structure, it is important to understand the available options and how they might be used to maximize flexibility for the developer during the development process and long-term community operation.

A structure and program for community management are essential to the implementation and protection of the developer's master plan. A carefully designed community management structure provides a mechanism for:

- ensuring the preservation of common areas, including those that buffer the community and set it apart from surrounding areas;
- long-term ownership, maintenance, and operation of amenities that benefit property owners and increase the community's attractiveness to visitors and prospective purchasers;
- fulfilling long-term and continuing obligations undertaken by the developer as a condition of obtaining development approval; and
- establishing and enforcing community-wide standards of maintenance, architecture, and design.

A variety of community management structures may accomplish these objectives; indeed, no single structure works best for all communities. In many cases, two or more structures may need to be combined to address a particular community's needs. In determining which option or combination of options is most appropriate for a given community, the developer should consider the community's particular characteristics, goals, and constraints:

- the types of uses planned for the community and the approximate area and acreage to be devoted to each use;
- the proposed location of different land uses in relation to each other;
- the types of amenities proposed for the community and the extent to which they benefit each of the various land uses;
- the development timetable and phasing plan;
- the extent to which the developer intends to retain long-term ownership or control of one or more components of the community;
- the nature and scope of responsibilities to be fulfilled by the governing entity or entities;
- the nature and scope of services to be provided to the various land uses that make up the community;

- the legal foundation and "tools" made available by the jurisdiction where the community is located;
- the relationship with local government; and
- the targeted market.

The basic organizational options fall into three major categories: governmental and quasi-governmental bodies, nonprofit tax-exempt corporations, and community associations. These options may be varied and combined to maximize control and flexibility for the developer during the development process and to enhance community marketability.

When and why would someone choose to create and to be part of a common interest community with these governance mechanisms? The most practical reasons from an owner's perspective are shared costs, a pooling of resources, and economies of scale.

Three key words in determining whether a particular project needs a community association are *maintenance, preservation,* and *sharing.* A common interest community and association are appropriate whenever facilities and services are shared coupled with the obligation to pay for those services; however, much more is possible if the emphasis is on the opportunity to build *community.*

These theoretical, more generalized reasons for using community governance overlay four specific, real-world reasons. First, a community association provides a vehicle for the maintenance and ownership of common property, including infrastructure, parking, open space, recreational facilities, and maintenance facilities—components that otherwise do not fit in any for-sale parcel. All of them and more can be conveyed, either for a price or not, to the community association. The association then becomes the operating entity that assumes the responsibilities that would otherwise be the developer's, even after the development is completely sold.

Second, the community association, in its governing role, provides the vehicle to preserve and enforce the land use plan through architectural, environmental, design, land use, occupancy, and other restrictions. These preservation and enforcement opportunities and powers are multiple and varied. Implicit in the responsibility to preserve and enforce the general plan of development is the power to impose assessments on all benefited owners. The community association thus becomes an entity that accepts the developer's responsibilities and has the legally recognized power, coupled with a legally enforceable funding mechanism, to discharge those responsibilities.

Third, the community association affords wide flexibility in land planning and use, because by definition it is an entity that can take title to open space, common properties, and other portions of the community subject to legally recognized restrictions and easements. *Planned unit development* is a zoning term that allows massing of development on one portion of land by virtue of the preservation as open space of other portions within the

Maintaining open space is one concern of community associations.

boundaries of the community association's jurisdiction. Developmental flexibility is undoubtedly one of the most vital ingredients in a successful development. The community association as an adjunct to land planning and land use is the single greatest contributor to maximizing and preserving that flexibility.

Fourth, using a community association form of ownership gives the developer a realistic exit strategy. Issues inherent in such a strategy can include ownership or responsibility for remaining pieces of land, settlement of financial and other matters, long-term compliance with local government mandates on the developer, and many other issues. The exit issues are as myriad as the types of potential development; however, these strategies must be both workable and fair to the owners who accept these responsibilities.

The governing structure serves diverse land uses and perspectives yet is intended to unify this diversity into a sense of community. The best governance structure has the capacity to address both development-wide needs and activities and, at the same time, the specific concerns of disparate product types. The word *community* in this context is defined broadly to signify the sharing of common interests, whether the interest is infrastructure, maintenance, or something else. A properly structured community governance system contains both the unifying and separating factors that permit both independence and interdependence.

The Importance of Community: New Applications, New Realities

A community is based on sharing, participation, and common interest. It should be autocratic; it is not corporate in mind-set, even if it is corporate in structure. Communities—vibrant communities where people want to live—are not highly or overly regimented, and they are certainly not overly regulated. Communities are not bland or compulsive or contrived. They are not places where ownership is more important than relationships.

But all too often, these characteristics are the very ones that traditional governance mechanisms have compelled or created in common interest communities.

How can a community association exercise properly the power of governance while maintaining a sense of community among residents? Any discussion of governance systems must recognize the impact that governance has on various facets of community association activity. First is an obvious concern: the balance between the rights of the community and the rights of individuals residing in that community. Although simplicity and flexibility are desirable, individuals are entitled to expect a degree of certainty regarding what the rules are and reasonable assurance that the rules will not change so drastically as to make ownership no longer desirable.

Beyond those matters that are directly and naturally involved in the running of community associations are broader societal concerns. If the public should become convinced that community association living means conformity, control, and constraint, buyers will avoid this form of community. Eventually, this perception will significantly reduce the available housing stock because the relative unpopularity of such existing and ongoing projects will mean that their units are in effect no longer part of the "available" stock. This outcome would have a negative impact on housing producers, owners, and local governments. And these effects would have no compensating benefit, because no technical or anecdotal evidence exists that the more highly regulated a community is, the better or more desirable it is. Indeed, evidence increasingly suggests that excessive regulation diminishes the quality of life.

Quality of life and lifestyle present another area of concern. The highly individualistic person perhaps does not belong in a place where his interests run strongly counter to the degree of conformity required in a planned community. By the same token, *community* is not synonymous with *conformity,* and making this differentiation is a challenge for developers and operators of

A community is based on sharing, participation, and common interest.

John Connell

Governance should be concerned with building and sustaining community.

Looney Ricks Kiss

community associations. Highly regulated and formalized governance structures are perhaps inconsistent with the amount and type of flexibility necessary to make a community successful.

Guideposts for documentation intended to facilitate the creation of community are included later in this chapter, but here it is appropriate to make a few brief observations about governance if one is to follow a strategy intended to create community.

First, developers and their counsel must abandon the command-and-control mentality and methodology to structure and operate communities. Second, the emphasis must shift dramatically from a focus on people and property *management* to one of building and sustaining community.

Governance must be as concerned with relationships as ownership. This does not mean that the ultimate decision about the care and upkeep of property and the financial responsibility should shift from those who own the property and who have the ultimate obligation to meet the financial responsibility. It does mean that opportunities for involvement, participation, and voice need to be provided for those who reside in the community and who, if community is to exist, must be meaningfully included.

This shift must also involve the creation of systems, documents, and design approaches that empower, not impose. It can be as simple as a mechanism that sets forth fundamental governance at the time the project is created and contains an empowering mechanism that allows the community to evolve in a meaningful way as its physical, practical, and demographic circumstances change. Empowering, not imposing, puts the focus on regulation, not prohibition, which makes a substantial difference in the importance and perception of restrictiveness in the community's development.

Last, a strategy to create community seeks governance that maximizes opportunity for choice that is flexible and transparent.

The Developer's Role

The developer plays many roles in the creation and implementation of community governance, but three are paramount—visionary, creator, and governor/operator.

The developer must understand what he or she wishes to create in the way of community governance and why. To do so, the developer must ensure that governance fits the site and that it satisfies the specific developmental needs of the project rather than simply being an imitation of some other successful project down the street or across the country. Governance must reflect the nature of the common interest involved and the common ownership requirements. Most important, it must reflect the developer's vision of what type of community he intends to create.

All these aims are best met through use of a development team. The goals of this team are coordination, communication, and control over the development process. The team seeks to meld what the developer and the planners conceive with what the attorney can deliver and what the association can perform. In other words, it seeks to tie down what is expected of whom and when. This coordination is vital if governance is to unfold in the same structured, orderly way as the physical product. An important caveat is that those persons who participate in planning the project should be the same ones who are responsible for the plan's execution. And too frequently ignored is that this position is a "command responsibility" for the developer. Decisions about governance should not all be left to very junior staffers who may not understand the developer's vision.

Creating a common interest community and its community association is a process that takes time, thus placing the developer in evolving roles over the development of the community. During the *creation stage*, governance is structured and documents are drafted. At this point, no homes have been sold, and the parties involved are the developer/declarant, the developer's attorney, and

Creating a community association takes time. Documents are drafted before any homes are sold.

other consultants. At this point, the association exists only on paper.

The *control period* begins concurrently with home sales. The declarant is in control of the association and operates it in accordance with its documents and state law. Governance evolves from paper to reality. The *transition period* (a period of time, not an event) occurs over the course of development and sales as the declarant increasingly involves the homeowners in governance of the association and ultimately exits from the operational role. Last, the *period of owner control* begins when the declarant's operational control ends and owners control the association for the life of the development. The declarant may still have inventory to sell and thus may still have a genuine interest in the common interest community, but it is no longer empowered to control the community association.

Creating Governance

Options and Opportunities
Governmental and Quasi-Governmental Bodies. Municipal corporations (cities or towns) and community improvement districts (special tax districts of many types) can both play a valuable role in the development and operation of a master-planned community. As stand-alone entities, however, they have disadvantages that generally make them inadequate for addressing all the project's needs. Therefore, they are most helpful when used in combination with other options.

Municipalities and special taxing districts generally have the power to tax and the power of eminent domain. They usually have access to public funds for various projects and services and may issue debt to finance certain activities, thereby offering a lower-cost method of financing public infrastructure and facilities than traditional means based on tax revenues. Generally, the taxes paid by property owners are deductible, making creation of a

community improvement district an attractive vehicle for undertaking many "public" functions in the community.

Governmental bodies are, however, subject to constitutional restraints and must operate in accordance with the demands of state and federal law, which generates additional cost for property owners. For example, governmental bodies cannot restrict public access to parks, streets, and other property and thus do not have the flexibility to operate or maintain private amenities for the exclusive use of the community's property owners and their tenants and guests.

Perhaps the most significant factor to consider is that of control. In both a municipality and a community improvement district, most decisions rest with an elected body. Few if any decisions require a vote of the property owners, and the developer has no basis on which to retain veto power. In fact, a municipality's residents elect the governing body from the outset; thus, the developer does not enjoy even an initial period of control. From the developer's perspective, this lack of control means that he has no assurance that the municipality will accept ownership of or maintenance responsibility for the open spaces, parks, and other amenities created for the community.

Although the election provisions under enabling statutes for community improvement districts vary, the developer, as the major landowner, may be able to control the election of the district's governing board for several years. In some jurisdictions, though, the enabling statutes require the eventual election of the district's governing board by the "qualified electors" of the district, that is, those residents who are eligible and registered to vote. This requirement may exclude property owners who do not reside in the district, including the developer. In a resort or second-home recreational community with few permanent residents, the vast majority of property owners might not be represented at all.

Even if the developer resides in the community improvement district, voting is based on a one-resident, one-vote system, so his or her vote is equal to that of a resident who does not own property. Thus, control may be taken out of the developer's hands long before the community is built out. Therefore, the developer must carefully consider the nature of the facilities to be handled through the community improvement district and the degree to which the eventual loss of control could affect development of the overall project and the marketing of the balance of the community.

Nonprofit Tax-Exempt Organizations. A nonprofit corporation structured to meet the requirements of a civic league under Section 501(c)(4) of the Internal Revenue Code can, in part, address the control issue. To qualify for tax-exempt status, the nonprofit corporation must serve "the common good and general welfare of the people of a community," and the "community" must bear a reasonable relationship to an area ordinarily identified as a governmental area. Thus, like for a municipality, the corporation's property must be available for use and enjoyment by the general public. The corporation is not, however, required to have members; it may be guided solely by its board of directors.

The code grants wide discretion in determining the mechanism for establishing the corporation's board. Thus, the developer may indefinitely control the appointment of the board and convey to the corporation such community facilities as roads, open space, wetlands, and conservation easements that are intended to benefit the entire community. In this way, the developer can ensure that facilities are maintained at an acceptable level.

A 501(c)(4) corporation may engage in a wide variety of activities without losing its tax-exempt status. Such activities include maintenance of roadways, parkways, sidewalks, streetlights, and similar infrastructure, and enforcement of covenants. A declaration of covenants may give the corporation the authority to exercise architectural control over all property subject to its terms as well as the power to assess such property for a share of the corporation's expenses.

It may also be desirable to establish one or more 501(c)(3) organizations to solicit and accept tax-deductible/tax-exempt contributions for such purposes as environmental and conservation activities, provision of low-income housing, educational and cultural activities such as art festivals and concerts, and facilities such as art centers and nature centers. Neither 501(c)(4) nor 501(c)(3) organizations can perform maintenance on private property owned by a third party, however. As a result, these entities lack the flexibility to provide certain services to property owners as well as the authority to enforce covenants by performing maintenance if the owner fails to do so, both of which may be desirable in a master-planned community. Therefore, the tax-exempt organization is best used in combination with other options that can provide the developer greater flexibility in the development and operation of the community.

Community Associations. A community association structure, either alone or in conjunction with the options discussed previously, may provide the greatest flexibility. Although membership in a community associa-

Keene's Pointe in Windermere, Florida, is made up of 14 separate neighborhoods.

Castle & Cooke

tion extends to all property owners, the association may be established with multiple classes of membership to vest control in the developer for an extended development period while providing for transition of control to homeowners at a future date.

A community association generally provides broad flexibility in allocating voting rights and economic burdens among property owners, allowing for the assessment of property owners in accordance with benefits received rather than strictly on the basis of property value. Moreover, a community association may own and maintain property not intended for public use. Thus, a community association is able to provide varying levels of service to property owners, maintain private amenities for the primary use and benefit of particular areas in the community, and maintain private property if the owner does not maintain it to an acceptable level.

A community association is a mandatory membership entity responsible for performing various functions within any of the developmental approaches discussed in this section. Each property owner automatically becomes a member of the community association upon acceptance of a deed to his property in the development. The mandatory membership aspect of the community association sets it apart from a civic association, social or business club, or other volunteer organization. The community association has long been used in purely residential developments but is increasingly becoming the norm in mixed-use projects as well.

A community association is an appropriate mechanism for any development characterized by:

- individually owned parcels of property ("units") and common features and facilities benefiting all the individually owned parcels;
- common services such as common maintenance or security provided to two or more parcels within the development; or
- a need or desire for regulation and enforcement of community-wide standards of maintenance, architecture, use, and conduct for the enhancement and protection of property values.

The community association, like a corporation, has a perpetual existence separate from any individual or group of individuals. Like a corporation or municipal government, it acts on behalf of its member owners—its "citizens." It is a separate entity from the developer, governed by a set of legal documents and applicable law.

A community association can own and/or maintain various property and improvements that benefit the entire community such as stormwater drainage facilities, open space, community signage, parks and recreational facilities, and landscaping in public rights-of-way. The community association is also an ideal entity to take on any continuing obligations that the developer may have undertaken as a condition of development approval, such as maintaining conservation areas or parks and monitoring traffic patterns.

Community associations regulate standards of maintenance, architecture, and use.

Community associations have a dual role: a business in managing and maintaining private property and a government in delivering services and enforcing covenants and rules. In many developments, the association exercises architectural control over, and may provide some level of maintenance on, individually owned property. It often provides all or some of the utility services, common area maintenance, street lighting, refuse removal, security services, and other such municipal services. It may sponsor various forms of communication within the community, such as newsletters or an intranet. It may also offer cultural, educational, and recreational programs and activities and sponsor special events such as festivals, parades, and concerts to create synergy and a sense of community.

Acting through its board of directors, the association is charged with enforcing any specific covenants and restrictions set forth in the declaration. It is typically authorized to make and enforce additional rules and regulations as well. Such restrictions and rules may include restrictions on land use, prohibitions on certain types of activities, restrictions designed to control architecture and aesthetics within the development, and regulations regarding use of the common areas and individually owned properties.

Two powers granted to the association—the power to levy and the power to control property—reinforce the governmental aspect of the association's role. These powers are usually created in the declaration (in some cases by statute) and are enforceable through state courts.

The power to levy is the association's power to assess property owners for their prorated shares of the association's expenses. Clearly analogous to the municipality's power to tax, the power to levy includes the obligation of the association or its board of directors to develop a fiscal plan, to assign a share of the cost of that plan to the property owners as a charge against their individual properties, and to collect the assessment through lien rights and state court action in the event that the assessment is not paid as scheduled. The assessment is not equivalent to membership dues or some other discretionary charge but is in fact a proportionate share of the expenses incurred to fund the association's business and governmental services.

The power to control the use and enjoyment of property through the exercise of architectural and environmental controls, use restrictions, and rule-making authority allows the association to exert tremendous influence over the bundle of rights normally enjoyed as a concomitant part of fee simple ownership of property. This relatively high degree of control is vested through, and must be exercised in accordance with, the recorded declaration and applicable law.

Layered Associations in Large and Master-Planned Communities. Large master-planned communities almost always contain sufficient and sufficiently different structures to justify suborganizations. Such suborganizations can be treated in different ways. One approach is to create one "master" association with one or more "subassociations," perhaps one for condominium owners and one for other owners. A preferable approach is to have a single association and multiple "cost centers," often called neighborhoods, villages, or some other market-friendly term, to provide targeted services to different portions of the community. This approach avoids the necessity of multiple associations with the attendant costs and other negative factors they can bring.

This section discusses governance in large communities, that is, projects of more than 500 acres (200 hectares) or 500 units, generally with various housing products and other uses. Project size is important but not as important as the number and mix of units in the community. That mix may include single-family attached housing and detached housing on various lot sizes and configurations, multifamily rental housing, and nonresidential components.

A large community is likely to include discrete areas of substantially dissimilar components. Generally, the community association assumes more "governmental" activities (for example, fire and security services). These unique aspects of large projects call for specially tailored governance applications.

In a large community, size creates problems. For example, a high percentage of one type of housing may result in those residents' dominating the governance process because they have sufficient votes to control the election of the board. This dominance would be to the detriment of broadly based representation generally and to other areas of the community that have an important economic interest in the operation of the association specifically. Challenges to homogeneity arise from differences in owners' housing type, needs, demographics, economic capabilities, desires, and other factors.

The local components in a large community, that is, the groupings of different types of residences, have their own localized needs, and the governance structure must be empowered to satisfy those needs. For example, a single-family detached dwelling may need no exterior building or ground maintenance, but a single-family attached dwelling may require such services. The governance structure and the service delivery systems must be able to meet both needs. A governing structure with many different subassociations may impose assessments, but the duplication of services means unnecessary expenditures and unnecessary charges to owners. Thus, the governance structure for a large community seeks ways to deliver different services cost-effectively, such as differentiated charges for the community (either through

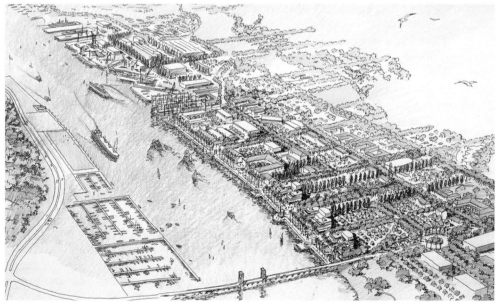

In very large master-planned communities, the community association generally assumes more "governmental" responsibilities. Mare Island in Vallejo, California, is a 5,000-acre (2,025-hectare) conversion of a naval shipyard to a mixed-use development.

SWA Group

figure 7-1
Comparison of Community Association Structures

Type of Association	Advantages	Disadvantages
Single community association with service area structure	• Simplicity; minimizes administrative burden of managing multiple associations. • Provides unifying body to maintain a community-wide standard.	• May be a perception that separately incorporated service area associations have greater autonomy. • Subjects nonresidential owners to control of residential owners or vice versa, which can affect marketing of properties.
Single residential association with neighborhood structure and covenant to share costs on nonresidential properties	• Provides autonomy to owners of nonresidential properties by not involving them in administration of primarily residential community.	• Can be cumbersome in projects characterized by multiple nonresidential parcels and nonresidential uses geographically interspersed with residential properties. • Provides little protection for residential owners concerned about use and appearance of nonresidential properties.

assessments or user fees) based on different benefits or services received. This differentiation gives the association's board greater flexibility to accommodate residents' desire for different levels of services (based, for example, on different income levels). A successful governance structure for a large community provides for the sharing of responsibility with the maximum appropriate degree of autonomy.

The *umbrella with subassociation* was for years the usual governance model for a large community; that form is now changing. The umbrella is the "master" association that governs the entire community. It is empowered to deal with community-wide matters and has powers of design review, assessment, and rule making over all components of the community. The subassociations are established for individual neighborhoods or types of housing. The developer creates subassociations as individual subdivisions are built in the community. The result could be dozens of subassociations within the overall jurisdiction of the master association. Each subassociation has a board of directors, a management structure, an insurance policy, and all the other indicia of association governance and operation. The result is a dramatic demand on time, volunteers, and cost. Figure 7-2 shows a typical model for a master association and subassociations.

A much more feasible alternative is the "consolidated government" model, which has one community-wide association and no subassociations except as may be required by law (for example, a subassociation would be necessary for a condominium because of state law requirements and ownership issues). In all other circumstances, individual developments are semiautonomous local units for both cost accounting and decision making, those "service areas" mentioned earlier.

A consolidated association structure is generally efficient, economic, market-wise, and risk averse. It provides a unified system for assessments, architectural control, meetings, regulations, insurance, and so on. It provides a centralized organization with one board, one management contract, and far fewer meetings, resulting in cost reductions and a systematic maintenance standard. It can enhance developer control and reduce the problems that arise with subassociations, including litigation. Accordingly, drafters should be mindful to protect the interests of these diverse groups in the community and build in methods for meaningful participation during the control period.

A consolidated government association for a large community allows for the provision of neighborhood services and market segmentation. Owners of attached housing, detached housing, and nonresidential buildings and tenants are able to receive the services they need and for which they can pay. An owner participates in community governance through a centralized communication structure with the capacity for "local" services. A consolidated government association also provides opportunities to participate without the necessity of multiple corporate structures; it controls costs by avoiding duplication.

A consolidated government association for a large community must have a well-considered mechanism for representative government. The mechanism normally involves grouping the neighborhoods into voting groups or electoral districts, permitting representative voting, and ensuring that different groups all participate in selecting directors (see Figure 7-3).

The neighborhood (which in the master and subassociation model is the subassociation) may be the same as or different from a voting group, depending on project size, configuration, housing type, neighbor-

figure 7-2

Typical Umbrella Community Association Structure

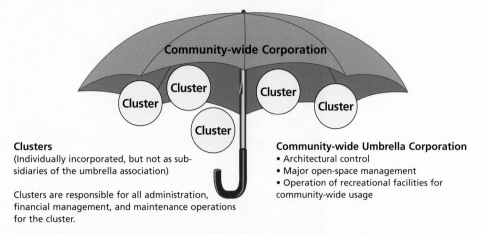

Clusters
(Individually incorporated, but not as subsidiaries of the umbrella association)

Clusters are responsible for all administration, financial management, and maintenance operations for the cluster.

Community-wide Umbrella Corporation
• Architectural control
• Major open-space management
• Operation of recreational facilities for community-wide usage

In comparison with the unified community association, the umbrella association structure lacks:
• The better controls of centralized administration and financial management
• Centralized communications
• The economies of scale of centralized maintenance operations
• Uniform quality control of community appearances
• Effective centralized community code adoption and enforcement.

Source: Wayne S. Hyatt, *Condominium and Homeowner Association Practice: Community Association Law,* 3d ed. (Philadelphia: American Law Institute–American Bar Association, 2000). Reprinted with permission. Further reproduction is strictly prohibited.

figure 7-3

Model for Community Governance

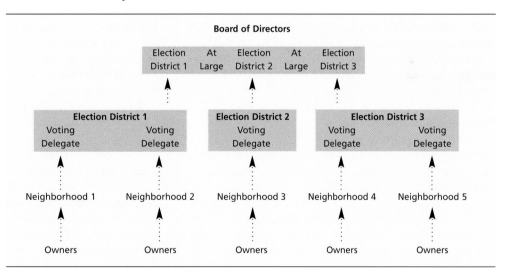

hood size, and other such factors. A voting group may consist of one or more neighborhoods. The developer/declarant must be able to create and change neighborhoods and voting groups as the project grows. Generally, neighborhoods comprise the same kinds of dwellings or nonresidential buildings in the same geographic area.

The developer/declarant assigns neighborhoods to voting groups. This assignment might reflect geographi-

cal area, similar housing type, approximate unit density, desired maintenance or service levels, and other such matters. The voting groups need not be equal in population, although similarity in size is certainly a desirable characteristic. Once voting groups are established, owners of residences within a voting group should have a say in any changes to the composition of their voting group.

The voting process is further simplified by each neighborhood's selecting a voting delegate. This person is

Shady Canyon is a 1,000-acre (405-hectare) community offering luxury resort living in Irvine, California.

SWA Group

frequently the head of the neighborhood committee, which is responsible for notifying the association's board of directors of desired levels of service for that neighborhood. The person also acts as that neighborhood's representative and casts the number of votes equal to the number of units within the neighborhood when all voting delegates come together to cast votes on association business.

Frequently, a voting delegate meets with his or her constituents before voting. Sometimes governing documents require such a meeting on some or all issues. More commonly, the voting delegate is charged with voting as he or she deems appropriate but also has the power to poll the constituents. The result is a simplified, cost-effective system that still affords a significant degree of autonomy and participation in governance.

Documentation

The governing documents must accomplish the basic objectives necessary for the successful formation and operation of any community association. The objectives, both general and specific, are very important to an understanding of the overall community association process. As one considers what the documents are, it is helpful to understand what they do.

First, from a general or theoretical perspective, the development plan and the governing documentation must fit the project, must be clear in application and enforcement, and must embody the "law of the project." This last point is often overlooked when the lawyer who drafts the documents simply replicates document packages from previous projects. Each project is different, and the legal principles governing that project, both of an external and internal nature, must vary as project facts and circumstances vary. Consider how they might change with variations in the size of the development, the nature of common property, and the uses of property in the development.

In addition, the governing instruments and the development plan must meet certain specific legal objectives for the project itself to be workable:

- Specifying who owns what, which includes defining what is owned as well as by whom. It requires delineating the common area, limited common area, and privately owned property;
- Establishing a system of interlocking relationships among and between owners, which includes the mandatory nature of membership in the association as well as its structure;
- Creating an array of protective standards and restrictions that institutionalize the land development plan. The objective is the delicate balancing act of creating provisions that are flexible yet specific, reasonable, and enforceable;
- Determining the scope of and creating the necessary administrative vehicle to maintain and preserve the project;
- Implementing an association funding plan that is adequate, enforceable, and changeable, which involves both the power to assess and the procedures and mechanisms to collect funds;
- Anticipating the need for and creating a plan to transfer control of the association at some point in the future from the developer to the various owners; and
- Creating and preserving developer/declarant rights with respect to the ongoing development and sale of the project.

The last point illustrates one other essential consideration in approaching a discussion of project creation: within every successful common interest community, no matter what type, the disparate interests of the parties must be balanced.

Well-drafted documents involve a thorough analysis of the project and its peculiarities, including geography, demographics, amenities, interrelationships, and perceived market demands and limitations. They answer such questions as who will own and use what, and how common expenses will be funded. They are sensitive to the levels of participation that might be appropriate in the particular community.

The Essential Documents. Creating a community association requires a set of documents that generally includes a declaration, bylaws, articles of incorporation, plats, and deeds. A community association for a condominium or some other attached housing development also requires floor plans.[1]

The first creating document in a community association is the *declaration*. For a condominium, it might be called the *declaration of condominium* or the *master deed,* depending on state law. For other types of owners associations, the document is generally referred to as the *declaration of covenants, conditions, and restrictions, or CCRs.* The declaration is a document containing the plan of development and the essentials of ownership, the method of operation, and the rights and responsibilities of the association and the owners within the association. It is a covenant running with the land, recorded in the land records, and binding upon every person who becomes a property owner in the project. The declaration is also the enabling document that establishes the role and authority of the community association, much like a city's charter.

The length of time a declaration remains in force depends on the terms of the declaration and state law. The declaration can set forth a definite term and the procedure for extending or ending the term. Although it might have perpetual duration, the declaration for an owners' association generally is effective for at least 20 years. State law and custom affect the duration.

The second legal document essential to the community association is a set of *bylaws*, which establish procedures for the internal government and operation of the association. In contrast to the declaration, which deals with ownership and property rights, the bylaws typically contain procedures for communication with the members, voting, election of the board of directors, meetings of the membership and board, and management procedures.

Often, but not always, the bylaws are recorded in the land records as an exhibit to the declaration. Some attorneys believe that unrecorded bylaws are easier to amend. Others believe that having one complete, official set of records puts everyone on notice of the governing provisions and ensures that these important provisions are available to everyone.

The third necessary document, if the association is incorporated, is the *articles of incorporation* or other instrument that, under state law, creates or charters a corporation. This instrument contains the provisions required under state corporate law, tailored to reflect the realities of community association operation. For example, the association is typically structured as a nonprofit corporation. It has no shareholders, and most associations have no traditional business purpose.

The fourth legal document is the *plat*. The plat shows the boundaries of the land in the development; locates the buildings or building sites on that land; and locates, identifies, and distinguishes between units or lots and common elements or areas. Plats are visual representations of the property descriptions contained in the declaration; they are essentially maps that are drawn to scale to include scattered sites as well as contiguous pieces of property. A common interest community can include noncontiguous property and, depending on the state condominium statute, so might a condominium. The plat depicts what is in the common interest community and the territorial jurisdiction of the community association.

The fifth document, the *deed*, is the document used to transfer title in the unit or lot. It is essentially the same as any other deed except to the extent that it refers to mandatory membership in the association and makes the conveyance subject to the terms of the declaration.

Condominiums typically are governed by community associations.

RTKL/David Whitcomb

figure 7-4
Governing Documents

Articles of Incorporation (filed with the Secretary of State)	Establish the association as a nonprofit corporation under state law
Bylaws (board of directors adopts)	Govern the association's internal affairs, such as voting rights, elections, meetings, and officers
Declaration (recorded)	Creates obligations that are binding on the association and all present and future owners of property
Supplemental Declaration (recorded)	Adds property; may impose additional obligations or restrictions on such property
Architectural Guidelines (declarant adopts)	Establish architectural standards and guidelines for improvements and modifications to units, including structures, landscaping, and other items on units
Restrictions and Rules	Govern use of property, activities, and conduct
Board Resolutions (board adopts)	Establish rules, policies, and procedures for internal governance and association activities; regulate operation and use of common area

For a condominium, the deed conveying a unit also sets forth the specified undivided interest in the common elements that pass with title to the unit.

Design Guidelines or Standards.[2] One of the major selling points of a planned community is the consistency of quality, design, and compatibility provided through a system of architectural controls not typically found in a traditional subdivision. Architectural controls help to keep a community attractive for the enjoyment of residents and protect the property values within the community.

Although the advantages of architectural controls are widely recognized, the methods used to impose, implement, and enforce them are quite varied and often fall short of providing the full benefits they should provide to the developer and the community. For years, many developers imposed architectural controls by setting forth specific requirements and restrictions on the subdivision plat or in recorded covenants on the property in their developments. This approach often results in a relatively inflexible set of requirements that are unable to accommodate the characteristics of each lot, changes in market demands, or changing technology.

If a list of requirements and restrictions is the only mechanism of architectural control employed, the architectural control process contains no element of subjectivity. If property owners meet all the stated requirements and avoid all the prohibitions, they may undertake their proposed construction, regardless of how unattractive or incompatible with the surrounding improvements it may be. At the same time, no means is available of obtaining a variance for proposed construction that may technically violate a recorded standard but that might otherwise be perfectly acceptable. Such an approach makes it incumbent on the developer, before the first piece of property is sold, to think of every possible condition that might be found objectionable and proscribe

it on the plat or in the covenants, while carefully avoiding overly broad prohibitions that might limit the flexibility to address special circumstances such as distinctive topography.

An alternative and more flexible approach is to establish the authority and framework for the exercise of architectural control in the recorded covenants, vesting authority to review and approve or disapprove plans for proposed construction in an entity that can exercise judgment while leaving the specific design criteria on which such review will be based to a separate, unrecorded set of design guidelines and aesthetic standards. That document should be prepared as a joint effort of the developer, the design team (architect, landscape architect, engineer, and other design professionals), the attorney, and the association's consultant or manager. It may include more detailed procedures for submitting and processing applications for approval and supporting documentation so long as they are consistent with the procedures established in the recorded covenants.

The design guidelines may address site and building design, including architectural styles, building materials, colors, accessory buildings, fences, walls, landscaping, and other elements of site development and construction, but they should do so in a manner that sets the theme and tone for what the reviewer is seeking rather than appearing to be simply an additional list of requirements or restrictions. The design guidelines may also address other matters of aesthetics, such as signage, sports and play equipment, and screening of garbage cans and air-conditioning equipment, but should again leave some room for the reviewer to exercise its discretion and judgment to provide for a level of reasonableness in application and enforcement. Design and aesthetic matters relating to improvements to the property should not be confused with matters of use (e.g., parking vehicles in driveways, trash collection), as the former are more

Architectural controls require a careful balancing of conformity and diversity.

appropriately included in the rules of the association administered by its board of directors rather than in the design guidelines.

The goal of the design guidelines should be to provide guidance to an owner or builder in developing plans for proposed construction and improvements to the property by highlighting areas of concern to the reviewer, thereby facilitating the review and approval process. The design guidelines should not appear to be an all-inclusive list of requirements, limiting the reviewer's ability to reject plans on other grounds, nor should they be cast in stone so as to prevent the reviewer from granting minor variances when special circumstances warrant. If properly drafted, however, they will provide criteria for consistent decisions by the reviewer and from one reviewer to the next as that responsibility changes hands over time.

Such a system of architectural control requires the designation of one or more persons to exercise the power to review and approve or disapprove proposed construction and modifications to existing structures. It also requires the designation of someone to enforce the design standards and approval requirements, which power may, but need not, be vested in the same persons who hold reviewing authority. These powers may be granted to a committee or committees of the owners' association or to an independent committee appointed by the developer or elected by the property owners, or reserved to the developer with the right to delegate some or all

of its architectural control power to another entity in the future.

Typically, the developer will want to maintain control over the architectural review process during the development period to ensure that his or her vision for the community is carried out and that nothing gets built in the development that could hinder the ability to market the remaining inventory. In addition, the developer will want to be able to assure builders that their plans will not be subjected to an unreasonable level of scrutiny by property owners who may have very different ideas as to what is acceptable or interests that conflict with the developer's or builder's interests. Nevertheless, managing the architectural review process for a large community can impose a heavy administrative burden on a developer and its staff. Thus, once the general theme and standards for the community are established, the developer may wish to delegate all or a portion of his or her authority in developed areas of the community, or with respect to certain types of approvals, to a committee comprising property owners to lessen his or her burden.

This transition can be accomplished in several ways. For example, the recorded covenants might establish a two-committee system under the auspices of the association, with one committee appointed by the developer to exercise exclusive jurisdiction over new construction and a second committee appointed by the association's board of directors to exercise jurisdiction over modifications

Design guidelines may address architectural styles, materials, colors, and other elements.

to developed property. This approach gives the developer control over that aspect of design review about which it is most concerned (new construction) and allows the control of the modifications committee to be transitioned to the owners at the same time as control of the board of directors, with a reserved veto power in the developer-controlled new construction committee.

This approach makes available the association's assessment power to fund the administrative costs of architectural review and enforcement and extends the protection of the association's insurance coverage if sued in connection with any architectural matter. It also imposes on both committees, however, certain fiduciary duties to exercise their powers and fulfill their responsibilities in a manner that serves the best interests of the association's members. This approach may at times create conflicts for the developer.

An alternative approach is for the community's recorded covenants to reserve exclusive authority over architectural matters directly to the developer, with the right to delegate all or a portion of architectural control power to the community association or a committee of the association at a future time. This approach removes the developer's activities from the realm of association business and, as a result, requires the developer to fund the costs of its architectural control activities. If this reserved power is properly drafted, however, it may give the developer broader discretion and flexibility in reviewing and approving proposed construction by negating any inference that the developer has a duty to act on behalf of the association or in the best interests of other owners as it would have if exercising such powers through a committee under the auspices of the association.

The design guidelines should set forth the application and review procedures for the architectural control process, addressing the required submissions, the steps in the review process and timing of review at each step,

Construction Warranties

Traditionally, a builder's or developer's reputation was the main vehicle for delivering construction warranties to consumers. Until the early 1990s, builders and developers often simply provided homebuyers with a gentleman's agreement to repair or replace defects found before closing, and to guarantee repair of defects in materials and workmanship for one year after closing. The buyer also had recourse through the warranties offered by the manufacturers of installed equipment and appliances. Where applicable, local building codes also provided homebuyers with additional protection, guaranteeing specific levels of workmanship and adherance to local construction standards.

This system ran into problems as some developers failed to honor warranties. The consumer also had virtually no recourse if the builder or developer went out of business or if the developer was a shell corporation set up to only complete one development, ceasing to exist thereafter.

Many new homes now come with limited warranties issued by third-party insurers. With such warranties, the builder buys warranty coverage for the home and passes the cost through to the buyer, buried in the sale price. If the buyer discovers a defect, the builder must make the repairs. If the builder is unable to do so, then the warranty company performs the repairs.

The standard warranty program for new houses today is ten years of coverage for structural defects (faults in load-bearing elements that support the weight of the house), two years of coverage on mechanical systems (plumbing, heating, electrical), and one year of coverage on materials and workmanship. The decision to provide warranty coverage by a builder or developer should be done in conjunction with legal counsel, taking into account local and state warranty laws, typical arrangements in the local market (buyers' expectations), and the potential legal options available to community associations (if applicable). Rules for resolving disputes and the role of arbitration are also important components under the larger topic of warranties.

Many states have very general implied warranty laws that are subject to interpretation, leaving it to the courts to determine what is implied to be warrantied. Thus, homebuilders and developers are exposed to a significant, yet uncertain, level of liability. In response to complaints of excessive exposure to liability by builders associations, some states have enacted legislation allowing the waiving of implied warranties when a builder and buyer agree on an expressed warranty. Consumers too often have problems with general state warranty laws, with advocates often arguing that limitations on these laws are significant and greatly reduce the value of such policies.

Consumers today expect a full level of recourse to remedy defects in their new homes. Sound warranty programs are a good idea for responsible builders, as they are yet another way to offer valued consumer benefits. ■

Design guidelines must be flexible enough to anticipate innovations in building materials and other technologies. Cement fiber siding and manufactured stone are relatively new products that closely resemble traditional materials.

the scope and basis of review, and the reviewer's authority to grant variances. In addition, they should address procedures for appeal, if any, and the authority of the reviewer to impose, as a condition of approval, a time frame during which proposed work must be commenced and completed.

The nature and extent of the design guidelines dictate the degree of detail needed in the required submissions, including site plans, elevations, and construction plans and specifications. The required submittals should be sufficiently detailed and accurate to permit a fair evaluation of the acceptability of proposed construction or modifications and to confirm upon inspection after completion that such work has been undertaken in accordance with the approved plans.

The design guidelines should specify the amount of time the reviewer will have to approve or disapprove the plans (if not set forth in recorded covenants). The time period should be sufficient to allow the reviewer to determine whether the plans are in compliance with the guidelines but not so much time as to delay or hinder the development process. Failure of the reviewer to approve or disapprove within the specified time period should be deemed an approval of the plans. The guidelines should also set forth the procedure and timing for resubmitting plans in the event they are initially disapproved and should set a maximum amount of time that an approval is valid if construction is not begun immediately (consistent with covenants).

Review and approval of any application should be made on the basis of aesthetic considerations only. The reviewer of the plans should not be responsible for ensuring that the plans and specifications are in compliance with applicable laws and building codes, and the guidelines should thus disclaim any liability of the reviewer based on the adequacy of the plans and specifications in that regard. The guidelines should require that all plans and specifications contain a certification by a registered architect or engineer that such plans comply with all applicable federal, state, and local codes, regulations, restrictions, or any other stipulations.

Some circumstances such as topography, natural obstructions, hardship, and aesthetic or environmental considerations may require deviation from the guidelines. In such cases, the guidelines should authorize the reviewer to grant variances from strict compliance as long as such a variance would not materially violate the intent of the guidelines.

In adopting and enforcing architectural controls, the developer must balance his desires with the knowledge that excessive controls on the reasonable use of privately owned property will not be enforceable. Reasonableness, fairness, and need should be the measures of four conditions: 1) whether a requirement for design guidelines or design review is desirable to preserve and protect the developer's and the owners' interests; 2) whether it is likely to be enforced diligently and therefore not lose its effect through failure to enforce it; 3) whether the association and the owners can reasonably interpret it; and 4) whether it is so rigid that changing circumstances requiring modifications cannot be accommodated.

Some Important Principles. If one is to create governance that works and that institutionalizes community, one must embrace some important principles. The developer and the development team must acknowledge that governance is a strategic tool and not an end in itself. The developer and his or her attorneys must acknowledge that governance is something more than a necessary evil that can simply be memorialized by reliance on forms, particularly outdated forms. Moreover, the development team must embrace the principle that community governance is a system of thinking and acting and that it requires new approaches to viewing governance. The developer and the drafter of governance documents must take a holistic approach that considers all aspects of planning, governing, and living in the common interest community.

One of the roles of the developer is to be the visionary for the common interest community. This vision extends not only to the product but also to the process; thus, it is important to note that having a vision for each community and for "community" at each development is vital.

All governance documents need to be user-friendly. They need to be clear and readable. The consequences of unintelligible documentation are substantial, as summed up by a recognized critic of common interest communities, Evan McKenzie, who says that current documents, because of their lack of clarity, create confusion, distrust, and disobedience.

Drafters must soften the corporate edges and reduce the regimentation and restrictiveness, which can be done by relying more on standards and less on rules, by seeking to strike balance, by asking whether the restriction is necessary and why. Perhaps most important, the development team and the drafter can provide and encourage an appropriate degree of autonomy for the community within the governance structure consistent with the vision and the purpose that have been articulated. To do so involves legalizing and encouraging the use of discretion and the exercise of judgment.

Making Governance Work

The Developer's Role Revisited

The third role of the developer is that of *governor/operator.* The operation of the association is too frequently a task that is the least understood and has the smallest commitment from the development team, yet it is one that can produce the greatest liability and can have a profound impact on the marketability of present and future projects. If a developer is to understand governance, he or she must understand this third role. It is important to ask how the developer sees his or her relationship to the community association and to acknowledge that the community association has an existence separate from the developer. The association exists from the time the documents are recorded, that is, from the outset of the development itself. Although the developer has the ability to control the association, this control comes with a price.

Rather than "being the association," the developer is in the position of a majority stockholder in a corporation or the managing partner in a partnership. The developer in control of a community association must be concerned with the fact that the developer is a fiduciary whose duty is to both the association and its members. Therefore, in the exercise of his rights to control, the developer must at all times be sensitive to the needs of the association as well as to the interests and needs of the developmental entity. The failure to maintain a sense of balance or conduct the association's affairs with fairness and in good faith can subject the developer to substantial liability.

Because of the roles and functions filled by the association, it is important that the association begin to

At Anthem in Arizona, the multiple homeowners' associations are all subordinate to the Community Council, the overall association that owns and maintains all common assets.

operate as soon as the developer sells the first parcel of property, if not before. Doing so permits the developer and the other association members, working within the framework established by the declaration and bylaws, to develop and implement the policies and procedures necessary to ensure that the association functions smoothly and efficiently both during and after the period of developer control. A clear understanding of those roles and functions and a commitment by its developer, officers, directors, and members to work together for the common good within the framework of the association's governing documents are essential to the successful self-government of the common interest community.

Operation of the Association

The long-term success of a for-sale residential development hinges on the quality and effectiveness of its management; the community association is the most prevalent tool used for this purpose. Small associations can be managed and governed by volunteers. Larger ones may wish to retain professional managers. The growth of associations has brought about corresponding growth in the number of qualified managers for community associations and firms that specialize in providing management services to community associations.

Early in the development process, developers need to establish competent association managers within their own organizations or seek outside management services. Many experienced professionals believe that developers should undertake management only when they have experience in the management business. Management is a service-oriented function that is quite different from the business of residential development. Management should not be left as a subordinate function. Further, early participation of the owners in the association and their training in the proper methods of management and operation will help make the transition from the developer's to the owners' control go more smoothly.

Whether controlled by the developer or by homeowners, the community association board has four options for management: 1) self-management by volunteers, 2) self-management by employees on the association's payroll, 3) contract management by an outside management company, and 4) a combination of these methods. Developers must think through the kind of management most suitable for a particular project and must plan the management program in conjunction with initial planning for the project. Ideally, independent professional management is the best course of action to follow. Most regions of the country are now home to companies that can competently perform the functions of professional management.

Self-management is most typical of small associations (50 units or fewer) and associations that are several years old where the developer is no longer involved. With a staff paid by the association, the association board identifies responsibilities and hires the necessary employees. Under management by a third party, a totally independent management firm provides all services, with minimal participation by the developer or the association. Some developers choose to contract with a third-party contractor for certain specific services, such as lawn maintenance, while the developer or the owners han-dle general governance, depending on the stage of the association.[3]

Transferring Control from the Developer to Property Owners

As explained earlier, the transfer of control from the declarant to the homeowners or unit owners is a transition, and a successful transition is a *process*, not an event. Often the focus is on the actual point at which control is turned over, with the resulting misperception being that all activities begin and end at that particular point. That misunderstanding gives rise to many problems.

This section looks at the issue of control by the declarant as well as the actual passage of that control to the owners. These topics are inextricably linked. The extent and methods of control and the way that control is exercised and ended collectively provide the basis for a significant area of potential declarant liability and association dysfunction.

Control in a community association is manifested in a variety of ways. In the early years of development of common interest communities, and sometimes today, developers asserted in their documents, marketing materials, and management practices that the association did not exist until all or substantially all of the units were sold. In the meantime, the declarant was the association. Such assertions not only are incorrect but also cause potential problems and liabilities—and not just for the declarant.

Sometimes the documents state that the association exists from the beginning but that the declarant is in a position of dominance over the association. Frequently, however, the documents are silent regarding how to effect transition. This omission presents a problem, because, in some cases, the owners are reluctant to take over control but in others are extremely eager to do so.

Many documents do not provide for an orderly or phased transition that allows increased owner participation at various stages. Transition in phases raises the understanding and technical confidence of the owners as they move from being merely owner/members to members in control. The Uniform Common Interest Ownership Act and various state statutes mandate a phased transition.

The declarant wants control because of basic business needs, such as flexibility to adjust to changing circumstances and markets and ability to enforce developmental standards and guidelines to ensure product quality. The developer also needs assurance that the budget will remain at a level necessary to fund operations of the project at the expected stage. This assurance is impor-

At Celebration, Florida, a strong community association helps to maintain neighborhood quality.

Torti Gallas and Partners

figure 7-5

Key Decisions or Activities Affecting a Community Association

Association Phase	Predesign			Design	
Development Phase	**Choice and Evaluation of Site**	**Design Assessment**	**Market Approach**	**Financing the Project**	**Marketing the Project**
Association-Related Decisions or Activities	Assess natural features of barriers and of common property.	Select common areas and open space.	Determine market's acceptance of design and project.	Complete the preparation of the legal documents.	Explain the association concept as a sales tool.
	Decide clustering and land conservation.	Determine common facilities.	Explore alternative approaches to ownership of common property for the association:	Make sure the project conforms with requirements of FNMA, FHLMC, VA, FHA, and other lending-related institutions.	Inform the sales force about the legal aspects of selling a house with an association.
	Decide housing types.	Decide major capital items requiring long-term maintenance.	• Joint ownership • Private club • Dedication to local entity • Funded trust	Prepare initial association budget and management procedures.	Prepare brochures for homebuyers and homeowners.
		Decide whether to develop all at once or in phases.	Decide on condominium or homeowners' association.	Submit preliminary association management and sales program to lender.	
			Municipal officials accept design and development.		
			Assemble team.		
			Initiate preparation of association's legal documents.		

Source: C. James Dowden, *Creating a Community Association: The Developer's Role in Condominium and Homeowner Associations,* 2d rev. ed. (Washington, D.C., and Alexandria, Virginia: ULI–the Urban Land Institute and CAI–Community Associations Institute, 1986), pp. 22–23.

Startup		Transition		Governance	
Management	**First Phase of Construction (presale and sales) up to 25 Percent of Closings**	**Second Phase of Construction with 26 to 75 Percent of Closings**	**Final Phase of Construction with 76 to 90 Percent of Closings**	**Operational Project with Construction Completed and 91 to 100 Percent of Closings**	**Operational Project with Sales Completed**
Finalize management procedures and program.	Advise prospects of the nature and requirements of association living.	Continue association-related sales activities.	Continue sales program.	Continue sales program.	Owners prepare annual budget and set assessments.
Designate the management approach.	Distribute homebuyer brochure with appropriate data and documents.	Ensure management functions as follows: • Owners on committees • Annual membership meetings conducted • Officers and board members elected • Some, if not a majority, of owner seats on board • Assumption of most administrative and financial functions by owners.	Owners control association and proceed with management, with increasing emphasis on: • An architectural review committee • Firm administrative procedures and systems • Owner-controlled committees • Owners' review of budget and assessments • Finalization of transition process with common area inspections and transfer of books, records, plans, and specifications. Developer continues minority position on board and key committees.	Owners assume all management function. Owners control all financial, physical, and administrative functions.	All committees are owner controlled and functioning. Owners control capital improvement programs.
Refine the initial budget and set initial assessments.	Distribute homeowner information, including association legal documents, budget, and brochure.				
Arrange for maintenance.	Solicit homeowners for involvement and participation in association.				
Prepare financial and administrative management programs.	Identify potential association leaders.				
Record the legal documents.	Initiate association committees.				
Appoint or elect initial board, which will meet to adopt the budget, management approach, assessments, and rules.	For a homeowners' association community, deed the common elements before the first closing.				
Let outside contracts (by the board) for maintenance, insurance, and so on.					

tant not only to the developer for purposes of long-term marketing but also to initial buyers who buy a product relying on marketing representations.

The developer needs a sufficient level of control over the association to protect its rights to develop in accordance with the basic development plan. Often the declarant wants control because of lack of trust in the owners or because the declarant simply does not understand the positive attributes of sharing or transferring control.

The transition process begins when the documents are drafted, because the documents establish the transition system, specify the association's operations, and detail the owners' and developer's relationship to the association. The transition process takes a long step forward when sales are first made, not only because the homeowners start to inhabit the community but also because the developer or sales team can begin communication with, and education of, community association members. This step is the builder/developer's opportunity to explain what the association is and does.

A successful transition requires trust and understanding among the developer, the association manager, and the owners. The manager facilitates the transition process and assures that it proceeds in accordance with the documents and the operational plan. The attorney and other professionals are merely supporting cast members in the process.

Certain problems arise frequently in the transition process. First is the failure to communicate. Failure to educate the new owners, coupled with rumor, can result in a developer who is afraid to relinquish control of the association and homeowners who are afraid to accept it.

Second is the failure to recognize and to appreciate what the association can and will do for all the parties. The association is not a necessary evil that must be used because of advantages in land planning. The association can enhance the livability of the development to the advantage of all concerned.

Third is the failure to act—the do-nothing approach to association transition. The declarant allows matters to slide along with no plan or purpose and with no control over what the homeowners understand and how the association is to operate. This approach reflects a mistaken belief that the best policy is no policy at all.

The fourth cause of problems in transition is the dichotomous companion to the do-nothing approach: the paternal builder/developer who seeks to do everything on behalf of the association with no association involvement, no education, and no training. Both problems reflect inadequate planning and documentation (or failure to implement the documents as drafted).

Fifth is the failure to deliver on promises made. The frustration of unmet expectations is a serious and significant cause of litigation. A successful transition—with no disputes and no litigation—is likely when the developer has been forthright from the outset, saying what it will and will not do, and then living up to those self-imposed standards.

Last are unrealistic expectations on behalf of the owners and an attitude that the developer is the ultimate landlord. Expectations and attitudes should realistically reflect the fact that the developer/declarant is in business and has a legitimate desire to stay in business and earn profits. Unrealistic expectations can permeate the transition process when the homeowners believe, to quote Groucho Marx, that it is the "last chance to beat the other couples." Such an attitude and such unreasonable expectations are clearly wrong, and all parties involved in the process should work to avoid them.

The developer/declarant can set the stage for a successful transition with three activities: good communication, full operation of the association, and prompt attention to defects in construction.

Communication

Communication should be structured to fit the particular project: a 10,000-unit development requires communication strategies that are considerably different

At Farrcroft in Fairfax, Virginia, the developer created a strong homeowners' association that maintains covenants and operates social activities.

Hugh Broadus

Looney Ricks Kiss

from those of a 20-unit project. Regardless of the size of the community, however, communication activities fall into at least three areas:

- Development Documents—The original development documents, including the declaration of condominium or the declaration of CCRs and the bylaws, are communication tools. Development documents establish the fundamentals of the association and the transition process. Therefore, the documents should be drafted with solving and preventing problems in mind. Good disclosure documents and disclosure statements are also good communications adjuncts to the document package.
- Sales Representations—The sales staff is a communication tool, and it should have a well-developed program and operational plan. The operational plan is an internal document explaining to the sales staff how the transition will be effected and how the association will operate. The sales staff communicates these messages through sales presentations and programs for new owners. The sales staff can ensure that homebuyers understand what the developer will do and what it will not do. When buyers know from the beginning not to expect certain types of activity, the developer is more likely to avoid unfulfilled expectations.
- Community News—Newsletters, E-mail listservs, and ad hoc communications are communication tools.

The type of newsletter or ad hoc communication, the frequency of the publication, and the content generally depend on the size of the association, the nature of the association, the nature of the membership, and the nature of the personnel and financial resources available for production. Whatever the form of the newsletter, the developer should ensure that some method of community-wide communication is available—not only to promote sales but also to promote association activity and to ensure continuing education of the association members.

Full Operation of the Association

The second major activity that sets the stage for successful transition is to have the association operate fully from the outset. Involving owners in the operation of the association, however, should not begin when there are too few owners to have a meaningful pool of talent and volunteers. At the very least, the association should be fully operational when transition approaches. The developer should recognize the importance of orienting the owners to the nature, purpose, and function of the association but should not delay their involvement until there are so many owners that ad hoc organizations have sprung up.

Prompt Attention to Defects and Problems

The third area of activity is to fix or cure all defects and problems as they arise. Cost-effective, preventive

Rancho Viejo near Santa Fe, New Mexico, will eventually include more than 1,000 homes in a compact, village-like plan that preserves open space.

work to correct construction defects and other "small" problems will avoid the large problems. Establishing an aura of good feelings within the association can lead to good results.

Leadership is action, not position. Leadership begets leaders, and the process of *developing* rather than selecting leaders is important. A successful transition requires finding ways to allow the members of the association to participate meaningfully in community governance even as the declarant retains ultimate control.

Remember what transition is not. Transition is not a time to resolve disputes. It is not a time for a release of liability. Such a release is of questionable validity, and the process of negotiating and executing the release would vitiate the political process of transfer of control and would tend to polarize the parties. Both sides—the association members and the declarant—are protected if transition is accomplished before any issues of the declarant's liability are resolved. Do not inject legal issues into the political process if the process is ultimately to be successful.

James Chaffin, former ULI chair, says that transition is actually a process of executing the developer's "sense of stewardship." He points out that one must start with good documents that set forth quality governance and articulate a vision. Transition is also a reflection of the developer's attitude about dealing with property owners; a positive attitude that allows the identification and involvement of potential leaders is vital. Chaffin adds

that in identifying potential leaders, one should identify both advocates and adversaries so as to have meaningful feedback.

Moreover, he says, transition works when the developer listens and is not automatically defensive yet remains in a leadership position. As the developer moves toward transition, he or she should choose from that group of potential leaders and involve them in the transition process. Chaffin finds that having various forms of communication, including a seminar for the owners to jump-start the transition, is vital. A comprehensive guide to the transition from developer to owner is *Transition from Developer Control* by the late Amanda G. Hyatt.[4]

Conclusion

It would be remiss not to alert developers that community governance carries with it the potential cost of litigation with owners, associations, or others. Experience indicates that the most common sources of litigation for the developer in a common interest community arise from the operation of the association, representations made in marketing the community to purchasers, and construction defects.[5]

ULI's *Trends and Innovations in Master-Planned Communities* explores new approaches to creation of common interest communities.[6] The chapter on governance observes that community associations have evolved dramati-

208 **Residential Development Handbook**

cally from a seldom heard concept to one of the most significant factors in modern real estate development. Governance has evolved, but it also has both the need and the opportunity for additional evolution. Developers should look at community governance not as a necessary evil but as an opportunity to enhance their projects, to empower their residents in very positive ways, and to shift the focus so as to allow all concerned to do good and to do well at the same time.

The capacity for future application of community governance is limited only by the imagination of developers and the skill, creativity, and commitment of drafters. Community governance can become a positive force that will allow the process to enhance the product greatly.

Notes

1. Because this chapter is about community governance, the specific details of condominium development are left to other sources. See, e.g., David Clurman, F. Scott Jackson, and Edna Hebard, *Condominiums and Cooperatives,* 2d ed. (New York: John Wiley & Sons, 1984); Wayne S. Hyatt, *Condominiums and Home Owner Associations: A Guide to the Development Process* (Colorado Springs: Shepard's/McGraw-Hill, 1985); and Wayne S. Hyatt, *Condominium and Homeowner Association Practice: Community Association Law,* 3d ed. (Philadelphia: American Law Institute–American Bar Association, 2000).

2. This section is excerpted from Jo Anne P. Stubblefield, "Using Architectural Guidelines in the Planned Community," *The Practical Real Estate Lawyer,* November 1996, pp.83–88.

3. Community association management is an industry unto itself, and the wealth of information and materials available for the developer cannot adequately be covered in the limited space of this chapter on governance. The Community Associations Institute, headquartered in Alexandria, Virginia, is the leading nonprofit research and education organization in the field of community association management and operation. It has an extensive library of materials, training courses, and programs available for the developer, developer's counsel, other team members, and, perhaps most important, board members, whether appointed by the developer or elected by the homeowners. It is well worth the developer's time and a modest financial investment to use the resources available through the Community Associations Institute.

4. Amanda G. Hyatt, *Transition from Developer Control,* 3d ed. (Alexandria, Virginia: Community Associations Institute, 1998).

5. For more information on this topic, see Wayne Hyatt, *Protecting Your Assets: Strategies for Successful Business Operation in a Litigious Society* (Washington, D.C.: ULI–the Urban Land Institute, 1997).

6. Adrienne Schmitz, et al. *Trends and Innovations in Master-Planned Communities* (Washington, D.C.: ULI–the Urban Land Institute, 1998).

8. Specialized Niche Opportunities

The typical nuclear family—a working father, stay-at-home mother, and two or more children—constitutes less than one quarter of all households today. As population and household types become increasingly diverse and demand housing appropriate for their lifestyles, a broader range of housing types is needed. Other demographic trends such as the continuing migration to the Sunbelt, the aging of baby boomers and the coming of age of the echo boomers, immigration, and the resurgence of downtowns as livable places have all created substantial opportunities for residential developers. No longer is there a singular demand for detached homes in the suburbs: new housing types are being sought and developed at remarkable rates. Developers who choose to respond to these changes by offering attractive and creative housing opportunities should fare well in the coming decades.

This chapter offers an overview of some of the current development types that have been spurred by demographic and cultural changes and have filled niches to supply both upscale and affordable housing. It explains some of the ins and outs of developing infill housing, seniors' housing, manufactured housing, workforce housing, condominium conversions, and brownfield and greyfield sites. The categories overlap; for example, brownfield development is often a subset of adaptive use, which is often a subset of infill development. Each type of development contains specific characteristics that are illustrated here by examples and suggestions. These housing types will almost certainly continue to be popular in the coming decades.

The key to succeeding in these markets is to be able to identify a suitable geographic location and appropriate market segment. Usually niche market buyers are looking for a distinctive yet reliable kind of housing that meets their needs. Satisfying these needs requires good market research and the ability to supply an attractive product at a reasonable price. Developers pursuing these housing options usually must have a proven track record to gain lenders', the community's, and buyers' confidence. As these types become more prolific, however, the market will break open, providing chances for those who seek to expand their reputations and develop creatively.

Infill Development

The combination of growth controls and the increased desirability of living in downtowns has created an interest in infill development—building on unused or underused urban land where markets and infrastructure already exist. Infill development will likely become even more important as the population grows, local governments reign in sprawl, households continue to change, and the building stock ages. In 2000, the national housing stock included 115.9 million residential units, and based on growth rates, it is estimated that it will

The Academy, Boulder, Colorado.

Infill sites offer tremendous potential. Playa Vista in Los Angeles, California, is one of the largest infill sites in the United States.

Playa Vista

increase toapproximately 154.8 million units by 2030.[1] It is likely that a good share of this tremendous amount of new building will not take place in undeveloped suburbs without supporting infrastructure (also known as greenfield development). The development model that has been dominant since the late 1940s—that of growth pushing farther out from the city and the proliferation of single-family detached homes in suburban communities—will perhaps give way to new types of urban and suburban infill development. Infill development encourages a variety of design and housing options—accessory units, townhouses, condominiums, studios, rental apartments, and co-housing. Infill housing can offer buyers a locational advantage over greenfield development in that it is often closer to jobs, amenities, and services.

Although suburban areas are increasingly home to infill and redevelopment, most of the innovative infill projects have taken place in established cities and older, inner-ring suburbs. Such areas usually welcome infill development, and many offer tax abatements, tax increment financing, flexible zoning, density bonuses, fast-track permitting, writedowns (lowering the cost of the land), and assistance with land assembly. Developers used to avoid infill projects, citing impenetrable issues such as fragmented land parcels, expensive and difficult environmental cleanup, intractable community opposition, and the inability to obtain financing for nontraditional projects. Local governments, eager to gain tax revenue, are now more willing to work with developers and are increasingly sensitive to these barriers. As the number of infill projects increases, the number of appraisal comparables increases, and lenders therefore are becoming amenable to supplying capital. Developers with proven track records and projects demonstrating that they are meeting a proven need tend to obtain financing more easily than those new to the field.

Community Concerns

Infill projects are located in existing neighborhoods, and the developer must therefore be sensitive to community concerns. Frequently, infill developers need land to be rezoned to more intensive uses to make a project financially feasible. Surrounding residents may oppose higher density, even if the project will increase property values.[2] Infill projects may also be perceived as gentrifying a neighborhood and therefore leading to the displacement of lower-income residents. This situation can be especially problematic if the city chooses to use eminent domain to condemn structures forcibly. Developers must work with the community and local officials from the beginning to create good will and, if possible, create a range of prices for their units so they can accommodate a range of incomes—particularly those from the surrounding neighborhood who would like to buy into the new development. Objections of NIMBY (not in my backyard) can also be quelled by sensitive architecture and design that enhances rather

Brownfield sites can be challenging for residential development, but a slag heap in Pittsburgh, Pennsylvania, has yielded Summerset at Frick Park.

Looney Ricks Kiss/Nicholas Traub

Established suburban communities may offer well-located, highly desirable infill or redevelopment sites.

Adrienne Schmitz

than clashes with the community's character. Good design also creates added value and can become a marketing tool. The most successful infill communities are architecturally integrated into the community and are pedestrian friendly, compact, and accessible by public transportation.

Parcels in central cities tend to be the leftovers from previous neighborhood development that are difficult to build on. They may be small, oddly shaped, on steep terrain, or with limited access. Therefore, city officials and developers look for large-scale underdeveloped sites owned by one or several entities. They may be abandoned housing developments, factories, warehouses, schools, dump sites, parking lots, military bases, or formerly industrial waterfronts. Usually, these sites contain some sort of contamination or necessitate environmental cleanup. Such areas are called *brownfield* or *TOAD* (temporarily obsolete abandoned derelict) sites.

Environmental Issues

Developing environmentally impaired real estate increases risk and adds to project costs, but local and federal governments offer a wide array of incentives to mitigate these negative factors. In 1997, the federal government passed the Taxpayer Relief Act, which contains the Brownfields Tax Incentive. Under this law, environmental cleanup costs are fully deductible in the year they are incurred rather than having to be capitalized. The government estimates that although the tax incentive costs approximately $300 million in annual tax revenue, the tax incentive is expected to leverage $3.4 billion in private investment and return 8,000 brownfields to productive use.[3] Congress also passed the Asset Conservation, Lender Liability, and Deposit Insurance Protection Act in September 1996. This act creates safe harbors for lenders against environmental liability arising from property on which the lender holds a security interest. The U.S. EPA provides grants for cleanup, a revolving loan fund,

liability protection, and brownfield development assistance information.

Developers must also conform to state environmental agency regulations, which, like federal regulations, have become more flexible. State programs provide some form of liability protection to the owner of brownfields property, often in the form of a covenant not to sue from the state or a release of liability for further remediation once the above remediation standards have been achieved.[4] Some local governments also provide such incentives as land writedowns and gap financing to lessen the cost of cleanup and site preparation.[5]

In addition, developers must make a full disclosure of environmental hazards to potential purchasers. Assuming a developer remediates a property's contamination to a risk-based cleanup standard or to numerical residential cleanup standards promulgated by the state, the developer faces the dilemma of what to disclose to potential purchasers. An obvious tension arises between the lack of disclosure, which can result in future claims of concealment or misrepresentation, and too much disclosure, which is fundamentally inconsistent with marketing the property. Developers must find an acceptable middle ground. Despite the risks involved with brownfields, developers continue to pursue them because they are often located on potentially valuable well-located real estate parcels, and once they are developed, they can yield high returns and generate positive publicity.

Suburban Infill

As a result of the success and demand for urban residential infill, suburban infill development is quickly gaining acceptance. Many of the same issues and concerns exist for suburban infill as for urban infill, but suburban infill projects do have a separate set of complications: they are much rarer than urban infill projects and therefore harder to finance, NIMBYism can be just as virulent in suburban locations, zoning is often rigidly uniform, and proximity to transportation and other services is not as

In 2004, about 25 million home-based businesses exist nationwide, up from 17 million in 1990, reports the Home-Based Business Council in Neptune City, New Jersey. Live/work communities, where residences are combined with offices or other work spaces, began to make a comeback during the early 1990s, when developers built new multistory structures with commercial uses on the ground floor and loft space above. In the next stage of the live/work resurgence, planned communities pushed the boundaries of the concept with townhouse-type structures, again with commercial space on the ground floor. One community offering this type of unit is Kentlands, located in Gaithersburg, Maryland.

The first homes in Kentlands were built in 1989, but construction has been ongoing, says Diane Dorney, proprietor of *The Town Paper*, a newspaper whose headquarters occupies the ground floor of one of the 60 live/work buildings at Kentlands.

Originally, Dorney put a downpayment on a live/work unit, thinking it would be a good rental property, but during its construction, she became enthusiastic about being right in the town center rather than a 15-minute walk away. Moreover, the work area gave her more space and a better image. "The visibility of a storefront does add value to your business, as opposed to working out of your den," she says. "Now I have more visitors."

Developers on the West Coast also have been developing live/work buildings. Development of Orenco Station began in the late 1990s along the light-rail line that runs into Portland, Oregon. When creating the 200-acre (80-hectare) mixed-use community, the developer, Portland's Pacific Realty Associates LP (PacTrust), was looking for a way to bridge a town center with surrounding detached housing, so it created live/work townhouses. "They look like Boston brownstones," suggests Dick Loffelmacher, PacTrust's director of retail development. "The 28 buildings are three stories. The front of the buildings have a split entryway: the lower level is the work component, with two upper levels of living space." Among the many types of businesses occupying the ground floors of the townhouses are an art gallery, a hair salon, and offices for a lumber brokerage, financial analysts, and an accountant.

A need to increase the density of its suburban development prompted PacTrust to create a live/work project. The buildings at Orenco Station were designed from scratch, as PacTrust had no model for them. "It is unique for this area," says Loffelmacher. "When we started this project, there were really no developments around that had these features."

Rancho Mission Viejo, a San Juan Capistrano, California, developer, saw no need for density. In fact, the developer decided that it had to take a giant leap of faith and create a live/work environment, even though its 4,000-acre (1,620-hectare) Ladera Ranch could easily have remained a single-use residential project.

"What we wanted to do was integrate a working environment in a residential component," explains Paul Johnson, a senior vice president with Rancho Mission Viejo. "There are a lot of places in the country where the live/work idea is alive and doing well, but it's usually in a mostly urban environment. We decided to experiment and figure out a way to do it in a suburban setting."

Within Ladera Ranch, the developer created a 22-home enclave called the Front Street neighborhood, built by Standard Pacific Homes. "Rancho Mission Viejo identified the plan but didn't know how to configure it," says Ralph Spargo, a general manager with Irvine, California–based Standard Pacific Corp. "We came up with the concept."

The difference between Front Street and other live/work communities is not only that the neighborhood has the traditional look and feel of the suburbs but also that the work space is on the same level as the residential space. This feature was accomplished in two ways: the front of the home faces the street and the office faces the back, and additional common-area parking was created. To casual passersby on the street, the presence of a home-based business is subtle, noticeable mostly by the "shingles" that announce the business and by the larger windows, which can, if needed, be used as display windows. The objective was to maintain as much of the street's residential character as possible, partly because, says Spargo, if the concept did not prove popular, the live/work units could always be marketed as purely residential properties. "Other than the signage that hangs from porches and balconies, one would never guess that the Front Street homes are in fact home-based businesses," says David Kosco, a Newport Beach, California, architect who designed the structures.

"The biggest challenge was to resolve the entries to the homes," says Kosco. "Creating an interior lane to the community gave us the ability to have front doors on opposite sides of the homes." The living space in the residences runs from 2,517 to 3,175 square feet (234 to 295 square meters), and the work space ranges from 450 to 696 square feet (42 to 65 square meters). "These are not ten- by ten-foot (3- by 3-meter) dens that someone calls an office. These are significant spaces designed in a multitude of arrangements, depending on individual home-based business need," he notes.

Many people in Orange County work from home, observes Spargo, and the county has regulations for home businesses. For example, someone who works out of his or her residence cannot have signage or employees, or invite the public to the house to execute business. Front Street does allow moderate signage.

The first step in constructing Front Street was working on zoning with the county, which proved very flexible in meeting the developer's needs. Out of the give-and-take between Rancho Mission Viejo and the county emerged regulations for home-based business enclaves, which allow small, entrepreneurial business owners to operate out of their homes or in facilities located on the same lot as their homes, in the context of a neighborhood geared toward the special needs of home-based business owners.

Specifically, Orange County's new regulations:

- Allow uses that include, but are not limited to, tax preparation, accounting, financial, architecture, graphics and arts, legal, Internet- or Web-oriented business, or any other similar uses that do not require intensive customer traffic.
- Prohibit such uses as medical and dental offices, veterinarians, tattoo parlors, fortune tellers, and all uses prohibited by Ladera Ranch. In addition, no hazardous materials are allowed.
- Require that a signage program be submitted as part of the site development permit application package, addressing proposed monument, ladder, and/or individual property signage.

"It's really not much different from what any other resident in a single-family or multifamily dwelling in Orange County can do. The only difference is that we provided for some exterior signage and allotted business parking in addition to residential parking requirements," says Chad Brown, chief of the site planning and consistency section of Orange County's Resources and Development Management Department.

Real estate agencies, property management companies, insurance offices, daycare centers, a hair salon, a magazine office, a software development firm, and a commercial photography studio are some of the many businesses in the Front Street neighborhood.

"When we started working with the county, we wanted to look at specific issues: noise, lights, traffic generation, and what the houses would look like," recalls Johnson. "After many months, we were able to work through these major issues and develop home-based business enterprise zoning."

One result was an increase in the parking ratio, allocating space inside the project that would not be seen by the adjacent neighborhood and that could accommodate additional employee or delivery parking. The homes form the outside edge of the square, while the inside common area is dedicated to parking; thus, those driving by see only the buildings' residential facade. "We have not had any negative feedback from adjacent neighborhoods," says Johnson.

In a newer development at Ladera Ranch called Banister Street in Terramor, Standard Pacific is building 24 live/work residences in the style of townhouses, with a two-story living area atop a ground floor that is mostly work space but also includes a garage and a foyer. The Banister townhouses will be priced around $500,000, while the Front Street homes were priced in the mid-$800s. "It is really a more vertical version of Front Street, with the business at the bottom of the house," says Spargo. In addition, the homes are smaller and are expected to attract smaller businesses and younger buyers. Banister Street is currently under development.

Underway on the East Coast is Afton Village, a 170-acre (70-hectare) mixed-use community going up about 20 miles (32 kilometers) from downtown Charlotte, in Concord, North Carolina. Afton Village eventually will consist of 700 residential units and 300,000 square feet (28,000 square meters) of commercial space. A "main street" is also being constructed, which is one of the reasons live/work townhouses will be offered. "It fits between the straight townhouses and the straight commercial retail," says David Mayfield, president of Charlotte-based Mayfield Development Corp.

These units will be three-story buildings with the storefront on the first floor and the upper floors for residential use, explains Mayfield. "It makes for a nice transition between an area that is completely residential and one that is completely commercial." Afton Village's live/work homes will include two-car garages, private courtyards, and 2,700 square feet (250 square meters) of space. The primary entrance to the commercial area is in the front, while that to the residential portion is at the rear.

The National Association of Home Builders reports that nearly a quarter of the houses built in the country today have home offices. The next step is for the home to have its own business space, which is what Kentlands, Afton Village, Orenco Station, and Ladera Ranch have attempted to do. ∎

Source: Adapted from Steve Bergsman, "Suburban Live/Work Communities," *Urban Land*, May 2004, pp. 60–61.

readily available. But the lack of undeveloped land and demand for new types of housing will fuel suburban infill development.

In the most desirable metropolitan areas, older suburban communities with tract housing are being razed to make way for higher-density communities with a mix of housing types. In suburban Washington, D.C., for example, 100 single-family houses in a Fairfax County development dating from the 1950s were demolished to make way for 1,000 townhouses, apartments, and detached houses.[6] After many years of negotiation, a national builder bought out residents for a total of about $36 million. Residents were hesitant to sell at first but changed their minds after years of encroaching development and difficulty reselling their aging and obsolete homes.

Older communities in the middle of high-growth areas are often hemmed in by new development; local governments may see them as not dense enough and seek to redevelop them. The localities gain more housing and tax revenues, and developers sometimes proffer schools, infrastructure improvements, and recreation space. This type of development can be very successful and rapidly growing municipalities tend to support it as part of a smart growth initiative, yet it also can be politically controversial and costly. Developers must be prepared for years of working with the community and must have the support of local officials. The redevelopment of tract housing usually appeals to a different demographic from that of urban infill; its target market is those who are looking for high-quality schools, the security of the suburbs, convenience to jobs, and access to major highways.

Another form of suburban infill development that is causing controversy is the building of disproportionately large homes in established residential communities. These homes, sometimes called "McMansions," are most common in high-cost major metropolitan areas and in some resort communities. They appear most frequently in older parts of high-growth areas, prestigious mature neighborhoods, and high-tech belts.[7]

The exact definition of a McMansion is subjective, but the size of the American home is continually expanding. According to the 2000 Census, median house size increased in the last decade from 5.2 rooms to 5.8 rooms. The Census Survey of Construction also shows that the average new home jumped from 1,500 square feet (140 square meters) in 1970 to 2,266 square feet (210 square meters) in 2000. According to data collected by the National Association of Home Builders, only 7 percent of new houses exceeded 3,000 square feet (280 square meters) in 1984; by 2000, the figure stood at 18 percent. Mature suburbs offer scenic landscaping, good schools, and access to services and amenities, but often the existing homes are too small to meet the demands of today's buyers. Therefore, outdated housing is torn down and larger single-family houses with more up-to-date features are constructed in their place. Critics state that oversized houses change a neighborhood's character, overwhelm the smaller houses, and reduce the supply of more affordable housing units.

Many localities, especially those that are struggling financially, are often tempted to allow the building of large homes that will bring greater tax revenues than the current stock. Overall, it is better for a community to include both—a mix of housing types for a mix of incomes—and compromises are possible. The city of Naperville, Illinois, worked with residents to develop a guidebook meant to sensitize would-be developers and owners of oversized homes to their neighborhood's character and prominent features, including typical house size. To ensure maximum flexibility, Naperville does not use formulas to determine lot coverage, and the guidebook fits existing zoning codes. The idea is to have the developer and the prospective homeowner consider the neighborhood context in which they are building.[8]

Greyfields could be considered the suburban counterpoints of brownfields. Instead of vacant industrial sites, greyfields are failed suburban shopping centers. The Congress for the New Urbanism estimates that there are

Once a surface parking lot for an obsolete Sears store, Market Common Clarendon in Arlington, Virginia, is now a mixed-use development that includes housing, shopping, and entertainment.

as many as 140 regional malls in the United States that would qualify as greyfields, with another 200 to 250 malls approaching greyfield status.[9] Greyfield sites are, on average, about 45 acres (18 hectares) and not well connected to regional transportation systems. They are usually not far from residential neighborhoods, which usually makes them ideal for additional residential and green space development. Often the malls themselves are too inadequate to be repositioned as new commercial centers. So rather have them sit vacant, many communities have worked to redevelop them into mixed-use centers with a range of housing types. Santana Row in San Jose, California, referred to as a "lifestyle center," is a mix of rental housing and retail space aimed at aging baby boomers. Local governments welcome the redevelopment of these centers and generally like to see a balance of commercial and residential uses so as to achieve a balance between the cost of services and revenues. Successful greyfield development shifts away from its previous monolithic footprint and employs place-making techniques that bring together considerate composition of physical forms, pedestrian scale, connectivity and access, distinctive open spaces, and appropriate landscaping.[10]

Condominium Conversions

Condominiums became popular during the late 1970s and early 1980s, when interest rates and housing costs were high. They were an easy way for those who could not afford or did not desire single-family homes to begin to build equity. The market grew, and, as a result, thousands of multifamily rental units were converted to for-sale condominiums. As interest rates dropped, sales slowed, and for years, they remained a relatively stagnant sector of the housing market. But the recent resurgence of many older cities and downtowns has brought with it a renewed interest in for-sale multifamily housing, including condominium conversions. Classically styled apartment buildings that were once considered at the urban fringe and charged moderate rents have been bought, remodeled, and repackaged as stylish condominium units. This practice has been embraced by those seeking low-maintenance housing but has also been a long-standing source of ire to affordable housing advocates who see conversions as sapping the supply of rental apartments.

Despite the possibility of community opposition, the benefits of condominium conversion to the developer are many. Often, little environmental mitigation is required, profits from sales tend to be high, local and federal governments may offer incentives, and, as the lack of developable land in desirable areas in cities shrinks, conversions provide an answer to the shortage of housing. The period of sustained economic growth in the late 1990s combined with the stabilization and growth of urban populations made condominium conversions even more attractive, especially during a tight rental market. The sales of condominiums overall grew by 10 percent in the United States from 1999 to 2001, with the

New Biscuit Lofts in Evanston, Illinois, is an adaptive use loft conversion of a Nabisco cookie factory.

biggest gains in the South (16 percent) and largest jump in price in the Midwest (18 percent).[11]

Since the late 1990s, condominium conversion rates have skyrocketed in cities such as Atlanta, Chicago, and Los Angeles. Even during the economic slowdown of the early 2000s, condominium conversions managed to maintain their market appeal. Cities such as San Francisco that saw their downtown office markets boom face drastic cuts in office lease rates, partly because of the dot-com bust. Bay-area developers are now looking to retool Class A office buildings in such high-profile places as the Embarcadero into residential space.[12] Cities are usually open to these approaches, but developers have been known to first make the conversions and then comply with city codes, instead of wading through an approval process that may take years and cost thousands of dollars. Planners are working with developers, however, to streamline the approval process and reach accord on what has been perceived as an unnecessarily complex process.

Not only have larger, older urban areas seen an increase in conversions: smaller cities such as Portland, Maine, have participated, going from zero condominium conversions in 1999 to 50 in 2001.[13] Although a relatively small number, local developers see a growing trend, especially after the events of September 11, 2001, and the burgeoning population of retirees. Upper-middle-class Bostonians, New Yorkers, and other out-of-towners have recently flocked to lower-profile cities like Portland in search of peace, quiet, and a second or retirement home. Local Portland residents, who were paying an average of $800 per month in rent, found that they could obtain a condominium for a monthly payment about equal to their rent.

Taking on condominium conversions can be difficult as a result of community opposition, slow or difficult permitting, quality of the neighborhood, and availability of local amenities. A marketing plan should build good will in the neighborhood and among current tenants, appeal to those wanting to live in a downtown environment, and differentiate itself from the bulk of urban

Casa de les Punxes, in one of Barcelona's finest neighborhoods, was built in 1905 and refurbished in 2003. It includes residences, offices, and commercial space.

Joan Rodon Arquitectes Associats SA

Adaptive Use

Similar to condominium conversions, adaptive use provides new residential opportunities from existing structures. Adaptive use is the imaginative reworking of buildings that are no longer suited to their original use but, unlike condominium conversions, usually occurs in buildings that contained nonresidential uses. Adaptive use projects involve former school buildings, train stations, hospitals and other public buildings, warehouses, offices, and industrial buildings. Abandoned "white elephant" inner-city properties are now being retooled into all kinds of residential products—upscale and affordable, rental and for-sale. Although redeveloping properties can be costly and time-consuming, it is usually a worthwhile task that promotes efficiency and the conservation of historic resources and often yields high returns on investment.

Cities are usually amenable to this type of development as a way to introduce housing into formerly nonresidential areas, to restore buildings to a useful purpose, and to bring properties back onto the tax rolls. Often cities offer tax relief, grants, and loans and implement flexible zoning to spark such projects. The Lofts on St. Clair—a former produce warehouse in Dayton, Ohio, that now contains 108 units—qualified for a national historic tax credit and received a 12-year abatement on local taxes. When public buildings are involved, cooperation with public officials is important to expedite property transfer, save costs, and generate support and good will for the life of the project.

Developers considering adaptive use must take into account the building's architectural significance, location, age, configuration, and structural condition. Lenders, because the demand for downtown housing has been so high, also consider these factors and are generally supportive of such projects. Because these projects usually take place in neighborhoods that have declined or are recently experiencing an upsurge, investment is usually tied to anticipated future neighborhood stability once the building is adapted. During economic downtimes, however, lenders scrutinize a project regardless of demand or a developer's track record.[14] Lenders are especially cautious about luxury rental projects, because vacancy rates tend to rise during a slow economy. Lenders generally do not grant financing for site acquisition or initial site work if the property needs environmental remediation.[15]

School buildings are a favored type to be converted into housing, as they are usually in residential neighborhoods and do not require extensive environmental cleanup. Many also include outstanding architectural features that buyers looking for distinctive dwellings appreciate. Examples exist in many cities. In Atlanta, a 1920s-era high school was converted to Bass Lofts, a luxury condominium project of 103 units. The project takes advantage of many of the school building's original features, such as classroom doors with transoms, blackboards, and wood floors.

condominium projects. Certain developers have been selling condominiums "as is," that is, redeveloping the outside and leaving the interiors unfinished, an innovative yet risky approach that should be tested through focus groups before proceeding. Other developers find that little renovation needs to be done to convert a rental property to condominiums: perhaps repainting, recarpeting, and cleaning out remnants of the building's former life. Either method brings the units to market much more quickly than a full renovation.

Many converted buildings also have historic significance, which can aid in their marketability as well as their financial viability. The city of Chicago, which experienced more than 8,500 conversions from 1993 to 1998, provides an eight-year freeze on property taxes to buyers of historic landmark properties. Chicago has also used tax increment financing districts, which provide financial assistance for building rehabilitation and facade work. Many cities offer an array of incentives, although they may be balanced with legislation limiting conversions that are perceived as cannibalizing the affordable rental market.

Conversions often support only what the rents will bear: rushing toward trends may work in some cities such as Denver, where loft conversions are popular, but not yield the same results in a city like Kansas City, where small-scale conversions may be more appropriate. In general, traditional units priced in the middle range tend to attract the largest number of buyers and hold their selling appeal during market fluctuations.

Residential lofts are common products in all kinds of adaptive use and have become tremendously popular in recent years. Their appeal comes from their typical architectural features: high ceilings (from 10 to 25 feet [3 to 7.6 meters]), large open spaces without walls, huge windows to let in lots of natural light, seasoned wood floors, exposed beams, brick walls, arches, and skylights. New features can include granite-accented kitchens, marble baths, sophisticated lighting, and high-tech wiring, all in contrast to the industrial textures. Courtyards, rooftop gardens and swimming pools, decks and walking areas are common. With purchase costs from $100,000 to more than $1 million, most lofts are marketed to upscale consumers. Loft purchasers tend to want an urban environment and want to be near shops, entertainment, and transportation. They are usually young professionals (rarely with children older than four) or empty nesters. The lofts built during the 1970s and 1980s in Manhattan's SoHo and Tribeca districts set the standards and have forever associated the concept with hip urbanity.

Marketing adaptive use properties is usually clear cut. The building's historic significance, its architectural details, and the story of its redevelopment all contribute to an effective marketing plan. Units in restored historic properties typically command some of the highest rents and sale prices in their market.[16] Market studies should of course be undertaken to determine the product type and price structure that will match potential purchasers.

Workforce Housing

The term *affordable housing* has long been an industry buzzword, but observers agree its meaning is relative. What may be considered affordable in San Francisco may not be considered affordable in Cleveland. Moreover, people often assume that affordable housing means

The Academy in Boulder, Colorado, is an adaptive use project: a former girls' school converted to 38 seniors' apartments and seven assisted living units.

Ed LaCasse

In a neighborhood that needed housing, Fifth Avenue Lofts in San Diego, California, is the conversion of a vacant office building into loft condominiums. Redevelopment of surface parking provided space for units with large patios.

Loft-style units are so popular that developers are creating new buildings that replicate the industrial look of warehouse conversions.

only low-income or public housing. Now, however, low-income and middle-income housing are differentiated. *Workforce housing* is used when discussing housing for middle-income workers such as police, teachers, firefighters, nurses, or any job holders who earn a high percentage of an area's median income but are shut out of the existing housing market. Housing for these households is a growing crisis in many regions, especially among vital municipal employees. Often, they must pay more than 50 percent of their income toward housing costs instead of the ideal 25 to 30 percent. Increasingly, the only housing they can afford is located in old, deteriorating neighborhoods in central cities and inner-ring suburbs or at the far outer fringes of urban areas. This situation forces households to "drive to qualify," that is, to drive farther and farther out from their jobs to find suitable housing they can afford.[17] The lack of affordable housing near employment centers exacerbates traffic congestion, sprawl, and an uneven jobs-to-housing ratio.

For decades, federal and local governments have been responding to the housing needs of its poorest citizens, assuming that those with moderate incomes could afford to pay for housing without assistance. Over time, redevelopment and gentrification pushed out moderately priced units, leaving consumers with fewer choices in their income bracket. Local governments responded with inclusionary zoning policies that mandate or provide incentives for the development of moderately priced units in market-rate developments. Incentives can include increased density allowances, reduced impact fees, tax abatements for affordable units, and accelerated permit processing.

At the federal level, the U.S. Department of Housing and Urban Development's HOPE VI program redevelops former public housing projects into mixed-income communities. Private sector and nonprofit developers team with local governments, with the assistance of federal money and low-income housing tax credits, to create housing for a range of incomes. The HOPE VI program has been controversial because of gentrification and displacement issues, but the completed projects have been well received by the public and housing sales have been brisk overall. The projects are often located in desirable urban areas; with the right design and marketing, they can be highly successful. At this writing, federal funding for the program is at risk.

As housing prices increased along with interest rates during the 1990s, municipalities, universities, and large companies noticed that they were having difficulty maintaining and recruiting employees because of the high costs of housing in their areas. Employers began offering housing assistance (providing downpayment subsidies and secondary loans and guaranteeing mortgages) as a benefit to employees; some have even partnered with developers to build housing. Land-rich employers such as universities and municipalities are finding that site-assisted housing can be a way to house employees as well as a way to generate revenue. Em-

First Ward in Charlotte, North Carolina, is an example of an urban revitalization project using federal HOPE VI funding.

Urban Design Associates

ployers retain ownership of the land (land costs are often what make housing so expensive) but sell the housing units to the employees. As long as the land remains under the employer's control, the housing remains affordable even as it is resold. In response to employee recruitment problems as a result of high housing prices in the area, the University of California at Irvine teamed with a private developer to create a faculty housing community based on the land lease model. Davidson College in North Carolina used a similar model. The college developed a 202-unit residential community with a mix of subsidized housing to meet faculty and staff needs, and market-rate housing to sell to the general public.

Developers may also want to team with employers (who could provide loan guarantees) and offer discounted sale prices during preleasing to those employees. *Employer-assisted housing* is increasingly a specialized opportunity in those parts of the country where housing prices have outpaced incomes and threaten economic competitiveness.

Seniors' Housing

In the first decades of the 21st century, the population cohort aged 55 to 64 will be the fastest-growing segment of the homebuying public. As they retire, these aging baby boomers, with needs and expectations different from their parents' generation, will make up a significant share of the homebuying market. They are predicted to live longer, be healthier and more active, work well past the typical retirement age, and start second careers. A recent survey by the Del Webb Corporation, a large developer of retirement communities, indicates that half the "boomer-zoomers" claim that their retirement lifestyle will include working part time and that they will want offices in their retirement homes.[18] The survey also in-

---

Employer-Assisted Housing Partnerships

Cash Participation
Employers can encourage the development of rental or ownership units by partly funding projects, essentially subsidizing the project to lower the ultimate cost of housing to the employee and to ensure that a percentage of units is made available for rental or sale to employees.

Provision of Development Sites
Employers can donate, sell at below-market rates, or offer long-term leases on land or buildings to use as development sites. In return, employers can negotiate concessions on rent or sale prices from developers or secure commitments that a certain number of units will be made available to employees.

Donation of Services
Some larger firms with in-house legal, architectural, engineering, and property management capacities could provide valuable technical assistance, particularly to nonprofit organizations.

Construction Financing
Employers can provide construction financing for new rental or ownership units. Employers, especially large corporations that can access short-term capital at low rates, can provide construction financing at low rates or guarantee construction loans. In exchange, employers can obtain reduced rents or sale prices or guaranteed units for employees. Another option is to trade construction financing for shares in cooperatives.

Purchase Guarantees
Purchase guarantees are development incentives that come into effect once development is complete. Employers guarantee developers that they will purchase a designated number of units if they are not sold on the mar-

ket by a predetermined date. In return, the developer agrees to sell the unit at a lower price. If the units sell within the time limit, the guarantee costs the employer nothing. If the units do not sell, the employer is liable for the cost of carrying the units until they do.

Master Leases
Employers can enter into master leases with property owners for new and existing rental properties. Employers then sublease these units to their employees. A master lease guarantees income for the developer and lender, easing project financing. In exchange, employers can expect to gain concessions on affordability and assurances that housing units will be available to their employees. The cost of a master lease to the employer can be minimal, for there is no cost as long as the unit is actually rented by an employee or other renter. ∎

Source: Joint Center for Housing Studies of Harvard University and the Neighborhood Reinvestment Corporation, *Employer-Assisted Housing: Competitiveness through Partnership,* September 2000.

figure 8-1

Projected Growth of the Population 65 and Older, 2000 to 2050

Year	65 to 74		75 to 79		80 to 84		85 and older	
	Number (000)	Percent of Total Population	Number (000)	Percent of Total Population	Number (000)	Percent of Total Population	Number (000)	Percent of Total Population
2000	18,136	6.6	7,415	2.7	4,900	1.8	4,259	1.6
2010	21,057	7.1	7,124	2.4	5,557	1.9	5,671	1.9
2020	31,385	9.7	9,435	2.9	5,940	1.8	6,460	2.0
2030	37,407	10.8	13,962	4.0	9,555	2.8	8,455	2.4
2040	33,013	8.9	16,004	4.3	12,664	3.4	13,552	3.7
2050	34,731	8.8	13,927	3.5	11,977	3.0	18,223	4.6

Source: U.S. Census Bureau, Population Projections of the United States by Age, Sex, Race, and Hispanic Origin: 1995 to 2050, *Current Population Reports,* Series P-25, No. 1130 (Washington, D.C.: U.S. Government Printing Office, 1996).

dicates that boomers eschew formal living spaces and prefer homes with centrally located gourmet kitchens, exercise rooms, and energy-efficient systems. About half the people surveyed want to retire to a house similar in size to their current one. Many want resort-like active adult communities that offer active sports like golf and tennis rather than the stereotypical pursuits of bingo and shuffleboard. No single product or solution exists to housing all seniors, and the market will become increasingly diverse.

Figure 8-1 shows the projected growth in the senior population, with the population of 65- to 74-year-olds peaking around 2030. The oldest of seniors, those 85 and beyond, made up only 1.6 percent of the total U.S. population in 2000, but by 2050 they will account for approximately 4.6 percent of the total population, a tripling of market share. Obviously, seniors in these categories will have different needs and lifestyles; not all will be physically healthy or financially prepared for retirement. Despite all that has been written about intergenera-

tional wealth transfers from the baby boomers' parents, the median income (including income from social security, pensions, and assets) for persons 65 and older was only $13,769 in 2000.[19] Living arrangements and marital status will also affect an older person's income and housing preferences. Among women 75 and over, half live alone, according to the 2000 Census. These women tend to be poorer than their male counterparts and make up a larger share of the seniors' housing market.

In the past, seniors had limited housing options when they retired or were no longer able to manage a household. They often relied on family members or moved into rooming houses or nursing homes. But options have expanded; five types of seniors' housing now exist, as shown in the feature box on the facing page.

The late 1990s saw a boom in construction of housing for seniors, mostly fed by the interest of Wall Street investors. Previously, few developers had built seniors' housing because of the complex government regulations and multiparty management requirements. Moreover,

Solavita, Avatar's active adult community in Poinciana, Florida, is developed around a vibrant town center that encourages social interaction.

Canin Associates

- Active Adult Communities—These communities comprise houses and/or apartments, usually for sale, in resort-style settings; they are usually restricted to those aged 55 and older. According to federal fair housing laws, developers must furnish facilities and services targeted for an older population, and at least one person per household must be that age or older. These communities tend to focus on recreational amenities; they are generally attractive and well situated enough to entice retirees to sell their current homes and relocate. Active adult communities attract empty nesters and those who want to continue to be active during retirement, surrounded by those of their own generation in a maintenance-free home. Larger homebuilders and development companies once dominated this category and built thousands of units of "destination" housing, mainly in the Sunbelt, for those who were already retired. Now small and medium companies are building more modestly sized communities in different parts of the country. Very little special regulation applies to this category.

- Congregate Care or Independent Living Housing— These projects are targeted to those who are in relatively good health but may desire some support with meals and housekeeping. They are usually multifamily mid- to high-rise buildings, and units are offered either for rent or for sale. The typical age of residents varies, but the core group, sometimes referred to as the "dependently active," usually moves to this type of housing upon the death of a spouse or a somewhat debilitating injury. Therefore, amenities focus on common space for increased social interaction, and facilities are designed to accommodate those who are not fully mobile. Residents usually bring their own furnishings for their units, which typically include a small kitchen.

- Assisted Living—Assisted living facilities are similar to congregate care facilities but offer a higher level of assistance with daily activities and medical needs. Typically, they house fewer than 100 residents in private to semiprivate rooms. Assisted living facilities provide prepared meals, 24-hour security, transportation, access to health care and special social and recreation programs. Residents are usually in their early to mid-80s, and most are female. These facilities also offer care for Alzheimer's disease or other forms of dementia.[1]

- Nursing Homes—Nursing homes offer the most comprehensive care, as their residents tend to have the most medical needs. They require skilled nursing care and are similar in nature to hospitals. The number of beds can range from three to 500, but the average number is around 100. They are subject to the most stringent forms of regulation and usually must be certified by Medicare or Medicaid or licensed by a government agency.

- Continuing Care Retirement Communities (CCRCs)— These communities provide a range of housing for seniors, including at least two of the categories listed above. With several facilities on the same grounds, they accommodate older people who are relatively active as well as those who have serious physical and mental disabilities. Residents usually sign long-term contracts and are guaranteed to be housed and cared for as their medical needs increase as they age. The cost of living in these communities can be quite high and unaffordable to those with low or moderate incomes and few assets. Most communities require an entrance fee and monthly payments. These fees can range from $20,000 to $400,000. Some require that a resident turn over his or her entire estate as a downpayment, but this approach is becoming less common. Monthly payments may range from $200 to $2,500. In some communities, residents own their living space; in others, the space is rented.[2] ■

Notes

1. Douglas R. Porter, "Developing Housing for Seniors," *Urban Land*, February 1995, pp. 17–22.
2. "Continuing Care Retirement Communities," AARP Web site, www.aarp.org.

building and managing such housing requires a complex mix of residential, hotel, and medical facility development and ongoing services. But demographic projections drove much of the building and opened up new opportunities for financing. Commercial banks, HUD, insurance companies, affordable housing tax credits, tax-exempt debt, and health care REITs all supported much of the new seniors' housing construction. Developers have entered into joint venture partnerships with hospitals and colleges to provide seniors' housing, as both types of institutions tend to have available land and strong community ties.

According to the American Seniors Housing Association, construction rates are currently declining; overbuilding has occurred in the assisted living category, while relatively few CCRCs have been built. From 1996 to 2001, the independent living category had the highest median occupancy rates and operating margins, while occupancy rates and operating margins for assisted living facilities dipped. The biggest challenges facing the industry are increased regulation and staffing shortages, but real estate transaction values have been consistently high for Class A facilities.[20]

The location of seniors' housing tends to vary according to category and income of residents. The top five metropolitan areas for seniors' housing from 1999 to 2002 were Baltimore/Washington, D.C., Los Angeles, New York City, Chicago, and Dallas.[21] Seniors' housing, especially active adult communities, tends to flourish near larger metropolitan areas. Although many active communities were built in the traditional Sunbelt locales of Miami and Phoenix, recent studies reveal that some seniors prefer to retire where they vacation—mountains, beach, islands, and college towns.[22] Conversely, many retirees have stayed close to home to maintain social connections and to be close to their families. Many seniors' housing projects are increasingly built "close to home" rather than in vacation destinations, and local communities increasingly are interested in finding ways for their older residents to remain active, work at home, and stay connected to family and peers at an affordable price. Typically, middle- to lower-income retirees prefer to "age in place," and developers, municipalities, and long-term health care organizations are beginning to collaborate on facilities.

When marketing seniors' housing, it is important to offer a range of amenities. Senior residents usually seek social activities to avoid isolation, and suppliers now offer a range of on-site activities and provide access to off-site services. Facilities should include transportation options that assist those residents who are unable to drive and should be located close to retail facilities, banks, colleges, and churches. In the past, seniors' housing had been based on the hospital model, and the environments were often unwelcoming and spartan. Facilities now contain more appealing options that are similar to those of hotels and upscale apartment communities. Site and building designs should accommodate residents who are not entirely mobile and should offer supportive devices, places for social interaction, outdoor recreation space, and concierge services.

Factory-Built Housing

The majority of houses in the United States are now built with some prefabricated components; for example, nearly all windows and doors are preassembled and in their frames, and many are prefinished. Roof trusses, staircases, and other components are also increasingly delivered to the site already assembled. Factory-built housing takes this trend a step farther; it may consist of panels, rooms, or entire houses delivered to the site and installed on already poured foundations.

Factory-built housing is often considered synonymous with trailer parks and the attendant stereotype

Factory-built housing has come a long way. At the Mills of Carthage in Cincinnati, Ohio, modular homes were erected on reclaimed brownfields.

On an urban infill site in Oakland, California, a manufactured home is compatible with surrounding single-family and multi-family homes.

of dereliction. It is, however, one of the fastest-growing housing markets in the United States. The Manufactured Housing Institute estimates that, as of 2001, 22 million people lived in 10 million manufactured homes. Producers have been working to change the associated negative perceptions and now offer more product types than ever before. Units can range from small single-section homes to traditional two-story houses to energy-efficient "green" homes. The manufactured housing industry dropped the term *mobile home* in the early 1980s and has established a distinct vocabulary to go with its new image.

Four broad types of preengineered structures are available: panelized, precut, manufactured, and modular. Panelized homes are factory-built homes in which whole walls with windows, doors, wiring, and outside siding are transported to the site and assembled. Precut homes are factory-built housing in which the separate elements are cut to design specifications, transported to the site, and assembled. Precut homes include kit, log, and dome homes. Both these types must meet local and state building codes.[23]

Modular homes are built in the factory to comply with codes in the locality where the home will be delivered. They are transported to the site and installed, although they may be delivered in multiple sections. HUD regulates the design, construction, strength, transportability, fire resistance, energy efficiency, and the heating, cooling, electrical, and plumbing systems for all manufactured homes through the National Manufactured Housing Construction and Safety Standards Act. Any on-site additions such as garages, decks, and porches must meet local, state, or regional building codes. Modular homes, because of their uniform standards, are often thought to be more desirable than manufactured units. In 2001, about 13 percent of all new single-family housing starts were manufactured homes; manufactured housing retail sales were estimated at $9.5 billion.[24]

Advantages

Manufactured and modular homes are usually more affordable than houses built on site. A manufactured house, without including the price of the land, can cost one-third the median price of a new site-built home. According to the Manufactured Housing Institute, the average sale price for a manufactured home was $48,800 in 2001, compared with the national average of $175,200 for a site-built house. Because of their affordability, the bulk of buyers are senior citizens or young families making their first home purchases. Although many manufactured homes are built on leased or rented land, increasingly they are part of fee simple communities. Such housing has other advantages:

- Manufactured homes are assembled by the manufacturer, which reduces the need for subcontractors and therefore saves time and money. Costs are also kept low on the production side because the factory setting ensures that construction can take place year round, regardless of weather conditions, and the housing units can be shipped to various markets across the United States.
- The factory setting allows for better quality control than site-built construction, where quality depends on the experience and quality of the contractors and subcontractors. This advantage is even greater in areas with a shortage of skilled labor.
- Manufactured homes can be assembled and ready for occupancy in less than five weeks once they arrive from the factory, much less than for site-built homes.
- Standardization allows manufacturers to lower their material costs through high-volume buying, while the nationally known HUD code streamlines the building process by applying one standard nationwide.
- Because building materials are not left on site, vandalism and weather damage are nonexistent.

Buyers can often obtain mortgage financing for manufactured homes identical to the rates, terms, loan-to-value ratios, and nonrecurring closing costs of any new site-built home. A wide range of Freddie Mac and Fannie Mae loan products are available to buyers of manufactured homes, and HUD's Title I program offers financing from approved lenders. Some states, however, treat factory-built housing that is not secured by land as personal property rather than real estate and do not allow such homes to be financed through a conventional mortgage. The appreciation on manufactured homes can be slower than on site-built homes, but the gap can be narrowed through proper maintenance, a quality site, and attractive landscaping. Modular and kit homes allow for more customization and are therefore more expensive, but may increase in value more rapidly.

Although many manufactured homes are bought and sited for fee simple settings, developers have been building communities of manufactured housing, also known as land-lease communities, with success. In these situations, homebuyers own and maintain their homes, and the property owner owns and manages the site where the homes are located as well as common facilities and amenities. The city of Cincinnati, Ohio, recently paired with a private developer to create a community on a brownfield site. The costs of environmental remediation were offset by the lower building costs, and the developer was still able to provide affordable, modern homes in a master-planned community.[25] The city of Poway, California, spent $12 million to redevelop a downtown trailer park dating from the 1940s into an affordable manufactured housing community and commercial center.[26]

These communities are especially popular in areas where housing costs outpace incomes and in states such as California where regulatory barriers have been reduced. Overall, manufactured housing units are most numerous in the southern and western regions of the United States. Nine of the top ten states for manufactured housing shipments are located in those regions, along with eight of the top ten states where homes are manufactured.[27]

Regulation and Financing

Manufactured housing has long been subjected to restrictive zoning and considered an undesirable use that lowers adjacent property values. Local governments are gradually realizing, however, that manufactured housing increasingly consists of affordable multisection units that resemble single-family homes complete with features like pitched roofs, high ceilings, and front porches. The city of Elkridge, in Howard County, Maryland, contains a gated manufactured housing community on land zoned for mobile homes. The purchase price for one of the 236 units is about $100,000—60 percent of the county's median house price. Howard County not only encouraged the establishment of a manufactured home community, it even bought 11 units to add to its affordable housing inventory.[28] As the product evolves and pressure for affordable housing increases, it is likely that communities will abandon zoning policies that categorically prohibit manufactured housing.

East Village: Mixed-Income Housing in the Twin Cities

"Location, location, location" has special significance in affordable housing because it can either limit or expand residents' options for employment. Located at the edge of downtown Minneapolis, the newly opened, $29.5 million East Village mixed-use, mixed-income development is a giant stride toward revitalization in Elliot Park, one of the city's oldest and poorest neighborhoods. It lies within walking distance of jobs in downtown and at the University of Minnesota, two major employment bases.

Developed by the nonprofit Central Community Housing Trust (CCHT), East Village has been recognized with a Most Innovative Housing Project award by the Minneapolis Neighborhood Revitalization Program, as well as a Committee on Urban Environment award from the Minneapolis Planning Department. The community blends affordable housing with the first market-rate housing built in the neighborhood in more than 70 years. In addition to 180 aesthetically appealing rental apartments and townhouses, the project includes 6,500 square feet (605 square meters) of first-floor retail space—a neighborhood restaurant, a minimarket, and an upscale coffee establishment are among the tenants—as well as a 350-space, two-level underground parking garage. The garage replaced surface parking, which allowed the creation of a pedestrian greenway. One hundred parking spaces are leased for employees of a nearby senior care facility.

Before construction, the 2.9-acre (1.2-hectare) site—only a few blocks from the Hubert H. Humphrey Metrodome, contained, in addition to the surface parking, several deteriorated rental homes and commercial buildings. CCHT's collaborators on the project included Augustana Care Center (which owns the senior care facility), the Minneapolis Public Housing Authority, and

Elliot Park Neighborhood, Inc. Funding was through 14 private and public sources.

Miller Hanson Partners, a Minneapolis architecture and planning firm, worked closely with CCHT in designing and planning the three- and five-story project, which consists of a north building and a south building surrounding the greenway that leads to a city park across the street. Brick and horizontal siding, bay windows, French balconies, and high brick parapets complement the character of the neighborhood's older housing stock. The buildings themselves are divided into small neighborhoods so that residents will be able to get to know their neighbors.

The design team worked with the city of Minneapolis to vacate an adjacent street that separated the East Village site from neighboring housing towers. It also worked with the U.S. Department of Housing and Urban Development and the Minneapolis Public Housing Authority, both of which were enthusiastic about developing a pedestrian link through the site from the towers to retail uses and to the city park. ∎

Source: Kathe Stanton, St. Paul, Minnesota–based writer and media relations consultant.

Houses back the golf course at Stonebridge Golf Community in Aurora, Illinois.

Because of reservations consumers may have about manufactured housing, it must be carefully designed, constructed, marketed, and managed. Communities should look and feel like well-planned conventional housing developments that are aesthetically integrated with their surrounding communities. Marketing materials should emphasize amenities and how sophisticated manufactured housing has become. Often, manufacturers can provide assistance with marketing and installation. With this approach, the developer forfeits some sales profits, but the manufacturer assumes most of the risk. Some developers, working in strong markets, have financed project costs through the rapid sale and placement of new manufactured homes.[29] Management of communities by professional property managers is typical and helps waylay concerns that property will become derelict.

Financing for land-lease communities typically comes from commercial banks. The developer should provide as much information as possible about market demand, the housing product, and past and projected financial performance. The borrowed amount is typically 75 to 80 percent of the value of the completed development.[30] The Federal Housing Administration's 207(m) program offers a HUD-insured source of capital from commercial lenders to finance the construction of new manufactured housing land-lease communities and to expand and improve existing communities. When used to produce homes that are affordable to targeted income groups, manufactured housing developments may also be eligible for financial resources offered by other federal, state, local, and private groups.

Themed Recreational Communities

Golf Course Communities

Because of the popularity of golf, many developers are too quick to assume that their development should contain a golf course. This assumption is risky, because golf courses require a large capital investment, consume a large amount of land, and once built are difficult and costly to change. Moreover, aside from initial costs, developers must take into account the possibility that they will have to assume the expense of maintaining and operating the course for some years.

A golf course does add three basic benefits to a residential development. It provides 160 to 200 acres (65 to 80 hectares) of maintained open space to a community and thus may be beneficial during negotiations with local officials. Second, it permits an additional activity to property owners in a sport that is in great demand and short supply. And, third, golf courses add substantial value to lots or houses fronting the course and some value to houses located in the community but without direct frontage.

Economic feasibility is the most important factor to consider in the decision about whether or not to build a golf course. Are the benefits to be derived offset by the cost, time, and responsibility involved in constructing and operating a golf course? In part, the benefits derived from a golf course are intangible. A golf course can be a great selling point for the developer, but whether it sells enough lots with higher premiums to justify the expense, especially in areas where play is restricted to six months or fewer, should be evaluated. In general, a golf course may be an amenity to consider if:

- Few golf courses are in the area, and public courses are overcrowded.
- The development contains luxury housing.
- Land costs are relatively low.
- The golf course can be amortized over several years and several hundred dwelling units.
- The site is appropriate for use as a golf course, especially in terms of its configuration and terrain.

Developers should study the feasibility of a course, including the number of courses in play in the area, increases in population, and per capita income. In addition, the study should look at existing clubs in the area, their size and classes of membership, existing initiation fees and annual dues, their waiting lists for membership, and the volume of players. The study should also look at causes for successes or failures in similar local projects.

Developers should remember that a quality course requires a substantial amount of time to construct and for the turf to mature before the course is playable: at least two full growing seasons in northern climates (18 to 24 months) and 12 to 15 months in southern climates. Moreover, a minimum membership of 300 or more is typically required to break even for a golf course/country club. About 450 to 500 active players is the capacity of a regulation 18-hole course.

The development of a golf course is a large undertaking. The success of the course and the surrounding development is determined by many factors: economic feasibility, the site's suitability and location, selection of a capable golf course architect, detailed cost estimates for the course and for the clubhouse, financing, maintenance, and management. If a golf course is deemed feasible, developers should try to build an 18-hole regulation course with a par of 72. But developers should never insist that their developments contain only a championship course; they should investigate other types of public and private courses as well. If adequate property or money is not available for a regulation 18-hole golf course but including golf in the development seems to be warranted, then developers should consider the alternatives: a nine-hole regulation course, a nine-hole course with multiple tees, an executive golf course, or a par-three course.

A nine-hole regulation course is a possibility, but they are not as popular with golfers because they must replay the course to get in 18 holes. A nine-hole course with multiple tees saves land area yet still offers golfers a variety of shots, choices of clubs, and visual excitement. But

this type of course should be considered only if land and anticipated play are limited. An 18-hole executive golf course is generally built on 90 to 120 acres (36 to 48 hectares) and can be played in half the time of a regulation course. Its main function, however, is typically as a supplementary course. An 18-hole, par-three course uses only 60 to 90 acres (24 to 36 hectares).

Because of the premium prices paid for lots fronting on a golf course, a single fairway system may be used. If land is limited, a double fairway system is possible, with fewer lots fronting the course. Siting multifamily dwellings next to a golf course is a better option. Multifamily units overlooking a course can sell for 10 to 20 percent more than the same units on interior lots.

As the design of golf courses has become more sophisticated, so has the planning of residential units around a course. Innovative planning can provide a consistent base price for units with direct frontage, increase premiums for off-course parcels and lots, and help to pick up the pace of sales. The 1950s and 1960s emphasized lining up lots along golf fairways, but today designers maximize premiums by opening "windows" to the course that allow a greater number of residents to view it.

Residential developers should remember, however, that all residential areas fronting a golf course are not valued alike. That is, premiums vary in accordance with interest, attractiveness, activity, and creativity of the design at any given location. To boost the value of off-course parcels (parcels near the course but without direct frontage), the project's entry roads can be located to provide views onto the course.

Generally, it is better to construct the course before the houses on lots adjacent to it. Doing so not only helps with sales but also makes it easier and more economical to establish the course before houses are built. In addition, maximum benefit from the natural features—topography, drainage, vegetation, soil, water—can be incorporated into the course.

Whenever possible, golf courses should be located in valleys or lower, flatter areas. If a site can be used to a large degree with minimal grading, the cost of the course is relatively low; if much earth moving and grading are necessary, the expense is greater. For a minimum amount of grading, developers should figure on 100,000 cubic yards (76,500 cubic meters) to elevate tees and greens and perhaps another 150,000 cubic yards (114,800 cubic meters) to create the fairways.

Totally flat sites make uninteresting golf courses, and drainage must be improved by grading. Gently rolling terrain with some trees is preferable. It is usually desirable to locate golf courses in those areas unsuitable for buildings, but construction in floodplains or around wetlands may be expensive as well as environmentally challenging.

Marinas

A marina can be a community pier with a handful of boats or a large commercial enterprise with several thousand boat slips. The rising popularity of boating and the

Golf is a popular amenity for active adult retirement resorts like Solavita in Poinciana, Florida.

Canin Associates

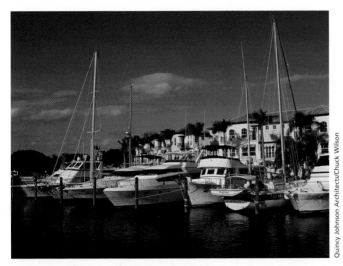

Marina Gardens is a townhouse community located on the Soverel Marine Harbor in North Palm Beach, Florida. Boat slips accommodating boats up to 65 feet (20 meters) are available.

increase in boat owners have not seen a corresponding increase in the number of marinas and docks, however.[31] Much of the growth has occurred in smaller craft, which can be easily launched from a car trailer and therefore stored anywhere. At one time, a marina was merely a place for berthing recreational boats where the boater could obtain fuel, water, and sometimes other supplies. They have evolved, however, into facilities offering more services—restaurants, sleeping accommodations, repair facilities, and boating supplies.

More complex commercial marinas are being built on inland waterways and oceanfronts, although marinas can be simple buildings with a parking area, docks, and rental boats. A complete marina furnishes docks with water and electricity piped to the berths, launching ramps, winter storage, marine railways, marine repair and supply shops, charter services, a sales agency, auto parking space, auto rental services, showers and dressing rooms, offices, a clubhouse, restaurants, a water travel bureau, complete shopping services, and a motel.

Because marinas are a service for boat owners, their designs vary according to the size and type of boats in the area. In areas with mostly outboard motorboats, services are specialized—smaller berths, large launching facilities, and parking areas for boat trailers. Services for sailboats, boats with high-horsepower motors, and yachts vary accordingly.

Shoreline property is some of the most highly prized real estate, yet it also contains some of the most sensitive natural resources. Management and development of the coast therefore present great challenges to developers and regulators alike. Thus, several items must be considered when evaluating the feasibility of a marina:

- Market Acceptability—Demand characteristics, existing supply, facilities capacity, and quality;
- Technical Feasibility—Water depth (ideally at least 8 feet [2.4 meters] below the historic low water datum,

water level fluctuations, soil characteristics, bottom material, environmental constraints, wind and wave action, storm surges (particularly for offshore marinas), water quality/flushing action (critical in land-locked, inland basins);
- Community Compatibility—Uses closely integrated rather than segregated;
- Financial Viability—Construction costs, gross sales, cost of sales, indirect costs, gross profit from sales, net profit from sales, return on investment.

Like those on golf courses, houses located adjacent to marinas can command large premiums because of the views and access to the valued recreational activity they offer. Marinas are costly to build and operate, however, and are not always suitable for residential developments. Before a marina is developed, a feasibility study is absolutely necessary.

Ski Resort Communities

Although skiing continues to increase in popularity, residential projects with ski facilities are largely limited to resort and second-home developments. The cost of building ski resorts depends primarily on slope, tree cover, terrain, soil conditions, and market characteristics. Where the operation can be kept small and informal and mainly for local residents, surface lifts should be adequate, and snowmaking equipment may not be necessary. If the market shows that snow skiing would be desirable but the cost of Alpine facilities is prohibitive, developers should not overlook the value of creating trails that can be used for bicycling or horseback riding in the warm months and cross-country skiing in the winter. Equipment costs are lower for this type of skiing, and the sport can be learned with relatively little practice, thus broadening its appeal.

Perhaps the most important means of ensuring the long-term growth of mountain, ski-oriented residential developments is to extend their seasonality. By adding

Mont Tremblant in Quebec is a 2,000-acre (810-hectare) four-season ski rsort with 3,000 residential units.

On the site of an abandoned cement plant along Lake Michigan, Bay Harbor is a luxury community that includes an equestrian center.

year-round attractions such as golf courses, conference centers, theme-oriented commercial uses, and summer activities, ski resorts can expand their potential for growth in the residential market.

Equestrian Communities

Equestrian communities have been most successful in areas where a "horse culture" already exists: southern California, Florida, Kentucky, Texas, and parts of Virginia. In fact, this culture seems essential to the success of equestrian communities, although many lots in such communities are sold to households that simply like the atmosphere of the horse world. Some estimates show that only about a quarter of homebuyers in equestrian communities actually own and board horses. Typically, equestrian communities include communal barns and riding centers, storage areas for horse trailers, riding trails (many such projects are located adjacent to parks and forests), pastures, and other accessories. By

putting facilities like barns and stables in a central location, expenses can be shared among homeowners and annoyances associated with odors and insects confined. In some instances, horse stables and care facilities can be operated by a community association, but this option is complicated by homeowners who do not own or board horses. Another option that should be explored is privatizing stables, operating them for profit for the benefit of community residents as well as others who may live outside the community but board their horses there.

Developers considering an equestrian-themed project need to carefully explore market potential and consider various options for financial structure of the community and the equestrian facilities. Further, targeting equestrian communities to other than high-income markets is risky. Even if market opportunities appear strong, the hardest part of the development process may prove to be obtaining financing.

Conclusion

The standard four-bedroom center-hall colonial house on a quarter-acre (0.1-hectare) suburban lot suits a shrinking portion of the housing market. As the population continues to age and become more diverse and households are smaller, busier, and more demanding, homebuyers will require that their housing needs be met with more custom-tailored solutions. What are currently viewed as niche product types will, in the coming decades, make up an increasing share of new units. Homes and the communities they occupy will be developed to meet the needs of the broad range of homebuyers.

Notes

1. Arthur C. Nelson, "Towards a New Metropolis: The Opportunity to Rebuild America," unpublished manuscript, Urban Affairs and Planning Program, Virginia Polytechnic University, 2004.

2. J. Terrence Farris, "The Barriers to Using Urban Infill Development to Achieve Smart Growth," *Housing Policy Debate*, Volume 12, Number 1, pp. 1–30.

3. U.S. Environmental Protection Agency, http://www.epa.gov/brownfields/index.html.

4. Robert D. Fox, "Brave New World: Residential Development on Brownfields Property," *The Legal Suburban*, April 6, 1998.

5. Farris, "The Barriers to Using Urban Infill Development to Achieve Smart Growth."

6. Sandra Fleishman, "In Fairfax, High-Density Suburban Renewal," *The Washington Post*, September 3, 2002.

7. Robert Lang, Karen Danielsen, and Mark Hinshaw, "Monster Houses? Yes! No!" *Planning*, May 2002, pp. 24–27.

8. Ibid.

9. Congress for the New Urbanism and PricewaterhouseCoopers, *Greyfields into Gold*, February 2001, http://www.cnu.org/cnu_reports/Greyfield_Feb_01.pdf.

10. Lee S. Sobel with Steven Bodzin, *Transforming Suburban Business Districts* (Washington, D.C.: ULI–the Urban Land Institute, 2001).

11. National Association of Realtors, *Sales of Existing Apartment Condos and Co-ops*, www.realtor.com.

12. Steve Ginsburg, "San Francisco Office Owners Rush to Convert Housing," *San Francisco Business Times*, August 12, 2002.

13. Mary Ruoff, "Condominium Conversions Gain Popularity," *Maine Today*, November 16, 2001.

14. Beth Mattson-Tieg, "Financing Urban Revitalization," *Urban Land*, March 2002, pp. 74–75+.

15. Scott Hartstein, "High Yield Lenders Play Role toward Adaptive Reuse," *Real Estate Weekly*, October 25, 2000.

16. Richard M. Haughey, "Fitting In," *Urban Land*, January 2002, pp. 50–56.

17. John McIlwain, "The Crisis in Workforce Housing," http://experts.uli.org/Content/ResFellows/McIlwain/McIlwain_C04.htm.

18. Dena Amoruso, "Baby Boomers Debunk Retirement Myths," *Realty Times*, February 8, 2000.

19. U.S. Administration on Aging, *A Profile of Older Americans: 2001* (Washington, D.C.: U.S. Administration on Aging, 2001).

20. Mel Gamzon, "Seniors' Housing for the 21st Century," *Urban Land*, June 1999, pp. 74–77+.

21. American Seniors Housing Association, *Housing Washington*, www.seniorshousing.org.

22. "A New Dawn," *Builder Magazine*, January 2000, p. 178.

23. Cryss Cada, "Manufactured Housing Sheds Stereotype," *Northern Colorado Business Report*, June 14, 2002.

24. Manufactured Housing Institute, www.manufacturedhousing.org.

25. Steve Hullibarger, "City at the Mills of Carthage," *MHD*, Winter 2003, www.manufacturedhousing.org.

26. "Haley Ranch Estates Redevelopment," Manufactured Housing Institute, www.manufacturedhousing.org.

27. Manufactured Housing Institute, www.manufacturedhousing.org.

28. Mary Otto, "Area Housing Boom Drives Out Mobile Homes," *The Washington Post*, December 27, 2002.

29. George Allen, "Developing and Financing in Land-Lease Communities," *Urban Land*, January 1996, pp. 35–39.

30. Ibid.

31. Patrick Phillips, *Developing with Recreational Amenities* (Washington, D.C.: ULI–the Urban Land Institute, 1986), Chapter 6.

9. Case Studies

Britannia Mills, Manchester, United Kingdom

A six-building complex that was once a sandpaper factory now houses 125 loft-style residential units. The industrial character of the factory makes for edgy, high-style units that appeal to young buyers.

Cherry Hill Village, Wayne County, Michigan

A traditional neighborhood development located on a green-field site creates the feeling of a small town with a mix of housing types. The community's focus is a core of commercial and civic uses.

The Dakota and Essex on the Park, St. Paul, Minnesota

A 75-unit urban townhouse and condominium project located on an urban infill site was the catalyst for the revitalization of the neighborhood. The project is part of a larger development that includes apartments, a public park, and 10,000 square feet (930 square meters) of retail space.

Highland's Garden Village, Denver, Colorado

An urban infill project, Highland's Garden Village combines housing for seniors, live/work units, co-housing, and more conventional housing types with a series of environmentally sensitive parks and gardens.

I'On, Mt. Pleasant, South Carolina

A 700-unit community based on concepts of the new urbanism and classic Lowcountry architectural styles, I'On features a pedestrian-friendly, relatively high-density environment with tree-lined streets, natural open areas, marshes, lakes, and recreational facilities for residents.

Maple Trace, Fairfax, Virginia

On a small infill site surrounded by established residential neighborhoods and straddling two jurisdictions, 23 single-family units use two different concepts. A landscaped village square at the entrance of the development sets the tone and provides a gathering place for residents.

Newington Village, Sydney, New South Wales, Australia

Newington Village, a legacy of the 2000 Olympic Games in Sydney, is now a medium-density neighborhood with an expected population of 5,000 residents at completion. The development uses "green" technology to promote environmental sustainability.

Nicholas Court, Seattle, Washington

Nicholas Court brings an urbane, modernist sensibility to an older neighborhood in Seattle. Nine condominium units with distinct shapes and identities are fitted into three three-story buildings on a double lot.

One Ford Road, Newport Beach, California

The emphasis of this upscale master-planned community of 370 houses is on community and neighborhood. Small lots are offset by the project's substantial investment in community facilities and common open space.

Playa Vista, Los Angeles, California

After a 20-year battle for approvals, Playa Vista is taking shape, providing high-density housing on a large infill site in Los Angeles. The development balances a broad mix of uses in a pedestrian-oriented environment.

Ravenna Cottages, Seattle, Washington

A model for leveraging low square footage provides privacy, community appeal, and environmental responsibility. Nine units fit neatly on a lot designated for two single-family houses in a traditional single-family neighborhood.

Rivermark, Santa Clara, California

The collaboration of three large production homebuilders resulted in Rivermark. The development incorporates a full array of housing types, from rental apartments to for-sale townhouses to high-density detached homes.

Rollins Square, Boston, Massachusetts

Creative financing and a public/private partnership resulted in this innovative mixed-income urban development. With 147 condominium units, 37 rental apartments, and 6,000 square feet (560 square meters) of ground-floor retail space, Rollins Square provides affordable housing in a rapidly gentrifying urban neighborhood.

Sailhouse, Corona del Mar, California

This pedestrian-oriented infill development of 89 units features a network of wooden walkways with no walls or gates, encouraging pedestrian traffic out of the development and into the surrounding neighborhoods.

Stapleton, Denver, Colorado

Currently the largest infill development project in the United States, Stapleton is a mixed-use master-planned community on the former site of Stapleton International Airport in Denver, Colorado. The development will include 12,000 homes of all types and eventually house more than 30,000 residents and 35,000 workers..

Britannia Mills
Manchester, United Kingdom

Urban Splash Chair Tom Bloxham had a vision: that a former factory in a depressed suburb of Manchester could become a sophisticated residential scheme. He paid for the Britannia Mills development using privately raised funding and his own cash. Work on Britannia Mills, in the Castlefield/Hulme area of Manchester, started in 1996. In those days, Urban Splash was a three-year-old development company incorporating its own architecture department and its own construction team. Contractors working on Britannia Mills were usually subcontractors closely managed from within Urban Splash.

The Site
The history of Britannia Mills, formerly the English Abrasives sandpaper factory, goes back to the 1830s, when it was beginning to become a collection of wharves and timber mills associated with the Bridgewater Canal, which runs along one side of it. Then came the slump in U.K. manufacturing industries in the 1970s and 1980s. By 1996, the site had been vacant for more than five years.

When Urban Splash took it on, the site consisted of vandalized mid-19th century brick-vaulted warehouses with big timber windows and mid-20th century warehouses with steel frames and timber floors. Other buildings from the 1950s had been put up on the site of World War II bomb damage.

"Nobody wanted the site," says Simon Marsh, then an Urban Splash architect. "Although it is only a 15-minute walk from the city center along the canal towpath, it was cut off from the city center. It was in Hulme, a depressed suburb. When Tom Bloxham purchased the long lease-hold, everyone thought he was mad."

The Plan
Urban Splash started work on the project in October 1996. It originally planned to build 85 apartments. It applied for grant aid in April 1997 and was given a decision within a week, but the grant available was too small for that size scheme. The architecture department then bumped up the number of apartments to a more profitable 125.

Hulme was such a depressed area that English Partnerships, the U.K.'s national regeneration agency, agreed to fund about a third of the building costs of the scheme. English Partnerships is a key delivery agency for urban renaissance and the government's new sustainable communities agenda. It helps depressed local communities through initiatives such as Urban Regeneration Companies and the National Coalfields Programme; it works together with partners such as the Housing Corporation to relieve housing market pressure, increase affordability, and tackle housing abandonment; it develops and maintains a national brownfield strategy, including acquiring and redeveloping public and private sector brownfields; and it creates forums for sharing expertise in regeneration and development—particularly good urban design—to inspire new approaches and a better way of life. It has its own sites, and it works with others in the private sector.

Britannia Mills now comprises the six original mill buildings typical of those built from the mid-1800s and located on the edge of the Bridgewater Canal. Inside, Urban Splash created a complex of 125 for-sale loft-style apartments, with the landscaped surroundings designed to complement the industrial setting. The project also incorporates parking.

At the time, it was a unique development for Manchester. Three-quarters of the flats include mezzanine areas. In an early stage of design, Urban Splash agreed to retain the original structures despite their poor condition and to apply to demolish several single-story factory buildings. A series of hard landscaped gardens surround the car parking.

Typical of their age and size, the retained mill buildings at Britannia have the natural light, high ceilings, cast-iron columns, and timber floors that lend themselves to the creation of airy, open-plan spaces. The sturdiness of the existing structures has allowed for the insertion of new gallery or mezzanine floors to most apartments, the construction of additional floors that allow views of the city, and the creation of a new "wing roof" overhanging the building-covered courtyard to allow light into the rear of the apartments.

Planning
Urban Splash went to the local authority for planning approval in April 1997. That part of Hulme is not residential, and only one objection was raised, from the site's owner, a property speculator. (The "owner" is actually a freeholder with a 999-year lease on the property, common in the U.K.) Urban Splash was able to silence the objection by buying the freehold for a sum reflecting a low yield but still an insignificant portion of the cost of construction.

Despite Bloxham's eagerness to deliver urban regeneration, he did not have a completely easy ride. Planners wanted more access for local people to the canal. Yet Bloxham realized that to appeal to his security-conscious buying public in the unproven area of Hulme, Britannia

Britannia Mills began in the 1830s as a factory. The six-building complex now houses 125 loft-style residential units.

The industrial character of the factory makes it appealing to young loft buyers.

New exterior stairs lead to residences. Their style plays up the original character of the buildings.

Mills needed to be a gated development. "Closed-circuit TV was necessary," says Marsh. "Each apartment has videophones, but security is not overwhelming."

Planning policy required all new developments along the Bridgewater Canal to provide access for the disabled to the towpath; further conditions on access onto and around the site were met following further consultation with the Planning Authority and Manchester Ship Canal. The planners agreed to a new ramp providing access to the canal-side towpath from the street but behind a gabion wall with basalt infill. This solution blocked the view of the canal from the ground-floor apartments, but by this time, Bloxham knew he was developing low-budget warehouse-style living space, not apartments that would attract a premium for waterfront access.

The main concerns regarding the retained buildings were the replacement of windows and the rebuilding and cleaning of the brickwork. Each of the six remaining mill buildings was of a different time period and construction type, so they were treated accordingly with replacement windows in metal and timber to suit both sight lines and acoustic specifications. A railway runs nearby; thus, the flats needed an air supply that did not require opening windows and hearing the trains go past.

Liaison with the Planning Authority was carried out at an early stage because of the proposals to reintroduce residential development to this area for the first time in years. "On the whole, the planners were very encouraging," says Marsh.

The site is located in the Castlefield Conservation Area; it contains many prime examples of structurally innovative mill buildings from the 19th century. A comprehensive photographic record was taken of the existing buildings before demolition of redundant structures. It was also used to enable the rebuilding of elements such as the intricate brickwork parapet wall to the Emery Warehouse. In July 1997, the Manchester City Council granted Urban Splash planning permission for the project.

Construction

After obtaining approvals, Urban Splash demolished the one-story buildings and a 19th-century office building to make parking for 80 cars and open space. It kept some buildings Marsh admits it should have demolished. The old boiler works cost more to refurbish than it produced in sales, but that building makes a good centerpiece for the scheme.

Following demolition, six buildings remained on the site, and Urban Splash's architectural team split into two teams to design the first and second phases. They were to complete the second phase in July 2000.

Major work was carried out in the two main warehouses. Timber floors were replaced with a composite flooring system to upgrade acoustic performance without propping up the remaining structure. Additionally, the existing steel lintels were deteriorating and required extensive refurbishment by exposing them from within the brickwork on all facades of the Emery Warehouse.

An interior courtyard provides private open space for residents.

The parapet wall had to be reconstructed and a new roof structure built.

Among the more challenging aspects of the work was the Sand Building. It had a rotten floor and no roof, so Urban Splash rebuilt it from the bottom up. "We could have pushed the planners to allow us to knock the whole thing down and start again," says Marsh. In retrospect, it might have been more profitable to do just that.

"Wherever we did anything new to the old buildings, we consciously tried to make it look new. When we added a new window, for example, we made it a different style from the existing windows because the whole site has been developed over 150 years and nobody before us cared what any of the buildings looked like in relation to any of the other buildings."

The initial work consisted of foundations, substructure, and brickwork, followed by floors, partitions, and internal fitouts for Phases I and II. The design includes a mix of original brick vaulting and new timber floors. Urban Splash reused old timber from the floors to make the gallery floors in the apartments. In one building, it installed an enclosed light well, which provides a public atrium. In the canal inlet, landscape gardeners put in a basic marsh garden, which allows nesting sites for local swans.

The materials use reclaimed York stone and cobblestones from the site and are supplemented with new Pennant stone, cast concrete paving, timber decking, and gravel. The inset lighting leads people around the pathways located away from vehicular routes. The canal arm coming into the development from the main Bridgewater Canal gives a strong attractive boundary to the site. It requires extensive management, bringing no obvious return but useful as a marketing tool.

The materials used for all the new elements in the buildings themselves are strong industrial-grade materials used innovatively and cost-effectively. One detail in particular is the gallery deck level, which is formed from reclaimed timber. This structural flooring also becomes the timber floor finish and ceiling finish to the underside, allowing all new support steelwork to be on view. The design approach has been taken through all the new entrance areas, forming a sequence of circulation routes into individual buildings. A new vertical circulation core has been inserted between the two largest mills. Designed to create a gap between them, it features a suspended steel and timber staircase hung in the space.

The one new building on the site uses high-quality modern materials, which complement the existing architecture and form a clear marker for the new pedestrian entrance to the site. The lower floors reflect the solidity of the existing mills, juxtaposing large load-bearing brick openings with lighter composite aluminium and timber windows with timber strip infills. Above the existing roof level, this arrangement develops into a lightweight glazed structure to take advantage of spectacular views over the city.

New load-bearing walls were constructed in the existing structure of the Sand Warehouse, allowing an additional floor to be added at roof level, where a terne-coated stainless steel barrel-vaulted roof is supported on a lightweight steel frame enclosed by fully opening concertina-glazed doors.

Having an in-house architectural team made this job easier. Instead of sticking to an exact tender plan, Urban Splash architects were able to react quicker when problems cropped up. Urban Splash kept two architects on site in the builders' hut at all times during working hours for just this situation. For example, just before starting work on the former Emery Building, Urban Splash changed the design plan to include a full-height atrium through the building.

Marketing

Sales at Britannia Mills began early in the development process; the project sold entirely based on plans eight months before completion. The pioneering purchasers who bought early have seen a return of as much as 50 percent on their investment. Most important, however, residents find it a pleasant place to live, with well-designed spaces and surroundings, easy access to the city, and value for money.

A temporary wall down the middle of the site separated the two phases. Practical completion of the 35 apartments in Phase I came in October 1998. Even by the time the apartments came to market, Urban Splash sales and marketing director Fiona Woodward confirms that there was little appetite to invest in property in a regeneration area. Most buyers chose Britannia Mills because they liked the scheme and wanted to live in it themselves. Today, the reverse is true. "At the time, people were only beginning to see that investing in property was a prudent thing to do," she says.

Even without investors, all those apartments and the other 90 in Phase II had sold by the middle of 1999, a year before the whole project was topped out. "People were lining up in October 1998 to reserve space," says Marsh. "The apartments were cheap for Manchester. Those buyers have easily doubled their investment in the three or four years they've been there."

The land and construction costs came to £80 per square foot (£860 per square meter),[1] "taking into account that it was a difficult site and we never knew the condition of each building until we got into it," explains Marsh, "against a sale price of around £125 per square foot (£1,345 per square meter). Six years later, this real estate is now selling for at least £200 per square foot (£2,152 per square meter)."

The properties sold on 999-year leases with no incentives. The 999-year lease makes it easier for interested parties to enforce the terms of a lease against a leaseholder than if the properties had been sold on freehold. Urban Splash offered no buyer incentives. Service charge at the time was £1 per square foot (£10.80 per square meter) but has since risen to around £1.20 per square foot (£12.90 per square meter).

The scheme included 80 parking spaces, which were sold at £12,000 for a covered space and £9,500 for an external space. The area lacks good public transport. Local bus service is available, but the nearest tram stop is half a mile (0.8 kilometer) away. Nevertheless, buyers do not seem to mind.

Britannia Mills has won numerous awards, including the 2002 Civic Trust Award, the 2001 RIBA (Royal Institute of British Architects) Award for Architecture, and the 2001 Best Restoration and Conversion Commendation from the National Homebuilder Awards.

Experience Gained

Britannia Mills was the start of a trend. It was the first of the warehouses converted by a variety of developers in an area called Britannia Basin. The area is not fully built out. Many local warehouses continue as sweatshops, but the ownership of most is for sale—at too high a price to tempt most developers.

Overhead walkways are made of rustic wood planks with industrial metal railings and beams.

Interiors feature original wood plank ceilings and rough brick walls balanced with sleek modern materials.

"The design was the first of its kind," says Woodward. "It was the start of Manchester's warehouse-to-loft conversion boom and . . . at the start of the city-center regeneration boom."

Urban Splash owns four more development sites in Britannia Basin and plans a phased development of them. It is looking at a greater mix of uses. Marsh says he would consider a convenience store but says he does not regret not including one in Britannia Mills, as it would have been hard to sell.

The success of Britannia Mills has encouraged other developers to bring many surrounding buildings back into use. Now a self-financing development company, Urban Splash is currently developing two other sites along the Bridgewater Canal toward the city center, which will provide a total of 370 new homes for this previously forgotten area.

Timber Wharf, the winner of a RIBA-sponsored competition, is the first innovative new construction in the city center. More conversion and new construction projects incorporating live/work units are about to begin, which will add to the creation of this new community and allow for the establishment of other uses.

Marsh would not design the buildings at Britannia Mills differently if he were doing it today. He says, however, that he would have better initial surveys done of the buildings. Because they are old, they produced some surprises that slowed the development process.

Note

1. As of August 2004, £1 equaled $1.82.

Site plan.

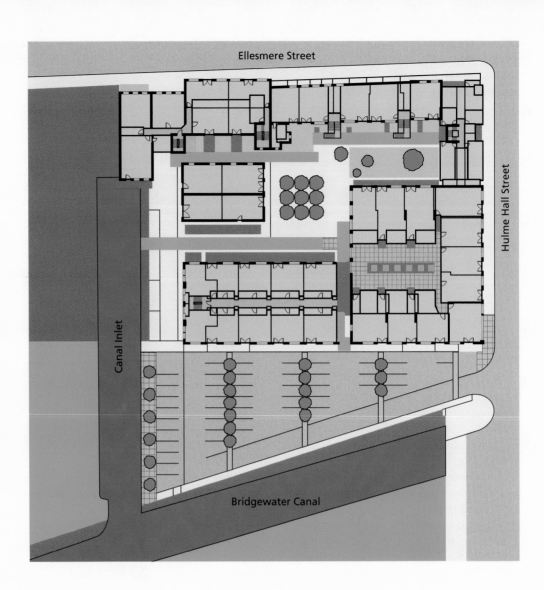

Ellesmere Street

Hulme Hall Street

Canal Inlet

Bridgewater Canal

Project Data: Britannia Mills

Land Use and Building Information

Site Area	0.5 acres (0.2 hectare)
Total Dwelling Units	125
Gross Density	250 units per acre (23 per hectare)
Average Net Density	500 units per acre (1,235 per hectare)

Land Use Plan

	Acres/ Hectare	Percent of Site
Attached Residential	0.35/0.1	70%
Common Open Space	0.15/0.06	30
Total	0.5/0.2	100%

Residential Unit Information

Unit Type	Unit Size (Square Feet/ Square Meters)	Number of Units	Sale Prices (Square Foot/ Square Meter)
2-Bedroom/1-Bath	2,000/185	125	£125/£1,345

Development Cost Information

Construction Cost	£80 per square foot (£860 per square meter)[1]

Developer

Urban Splash
Timber Wharf, 16–22 Worsley Street
Castlefield, Manchester M15 4LD
United Kingdom
+44 161 839 2999
www.urbansplash.co.uk

Site Planner and Architect

Urban Splash Architects (now Arkheion)
Unit 204, Tea Factory
82 Wood Street
Liverpool L1 4DQ
United Kingdom
+44 151 706 0932
www.liverpoolarchitecture.com

Development Schedule

1996	Site purchased, plan submitted
1997	Planning and grant applications submitted
1997	Approvals granted, demolition begun
1998	Main management contract started, model opened
1999	Phase I completed, sales completed
2000	Phase II completed

Note
[1] Grant supported.

Cherry Hill Village

Wayne County, Michigan

Cherry Hill Village is located in Canton Township, 15 miles (24 kilometers) east of Ann Arbor and 30 miles (48 kilometers) west of Detroit. The neotraditional community pays homage to the area's history, which dates to the early 1800s. The feel of a small town captured in the award-winning traditional neighborhood development (TND) resulted from the efforts of Biltmore Properties Corporation, an experienced Michigan family-owned residential developer; Looney Ricks Kiss (LRK), a nationally recognized architect; and Canton Township trustees, planners, and residents. When complete, the 338-acre (137-hectare) traditional neighborhood development will contain 1,291 housing units—a mix of condominiums, townhouses, and single-family homes interspersed with parks and walking trails. Residents will be within walking distance of the village square—the site of restaurants, shops, and a performing arts center. The master plan also includes municipal offices, a fire station, an elementary school, a daycare center, and a grocery store.

The Site and Its History

One of the fastest-growing communities in southeast Michigan, Canton Township's burgeoning population of 83,000 is fueling residential and retail development in areas once occupied by farmland. Although much of the growth during the 1980s and 1990s consisted of large-lot subdivisions, residents of Cherry Hill had a different vision for their township—retaining the historic village's sense of community and place. Established in 1834, the village's heritage is visible in several historic structures, including an inn constructed in 1860, a schoolhouse built in 1876, and a Methodist Church dating back to 1882.

When Biltmore Properties approached Canton Township in 1998 with the idea for developing Cherry Hill into a TND, its timing could not have been better. The township was in the middle of revising its master plan and assessing development options for Cherry Hill. The proposed TND captured the land use and neighborhood elements the community wanted to promote: a mix of housing types and prices, preservation of the area's cultural history and sense of place, and creation of a downtown corridor within walking distance of residences.

Although the township was very interested in the concept, it did have some reservations. Biltmore had more than 75 years of experience developing subdivisions, but residents wondered whether that experience could be translated into creation of a successful TND. During the planning and design stages, Biltmore was able to allay

the concerns by forming a true public/private partnership with the community. Biltmore also teamed with LRK, which had extensive experience with TNDs, including Harbor Town in Memphis, Tennessee, one of the first TNDs in the United States.

Development Process and Design

In 1998, Biltmore Properties and the township convened a five-day charrette to begin defining the concept plan for Cherry Hill Village and the surrounding area in keeping with Canton Township's master plan. During the meetings, the developer, township trustees, planning officials, and community residents worked with LRK to put the community's vision on paper. In creating the plan, participants walked the site, reviewed results of the community visual preference survey, and communicated their ideas of how the community should look. The interactive process allowed both the developers and community members to voice concerns and create a workable community plan.

Results of the visual preference surveys proved instructive for the working group. The survey, which was implemented through computer kiosks located at several civic and residential locations throughout Canton and at area home shows, captured consumers' reactions to factors such as housing type, design, and scale, and commercial design and integration with residential uses. Overwhelmingly, residents and nonresidents confirmed that a market exists for traditional neighborhood design by indicating a preference for walkable, urban-scale neighborhoods.

These elements were incorporated into Cherry Hill Village, and the project was approved as a planned unit development by the township. The plan, which received an outstanding project award from the Michigan Society of Planning in 2000, incorporates commercial and residential uses connected by sidewalks and narrow streets and small and large parks integrated throughout the neighborhood. Formerly a no-growth area, an overlay zone was created that allows for an average density of four units per acre (10 per hectare). Like many small towns, density is higher—six units per acre (15 per hectare)—closer to the village square.

To create a traditional village center, the community plan calls for commercial and cultural uses along Cherry Hill Road. Current residential development is located on the south side of Cherry Hill Road. The overall plan incorporates an apartment complex and additional single-family houses and townhouses on the north side of the

With its traditional architecture and site plan, Cherry Hill Village evokes a traditional midwestern small town.

A neighborhood square offers usable open space and views for residential units.

village square. Biltmore started construction of the 600-unit apartment complex (Uptown) at the end of 2003. Uptown flanks the Plymouth/Canton Performing Arts Center, which is sited on the northeast corner of the village square. The township recently started construction of the arts center, which is expected to open in October 2004.

Creating a distinctive, welcoming sense of place was important to all those involved in the development. To achieve a pleasing and diverse streetscape, housing types are dispersed throughout the development. The manor homes (condominiums) and townhouses are sited next to both the smaller cottage homes (1,100 to 3,000 square feet [102 to 280 square meters]) and the larger estate homes (3,000+ square feet [280+ square meters]). To maintain the human scale and street aesthetics, homes have tight setbacks and are sited along connecting narrow streets lined with sidewalks. The condominiums, townhouses, and cottage homes come with alley-loaded

garages, and efforts are made to minimize the impact of front-loaded garages.

At the completion of the charrette, support for Cherry Hill Village was clear, and the township very quickly approved the project. Construction started in 2000, and the first homes were completed in 2001. Biltmore chose initially to work with three builders—Curtis Building Company, Ivanhoe-Huntley Homes, and Biltmore Building Company—to implement the plan. A fourth builder, Mill Creek, was added later. To encourage architectural diversity, each builder worked with a different architect, and they were assigned various lot sizes at locations throughout the development.

In keeping with its goal of variety in design, Biltmore chose not to require a specific type of architectural style; instead, it developed a pattern book that includes examples of appropriate types of architecture to achieve the appropriate scale and feel. An architectural review board, which includes the village architect (LRK), reviews

Houses reflect traditional American architectural styles. White picket fences appear throughout the community.

Public spaces include natural wooded areas and more formal squares.

and approves plans. The attention to design detail, housing type, and location of houses has resulted in a colorful palette of homes, with no two streets alike.

Financing, Marketing, and Operations
Site acquisition, development, and construction of Cherry Hill were financed through private loans and $7 million in equity. Biltmore raised $3 million in private equity from its partners and $4 million through syndication. Comerica Bank, headquartered in Detroit, served as the primary lender, providing acquisition loans and residential and commercial construction loans for the project.

Before the much-anticipated opening, people began calling about purchasing lots. A lottery held in January 2001 provided interested buyers an option to purchase one of the first homes. Construction of Phase I was completed in 2001. Construction of Phase II started in January 2003, and completion is slated for 2014.

Regular articles in the local press and word of mouth have attracted a steady stream of potential buyers. Nevertheless, Biltmore and the homebuilders are refining the home designs and the development plan for the remaining phases based on market conditions. Although absorption ranges from 100 to 150 units per year, Biltmore would like to reach 200 units per year. Because the large estate homes are selling slowly, Biltmore is reconfiguring the lot sizes in Phase IV by replacing some estate homes with cottage and village homes. More townhouses are also being added. As approved by the township, this reconfiguration will increase the density to six units per acre (15 per hectare) and help bring more of the popular cottage units online.

Experience Gained
The project would not have been possible without community input and support. Working closely with the township trustees and the planning commission helped facilitate better understanding between the developer and the community so that the Cherry Hill Village plan matched the community's vision.

Although Biltmore had years of experience developing subdivisions, Cherry Hill was its first TND. The developer suggests that imparting the sense of place that is the hallmark of TNDs requires patience and a different mind-set. Connecting with an architectural firm that had experience developing a TND and working with the community was key.

One of the more controversial elements of a TND is the dispersion of housing types throughout the project. At Cherry Hill Village, extra efforts were made to disperse housing types to maintain a visually appealing development. Each builder was assigned various lot types in each phase. Although this approach gives the village a welcoming feeling, it has made coordinating unit construction difficult. In the future, the developer would consider some clustering of lots by each builder.

Cherry Hill Village includes a mix of housing types, parks, and a town center.

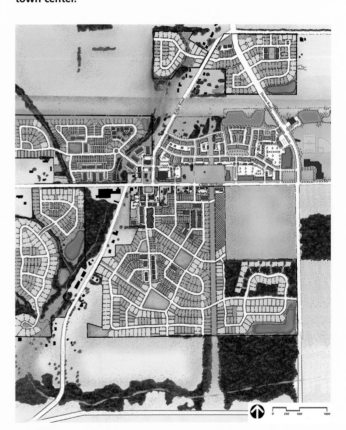

Site plan.

Project Data: Cherry Hill Village

Land Use and Building Information

Site Area	338 acres (137 hectares)
Total Dwelling Units Planned	1,291
Gross Density	4 units per acre (10 per hectare)

Land Use Plan

	Acres/Hectares	Percent of Site
Detached Residential	151.0/61	44.6%
Attached Residential	22.6/9	6.7
Roads	78.6/32	23.2
Common Open Space	78.8/32	23.2
Commercial	2.9/1	0.8
Other	4.9/2	1.4
Total	338.8/137	100.0%

Development Cost Information

Site Costs

Site acquisition	$17,600,000
Site improvement	28,400,000
Total Development Cost Expected at Buildout	$46,000,000

Developer

Biltmore Properties Corporation
2025 West Long Lake Road
Troy, Michigan 48098
248-641-3900
www.biltmore-homes.com

Site Planner/Architect

Looney Ricks Kiss
19 Vandeventer Avenue
Princeton, New Jersey 08542
609-683-3600
www.lrk.com

Residential Unit Information

Unit Type	Lot Size (Square Feet/ Square Meters)	Unit Size (Square Feet/ Square Meters)	Total Units/ Units Sold	Initial Price Range
Estate Lot	7,500–9,000/697–836	3,000+/279+	313/25	$450,000–800,000
Village Lot	5,500/511	2,000–4,000/186–372	369/56	$375,000–600,000
Cottage Lot	4,000/372	1,100–3,000/102–279	249/62	$275,000–400,000
Manor Unit	N/A	1,300–2,200/121–204	248/30	$225,000–300,000
Townhouse	N/A	1,100–2,000/102–186	112/38	$170,000–220,000
Total			1,291/211	

Architects

Dominick Tringali Associates
1668 Telegraph Road
Bloomfield Hills, Michigan 48302
248-335-8888

Barton & Associates
700 East Main Street
Norristown, Pennsylvania 19401
610-930-2800
www.bartonpartners.com

Peter Brown
2136 Kipling
Houston, Texas 77098
713-520-6606

Shapiro and Company Architects
4646 Poplar
Memphis, Tennessee 38117
901-685-9001

Homebuilders

Curtis Building Company
2992 Northwestern Highway
Farmington Hills, Michigan 48334
248-737-3380
www.curtisbuilding.com

Ivanhoe-Huntley Homes, Inc.
7001 Orchard Lake Road
West Bloomfield, Michigan 48332
248-851-9951
www.ivanhoehuntley.com

Millcreek Building Company
70 West Long Lake Road
Troy, Michigan 48098
248-828-7200

Biltmore Building Company
2025 West Long Lake Road
Troy, Michigan 48098
248-641-3900

Development Schedule

1998	Planning started
1999	Site purchased
2000	Construction started
2001	Sales started
2001	First closing
2014	Estimated completion

The Dakota and Essex on the Park
St. Paul, Minnesota

The Dakota and Essex on the Park is a 75-unit urban townhouse and condominium project located on an infill site in St. Paul, Minnesota. Built in two phases, it is the catalyst for the emerging North Quadrant neighborhood on the northeastern fringe of downtown. The Essex, built first, has 38 units, the Dakota 37. Each comprises four-story buildings, with two-story townhouses and two stories of flats above.

The Dakota and Essex is part of a larger, two-phase development that includes 236 apartment units, a one-acre (0.4-hectare) public park called Wacouta Commons, and 10,000 square feet (930 square meters) of retail space. The success of the Dakota and Essex has spurred other developments in the North Quadrant.

The Site and History
The North Quadrant was the location of St. Paul's first mansions from 1850 to 1880, as the city established itself economically. The mansions gave way to primarily four- to six-story brick warehouses as railroads impacted industrial development from the 1880s to the 1920s. The third phase of development in the neighborhood was the demolition of a vast majority of the warehouses to make room for surface parking for the downtown office core.

The fourth phase of development is the reestablishment of a residential neighborhood, complete with a variety of uses: owner-occupied and rental housing, retail space, office buildings, and hotels. As the catalyst for development in the North Quadrant, the Dakota and Essex on the Park is the first project to be constructed in the fourth generation of development in the neighborhood.

Before development, the site was primarily used for parking, and, in fact, no buildings were removed for the construction of the Dakota and Essex. An automobile service station was removed to make way for Wacouta Commons, which serves as a focal point and neighborhood amenity for area residents.

The North Quadrant presented a good opportunity for the redevelopment of a residential neighborhood. It is nestled between the office core of downtown St. Paul and I-94, adjacent to the historic Lowertown neighborhood and less than one mile (1.6 kilometers) from the Mississippi River.

Development Process
The developers, the Lander Group and Sherman Associates, both of Minneapolis, formed a team for the Dakota

and Essex project; they have collaborated on other projects since. The Lander Group has been developing high-quality residential and commercial buildings, mostly for-sale housing on urban infill sites, since the 1980s. Sherman Associates has developed and rehabilitated more than 3,500 single-family and multifamily housing units, from tax-credit apartments to luxury homes, since 1978. For collaborations, they are known as Lander Sherman Urban Development.

In the late 1990s, the city of St. Paul hired Ken Greenberg, who was at the time with Urban Strategies of Toronto, to create a master plan for the North Quadrant as part of other work in downtown St. Paul. Greenberg worked closely with city staff and community leaders to create the plan, which has guided neighborhood development for a variety of uses, including retail buildings, hotels, and as many as 1,000 units of housing. The North Quadrant Precinct Plan, which served as the general use plan, was competed in January 2000; it was followed by the North Quadrant Urban Village Design Guidelines, which offered specific guidelines for buildings, streets, and public spaces, in June 2000.

Lander Sherman knew the city had the support of the neighborhood and other stakeholders, and with a master plan in place, it was allowed to develop the first two phases of development in the North Quadrant. The city chose Lander Sherman for its combined reputation and its willingness to be involved with the city and community during the planning process. Lander Sherman understood the city's desire to create a vibrant neighborhood in the North Quadrant.

The city of St. Paul understands that quality design and planning can attract development and, partly because of competition for investment from Minneapolis, in recent years has pursued quality development through strong public/private partnerships. To this end, the St. Paul Riverfront Corporation, a private nonprofit organization providing leadership for St. Paul's redevelopment efforts, was created in 1994 as an offshoot of previous organizations. Its in-house Design Center, created in 1997, acts as a public face for potential investors, providing a link between the city of St. Paul's Planning and Economic Department and the developer.

The Design Center, as "keeper of the plan," worked closely with Lander Sherman to bring the Dakota and Essex to fruition, taking a proactive approach to solv-ing problems and issues that arose during the process. Michael Lander, president of the Lander Group, points out that the development process can be likened to that

The Dakota and Essex on the Park comprises two phases of a larger urban infill development of townhouses and condominiums.

of large master-planned communities, except that in this case the master developer was a municipal body, the city of St. Paul.

Financing

Financing was a challenge for the Dakota and Essex project, because much of it was tied to the Sibley Park and Court Apartments, which contain both market-rate and affordable apartments as well as 10,000 square feet (930 square meters) of retail space. The mixed uses were a challenge, requiring multiple funding sources.

Another specific obstacle to acquiring conventional financing for the Dakota and Essex was that downtown St. Paul contained no recent comparable for-sale multifamily housing developments. As a result, the project was considered riskier than more conventional development such as single-family housing.

When separated from the apartment buildings, the Dakota and Essex each received conventional financing to cover approximately two-thirds of the project, with the remainder coming from developer equity, grants, land loans, and tax-increment financing.

Approvals

The approval process was relatively easy for the developer, mainly because the North Quadrant Precinct Plan was already in place. Thus, the approval process essentially occurred during the planning phase, saving the developer time in front of the zoning commission.

Planning and Design

It was important to the city of St. Paul and Lander Sherman that the design of the buildings fit well with the overall plan for the neighborhood. Lander Sherman convened regular meetings of the developer, architect, engineers, city staff, and neighborhood group to receive input on the project. They also hired two firms, Close Associates and Paul Madson & Associates, both of Minneapolis and together known as the Town Planning Collaborative, to create the specific site plan, which merged the more general neighborhood plan created by Ken Greenberg into the details of the Dakota and Essex buildings. Paul Madson & Associates also was the architect of the Dakota and Essex; it ensured the focus of the buildings was on fitting into the neighborhood. This approach fits the Lander Group's philosophy of context-sensitive design, where buildings are well proportioned with relation to their surroundings and use quality materials.

The Dakota and Essex fully embraces the principles of new urbanism, with buildings designed to emulate the vernacular of the remaining warehouse buildings in the area. For example, the Dakota and Essex buildings are four stories, incorporate brick in their exteriors, and are built up to the public sidewalks rather than being set back. No off-street surface parking is available in the development. The orientation of the buildings is toward the street and the public realm. The courtyard, for example, is located on the Essex site and is privately owned, but public

The buildings are designed
to fit into the neighborhood.
Buildings echo the nearby warehouses in style and materials.

Residents of the Essex and
adjacent apartments share
a courtyard.

Wacouta Commons is a
one-acre (0.4-hectare) park
that provides open space
for residents.

access is allowed. Balconies were installed on the rear of the buildings, with only French, ornamental balconies (not for human occupancy) on the front of buildings.

Although building exteriors are traditional, the interiors of the units feature modern floor plans and include the amenities that buyers of a $400,000 multifamily unit would expect in a single-family home. Units include open floor plans, with kitchens and living rooms flowing into each other to maximize the use of space, modern wiring for cable television and high-speed Internet service, large master suites, and luxurious bathrooms. Kitchens offer optional stainless steel appliances, a selection of designer cabinetry, and high-pressure laminate countertops; bathrooms have ceramic tile flooring, soaking tubs, and separate showers.

Construction

With groundbreaking in 2000, the Essex on the Park saw its first closing in December 2001; it was completed in March 2002. It was part of the first phase of the development, sharing a block with the Sibley Park Apartments, a 114-unit apartment building containing 10,000 square feet (930 square meters) of ground-level retail space, also completed in 2002. Units on the north side of Essex on the Park face Wacouta Commons, and units on the south side of the building face a courtyard shared with Sibley Park Apartments.

The Dakota on the Park was completed in March 2003.

Marketing/Buyers

At the time of initial marketing in summer 2000, the urban loft and condominium market was new enough in the Twin Cities that savvy marketing firms had not yet established a presence. As a result, Lander Sherman marketed the project itself. A sales trailer with marketing materials was set up on the site. A Web site was also created that includes price lists and detailed floor plans.

The development team held a series of promotional events, including the groundbreaking, to create exposure for an area of the city that had no other housing to speak of. Marketing emphasized a centralized location within walking distance of downtown St. Paul employment, multimodal transportation access, proximity to the charming Lowertown neighborhood, and access to the nearby Mississippi River.

Initial demand came from buyers who simply wanted to live downtown, and 15 units sold shortly after the sales trailer opened. Overall, sales were healthy, and units sold at an average rate of more than two per month. Units priced under $200,000 sold the fastest, but townhouse units priced as high as $429,000 also sold well. Buyers slightly favored units that face the park, as opposed to those that face the courtyard, despite those units' being more expensive and lacking usable balconies.

An especially popular unit is one that is relatively small (1,050 square feet [98 square meters]), in which the living room stretches across the width of the unit and the single bedroom has a sliding door. The wide living room maximizes natural light, and the sliding door, when open,

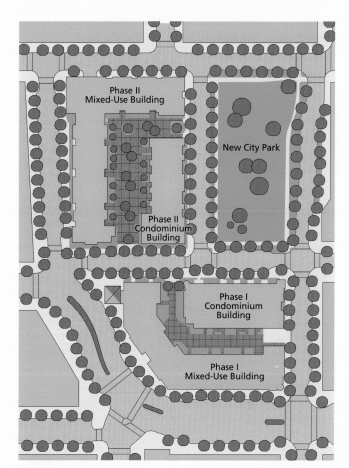

Site plan.

provides additional light to the bedroom, which has no windows. Two-story townhouse units, although more expensive, have also been popular.

Experience Gained

A thoughtful master plan with input from stakeholders is an important first step in development. The North Quadrant Precinct Plan and the guidelines led to a building design that celebrates the street and fits into the context of the neighborhood.

A quality public/private relationship is essential to move the process along. A proactive approach by the public sector in particular can save time and headaches. The St. Paul Riverfront Corporation's Design Center acted as the keeper of the master plan, keeping an eye toward the future while dealing with the issues of the present.

The economic diversity of the Dakota and Essex with the more affordable Sibley Park and Court Apartments has been an important aspect of the overall project, because Lander Sherman and the city agreed that mixed-income housing was an essential part of urban life. They never intended to wall off the expensive for-sale units from the tax-credit rental units.

An important consideration is that the project consists of only 75 units, out of potentially 1,000 units planned for the neighborhood. Neighborhood building is very incremental.

Project Data: The Dakota and Essex on the Park

Land Use and Building Information

Site Area	2.2 acres (0.9 hectare)
Total Dwelling Units	75
Gross Density	35 units per acre (86 per hectare)
Average Net Density	54 units per acre (133 per hectare)

Land Use Plan

	Acres/ Hectares	Percent of Site
Attached Residential	1.4/0.6	64%
Common Open Space[1]	0.8/0.3	36
Total	2.2/0.9	100%

Residential Unit Information

Unit Type	Unit Size (Square Feet/ Square Meters)	Number of Units	Price Range
Townhouse	1,661–2,809/154–261	27	$259,000–429,000
Condominiums	895–1,904/83–177	48	$159,000–379,000

Development Cost Information

Essex on the Park

Site Acquisition Costs	$151,000

Hard Construction Costs

New construction	$5,837,600
General conditions	281,900
Contractor overhead	116,800
Contractor profit	116,800
Construction contingency	473,000
Subtotal	$6,826,100

Professional Fees

Architect—design	$200,000
Architect—supervision	36,000
Attorneys for owner	170,000
Survey, engineering	40,000
Appraisal, market feasibility	12,000
Environment studies	25,000
Subtotal	$483,000

Developer Fees

Developer overhead	$150,000
Developer profit	900,000
Subtotal	$1,050,000

Soft Costs

Hazard and liability insurance	$15,000
Real estate taxes	10,000
Cost certification/accounting	5,000
Broker fees and advertising	340,000
Marketing materials	110,000
Subtotal	$480,000

Construction Financing Costs

Construction interest	$450,000
Loan origination fee	65,000
Inspecting architect	4,000
Attorney for lender	10,000
Title and recording	15,000
Insurance costs	64,000
Subtotal	$608,000

Total Development Cost	**$9,598,100**

Sources of Funds

First mortgage loan	$6,485,000
Grant proceeds	900,000
Commissions and buyer deposits	848,000
Equity	539,000
Land loan	115,000
Deferred developer fee	900,000
Total	$9,787,000

Dakota on the Park

Site Acquisition costs

Land	$115,000
Site work	237,000
Interest on land note	9,500
Subtotal	$361,500

Hard Construction Costs

New construction	$5,247,900
General conditions	306,900
Contractor profit	116,200
Construction contingency	180,000
Subtotal	$5,851,000

Professional Fees

Architect—design	$135,500
Architect—supervision	28,000
Attorneys for owner	150,000
Survey, engineering	50,000
Appraisal, market feasibility	10,000
Environmental studies	40,000
Subtotal	$413,500

Note
[1] Shared courtyard with Sibley Park Apartments considered the common open space.

Developer Fees	
Developer overhead	$280,000
Developer profit	1,520,000
Subtotal	$1,800,000

Soft Costs	
Hazard and liability insurance	$35,000
Real estate taxes	15,000
Accounting	15,000
Broker fees and advertising	440,000
Marketing materials	250,000
Subtotal	$755,000

Construction Financing Fees	
Construction interest	$400,000
Loan origination fee	64,300
Inspecting architect	7,200
Attorney for lender	20,000
Title and recording	35,000
FNMA fee	10,000
FNMA interest	55,000
Contingency	32,300
Subtotal	$623,800

Reserves	
Decorating	$125,000
Subtotal	$125,000

Total Development Cost	$9,929,800

Sources of Funds	
First mortgage loan	$6,430,000
TIF bond proceeds	719,100
Commissions	440,000
Deferred developer fee	1,520,000
Deferred TIF note proceeds	179,800
HRA land loan	100,500
Equity	539,000
Total Sources of Funds	$9,928,400

Total Development Cost Expected at Buildout	$19,539,800

Developer

Lander Sherman Urban Development
3346 Hennepin Avenue South
Minneapolis, Minnesota 55408
612-825-4954
www.landergroup.com

Site Planner

Town Planning Collaborative
3346 Hennepin Avenue South
Minneapolis, Minnesota 55408
612-825-4954

Architect

Paul Madson & Associates, Ltd.
420 North Fifth Street
Minneapolis, Minnesota 55401
612-332-7026

Public Developer

City of St. Paul Department of Planning and Economic Development
25 West Fourth Street
St. Paul, Minnesota 55101
651-266-6616

Environmental Engineer

Braun Intertee
245 East Roselawn Avenue
St. Paul, Minnesota 55117
952-942-4802
www.brauncorp.com

Civil Engineer

Loucks Associates
7200 Hemlock Land
Suite 300
Minneapolis, Minnesota 55369
763-424-5505

Landscape Architect

Close Landscape Architecture
275 East Fourth Street
Suite 610
St. Paul, Minnesota 55101
651-222-5754

General Contractor

Kraus-Anderson Companies
525 South Eighth Street
Minneapolis, Minnesota 55404
612-332-7281

Development Schedule

10/1999, 9/2000	Site purchased
1/2000	Planning started
10/2000	Construction started
11/2000	Sales started
12/2001	First closing
2/2003	Project completed

Highland's Garden Village

Denver, Colorado

Highland's Garden Village is an urban infill project that combines a wide variety of residential types—rental housing for seniors, live/work units, co-housing, and other more conventional types—with a series of environmentally sensitive parks and gardens and other amenities. The project has garnered national attention for its preservation efforts and the site's numerous green features, including use of recycled materials.

A garden community three miles (4.8 kilometers) northwest of downtown Denver, Highland's Garden Village is located on a 27-acre (11-hectare) infill site. Originally the site of Elitch Gardens Amusement Park, the project features a number of housing types and 3.2 acres (1.3 hectares) of parks and gardens, reminiscent of the former amusement park. The project includes the connection of surrounding street grids and the addition of 82,400 square feet (7,660 square meters) of traditional main street retail uses and restaurants. Effective recycling and reuse programs have made Highland's Garden Village a national model for environmentally conscious development. The site uses wind to generate electricity for community buildings and relies on existing city water, sewer, and stormwater infrastructure surrounding the site.

The Site and Its History

Elitch Gardens Amusement Park opened in 1890, serving as an escape from what was then a seemingly remote, bustling downtown Denver. For more than a century, the amusement park offered the public entertainment in the form of carnival rides, live shows, wild animals, and botanical gardens. The Elitch Theater was one of America's longest-running summer showcases; it was where the first movies in Denver were shown and where stars such as Grace Kelly and Sarah Bernhardt appeared.

While Elitch Gardens Amusement Park stayed much the same over the years, Denver continued to grow as a metropolitan area, and housing was eventually developed around the park. In 1994, the amusement park shut down, leaving a gaping hole in what had become a working-class neighborhood. Chuck Perry, a local developer and restaurateur, decided to redevelop the former amusement park into a viable mixed-income community. Partnering with Jonathan Rose, a developer based in Katonah, New York, the Perry/Affordable Housing Development Corporation was formed and plans for the Highland's Garden Village developed.

Development Process and Design

Rose and Perry bought the Elitch Gardens Amusement Park in 1998 and soon developed a plan for the $50 million mixed-use project. Much of this plan came out of a community-based planning process in which the developers met more than 50 times with local residents and groups such as the West Highlands Neighborhood Association, the civic association for the neighborhood that surrounds the development.

Although the parties did not all agree about what should replace the amusement park, in the end the planning process was beneficial. One main point of contention was that the neighborhood wanted the new development to include housing for seniors. Perry and Rose eventually agreed, and the city of Denver awarded a density bonus for the project. The major obstacle faced during the planning process was the site's zoning regulations. The site was formerly zoned A-1, which allows only a few uses such as a prison or an amusement park.

After two years of negotiation, the area was rezoned as a planned unit development. In Colorado, a PUD provides developers with higher densities that can be changed quickly to respond to demographic conditions and fluctuating housing markets. Original plans for the development called for 30-foot (9-meter) or narrower streets. During the planning process, however, the city of Denver changed its requirement; new streets had to be 36 feet (11 meters) wide. Perry and Rose eventually compromised with the city, making streets 32 feet (10 meters) wide. With narrower streets, Highland's Garden Village exhibits a more intimate, human-scale character that promotes pedestrian activity, reduces vehicular traffic speeds, and also saved money on construction costs.

Dismantling much of the old amusement park, including the "Twister" roller coaster, was necessary, but Rose and Perry wanted to retain some aspects that would give the new project an identity and pay tribute to Elitch Gardens. The centerpieces of Highland's Garden Village are two historic structures from the old park: the century-old octagonal, two-story Elitch Theater; and the Elitch entrance gardens, featuring a 1926 carousel pavilion.

The gardens, carousel pavilion, and theater all have undergone major restorations; they play important roles in the community. The actual theater building is 5,890 square feet (550 square meters); a "fly building" attached to it houses backstage operations. Future development plans include demolishing this dysfunctional structure and replacing it with an updated 9,700-square-foot (900-

Highland's Garden Village includes a mix of product types: co-housing (left), rental apartments (rear), and townhouses (right). The community gardens are reminiscent of the gardens that graced the Elitch Gardens Amusement Park that once stood at this site.

square-meter) fly house. A variety of performing arts groups use the Elitch Theater, and the gardens serve as attractive open space. The floor of the former carousel features a meditative walking labyrinth, designed to the "golden mean" ratio of 1.68:1, which has been used in architecture since classical times to strike a harmonic balance between the constructed and the living worlds. The carousel itself, along with most of the other rides from Elitch's, were moved in 1995 when the owners relocated closer to downtown Denver in the Platte River Valley.

The residential units vary in design and price, making Highland's Garden Village a socioeconomically diverse community. The master plan, designed by Calthorpe Associates, strives to blend the new homes and buildings with the existing older neighborhood that surrounds the amusement park site. The 52 single-family houses have all been sold; they each contain two to four bedrooms and one to two and one-half bathrooms. Prices ranged from $211,996 to $429,666. Homes, built in craftsman and Denver Square styles with dormer windows and embellished trim details, face outward toward existing homes. The houses have front porches and alley-loaded garages, with a few of the residences having wraparound porches. Twenty of the homes have carriage houses built above the garage that can be used as a home office or living quarters for family members or rented out to help cover mortgage payments. The carriage units are rented from $600 to $800 per month and measure approximately 400 to 480 square feet (37 to 45 square meters). All homes in Highland's Garden Village received a five-star rating from the Denver Home Builders Association's Built Green Program and are E-Star certified by Energy Rated Homes of Colorado.

Cottage Hill Senior Apartments comprise 63 rental apartments ranging from $604 to $1,250 per month in a three-story complex constructed around a private courtyard. Currently, 87 percent of the units are occupied, with 40 percent of all the apartments having been designated as affordable units ranging from $450 to $1,065 per month. In addition to housing for seniors, the project includes a four-building, 74-unit apartment complex, 38 rowhouses, and 19 live-work units intended for artists.

Offering a cost-saving and lifestyle alternative to single-family homes, Hearthstone is Highland's Garden Village's 33-unit co-housing complex. Families live in one- to four-bedroom homes but share certain living spaces, such as outdoor children's play areas and a common house. The 4,800-square-foot (446-square-meter) common house is equipped with a catering kitchen, a playroom, dining and sitting rooms, and a guest suite. Traditionally, co-housing has front entrances that open onto a community courtyard. One request made for Hearthstone was for a presence on the community's streetfront. As a result, several of the residences have both front and rear entrances. The houses that face a public street have access from both the front and the rear, while those that front

A row of single-family houses faces the gardens, which were recreated using native drought-resistant plants. The gardens are maintained by the homeowners' association.

Hearthstone is the co-housing component of Highland's Garden Village. The homes line a central courtyard that provides play space where children can be easily supervised.

the courtyard have only one entrance and private back-yards or back entrances into their garages. Co-housing units are priced between $153,795 and $267,817, with each house bought under a condominium ownership structure because of the shared spaces.

Preserving open space and rehabilitating the amusement park's attractive gardens were emphasized throughout the development process. The project includes 3.2 acres (1.3 hectares) of community parks that encourage walking and jogging. Various gardens feature edible plants; in many cases, existing trees and plantings were preserved or transplanted. For example, honey locust trees were transplanted around the single-family homes, and tulip bulbs were saved for use in the gardens.

A number of green features have garnered Highland's Garden Village national attention: 30 tons (27.3 metric tons) of concrete from the old site was crushed and re-used as road base; the project uses alternative energy sources such as wind-generated electricity for parks, civic

buildings, and apartment buildings; and various recycled products such as wood, insulation, and siding were used in construction of the homes.

Financing, Marketing, and Operations

Located within an urban renewal area, Highland's Garden Village is eligible for city tax increment funds. Over a 20-year period, the project can receive upward of $4.2 million for sewers, roads, and other infrastructure. This amount depends on increases in property taxes and sales taxes, with property taxes on the average home currently around $1,500 per year. The theater, carousel, and Elitch Gardens will also receive $4.6 million in tax increment funds for renovations.

The development cost for the project is expected to total $69 million, though the property was broken up into smaller parcels, of $10 million to $15 million, to make financing more manageable. The first phase of development included the construction of the seniors'

The 1926 carousel pavilion is used for community functions. The floor now features a walking labyrinth.

apartments and the single-family houses. A joint venture between Wonderland Homes and Perry/Affordable Housing Development Corporation purchased the land and used a loan for the development of the single-family residences. The seniors' and multifamily housing units were financed through a tax-exempt bond offered through the U.S. Department of Housing and Urban Development, a Denver 4 percent home loan, and a Colorado state home loan. Perry sold lots to Wonderland Homes for construction of the co-housing, with Wonderland using a straight construction loan for development of those homes. Wonderland and Perry split the profits from sales of the co-housing units. Perry/Affordable Housing Development Corporation owns the multifamily and seniors' housing units, both of which are managed by a third-party management firm.

Experience Gained

In terms of financing, Rose and Perry would not do anything differently. By avoiding "Wall Street–like" money, the project was not rushed and could be developed at a manageable and rewarding pace.

Throughout the different phases of development, Rose and Perry made it a point not to build more infrastructure than was required. Constructing roads, sewers, and sidewalks before they were needed would have left the project financially strapped.

By making the streets narrower, developers were able to widen sidewalks, promote pedestrian traffic, reduce

One of the original amusement park buildings is now used as a community theater.

vehicular traffic speeds, and save money on construction costs.

Developers of Highland's Garden Village did not adequately plan ahead to match various models of homes to their respective lots. Rose and Perry left this decision to homebuyers, and they believe the project ended up not being diverse enough on some streets.

Site plan.

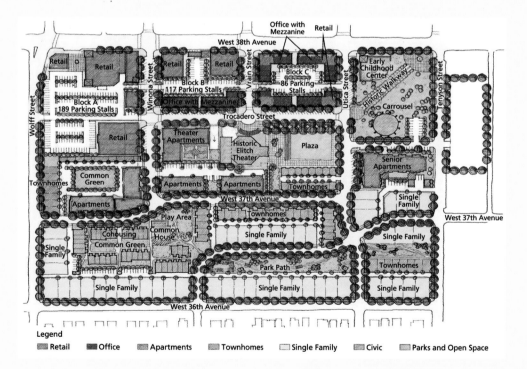

Project Data: Highland's Garden Village

Land Use and Building Information

Site area

27.39 acres (11 hectares)

Gross Building Area

Use	Square Feet/ Square Meters
Office	14,000/1,300
Retail	82,400/7,660
Residential	376,000/35,000
Parking	260,000/24,165
Open Space	145,000/13,500

Leasable Area	Square Feet/ Square Meters
Office Net Rentable Area	14,000/1,300
Retail Gross Leasable Area	82,400/7,660
Civic Buildings)	22,000/2,045

Land Use Plan

	Acres/ Hectares	Percent of Site
Buildings	13.5/5.5	49.3%
Streets/Surface Parking	8.9/3.6	32.5
Landscaping/Open Space	4.5/1.8	16.4
Civic Buildings	0.5/0.2	7.8
Total	27.4/11.1	100.0%

Residential Unit Information

Unit Type	Unit Size (Square Feet/ Square Meters)	Number of Units	Rent/Sale Range[1]
Single Family			
2-Bedroom, 1.5-Bath	1,100/102	6	$211,000–270,000
3-Bedroom, 2.5-Bath	1,512–2,331/ 140–217	30	$250,000–427,000
4-Bedroom, 2.5-Bath	1,957/182	6	$274,000–364,000
Carriage Units	400–480/ 37–45	20	$600–800/month
Rental Apartments	703–948/ 65–88	74	$604–1,250/month
Co-housing	1,304–2,114/ 121–196	33	$154,000–268,000
Seniors' Housing	395–995/ 37–92	63	$554–1,065/month
Townhouses			
2-Bedroom, 2.5-Bath	1,183/110	14	$190,000–244,000
3-Bedroom, 2.5-Bath	1,432–1,479/ 133–137	24	$207,000–275,000
Live/Work			
Plaza Lofts[2]	1,550/144	26	$275,000–300,000

Development Cost Information

Site Costs

Site acquisition	$2,416,000

Site Improvements

Excavation/grading	$345,000
Sewer/water/drainage	2,007,000
Paving/curbs/sidewalks	1,048,000
Landscaping/irrigation	188,000
Fees/general conditions	153,000
Dry utilities	769,000
Open space	1,668,000
Demolition	994,000
Environmental	$260,000
Total	$7,432,000

Construction Costs

Office	$1,204,000
Retail	7,100,000
Residential	38,000,000
Civic space	7,400,000
Total	$53,704,000

Soft Costs

Architecture/engineering	$1,072,000
Project management	2,429,000
Marketing	185,000
Legal/accounting	545,000
Taxes/insurance	342,000
Title fees	21,000
Construction interest and fees	432,000
Operating expenses	493,000
Total	$5,519,000

Total Development Cost	**$69,071,000**

Developer

Perry & Rose
910 16th Street
Denver, Colorado 80202
303-446-0600
www.rose-network.com

Notes

[1] Initial prices and rents.

[2] Two bedrooms, study, three bathrooms.

Master Site Planner

Calthorpe Associates
739 Allston Way
Berkeley, California 94710
510-548-6800
www.calthorpe.com

Site Planner

Civitas
1250 Bannock Street
Denver, Colorado 80204
303-571-0053
www.civitasinc.com

Architects

Single Family and Townhouses

Wolff/Lyon Architects
777 Pearl Street
Suite 210
Boulder, Colorado 80302
303-447-2786
www.wlarch.com

Seniors' Apartments

Oz Architecture
1580 Lincoln Street
Suite 1200
Denver, Colorado 80203
303-861-5704
www.ozarch.com

Harry Teague Architects
412 North Mill Street
Aspen, Colorado 81611
970-925-2556
www.harryteaguearchitects.com

Co-housing

CoHousing Company
1250 Addison Street
Suite 113
Berkeley, California 94702
510-549-9980

Synergy Design

917 Cottonwood Circle
Golden, Colorado 80401
303-278-1880

Landscape Architect

Lee Weintraub Landscape Architecture
59 Edgecliff Terrace
Yonkers, New York 10705
914-965-6540

Development Schedule

7/1996	Planning started
8/1998	Site purchased
10/1998	Construction started
1/1999	Sales/leasing started
1/2001	Phase I completed
12/2003	Phase II completed
12/2005	Project completion date

I'On

Mt. Pleasant, South Carolina

I'On is a 760-unit community based on new urbanist design concepts and classic South Carolina Lowcountry architectural styles. The pedestrian-friendly development is relatively high density. The community also protects its natural environment, with tree-lined streets, natural open areas, marshes, lakes, and recreational facilities for residents.

I'On encompasses 244 acres (99 hectares) in Mt. Pleasant, South Carolina, six miles (10 kilometers) east of Charleston. At buildout, it will include more than 700 single-family custom-built homes as well as community facilities and a small-scale commercial area near its entrance. The development is divided into six residential boroughs, each of which is planned around a community space.

The classic Lowcountry style of the region serves as I'On's architectural reference. The I'On Code, a set of simple architectural principles that aims to encourage good design rather than discourage bad design, promotes flexible conformance to this model. Lot sizes are varied to accommodate a mix of house sizes and types.

The Site

Located three miles (4.8 kilometers) northwest of the center of Mt. Pleasant and six miles (10 kilometers) east of downtown Charleston, I'On is accessed at its southern border by a main entrance off Mathis Ferry Road. Residential subdivisions flank the site to the east and west, deep-water marshes and tidal creeks to the north.

The original owner of the land, Jacob Bond I'On (1782–1859), was a planter, U.S. Army and militia officer, and state legislator. A contemporary of John C. Calhoun at Yale University, he went on to represent St. James Santee Parish in the South Carolina House from 1810 to 1812. In 1816, he began serving in the South Carolina Senate, representing St. James Santee Parish first, then Christ Church Parish. He was president of the Senate from 1822 until 1828.

More recently, this generally flat infill site was used for construction storage and soil mining. Just before its purchase by the I'On Company, about 60 percent of the site comprised agricultural fields, 30 percent was old-growth hardwoods, and 10 percent took the form of manmade lakes.

The master plan for the development dictates the preservation of natural features such as stands of trees, marshlands, and lakes that were originally created as borrow pits by the previous owner. The Rookery, a seven-acre (3-hectare) pond actively used by wading birds as a nesting site, was enhanced as a freshwater wetland preserve. Careful planning and monitoring have protected the area, enabling the nesting population to increase while providing residents with the opportunity to view the birds from blinds without disturbing them. Sensitive freshwater ecosystems have been preserved through the dedication of wetland areas and the undisturbed buffers surrounding them. Other on-site green areas include a two-mile (3.2-kilometer) walk along the Hobcaw and Shelmore creeks, a soccer field, and intimate pocket parks scattered throughout the development.

Planning and Design

In early 1995, the founders of I'On began with a concept of a mixed-use development that would include single- and multifamily housing units, commercial space, and public areas. They retained two recognized architecture and planning firms, Duany Plater-Zyberk & Company and Dover, Kohl & Partners. As a first step in the master planning process, the design team visited recognized models of city planning and architecture in the region, including Savannah, Georgia, and Charleston, South Carolina, as well as less-well-known South Carolina coastal towns such as Beaufort, Rockville, and Mt. Pleasant.

Observations at these communities led the designers to choose the Lowcountry vernacular style for the new neighborhood. This style, borrowed from Mt. Pleasant Old Village and Historic Charleston, features deep front porches, tall windows, and houses taller than they are wide. The style also embraces historic exterior finishes such as wood clapboard, brick, and stucco; balconies; shuttered windows; simple, symmetrical rooflines; picket fences; garden walls and gates; and outbuildings such as garages, potting sheds, and workshops.

The I'On Code upholds adherence to the Lowcountry style. The code is supplemented with an architectural primer, *Principles of Lowcountry Vernacular Architecture,* and a set of *Community Patterns* that provide design concepts for specific situations such as corner lots. An I'On design coordinator on staff works with homebuyers, architects, and builders to convey the vision for the community and provides advice on architectural design. This person also administers the I'On Design Committee, the architectural review body for the neighborhood.

I'On is divided into six residential boroughs: Shelmore, Eastlake, Ponsbury, Ionsborough, Westlake, and Montrose. Boroughs are connected by a network of narrow streets and view corridors. Each borough is planned around a preserved civic space such as a lake,

I'On is a pedestrian-friendly, relatively high-density development that pays attention to the natural environment, with natural open areas, marshes, lakes, and tree-lined streets.

park, or square and contains 80 to 150 homes. Lots range from 3,500 to 12,000 square feet (325 to 1,115 square meters), and houses range from 960 to more than 6,000 square feet (90 to 560 square meters), with the average house measuring about 2,400 square feet (225 square meters).

The streets in the six neighborhoods are narrow (17 to 22 feet [5.2 to 6.7 meters]) and designed with twists and turns to add visual interest and to slow vehicular traffic. I'On's connector streets are wider (30 feet [9.1 meters]), but curbs of granite blocks are used to narrow the size of intersections so that drivers slow down in response. At the main entrance, a traditional roundabout introduces the neighborhood, further enforcing the image of a pedestrian-oriented environment.

The natural environment played an important role in the design of I'On. Taking advantage of existing vegetation and water features, the master planners were able to create a variety of natural settings. Natural land-scaped parks and marsh-front paths and wetlands can be found throughout the development. The Rookery is a five-acre (2-hectare) wildlife preserve that is home to migratory birds and native mammals and fish. It is sheltered from houses by a buffer of wetlands and vegetation. Sensitive freshwater ecosystems have been preserved through the dedication of wetland areas and undisturbed buffers surrounding them. These fresh-water springs are the headwaters of I'On's tidal creeks and home to a wide variety of Lowcountry plants and wildlife. Canals that provide opportunities for water-front homes separate the two lakes of the development. In 1999, I'On's creators were given the Stewardship Award with Full Recognition from the South Carolina Department of Natural Resources for its protection of wildlife habitats and water quality, and its environmen-tally sensitive site plan.

Eight sites throughout I'On have been reserved for civic buildings to be built in the future, including small

The regional Lowcountry architectural style, characterized by deep front porches, tall windows, and natural exterior finishes, serves as I'On's architectural theme.

churches and other community buildings. I'On Square, a commercial center with retail and office uses, will eventually house just over 30,000 square feet (2,790 square meters) of commercial space. The first phase, which has been completed, includes a gourmet food-to-go shop, a restaurant, a salon, a spa, the I'On Company's sales office, and several professional offices. Other amenities include a multipurpose athletic field; playgrounds and parks; I'On Club, a private swim and tennis club; and the Creek Club, a 5,000-square-foot (465-square-meter) facility for parties and community gatherings.

Approvals Process

The I'On Company faced many hurdles in its 30-month pursuit of rezoning and permitting. Despite the developer's experience in creating new urbanist communities in the region and a design team comprising some of the most recognized names in the new urbanist movement, considerable opposition arose from local resi-

dents who objected to the scale and density of the proposed development.

In spring 1995, Vince Graham and his father, Tom, contracted to buy the property in Mt. Pleasant, a bedroom community of Charleston. With the exception of its historic Old Village, the town is characterized by suburban-style residential neighborhoods from the 1950s to 1980s. In 1992, the town of Mt. Pleasant adopted a master plan for the town incorporating traditional neighborhood principles. At that time, well in advance of the approvals process for I'On, the undeveloped I'On site was identified in the plan as an ideal location for a traditional neighborhood development. Unfortunately, the town's zoning regulations were not consistent with the master plan. Because the underlying zoning for the site was R-1, which specifies 10,000-square-foot (930-square-meter) minimum lots and conventional subdivision requirements, it was necessary to seek a zoning change to Planned Development to create a more traditional

I'On is divided into six residential boroughs, ranging from 80 to 150 homes, which are connected by a network of narrow streets and view corridors and focused around an amenity such as a lake, a park, or a square.

neighborhood development with smaller lots and higher densities.

The design code and preliminary plan for I'On, created by architects Dover, Kohl & Partners and Duany Plater-Zyberk and Company, was presented to a standing-room-only crowd in mid-May 1995. This plan, which included 800 single-family lots, 440 multifamily units, and 90,000 square feet (8,365 square meters) of commercial space, was fine-tuned over the next several months in preparation for the rezoning application submitted in August 1995. After several public hearings, the planning board approved the application. Before review by the Mt. Pleasant Town Council, compromises were made to the zoning application to reduce the number of single-family lots to 730 and the number of multifamily units to 120. The Mt. Pleasant Town Council rejected this application by a vote of five to four in December 1995.

Despite this setback, the developer elected to continue with option payments to the landowner to ensure that the land would be available once approvals were received. Efforts were also made to determine what type of plan the town council could approve. The architects further modified the plan by eliminating the multifamily component, reducing the number of thoroughfare types from 11 to four, reducing the commercial component to 30,000 square feet (2,790 square meters), and decreasing the total number of residential units to 759. This new plan and rezoning application was submitted in December 1996. The planning board recommended approval in January 1997, and the Mt. Pleasant Town Council approved it in March 1997.

The founders then worked directly with the project engineers to define the first subphase of the project—45 lots, three parks, and three street types. The intent was to enter the market quickly with a small phase of diverse homesites that could illustrate the design concept, a traditional neighborhood, to prospective buyers. Infrastructure construction began in summer 1997, and ground was broken for the first house in March 1998.

I'On Square includes over 30,000 square feet (2,790 square meters) of retail and office uses.

Homes built in this first subphase in 1998 sold for $160,000 to $625,000.

During that time period, from February 1997 to summer 1997, local opponents of the project gathered a petition of 3,500 registered voters, which they presented to the town council. The petition requested that the approved ordinance be overturned or that a referendum be held on the issue. The developer challenged this action, and a circuit court judge placed a temporary restraining order

Rear alleyways provide off-street parking and an additional place for neighbors to socialize.

on the town, prohibiting it from acting on the petition. The restraining order was subsequently lifted. Although the town council voted against overturning the rezoning, it did agree to a town-wide referendum to be held October 1997. One week before the scheduled referendum, however, the circuit court ruled that a municipality could not hold a referendum on zoning issues. Opponents appealed this decision, but in January 2000, the South Carolina Supreme Court upheld the lower court's decision.

Development and Construction

Despite the legal challenges, site work at I'On continued unabated. As of summer 2003, 70 percent of the total number of homesites had been sold or are under contract. Plans call for all homes and commercial areas to be completed by 2006.

Individual residences at I'On are built by members of the I'On Guild, a group of 17 builders who have been selected based on experience, craftsmanship, client and trade references, financial strength, and enthusiasm. The purpose of the guild is to ensure high-quality, sustainable construction. By inviting a variety of builders and craftsmen to participate in the development process from the very beginning, the community has acquired visual diversity and a sense of authenticity in an unusually short period of time.

Marketing and Operations

Sales began in January 1998. By summer 2003, 529 of 568 developed lots had been sold or were under contract. A total of 350 homes were occupied, with approximately 75 under construction. Sale prices range from $309,000 to $1.75 million.

Helped by a strong housing market in its early years, I'On has seen impressive increases in real estate values. In just two years, resale of homes appreciated as much as 50 percent. During that period, prices of premium marshfront and lakefront homesites more than tripled.

The homes at I'On are built by members of the I'On Guild, a group of 17 builders selected based on their experience, craftsmanship, and client and trade references.

By using a variety of builders, the community has acquired a level of visual diversity and a sense of authenticity in a short period of time.

The Eastlake Boathouse, I'On's first civic building, offers residents a place for social gatherings along the lakefront park.

Publicity and word of mouth play an important role in marketing the development. I'On has received numerous awards and has been featured in a variety of publications. Innovative ideas such as the "life-point house," which illustrates ways for homebuilders to meet the needs of a growing family in one location, have also helped the community earn national recognition. Through this project, a team of architects, builders, and designers led by architect Andrés Duany built and enlarged a model home in stages from a 780-square-foot (72.5-square-meter) starter cottage to a spacious 3,700-square-foot (345-square-meter) family-sized home.

Residents also play an important part in marketing the development. To reinforce the values of a tightly knit community and to encourage interaction with its neighbors, the I'On Company helped establish two groups: the I'On Trust and the I'On Assembly. The trust's executive director, Caroline Bennett, says, "The trust is designed for interaction between I'On residents and the East Cooper portion of Charleston. Its goal is to enliven the human spirit and enhance the quality of our lives. We want to the bring the Charleston area into I'On." The trust organizes events for both I'On residents and neighbors from surrounding developments. It provides cultural enrichment programs such as educational seminars and workshops.

The I'On Assembly serves as the homeowners' association. It is responsible for common area maintenance, street landscaping, and providing insurance coverage for the development.

Experience Gained

The early design process should focus on conceptual plans that can evolve throughout the development phases. Rather than attempting to create detailed plans for the entire development at the beginning, it is more efficient and realistic to focus design energy on the first phases.

Rezoning can be a highly charged political process that requires a careful strategy and potentially a great deal of time. Developers should not assume that citizens or elected officials understand or appreciate the concept of new urbanism. They may need to be educated about the concept.

The success of the early stages of I'On has proved that consumers will accept higher-density neighborhoods built with architectural integrity, quality construction, and consideration of local conditions.

The effort made to preserve the area's natural elements also proves that compact development can work without compromising the surrounding environment.

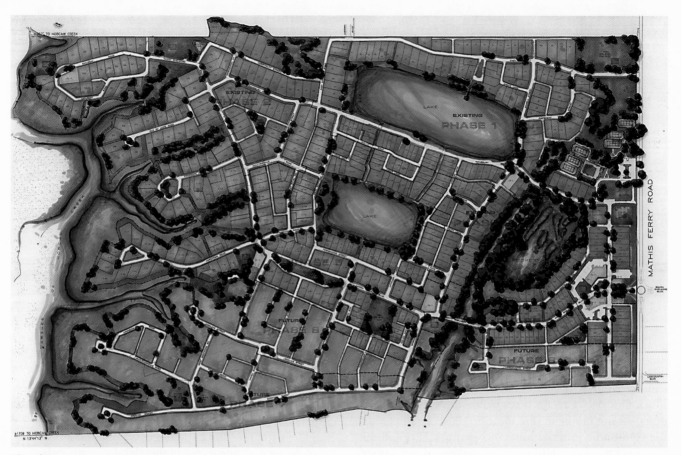

Site plan.

Project Data: I'On

Land Use and Building Information

Site Area	243 acres (98 hectares)
Gross Density	3.2 units per acre (8 per hectare)

Land Use Plan

	Acres/ Hectares	Percent of Site
Detached Residential	121.7/49.3	49.9%
Streets/Surface Parking	45.8/18.5	18.8
Landscaped Areas/Open Space	60.3/24.4	24.7
Civic and Common	16.1/6.5	6.6
Total	243.9/98.7	100.0%

Residential Unit Information

Detached Single-Family Homes	762 planned
Home sizes	960–6,000 square feet (90–560 square meters)
Lot sizes	3,500–12,000 square feet (325–1,115 square meters)
Average Home Size	2,300–2,400 square feet (215–225 square meters)
Home Prices	$309,000–1,750,000
Lot Prices	$69,000–469,000
Average Cost of Construction (Without Land)	$165 per square foot ($1,775 per square meter)

Commercial Space Information

Total Area

Existing (Square Feet/Square Meters)	14,000/1,300
Planned (Square Feet/Square Meters)	16,000/1,490
Percent Occupied	90%
Number of Tenants	12 (retail and office)
Average Tenant Size	1,200 square feet (110 square meters)
Annual Rents	$18–24 per square foot ($85–260 per square meter)
Average Length of Lease	1–5 years
Typical Terms	Triple net

Development Cost Information

Site Costs

Site acquisition	$11,000,000

Site Improvements

Residential site development, landscaping	$11,000,000
Total Development Cost to Date	$30,000,000
Total Development Cost at Buildout	$37,000,000

Development Schedule

1994	Planning started
6/1997	Site purchased[1]
8/1998	Construction started
2/1998	Sales started
6/2006	Estimated date of completion

Developer

The I'On Company
159 Civitas Street
Mt. Pleasant, South Carolina 29401
843-971-1662

Site Planners

Duany Plater-Zyberk & Company
1023 Southwest 25th Avenue
Miami, Florida 33135
305-644-1023
www.dpz.com

Dover, Kohl & Partners
1571 Sunset Drive
Suite 1
Coral Gables, Florida 33143
305-666-0446
www.doverkohl.com

Seamon, Whiteside & Associates
503 Wando Park Boulevard
Suite 100
Mt. Pleasant, South Carolina 29464
843-884-1667
www.swasc.com

Note

[1] First purchase of rolling takedown.

Maple Trace

Fairfax, Virginia

Maple Trace is a small infill development surrounded by established residential neighborhoods. The development straddles two jurisdictions: the city of Fairfax and Fairfax County, Virginia, about 15 miles (24 kilometers) west of Washington, D.C. Despite the project's small size—only 19 single-family units on the main parcel—it has the feel of a distinct community. Enough land was conserved to provide a landscaped square at the entrance of the development that sets the neighborhood's tone and provides a gathering place for residents.

Most of Maple Trace's plan is based on a modified grid pattern that lends a village character to the community and pays homage to the nearby historic district of the city of Fairfax. The homes are reminiscent of the earliest colonial homes of Virginia, a style that continues to be very popular in this region. Units range from 2,832 square feet to 3,600 square feet (265 to 335 square meters). Sale prices ranged from $405,000 to $637,000.

The Site

Maple Trace is located along Little River Turnpike/ Main Street, straddling the city of Fairfax and Fairfax County. The smaller piece extends into the county and was developed as an outparcel, separate from the main portion of the project.

The city of Fairfax, a colonial-era town that now is part of the burgeoning northern Virginia suburbs of Washington, D.C., has seen a revival in its appeal in recent years as a result of its desirable location, amenities, and historic, small-town character. The historic core has been undergoing revitalization, including the restoration of several homes and commercial buildings dating from the 1800s to be used as museums and other facilities. New commercial developments have brought stylish restaurants and shops, increasing the community's desirability. Residential developers have taken advantage of the city's growing popularity and have snapped up any infill sites available.

The area that is now the city of Fairfax was settled in the early 1700s. The first county courthouse, completed in 1800, was located on Little River Turnpike not far from the site of Maple Trace. Up until the second half of the 20th century, Fairfax remained relatively rural except for the few blocks surrounding the courthouse. In 1961, following a decade of tremendous regional growth, the city was incorporated and its boundaries set to include the 6.4 square miles (16.5 square kilometers) it comprises today. By the 1970s, the population had stabilized at about 21,000; today's population is an estimated 21,500.

Maple Trace is convenient to commuting routes, bus lines, and a Metro subway station, providing excellent access to downtown and suburban employment centers. It is less than two miles (3.2 kilometers) from George Mason University and Northern Virginia Community College and a short walk to the local middle school and high school. A daycare center is adjacent to the property.

The larger portion of the Maple Trace site (located in the city of Fairfax) is rectangular and relatively flat and is about 2.4 acres (1 hectare). The county portion is sloping, comprising about 1.4 acres (0.6 hectare). The Christopher Companies purchased the two sites for a combined price of just under $1.3 million. It was undeveloped at the time and included several large trees, which were preserved during construction and transplanted to appropriate locations on the site.

Planning and Design

Development was complicated by having to deal with two jurisdictions with different regulations and their failure to agree on a development concept for the combined site. The proposed plan was for a small-lot, village-style neighborhood. But although the city embraced the plan, the county rejected that concept. As a compromise, the developer ultimately built two distinctly different communities: a compact, 19-unit village on the large rectangular portion in the city and a subdivision of four third-acre (0.1-hectare) lots served by a private drive in the county.

Maple Trace's main plan is designed along the general principles of the new urbanism, with small lots, narrow setbacks, and garages removed from the street. A loop road runs through the development, with most houses fronting it. The loop road is narrow to maintain the intimate character of the community, and no parking is permitted along it. A small alley cuts through to provide rear-access garages for six of the houses. An interesting aspect of the plan is the paired driveways that serve the 13 houses along the site's perimeter and lead to integral garages at the rear of each house. By combining the driveways of two houses, curb cuts are minimized and the streetscape improved. Ownership of the driveway is split down the middle.

Like most developments in the Washington, D.C., area, Maple Trace is not gated. It was designed to allow maximum mobility with sidewalks that connect the neighborhood to its surroundings. The entrance to the development is from Maple Avenue, a quiet side street that gets little traffic. The busier Main Street perimeter of the development has no access point and, with a buffer

An old-fashioned square at the entrance of the development provides a gathering place for residents.

Maple Trace's plan incorporates narrow setbacks and rear garages to improve the streetscapes.

Adrienne Schmitz

Every house includes a covered front porch.

Adrienne Schmitz

of trees, backs the rear of a row of houses. Living space inside those houses is further buffered from street noise by the integral rear two-car garages.

By consolidating open space, the developer was able to reserve about one-third acre (0.1 hectare) to be used as a village square at the entrance of the neighborhood. The square is landscaped with mature shade trees and features a gazebo that lends an old-fashioned flavor and serves as a signature for the community's marketing ma-

terials. It is a gathering place for residents and provides an attractive view from many of the homes as well as for passersby.

Lots average 4,600 square feet (430 square meters) and measure an average of 46 feet by 100 feet (14 meters by 30 meters), with the narrow dimension facing the street. Front setbacks are narrow, only about ten feet (3 meters) from the sidewalk. Land between the house and the street is owned and maintained by the home-

Homes are colonial in style, with fine detailing.

Adrienne Schmitz

owners' association as a way to keep landscaping consistent and properly cared for. Ownership of side yards is evenly split between each two houses.

Two floor plans and eight colonial-style elevations were offered for Phase I; the wide selection of exterior designs gives the appearance that no two homes are identical. Both floor plans, at 2,832 and 2,912 square feet (265 and 270 square meters), include four bedrooms and two and one-half baths. An optional loft with an additional bath is also available. The elevations are a mix of red brick and neutral-color clapboard siding with white or beige trim, unifying the color scheme throughout the development. Every house includes a covered front porch, ranging from generous colonial-style pillared porches that run the width of both stories to smaller covered stoops with nonfunctioning balconies above. One model with a variety of elevations was offered in Phase II.

The Developer

The Christopher Companies is a privately held company, founded in 1974 by Frederick Kober. It is a regional developer and homebuilder and has built both large and small projects totaling more than 4,000 homes in northern and southeastern Virginia. Products include single-family houses, townhouses, and condominiums. In recent years, the firm has concentrated on developing small infill sites that demand distinctive approaches. The Christopher Companies has won more than 50

homebuilding awards over its 30-year history. Maple Trace won a Best in American Living award for smart growth.

The Christopher Companies has made philanthropy a part of its mission and has sponsored a number of charity events. The firm often designates the first home in a development as a charity home and donates the profits to charity. At Maple Trace, the firm combined efforts with many of its contractors and suppliers and donated the net proceeds from the first home sold, $67,000, to several local outreach groups.

The project began selling in April 2000 at base prices of $380,000 and $384,500 and increased by about 7 percent during the year. Options and upgrades raised sale prices as high as $617,900. The four larger homes on the outparcel lots had sale prices, including options, ranging from $602,600 to $636,700. All 23 homes were sold by November 2001.

Experience Gained

Maple Trace is a successful example of a small, well-designed infill development that offers a high-end product on small lots. The developer has used the project as a model for more recent development. Christopher Company's Morgan Chase, located on another infill site, uses the home plans from Maple Trace as its rear-garage homes.

Site plan.

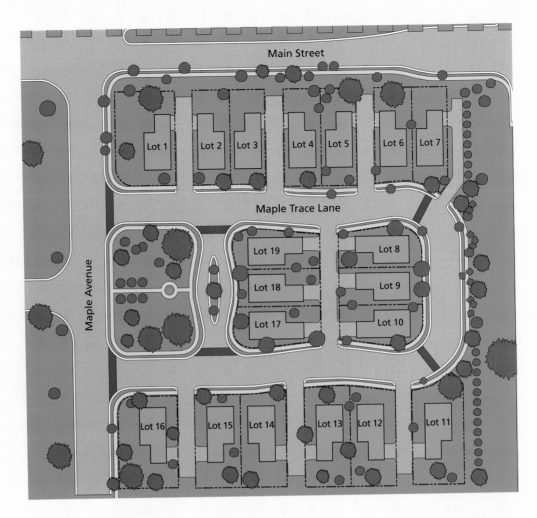

Standard floor plans.

Land Use and Building Information

Site Area	3.87 acres (1.6 hectares)
Dwelling Units	23
Gross Density	4.9 units per acre (12 per hectare)—county portion
	7.8 units per acre (19 per hectare)—city portion

Land Use Plan

	Acres/Hectares	Percent of Site
Residential Lots	2.013/0.8	52%
Roads	1.406/0.6	36
Open Space	0.451/0.2	12
Total	3.87/1.6	100%

Residential Unit Information

Unit Type	Unit Size (Square Feet/ Square Meters)	Number of Units	Base Price Range
Parkland	2,912/270	8	$413,500
Grove	2,832/265	11	$406,500
Madison	3,600/335	4	$554,900–581,400

Development Cost Information

Site Costs

Site acquisition	$1,276,615

Site Improvements

Excavation/grading	$102,157
Sewer/water/drainage	234,486
Landscaping/irrigation	131,210
Paving, landscaping, other	311,428
Demolition	39,886
Fees	305,007
Total	$1,124,174

Construction Costs

Superstructure	$56,934
HVAC	44,128
Electrical	91,103
Plumbing/sprinklers	321,708
Finishes	128,114
Graphics/specialties	616,370
Fees	150,890
Total	$1,409,247

Soft Costs

Architecture/engineering	$150,640
Project management	422,013
Sales/marketing	721,187
Legal/accounting	293,364
Construction interest and fees	203,054
Title fees	20,361
Total	$1,810,619

Total Development Cost	**$5,620,655**

Developer/Homebuilder

The Christopher Companies
11150 Main Street
Fairfax, Virginia 22030
703-352-5950
www.christophercompanies.com

Site Planner (Phase I)

Rinker-Detwiler
9240 Mosby Street
Manassas, Virginia 20110
703-368-7373
www.rinker-detwiler.com

Site Planner (Phase II)

Urban Engineering
7712 Little River Turnpike
Annandale, Virginia 22003
703-642-8080
www.urban-engineering.com

Architect

Snyder-Egbue Associates, Inc.
3959 Pender Drive
Fairfax, Virginia 22030
703-218-8404

Interior Merchandiser

Interior Concepts
2560 Riva Road
Annapolis, Maryland 21401
301-970-8009
www.interiorconceptsinc.com

Development Schedule

3/2000	Site purchased (Phase I)
5/2001	Site purchased (Phase II)
1999	Planning started
6/2000	Construction started
4/2000	Sales started
9/2000	First closing
12/2001	Project completed

Newington Village
Sydney, New South Wales, Australia

When it hosted the 2000 Olympic Games, the city of Sydney made a commitment that this event would use ecologically sustainable practices wherever possible. Located less than 9.5 miles (15.3 kilometers) west of Sydney's central business district, Newington Village is a lasting legacy of those "green games." Before becoming one of the premier residential suburbs in Sydney, Newington Village played host to more than 15,000 athletes and officials for the five weeks of the games. The end of the Olympics brought in a new set of temporary guests as Newington became home for the more than 7,000 athletes and officials of the 2000 Paralympic Games. Occurring after the Olympics and using the same sporting facilities, the Paralympic Games provide an international forum for world-class athletes with physical or intellectual disabilities to compete with each other. Newington Village is now a medium-density neighborhood; when construction is complete, it will have a population of 5,000 residents.

Mirvac Lend Lease Village Consortium (MLLVC), a partnership of two of Australia's largest developers, built 513 houses and 355 multifamily units and assembled 330 temporary modular homes using ecologically sustainable practices. Many of these houses were sold to the public even before the games started. Afterward, MLLVC retrofitted the village to serve as a residential neighborhood for Sydney. Structures that once housed up to 16 athletes were transformed into comfortable three- and four-bedroom houses. Units that once housed eight athletes were transformed into two-bedroom apartments. New permanent houses were built to replace the temporary modular housing.

When complete, the 222-acre (90-hectare) Newington Village will include 2,009 dwelling units (921 apartments and 1,088 houses), a 38,750-square-foot (3,600-square-meter) retail component that already is the site of a grocery store and 12 specialty shops, and a 581,250-square-foot (54,020-square-meter) commercial business park. Located in the center of the village is a primary school that used to be the athletes' clinic.

Although the transformation from Olympic Village to residential development is by itself quite a feat, the high environmental standards to which Newington Village was constructed add further merit to this project. Solar panels on the northern-facing roof of every house help to power hot water heaters and generate a large portion of each house's electricity. Standards for construction included use of passive solar power to help heat and cool the structures, careful selection of green or environmentally friendly building materials, and the use of only native plants in the landscaping.

Site and Development Process
The site of Newington Village and the surrounding areas near the Parramatta River played an important role in shaping how this land was used. Industrial products could be produced upriver where the land was cheaper and then shipped downriver to Sydney. In 1882, the land that is now Newington Village became an armaments depot for the Royal Australian Navy. The depot grew over time, eventually to more than 200 munitions bunkers, many of them still standing. Out of a need for security and to create a buffer between the depot and the residences in the area, the northern part of the site was left relatively untouched. Some of the few remaining tidal wetlands and eucalyptus forests in the Sydney region can be found on or near this site. Adjacent land in the area was used for a prison, a slaughterhouse, and a brickyard.

By the early 1990s, the site's location near downtown Sydney and its proximity to a number of transportation modes (freeway, bus, train, ferry) made it ripe for redevelopment. The organizers of the 2000 Olympics wanted to create a village for the athletes that was within walking distance of most venues, close to multiple modes of transit, and built using ecologically sustainable practices. In 1995, the Olympic Coordination Association purchased the land for Newington Village from the commonwealth government. By 1996, the Mirvac Group and Lend Lease Development formed MLLVC and won the contract to finance, design, and construct Newington Village. MLLVC started construction in May 1997 and completed the Olympic Village in early 2000. The end of the Olympics brought a new phase of construction. Construction in Newington Village is expected to be completed in 2005.

The Olympics completely reshaped and revitalized the area. The southern portion of the depot became Newington Village, and the northern half, with many of the original munitions bunkers intact, became part of Millennium Parklands, Sydney's largest city park. To the northwest of Newington Village is the Silverwater Prison complex; to the east is the Narawang Wetland and Halsam's Creek, an offshoot of the Paramatta River; to the south is the Western Motorway (the M4), one of the busiest freeways in Australia; and to the west are numerous industrial uses in the Silverwater neighborhood.

Previously a concrete channel, Haslams Creek was reconstructed and its natural ecology restored; it is connected directly into Newington's parks and pedestrian trail system, with native plants maximizing sustainability.

Planning, Design, and Construction

A key concern in designing Newington Village was accommodating the Olympic and Paralympic athletes in a space that is accessible to the physically disabled, walkable, ecologically sustainable, and convertible to a medium-density suburb after the games ended. The Sydney Olympics were the first games to provide all of the athletes' housing in the same area and within walking distance of most of the venues. Many officials and athletes from the Paralympics and the Olympics rated the Olympic Village "the best ever."

The plan for Newington calls for five separate areas or precincts. Precincts 1 through 3 are residential, each with its own identity and separated from each other by green spaces. In the center of each residential precinct, a park acts as a focal point. Housing in each precinct is a mix of apartments, townhouses, and single-family homes. The roads in each precinct form grids that have been modified to take advantage of the views and to create visual appeal. One main boulevard connects the largely self-contained residential precincts, creating a sense of unity among the three distinct communities of Newington Village.

Precinct 5, in the northwestern edge of the project, is a business park. Located between the historically industrial areas of the Silverwater neighborhood to the west and the homes of Newington to the east, Precinct 5 creates a comfortable transition, linking these different uses. An Australian firm, Cox Richardson Architects, master planned the 23.5-acre (9.5-hectare) precinct

with the same environmentally sensitive values as the rest of Newington Village. The buildings in this precinct contain more than 580,000 square feet (53,900 square meters) of office space.

Precinct 4 serves as the village retail center and a nexus for Newington Village. With the exception of Precinct 1, all the precincts border Precinct 4. Residents of Newington Village and employees at the business park can shop at the supermarket, cafés, bakery, newsstand, and other specialty retail shops in Precinct 4. A daycare center with space for 40 children is also located in this area. The location and combination of these services have made Precinct 4 the de facto town center and informal meeting place of the village.

MLLVC commissioned 15 architectural and design firms to work on Newington Village. The different firms managed to create diverse styles while retaining a sense of visual coherence and compatibility between buildings. Aesthetic considerations were not the only design challenges. Addressing the needs of the wheelchair-bound athletes in the Paralympics helped Newington Village set higher standards regarding the physical accessibility of master-planned communities in Australia. Hallways in houses were made wide enough to accommodate people in wheelchairs, street curbs were specially designed, paving materials were carefully chosen, a 1:20 gradient was used throughout Newington Village, accessible street furniture was created, and special attention was given to the levels of lighting and signage.

A variety of multifamily housing types are offered at Newington Village.

Newington Village has Australia's largest concentration of solar housing constructed to date.

One of the signature design features of Newington Village is its commitment to ecological sustainability. Like physical accessibility, environmentally friendly values are embedded in every aspect of Newington Village. Artificial wetlands are used to collect and reclaim stormwater, which is then used for toilets and landscaping. Other ecologically sustainable practices used in the construction of Newington Village include limiting the use of building materials whose manufacture uses or creates toxic pollution as a byproduct, using nontoxic termite prevention methods, limiting the use of polyvinyl chloride (PVC), buying much of the lumber from sustainable forest farms, choosing energy-efficient appliances for the residences, and using more than 90 percent local native plant species in the public areas. The houses were designed to take advantage of passive solar heating, and windows were strategically placed to facilitate cross ventilation. As a result, none of the houses were built with air conditioners, providing a savings in initial housing costs and in the energy expenditure involved in operating an air conditioner.

Among these practices, Newington Village's use of solar power is notable. As of 2002, Newington Village was one of the largest solar-powered communities in the world. The use of solar power allows Newington Village to consume 75 percent less electricity from the main grid than a nonsolar suburb of the same size. The north/south orientation of the project and placement of most of the houses on their southern borders help to maximize solar exposure.

Marketing, Management, Tenants, and Performance

MLLVC's market research uncovered a strong demand for quality housing within the 6.2-mile (10-kilometer) catchment area. Research revealed that people in the area want an alternative to low-density suburban development and value ease of maintenance and open spaces. Given the differences between Newington Village and most other residential developments in Sydney, MLLVC did not want to rely solely on conceptual drawings to sell units. For this reason, one of the main marketing strategies was the use of Precinct 3 as a demonstration area. During the initial construction phase, 66 houses were built in this precinct. Consumer feedback on these houses shaped and refined the construction of houses in later phases of development. Precinct 3 thus helped to set design, construction, and marketing guidelines for the rest of Newington Village. Further, Precinct 3 became a showcase for what potential homebuyers could expect when the rest of Newington Village was completed. Sales of these units also helped to finance later construction and development. Precinct 3 was responsible for selling many of the units in the Olympic Village before the games and the houses' conversions to single-family uses.

Demand for property in Newington Village has been overwhelming. From 1999 to 2002, consumers bought an average of eight units a week. Houses that initially sold for AU$400,000 in 1999 sold for AU$650,000 in

Neighborhood parks are the centerpiece for each of the three villages of Newington.

©2000 EDAW/Dixi Carrillo

Higher-density housing and walkable neighborhoods are key elements of the project's green design.

©2000 EDAW/Dixi Carrillo

2002.[1] For multifamily units, the price increased from AU$250,000 in 1999 to AU$390,000 in 2002. At times during the development process, the demand for Newington Village properties was so high that houses and apartments were sold before their construction.

Experience Gained

Newington Village has demonstrated that ecologically sustainable development can be successful in terms of helping the environment, exceeding government regulations, and fulfilling consumer demand for more environmentally friendly homes.

The installation of solar panels on all houses in the village has made Newington Village the largest solar-powered community in the world. The electricity generated by these panels has prevented 7,000 tons of carbon dioxide a year from being released into the atmosphere.

Newington Village has also set new standards in environments for the physically challenged. Wheelchair-navigable curbs, streets, and intersections were successfully and seamlessly integrated into the development.

The state of New South Wales and the Australian federal government are using the lessons learned from Newington Village to create new guidelines and benchmarks for future developments.

Note

1. As of August 2004, the exchange rate was 1USD = 1.42AUD.

Master plan.

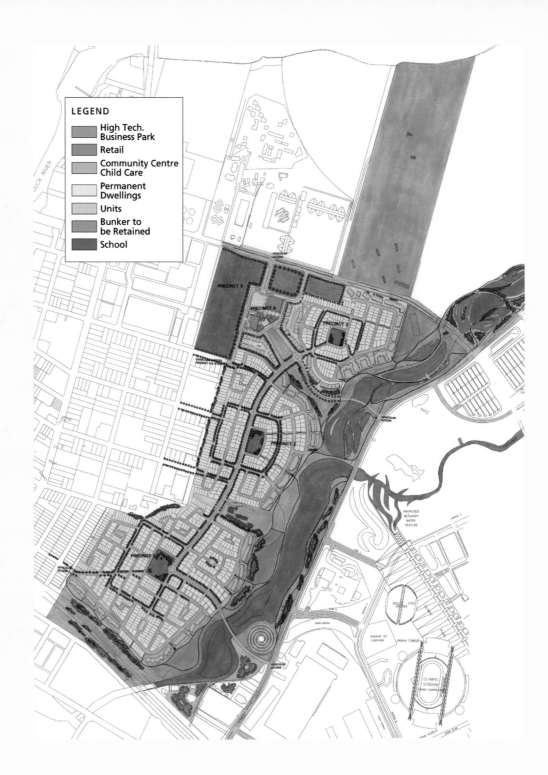

LEGEND

- High Tech. Business Park
- Retail
- Community Centre Child Care
- Permanent Dwellings
- Units
- Bunker to be Retained
- School

Project Data: Newington Village

Land Use and Building Information

Site Area	222 acres (90 hectares)
Dwelling Units Planned	2,009
Gross Density	74 dwelling units per acre (30 per hectare)

Land Use Plan

	Square Feet/ Square Meters
Commercial/Office Space	581,251/54,020
Retail	38,750/3,600
Public Open Space, including Roads	64.0 acres (25.9 hectares)

Residential Unit Information

For-Sale Apartments

	Unit Size (Square Feet/ Square Meters)	Current Prices
2–Bedroom	970–1,020/ 90–95	Mid- to high AU$400,000s
3–Bedroom	1,130–1,185/ 105–110	Low AU$500,000s
3–Bedroom Maisonettes	1,345–1,560/ 125–145	High AU$500,000s– low AU$600,000s

Houses

	Lot Size (Square Feet/ Square Meters)	Unit Size (Square Feet/ Square Meters)	Current Prices
3-Bedroom Townhouse	2,150/200	1,615/150	Mid- AU$500,000s
3-Bedroom House (Type 1)	2,150–3,230/ 200–300	1,720–1,830/ 160–170	Low to mid- AU$600,000s
3-Bedroom House (Type 2)	2,690–3,230/ 250–300	1,935/180	Mid- to high AU$600,000s
4-Bedroom House	2,690-4,305/ 250–400	2,045-2,365/ 190-220	Mid-AU$700,000s to mid-AU$800,000s

Development Schedule

5/1997	Construction started
1998	Phase I (Precinct 3) completed
2005	Project completion date

Developer

Mirvac Lend Lease Village Consortium
6 Monterey Street
Newington, New South Wales 2127
Australia
(02) 9748 0166
www.mirvac.com

Master Planner

HPA Architects
The Mirvac Group
40 Miller Street
North Sydney, New South Wales 2060
Australia
(02) 9080 8000
www.mirvac.com

Architects

Lend Lease Design Group Limited
Plaza Building
Australia Square
Sydney, New South Wales 2000
Australia
www.lendlease.com

Cox Richardson Architects & Planners
204 Clarence Street
Sydney, New South Wales 2000
Australia
(02) 9267 9599
www.cox.com.au

Landscape Architect

EDAW
211 Pacific Highway
St Leonards, New South Wales 2065
Australia
612-9906-6899
www.edaw.com

Nicholas Court
Seattle, Washington

Part of a small wave of multifamily infill housing in Seattle, Nicholas Court brings an urbane, modernist sensibility to an older neighborhood. Nine market-rate condominium units with distinct shapes and identities are fitted into three three-story buildings on a double lot. Nicholas Court combines small studio flats with single and multi-level townhouses and partially below-grade parking for 11 vehicles. The project is a bold experiment in infill housing that places high emphasis on quality design, environmental responsibility, and low maintenance. It is also a response to the city of Seattle's long-range plan to add greater density to city neighborhoods in the form of new and traditional housing types.

Nicholas Court was designed to attract buyers who choose to live in the city and are willing to trade a space-heavy, highly auto-dependent lifestyle for the advantages of urban life. It is decidedly modern in character but offers the community appeal of a small number of units with shared circulation and distinct identities. The project leverages small square footage with intensively designed interiors and building envelopes. Personal balconies, patios, and decks and shared outdoor circulation spaces effectively balance privacy and neighborly interaction.

The developer and architect set out with the common goal of creating a new multifamily housing design that would respond to the potential of zoning overlays and the anticipation of a new generation of buyers typical of the software, e-commerce, and biotech industries prevalent in the Seattle area. If successful, the experience of Nicholas Court will have applications all over the city, where whole neighborhoods have been rezoned to accept more density in the form of accessory units, cottage housing, and small-scale multifamily developments.

The Site
Nicholas Court is located on 15th Avenue, near Capitol Hill in Seattle, in an area zoned for low-rise and residential buildings. The site was carefully chosen for its adjacency to transit and to cultural and educational facilities. It is a few blocks from Seattle University and a close neighbor to Seattle Academy of Arts and Sciences. Buses are available within a block in two directions. Downtown Seattle is a 20-minute walk.

Two 30-foot by 125-foot (9-meter by 38-meter) lots were purchased for the development, for a total site area of 60 feet by 125 feet (18 meters by 38 meters). The site is bracketed by two single-family homes of soapbox revival style, each bordering on large-scale traditional brick apartment buildings. The extended streetscape, with structures spanning the entire 20th century, mixes apartment buildings with single-family homes. But it is dominated by the three-story facade of the beaux arts–style Temple De Hirsch Sinai across the street.

The site was last occupied by one large house, which had burned to the ground years ago and left a sizable depression in the ground where the foundation had been. One of the challenges of development on the site was the Seattle building code's requirement that height limits for the site be based on ground level at the former foundation. To overcome this limitation and take better advantage of views of downtown Seattle, it was necessary to win a departure from the code.

Development Process
Because of its emphasis on cutting-edge design and the creation of a new market for in-city living, the development of Nicholas Court was a close collaboration of two developers—Mike Conte of Better Neighborhoods and Peter Erickson of Urban Developments—and designers Gordon Walker and Colin Walker. Urban Developments, which was formed in 1973 for the purpose of acquiring, developing, and managing quality real estate investments for limited liability companies (LLCs), is the managing entity in Better Neighborhoods, LLC.

Peter Erickson, president of Urban Developments, is educated in architecture and urban planning and is licensed and experienced as a contractor. For the last two decades, Urban Developments has developed a portfolio of urban projects, ranging from renovation and reuse to historic renovation to new infill construction. It includes several multifamily loft projects, an office building, and a school. Nicholas Court is in keeping with the company's continuing interest in infill development.

Nicholas Court deliberately challenges the notion that great architecture is affordable only to public institutions and wealthy individuals. Award-winning architecture has become a trademark for Urban Developments and Better Neighborhoods, entailing a number of risks and costs that must be managed through a strategy of value engineering and careful market research.

Since the company's inception, Erickson has developed some guiding principles for success in infill projects:

• Value Added—Identify underused properties or sites in the path of growth. Innovative design and good development will vitalize neighborhoods and ensure profitability for investors.

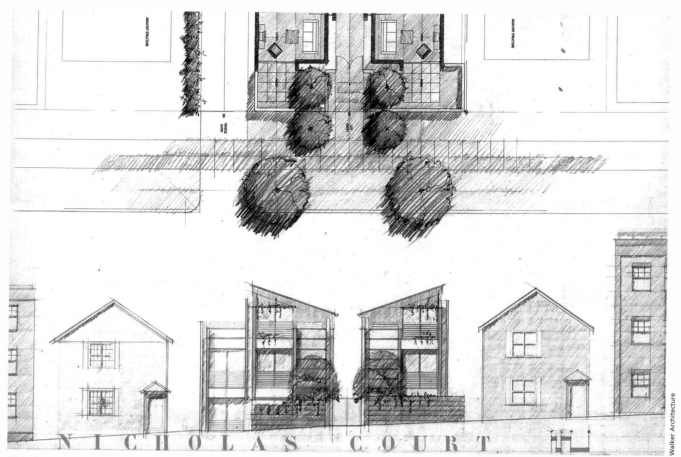

Nicholas Court in Seattle is an infill project of nine condominium units.

- Niche Market—Integrate pragmatic space planning with the best architecture available to generate distinctive niche projects that rise to the top of any market.
- Sound Financing—Maintain solid equity positions and modest debt coverage in real estate developments to ensure performance during downturns of economic cycles.
- Landbank—When investing in emerging neighborhoods where development timing is uncertain, target acquisitions with existing cash flow to provide interim returns on investment while waiting for market maturity. Use the interim period to go through the architecture, engineering, and entitlement processes.

At Nicholas Court, architect Gordon Walker pursued his own longstanding interest in the possibilities of urban infill architecture and housing. His 39-year career includes a mix of architecture, urban planning, development, teaching, and community advocacy. His son and partner in Walker Architecture, Colin Walker, brought to Nicholas Court a cutting-edge design sensibility honed in the late 1990s at Studios Architecture in San Francisco, where he was designer and job captain for a variety of urban projects.

Erickson defined the appropriate product for the neighborhood by surveying adjacent property owners and by retaining Michael Nelson, a real estate broker specializing in the neighborhood. As a result of the surveys, Urban Developments was able to identify pricing thresholds, spatial requirements, transportation issues, and a necessary amenities package. The same broker developed and managed the marketing and sales program for Nicholas Court.

After receiving basic approvals from the city, the development team entered into a three-month cost evaluation, an iterative process involving architect, contractor, and developer. They shared a determination to defy the assumption that high-quality architecture is usually affordable only to government agencies, colleges, and wealthy individuals. To meet budget criteria established at the outset by careful market research, the architect, engineer, and contractor worked creatively with the developer at this phase. The building permit was obtained in fall 1999. Construction of Nicholas Court began immediately and lasted 16 months.

Financing

Construction financing was arranged through Better Neighborhoods, LLC, the development and investment holding company of Mike Conte and his wife, who were equity partners. Urban Developments arranged takeout financing through Wells Fargo, and the Contes were paid back through sales.

Approvals

The project that became Nicholas Court was first seen in 1998 in the Design Demonstration Program, a juried collection of architect-designed urban infill projects that

Nicholas Court brings an urbane, modernist sensibility to an older neighborhood.

would not be permissible under Seattle's then-current zoning code. The purpose of the program, a cooperative venture between the city of Seattle and a group of local architects, was to show the way toward small-scale design that appeals to owner-occupants and neighborhoods while helping achieve greater density in the city. Nicholas Court was the first of 20 projects picked, which allowed it to go through a neighborhood design review process and seek departures from an existing code. Without this special designation, the project would have been impossible to approve, partly because of its slanted rooflines and unusual approach to height calculations.

Going through the program allowed some departures from code. One departure allowed the courtyard space to be included in the total square footage of landscaped area on site. Another increased the density by one unit, from an allowable eight to a granted nine units. Because it was the first project through the program and the process took nine months, it was a financial hardship for the developer. Today, the same process would take only four to six months.

Planning and Design

The ambitious urban design goals of Nicholas Court included sensitivity to the scale of surrounding structures—a very mixed group—and the perception of distinct and recognizable units. At the same time, the development team wanted to present an aesthetic reflecting our time and not a knockoff of existing housing typologies. In

general, the designer and developer wanted to provide an example of what "home" can be to the urbanite of the 21st century.

In addition to resetting the uneven rhythm of a single- and multifamily residential neighborhood, Nicholas Court achieves a sense of human scale and distinct identity in contemporary multifamily units. It also helps to redefine the meaning of open space, light, and air, all basic needs that drive setback and open-space requirements in building codes.

The design concept is grounded in the courtyard bungalow housing tradition of early 20th-century Los Angeles. The composition is planned around an open-air garden courtyard that extends without a barrier from the public sidewalk. Each unit has at least three sides that are outer walls as well as its own front door, accessible from the outside. Its visual appeal from the street is based on a combination of factors. It has an enveloping perimeter that meets the sidewalk in a low wall, and it demonstrates new construction technologies on the exterior.

The project includes two three-story buildings on the street side and one long three-story building, stepped down to one floor, at the opposite side of the sloping site. The three buildings are connected only by bridges between the upper levels and by a terrace over the parking. Nicholas Court mixes small studio flats with single-floor apartments and multilevel townhouses. The floor plan integrates circulation and living spaces to diminish the typical 17 to 20 percent load factor for circulation areas in condominiums. No square footage is lost: all exterior and interior spaces are multiuse.

The height, bulk, and scale of the project push the limits of the allowable envelope, enabling Nicholas Court to accommodate a generous network of common and private outdoor space inside the perimeter of the development. At the same time, it establishes an urban armature along the street. The courtyard layout is a direct extension of the public sidewalk, thereby integrating the structure into the urban infrastructure. The head-high cinderblock wall in front provides a strong boundary and clear entrance on the street. The wall opens in the center to a passage that leads to the inner courtyard. The courtyard allows glimpses to downtown Seattle enjoyed by the highest units on the side opposite the street.

This courtyard is an active multilevel circulation area, with front doors on two levels and old-fashioned mailboxes lined up along a rail. In plan, the open space at street grade is cross-shaped. The courtyard is at the cen-ter of the units, which are grouped in three clusters and connected above with walkways and landings and below on the base that contains parking. Personal outdoor areas include a mixture of roof terraces, garden patios, balconies, and decks.

Cars are out of sight, tucked beneath the complex along with a storage locker for each unit. At one side of the streetfront, a ramp down to the parking level passes under the balcony of one of the units, one of many design features that brings an urban complexity to the composition, enhances the identities of the units, and adds special appeal from the street.

Signatures of modernist sensibility are everywhere at Nicholas Court. Inside and out, industrial elements and inexpensive, conventional building materials are exploited for visual effect and durability. Cement board, laid horizontally with small breaks between, is attached with a small margin over a European-manufactured moisture barrier. The system, engineered by Exterior Research

The project features dramatic spaces and contemporary materials.

Stefan Coe

©Under the Light

and Design, provides depth and bold detail to exterior surfaces while promising a long-lived, breathable, and waterproof envelope.

The high-ceilinged interiors are tightly orchestrated to receive natural light and capture views. In the spirit of early modernism, the glass is set into full-height openings that emphasize views of the street and the city skyline. In another design feature carried over from early modernism, windows meet outer walls at right angles without returns. In this way, the visual flow between interior and city is unhampered, and the perception of spaciousness is heightened.

The designers have perfected the modernist character of Nicholas Court in the careful cutting and shaping of kitchen cabinetry, stair steps, shelving, and doors. They are all made of particleboard and coated with a clear finish or painted. In the townhouses, particleboard shelving and a stairway to the second floor are fused into one carefully fitted structures, adding architectural drama and finish to the high-ceilinged living and dining areas of the first floor. Radiant hot-water heating is built into the stained concrete floors throughout the first level, with hardwood or carpet on upper floors.

Marketing and Sales

Sales at Nicholas Court began with an open house in February 2001. With Better Neighborhoods keeping one unit for its portfolio, the other eight sold within six weeks. The project sold out quickly in a falling real estate market in which other projects were not selling, largely because of Nicholas Court's distinctive and appealing design. Buyers are singles and couples, age 28 to 74. Three buyers are architects, and two are associated with high-tech industries.

Prices ranged from $215,000 for a 652-square-foot (60-square-meter) flat with a study, garden patio, covered parking, and garage to $471,584 for a 1,229-square-foot (115-square-meter) unit with study, balconies, covered parking, and storage.

Based on the developer's past experience, feedback from the successful marketing and sales effort for Nicholas Court, and comments gleaned from meetings of the homeowners' association, the project's market success can be attributed to several factors:

- Light and Air—Given their desire to live in more dense urban environments, buyers of units are prioritizing a sense of expansiveness in their units, a sense en-

Unit interiors are spacious and modern.

hanced by high ceilings, open space, light, and air. These features are often as important to buyers as the gross square footage.

- Design—Buyers attracted to an urban environment are sensitive to design. They want to take pride in the uniqueness of their project and their unit.
- Flexibility—Buyers increasingly want less defined spaces and more ability to structure the space according to their needs. Flex-space or space with an ability to accommodate several functions is an important element.
- Buyers' Sophistication—Urban buyers are more sophisticated and actively seek information about a project. They want to know about noise transmission, ability to control energy costs, envelope technology specs, and "connectivity."
- Community—Because they are buying into a densely populated, rapidly moving city, buyers are highly responsive to the sense of community and security engendered by a project.

Experience Gained

Producing a test project for a new zoning application is difficult and time-consuming, and bold departures from traditional infill housing typologies require a high level of commitment. Changing the marketplace for housing in a way that is environmentally responsible and aesthetically adventurous is satisfying to the project team, but it makes sense to investors only if the concept is replicable and the lessons learned reduce costs in future applications.

Nicholas Court was a prototype for projects with a targeted return on investment of 20 percent. It achieved 14 percent. Even with first-time development costs, it was a profitable endeavor for the owner and development team.

The project has helped to make the case for high-density infill development in existing residential neighborhoods. It has brought new definition to a neighborhood with a mix of low-rise buildings and single-family homes.

The homeowners' association for Nicholas Court was established in June 2001. Based on feedback at the monthly meetings, the project has been a success. Residents frequently refer to the unanticipated benefits of both private decks and public walkways for neighborly gatherings and encounters. The blend of private and public spaces provides light, air, and a sense of community to Nicholas Court, elements often missing in enclosed and compartmentalized projects.

After only two years, it became clear that the judicious use of carefully detailed, basic industrial materials has added value to the project in the form of reduced maintenance costs. It is now a demonstrable benefit to each resident owner and to future buyers of similar properties.

Quality architecture, in conjunction with market research and disciplined management, can generate

Rear view. Decks and enclosed patios provide outdoor living areas.

Stefan Coe

affordable projects with a great deal of public appeal. Public appeal eases the review process, attracts lenders, and brings buyers to the project. One of the most important lessons learned in the development of Nicholas Court is that great design, if cost-effective, is always a hedge against a falling real estate market.

Site plan.

Walker Architecture

Project Data: Nicholas Court

Land Use and Building Information

Site Area	7,552 square feet (700 square meters)
Total Dwelling Units	9
Gross Density	54 units per acre (133 per hectare)

Land Use Plan

	Square Feet/ Square Meters	Percent of Site
Common Open Space (Including Courtyard)	3,127/290	30

Residential Unit Information

Unit Type	Unit Size (Square Feet/ Square Meters)	Final Sale Price
1-Bedroom/1-Bath	644–662/60–62	$235,000–250,000
1-Bedroom/1.5-Bath	753/70	$225,000
2-Bedroom/2-Bath	1,025–1,229/95–115	$315,000–395,000
2-Bedroom/2.5-Bath	1,103/103	$355,000
3-Bedroom/2.5-Bath	1,262/117	$375,000–385,000

Development Cost Information

Site Costs

Site acquisition	$ 142,500

Site improvement

Excavation/grading/sewer/water/drainage/ paving/curbs/sidewalks	$ 151,000
Landscaping/irrigation	24,000
Total	$175,000

Construction Costs

Superstructure	$325,000
HVAC	142,000
Electrical	114,000
Plumbing/sprinklers	145,000
Finishes	325,500
Windows/doors/roof/siding/insulation	270,000
Graphics/specialties	5,000
Fees/general conditions (9%)	265,000
Other	394,300
Total, Including Tax	$1,985,800

Soft Costs

Architecture/engineering	$120,000
Project management	47,000
Marketing, legal/accounting, taxes/insurance, title fees	129,700
Construction interest and fees	147,000
Total	$443,700

Total Development Cost	**$2,747,000**

Developer

Better Neighborhoods LLC
(a partnership of Inagua and Walker Architecture)

Inagua Enterprises
1411 4th Avenue
Suite 1324
Seattle, Washington 98104
206-623-1234
www.peter-erickson.com/

Site Planner and Architect

Walker Architecture
2301 Western Avenue
Seattle, Washington 98121
206-443-1791
www.walkerarch.com

Development Schedule

9/1997	Site purchased
10/1997	Planning started
9/1998	Construction started
3/2000	Sales started
3/2000	First closing
4/2000	Project completed

One Ford Road
Newport Beach, California

One Ford Road is a 370-unit master-planned community located in the heart of fashionable Newport Beach, just down the road from Newport Center/Fashion Island and the University of California, Irvine. With sale prices mostly above $1 million in the final phase, the project clearly has high-end appeal. But unlike many such developments, the emphasis at One Ford Road has been on community and neighborhood as much as on individual houses and lots. Although lot sizes are relatively small for such high-end housing—ranging primarily from 3,600 to 7,000 square feet (335 to 650 square meters)—the smaller private open spaces are offset by the project's substantial investment in community facilities and common open space. To further reinforce the neighborhood orientation of the project, the developer, Pacific Bay Properties, has experimented with alley-accessed parking and a mix of product types, both of which are relative rarities in upper-income housing.

Site Planning and Design
The 100-acre (40-hectare) site of One Ford Road was one of the last remaining close-in undeveloped housing sites in Newport Beach. It is surrounded on all sides by existing housing developments. Originally owned by the Irvine Company, the site was initially mapped for more than 500 dwelling units. The Ford Motor Land Company later acquired the land and then enlisted Pacific Bay Properties to develop the site.

Under the guidance of Pacific Bay's president, John Markely, the architectural firm MVE & Partners undertook master plan studies, with input from Kenneth Agid of the Marketing Department, marketing consultants. From the start, Markely's goal was to create a sense of neighborhood cohesion. He wanted the master plan to emphasize social values and interaction, unlike the many affluent communities with high walls and inward-oriented housing. One result was an initial reduction in the number of planned dwellings from 500 to 387 units. The land taken out of production was used for community facilities and open space. As the project—even the models with smaller yards—began to attract more and more families, Pacific Bay reduced the lot count to 370 units and used the reclaimed land for pocket parks and other community facilities.

Two entrances to One Ford Road, at the north and south, lead past manned gatehouses to Old Course Drive, a loop road that forms the circulation spine of the community. Secondary loops and culs-de-sac emanate from the primary loop road. The community's recreation facili-

ties visually anchor the two entry drives. Terminating the view from the north entry is the main clubhouse and pool complex, and anchoring the southern entry is an elaborate pergola and a second pool. A one-third-mile-long (0.5-kilometer) pathway and recreation area, dubbed "the Paseo," connects these community facilities, providing an off-street pedestrian walkway for the community.

Although it is just a few years old, One Ford Road already has much of the feeling of a mature community. Considerable attention has been paid to the streetscape. Larger street trees were installed along the main loop street at relatively close intervals, 30 feet (9 meters) on center. Camphor trees were selected for the loop road because of their large size and spreading canopy at maturity. Tree species on the local streets include bay laurel, Bradford pear, and glossy privet, typically spaced at 25 feet (7.6 meters) on center. To further heighten the sense of a mature landscape, the developer installed most of the front yard landscaping for houses facing the loop road and most of the landscaping for the alley-backed Balboa units. Adding to the project's sense of permanence and historical recall is the extensive use of cultured stone for the gatehouses and running walls and the use of large trellised shade structures and decorative details.

Most community amenities and facilities are connected to each other via the Paseo. The pool at the northern end, constructed to Junior Olympic size and standards, is home to One Ford Road's swim team, which competes against other local community teams. In addition to the clubhouse, the complex includes a 2,500-square-foot (230-square-meter) workout facility, with equipment comparable to a small commercial gym. Trainers are on site two days a week to show residents how to use the equipment. The workout facility "is a very social thing," notes Markely. "People are there at five-thirty in the morning" and socialize just like at a commercial gym. The pool complex also has basketball courts and a playground for younger children.

Farther along the Paseo is an 18-hole putting green and a "secret garden" for children. At the southern end of the development are a large open green, a terraced pergola with barbecue facilities, and the community's second pool, which is geared more to adults than the main pool. In addition to the Paseo, several small themed open spaces—among them a croquet garden, a volleyball court, and a rose garden—are dispersed throughout the community. Typically a half-acre (0.2 hectare)

One Ford Road offers an attractive streetscape, created by eliminating driveways and relegating garages to the rear. Deep planting strips at the curb, raised front porches, and fine architectural detailing further enhance the streetscape.

or smaller, these pockets of greenery provide further active and passive recreational opportunities.

Managing all these facilities and the social life of the community as well is the community concierge, a full-time paid staff person, funded through homeowners' association dues. The community concierge handles reservations for private use of the clubhouse (for weddings, parties, classes, and so on) and other facilities and coordinates catering services. The concierge also organizes community events such as the back-to-school sleep-out on the green, the traditional Fourth of July celebration, and other holiday events.

One Ford Road maintains a Web site for the community. The site is partitioned into a public side for non-residents who want to know more about the community and a password-protected side for community residents. The residents-only part of the Web site includes a calendar of community events maintained by the community concierge and a resources section that includes listings of baby-sitters and other contacts and resources. The site also includes photos of community events.

Housing

Pacific Bay not only developed One Ford Road's site infrastructure but also developed and built all the community's housing. Unlike most planned communities, which include a variety of merchant builders recruited to build the housing and provide diverse products, Pacific Bay decided to keep this function in house to maintain

maximum control of the community's appearance and buildout. It also allowed the developer more control over the interrelationships between the various housing types in the community and provided the opportunity to carefully mix housing product.

Five unit types were designed for the project, ranging from approximately 2,400 square feet to 5,000 square feet (225 to 465 square meters). The smallest is the Balboa, a two-bedroom/2½-bath unit. Designed to maximize the usable street-facing frontage, the Balboa units feature raised, covered front porches. Inspired by nearby Balboa Island, a historic island community in Newport Harbor, the Balboa features garages that are accessed by rear-facing alleys. Notes architect Carl McLarand, principal of MVE & Partners, the 20-foot (6-meter) width of the alleys comprises ten feet (3 meters) taken from the 100-foot (30-meter) depth of typical lots to either side, maintaining efficient land use.

The remaining unit types have more traditional street-access garages, though some of the units have side-loaded garages, that is, garages with doors turned 90 degrees perpendicular to the street to minimize the visual impact and bulky massing of, typically, three-car garages.

Some of the larger models feature master suites on the main level targeted to older buyers. Bonus rooms above garages and home offices with separate entries have proved to be popular options. Chris Yelich, senior vice president of Pacific Bay Homes, says that use of such

The Paseo, a landscaped pedestrian walkway, winds through the center of the site, connecting the project's community facilities at either end and along the way.

Extensive use of stone walls and wood trellises provides landscape continuity throughout the project. These elements, as well as large, closely spaced trees, give the project the look of a more mature community

space runs from guest bedrooms to in-law residences to studios to recreation space to rental units.

Stylistically, the housing at One Ford Road takes its design cues from California and Cape Cod beach cottages, craftsman-inspired elements, and similar period influences. Roofs are typically cedar shingles, siding a cement fiber composite board. Common to all the units is a high level of exterior detailing, with highly developed railings, moldings, and trim.

Although most of One Ford Road was developed with a single housing type on each street, Pacific Bay experimented by varying product types on individual streets, particularly along the north and south entry roads and on a few additional locations interspersed throughout the project. The intent, according to John Markely, was to reflect the diversity of some premier older neighborhoods around the United States.

In addition to the five unit types making up the bulk of the project, One Ford Road includes eight custom

home lots ranging from 18,000 to 40,000 square feet (1,675 to 3,720 square meters). Pacific Bay built speculative homes on the first two of these lots to set the tone for the remaining six lots. These first two houses are approximately 8,400 square feet (780 square meters) and are expected to sell for approximately $5 million. The remaining lots will be sold with architectural plans for residences ranging up to 12,000 square feet (1,115 square meters). Buyers for these lots will select and contract with their own builders.

Marketing and Sales

Sales at One Ford Road started in 1998 and averaged almost ten units per month. About 90 percent of the buyers have come from within a ten-mile (16-kilometer) radius, the majority from within a radius of five to seven miles (8 to 11 kilometers). According to Yelich, the marketing program for One Ford Road was not elaborate. In the early stage, it consisted primarily of a project sign

Design cues come from California and Cape Cod beach cottages. Variations of craftsman and cottage-style elevations are applied to six unit types available at One Ford Road.

and a phone number backed by a temporary design center. Later, model units were added. Rather than host large events and open houses, Pacific Bay required appointments from interested parties so that the sales staff could meet one on one with potential buyers to fully explain the community's virtues. Over time, the predominant force driving marketing was referrals, according to Markely.

The market response to One Ford Road has been wider than initially expected. The Balboa units were expected to generate the greatest interest from childless couples because of their small lots, but they have drawn an additional component of families with children. Despite the smaller private yards, many families, attracted by the community facilities and overall environment, purchased the Balboa units just to get a foothold in the community. Some of these families have since traded up to larger homes in the community.

Another strong market segment has been move-down buyers: well-to-do empty nesters who are ready to trade their 5,000 to 10,000-square-foot (465- to 930-square-meter) homes for the still large but more manageable houses at One Ford Road. Among this group, the first-floor master suites have proved to be desirable because of their increased accessibility for older persons.

Price appreciation at One Ford Road has been quite strong. Started during the recession of the mid-1990s, expected sale prices for the first of four phases were limited. The strong market response to the project, coupled with inflation in the housing market in the late 1990s and early 2000s, has resulted in prices that have more than doubled for the final phase of the project over the initial 1998 prices.

Experience Gained

Although alley-loaded projects have more often been constructed as moderately priced housing, alley units were highly successful at One Ford Road. According to Pacific Bay's John Markely, alley-accessed units

could well have been successfully developed at even higher prices.

Mixing unit types has also been successful at One Ford Road. Buyers offered little resistance to the mixing of house sizes and prices within the range offered at One Ford Road.

The extensive community facilities offered at One Ford Road were found to be a considerable inducement to buyers, effectively offsetting the smaller lots, even for families with children.

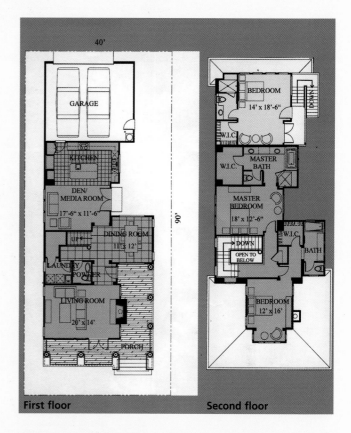

First floor   **Second floor**

Floor plans.

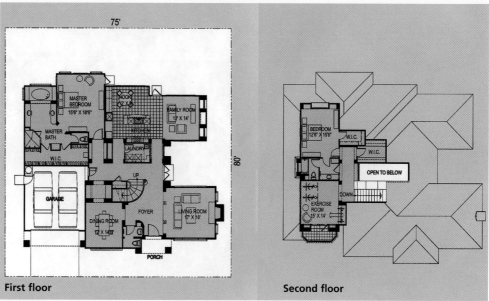

First floor   **Second floor**

Rear alleys provide access to
the Balboa units. The developer installed all the yard
landscaping for these units to
ensure the desired standards.

Site plan.

Balboa

Carmel

Stonybrook

Pacific
Heights

Summer
House

Providence

NORTH

Project Data: One Ford Road

Land Use and Building Information

Site Area	100 acres (40 hectares)
Total Dwelling Units	370
Gross Density	3.7 units per acre (9 per hectare)

Land Use Plan

	Acres/ Hectares	Percent of Site
Detached Residential	65/26	65%
Roads	5/2	5
Common Open Space	25/10	25
Recreation Facilities	5/2	5
Total	100/40	100%

Residential Unit Information

Unit Type	Lot Size (Square Feet/ Square Meters)	Unit Size (Square Feet/ Square Meters)	Number of Units	Sale Price Range
Balboa	4,000/370	2,400–3,100/ 225–290	103	Low 900,000s
Carmel	5,000/465	2,750–3,200/ 255–295	57	$1,000,000
Stonybrook	6,000/560	3,100–3,850/ 290–360	80	$1,300,000
Summerhouse	6,000/560	3,100–3,800/ 290–355	63	$1,350,000
Providence	7,000/650	4,000–5,000/ 370–465	59	$1,750,000
Pacific Heights	8,000–40,000/ 1,675–3,715	8,400–12,000/ 780–1,115	8	$5,000,000 +

Development Cost Information

Site Costs

Site acquisition	$38,000,000
Common areas	25,000,000
Site improvement	47,000,000
Total	$110,000,000

Construction Costs

	$145,000,000

Soft Costs

	$45,000,000

Total Development Cost

	$300,000,000

Developer

Pacific Bay Properties
4041 MacArthur Boulevard
Suite 500
Newport Beach, California
949-440-7216

Site Planner and Project Architect

MVE & Partners
1900 Main Street
8th Floor
Irvine, California 92614
949-809-3300
www.mve-architects.com/

Landscape Designer

Burton Associates
307 South Cedros
Solana Beach, California 92075
858-794-7204
www.burtonassociates.com/

Marketing

The Marketing Department
4041 MacArthur Boulevard
Suite 140
Newport Beach, California 92660
949-476-1895

Development Schedule

1995	Site purchased
1995	Planning started
8/1997	Construction started
5/1998	Sales started
11/1998	First closing
3/1999	Phase I completed
12/2001	Project completed

Playa Vista
Los Angeles, California

Playa Vista is a new master-planned community that finally succeeded—when two decades of other plans had failed—by building a new model of urban infill place making based on the Ahwahnee principles (see the feature box in Chapter 4). Playa Vista balances nature with a broad mix of uses, including a wide variety of housing, workplaces, shops, recreational facilities, new technology, transportation, and community services in a pedestrian-oriented environment. Approximately 70 percent of the site has been set aside as open space.

To help create a vibrant urban environment, housing is built at densities ranging from 14 units to 85 units per acre (34.5 to 210 per hectare), with an average density of 24 units per acre (60 per hectare)—compared with typical densities in southern California of four to 12 units per acre (10 to 30 per hectare). Playa Vista has become the new urban development model of its decade, attracting attention from architects, planners, government officials, and developers from across the United States and from as far away as Japan.

Master developer Playa Capital Company—a group that includes investment banks and a union pension fund—is constructing Playa Vista on a flat, long, generally rectangular 1,087-acre (440-hectare) site that runs west to east from near the Pacific Ocean inland to I-405 (the San Diego Freeway) in Los Angeles's popular but housing-starved Westside. The master plan divides Playa Vista into four basic zones: open space, a multiuse community, the Village at Playa Vista (a mixed-use town center), and the Campus at Playa Vista (office and commercial uses). Playa Vista is bordered on the north by Marina del Rey and on the south by Westchester; it is approximately three miles (5 kilometers) north of Los Angeles International Airport. The site, which was the last large developable piece of land in the city of Los Angeles, contains parts of the Ballona wetlands, one of the last large wetlands in southern California. More than 700 acres (280 hectares) of open space includes extensive wetlands and more than two dozen parks.

Under construction since 1998, Playa Vista is expected to reach buildout in 2010, when it is projected to include 5,846 residential units comprising 17 different product lines with 76 floor plans. The project will also include 3.4 million square feet (316,000 square meters) of office space and 185,000 square feet (17,200 square meters) of retail, restaurant, community, and commercial uses. The community also includes a branch of the Los Angeles public library, the 26,000-square-foot (2,415-square-meter) CenterPointe Club social and activity community center,

a fire station, and a police drop-in station. The streets and buildings are scaled to create a pedestrian-friendly environment. No building is taller than six stories.

The Site and Its History

In 1839, Rancho La Ballona was established on the Playa Vista site, where cattle ran for 40 years. After the ranch was broken up in 1880, the Playa Vista portion was used as a large dairy and agricultural farm. During World War II, Howard Hughes bought the Playa Vista site and built his Hughes Aircraft plant, a runway, and several hangars, including the 315,000-square-foot (29,000-square-meter) hangar where he designed and constructed the legendary *Spruce Goose,* a wooden cargo flying boat that remains the largest aircraft ever built.

In 1978, Hughes's Summa Corporation released its plan to develop a new community on the property with high-rise office buildings, 8,800 residential units, a golf course, and the 175-acre (70-hectare) Ballona wetlands preserve. For more than 150 years, the Ballona wetlands had been grazed, developed, drained, dredged, and cut off from the Pacific Ocean and its rejuvenating tidewaters. Nevertheless, in a county that had destroyed 95 percent of its wetlands, the Ballona wetlands remained one of the last large wetlands in southern California. As a result, environmental groups and other organizations sued to stop the Summa Corporation development.

In 1989, Maguire Thomas Partners–Playa Vista took over the project, scaled back the development program, provided greater wetlands preservation, and, in 1993, secured Phase I entitlements. But the surrounding community was still concerned that the project would generate additional traffic congestion, overburden the sewer system, pollute the Pacific Ocean, and consume too much of the Ballona wetlands.

In 1997, the Playa Capital Company acquired the property and became the master developer. The surrounding Westside community was job rich but housing poor and eager for an urban environment with abundant open space; at the same time, a wide variety of environmental and community groups wanted to preserve and rehabilitate the Ballona wetlands.

Playa Capital Company had its own objectives. First, it wanted to build a balanced community with a strong and distinctive identity that adheres to the Ahwahnee principles, a set of guidelines drafted by the founders of the new urbanism movement. Second, and of equal importance, the company wanted to implement extensive environmental programs, incorporate a wide variety

Playa Vista is a 1,087-acre (440-hectare) urban infill site that brings a broad range of new housing to Los Angeles.

Playa Vista

of open-space venues throughout the development, and provide a "natural" stormwater management system.

To resolve continuing opposition and litigation and to answer community concerns, Playa Capital partnered with one of the oldest and largest local environmental groups, Friends of the Ballona Wetlands, as well as leading planners, architects, and landscape architects to create a new $2.7 billion urban infill community master plan. The company also forged an option agreement with the Trust for Public Land that sets aside 70 percent of the site as dedicated open space, creating a natural oasis in the midst of sprawling Los Angeles. The master plan limits construction to land previously developed by Howard Hughes, avoiding the remaining wetlands, and it has earned the support of most mainstream activists and environmental groups.

Development and Design Process
Summa Corporation's 1978 master plan to redevelop the Playa Vista site with high rises and a golf course had been created in house. Maguire Thomas Partners–Playa Vista's 1993 plan, however, was based primarily on three days of design charrettes held in June 1989 that drew on the ideas and feedback from nationally recognized urban planners, architects, and consultants, as well as the surrounding community.

While adopting most of Maguire Thomas's concepts, Playa Capital Company refined its Playa Vista urban infill master plan based on the 23 Ahwahnee

principles. Those principles stress, among other things, that a community should have the housing, shops, workplaces, schools, parks, and civic facilities essential to the daily life of its residents and that those uses should be within easy walking distance of each other. A community should also include diverse housing products to serve residents from a wide range of economic levels, age groups, and lifestyles. Finally, development should be compact and high density, complemented by abundant open space.

Playa Capital designed and constructed Playa Vista's public streets and landscapes. Residential and commercial builders are required to follow the master plan's building and block concepts.

Open Space
Playa Capital Company is under contract to the state of California to sell 193 acres (78 hectares) of Playa Vista and to donate or waive its rights to an additional 415 acres (168 hectares) for wetlands restoration and preservation. The company is also spending $40 million on three major on-site wetlands and wildlife habitat restoration and enhancement programs encompassing an additional 290 acres (117 hectares), each of which is accessible to some degree to Playa Vista residents. It has created funding mechanisms to preserve, monitor, and maintain these projects in perpetuity. The Ballona wetlands is considered one of the largest natural restoration projects undertaken in U.S. history.

Villa d'Esta luxury condominiums were inspired by the Spanish Colonial revival mansions of the 1920s.

In 2002, the company completed the 18-acre (7.3-hectare) first phase of the new 26-acre (10.5-hectare) Ballona Freshwater Marsh, which will have a riparian ecosystem of 3,000 trees and nearly 10,000 native grasses, shrubs, and plants bordering open water. The marsh provides flood control and the first natural stormwater management system in Los Angeles County; helps prevent flooding by capturing stormwater runoff and releasing it slowly into the ocean; and helps to cleanse the water by filtering out pollutants and toxins. The company deeded the marsh to the state in 2004.

The company will also restore and enhance the 40.7-acre (16.5-hectare) Westchester Bluffs coastal sage scrub community. In addition, Playa Capital is replacing the concrete-lined Centinela storm ditch with the new 1.5-mile (2.4-kilometer), 25-acre (10-hectare) Bluff Creek Riparian Corridor, which will run along the base of the Westchester Bluffs and provide wildlife habitat, treat stormwater, and support flood control.

Playa Vista will also have more than two dozen parks united in a community-wide system. Parks for Phase II will include design input from Edwin Schlossberg, founder of New York City–based ESI Design, and his five-person team.

A Multiuse Community

In Los Angeles's job-rich but housing-limited Westside, Playa Vista plans to add 5,846 residential units incorporating diverse architectural styles, floor plans, and prices, primarily in the multiuse community zone. The multiuse zone is also planned for 400,000 square feet (37,200 square meters) of office space, 35,000 square feet (3,250 square meters) of retail space, and a wide variety of services and amenities.

The buildings reflect Los Angeles's varied streetscape with architecture inspired by Art Deco and Retro styles, Frank Lloyd Wright, and neoclassical European buildings. Each neighborhood includes a mix of building styles.

Paseos provide access for pedestrians between buildings.

Rich architectural detailing recalls the Spanish heritage of Los Angeles.

Although some architectural purists have objected to these predominantly mainstream choices, Playa Capital Company selected these styles because of their enduring popularity among southern California renters and homebuyers.

Although the parcels and buildings vary in size and dimensions, the typical block has a building footprint of about 220 feet by 300 feet (67 by 91 meters). But because the buildings are subject to a 55 percent lot coverage ratio, most have substantial open space in inner courtyards, and many of the buildings are broken up for greater visual interest.

Playa Vista's compact neighborhoods have active connections to the streets and sidewalks through underground parking, street-level units, and extensive landscaping. Rather than sitting atop an above-ground parking garage, for example, the community's multifamily residential units start at street level, with their doors, patios, or porches providing direct entrances as well as architectural interest to sidewalks and streets. Courtyards connect buildings to each other and to neighborhood amenities, such as parks.

The many different kinds of housing and neighborhoods are clustered into several different districts, each of which has at least one major park. The Fountain Park District, for example, has two parks as well as the Fountain Park Apartments complex (705 apartments in five buildings with interconnected courtyards), Bridgeway Mills (80 industrial loft–style townhouses), Playa Vista's 6,600-square-foot (615-square-meter) visitor center, and Water's Edge, a 6+-acre (2.4-hectare) high-tech contemporary business center. Water's Edge will be home to Redwood City–based Electronic Arts's state-of-the art game development studio.

The Concert Park District, on the other hand, is laid out like a traditional town square with mixed-use buildings. Its diverse housing includes the Lofts (63 loft-style condominiums) and East Concert Park Condominiums, both with ground-floor retail shops, and Citi-Homes (ten detached 3,500-square-foot [325-square-meter] single-family homes).

The Village at Playa Vista

The heart of Playa Vista will be a 111-acre (45-hectare) pedestrian-oriented village that connects the multiuse community to the west with the commercial Campus at Playa Vista to the east. The village will have a balanced mix of uses, including approximately 2,600 new residences comprising a variety of housing products, 150,000 square feet (14,000 square meters) of commercial space (shops, restaurants, coffee houses, a pharmacy, a grocery), 175,000 square feet (16,300 square meters) of neighborhood-scale office and commercial space, and approximately 40,000 square feet (3,700 square meters) of space dedicated to community-serving uses. The village will also have approximately 12 acres (5 hectares) of open space, including preserved wildlife habitat, a town green, and five other parks connected by a network of pedestrian paths, sidewalks, and nature trails.

A variety of public parks and squares enliven the outdoor areas at Playa Vista.

The Campus at Playa Vista

When fully built, the 114-acre (46-hectare) Campus at Playa Vista on the eastern side of the community—part of the 1993 Maguire Thomas entitlements approved by the city of Los Angeles—will have 3.2 million square feet (297,400 square meters) of commercial office space, studios, studio support space, a child care center, stores, and restaurants in both historic and new buildings with landscaped open spaces. Several of the site's existing historic build-

Community swimming pools are part of the suburban-style recreation package.

The Metro, a luxury condominium development, overlooks one of the parks at Playa Vista.

ings, including the *Spruce Goose* hangar, are slated for permanent preservation and are being reused on an interim basis. In the mid-1990s, for example, the former Hughes aircraft hangars were converted into motion picture and television sound stages. Scenes from a number of major motion pictures have been filmed at Playa Vista.

Transportation

Playa Vista's $100 million traffic plan includes improving local traffic flow by adding much-needed capacity. Playa Vista is contributing to improvements to the state highway system, including the Jefferson Boulevard on- and off-ramps to the San Diego Freeway. It also is providing 11 new buses for the Santa Monica and Culver City bus lines to connect the community to major Westside employment centers.

Within the community, the overall street design uses an urban-style grid of landscaped parkways and comparatively narrow streets to create a cohesive and walkable

framework for the community that discourages high-speed traffic. Approximately 90 percent of Playa Vista's parking will be underground. Landscaped pedestrian pathways and bike trails are designed to connect residents and workers to all of the neighborhoods, commercial districts, and parks and open space throughout Playa Vista. Hiking trails will be constructed along the Bluff Creek Riparian Corridor.

The master plan's transportation strategy is to reduce automobile use in Playa Vista—and between Playa Vista and neighboring communities—by providing an extensive system of alternative transportation choices, including bus shuttles, bikeways, and a community-wide, clean fuel "smart tram" system that will run on electric power and will transport residents within Playa Vista and to nearby businesses, stores, and transit centers. Playa Vista's residents and businesses can also purchase zero-emission, virtually silent all-electric vehicles through a partnership with DaimlerChrysler's Global Electric Motorcars LLC (GEM) subsidiary.

A Technological Foundation

Each Playa Vista residence has been prewired with a comprehensive technology package that includes entertainment, high-speed data, telecommunications, electronic access control, and other customizable features. Every business has built-in dedicated high-speed cable Internet access. Wireless capabilities will be added to selected parks and public spaces throughout Playa Vista, enabling residents to gain Internet access while sitting on a park bench.

PlayaLink.net, the community Web site, enables residents to monitor their home security while away from home. The community's technology design center, staffed by a full-time CompUSA employee known as a "Connectivity Concierge," provides information and help on anything related to technology, from hardware and software to home theaters and lighting controls.

Financing, Marketing, and Operations

Playa Vista is a $2.7 billion project. Bank of the West provided a total of $386 million in financing. Although not yet fully built, Playa Vista is already highly sought after. Of the 552 for-sale units released as of December 1, 2003, 518 had either been sold or reserved with a deposit, and 591 of the 705 released Fountain Park Apartment complex rental units had been leased. As of this writing, Playa Capital Company has a waiting list of 7,000 people for 2,000 residential units.

The marketing program focuses less on Playa Vista's 76 different residential floor plans and more on the community as a whole, particularly its warm, close-knit, neighborhood feel, its desirable Westside location and proximity to jobs, and the pedestrian-oriented urban lifestyle.

Each Playa Vista residential neighborhood has its own homeowners' association that oversees the maintenance and improvements to its respective area. Playa Vista Parks and Landscaping is the community's master residents association responsible for the day-to-day operations of the overall community, including landscaping, common area maintenance, trash and recycling, and the patrol service. It works closely with each homeowners' association and is funded by residential assessments.

Experience Gained

Playa Capital Company faced several challenges in planning and winning approval for Playa Vista. By studying the experiences of its predecessors, Playa Capital Company learned the importance of turning opponents into allies by working with them. Playa Capital, for example, worked with Friends of the Ballona Wetlands to create the master plan and environmental plans for Playa Vista. That kind of collaboration has continued throughout the community's development process. Experience Ballona, for example, is an ongoing initiative between Loyola Marymount University, Friends of the Ballona Wetlands, and Playa Vista focused on bringing awareness, restoration, and appreciation of Playa Vista's ecosystem to the locality and the region. Audubon scientists have developed interpretive signage for the Ballona Freshwater Marsh.

Some architects and planners have criticized Playa Vista for its design and density choices. But Playa Vista celebrates higher-density development as a vital tool for creating a strong sense of community. The higher densities create greater pedestrian activity, which enhances the vibrancy of the streetscape, supports transit, and allows more room for precious open space. And the community's 17 different residential products in a broad range of architectural styles help to creating a diverse and attrac-

tive whole that relates contextually to other southern California streetscapes while meeting the design preferences of a diverse marketplace.

In 1999, Playa Vista received the Ahwahnee Award, given annually by nationally renowned architects and urban designers in recognition of projects, plans, and programs that help create more livable pedestrian- and transit-friendly communities in the western United States. The strong residential sales and leases the community has enjoyed thus far, the continuing and overwhelming demand from prospective homebuyers and tenants, and the signing of major commercial tenants also prove not only the wisdom of Playa Capital's decisions but also the success of Playa Vista as a whole.

Site plan, aerial view.

Project Data: Playa Vista

Land Use and Building Information

Site Area	1,087 acres (440 hectares)
Total Dwelling Units Planned	5,846
Total Dwelling Units Completed	1,380
Gross Density	23 units per acre (57 per hectare)
Average Net Density	12–80 units per acre (30–200 per hectare)

Land Use Plan

	Acres/ Hectares	Percent of Site
Detached Residential	24/9.7	2%
Attached Residential	9/3.6	1
Mixed-Use Residential/Retail	16/6.5	1
Multifamily Residential (including Assisted Living)	72/29.1	7
Residential Apartments	25/10.1	2
Roads	93/37.7	9
Office	82/33.2	8
Community Serving	9/3.6	1
Parks	46/18.6	4
Open Space	711/287.9	65
Total	1,087/440.0	100%

Developer

Playa Capital Company
5450 Lincoln Boulevard
Playa Vista, California 90094
800-530-7768
www.playavista.com

Site Planners

Moule & Polyzoides
180 East California Boulevard
Pasadena, California 91105
626-844-2400
www.mparchitects.com

Moore Ruble Yudell
933 Pico Boulevard
Santa Monica, California 90405
310-450-1400
www.moorerubleyudell.com

Residential Unit Information

Unit Type	Units per Acre/ per Hectare	Unit Size (Square Feet/ Square Meters)	Number of Units (Planned/Built)	Opening Sale Price/ Rent Range
Detached	12–16/30–40	2,100–3,500/195–325	307/23	$750,000–1,500,000
Attached	20/50	1,600–2,800/150–260	164/25	$525,000–900,000
Mixed Use	55	TBD[1]	354/0	TBD[1]
Multifamily	35–80/85–200	625–3,500/60–325	2,868/413	$218,000–1,100,000
Assisted Living	68–80/170–200	TBD[1]	280/0	TBD[1]
Apartments	70–80/175–200	525–1,400/50–130	1,873/919	$500–3,400 per month

Note
[1] To be determined.

Duany Plater-Zyberk & Company
1023 SW 25th Avenue
Miami, Florida 33135
305-644-1023
www.dpz.com

Legorreta Arquitectos
3440 Motor Avenue
Second Floor
Los Angeles, California 90034
310-391-9976

Park Design Consultant
ESI Design
641 Sixth Avenue
5th Floor
New York, New York 10011
212-989-3993
www.esidesign.com

Landscape Architects
EDAW Los Angeles
3780 Wilshire Boulevard
Suite 250
Los Angeles, California 90010
213-368-1608
www.edaw.com

The Olin Partnership
150 South Independence Mall West
Suite 1123
Philadelphia, Pennsylvania 19106
215-440-0030
www.olinptr.com

Fong Hart Schneider + Partners
930 West 16th Street
Costa Mesa, California 92627
949-645-9444

Mia Lehrer + Associates
3780 Wilshire Boulevard
Suite 1100
Los Angeles, California 90010
213-384-3844
www.mlagreen.com

Collaborative West, Inc.
100 Avenida Miramar
San Clemente, California 92672
949-366-6624
www.thecollaborativewest.com

Development Schedule

1989	Planning started
1997	Site purchased
1998	Construction started
1999	Sales started
2002	First closing
2006	Phase I estimated completion
2010	Project completion

Ravenna Cottages

Seattle, Washington

Ravenna Cottages is a courtyard cluster of nine market-rate owner-occupied housing units tucked into a large mid-block lot in Green Lake, a single-family Seattle neighborhood that built up over the first half of the 20th century. The development includes six two-bedroom, $1^1/_2$-bath detached cottages and three two-bedroom, one-bath loft carriage units above a base containing nine separate garages, all on commonly held land. Ravenna Cottages is one of the few infill cottage home developments built in contemporary times and the only one in the region that features carriage units over the garage.

As the revival of a traditional housing type, cottage clusters satisfy the public environmental agenda by increasing density and furthering growth management goals for cities concerned about sprawl. In addition to conserving energy and making efficient use of existing infrastructure, Ravenna Cottages adds nine units at the effective density of 37 units per acre (91 per hectare) into a neighborhood context of six to eight units per acre (15 to 20 per hectare). The project provides a model for offering more housing options and raising density incrementally when applied to disbursed sites and adapted to neighborhood and site conditions.

Cottages also satisfy the market, where the desire to own a single-family, detached house is deeply and widely held. Because of the finite nature of single-family lots in any city and the general scarcity of land inside urban centers, homebuyers typically are forced to choose from among a shrinking supply of single-family homes, with their attendant high cost, overadequate square footage, and high maintenance. Or they must choose the anonymity of multifamily housing or the impracticality of commuting to a home in the suburbs.

Along with the privacy of a detached unit, well-designed cottage housing offers an intensified sense of community. It also shares the advantages of a multifamily unit: low square footage, low maintenance, and lower cost. Ravenna Cottages offers an important model for this housing type.

The Site

Ravenna Cottages is located in a single-family neighborhood about ten minutes driving distance north of downtown Seattle, to the north and west of the University District. The area called Green Lake began to build up from a rural area to a city neighborhood after 1910, and the housing stock is a typical Seattle mixture of prewar bungalows and postwar housing with a small number of turn-of-the-century farmhouses.

It is now populated by two-worker couples and a scattering of families with children. Property values have gained substantially in the last two decades. Ravenna Cottages is just a block from a Metro express bus stop and $1^1/_2$ blocks from Green Lake, a very popular outdoor destination for shopping, dining, exercise, recreation, and relaxation.

The site is an unusually large, 10,500-square-foot (975-square-meter) mid-block lot that slopes a challenging 12 feet (3.6 meters) diagonally across the site.

Development Process

Recognizing the importance of the demographic trend toward smaller households as well as economic and political conditions of our time, developer Threshold Housing translated the cottage cluster from a historic form of building to a contemporary option in housing.

Several clusters of small cottages were built throughout the city before 1925. Yet until very recently, they could not be built under Seattle's land use code, primarily because of neighborhood fears that this type of housing would threaten the value of their single-family homes. With the redevelopment of Pine Street Cottages in 1991, a set of ten one-bedroom craftsman-style cottages built in 1916, the perception began to change. The renovated cottages not only made money and jumped in value but also became a leveraging tool for marketing the neighborhood.

In the meantime, the passage of the Washington State Growth Management Act in 1990 led to calls for higher-density housing in existing urban areas. In 1991, the King County Housing Partnership founded Threshold Housing, with the goal of developing demonstration projects to test new housing forms. Directors John Kucher and Marcia Hadley had been involved in the redevelopment of Pine Street Cottages, Kucher as developer and Hadley as architect.

Threshold is a small nonprofit housing corporation that owns and manages low-income rental housing targeted to families with children. It has built 66 homes in single-family or cottage-style developments near Seattle, most without government subsidy and sold on the open market.

As a developer, Kucher is responsible for more than 770 apartment and condominium units throughout Seattle, some in conjunction with the city of Seattle as part of the city's low-income housing programs. Hadley is an architect, housing policy specialist, and founding executive director of the King County Housing Partner-

The entrance to Ravenna Cottages provides enclosure and separation between the public sidewalk and the private courtyard in the center of the community.

ship, a business-based nonprofit company. She was closely involved in the concept and planning for Ravenna Cottages, which was designed by Paul Pierce.

After the success of Kucher's Pine Street Cottages, the King County Housing Partnership worked to help write an ordinance that would allow for clusters of small houses to be built in single-family zones. The city made this new option available only in low-density multifamily zones, but no projects were built. City officials then im-

plemented a program that would allow cottages on a selective and limited basis in single-family zones. Ideally, these developments would meet with the approval of surrounding residents concerned about neighborhood character and property values while showing the public new, attractive choices in housing. The Ravenna Cottages site became available when owner Jim Hammock, who had built Pine Street Cottages as a boy with his father, offered the site to Threshold for another cottage proj-

Ravenna Cottages, as seen from the street and sidewalk.

ect. After the development was substantially designed, a distinguished panel of judges selected Ravenna Cottages to receive one of 23 "Should Be Built" designations from Housing Seattle: Design Demonstration Projects jointly sponsored by the Office of the Mayor of Seattle and the Seattle Chapter of the American Institute of Architects. The intent of the program was to make possible a limited number of projects that would otherwise violate zoning in their neighborhoods. Selected projects would go through a special approval process and serve as examples that might support changes to the code and the permitting process.

Cottage cluster housing was one of several distinct housing types cited for inclusion in traditional single-family neighborhoods through the program; others included irregular apartment buildings, detached accessory dwelling units, combinations of parking and open space, garage conversions, and co-housing. Under the terms of the Should Be Built designation, final permitting required support from the surrounding community in the form of an explicit endorsement from a community group. As a designated project, Ravenna Cottages entered the final stages of design, gaining neighborhood sponsorship and winning the necessary departures from code to get a building permit.

Construction began in February 2000 and continued for a year. The difficulty of staging material and equipment for the tightly planned construction, the newness of the housing type to inspectors, and the desire not to block the neighborhood street all lengthened the construction schedule.

Financing
Conventional financing for Ravenna Cottages would have been difficult, because a new housing type has no track record to aid in qualifying loans. Threshold board members' links to financial networks were essential to the project.

Washington Federal Savings and Loan provided the construction financing. It previously had loaned funds for an earlier award-winning Threshold project, Malden Court, and the relationship between the bank and the developer helped the loan process for Ravenna Cottages. One board member provided project equity of $300,000 for Ravenna Cottages, and other members contributed smaller amounts. All were paid back from proceeds of sales.

Approvals

As a designated Design Demonstration Project, Ravenna Cottages had an opportunity to obtain permit approval but would have to gain neighborhood support even as the necessary departures from code were sought. Neighborhood fears and values were an important focus of the design process. Key residents were kept apprised of design decisions and the resolution of critical issues like parking and construction staging.

Current zoning would allow two to three large homes with mother-in-law apartments on the site, for a total of four to six units. The departures necessary to build more units were justified primarily in environmental terms. Ravenna Cottages would house nine households at one-third the total heated square footage that would fit in the allowable building envelopes. At the same time, it would house nine small families instead of six and provide off-street parking for nine cars, all of which decrease the environmental burdens of development and advance growth management goals.

The permit application process for Ravenna Cottages began with the "cottage ordinance," a set of special regulations for cottage development in the city that was added to the building code after the renovation of the Pine Street Cottages in 1991. The ordinance, which was applicable only in multifamily zones, had never been used until Ravenna Cottages came along.

Ravenna Cottages, as designed, required four departures from code as set down in the cottage ordinance. Two of them, which had to be approved by a standing design review board, had to do with lot coverage and open space. The ordinance limits lot coverage to 40 percent. The garages included in the plan for Ravenna Cottages, which were not contemplated in the cottage ordinance and pushed lot coverage up substantially, were defended as responsive to neighborhood concerns about parking and to market demand. Open-space requirements were adjusted to shift a small percentage from private to common areas. Private open spaces, which include 184 square feet (17 square meters) of deck area or usable private open space per cottage, will accommodate seating for up to six people in each space—less than the 200 square feet (18.5 square meters) required, however. To obtain approval, Threshold argued that the usefulness and perceived privacy of the individual open spaces and the size and intimate community atmosphere of the court and common areas compensated for any lack of private space.

A second departure from code was needed to build a full second floor on the cottage units to accommodate a

Rather than individual yards, homes open onto the shared courtyard that is the focal point of the neighborhood.

The interior courtyard provides a range of outdoor environments in a very small space. Shown here is a sheltered place for sitting.

Residents can use the courtyard for socializing.

spacious master bedroom and a second bedroom/office within the standard cottage footprint. This addition would help expand the market from single adults to couples and single parents. Permission was also sought for the construction of a large common basement for storage. The basement storage takes pressure off storage requirements in individual units and makes garage clutter and on-street parking less likely.

Planning and Design

The design of Ravenna Cottages redefines the possibilities of an oversized parcel in an established single-family neighborhood. Along with fitting nine housing units on the site, the design goal was to achieve an exceptional combination of privacy, practicality and convenience, affordability, and community.

The arrangement of the cottage cluster in plan is formal and traditional. The cottages face the courtyard, three on each side; the combination garage/carriage house is on the inside of the courtyard, with garages facing onto an alley. The massing of the carriage house with garage, which blocks freeway noise, is visually broken down with three different roof heights and contrasting dormer shapes.

Along the street, the length of the lot is divided into three sections representing roughly 30-foot-wide (9-meter) lots, with the sides of two of the cottages taking up the outer sections and echoing the typical widths of the homes on the street. Decks and French side doors face the street on the two outer cottages, inside a wrought iron perimeter fence. Centered in the middle section is a welcoming gazebo with benches just outside the gracefully traditional metal security gate. Thus, the rhythm of the streetscape is preserved and the pedestrian experience along the sidewalk enhanced.

The multilayer courtyard plan offers three levels of privacy between street and dwelling interior, compared with just one or none in a typical single-family home. Just inside the gate is a perennial garden designed to be seen and enjoyed by pedestrians. A series of well-defined and carefully appointed outdoor "rooms" define the community connection of the cottages. The porches of the cottage units themselves and the stairs and balconies at the entrances to the carriage units connect to a paved walkway that rings the courtyard.

Tucked into the center of the lot, the courtyard itself is defined by a low concrete sitting wall and paved in exposed aggregate. It is furnished with sturdy teak chairs and tables for community use. A stepped, trellis-covered walkway and water feature divide the courtyard from the outer planting garden, which lies just inside the gate. Planting wells and recesses soften the armature of the open space.

The difference in elevation from one side of the block to the other is resolved between the enclosed rooms of the landscape, with the courtyard serving as a table between the high side and the low. The steps between the two sides of the courtyard add interest to the composition.

Roof pitches and overhangs are similar to those in the surrounding houses. Roofing material also reflects the predominant composition roofing in the area, and different colors of roofing are used on each unit to provide variation and to blend with the neighborhood roofscape. Composition concrete plank siding, paint colors, and plant palette all borrow from surrounding visual samples. As a result, the cluster of cottages is virtually indistinguishable from surrounding vantage points, blending seamlessly into the neighborhood.

The cottages themselves are designed with traditional craftsman-inspired forms and features, with front porches, gables, dormers, lap cement-board siding, and trellises. Floor plans of the six two-story, 930-square-foot (86-square-meter) cottages are the same or are mirror images, with a great room, kitchen, and half bath on the first floor and two bedrooms and full bath on the second. Each floor has operable windows on all four sides. Floors on the first level are all hardwood, and each unit has a gas fireplace in the great room. French doors open to a small deck of long-lasting wood/plastic composite material, and a back door from the kitchen opens to a small concrete patio wrapped around the rear of the cottage. Added touches such as ceramic tile surrounds for the tub and spindled railings on the stairs reinforce the perception of single-family quality. Cottages are heated with a radiant hot water system. Three 900-square-foot (84-square-meter) carriage houses each have a two-story vaulted great room overlooked by a 20- by 12-foot (6- by 2.6-meter) loft tall enough for a person to stand in. One bedroom and a bath are also on the first floor. All are heated by radiant heat under hardwood flooring.

Because of the limited storage space in the living units and the desire to keep the garages free of storables, each unit has an individual eight- by ten-foot (2.4- by 3-meter) heated storage space located in a common basement under two of the cottage units, constructed using the void left when the basement of the house was demolished for the cottage project.

Marketing and Buyers

Unlike many other successful housing developments, none of the units at Ravenna Cottages were presold. Because the developers believed that the common spaces and the interior and exterior details and finishes are all critical for market appeal in cottage units, sales were postponed until the entire development—including the courtyard and all common outdoor areas—was complete. Once they went on the market, however, all nine units were sold within nine weeks. Several were sold in the first week after the project got extensive coverage in the *Seattle Times;* 2,000 people attended the associated open house. Street signs drew many prospective buyers.

Threshold decided not to list the property with an agent. Instead, the group hired a sales person and paid a flat fee per unit sold. Real estate agents were given a commission of 3 percent on the first $100,000 and 1.5 percent on the remainder of the sale.

Sale prices for the cottages ranged from $255,000 to $310,000. Four of the units went to singles and one couple, all in their 20s and 30s and employed in high-tech fields. Two went to doctors, one to a lawyer, and two to retirees. In all, seven units are owned by single people and two by couples. For all but three of the buyers, it was their first home purchase. The units were priced for income levels of 130 to 180 percent of the median for the area.

Experience Gained

As an unusual and particular type of development, cottage cluster housing is likely to fall between the cracks in a code that distinguishes rigidly between multifamily and single-family housing, which can be confusing for reviewers and inspectors. For instance, because the storage locker area at Ravenna Cottages has community access, it must have one-hour fire separation, whereas a conventional basement would not need that separation. Even though none of the cottages are far from the street, fire access must be provided between each of the cottages.

Each cottage development must have on-site stormwater retention like that required for multifamily housing, even though the cluster plan has less impervious surface (and less need for filtration) than the three typical single-family homes that would have been allowed on the site with no such requirement.

Because each one is owned separately, units must have individual utility hookups. This requirement not only added to the costs of construction but also raised the risk of damaging utility lines laid previously on the same project. In retrospect, one way of simplifying the problem would be to build a utility vault under the courtyard and dig clear paths to each unit.

The city allowed the project to have a single sewer connection; nine separate sewer connections would have meant digging a large part of the street at great expense. Because units are owned as condominiums, the development has a single primary water meter and submeters for each unit, allowing the owners' associa-

A postage stamp–sized garden at one side of the interior courtyard.

What the cottages lack in space they make up in style. Large panes of glass allow maximum light.

tion to bill residents for water and sewer service based on actual use.

Such problems, which accrue to a housing type that may be politically desirable and in demand but not yet familiar to the local bureaucracy, will iron out over time. Most codes are not written to anticipate urban infill development in single-family neighborhoods. Much can be done to streamline and unburden the approval process. Plan reviewers should have a clear mandate, adaptable guidelines, and the discretionary authority to apply them.

Because of the small scale and fine-grained urban fabric of cottage-style units, success depends on special attention to detail and the way the entire development presents to the street and to a potential buyer. A cottage standing alone does not have the same appeal as one in a cluster, and because it is difficult for buyers to visualize the finished product, it is important for the composition to be complete. To help cottage housing sell on its own terms and achieve the best market prices, the courtyard and community landscape must receive finishing touches before the project goes on the market.

A direct tradeoff exists between quantity of space and quality of detail and finishes. In other words, it is very important to invest in surfaces, architectural features, and fixtures that contribute to character, livability, and ease of maintenance. And it is important to have these things in place before units are shown. Furnishing a model unit will pay off in sales. As with any residential

space, if planning has been careful and well conceived, the furnished unit will look and feel larger than an unfinished unit—an especially important factor in a house with less square footage.

In part because of Ravenna Cottages, popular interest in and awareness of cottage housing as a choice of housing is clearly growing. A handful of cottage cluster developments in the Northwest are now complete or on the boards. In the meantime, more than 2,500 visitors from the United States and Canada have toured Ravenna Cottages.

Alley

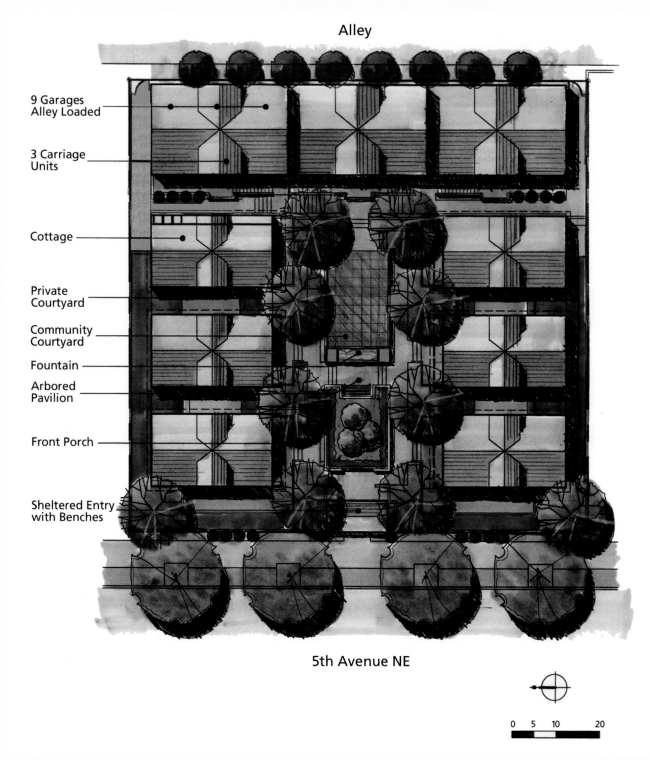

9 Garages
Alley Loaded

3 Carriage
Units

Cottage

Private
Courtyard

Community
Courtyard

Fountain

Arbored
Pavilion

Front Porch

Sheltered Entry
with Benches

5th Avenue NE

0   5   10   20

Site plan.

Project Data: Ravenna Cottages

Land Use and Building Information

Site Area   10,500 square feet (975 square meters)

Total Dwelling Units Planned
and Completed   9

Gross Density   37 units per acre (91 per hectare)

Land Use Plan

	Square Feet/ Square Meters	Percent of Site
Attached Residential (Carriage Houses)	1,900/175	18%
Common Open Space/Walks	4,244/395	40
Detached Residential (Cottages)	2,688/250	26
Private Open Space	1,668/155	16
Total	10,500/975	100%

Residential Unit Information

Unit Type (Bedrooms/Baths)	Number of Units	Unit Size (Square Feet/ Square Meters)	Current or Final Sale Price Range
2/1.5	6	928/86	$290,000–310,000
2/1	3	1,020/95	$255,000–265,000

Development Cost Information

Site Costs

Site acquisition	$199,000
Site improvement	
Excavation/grading	73,185
Sewer/water/drainage	84,406
Paving/curbs/sidewalks	43,267
Landscaping/irrigation	41,577
Fees/general conditions	20,598
Natural gas/underground electrical	3,103
Total	$465,136

Construction Costs

Superstructure	$626,795
HVAC	33,617
Electrical	124,019
Plumbing/sprinklers	71,266
Finishes	364,652
Graphics/specialties	598
Fees/general conditions	173,976
Appliances	29,573
Exhaust duct	7,702
Punch list/warranties	47,040
Total	$1,479,238

Soft Costs

Architecture/engineering	$ 43,047
Project management	60,266
Marketing	17,902
Legal/accounting	12,026
Taxes/insurance	5,590
Title fees	2,796
Construction interest and fees	145,306
Miscellaneous	14,200
Total	$301,133

Total Development Cost $2,245,507

Developer

John Kucher
Threshold Housing
3425 East Denny Way
Seattle, Washington 98122
206-322-0989

Site Planner

Marcia Gamble Hadley
5641 Beach Drive Southwest
Seattle, Washington 98136
206-234-5599

Architect

Paul Pierce
1352 North 78th Street
Seattle, Washington 98103
206-387-7570

Landscape Designer

Suzanne Edison
Edison Landscape Design
1511 37th Avenue
Seattle, Washington 98122
206-322-2475

Interior Designer

Sheila Thomas
3832 Eastern Avenue North
Seattle, Washington 98103
206-634-1013

Development Schedule

1/1998	Planning started
3/1999	Site purchased
2/2000	Construction started
2/2001	Sales started
3/2001	First closing
3/2001	Project completed

Rivermark

Santa Clara, California

Silicon Valley is best known for its innovation in the technology sector. But while hardware, software, and Internet businesses cycled down since the turn of the century, northern California's community developers picked up the innovation gauntlet with Rivermark, a 1,889-unit multiuse master-planned community in Santa Clara, at the southern end of the San Francisco Bay. The project is cutting edge in land planning and housing product and in the collaboration among community builders Centex Homes, Shea Homes, and Lennar Communities (Greystone Homes).

Rivermark incorporates many elements of traditional neighborhood design, offering a full array of housing options from rental apartments to for-sale townhouses to high-density detached homes reaching 14 units per acre (35 per hectare). Adjacent to the new Sun Microsystems corporate campus and within walking distance to light-rail service, the residential community is oriented to a 140,000-square-foot (13,000-square-meter) retail town center. It is master planned down to the last detail, with land planning, architecture, and even the community color palette carefully coordinated and implemented collectively.

Site Context, Land Acquisition, and the Joint Venture Partnership

Rivermark was developed on the site of the former Agnew State Hospital, a quintessential infill location underserved for both housing and retail. The city of Santa Clara, directly north of and abutting the city of San Jose, is home to 100,000 high-income residents and about 140,000 jobs. The city is headquarters to Intel, National Semiconductor, and Applied Materials, and, even after the recent layoffs, close to 1 million jobs are located within a ten-mile (16-kilometer) radius.

Sixty acres (24 hectares) of the Agnew site was sold to Sun in 1997 for a 1 million-square-foot (93,000-square-meter) corporate campus. The state of California issued a request for proposals (RFP) in August 1998 for an additional 154 acres (62 hectares), with the balance of the land set aside for affordable housing and preservation of a cemetery and physical rehabilitation facility. The state had worked closely with the city of Santa Clara in identifying the land use goals for the community—a grocery-anchored shopping center, sites for a school and a fire station, parkland, and affordable housing—which were outlined clearly in the RFP.

Centex took the lead in organizing the joint venture partnership with Shea and Lennar, a group with strong

northern California relationships. Cooperation and the ability to leverage each corporate entity's strengths were of critical importance in the planning process. Centex took the lead in getting the property entitled, negotiating with the city and doing master land development, Lennar was instrumental in refining the community business plan and housing segmentation and positioning strategy, and Shea (with its commercial wing Shea Properties) spearheaded the retail/commercial development. The agreement was that commercial and multifamily sites would be sold and each partner would act as homebuilder for two projects in each phase of for-sale development.

The partnership retained the Dahlin Group to prepare the community land plan and the residential architecture that would be used by all the homebuilders. After the partnership's winning response to the RFP, it worked closely with the city to refine the community land plan, to change the city's planned development ordinance to allow for the creation of a planned development master community (PD-MC zoning), and to establish a new zoning district with design guidelines and development standards that supported the community concept. Following toxic cleanup of the site, the land was taken down in August 2001. The partnership's ability to fulfill most of the community's objectives ensured limited resistance to the project from neighbors.

Site Planning and Design

The Rivermark Partnership would ultimately control 154 acres (62 hectares) for for-sale residential development, but it master planned the entire 225-acre (91-hectare) site (which excludes Sun's campus). Within that larger master-planned area were several sites for affordable multifamily and seniors' housing developments, allowing the total site to accommodate 15 percent affordable housing, although none of the partnership's for-sale program would be dedicated to that use.

The eastern boundary of Rivermark is formed by the Guadalupe River, which the partnership will enhance with landscaping on both banks. The river will eventually be bridged, providing pedestrian access to the River Oaks light-rail station, approximately one-third mile (0.5 kilometer) from the center of the community. It serves downtown San Jose and other Silicon Valley employment centers.

The community's preference was for commercial uses, including a retail center to be located on Montague Expressway, a major east/west collector road and the southern boundary of the site. An 11-acre (4-hectare)

retail parcel was created and transferred to Rivermark Villages for creation of a retail center that mixes a main street with a more suburban-style, grocery-anchored design. The 140,000-square-foot (13,000-square-meter) center includes a Safeway and in-line stores heavily weighted toward restaurants and lifestyle stores in a single building with storefronts on all four sides. At-grade parking is limited, but a two-story parking structure is located at the back of the site. The original entitlements included office space above the retail space, which may still be developed when market conditions improve to support it. A site for a hotel was sold to LodgeWorks L.P. for an extended-stay Sierra Suites hotel.

A landscaped traffic circle to the rear of the retail center provides a direct link with the residential community. Three parcels surrounding the retail center were sold to multifamily developers; 782 market-rate rental housing units at an average density of 45 units per acre (110 per hectare) are under construction. This "tiered" approach clusters the highest-density product closest to the retail center to intensify activity there.

Between the commercial/multifamily concentration and the medium-density for-sale housing is an 18-acre (7-hectare) park site, which includes parcels for a branch library and a school serving kindergarten through grade 8. This large park and the retail center serve as key community amenities that invite city residents into the community, which is consistent with the development partnership's vision of a community "without walls."

The land plan relies to a great extent on traditional city planning, with a mostly regular street grid creating the residential neighborhoods and more suburban-style collector roads. Of the six product lines in the first phase, five are alley loaded, creating an effective hierarchy of main streets, neighborhood streets, and residential alleys. Although the development partnership has not yet quantified the cost of this alley-loaded configuration, it is understood to be higher. This configuration, however,

An 11-acre (4-hectare) town center includes a supermarket, shops, and restaurants.

A variety of housing types and architectural styles blend to create a town with a strong character.

allows maximum density for housing, mostly at the expense of rear yards.

Because the future homebuilders also oversaw land planning and land development, they were diligent in creating a plan that supported a finely segmented housing array and was flexible enough to change the mix of products in future phases as market conditions evolve. One bold decision was to avoid parceling the property into neighborhoods; in many instances, the highest-priced detached homes are across the street from more affordable attached housing.

Significant thought also went into creating vital, active streetscapes, with the goals of calming traffic, encouraging pedestrians' use, and achieving a vibrant social realm outside the home. All roads are lined with sidewalks separated by heavily landscaped planting strips that extend into the street and create parking bays. When they are mature, trees planted in these wells will create a canopy over streets and sidewalks. Small pocket parks are mixed throughout, and intersections are necked down to slow traffic. Streets are limited to a 46-foot (14-meter) right-of-way, resulting in 22-foot (6.7-meter) travel lanes.

The community is also interwoven with an extensive network of ten-foot-wide (3-meter-wide) walking paths (paseos). Many housing units face the paseos, providing access to the front door by path only and allowing vehicular access via the alley to rear garages. This design element was driven by the goal of clustering open space in front of houses rather than in strictly private spaces behind the homes.

To create a divide between the public and private realms, many homes are built on a raised pad, with the front door up half a flight of steps and a generous porch overlooking the paseos or sidewalk. The paseos and alleys are turned perpendicular to the street to create intimate spaces with regular home frontages. A community homeowners' association will maintain the paseo and park network and the extensive landscaping.

Housing

From the beginning of the planning process, architecture was understood to be critical in ensuring homebuyers' acceptance of the project density and land planning. Although future architecture was part of the master planning process and would be used by all homebuilders, diversity and an eclectic mix were emphasized above cohesiveness. The architecture relies heavily on prewar northern California styles such as Spanish, Mission, Monterey, Bungalow, French, English Cottage, and Victorian. Styles are mixed, even within product lines and attached building group, to reflect the irregular forms and rooflines of San Francisco and San Jose.

Two attached product lines were included in the first phase of development, representing just over 40 percent of the housing mix. Situated near the park and closest to the shopping district, the Park by Centex Homes is attached two- and three-story townhouses at 20 units per acre (50 per hectare). The units range from 16 to 21 feet (4.9 to 6.4 meters) wide and were designed to look like individual units built over time. Each attached unit has its own street address. Reduced front setbacks and half-flight front stoops create an urban feel. Most buildings front onto paseos and face each other. The units range from 1,400 to 1,700 square feet (130 to 158 square meters) in three floor plans with two or three bedrooms. Two of the plans have two-car tandem garages. With prices beginning in the high $400s, this is entry-level housing in northern California. At more than ten sales per month, this product line has been the most successful in the first phase, appealing predominantly to young buyers, most without families.

The Landings by Shea Homes is similar in configuration, with slightly wider fronts and an average density of 18 units per acre (44 per hectare). Two-car side-by-side garages are accessed by "carriage lanes," creating private space; units front the street or each other across paseos. Three floor plans range from 1,450 to 1,900 square feet (135 to 177 square meters); prices begin in

the mid-$500s. Finish levels are higher than in the Park, and more mature buyers have been attracted to the product. Sales are strong, at five to six units per month. Floor plans have a split half level between living room and kitchen/dining areas.

The Greens by Greystone Homes (a division of Lennar Communities) is the smallest detached product. The two- and three-story houses feature lots ranging from 1,700 to 2,700 square feet (158 to 251 square meters), achieving a density of 14 units per acre (35 per hectare). The architecture includes significant relief elements: stone facades with minibalconies and window shutters that deemphasize the buildings' verticality. The outdoor living areas comprise borrowed side easements and raised front patios. Units of 1,600 to 2,000 square feet (149 to 186 square meters) begin in the high $500s. Three-story plans have a bedroom/den on the lower level, the main living area on the second floor, and two bedrooms on the top level.

Centex Homes's the Arbors is built at a density of 12 units per acre (30 per hectare) on 35-foot (10-meter) lots, allowing side yards incorporating reciprocal easements. Traditional two-story homes range from 1,750 to 2,000 square feet (163 to 186 square meters) and are arranged in groups of eight on a regular grid with front entrances off the paseo. Three of the four floor plans include great rooms or modified great room living areas and are family oriented. Prices begin at $600,000 for this most popular detached product line.

At a density of nine to ten dwelling units per acre (22 to 25 per hectare), the Glen by Shea Homes is designed as "zero" lots with borrowed easements to provide private rear yards. All homes front the street; some garages are accessed by long, single-lane "Hollywood" driveways, pushing the garage to the back of the lot to minimize architectural impact and eliminate wide curb cuts. Homes range from 2,400 to 2,650 square feet (223 to 246 square meters) and begin in the $700s, typical for the regional market for new homes of this size. The number of bed-

The land plan is based on a traditional urban street grid. Many homes face pocket parks.

Streetscapes are vibrant with color and architectural detail. All streets are lined with planting strips and sidewalks.

Adrienne Schmitz

rooms is flexible, with the largest plan accommodating five bedrooms.

Greystone Homes's the Promenade includes the project's largest homes, 2,600 to 3,100 square feet (242 to 288 square meters), with prices beginning in the mid-$700s. Zero-lot-line design allows for side yards in a courtyard-style configuration. Building pads are raised two feet (0.6 meter) to allow for tighter setbacks and a density of eight to nine units per acre (20 to 22 per hectare). All homes are alley loaded; the largest plan includes a three-car garage. All plans feature generous living space on the first floor.

Marketing and Sales

Marketing and sales also reflect a combination of cooperation and individual effort. The partnership invested heavily in a coordinated branding and identity program, created with the help of San Francisco–based design and marketing firm Gauger Santy. The coordinated collat-

eral materials, Web presence, street signage, and advertising materials have a slightly edgy, modernist design with bright colors and bold graphics that give the community a youthful and exciting feel—just enough not to alienate more traditional homebuyers.

The partnership invested heavily in a community Web site to reflect the local market's technology orientation, which was less effective in generating actual sales than expected. During the first year of marketing, a centralized marketing facility handled marketing and sales; now, sales are handled by individual builders in their respective model complexes. All builders have invested heavily in product merchandising and have models of all floor plans.

A five-year buildout was projected for the community, and with 300 sales in the first year, Rivermark is near the goal for sales volume. Similar to the Silicon Valley housing market overall, prices have held although not appreciated significantly. Buyers are ethnically diverse, reflecting both the technology industry and its international draw, and diverse in age, attracting younger buyers, families, and move-down households.

Experience Gained

Working closely with the city and even helping to educate city staff helped create a development program that provided services and facilities to city residents and was sensitive to the economic realities of development and goals of the homebuilder partnership.

Integrated, thorough master planning allowed Rivermark to maximize project density, achieve an integrated, active community "without walls" and with active street scenes and aesthetic integrity and the flexibility to modify housing types between phases.

The strategy of delivering housing product that both draws on the history and architectural traditions of the Bay Area as well as represents the next generation in terms of configuration, density, and technical achievement has been validated by buyers' response.

Some housing units face paseos.

Site plan.

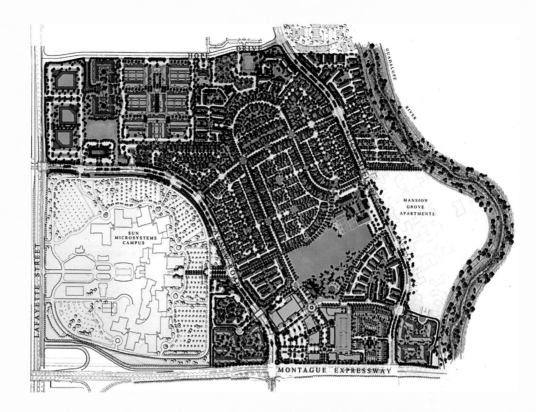

Plan detail, showing typical detached units with rear garages, front entries, and landscaped side yards.

Project Data: Rivermark

Land Use and Building Information

Site Area	225 acres (91 hectares), master plan; approximately 154 acres (62 hectares) for Rivermark Partners
Total Dwelling Units Planned	3,020 (master plan); 1,889 (Rivermark Partners)
Total Dwelling Units Completed	Approximately 900 in master plan area
Gross Density	13.4 units per acre (33 per hectare)
Average Net Density	19.5 units per acre (48 per hectare)

Land Use Plan

	Acres/ Hectares	Percent of Site
Detached residential	63/25.5	28%
Attached residential	31/12.5	14
Mixed use (high-density housing)	18/7.3	8
Commercial	15/6.1	7
Common open space	33/13.4	15
School, park, library	18/7.3	8
Fire station	1/0.4	0
Electrical substation	2/0.8	8
Cemetery	1/0.4	0
Multifamily residential (apartments)	18/7.3	8
Multifamily residential (affordable)	4/1.6	2
Medium-density (transitional housing)	3/1.2	1
High-density housing	16/6.5	7
Quasi-public	2/0.8	1
Total	225/91.1	100%

Developer

Rivermark Partners
1855 Gateway Boulevard
Suite 650
Concord, California 94520
925-356-7226
www.centexhomes.com

Site Planner and Residential Architect

Dahlin Group
2671 Crow Canyon Road
San Ramon, California 94583
925-837-8286
www.dahlingroup.com

Commercial Architect

SGPA
200 Pine Street
Studio 500
San Francisco, California 94104
415-983-0131
www.sgpa.com

Residential Unit Information

For-Sale Units	Lot Size (Square Feet/Square Meters)	Unit Size (Square Feet/Square Meters)	Number of Units Planned	Price Range
Park	Attached	1,450–1,750 (135–163)	290	$469,900–539,900
Landings	Attached	1,650–1,900 (153–177)	258	$540,900–606,900
Greens	1,700–2,700 (158–251)	1,600–2,000 (149–186)	187	$584,000–690,000
Arbors	2,625, 2,975 (244, 276)	1,750–2,100 (163–195)	81	$609,900–697,900
Glen	3,200 (297)	2,400–2,650 (223–246)	144	$700,000–790,000
Promenade	3,420 (318)	2,400–3,000 (223–279)	137	$757,000–853,000

Homebuilders

Centex Homes
1855 Gateway Boulevard
Suite 650
Concord, California 94520
925-827-8100
www.centexhomes.com

Lennar Homes
3130 Crow Canyon Place
Suite 300
San Ramon, California 94583
925-242-0811
www.lennar.com

Shea Homes
2580 Shea Center Drive
Livermore, California 94550
925-245-3600
www.sheahomes.com

Prometheus
350 Bridge Parkway
Redwood City, California 94065
650-596-5369
www.prometheusreg.com

Landscape Architect

Nuvis
5 Crow Canyon Court
Suite 110
San Ramon, California 94583
925-820-2772
www.nuvis.net

Civil Engineer

HMH Engineers
4456 Black Avenue
Suite 100
Pleasanton, California 94566
925-600-7335
www.hmh-engineers.com

Colorist

Colour Studio
1164 Bryant Street
San Francisco, California 94103
415-495-4760
www.colourstudio.com

Development Schedule

8/2001	Site purchased
1/1999	Planning started
7/2001	Land development started
12/2001	Housing construction started
6/2002	Sales started
9/2002	First closing
2006	Estimated completion date

Rollins Square

Boston, Massachusetts

A classic Bostonian streetscape and creative financing characterize this innovative mixed-income community. Containing a mix of 147 condominium units, 37 rental apartments, and 6,000 square feet (560 square meters) of ground-floor retail space, Rollins Square has successfully provided workforce housing in a rapidly gentrifying urban neighborhood. Workforce housing is affordable for middle-income workers such as teachers, nurses, and policemen who do not qualify for most housing subsidy programs but also do not have the income necessary to purchase housing in many high-priced cities. The Rollins Square project was developed by the Planning Office for Urban Affairs (POUA), Inc., a 501(c)(3) nonprofit housing developer affiliated with the Archdiocese of Boston. Established in 1969, POUA has developed approximately 1,690 units of affordable and mixed-income housing throughout the greater Boston market, with an additional 650 units currently under development. The project was also the result of Boston's "linkage ordinance." To balance commercial development with the housing demand that it creates, the city of Boston amended its zoning ordinance in 1983 to establish the linkage ordinance, which requires developers of major commercial, retail, hotel, and institutional projects to either pay a specified impact fee or develop an equivalent value of affordable housing on site (which the city defines as affordable to households whose income is at or below 80 percent of Boston's median area income [MAI]). The program has provided a predictable, long-term funding stream for the development of affordable and workforce housing while reducing the imbalance between jobs and housing in the central city.

Workforce Housing Program

With a particular focus on moderate-income units for first-time homebuyers, Rollins Square successfully meets the objective of providing entry-level housing for the area's growing workforce. The 73 affordable condominium units targeted South End residents who provide critical services to the community but cannot afford to live there.

The development provides housing opportunities for residents in a broad range of income levels. Twenty percent of the project's total units (37 units) are targeted to low-income residents whose income is 30 to 60 percent of area median income. Forty percent of the units (73) are for-sale condominiums targeted to moderate-income homebuyers whose incomes range from 80 to 120 percent of area median income. This component

of the project has provided significant homeownership opportunities to first-time homebuyers, a population severely underserved in Boston's South End. The remaining 40 percent (74) of the units were designed and marketed as high-end market-rate units selling for as much as $750,000.

Site, Surroundings, and History

Rollins Square is a diverse and vibrant urban neighborhood adjacent to Beacon Hill and Boston's Back Bay neighborhood. Once an old wharf district, the South End is characterized by a blend of low-income housing, newly constructed high-priced condominiums, and commercial office space that primarily serves educational and health care institutions.

Originally controlled by the Boston Redevelopment Agency, the Rollins Square site was awarded to POUA in the mid-1970s. POUA initially planned and programmed the 1.9-acre (0.8-hectare) site for an expansion of an adjacent Catholic high school. As time passed and the demand for affordable and moderate-income housing escalated, the developer changed the plans.

The agency, which retained a fee ownership interest in the property until construction was completed, also gave the developer an ultimatum to "use it or lose it," accelerating predevelopment efforts for the project. In the early stages of development planning, POUA worked closely with the office of Boston's Mayor Menino to craft a creative and attractive mixed-income development program for the site.

Like most urban infill sites, the Rollins Square property faced numerous challenges, including the need to build around three historic rowhouses and to solve significant environmental contamination issues. Considered a brownfield site, the property contained both lead and petroleum contamination. The Massachusetts Brownfields Fund provided $1 million to fund the project's environmental remediation.

Planning, Entitlements, and Development Program

Given the rapid gentrification of the South End and limited housing opportunities, serving a middle-income population was a major objective of the Archdiocesan Housing Office. Considerable neighborhood—and even citywide—support existed for the development of the Rollins Square site as a mixed-income community. Early in the approval process, the city of Boston identified local community groups for the developer to meet with and discuss the community's thoughts and concerns.

Rollins Square is an urban mixed-income community of condominium units, rental apartments, and ground-floor retail space.

The Washington Gateway Main Streets Association, a community-based group formed to preserve the historic and urban settlement patterns of the Washington Street Corridor in Boston's South End, facilitated this public meeting process. The newly created neighborhood group identified several important land use, urban design, and architectural issues for the developer to consider—including the use of traditional vernacular architecture, the creation of a streetscape and building massing consistent with the historic neighborhood's character, open space designed to ensure the safety of pedestrians, and retail uses on the ground floor. The developer shared the vision that the city and local community proposed, resulting in a remarkably efficient and effective approval process.

Financing

To accomplish a wide variety of public purpose objectives, POUA assembled a complex mosaic of debt, equity, and grants, totaling 13 financing sources. The developer's vision of creating an inclusive urban mixed-income community that contained both for-sale condominiums and rental apartments dramatically increased the complexity of Rollins Square's project financing. To succeed with this ambitious development program, which was unparalleled in the city of Boston, it was critical to have a highly committed, focused, and professional financing team. The key participants in that team were the city of Boston, the commonwealth of Massachusetts, Fleet Bank,

and the AFL-CIO. This partnership of public agencies and unusual private sector leadership focused on finding creative and flexible approaches to financing.

Because the proposed project included both for-sale and rental housing, a number of challenges emerged. First, it was necessary to apply for funds twice—once for each component. Other factors were the need to address issues of collateral and the difficulty of structuring the legal entities to cover all parties concerned. The application process significantly increased the project's predevelopment period.

The Boston Redevelopment Agency played an invaluable role in the project's site assembly and financing by writing down the project's land value to $1.5 million and deferring payment of that amount until construction was complete. This purchase price represented the market land value for 74 units of market-rate housing, while zero land value was attributed to the project's affordable units.

POUA secured several scarce financing resources available to developers of low- and moderate-income for-sale housing in the Boston marketplace: $1.17 million in state-administered HOME funds, $2 million in Massachusetts affordable housing trust funds, $2.9 million in permanent financing from MassHousing, $1.17 million in Leading the Way funds (a discretionary affordable housing fund controlled by the Boston mayor's office), and more than $2.5 million in funding from Boston's Neighborhood Housing Trust. The Neighborhood Hous-

Sixteen of the townhouses front directly on the new street and small park that were created in the center of the site.

Courtesy of CBT/Robert Benson Photography

Courtesy of CBT/Robert Benson Photography

ing Trust is directly funded by Boston's housing linkage program.

These funding sources financed only the portion of the development costs attributable to the for-sale workforce housing. POUA's mission and nonprofit status enabled the developer to internally subsidize the project's workforce housing condominium units. This internal subsidy was funded by the net revenue that was generated by the sale of the project's market-rate condominium units, representing approximately $11 million in forgone development fees.

Perhaps one of the most unusual elements of the financing was the prominent role played by a private sector commercial bank, FleetBoston, in this project with a very high public purpose. FleetBoston was the lead lender of the $52 million construction loan (with MassHousing as a 50 percent participating lender) and provided more than $3.8 million in tax credit equity. The unusual approach created underwriting challenges for the construction loan, which FleetBoston met by suggesting creative collateral for the loan.

In the early stages of the project's buildout, the lender required the developer to inventory and not sell a significant percentage of the project's moderate-income workforce condominium units. These "escrowed" units offered additional security that compensated for the limited guarantees the nonprofit developer was able to provide. Under this arrangement, the developer agreed to a discharge schedule that released workforce units for sale as market-rate units successfully sold over time. If the sale price of the market-rate units did not meet pro forma projections, some of the workforce housing units (whose sale prices were significantly written down) would have been sold at market rates. This creative approach allowed both the developer and the lender to recognize the unrealized economic value of the subsidized workforce housing units in the project financing.

Rollins Square's affordable rental units were spread throughout the project rather than consolidated in one building or on a single floor, creating a true mixed-income community. This component was central in the developer's mission not to isolate low-income households in only one area of the new community. Though the units were interspersed in the community, separate funding was required to finance them, and a limited partnership was formed to buy the 37 individual condominiums. POUA secured both low-income housing tax credits and Section 8 vouchers to finance the project's rental component.

To further assist with project financing, the developer used its status as a 501(c)(3) nonprofit organization and received an exemption from sales tax on all building materials, saving the project $1.5 million. This strategy required the developer to control all partnership entities during the construction period, thus maintaining the developer's nonprofit status. As a result, the project's limited partners placed their investments as debt that converted into an equity position upon completion of construction.

Rollins Square is made up of small buildings that form a series of open spaces.

Financing for Rollins Square became increasingly complicated after the events of September 11, 2001. As a result of uncertain market conditions and the loss of a significant number of presale commitments in the days immediately following, the developer was unable to close the construction loan committed to the project and was forced to seek bridge financing. POUA approached the AFL-CIO Housing Investment Trust, a national leader in pension real estate investment for the development of housing. The trust was able to design a customized $28 million bridge loan that provided the essential capital necessary to maintain construction progress during remarketing of the development. This arrangement also resulted in the creation of 644 union jobs during the project's construction.

Architecture and Design

The residences at Rollins Square occupy two city blocks bordered by Washington Street and Harrison Avenue on the north and south, Savoy and Waltham streets on the east and west, and the newly created Rollins Street through the center of the site. At the principal street corners, the project contains four six-story buildings and rows of four-story townhouses that fill in the street elevations between them. A small, well-landscaped park occupies the center of the site. The project includes a two-level underground parking garage with a total of 277 parking spaces.

Sixteen of the 20 townhouses front directly on the park. Adjacent pairs of townhouses share private front and rear entrances and have direct access to the garage below. The remaining 164 residential units are located in the project's four six-story buildings. Each of these buildings has a private ground-level entrance lobby and an elevator serving the residences and garage. Ground-floor residences facing the park include private raised patios, while many upper-floor residences include French-style balconies or roof terraces.

To maintain the street activity along the busy Washington Street commercial corridor, Rollins Square includes approximately 6,000 square feet (560 square meters) of ground-floor retail space, which is leased to a bank and a convenience store.

The project, with its varying building heights and diverse exterior materials, gives the appearance that it was constructed over time. Buildings are faced with a variety of materials, including brick, natural and synthetic stone, and precast concrete, and feature synthetic slate mansard roofs and metal-clad window bays. The result is an attractive streetscape that emulates and complements the project's historic surroundings.

A primary goal for the developer was to create a family- and neighborhood-friendly residential community in an urban setting. The design of Rollins Square achieved this end by avoiding long double-loaded corridors; instead, it is made up of small buildings constructed around a tighter core. The project includes 16 separate building entries rather than a central lobby and elevator core. The developers felt that the smaller building, which contains fewer units per floor, created a greater sense of community among the residents. This design concept resulted in the creation of seven building types and 24 different floor plans. While successful from the perspective of planning and design, however, this approach limited many of the considerable development and construction efficiencies often gained in multifamily production housing, thus increasing the overall cost of the project.

Each building's structural system is made of reinforced concrete block bearing walls and precast concrete planks.

The developer chose this "block-and-plank" method of construction over steel and concrete to differentiate its product in the marketplace. The significant marketing advantage achieved included greater sound attenuation and higher ceilings. This construction methodology, however, reduced design flexibility in the residential units and also limited the ability to combine units.

Marketing and Operations

Given the high demand for workforce housing, the developer established a lottery system to fairly market the subsidized units. Initial marketing for the project included advertising in neighborhood and minority newspapers. The result was more than 1,500 requests for applications. Five hundred prospects completed the application and submitted prequalification letters from lenders in time to participate in the lottery, and applications continued coming in long after the lottery. The city of Boston and commonwealth of Massachusetts oversaw the lottery, in which each of the 500 applicants was randomly chosen and assigned a number. The developer gave applicants with the lowest numbers first priority.

To ensure long-term affordability, a series of deed restrictions was established for Rollins Square's workforce housing units. Under these restrictions, residents are permitted to exceed affordability restrictions over time, but affordability covenants require that future residents who purchase Rollins Square workforce units have incomes that do not exceed 120 percent of area median income. The city of Boston enforces these deed restrictions and will also help residents to find and qualify income-eligible buyers for the resale of their workforce units.

Rollins Square's homeowners' association took into account the development's blend of low-income, workforce, and market-rate housing. Before completion of construction, the developer devised an assessment schedule for the homeowners' association in which each unit's owner pays a prorated share of operating expenses, based on the market value of the unit, regardless of a future

The project occupies two city blocks. It includes a two-level underground parking garage with 277 parking spaces.

resident's income level. Units were appraised to determine their market value, and each home's share of operating expenses and the association's budget was calculated per square foot, according to the appraised, not the subsidized, value. Thus, subsidized units pay condominium fees on the same basis that market-rate units do to avoid tension that could arise between income groups if operating expenses were not allocated equally across all units. The developer used projected association dues in calculating the monthly rent level and condominium sale prices for the low-income and moderate-income workforce housing units (keeping in mind that a resident's housing expenses, including association dues, should not exceed 30 percent of gross income).

Homeowners' association documents for Rollins Square also give the limited partnership that owns the rental apartments the same rights as condominium owners in the management and operation of the property. This arrangement addresses the concerns of low-income housing tax credit investors regarding the predictability and cost of future capital improvements and the resulting impact on investment returns. In turn, the limited partnership agreed to allow apartment residents limited rights to represent their interests in the operations of the association, including the right to vote for homeowners' association officers and trustees.

Experience Gained

As with many urban housing projects, parking was a critical design and development issue for Rollins Square and the surrounding neighborhood. The project included the development of 275 parking spaces, many of which were intended for sale to neighborhood residents to ease the pressure for parking in the area. Indeed, parking, which was sold separately, represented approximately 20 percent of the project's gross proceeds from sales. Although 98 percent of the residential units have been sold and occupied and the developer anticipates meeting both its social and financial goals for the project, the project's financial success was perhaps too dependent on the income derived from the sale of parking spaces to nonresidents of the development.

Income qualification for the moderate-income workforce housing units can be a time-consuming process. To avoid delaying closings, it is critical to allocate a reasonable amount of time for proper income qualification and documentation early in the process.

The mission of a nonprofit development entity can conflict with market dynamics. For example, the developers of Rollins Square could have accelerated the project's absorption by meeting the market's strong demand for one-bedroom units. POUA's development mission, however, is to create housing opportunities for families rather than single-person households. As a result, the developers chose to reduce the number of one-bedroom units while increasing the number of three-bedroom units.

The project's diverse and varied architectural styles resulted in seven building types and 24 different floor

Courtesy of CBT/Robert Benson Photography

The project, with its varying building heights and diverse exterior materials, gives the appearance that it was constructed over time.

plans, creating complications for the development, construction, and marketing teams. Limiting the number of unit types would have increased efficiency, decreased cost, and enhanced marketability.

The sale of market-rate units was initially spearheaded by a high-end "boutique-style" real estate sales and marketing group. The developer eventually changed marketing approaches and hired a marketing agency with significantly more experience in merchandising and sales of newly constructed housing, dramatically increasing preconstruction absorption. Approximately 50 percent of the market-rate units were presold early in the construction process.

The complexity of mixing uses (condominiums, apartments, and retail space) and incomes in a single condominium association has significant implications for both marketing and transactional expenses. In this instance, the high-quality design and amenities associated with the development and the developer's ability to forgo traditional development profits made this compromise work for all parties.

WASHINGTON STREET

Site plan.

Project Data: Rollins Square

Land Use and Building Information

Site Area	2.2 acres (0.9 hectare)
Multifamily Residential Units	184
Retail Space	6,000 square feet (560 square meters)

Land Use Plan

	Square Feet/ Square Meters	Percent of Site
Housing	249,337/23,173	71.5%
Parking Garage	99,488/9,246	28.5
Total	348,825/32,419	100.0%

Residential Unit Information

Multifamily Units

Unit Type	Unit Size (Square Feet/ Square Meters)	Sale Price/ Rent Range
Moderate-Income Condominium	600–1,900/56–177	$140,000–260,000
Market-Rate Condominium	600–1,900/56–177	$280,000–720,000
Low-Income Apartment	600–1,900/56–177	$354–1,022

Affordable Units

Unit Type	Number of Affordable Units	Targeted Income Group	Sale Price/ Rent Range
Condominium	25	80% MAI	$140,000–160,000
Condominium	48	120% MAI	$210,000–260,000
Affordable Apartments	37	30–60% MAI	$354–1,022

Development Cost Information

Site Acquisition Cost	$1,500,000
Construction Costs	53,000,000
Soft Costs	11,151,000
Total Development Cost	**$65,651,000**

Owner/Developer

Planning Office for Urban Affairs
185 Devonshire Street
Suite 600
Boston, Massachusetts 02110
617-350-8885

Architect

Childs Bertram & Tseckares
110 Canal Street
Boston, Massachusetts 02114
617-262-4354
www.cbtarchitects.com

Landscape Architect

CBA Landscape Architects
29 Manchester Road
Brookline, Massachusetts 02446
617-566-0834
www.CBALand.com

Structural Engineer

Weidlinger Associates
One Broadway
11th Floor
Cambridge, Massachusetts 02142
617-374-000
www.wai.com

Mechanical Engineer

Fitzemeyer & Tocci
206 West Cummings Park
Woburn, Massachusetts 01801
781-376-9600
www.f-t.com

General Contractor

Suffolk Construction
65 Allerton Street
Boston, Massachusetts 02119
617-445-3500
www.suffolk-construction.com

Marketing/Sales

Peabody Properties, Inc.
159 Burgin Parkway
Quincy, Massachusetts 02169
617-328-1313
www.peabodyproperties.com

Development Consultant

Peter J. Roche, Real Estate and Community Development
79 Quincy Avenue
Winthrop, Massachusetts 02152
617-846-5326

Development Schedule

2/2001	Site purchased
11/1999	Planning started
10/2000	Sales/leasing started
3/2001	Construction started
1/2003	First phase completed
6/2003	Project completed

Sailhouse
Corona del Mar, California

Sailhouse is a pedestrian-oriented infill development in Corona del Mar, California. With a total of 89 units, the project has become one of the premier residences in that part of Orange County. Sailhouse's design is based on the St. Augustine architectural style made popular in Florida's Seaside and Rosemary Beach developments. Units include a tightly knit mix of 25 bungalows, 12 carriage houses, and 52 cottages, ranging from 1,331 to 2,425 square feet (125 to 225 square meters). Sale prices range from $699,900 to $844,990 for a cottage, $771,990 to $849,990 for a bungalow, and $628,990 for a carriage house.

A winner of numerous awards, Sailhouse is designed using a style of architecture that is not traditional to California yet is consistent in scale and character with the already established neighborhood. Using walkways and other small communal open spaces, Sailhouse offers a sense of community not often found in newer developments typical of southern California.

Rather than isolating the development with walls and gates, as is common in southern California, John Laing Homes, the developer, chose to open the development and connect it to the surrounding neighborhoods and the larger community of Corona del Mar. Pedestrian traffic is encouraged out of the development and into the surrounding neighborhoods. The prime location lets the developer use the beach and local shops and restaurants as amenities, making the traditional recreation center unnecessary. In effect, the entire town becomes the amenity.

The developers of Sailhouse conducted extensive market research and, in a valiant departure from recent development in Orange County, responded to the documented demand for a pedestrian-friendly neighborhood. From start to finish, Sailhouse's development process offers an important model for the elements of a successful infill development.

The Site
Sailhouse is located on a narrow, 7.4-acre (3-hectare) parcel of land between the Pacific Coast Highway and MacArthur Boulevard in Corona del Mar, a small beach community in the coastal town of Newport Beach. Fronting the Pacific Ocean, Corona del Mar is located 70 miles (113 kilometers) north of San Diego and 50 miles (80 kilometers) south of Los Angeles International Airport. The Sailhouse site was originally developed in the 1960s as a 120-unit rental complex. John Laing Homes purchased the 40-year-old complex at the end of 2000 for $20.8 million and demolished it to make way for Sailhouse.

At the beginning of the 20th century, Corona del Mar was planned as a vacation resort. The concept changed, however, when vacationers liked the area so much that they began to take up permanent residence. The town's growth took off after the opening of Pacific Coast Highway in 1926. Translated as Crown of the Sea, Corona del Mar is noted for its high incomes and real estate values, with the median home price greater than $1 million.

The historic neighborhoods of Corona del Mar are typified by narrow lots with one- and two-story houses and rear garages. The community features many lifestyle amenities, including the beach and a downtown with stylish restaurants, coffeehouses, outdoor cafés, galleries, and specialty shops.

Development Process
The community is a result of six years of planning and development, from concept to buildout. First, legal issues involving the ownership of the property delayed the project for two years. Other predevelopment problems related to the sloping site, which ranges from seven to ten degrees off the horizontal. Following much dialogue with the civil engineer, Laing Homes concluded that grading individual lots on the steep slope would be prohibitively expensive. A more affordable solution was to level out six entire blocks and put the single-family homes on those blocks. At the same time, they would excavate around the blocks to create new streets and alleys, providing access to garages.

Meetings with adjacent homeowners revealed that neighbors living above the current project were concerned that the new project would rise too high and too close and would obstruct views, and that excavation would destabilize the bluff below. The developer responded by dropping the site elevation and reinforcing the bluff with a tall retaining wall. Computer renderings provided virtual evidence that views would actually be improved after construction of Sailhouse. Eventually, surrounding homeowners were won over, and they are pleased with the results.

The development process was further delayed because of the lengthy eviction of residents of the old apartment complex. Laing allowed families with children to remain in their apartments to finish the school year before being evicted. This delay also allowed the developer extra time to extensively examine the market and the community.

"Working with the city was a smooth process," says Laing's vice president of product development, Dan Nahabedian. "Newport Beach does not require official submittals, and developers can still receive feedback." A

Sailhouse is an 89-unit pedestrian-oriented infill development in Corona del Mar, California.

meeting is required of the planning director, fire commissioner, and head of public works. Partly because Laing had already held extensive meetings with neighbors and other community leaders, the planning commission requested no major changes to the project. "By the time we came in with a project, it was something the city was already looking for," says Nahabedian. "It was pedestrian friendly, it faced the street, and it did all the wonderful things they would have asked the developer to do. We were three steps ahead of them."

Planning and Design

With no preconceived design for the site, John Laing Homes invited three of the most noted architectural firms in southern California to present plans for Sailhouse; it selected Scheurer Architects, Inc., which envisioned a community reminiscent of some of the great beach towns from around the country. It was evident from the beginning that the development needed to be consistent with the size and scale of Corona del Mar's older homes and neighborhoods.

One option was to develop at the allowable scale of 121 units. To create that number of homes would have meant stacked flats with underground parking—a plan that was incompatible with the surrounding area and probably would have raised NIMBY issues among neighbors. The resulting plan for 89 units was economically feasible, better suited to its surroundings, and allowed larger and some detached units. At a density of 12.2 units per acre (30 per hectare), 44 percent of the site used for attached residences, 29 percent for roads, and 27 percent for open space, the developer kept with its vision of creating a pedestrian-friendly community that encouraged neighborly interaction.

Seeing a once-in-a-lifetime opportunity, the architects designed a product for the site that looked as though it had been part of Corona del Mar from the start. Using modern beach towns such as Rosemary Beach and Sea-

Using walkways and other small communal open spaces, Sailhouse offers a sense of community not often found in newer
developments in southern California.

side, Florida, as examples, the architect and developer
strove for a plan that accommodated site characteristics,
maintained the appeal of the surrounding areas, responded to the demands of upper-end buyers, and was
dense enough to be profitable.

With neither walls nor gates, Sailhouse was designed
to use the surrounding area to its advantage. With the
beach, restaurants, shopping, and galleries all within walking distance, the larger community is the major amenity

for residents of Sailhouse. The most notable design feature is the system of boardwalks and walkways that mean-
der through the complex, connecting neighbors with
each other and with an assortment of gazebos, perches,
and terraces, some with benches, fountains, or other
features. Eight feet (2.4 meters) above street level, this
separated system of boardwalks fulfills the goals of a
pedestrian-focused community, making public space
convenient and separated from vehicular traffic.

Despite being production housing, no two homes are
completely identical. Sailhouse comprises triplex and
detached buildings, and the builder has arranged the
89 units into two configurations: the 37 townhouses are
arranged in clusters in the site's interior, while the 52
cottages and small-lot single-family homes face the
perimeter street.

Detached units each provide 1,818 to 2,383 square
feet (170 to 220 square meters) of living space, two to
three bedrooms, and two and one-half baths. Adhering
to the basic design principles of new urbanism and em-
ulating the original Corona del Mar neighborhoods, the
garages are accessed from alleys at the back of the houses.
The bungalows are triplex units. Three plans, including
a carriage unit, range from 1,367 to 2,383 square feet
(125 to 220 square meters) of living space. These units
have up to three bedrooms and two or three baths. The
carriage house creates a triplex by straddling the back
garages of a duplex. At every third building, a pathway
connects the houses to interior circulation points.

John Laing Homes has been celebrated for introducing an innovative style of architecture to California. The
St. Augustine style features neutral-toned stucco on lower
levels, with boldly colored wood siding on upper levels.
The architectural detailing and the varied palette give the
illusion of detached homes. Most homes have small front
yards with low wooden railings that open onto the walkways. House plans are designed and placed so that major
living spaces receive maximum light. Detailing is rustic
and casual. The color palette, drawing cues from sand,
water, and sunsets, plays a major role in shaping the
warm and sophisticated but relaxed look of Sailhouse.

The palette, chosen by colorist Miriam Tate, was developed to complement the distinctive architecture and
to help coordinate and define the entire development
concept, including houses, signage, marketing materials,
and even a retaining wall. Looming over the Sailhouse
development and protecting it from a steep slope is a
massive concrete retaining wall reaching 25 feet (7.6
meters) at its highest point. Tate washed the formerly
unsightly wall in earth tones taken from the same color
palette as the rest of the development, creating a more
natural-looking wall that blends into the surroundings.
Eventually, as plantings mature, it will be further integrated into the natural landscape.

Financing and Marketing

The developer provided equity; Wells Fargo Bank was
the principal lender. More than 50 homes sold in the
first eight months despite deflation in the local high-end

Rather than isolating the development with walls and gates, the developer chose to connect it to the surrounding neighborhoods and the larger community of Corona del Mar.

market. The project's success has shown city officials that infill development can enhance the community and add to the economic base, which has helped to ease the way for other infill developments.

The Newport Beach area is considered a premier place to live. With its mild climate, attractive natural setting, and wealth of amenities, the region is appealing to a high-income, highly educated market. Buyers at Sailhouse range from the mid-20s to late 50s, with the majority between 31 and 45 years of age. Average household income is $208,588. For more than half the buyers, Sailhouse is at least their third home purchase.

By Orange County standards, the homes at Sailhouse, averaging 1,700 square feet (160 square meters), are small. The developer's market research suggested that more buyers than ever were willing to spend more money for a smaller amount of space if they were able to purchase a more manageable, appealing home in a pedestrian-friendly community.

Detailing is rustic and casual. The color palette, drawing cues from sand, water, and sunsets, plays a major role in shaping the warm and sophisticated but relaxed look of Sailhouse.

Experience Gained

Sailhouse is a step back in time compared with most southern California developments—largely single-use, low-density, walled and gated subdivisions that turn their backs on the surrounding streets. To fit into the already established Corona del Mar neighborhood, planners deemed it appropriate for the architects to go against the norm to create a higher-density, more pedestrian-oriented, human-scale community.

Sailhouse is a distinct and successful example of infill development. By meeting the needs of the local jurisdiction, a demanding market, and the developer's bottom line, it is one project that avoids sprawling into greenfields. As the recipient of the Community Development of 2003 award by *Coastal Living* magazine, the project was recognized for protecting the coastlines. Sailhouse introduced a new style of architecture to California yet still was consistent in scale and character with neighboring areas. Revered for creating a neighborhood that exemplifies the meaning of community spirit, John Laing Homes took care to plan and design an ideal environment. Taking a basic design of a costal town in Florida's panhandle, it then incorporated regional colors and design elements to blend the development into the surrounding community.

The developers used setbacks to their advantage. They used the delays they encountered because of complex entitlements and the case-by-case eviction of original tenants to their advantage by studying the market, the buyer, and the community. Developers learned of the need for a pedestrian-friendly community through research with the most successful brokers in Corona del Mar, tours of the area's old and new housing, conversations with locals, focus groups, and architectural studies.

Sailhouse is an example of a development that was successfully able to overcome the planning, design, and marketing issues of most infill developments, including complicated entitlements, difficult site characteristics, meticulous buyers, and high development costs.

Site plan.

Cottage floor plan.

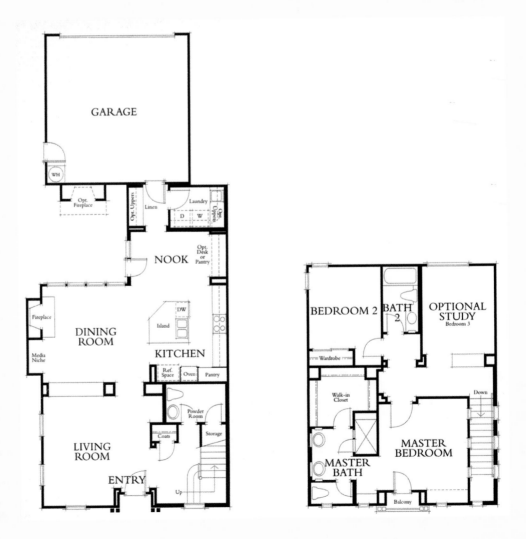

Project Data: Sailhouse

Land Use and Building Information

Site Area	7.4 acres (3 hectares)
Total Dwelling Units	89
Gross Density	12.2 units per acre (30 per hectare)

Land Use Plan

	Acres/ Hectares	Percent of Site
Attached Residential	3.3/1.3	44%
Roads	2.2/0.9	29
Common Open Space	2.0/0.8	27
Total	7.5/3.0	100%

Residential Unit Information

Unit Type	Unit Size (Square Feet/ Square Meters)	Number of Units	Sale Prices
2-Bedroom, 2-Bath Carriage	1,367/127	12	$628,990
2-Bedroom, 2.5-Bath Cottage 1	1,818/169	10	$699,990
3-Bedroom, 2.5-Bath Cottage 2	1,933/180	27	$709,990
3-Bedroom, 2.5-Bath Cottage 3	2,383/220	15	$844,990
3-Bedroom, 2.5-Bath Bungalow 1	1,757/163	13	$771,990
3-Bedroom, 3-Bathroom Bungalow 2	2,334/217	12	$849,990
Total		89	

Development Cost Information

Site Acquisition Costs	**$20,800,000**

Site Improvement Costs

Excavation/grading	$1,968,000
Sewer/water/drainage	791,000
Paving/curbs/sidewalks	834,000
Landscaping/irrigation	1,170,000
Fees/general conditions	333,000
Total	$5,096,000

Construction Costs

Superstructure	$13,580,000
HVAC	555,000
Electrical	632,000
Plumbing/sprinklers	1,515,000
Total	$16,282,000

Soft Costs

Architecture/engineering	$1,413,000
Marketing	4,324,000
Legal/accounting	152,000
Taxes/insurance	860,000
Title fees	36,000
Construction interest and fees	4,855,000
Total	$11,640,000

Total Development Cost	**$53,818,000**
Total Development Cost Expected at Buildout	**$64,616,000**

Developer/Builder

John Laing Homes
895 Dove Street
Suite 110
Newport Beach, California 92660
949-265-6800

Site Planner

Wagner Halladay
201 East Yorba Linda Boulevard
Placentia, California 92870
714-993-4500

Architect

Scheurer Architects
20411 Southwest Birch Street
Suite 330
Newport Beach, California 92660
949-752-4009

Colorist

Miriam Tate Company
2915 Redhill Avenue
Costa Mesa, California 92626
714-979-6900

Development Schedule

1997	Site purchased
1997	Planning started
2001	Construction started
2001	Sales started
2001	First closing
7/2003	Project completed

Stapleton
Denver, Colorado

Stapleton is a mixed-use master-planned community currently under construction on the former site of Stapleton International Airport. The site, ten minutes from downtown Denver and 20 minutes from Denver International Airport, will eventually house more than 30,000 residents and 35,000 workers. Stapleton was conceived as a sustainable community that seeks to integrate jobs, housing, and the environment. To create a vision for such a large undertaking, the stakeholders involved—the city and county of Denver, the Stapleton Redevelopment Foundation, and a citizens advisory board—devised the Stapleton Redevelopment Plan, "The Green Book," in 1995. The Green Book outlines a clear dedication to affordable housing, traditional neighborhood design, environmental conservation, minority participation in construction, and quality educational opportunities. In 1998, the Stapleton Development Corporation chose Forest City Enterprises as the master developer and began the largest infill redevelopment project in the country. The $4 billion development will take an estimated 20 years to complete. The project at buildout will include 8,000 for-sale homes, 4,000 rental apartments, 10 million square feet (930,000 square meters) of office space, and 3 million square feet (280,000 square meters) of retail space.

Stapleton is one of the most complex infill redevelopment projects in the United States. Soon after the city of Denver decided to close Stapleton Airport, the city and local citizens groups began planning for its reuse. Denver is home to numerous nonprofit housing groups, many of which sought involvement with the redevelopment process. The city, citizens, and nonprofits agreed that the Stapleton redevelopment must be underpinned by three principles: economic opportunity, environmental responsibility, and social equity. Almost 15 years later, construction is well underway. A regional big-box retail center, several office parks, a town center with offices and residences above retail, and 850 units of rental and for-sale housing had been constructed as of December 2003.

Forest City, which will develop much of the commercial space and rental housing, will buy the land from the city and county over time to eliminate costs and risks associated with holding the land for long periods. Forest City has agreed to pay $79.4 million over the next 15 years for the land and $15,000 per acre ($37,000 per hectare) to develop parks and open spaces. Project completion is estimated to be 2020.

Site Description and History

Stapleton is an enormous urban infill site—approximately 4,700 acres (1,900 hectares) of relatively flat prairie land. Stapleton International Airport served as Denver's municipal airport from 1929 to 1995. Denver Mayor Benjamin Franklin Stapleton rallied locals for the construction of the airfield, although some doubted the benefits of aviation and thought it an elitist practice. The 640-acre (260-hectare) site, known as "Rattlesnake Hollow," had been used for dairy farming and cattle grazing and appealed to the airport boosters because of its remote location and relatively cheap price. The airport, then known as Denver Municipal Airport, became an instant financial success and was heralded as the most modern airport in the United States during the 1930s.

Business and air traffic grew exponentially, and by the 1950s, Denver's airport (renamed Stapleton International in 1964) needed to expand. The city bought additional land from the nearby Rocky Mountain Arsenal, but the facility was soon being hemmed in by residential neighborhoods. By the 1970s, Stapleton had almost completely outgrown its site, and its runway layout was considered inadequate and potentially hazardous. Nearby residents became frustrated by the constant jet noise and filed suit. The combination of obsolescence and crowding forced the city to consider a new site northeast of Stapleton for what would become Denver International Airport. Denver was limited in its annexation powers and estimated that the reuse of the Stapleton site could provide for growth within the city.

The Stapleton site is surrounded by several racially diverse, middle- and lower-middle-class neighborhoods, the former Lowry Air Training Center (also being converted to a mixed-use community), the 27-square-mile (70-square-kilometer) Rocky Mountain Arsenal National Wildlife Area, a variety of retail, light manufacturing, and commercial uses, and the redeveloping Fitzsimons Army Medical Center. Interstate 70 runs east and west through the middle of the site, and additional highway and rail access points are nearby. Its location directly between Denver International Airport and downtown Denver brings additional advantage to the Stapleton site.

Many areas on the site enjoy views of downtown Denver and the Rocky Mountains. An existing lake, two streams, and a bluff complement the extensive open space that is planned in the semiarid sandhill and prairie environment. Developers will restore natural corridors to increase existing wildlife habitat.

Stapleton's plan is based on the design principles of new urbanism, providing physical and economic connections to the surrounding neighborhood.

As a former industrial site, Stapleton sustained some environmental damage. Initially, tests indicated ground-water contamination from petroleum products and chemical solvents in about 10 to 15 percent of the site. The city agreed to remediate the contamination to residential levels before selling any of the property to developers.

Planning and Development Process

When the decision to close Stapleton airport was announced in 1988, many citizens in the surrounding neighborhoods requested the opportunity to be involved in the redevelopment. Already sensitive to the problems associated with living next to an undesirable land use, a citizens group formed Stapleton Tomorrow to ensure a more harmonious development. In 1991, the Denver City Council adopted Stapleton Tomorrow's concept plan, which included input from a broad range of citizens. The group identified issues to be addressed such as social equity, job creation, and environmental preservation, and encouraged technical and social innovation.

Following the completion of Stapleton Tomorrow's input, the city and county of Denver entered into a partnership agreement with the Stapleton Redevelopment Foundation (SRF), a nonprofit 501(c)(3) corporation established by community leaders to assist the city and county in maximizing the opportunities at Stapleton. Together, they raised more than $4 million to create the Stapleton Redevelopment Plan (the Green Book). The SRF also agreed to assist the city and county in defining a long-term management structure for the Stapleton redevelopment program. A citizens advisory board worked with SRF during the formulation of the redevelopment plan; more than 100 community presentations took place. A team of technical consultants—planners, architects, urban designers, civil engineers, transportation planners, environmental scientists, market and financial analysts, and project managers—was brought in to develop the plan from 1993 to its completion in 1994. The Stapleton Redevelopment Plan was approved in 1995.

It won numerous national, state, and local awards, including the 1996 Outstanding Planning Award from the American Planning Association and the 1996 President's Award for Planning from the American Society of Landscape Architects.

The plan assigns 65 percent of the site to urban development and 35 percent to a variety of open-space uses. Development is organized into eight districts varying in density and uses. The districts each contain an identifi-

Courtesy of Forest City Stapleton, Inc.

Stapleton 335

Stapleton is the largest infill redevelopment project in the United States. At buildout it will include 12,000 homes, 10 million square feet (930,000 square meters) of office space, and 3 million square feet (280,000 square meters) of retail space.

able center and emphasize the integration of employment, housing, and a pedestrian scale. The plan also reinforces Stapleton's role as a regional employment center while creating strong ties between Stapleton and the surrounding neighborhoods. The open-space system links the eight districts and helps restore the ecological health of the site.

The plan also called for the creation of a private sector nonprofit organization that would be a vehicle for the dispersal of property at Stapleton. In November 1995, the Denver Urban Redevelopment Authority (DURA) signed a cooperative agreement with the city to form the Stapleton Development Corporation (SDC). The SDC is governed by 11 directors, who are business leaders and community activists (DURA appoints two members, and the mayor of Denver appoints nine). In 1997, the SDC funded a study to determine whether the Stapleton property should be considered blighted and therefore designated as an urban renewal area, a first step to determine Stapleton's eligibility for tax increment financing (TIF), a mechanism by which the increase in property tax and/ or sales tax revenues generated by the redevelopment can be used to help finance infrastructure construction.

In 1998, SDC entered into a master lease and disposition agreement with the city, which allows the SDC to maintain and lease Stapleton for 15 years and gives it an option to purchase the property and the authority to sell parcels for uses consistent with the Stapleton Redevelopment Plan. The SDC then began initiating transactions and encouraging support from employers and developers. Two years before, United Airlines agreed to build a $140 million expansion of its computer-simulation flight training facility at Stapleton. Other early clients were a grocery chain that opened a regional distribution warehouse and a 3.6 million-square-foot (335,000-square-meter) business park.

Later in 1998 after a competitive process to choose a master developer to oversee the entire parcel, SDC selected Forest City Enterprises, Inc., as its master developer. Forest City is a family-owned and publicly traded national real estate company with experience in mixed-use urban infill projects. Forest City offered expertise in all aspects of development, access to capital, marketing savvy, and a commitment to affordable housing, sustainable development, minority participation, and other principles of the Stapleton Development Plan.

Forest City entered into an exclusive right to negotiate with SDC for the purchase of Stapleton. SDC and Forest City finalized a purchase agreement in February 2000 that obligated Forest City to buy all developable land at Stapleton. As a condition of selling the balance of the property to a master developer, the Denver Department of Aviation agreed to undertake environmental remediation, substantially demolish unwanted buildings, and rezone the property for redevelopment. Over a period of 15 years, Forest City will pay $79.4 million for 2,935 acres (1,190 hectares), the amount of land that has not already been sold or set aside for regional open space, plus a "systems development fee" of $15,000 for each acre ($37,000 for each hectare) purchased, resulting in a total payment of $123.4 million. An FAA-approved appraisal process set the purchase price. Forest City is responsible for constructing all infrastructure and creating additional neighborhood parks. The developer advanced the front-end financing for regional infrastructure, with repayment through $30 million in TIF. Forest City bought its first land in 2001, agreeing to buy 1,000 acres (405 hectares) every five years until 2015, with the price stabilized at 2001 and increased according to the consumer price index.

Both Forest City and SDC had to go through lengthy due diligence processes before any sale could take place. In addition to Forest City and the SDC, other parties involved included the city of Denver, surrounding neighborhood groups, the Federal Aviation Administration, and the airlines that were former Stapleton tenants. Forest City's large, diverse portfolio (with assets exceeding

$5 billion) allowed it to sustain the extended due diligence process.

Financing

Stapleton is very much a public/private partnership. Creating TIF was key to funding the $600 million necessary in local and regional infrastructure costs. To accomplish this task, DURA, the only entity possessing such powers, became involved in the Stapleton redevelopment effort in 1995. DURA, created by the city in 1958, is responsible for conducting urban renewal activities throughout the city and county of Denver. TIF captures the net increase in property taxes in a redeveloped area and directs that sum toward specific public works projects. When a redevelopment project is being planned, DURA analyzes how much additional property and/or sales taxes will likely be generated once it is completed. That tax increment can then be used to finance bonds or to reimburse developers for a portion of their project financing. In either case, the new tax revenue must be used for improvements that have a public benefit and that support the redevelopment effort, such as site clearance, streets, utilities, parks, removal of hazardous conditions, or site acquisition.

All the additional taxes created by the redevelopment revert to the normal taxing entities once DURA has fulfilled its monetary obligations related to a project. Thus, the neighborhood benefits from the creation of revitalized, productive properties, and the tax-ing entities get new, permanent sources of revenue that would not have existed if DURA had not enabled the project to be undertaken. The TIF-based assessed value in 2001 was $28 million, the assessed value increment was $17 million, and the estimated incremental revenue was $800,000. Over the 25-year construction period, the annual property tax increment is estimated to grow to $93 million.

Forest City purchased $145 million in bonds from the Park Creek Metropolitan District to underwrite the initial infrastructure required for the redevelopment,

a transaction that was financed by Lehman Brothers. Forest City secured a $25 million loan from National City Bank for the initial land purchase, allowing it to bear much of the upfront costs. By assuming this risk, it will also reap most of the rewards. Forest City intends to deliver 500 to 600 single-family units, for different prices, per year.

Stapleton's affordable housing component has so far been financed in part by the Fannie Mae Foundation's American Communities Fund, tax-exempt bonds, and low-income housing tax credits, assisted by discounted land costs (from Forest City).

Design and Construction

Stapleton's plan is based on the design principles of new urbanism, providing physical and economic connections to the surrounding neighborhood. The project has abundant trails and open space for walking and biking. In addition, builders must comply with Energy Star standards and meet the minimum level of the Colorado Built Green program, which encourages energy efficiency, healthy indoor air, reduced water use, and preservation of natural resources.

Stapleton's master plan calls for the development to fit seamlessly into the patterns of the surrounding neighborhoods. The surrounding housing stock comprises mostly single-family homes with front porches; the development includes modest lots, pocket parks, and streets lined with sidewalks and mature trees. The homes in Stapleton will mirror these elements; other themes will relate to historic downtown Denver. Neighborhood streets will be relatively narrow to minimize the speed of traffic.

Within the eight districts are seven planning zones and plans for five mixed-use town centers. Each planning zone covers roughly 500 acres (202 hectares), which will be further divided into 100-acre (40-hectare) neighborhoods. The plan calls for a 1,116-acre (452-hectare) open-space system, which will traverse the site in a north/south

Stapleton includes a wide array of housing types: single-family homes, rowhouses, rental apartments, and four- and six-plex buildings (shown here) designed to look like mansions.

Courtesy of D. R. Horton

orientation. It will be maintained by the city and county of Denver.

Homes in the early phases are being designed as 12 typologies: seven single-family detached homes, two types of rowhouses, rental apartments (some of which will be live/work units), and four- and six-plex buildings designed to look like mansions. To ensure diversity in design and household profile, the housing types are mixed in each district. In the tradition of new urban-

Homes are designed to reflect Denver's architectural history. A pattern book details four primary styles: Victorian, craftsman, Colonial revival, and Denver foursquare.

Courtesy of John Laing Homes

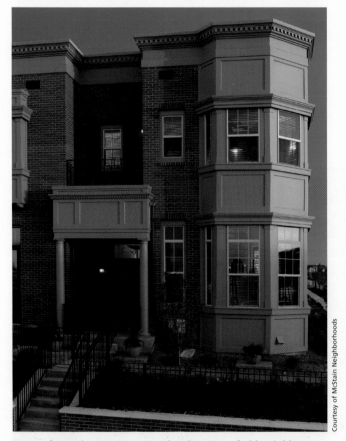

Rows of townhouses interpret the character of old neighborhoods of cities like Boston and Philadelphia.

Courtesy of McStain Neighborhoods

ism, the garages of a majority of homes are accessed from rear alleys.

Forest City worked with production homebuilders to design homes that are aesthetically pleasing and reflect Denver's architectural history. The Stapleton Design Book, created by EDAW, Wolff Lyon Architects, and Calthorpe Associates under the direction of Forest City Stapleton, recommends four primary styles—Victorian, craftsman, Colonial revival, and Denver foursquare— and two secondary styles—English revival and Mediterranean revival. The designs of larger homes reflect traditional Denver architecture and offer carriage units, broad front porches, and high-end finishes.

Office and retail uses will be within walking distance of residential neighborhoods. The first town center— East 29th Avenue—and a regional retail center—Quebec Square—have been developed in the first district. A main street lined with two- and three-story buildings is the prominent feature of each town center planned. Retail spaces and offices will occupy ground floors, while residential lofts and offices will be built on upper levels.

A goal of the Stapleton redevelopment project is to efficiently reuse some of the distinctive features of the old airport. The 264-foot (80-meter) control tower will be used as a visitors center. Old hangars and outbuildings have been recycled to house several businesses and the Denver Police Training Academy.

Stapleton is home to the world's largest recycling effort. The demolition of the remaining terminal buildings resulted in 50 percent of the concrete, rebar, and sheet metal's being recycled. The 1,100 acres (445 hectares) of old runways are being crushed to be used as road base and concrete aggregate for projects around Denver as well as for reuse in Stapleton's roads, trails, and sidewalks. More than 200,000 tons (220,500 metric tons) of asphalt from parking lots and the commuter runway has been transported north to the Rocky Mountain Arsenal National Wildlife Area, where it has been used to create road base. The first new bridge on the site was constructed out of StapleStone—otherwise known as old runway material. The terminal's 5,000-car garage has become the Stapleton Transit Center and is one of the busiest transportation hubs in the metropolitan area. Even some of the old carpeting from the terminal was recycled into carpet backing that is durable, cheap, and without any of the "off gases" that can cause indoor air pollution.

More than a third of the site is preserved for open space and parks. A new golf course will eventually be built on the northern half of the site. The 123-acre (50-hectare) Bluff Lake Natural Area serves as an outdoor classroom for thousands of children who study the wetlands and observe wildlife, including bald eagles, great horned owls, foxes, and a variety of aquatic fowl. When the network of recreation trails is complete, it will be part of the first loop of trails to surround a major U.S. city. Stapleton's bike paths will connect to Denver's Regional Bikeway and flow into the 27,000-acre (10,900-hectare) Rocky Mountain Wildlife Preserve.

All the homes at Stapleton are required to meet or exceed the minimum level of the Built Green Colorado program. Built Green Colorado is administered by the Home Builders Association of Metro Denver (HBA) and supported by the governor's Office of Energy Management and Conservation. It is a voluntary program that uses buyer demand, market education, and builder training to encourage builders to build homes that reduce pollution, are energy efficient, have healthier indoor air, reduce water use, preserve natural resources, have improved durability, and reduce the need for maintenance.

Forest City, the Stapleton Development Corporation, and the Regional Transportation District are jointly planning a future multimodal transit center to be incorporated into the regional retail center and office development to be built between Quebec and Yosemite streets. Currently, bus service runs along the edges of the site; stops will eventually be located in Stapleton.

Affordable Housing

Ten percent, or approximately 800, of the single-family homes sold at Stapleton will be built under the Home-Buyer Resource Program. The program was designed to put housing in reach of teachers, nurses, police officers, and other members of the community's workforce. A family needs to earn approximately $65,000 to afford the median-priced home in Denver, assuming good credit and the availability of funds for a downpayment and closing costs. Approximately 56 percent of Denver families earned less than $50,000 in 2000.

Forest City dedicated itself to establishing a comprehensive affordable housing program and established the Associate Developer Program to work with local nonprofit housing agencies and small development firms that wanted to build affordable housing at Stapleton. Forest City provides technical expertise and guidance to the developers chosen, many of whom do not have experience with the scale of or deed limitations associated with the project.

Affordable units must be developed in mixed-income areas and must adhere to minimum square footage guidelines (for example, a studio apartment cannot be smaller than 400 square feet [37 square meters], a three-bedroom apartment smaller than 1,100 square feet [102 square meters]); at least 15 percent of the units must have three or more bedrooms. The developers and Forest City must report to the city and the SDC their progress in fulfilling the affordable housing requirements.

To be eligible to purchase one of the affordable homes, a buyer's gross household income must be below specific target incomes published annually by HUD, and to ensure long-term affordability for future homebuyers, 30-year resale price restrictions apply to the homes. At the end of 30 years, a nonprofit entity created to control and monitor the for-sale units and supported by a 3 percent sales commission has the option of buying back the homes at the restricted price and re-restricting the units or letting them be sold on the open market and collecting the difference. The homeowner gets to keep a share of the appreciation, depending on how long he or she has been in the residence.

Marketing

Denver's ballparks, bike paths, microbreweries, and upscale boutiques help the city to promote a hip and culturally diverse image, and Stapleton hopes to capitalize on that image with its range of housing types and amenities.

Stapleton's initial sales were to large clients such as industrial park builders and corporations, but eventually smaller clients with specialized projects became interested and homebuilders showed tremendous interest in becoming part of Stapleton. Forest City is appealing to homeowners who are looking for a third choice in where they live—the first two being an old home in the city and a new house in the suburbs. Stapleton provides an urban feel but with greenery, open space, and parks often associated with suburban living.

The Forest City Stapleton Visitor Center welcomes visitors, buyers, renters, business owners, and the press. The center is a clear-span steel-frame building designed with energy-efficient materials that include special window glazing and carpeting made of recycled materials. The building can be "deconstructed" and moved to a new location for future use. It features a video wall that integrates actual aerial footage of the property with virtual reality images of the first neighborhoods built. Another highlight includes a network of pavilions that offer glimpses into the residential, office, retail, and open-space aspects of the new mixed-use neighborhoods. The pavilions also provide information about Stapleton initiatives, such as its sustainable development, educational environment, modern telecommunications links, and other elements that will create a walkable, whole-life urban community.

High-quality neighborhood schools make Stapleton appealing to families and able to compete with suburban developments. When the master plan was being developed, the Denver public school system was struggling to maintain standards, and it was thought that those moving into Stapleton would not want to send their children to the local public schools. Forest City, however, worked with the Denver public school system to establish first-rate public schools in Stapleton. Charter, private, vocational, and online learning schools will also be built. Current plans call for at least four elementary schools and two high schools as well as a number of early-childhood learning facilities.

Stapleton's Westerly Creek campus opened in 2003, the Denver School of Science and Technology, a charter high school, in 2004. Forest City donated ten acres (4 hectares) of land and $500,000 toward the construction of the latter school. Additional support came from contributions from the Bill and Melinda Gates Foundation, Hewlett Packard, and numerous other national and local foundations. The $14 million school will be a Denver public schools charter high school dedicated to increasing the proficiency of high school students in mathematics, science, and technology. Forest City has also committed funds to surrounding schools to increase Stapleton's positive impact.

Developers estimate that houses will be coming online at a rate of 50 to 75 new homes every month for the next 15 years. Most homebuilders have from two to four buyers for every home, so many are holding lotteries and other means of allocating homes. Stapleton's housing ranges from affordable workforce housing to urban estates priced up to $1 million.

Stapleton has tremendous appeal for retailers as a result of its location near I-70. Because of the variety of centers (big-box centers, town squares, and main streets), Stapleton can accommodate a range of retailers. Quebec Square, the 800,000-square-foot (74,350-square-meter) center, features big-box retailers. A 1.2 million-square-foot (111,500-square-meter) outdoor mall is scheduled to open in 2005 or 2006. Both planned centers will be located on I-70 to ensure good visibility.

The 57,000-square-foot (5,300-square-meter) East 29th Street Town Center provides a more pedestrian-oriented scale. It features neighborhood-oriented restaurants and stores and the Crescent Flats—66 one- and two-bedroom rental apartments above ground-floor shops. Main Street Office Suites offers 34,000 square feet (3,160 square meters) of executive offices overlooking 29th Avenue. Completing the town center will be additional apartments, townhouses, live/work lofts with attached garages, and a 100-unit affordable apartment complex for seniors. Forest City currently manages all rental properties.

The Stapleton Technology Master Plan was developed in part to equip Stapleton's housing with high-speed communications wiring and, in turn, increase its appeal to future residents. The master plan covers three integrated community communications aspects: home wiring, service providers, and community network. Stapleton allied with Qwest Communications and AT&T broadband to develop

Courtesy of Forest City Stapleton, Inc.

Town center buildings include shops on the street level with office space on upper floors.

High-quality neighborhood schools make Stapleton appealing to families. The Denver School of Science and Technology, a charter high school, opened in 2004.

Courtesy of New Schools Development Corp.

Stapleton residential wiring guidelines to ensure proper capacity. Stapleton also has its own intranet, where community members can browse through forums and newsgroups and learn about new stores, services, and events. Stapleton recently incorporated wireless technology, which resulted in lower construction costs. Installing and subsequently moving data cables for the construction trailers became problematic and expensive. Forest City decided to link the trailers to a wireless system, which would involve a one-time expenditure of about $50,000. Networking companies discovered that the former air traffic control tower could be used as a generation and transfer point for the signals. Stapleton's transfer to wireless technology will save the time of installing fiber-optic cable and approximately $2.2 million over the next 15 years.

Stapleton is marketed as a walking and biking community, but it also offers access to Honda Civic hybrids (gasoline-electric engines) that can be rented by the hour. A monthly or hourly fee covers gas, insurance, maintenance, and emergency service. The program is an attractive option for those who choose not to own a vehicle or who need a second vehicle for short trips.

Experience Gained

One of Forest City's greatest challenges has been the need to coordinate and implement a range of development activities that are nearly unprecedented in their scope. Forest City coordinated the work of 18 single-family builders to create housing that meets high standards of urban design and energy efficiency while being affordable to a wide range of incomes. A major hurdle was obtaining the permits, plat approvals, and zoning changes for such a large property.

Forest City credits its positive working relationship with city officials, local nonprofit groups, and the surrounding community as a major part of the project's momentum. Forest City respected the plans the city and citizens groups made and included minority- and women-owned business as contractors.

Another challenge was economically jump-starting the project so that retail, office space, and homes could be constructed simultaneously. The economic generator to start the project was the automobile-oriented regional Quebec Square. Citizens groups were taken aback by the scale of the proposed big-box center and pointed out that it was not in the spirit of Stapleton's neotraditional planning efforts. Designers approached this problem by educating all involved parties as to Stapleton's overall goals. The pedestrian-oriented neighborhoods and business districts must have an economic generator to be built successfully. Regional retail, while not traditionally consistent with pedestrian-oriented development, provides that economic security.

The developer also designed the regional retail site with the ability to evolve into denser uses once regional retail is gone. Specifically, the surrounding street grid was extended to Quebec Square, bringing with it pedestrian access and public transit, ensuring that it has street connections into it from the adjacent uses.

Although Stapleton has more than 15 years to go before buildout, its presence is already having a positive ripple effect in surrounding neighborhoods. The demolition of some of the large unsightly utility buildings, the restoration of open space, the elimination of aircraft noise, and the infusion of new retail businesses have ushered in increased neighborhood pride, property values, and tax revenues.

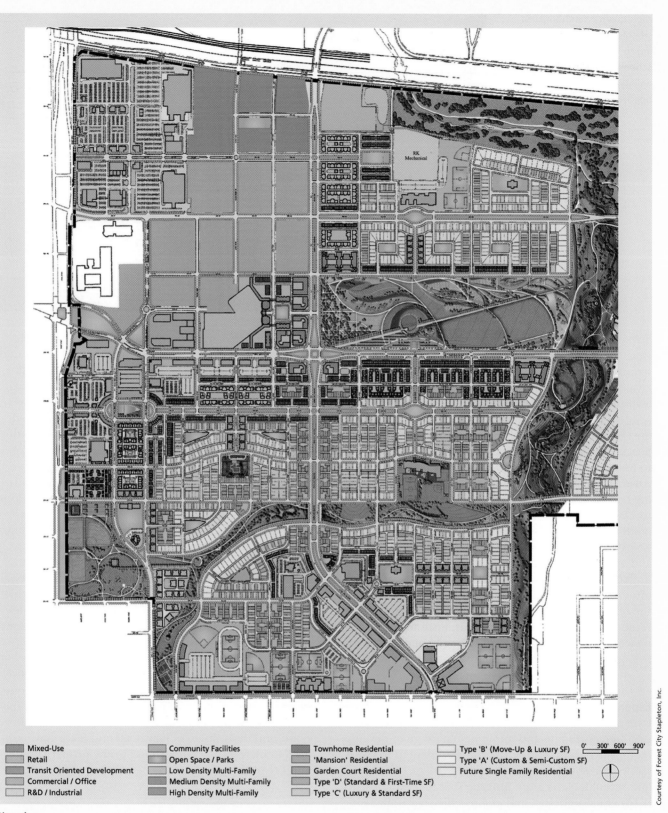

	Mixed-Use		Community Facilities		Townhome Residential		Type 'B' (Move-Up & Luxury SF)
	Retail		Open Space / Parks		'Mansion' Residential		Type 'A' (Custom & Semi-Custom SF)
	Transit Oriented Development		Low Density Multi-Family		Garden Court Residential		Future Single Family Residential
	Commercial / Office		Medium Density Multi-Family		Type 'D' (Standard & First-Time SF)		
	R&D / Industrial		High Density Multi-Family		Type 'C' (Luxury & Standard SF)		

0' 300' 600' 900'

Site plan.

Land Use and Building Information

Site Area	4,700 acres (1,903 hectares)
Office Space	10,000,000 square feet (930,000 square meters)
Retail Space	3,000,000 square feet (280,000 square meters)

Residential Unit Information

Unit Type	Unit Size (Square Feet/ Square Meters)	Number Sold	Initial Sale Price Range
Single-Family Detached			
Urban Estate Program	3,200–3,800/ 297–353	13	$650,000– 1,200,000
Sanford Homes	2,870–3,150/ 267–293	21	$495,900– 530,900
McStain Neighborhoods	1,812–2,875/ 168–267	76	$296,900– 432,900
John Laing Homes	1,950–2,750/ 181–256	157	$284,000– 385,900
New Town Builders	1,500–2,275/ 139–211	107	$264,900– 385,900
Parkwood Homes	1,730–2,250/ 161–209	57	$279,900– 427,900
KB Home	1,550–2,150/ 144–200	138	$222,995– 315,495
Infinity Home Collection	2,400–2,900/ 223–270	0	$400,000– 450,000
Wonderland Homes	1,185–1,770/ 110–164	85	$239,900– 334,900
KB Home (Green Court)	1,250–1,675/ 116–156	126	$179,995– 258,495
Single-Family Attached			
John Laing Homes	1,940–2,340/ 180–217	0	$325,000– 400,000
McStain Neighborhoods	1,340–1,650/ 124–153	94	$214,900– 279,900
Trimark Communities	1,035–1,575/ 96–146	101	$154,950– 236,950
Fullerton Company	668–1,500/ 62–139	27	$150,000– 321,000
TP Development	600–1,100/ 56–102	15	$123,775– 176,000
BMW	800–1,150/ 74–107	12	$135,000– 167,500

Development Cost Information

	To Date	Projected
Site Costs		
Site acquisition	$40,000,000	$125,000,000
Site improvement	80,000,000	620,000,000
Total	$120,000,000	$745,000,000
Construction Costs	$410,000,000	$3,470,000,000
Soft Costs	$220,000,000	$1,840,000,000
Total Development Cost	$750,000,000	$6,055,000,000

Developer

Forest City Stapleton, Inc.
7351 East 29th Avenue
Denver, Colorado 80238
303-382-1800
www.StapletonDenver.com

Master Planner

Calthorpe Associates
739 Allston Way
Berkeley, California 94710
510-548-6800
www.calthorpe.com

Architects

Design Guidelines
Wolff-Lyon
777 Pearl Street
Suite 210
Boulder, Colorado 80302
303-447-2786
www.wlarch.com

Mixed-Use and Commercial Buildings
Urban Design Group
1621 18th Street
Suite 200
Denver, Colorado 80202
303-292-3388

Elementary School
Anderson Mason Dale
1615 17th Street
Denver, Colorado 80202
303-294-9448
www.amdarchitects.com

Landscape Design Guidelines, Park Design

EDAW, Inc.
1809 Blake Street
Suite 200
Denver, Colorado 80202
303-595-4522
www.edaw.com

Development Schedule

2/2000	Purchase agreement signed
1989	Stapleton Development Plan started
5/2001	Construction started
1/2002	Sales/leasing started
2020	Estimated project completion

10. Emerging Trends

This final chapter discusses the future direction of residential development. The first edition of this handbook, published in 1978, correctly predicted a number of trends but erred on others; for example, homes did not shrink in response to smaller households. The second edition, published in 1990, correctly predicted many trends but once again predicted that house size would begin to decrease. This third edition will certainly miscalculate some predictions and correctly forecast others, but it will make no predictions about shrinking house size.

Demographics: Population Drives Demand

Although population has always been a major determining factor for residential development, recent changes in the U.S. population such as the rise in immigration, the growing number of seniors and nontraditional households, and changes in the American family will have a dramatic impact on housing needs. Realtors like to say the most important factors in housing are "location, location, location," but the most important element in predicting future housing trends is not the location of the housing but the location of certain population segments. According to Harvard University's Joint Center for Housing Studies, household growth—which determines housing demand—may exceed 12 million by 2010.

Nazca Buildings, Cordoba, Spain.

"Immigrants are expected to contribute more than one-quarter of this increase, and all minorities combined will represent two-thirds of growth. The growing influence of minorities on housing markets was already evident in 2001, when they accounted for 32 percent of recent first-time buyers and 42 percent of all renters."[1] As minorities gain affluence and become more integrated into the population, they will represent a growing segment of move-up buyers as well.

Immigration

The United States depends on immigrant labor to sustain its economy. In 2010, the U.S. population is expected to increase to about 300 million, partly as a result of immigration. Approximately three-quarters of the 1 million immigrants who arrive each year enter legally to work in the United States. These immigrants represent the extremes of the educational spectrum; most are either very well or very poorly educated.

According to demographer William H. Frey, new immigrants to the United States tend to "pile on" in specific parts of the country, joining previous immigrants from their home countries in 24-hour cities such as Washington, D.C., San Francisco, Chicago, New York, and Los Angeles. Hispanic immigrants, for example, tend to locate initially in Los Angeles or New York City, although the Hispanic population in Phoenix has doubled in recent years, from both spillover immigration from California and direct immigration. Asian immigrants often initially

The redevelopment of a neighborhood of 19th-century stone gate–style lane houses in downtown Shanghai not only preserves a historic district and its distinctive residential architecture but also creates land value by introducing a sophisticated leisure and entertainment center. Shanghai Xintiandi reflects modern China's rapidly progressing economic environment and the entrepreneurship that is fueling it.

Juxtapositions abound in post-Communist Shanghai's development scene. Before the 1949 revolution that made China a Communist country, Shanghai was renowned as the Paris of the Orient, largely because of its mercantile tradition. Its seaport was the most cosmopolitan of any in Asia, while it also hosted the parochial Chinese Communist Party's first congress in 1921. The site of that fateful meeting, a former school building, is a national historic shrine symbolizing the overthrow of capitalism. Today, the Revolutionary Museum is surrounded by Xintiandi, a recognizably western lifestyle center full of reminders of the recent ascension of a market-based economy.

Shanghai Xintiandi—pronounced "Shin-tien-dee" and translated "A New World"—is the first phase of the 72-acre (29-hectare) Taipingqia mixed-use redevelopment project in downtown Shanghai being led by Hong Kong–based Shui On Group. Starting with an investment in a Shanghai high-rise hotel venture in 1985, Shui On established contacts on the mainland that eventually led to an invitation from the district government in 1996 to redevelop a part of the central city adjacent to the business district, in what was once a French concession. Home to French expatriates during Shanghai's heyday, most of the buildings were in a particular Shanghai style known as *Shikumen*.

Shikumen—translated "stone gate"—houses were built along alleys, with each house, typically three stories, having a stone-framed entranceway. These elaborately carved ornamental stonework frames surround a lacquered door that opens to an interior courtyard. Originally built in the 1860s, they expressed a familiarity with western architectural styles, while, in typical colonial manner, they are constructed of local materials and with local techniques. With the Communist takeover, these homes were converted to tenements, housing as many as seven families, who shared a single kitchen and bathroom.

The government mandated that 2,300 households be relocated, that Shui On preserve the Revolutionary Museum and the buildings around it, and that the height of new construction be limited. With these precepts, Shui On was forced to depart from the usual formula of focusing on high-rise commercial and residential blocks and to concentrate instead on preserving the area's rich store of Shikumen houses, which were being razed elsewhere in the city to make way for new construction. Based on a master plan by the San Francisco, California, office of Skidmore, Owings & Merrill, the developer plotted a rehabilitation course that would preserve buildings and adapt them to accommodate the commercial necessities of a retail center.

Shui On brought in the Boston architectural firm Wood & Zapata, known for adaptive use of old buildings, to redesign the Shikumen houses for retail use. Wood & Zapata inventoried the buildings to determine which were worth preserving or moving. Most of the buildings

locate in New York, Los Angeles, or San Francisco but also may head to any city with a high-tech economy such as Dallas or Atlanta. According to Frey, "These concentrated gains for Hispanics and Asians reflect a 'chain migration' associated . . . with the need for interaction with co-nationals from countries of similar backgrounds, languages, and cultures that live in communities where they will receive both social and economic support."[2]

New "minority frontiers" are being established in parts of the Southwest and the Sunbelt where ample employment opportunities exist for immigrants of all skill levels. Minority frontiers for Hispanic and Asian immigrants include Atlanta, Charlotte, Orlando, Las Vegas, Phoenix, and Raleigh/Durham. Asian immigrants also are attracted to university towns and high-tech areas such as Austin, Tampa, Miami, and Detroit. According to Harvard's Joint Center for Housing Studies, "Minorities are on track to add 7.5 million households between 2000 and 2010, and another 7.8 million between 2010 and 2020."[3]

The influx of immigrants creating new minority frontiers outside gateway cities creates opportunities for all forms of residential development. Affordable housing, particularly rental, is needed to house new immigrants in gateway cities and other areas that function as initial ports of entry. By 2020, minorities are expected to make up more than half of all renters. Many immigrants then will look for housing in the suburbs as a result of their concerns over the quality of education and the rising costs of city living as well as the better housing and employment opportunities in the suburbs. Increasing numbers of immigrants are bypassing gateway cities altogether and moving directly to the suburbs, smaller towns, or rural areas. The influx of immigrants who buy houses vacated by older residents will encourage suburban growth. Immigrants and their children also are driving up demand for smaller or starter homes. Over the next two decades, they will constitute 64 percent of household growth, or 15.3 million households. As Anthony

were too deteriorated to restore, except for those parts of the outer shell that contained the distinctive stonework door frames and features such as lintels, eaves, and wooden windows. New buildings were designed around these highlights, and architectural features were cannibalized from other buildings. Where buildings had to be demolished, plazas were created. Alleys were retained and paved with the same century-old gray flagstones, and new walls were built with reused red and black bricks. (Such labor-intensive work could be accomplished in Shanghai, where labor costs are still low.) Where walls had to be removed, large glass panels fill in the spaces between the remaining architectural elements, forming storefronts at ground level. Throughout, new support structures and mechanical and electrical/communications systems have been installed, bringing the buildings up to contemporary standards.

After financing Shui On's purchase, the banks balked at the pioneering development scheme, and the developer had to proceed with its own money. When the construction costs ballooned, a loan of RMB372 million ($45 million) from a consortium of four banks enabled work on Shui On to continue. Xintiandi's North Block project cost RMB486 million ($58 million) and is returning an annual income of RMB72 million ($8.7 million). As leases come up for renewal, rental income increases substantially to reflect the surrounding area's escalating property values. Although citywide property values are increasing 33 percent, the values of the district property immediately surrounding Xintiandi are increasing 45 percent for commercial property and more than 50 percent for luxury residential property. As the rest of Shui On's Taipingqia project takes shape, the developer is accruing benefits from the increased values.

Internationals, who make up most of the clientele, liken Xintiandi to London's Covent Garden, San Francisco's Ghirardelli Square, and Hong Kong's Lan Kwai Fong. A wide variety of tenants and operators come from around the world: the Museum of Coca-Cola, an Australian couturier, Dior, Vidal Sassoon, Comme des Garçons, McDonald's, two Starbucks, and a Wolfgang Puck restaurant. There are 30 total food vendors.

With international tenants and prices to match, the redevelopment attracts Shanghai's young professionals and Shanghai-based Westerners who flock to Xintiandi as the place to see and be seen, SARS and avian flu scares notwithstanding. For this same reason, Xintiandi also attracts tourists from the interior of China, where *waiguoren,* or foreigners, are not yet common. Domestic tourists are mostly a daytime phenomenon, and 70 to 80 percent of Xintiandi's business is conducted in the evening. With the introduction of more such developments, the novelty and fame will diminish.

Shanghai Xintiandi would be a noteworthy leisure and entertainment center anywhere in the world. That it is located in the People's Republic of China, albeit in a city that has traditionally been regarded as China's gateway to the world, is all the more remarkable. In a booming high-rise-based real estate market, where the rehabilitation of historic structures for adaptive use was an unknown and where working with the government required hurdling barriers of corruption, bureaucracy, and general interference, Xintiandi represents a new way, a new product, perhaps even a "New World" in the front line of a business revolution that is accelerating the movement of a country toward a modern, open society. ■

Downs, a senior fellow at the Brookings Institution, points out, "Residential developers will have to adapt housing plans to accommodate immigrant groups with extended family households."[4]

Boomers Booming and Aging
As the number of Americans age 60 and over is expected to reach 88 million by 2030, baby boomers—those born between 1946 and 1964—continue to be trendsetters in many areas, including residential real estate. One-quarter of the population currently consists of boomers. The oldest boomers will not turn 75 until after 2020, and the greater need for housing for seniors will become more apparent after 2010, when boomers reach the peak of their wealth.

Communities in the Sunbelt and the West continue to be popular retirement options. On the other hand, the majority of retirees are choosing to remain within 50 miles (80 kilometers) of their previous residences or

are not moving at all. The choice to stay local has many contributing factors: the desire to remain within an existing social network rather than move and be forced to establish a new one, health insurance that can be used only in certain parts of the country, or the appeal of living in a house that is paid for and not take on a new mortgage. In some cases, NORCs, or "naturally occurring retirement communities," are being formed in neighborhoods of apartment buildings housing seniors who choose not to move.

Retiring baby boomers also may choose to stay local—or to move to or near a big city—to prepare for a stimulating retirement where they can work, start a new business, increase their knowledge, or establish other new goals. According to AARP, at least 80 percent of boomers plan to work after retirement, both for mental stimulation and to supplement their finances to live more comfortably. Even without the financial need to work, many seniors seek to meld employment and leisure opportunities to create a new way of retiring that meets their interests and needs. This interest in working will continue to change the way activities are planned in senior-oriented communities. More social events will be offered on evenings and weekends instead of during the day.

Developers are following these trends. Del Webb, a national developer that specializes in active adult communities, has opened a new prototype of an active adult, resort-style community in Fredericksburg, Virginia—a 50-mile (80-kilometer) commute to Washington, D.C.—to attract Washington-area boomers who want to stay near Washington. Falls Run is an age-restricted, retirement-oriented community that has a clubhouse, recreation center, and activities program, but, unlike nearly all Sunbelt retirement communities, it has no golf course.

Some boomers who choose to move to retirement communities opt for ones with traditional amenities that focus on healthy lifestyles, with activity directors to plan daily events and amenities such as gyms, swimming pools, and on-site health care facilities or wellness centers. At the Cliffs at Walnut Cove, outside Asheville, North Carolina, a full program of wellness services and amenities is available to residents, including personal fitness and nutritional assessments, sports conditioning, and medical services.

Some retirees choose communities with less traditional amenities, such as educational opportunities or environmental activities that bring them closer to nature, including mountain biking, rock climbing, rafting, and

kayaking. Another increasingly popular amenity is the business center with computers and high-speed Internet access. Many senior communities are now "themed": every detail, from marketing materials to architecture and furnishings, is carefully designed to create the atmosphere, ambience, and identity of a particular era, region, or setting, such as a rustic fishing village, a lakeside resort, a nature preserve, or a western ranch.

Intellectual opportunities draw boomers to university towns such as State College, Pennsylvania; Iowa City, Iowa; Bloomington, Indiana; and Madison, Wisconsin.[5] These college and university towns offer a wide range of cultural amenities that attract well-educated seniors. Many schools even welcome seniors back to the classroom, hosting tours, classes, and activities specifically designed to appeal to their interests.

The number of retirees living in the suburbs of major cities, including Atlanta, Dallas, and Washington, D.C., continues to grow. Boomers pioneered the suburban lifestyle and often lived in the suburbs their entire lives. Many intend to stay there during their retirement years. The growing number of boomers and retirees in the suburbs may lead to new debates about how local budgets should be spent, with health care facilities and golf courses competing with schools and playgrounds for funding. It also could lead to increased traffic from "senior gridlock" on the freeways. On the other hand, many communities actively try to attract retired seniors to their suburbs, because this age cohort typically con-

Retirees are choosing from a broad range of lifestyles. The Garlands of Barrington in Illinois offers independent living units in a campus-like setting for aging residents.

The majority of seniors do not choose age-restricted communities. At Esplanade Place, a 12-story luxury condominium in Phoenix, buyers range in age from the 30s to the 70s. Most are downsizing from larger homes.

tributes more money to the economy and the tax base than it costs in the provision of services.

Other Generations

The 78 million baby boomers now hitting retirement age are leaving behind only 40 million people age 25 to 34 to replace them. Although boomers continue to be the largest age cohort in the U.S. population, housing professionals should not make the mistake of discounting Generations X and Y—those born between 1965 and 1980 and those born after 1980, respectively. These postboomers will have the largest influence on future housing trends. They are drawn to the rapidly growing Sunbelt areas of Raleigh/Durham, Salt Lake City, Austin, and Dallas/Fort Worth, to places with large immigrant populations such as Salinas and Los Angeles, and to university towns such as Madison, Wisconsin; Lansing, Michigan; and Columbus, Ohio. The low cost of living in these areas attracts large numbers of both young adults and immigrants of all ages.[6] By 2010, the "echo boomers" —individuals born to the baby boom generation between 1977 and 1997—will range in age from 13 to 33. This group currently is enjoying its youth, but it also is beginning or bracing for the first steps into adulthood: college, first jobs, marriage or committed partnerships, setting up a household, and having children. The group is a racially and ethnically diverse group with a more open and global outlook than the boomers who preceded them.

Now in their 20s and 30s, many of the Generation X'ers have gotten a jumpstart on homeownership. Many members of this generation bought their first home at a younger age than their parents did, which has boosted the demand for starter and move-up homes. Today, approximately 1.5 million U.S. homeowners are under 25, the result, in part, of historically low interest rates and a wide variety of financing options. These younger homebuyers seek higher-density communities with pedestrian-oriented streets. The new urbanism movement will expand to meet their needs, as conventional subdivisions dominated by culs-de-sac, large lots, and wide roads continue to lose favor. Planners now advocate the development of neighborhoods with traditional grid street systems and businesses and services integrated into neighborhoods to encourage walking or biking and to reduce driving time.

Another interesting population note is the increasing number of single-person households and married couples without children. According to Harvard's Joint Center for Housing Studies:

> The number of people living alone is expected to rise by nearly 5 million in 2010 . . . and many of these single-person households will be relatively affluent, middle-aged baby boomers. The number of married couples over 55 without minor children living at home will be up 4.3 million during this decade and 6.1 million the next. As of 2002, 15 percent of married-couple households in this group included an adult child, while 11 percent of 25- to 34-year-olds still lived with their parents.[7]

Location: Cities versus Suburbs

With this general understanding of who is living where across the country, developers need to understand why certain population groups choose to live in the cities or the suburbs. A consumer preference survey of Generations X and Y in 2001 revealed a distinct preference for

Housing affordability is a continuing problem. Auburn Court in Cambridge, Massachusetts, includes units that are set aside for low- and moderate-income households.

Throughout the world, cities and suburbs continue to grow. In Bahrain, the Bandar A'Seef waterfront plan offers a resort-like lifestyle at urban densities.

urban and close-in suburban areas. Of those participating in the survey, 40 percent lived in an "urban suburb," and 34 percent lived in an urban area or city. Eighty-two percent planned to buy a home by 2006, and most (45 percent) planned to choose a close-in suburb or urban area. When looking for a new home, 61 percent of survey respondents cited proximity to restaurants and services as well as recreational amenities as important attributes to consider. On the other hand, 45 percent of Genera-

Loft-style housing appeals to many urban homebuyers.

tion X and Y respondents said they would be willing to live farther away from shopping, services, and entertainment to purchase a more affordable home.[8]

Suburbs Rising

Development continues to sprawl outward from cities into distant outer-ring suburbs and exurbs that are so far outside the urban core that they have little relationship with anything in the city beyond its media market, local ball teams, and airports. Forsyth and Paulding counties outside Atlanta and Douglas County outside Denver are examples of this type of growth. In between these counties and traditional suburbs lie "boomburgs" or "stealth cities"—areas of more than 100,000 residents that have maintained double-digit rates of population growth in recent decades but are not the largest cities in the metropolitan area. These places are where most new subdivisions are located, and commercial development is moving out to meet the built-in residential demand. Although the majority of growth is headed to these areas, a need still exists for residential developers who focus on mixed-use smart growth projects and projects near transportation, infill developments, and redevelopment in the inner-ring suburbs.

The traditional suburban middle-class household—Dad, Mom, 2.5 kids, and a dog—is declining in numbers. Yet the suburbs' lower cost of living appeals to both single parents—an enormous unrecognized constituency—and young adults, especially recent college graduates. The high divorce rate of the 1990s created many single-parent households. In addition, the percentage of one-person households in the suburbs grew from 17 percent in 1970 to 26 percent in 2002.

The number of nontraditional households—including young singles and elderly widows—living in the suburbs is quickly outpacing the number of traditional family households. Although the common suburban cry to reduce overcrowding in schools continues, demand also is rising for social services targeted to seniors. And the growing numbers of young-adult households—both singles and childless couples—who live in the suburbs to be closer to their jobs at suburban office locations want more nightlife and cultural venues. The possibility exists that the growing number of single suburbanites of all ages may be able to outvote families with children, further shifting suburban jurisdictions' spending priorities.

Downtowns Rebounding

Still, cities remain a popular choice with some baby boomers, Generations X and Y, and immigrants of all ages. Although the back-to-the-city movement has not been as large as originally anticipated and the number of higher-income households moving back to the city is modest, pockets of increased urban growth can be found around the country. Most of this growth is targeted to the needs of upper-middle-class boomers who can pay a premium to live in exciting urban areas near public transportation and within walking distance of cultural, retail, and entertainment options. Some empty nesters have decided to exchange the hassles of keeping up a suburban house and long daily commutes for the convenience of in-town living, often by renting or buying a luxury apartment.

Although young professionals and immigrants also are drawn to the cities for similar reasons, they often are priced out of the market. In addition, city living is not popular throughout the country. Patterns of urban growth and decline are uneven; some cities are losing residents, others are posting only modest increases, and still others are experiencing rapid population growth.[9] Many cities have become interested in attracting the nation's 23 million college-educated young professionals as a way of bringing in more businesses. Cities are doing so by promoting their funky neighborhoods, art galleries, coffee shops, restaurants and nightlife, and their diverse cultures. Second-tier cities such as Cincinnati, Memphis, Milwaukee, and Pittsburgh—among others—are adopt-

ing new, hipper images as a way to attract the young professionals who are now deciding where to live and work. These young professionals often have greater disposable income and require fewer of the expensive city services, such as schools and health care, than traditional family or senior households.

Many developers are creating new housing products to appeal to the young adult market. Urban developers seek out infill sites for loft housing, flats above commercial space, and other multifamily configurations. Suburban developers look for ways to attract young buyers to master-planned developments. Increasingly, town centers are used as an amenity to create an urban lifestyle beyond the urban core.

Inner-ring suburbs are also being revitalized. Suburbs originally developed between the 1940s and 1970s now occupy the best locations, but typically offer an obsolete housing stock. Some developers have made a specialty of redeveloping underused or overlooked sites. Such developments often prove to have wide market appeal and command high prices.

Housing Preferences: Design Trends

It is no surprise that the American home gets bigger every year. According to the U.S. Census, "Only 9 percent of the houses built in 1971 had 2,400 or more square feet [225 square meters] of living space. By 2002, 37 percent were that big—more than four times as many as 30 years earlier. [10] Although a backlash has occurred against big houses at a time when 2,000 square feet (185 square meters) is a starter home, the tide is not expected to turn anytime soon. William Frey believes the trend toward larger homes is similar to the 1950s migration to post–World War II suburbs. Those middle-class buyers who buy McMansions consider them a status symbol, just as a home in Levittown was the brass ring for middle-class families in the 1950s.[11]

Infill and revitalization occur in the best locations. Aqua, a dense urban mix of condominiums and townhouses, is being developed on a private island in Miami Beach.

Duany Plater-Zyberk & Company

Although the size of the typical American home is increasing, some market segments are influenced more by a home's location and finish than by the amount of square footage. Some families, for example, choose smaller homes with high-quality finishes in neighborhoods with great schools and other amenities over larger houses. A survey of potential Generation X and Y homebuyers discovered that they "value families over careers. They prefer informal floor plans and styling, require computing space, and value—and are willing to pay more for green building techniques. They are unconcerned about living in an ethically, socially, or economically diverse neighborhood."[12] Although members of Generations X and Y desire homes that are near restaurants and services, they may choose to live in a less appealing location to save money. This generation's ideal home would include office space in a multipurpose room, a big kitchen, and a large, informal dining area.

Single people look for homes in both urban and suburban areas. Regardless of location, they seek more common and less individualized space, nice built-in trim and moldings, and upgraded appliances.

Although trend-setting boomers still favor one-story, maintenance-free homes, they also require plenty of space in which to gather and socialize. Many choose smaller homes such as luxury townhouses and condominiums in amenity-rich communities that are being marketed specifically to empty nesters.

Popular Design Features

Buyers of new homes seek the following design features:

- A wide selection of exterior facades, styles, and interior plans;
- "Bonus" space such as a third story, a walkout basement, or a guest casita;
- An enhanced master bedroom suite;
- Gathering zones and private zones;
- Environmentally sensitive and responsible design, including the use of energy-efficient appliances, daylighting, alternative and/or recycled building materials, passive solar design, and native vegetation and xeriscaping;
- A focus on outdoor living, with multiple outdoor spaces and features—barbecue pits, pools, fountains, hot tubs, backyard fireplaces;
- Special areas for pets in laundry or mud rooms that feature outdoor access, automatic water fountains, and pet bathing areas;
- Resort-like amenities. ■

Floor Plans and Amenities

Since the 1980s, home designs have featured fewer formal living rooms and single-use kitchens and more informal multipurpose rooms. "More than one-third of 1,300 buyers in 2001 reported that they were willing to buy a house without a living room."[13] Today's living rooms typically are smaller than those of the past and are located at the front of the house; most "living" now takes place at the back of the house in a combined kitchen/family/entertainment room. Over the years, this transformation of the kitchen and family room into a multipurpose "great room" reflects the American family's new way of living: parents and children want to spend the small amount of spare time they have together.

Laundry rooms are expanding to include space for crafts and other "messy" activities. Dining rooms remain popular and are even expanding. Today's homebuyers plan to do more home entertaining, and some new homes feature dining rooms that can seat 12 guests. Dining rooms also are pulling double duty, often serving as a den, study, or library. Home theaters, on the other hand, are a trend that is fizzling out. Who wants to trudge down to a remote part of the basement just to watch a movie—no matter how nice the decor? Now that flat-screen televisions can be hung on a wall and upgraded surround-sound systems take up much less space, families have gone back to watching movies in the family room or great room, and couples might retire to the private master suite for a movie.

As for other trends in floor plans, builders—and their marketing departments—are capitalizing on children's input into their parents' decision to purchase a particular home by featuring appealing "children's wings" located in separate areas from the master bedroom that are designed with nooks and crannies for playing. Master-bedroom suites are expanding beyond the traditional sitting area and master bath to include his and hers walk-in closets, breakfast bars, exercise rooms, and offices/computer rooms. A hot feature for master baths is a large walk-in steam shower.

In-law suites or dual master bedrooms are gaining popularity for a variety of reasons. Traditionally used by visiting in-laws, these suites are becoming places for boomers to house and care for their aging parents, for a nanny or au pair, or for adult children who are returning to the family home (the boomerang generation). Dual master suites also can enable two single-parent households or young professionals to join forces to purchase a home. Some in-law suites are being used as separate home office space. More than 80 percent of homebuyers consider a home office a necessity, whether they work from home or not.

Universal Design

The AARP reports that 85 percent of people older than 45 would like to stay in their current homes as long as possible before moving on to a facility where they can receive assistance in daily living. The group also notes, however, that nearly 25 percent of those 45 and older

Courtyard Homes in Vero Beach, Florida, is an example of luxury homes that minimize maintenance.

Access for handicapped users was a consideration at Newington in Australia.

Crescent Club, a seniors' community in Orlando, has been designed for handicapped accessibility. For example, the swimming pool has a "zero elevation entry" that allows wheelchair access.

say they or someone they live with will have trouble maneuvering around their home in the coming years. In 2002, only about 10 percent of the nation's 100 million housing units were universally accessible. But that situation is changing. Both accessible design and visitability have been on the forefront of design trends in recent years, and solutions are reaching a critical mass. Accessible design makes homes usable by everyone, regardless of their mental or physical capabilities. Visitability allows those who are physically challenged to access at least the ground floor of a home. Both these design trends fall under the umbrella of *universal design,* which is defined as homes and other buildings that work for people of all ages, sizes, and degrees of physical or mental ability.

Universal design features can be relatively inconspicuous and easily incorporated into new homes, and do not need to raise construction costs more than 5 percent. It is important, however, to ensure that these features do not give a home the appearance of a nursing home or hospital. Until recently, universal design features were included only in nursing homes or in owner-commissioned homes. Naperville, Illinois, and Pima County (Tucson), Arizona, were among the first municipalities in the United States to require that all new homes be wheelchair accessible. While both jurisdictions require 32-inch-wide bathroom doors, Pima County takes the requirement a step farther by mandating that every home contain at least one entrance without steps. Universal home design features include not only wheelchair accessibility but also a variety of conveniences that can easily be built into homes without being noticeable and can add to the convenience and comfort of all residents, disabled or not. Some universal design elements include:

- Graded outdoor walkways in addition to or instead of stairs;
- Wheelchair ramps;
- A package shelf next to the front door;
- Handrails on all interior and exterior stairs;
- At-grade decks and porches at all entries;
- Grab bars on walls, especially in kitchens and bathrooms;
- Multiple-height work areas and kitchen counters;
- Raised dishwashers that can be loaded from a wheelchair or by standing without bending;
- Easily accessible storage spaces, shelves, cabinets, and washers and dryers—generally within an 18- to 54-inch (46- to 138-centimeter) reach;
- Roll-in showers;
- Raised toilets; and
- Wheelchair accessibility for each room of the house.

In addition, some builders include home elevators or plan spaces that can be converted to an elevator when needed and can be used as walk-in closets or wine cellars until then. They are must-have amenities in some regions of the South, especially Florida.

A 50-acre (20-hectare) site along the Tennessee River was developed as a second-home community of 33 lots with more than 40 acres (16 hectares) of open space. Lots are oriented to maximize river views and privacy.

Lifestyle Choices

Choosing a home based on luxury is out; "lifestyle choices" are in. Lifestyle amenities and traffic are most often the main drivers determining where people decide to live. Most people still want to live near their workplace. But workplace location is no longer the principal motivator for seeking housing; other lifestyle amenities are taking precedence. Even access to good schools, which used to be a major deciding factor, is generally not among the top reasons why people select their new home; the quality of the community and affordability are key for many households. For young adults, shopping and nightlife venues are important. Many baby boomers choose a new home based on the lifestyle it offers, such as a single-family home in a community with swimming pools, golf courses, nature trails, and fishing ponds or an urban townhouse that offers easy access to museums, theaters, and restaurants. Good medical facilities can be a primary motivator for older households.

Multigenerational communities that combine housing for all age groups as well as those that contain a mix of housing types at a variety of price levels are in demand, allowing residents to remain in the community as their housing needs change. All population groups, however, are attracted to areas that incorporate place-making techniques to create a sense of community and walkability. And denser, walkable neighborhoods are gaining popularity—and price premiums—over ones where houses are spread out on large lots.[14]

Second Homes

The number of second homes in the United States more than doubled, from 1.7 million in 1980 to 3.6 million in 2000, accounting for 3 percent of all housing. Florida is the epicenter of second homes, with 13.5 percent of all second homes located there. The baby boom generation virtually defines the second-home market, but GenXers have also been entering this market and will continue to do so throughout the next decade or so.

To find the best of both worlds, a growing number of retirees are trying to balance their desire to have a retirement lifestyle while still maintaining ties to their current home. They often choose to spend a portion of the year at the beach or on the ski slopes but continue to return home to spend time with family and friends. Sun City Huntley near Chicago is a popular second-home option for Midwesterners who seek this type of lifestyle balance. Preretirees are testing the water for such dual-home lifestyles as well, buying beach or lakefront homes within a short drive of their primary homes with the idea that they will eventually become their primary homes.

Baby boomers are at the forefront of the "lock-and-leave" lifestyle trend, which encompasses in-town luxury townhouses and condominiums as well as wilderness retreats and beachfront villas. Although boomers make up the majority of second-home owners, GenXers make up an increasing share of the market. Almost 80 percent

Baby boomers make up the majority of second-home owners.

Centennial City is a mixed-use urban district in Manila, intended to give visitors a vision of a modern 21st-century city.

of GenXers who own vacation homes are married couples, followed by single men, and then single women, all of whom have a median income of $68,800. The rise of telecommuting makes second homes more feasible for many, because it is increasingly feasible to work from home, no matter where that home might be. Also increasing demand are post-9/11 fears, fueling the desire for a sanctuary away from major cities.

Development Trends

Four interrelated issues affect trends for residential development: technology, the environment, affordability, and financing.

Technology

Technology affects residential development in two related ways. First, tech-savvy homebuyers bring new expectations to their search for a new home. No longer content with luxury finishes and grand spaces, many homebuyers also are looking for high-tech amenities like structured wiring to support satellite television and high-speed Internet access. Second, technology influences the way homebuilders and residential developers do business, affecting everything from design and construction to how they market their projects, communicate with prospective buyers, and keep residents happy.

Future-Proof Housing. How are residential developers and homebuilders future-proofing the products they build today? Web-based applications appear to be the technology wave of today and the future. Many young home shoppers will not even consider buying a home that does not have broadband Internet access. Today's homeowners use the Internet to communicate with friends and coworkers, shop for goods and services, manage their finances, listen to music, and work from home. Tomorrow's homeowners will find even more uses for it, including communicating with neighbors and

homeowners' associations via community intranets and managing their own home security, lighting, entertainment, and heating and cooling systems (see "Smarter Houses" below).

One pioneering project that is offering homeowners a way to manage such everyday tasks through the Internet is the Village at Tinker Creek, a 170-unit traditional neighborhood development in Roanoke, Virginia, that Roanoke-based Commonwealth Builders is developing in conjunction with IBM's Pervasive Computing Division. In addition to networking appliances and managing them remotely, homeowners will be able to access neighborhood information and bulletin boards, local news, shared calendars, and security and utility management systems. Many other developments have made good use of community intranets, including Ladera Ranch in Orange County, California, and Stapleton in Denver (see the case study in Chapter 9).

High-Tech Homebuilding. Residential developers and homebuilders also use new forms of technology to manage their businesses and to increase efficiency and productivity. Developers and homebuilders alike increasingly use interactive, Internet-based systems to manage a full range of business functions, from back-office tasks such as accounting to human resources and marketing. Although these technologies improve efficiency in the long run, they can be expensive to set up; allocations for technology are a growing item in many real estate firms' capital budgets.

The use of cutting-edge technology often begins early in the planning stages. Residential developers are starting to use sophisticated three-dimensional plans and animated presentations—created with the same software tools used to develop video games—to help win community support and obtain planning approvals for new projects. Such presentations enable viewers to visualize the completed project and the impact it will have on its surroundings more effectively than old-fashioned drawings and site plans. These types of presentations—sometimes known as virtual tours—also can be used to help secure financing and make preconstruction sales. Community-Viz™ is one such tool. This suite of software programs enables planners and developers to input a wide variety of data and produce highly realistic three-dimensional images that show the impact of their decisions on land development scenarios. Changes can be input, resulting in a different scenario instantly. CommunityViz™ was developed by the Orton Family Foundation, a non-profit organization.

Developers also are taking new and emerging technologies to the construction site to help them manage the development process. Forest City Stapleton, Inc., a division of Cleveland-based Forest City Enterprises, uses a wireless network to keep construction moving and costs down at its development of the former Stapleton International Airport in Denver. In addition to allowing easy communication on the construction site without the need to rewire trailers every time they are moved, the wireless system also gives homebuilders easy access to broadband connections at their model homes. Prospective residents, construction workers, and sales staff alike can access the Internet and communicate using PDAs (personal digital assistants) and laptop computers from anywhere on the 4,700-acre (1,900-hectare) site—and from desktop units in construction offices and model homes. The wireless network's estimated $50,000 cost is expected to lead to savings of more than $2 million during the first 15 years of the project.[15]

Web sites have changed the way many homebuilders market their products and communicate with prospective and existing customers. Sites geared toward attracting and keeping homebuyers are resulting in a doubling, tripling, and even quadrupling of filled-out contact forms requesting more information. Many homebuilders' sites now focus on keeping prospects coming back until they are ready to buy, with searchable databases, definitions of house-hunting terms, lists of options, floor plans, fi-

Kit homes come in a wide range of sizes and types. The 1,100-square-foot (102-square-meter) LV Home Kit, designed as a functional and low-maintenance vacation home, sells for about $30,000.

nancial worksheets, move-in checklists, personal folders, and detailed community information and maps. Others even allow homebuyers to monitor the construction of their new homes. Dallas-based Centex Homes gives buyers an identification number and a password they can use to check construction progress on the firm's Web site, which is updated as each construction stage is completed. Atlanta-based Beazer Homes USA was the first national builder to let customers track construction online in real time; its site allows homebuyers to view the current stage of building and its status—from the day work begins until the final inspection is held—using data gathered each day by site superintendents with wireless PDAs.

Soon, more homebuyers will be able to monitor the construction process using webcams, which builders already use for security and their own monitoring purposes. Orlando-based Regal Classic Homes has used a camera stationed on a pole to allow buyers to check the status of their new home online at any time, and the prospect of live updates as well as still photographs and movies that document a home's construction surely will appeal to more homebuyers. The cost of such technology varies greatly. Beazer spent about $1 million for its online tracking system, but the cost of a webcam system to monitor a single home can run from $2,000 to $3,000. Costs undoubtedly will come down as more and more developers begin to use these innovations.

Finally, coming advances in technology also should make tomorrow's housing more efficient, affordable, disaster resistant, and environmentally friendly. A public/private partnership launched in 1998 and funded by the U.S. Department of Housing and Urban Development, the Partnership for Advancing Technology in Housing (PATH) program seeks to achieve dramatic improvements in housing performance while maintaining affordability. The program's goals focus on improving the durability, energy efficiency, environmental performance, affordability, construction safety, and disaster resistance of the nation's housing. It also calls for new homes to be 50 percent more energy efficient by 2010. The partnership is investing in the development of a wide range of technologies to help the housing industry achieve these goals.

Smarter Houses. Although the 100 percent smart home predicted in the 1980s has not yet arrived, such houses probably will be commonplace within a decade or so. The amount of technology in homes has increased and will continue to do so. Large national retailers like Sears, Best Buy, and CompUSA are working with homebuilders to install structured wiring for cable or satellite television, audio, telephone, and computer traffic in almost every room of the house, and many homebuilders now include a structured-wiring network in their base price, although advances in wireless technology may make current wiring solutions obsolete. Several high-tech housing features are becoming common:

- A broadband Internet connection such as DSL, cable modem, or direct broadcast satellite;

Sponsored by the U.S. Department of Energy, the Solar Decathlon invites teams of college students to compete in designing, building, and demonstrating the advantages of a solar lifestyle.

- A home area network that allows all residents to share information and peripherals;
- Kitchen appliances with computer chips linking each machine to a central controller;
- Network hookups in every room leading to a central computer server in the basement or elsewhere;
- A computer-controlled home heating, cooling, lighting, security, and sound system that could even allow residents to raise and lower curtains and blinds remotely;
- A security system that sounds an alarm and reports to a central station and includes a closed-circuit television system that distributes video signals from surveillance cameras in and around the home;
- An integrated energy management system that maximizes energy efficiency and keeps heating and cooling costs down;
- An integrated ventilation system that helps improve energy efficiency and indoor air quality;
- Low-voltage dimming systems and computer controls that allow users to program the lights in a room to suit a given function, mood, or time of day;
- Interior and exterior lighting that turns on when someone approaches the house and warns residents if they leave the house without turning off an appliance;
- A panic button and/or sensors that can send a preprogrammed E-mail or phone message if someone has a heart attack or other emergency.

Green Building

Once thought of in simple terms of energy efficiency, recycling, and solar power, *green building*—now much more broadly defined as development that conserves resources—has become, according to NAHB, "one of the most significant developments in homebuilding in the past three decades" and is resulting in "a quiet revolution in the way that new homes and communities are planned and constructed."[16] Green building also is working hand in hand with another development trend—smart growth—with which it shares many goals. Smart growth typically is defined as a strategy that ensures that neighborhoods, towns, and regions accommodate growth in ways that are economically sound, environmentally responsible, and supportive of community livability; in other words, growth that enhances the quality of life.

Green development techniques include the use of land planning and design methods such as clustering homes that preserve trees, open space, and other natural amenities and minimize land disturbance; site development techniques that minimize erosion, paved surfaces, and runoff; the use of new and emerging materials and technology to make houses (and the systems and appliances within them) more energy efficient, reduce pollution, and improve indoor air quality; the use of energy and water conservation features; the use of materials that are durable, renewable, and recyclable; and the reduction of waste and the reuse and recycling of materials, both during construction and throughout the life of the house.[17]

Water supply is another major environmental issue that will continue to increase in importance for residential developers. Population growth and droughts have resulted in water shortages throughout the United States. Long an issue in the West, where "water wars" have been common for years, even eastern states and municipalities now are beginning to experience battles over water rights. The days when developers could take the water supply for granted are gone. A California law that took effect in January 2002 requires developers of 500 units or more to prove an adequate supply of water for the next 20 years. Developers in Florida and Las Vegas also cannot get building permits until they demonstrate that enough water will be available to serve their communities over the long term. Creative solutions include incorporating native drought-tolerant plants into landscaping and water reclamation systems that use treated sewer

Singapore's Green Public Housing

A long-term strategic plan for Singapore aims to create a livable city with a wide choice of housing locations and types, including additional public housing. To meet this objective, the four-acre (1.6-hectare) site of Duxton Plain will undergo redevelopment, eventually providing 1,800 new homes and becoming Singapore's tallest public housing development. Duxton Plain public housing, expected to be built by 2007, aims to transform the area into a vibrant urban place.

To plan for a projected 5.5 million people in Singapore and a reduction in household size, 800,000 new homes are needed in addition to the current 1 million dwelling units in the city. Because of the limited availability of land for new development, some of the needed new homes will come from additional high-density, high-rise structures. Currently, 3 percent of the population lives in 30,000 homes located within the central area; eventually this number will rise to 7 percent, or four times as many residents.

An international design competition resulted in a winning design by ARC Studio Architecture + Urbanism of Singapore, seven 48-story apartment blocks with a three-story parking garage, two stories of which are underground. Sky parks at the 26th story and the roof level will link the seven blocks, which are arranged to give most of the dwelling units unobstructed views of the city skyline. A variety of recreational and communal spaces are designed for the ground, 26th-floor, and roof levels. A communal garden is planned above the garage decks with cafés and convenience stores. Two jogging tracks will be located on the roof, along with gardens and pavilions for residents. ■

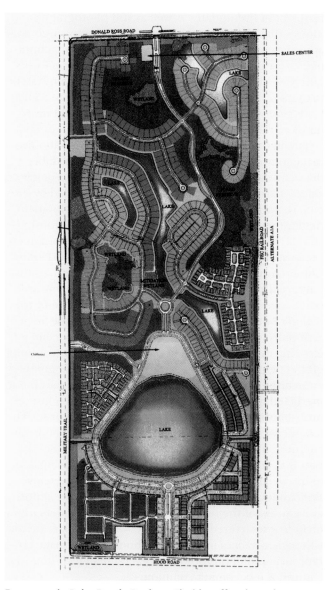

Evergrene in Palm Beach Gardens, Florida, offers homebuyers green technologies that optimize indoor air quality and energy efficiency, and employ recycled materials.

effluent for water features and irrigation.[18] Developers also are using greener stormwater management methods; decreasing the amount of impervious surfaces in residential communities by reducing the widths of roadways, building sidewalks on only one side of the street, and using pavers or other alternative materials for driveways; retaining larger portions of woodlands; and planting vegetation that removes pollutants and sediments while providing habitat for birds and wildlife.

Environmentally sensitive "green" homes and communities now can be found across the United States. Although no national standard for green housing yet exists, one is on the way. The LEED (Leadership in Energy and Environmental Design) for Homes Committee of the U.S. Green Building Council, which developed the LEED Green Building Rating System now used for commercial projects, is developing a LEED rating system to establish performance criteria for residential building owners, developers, and design teams working on new single-family and low-rise multi-family projects.

A variety of state associations currently certify green houses and communities. To receive this certification, a builder or developer typically must submit a worksheet specifying how a house or community meets certain environmental goals, follow a point system that quantifies how "green" the house or community is, and allow the house or community to be inspected during and/or after construction. The Florida Green Building Coalition provides a statewide green building checklist for builders that rates homes based on their energy efficiency, indoor air quality, water conservation and quality, and environmental impact. The Greater Atlanta Home Builders Association has been certifying environmentally sound and efficient EarthCraft houses since 1998 and is now certifying pilot EarthCraft communities. Built Green Colorado certifies both houses and communities. The California Building Industry grants builders who meet certain environmental standards its Green Builder designation.

Builders of green homes and communities are discovering that the investment in green building can pay off in fewer callbacks, reduced costs for supplies and waste disposal, a reduced risk of mold, and an increased market share. But they often must do more to sell buyers on the advantages of a green home. Most homebuyers today assume that all new houses are energy efficient and need to be educated about the distinction between energy-efficient, environmentally sound construction and standard homes. Norman, Oklahoma–based Ideal Homes includes a sample wall with the sheetrock cut away to show how it is constructed in its model homes and drills its sales staff to focus on the houses' green features. Bloomfield Hills, Michigan–based national homebuilder Pulte guarantees homebuyers' energy bills, promising purchasers of its Environment for Living homes that their utility bills will be less than $40 per month. Financing options such as Fannie Mae's green mortgages and other incentives also can help convince homebuyers.[19]

Modular Dwelling brings edgy style to prefabricated housing.

Affordable/Workforce Housing

Affordability continues to be a major issue throughout the United States, although the problem is more severe in some regions and metropolitan areas. As housing costs increase faster than wages, even modest housing remains out of reach for millions of Americans. An annual report released by the National Low Income Housing Coalition notes that the 2003 national "housing wage"—the amount a person working full time must earn to be able to afford to rent a two-bedroom unit at fair market rent while paying no more than 30 percent of his or her income in rent—was $15.21 an hour, or $31,637 a year, almost three times the federal minimum wage. Housing costs are an especially acute issue for those working in the service sector, which continues to represent a rapidly growing portion of the national economy.[20] A survey released in September 2003 by the National Association of Realtors® reports that two out of three Americans are concerned about the cost of housing in their communities, and

Recycling empty cargo containers that literally pile up at ports across the country into affordable housing units offers one solution to America's growing housing shortage. The winning proposal in a nationwide competition sponsored by the Boston Society of Architects would transform about 3,000 surplus shipping containers into 351 housing units; 170,000 square feet (15,800 square meters) of retail, office, and hotel space; and 27,700 square feet (2,575 square meters) of civic/cultural space. Containers would be stacked up to eight high in a crescent-shaped development around a central green at the rail station in Gloucester, Massachusetts. At-grade and below-grade parking for 593 cars would support the development and help meet commuters' needs.

From the time American industrialist Henry Kaiser sought to apply his success in rapid construction of World War II Liberty ships to building housing on the same scale for his Oregon shipyard workers, architects and planners have sought ways to industrialize housing. Coincidentally, one answer may come from the hundreds of thousands of full shipping containers that become surplus when insufficient exports force either expensive returns of empty containers or discounted disposal of them. Although the cargo containers are inexpensively built in low-wage exporting countries such as China for under $2,500, their heavy construction and large volume make them expensive to return. As a result, a standard 320-cubic-foot (9-cubic-meter) shipping container may be had for as little as $600, or less than $2.00 per square foot ($21.50 per square meter)—far less than the least expensive stick framing. Moreover, because all containers are of standard size and are made to be stacked up to ten high, Mark Strauss, principal in New York City–based Fox & Fowle Architects, who came up with the proposal, believes that interlocking them can create inexpensive and rigid high-rise construction. "Because the containers are designed and made to interlock at their corners, they can be linked in three dimensions," he says.

But questions arise as to how the narrow eight-foot-wide by nine-and-one-half-foot high (2.4- by 2.9-meter) windowless boxes, 20, 25, or 40 feet long (6, 7.6, or 12.2 meters), can be transformed into livable housing. As the containers are narrower than any room but a conventional bathroom, how can the modules be designed and combined to make livable units? The containers are built with a clear-span box frame within the edging of the containers, allowing sheathing to be removed from the shorter boxes without compromising the structural integrity of the container. By combining the containers and removing portions of the sheathing, spaces can be created that are 16, 24, or 32 feet (4.9, 7.3, or 9.7 meters) wide.

"For our competition project, we envisioned stacked duplexes that combine eight 25-foot-long (7.6-meter) containers to create a modular unit of 16 feet (4.9 meters) wide—or up to 1,600 square feet (150 square meters) in size," says Strauss. To bring light and air into the units, the sheathing would be removed from the end panels, and a modular window wall would be designed to be inserted in the frame.

Although the Gloucester project did not require participants to provide the level of engineering detail to address utilities and other mechanical services, Strauss envisions inserting modular kitchen, bathroom, laundry, and HVAC (heating, ventilation, and air-conditioning) components into the units. To take advantage of cost savings associated with recycling the shipping containers, much of the construction and installation of modular components could be done off site. The components then would be lifted into place with the container and connected on site.

The proposal planned a variety of sizes and mixes for the 351 units. They would include 184 live/work duplex lofts of 1,200 square feet (110 square meters) per unit that would include a modular kitchen and bath plus a sleeping loft; residents could modify the interiors. They also would include 61 ground-floor "shop houses" of 1,200 square feet (110 square meters), 53 duplex townhouse mews of 1,200 square feet (110 square meters), and 53 single townhouse mews of 600 square feet (55 square meters).

In the proposal, the high-rise units are connected on each floor by an independent exterior walkway at the rear of the units and by independent stair towers, also constructed from containers. An elevator core is planned to provide access to the exterior walkway. For the duplex townhouse mews, stoops are provided at the front of each unit. The single units are located on the ground floor.

Industrialized housing often has had trouble complying with local building codes, with the biggest issue being fireproofing, Strauss notes. He plans to use fire-rated gypsum board or possibly a fire-rated spray coating on the exposed steel to address the problem. Because the container units are designed to be combined both laterally and vertically to produce units of conventional widths and heights, insulation and sheetrock could be applied either off site or on site.

Strauss also predicts cost savings with his plan. "Because we are envisioning a modular construction with many of the components being built off site and possibly shipped from overseas, we could envision as much as a 25 percent savings over conventional construction," he explains. Considerable savings could also be realized over standard modular housing, he points out, because the units are already framed and sturdily constructed for transport by truck, rail, or barge, and can be easily moved and quickly placed by crane. And because containers can be stacked as many as ten high, raw inventory can be prepurchased and stored inexpensively in small areas, notes Strauss.

Containers have other benefits that allow creativity in design. They are structurally strong, spanning up to 40 feet (12 meters), so they can be used to form bridges inexpensively that create gateways to projects. Some containers are made with extensions at each end that can be positioned to cantilever over containers stacked below. They also can be placed in squares to create private courtyards, and rooftops of one container are sturdy enough to form terraces for upper units. In addition to multifamily housing of the type envisioned by Strauss, containers can be outfitted to create independent emergency housing modules that can be quickly trucked to disaster areas.

Challenges remain before this kind of project can actually be developed, however. "The problems associated with this project are the same as the problems with any modular housing project, including nonacceptance by building unions and nonuniform interpretation of building codes," note Strauss and Mark Ginsberg, president of the New York chapter of the American Institute of Architects and former chair of the AIA's housing committee. But Strauss argues that "if we are serious about wanting to provide affordable housing in this nation, we need to find ways to overcome these obstacles and be willing to embrace new ideas."

Recycling surplus containers into housing can be seen as the epitome of sustainable development. Not only are the materials and structures reused but also the energy that was consumed once to transport the containers full of imported goods replaces the energy and materials that would be consumed to build the housing that they replace. Moreover, the conversion of containers to low-cost housing building blocks creates a value-added product that could even be shipped back on the empty ships' return voyage to meet the housing crisis facing the vast populations of China and India that manufactured them. Use of the burgeoning trade deficit to help cure the affordable housing crisis may be a sustainable development solution whose time is near. ■

Source: William P. Macht, Solution File: Container Housing, *Urban Land*, May 2004, pp. 40–41.

The HOK Planning Group © 2004

The HOK Planning Group © 2004

Increasingly, multifamily housing will accommodate the world's growing population. In the rapidly growing city of Dubai, the Dubai Marina project will house up to 100,000 people.

71 percent would like to see government place a higher priority on making housing more affordable for renters and homeowners alike. Most also worry that their children and grandchildren will be unable to afford to live close to them and that the cost of a home is getting so unaffordable that it is hurting their local economy.[21]

Where affordable housing does exist, it often is located far from where most people work. This problem has led to a lack of *workforce housing*, which ULI defines as housing for households earning between 60 and 120 percent of area median income. These households often earn too much to qualify for federal, state, or local housing assistance but not enough to afford market-rate housing in locations convenient to their workplaces.

Although both public and private efforts to produce and support affordable and workforce housing have met with some success, the nation still faces a critical shortage of these types of housing, with no long-term solutions in sight. Affordability will be a continuing problem for

The greatest long-term threat to the greater Los Angeles economy is not the national recession: it is housing—or rather the *lack* of housing. California's current population of 34 million is expected to grow by 44 percent, or 15 million people, by 2020. And two-thirds of that growth will come from natural population increases, not immigration. In short, in less than 20 years, 49 million people throughout the state will need homes.

Much of that population growth will occur in southern California, which grew by 350,000 residents in 2001 alone. The demand for housing of any kind for southern Californians, whether for sale or rental, detached or attached, far outweighs the supply. To meet the demand over the next five years, Los Angeles County, for example, needs to build 25,000 to 30,000 new housing units each year and almost 50,000 homes a year after six years. But housing is not being built in those numbers. In 1998, 11,692 residential permits were issued in Los Angeles County; by 2002, that number had grown to only 19,364 permits.

Not only are insufficient numbers of homes being constructed but also many southern Californians cannot afford to buy what is being built. In 1998, the average price of a new home in Los Angeles County was $259,870. By 2002, the price had risen to $362,541—which means the qualifying income for the purchase of a new home in Los Angeles County must be almost $120,000 (based on the industry standard that qualifying income equals approximately 33 percent of the price of the home). According to Mill City, Oregon–based Western Economic Research Corp., however, the median family income in Los Angeles County in 2000 was $42,634.

The affordability gap is equally serious for resale homes. A California Association of Realtors® study in 2000 found that only 39 out of 100 Los Angeles County households could afford to pay the median price of existing homes, compared with a 54 percent affordability rate in Denver and a 55 percent rate in Seattle. In southern California, where resale housing prices rose steadily each year in the last half of the 1990s, the demand for housing is so great that prices continued to rise in 2002 and 2003 as the nation's and California's economies weakened.

Renters are also being priced out of the market. In the second quarter of 1998, the average monthly apartment rent in Los Angeles County was $916. By the second quarter of 2002, it had risen to $1,247.

Southern California's failure to build housing—particularly affordable homes near job centers—means that more employees will need to endure long (and therefore costly) commutes from less-expensive outlying communities, straining workers' budgets and the

Southern California's housing crisis is one of affordability and availability.

region's already-clogged roads and freeways, stealing hours from workers' lives every week, and creating unnecessary air pollution. Today, many companies base their location decisions on quality-of-life criteria, and a housing shortage, high housing prices, lengthy commutes, congestion, and pollution add up to a very poor quality of life. Many companies are not going to expand —much less relocate to greater Los Angeles—under those conditions. In the boom years of the late 1980s, rapidly escalating home prices were a major factor in stopping firms from expanding in—or relocating to— greater Los Angeles.

The Los Angeles housing crisis is considered a complex problem with many interconnected causes. First, unlike Atlanta or Houston or Dallas, each of which can spread ever outward, greater Los Angeles bumps up against the natural boundaries of the Pacific Ocean on the west and mountain ranges on the east. Intense development over the last century, and particularly during the last 50 years, has left little vacant land in much of the metropolitan area (and particularly in Los Angeles County) except in outlying areas such as the Santa Clara and Antelope valleys.

Second, because of Proposition 13, municipal governments often oppose housing, particularly moderate- and high-density projects, because they see housing as requiring new services for more residents, which drains already strained city budgets. These municipal governments would much rather have retail development like big boxes, power centers, and malls that generate sales tax revenues.

Third, it has become almost impossible to build high-density housing in existing urban and suburban areas. Often, developers are unable to increase density by constructing more single-family homes on smaller lots because suburban building codes insist on large lots.

NIMBYism also has generated strenuous opposition to higher-density housing that has frequently doomed proposed projects. Many residents believe that higher-density housing, particularly multifamily products, will lower their property values.

Finally, growth control measures in outlying areas limit the number of housing units that can be built and sometimes even prohibit housing construction.

How can southern California accommodate its predicted population growth and solve its housing crunch? First, it can change its building codes and zoning to support smart growth land use planning, which includes higher-density and multifamily housing as well as mixed-use development with a residential component. Multifamily housing is a large, often overlooked market. Families constitute just 25 percent of the American population, and many couples and singles want well-designed, well-constructed, easy-to-maintain apartments, condominiums, and townhouses located near transportation and employment centers.

Second, new schools, roads, water and sewer treatment facilities, and other public infrastructure must be planned and constructed in a timely manner to keep pace with both current and future demand for housing. Changes in state law allowing school bonds to pass with a 55 percent vote, for example, are a positive step toward encouraging construction of important new facilities.

Finally, the overly complex entitlement process and the California Environmental Quality Act process must be streamlined so that projects can receive a more standardized review. In particular, the approval process should be simplified to energize builders of small and medium-sized apartments and homes who could provide so much new housing, especially on small, close-in, infill sites that already are served by infrastructure.

The housing crunch in southern California is not going to disappear magically. If adequate housing is not provided for the state's growing population, including affordable housing near employment centers, companies will move out of state, potentially affecting California's economy as well as residents' well-being. California's crisis should be seen as an indicator for the future of many other markets in the nation. They too will surely face similar circumstances as the population of the nation grows by more than 130 million people by mid-century. ∎

Source: Adapted from Gary M. Cusumano, "The Southern California Housing Crunch," *Urban Land*, January 2002, pp. 44–45.

those at the lower income ranges and increasingly for middle-class households living in high-priced housing markets. New strategies and partnerships must be developed to create housing that is affordable and meets this growing need.

Notes
1. Joint Center for Housing Studies of Harvard University, *The State of the Nation's Housing 2003* (Cambridge, Massachusetts: President and Fellows of Harvard College, 2003).
2. William H. Frey, "Metro Magnets for Minorities and Whites: Melting Pots, the New Sunbelt, and the Heartland." (Ann Arbor and Santa Monica: Population Studies Center, University of Michigan, and Milken Institute, February 2002).
3. Joint Center for Housing Studies, *The State of the Nation's Housing 2003.*
4. Amanda May, "How Demographics Shape Development," *National Real Estate Investor*, September 1, 2002, pp. 16–22.
5. William H. Frey, "Seniors in Suburbia," *American Demographics*, November 2001, pp. 18–21.
6. William H. Frey, "Boomer Havens and Young Adult Magnets," *American Demographics*, September 2001, pp. 22–24.
7. Joint Center for Housing Studies, *The State of the Nation's Housing 2003.*
8. Christina Farnsworth, "Gen-X Files," *Builder*, February 2001, pp. 222–240.
9. Jennifer S. Vey and Benjamin Forman, *Demographic Change in Medium-Sized Cities: Evidence from the 2000 Census* (Washington, D.C.: Brookings Institution Center on Urban and Metropolitan Policy, July 2002).
10. *New One-Family Housing Units*, www.census.gov/const/C25Ann/soldsqft.pdf.
11. Bill Sharpsteen, "Keeping Up with the Jonesing," *Los Angeles Times Magazine*, April 27, 2003.
12. Christina Farnsworth, "Gen-X Files."
13. "Housing Hints," *Bowden's Market Barometer*, December 2002/January 2003.
14. Dowell Myers and Elizabeth Gearin, "Current Preferences and Future Demand for Denser Residential Environments," *Housing Policy Debate*, Volume 12, Number 4, 2001, pp. 633–660.
15. Dan Luzadder, "Forest City Stapleton: Air Port," *Baseline*, November 1, 2003, pp. 76–82.
16. National Association of Home Builders, *Building Greener, Building Better: The Quiet Revolution* (Washington, D.C.: Author, 2002).
17. Ibid.
18. Susan Brady, "Got Water?" *Big Builder*, February 2002, pp. 46–48.
19. Alison Rice, "Comfort Zone: Creating a Middle Ground for Green Building and Great Profits," *Big Builder*, March 2002, pp. 26–32.
20. National Low Income Housing Coalition, *Out of Reach: 2003* (Washington, D.C.: Author, 2003).
21. National Association of Realtors®, *National Housing Opportunity Pulse* (Washington, D.C.: Author, 2003).

Bibliography
and Index

Bibliography

Books

Altshuler, Alan A., and José A. Gómez-Ibáñez. *Regulation for Revenue: The Political Economy of Land Use Exactions.* Washington, D.C., & Cambridge, Massachusetts: Brookings Institution & Lincoln Institute of Land Policy, 1993.

Ames, Steven C., ed. *Guide to Community Visioning.* Chicago: APA Planners Press, 1998.

Barrett, G. Vincent, and John P. Blair. *How to Conduct and Analyze Real Estate Market and Feasibility Studies.* Second Edition. New York: Van Nostrand Reinhold, 1988.

Blakely, Edward J., and Mary Gail Snyder. *Fortress America: Gated Communities in the United States.* Washington, D.C.: ULI–the Urban Land Institute, 1999.

Bohl, Charles C. *Place Making: Developing Town Centers, Main Streets, and Urban Villages.* Washington, D.C.: ULI–the Urban Land Institute, 2002.

Brecht, Susan. *Analyzing Seniors' Housing Markets.* Washington, D.C.: ULI–the Urban Land Institute, 2002.

Burchell, Robert W., David Listokin, et al. *Development Impact Assessment Handbook.* Washington, D.C.: ULI–the Urban Land Institute, 1994.

Calthorpe, Peter. *The Next American Metropolis.* Princeton, N.J.: Princeton Architectural Press, 1993.

Calthorpe, Peter, and William B. Fulton. *The Regional City: Planning for the End of Sprawl.* Washington, D.C.: Island Press, 2001.

Congress for the New Urbanism, with the Great American Station Foundation. *The New Transit Town: Best Practices in Transit-Oriented Development.* San Francisco: Congress for the New Urbanism, 2003.

Council on Development Choices for the '80s. *The Affordable Community: Adapting Today's Communities to Tomorrow's Needs.* Washington, D.C.: ULI–the Urban Land Institute, 1981.

Dewberry & Davis. *Land Development Handbook: Planning, Engineering, and Surveying.* New York: McGraw-Hill, 2002.

Duany, Andres, Elizabeth Plater-Zyberk, and Jeff Speck. *Suburban Nation: The Rise of Sprawl and the Decline of the American Dream.* New York: North Point Press, 2000.

Fader, Steven. *Density by Design: New Directions in Residential Development.* Washington, D.C.: ULI–the Urban Land Institute, 2000.

Fisher, Robert Moore. *Twenty Years of Public Housing: Economic Aspects of the Federal Program.* New York: Harper & Brothers, 1959.

Funders' Network for Smart Growth and Livable Communities. "Real Estate Finance and Smart Growth Project Report, 2002." www.fundersnetwork.org.

Garreau, Joel. *Edge City: Life on the New Frontier.* New York: Anchor Books/Doubleday, 1991.

Hall, Kenneth B., and Gerald A. Porterfield. *Community by Design: New Urbanism for Suburbs and Small Communities.* New York: McGraw-Hill, 2001.

Hirschhorn, Joel S., and Paul Souza. *New Community Design to the Rescue: Fulfilling Another American Dream.* Washington, D.C.: National Governors Association, 2001.

Jacobs, Jane. *The Death and Life of Great American Cities.* New York: Random House, 1961.

Katz, Peter. *The New Urbanism: Toward an Architecture of Community.* New York: McGraw-Hill, 1994.

Kelbaugh, Douglas. *Common Place: Toward Neighborhood and Regional Design.* Seattle: University of Washington Press, 1997.

Kone, Linda D. *Land Development.* Washington, D.C.: BuilderBooks, 1999.

Kulash, Walter M. *Residential Streets.* Washington, D.C.: ULI–the Urban Land Institute, 2001.

Langdon, Philip. *A Better Place to Live: Reshaping the American Suburb.* Amherst: University of Massachusetts Press, 1997.

Mason, Joseph B. *History of Housing in the U.S., 1930–1980.* Houston: Gulf Publishing Co., 1982.

Miles, Mike E., Gayle Berens, and Marc A. Weiss. *Real Estate Development: Principles and Process.* Third Edition. Washington, D.C.: ULI–the Urban Land Institute, 2000.

Mulvihill, David, et al. *Golf Course Development in Residential Communities.* Washington, D.C.: ULI–the Urban Land Institute, 2001.

Mumford, Lewis. *The City in History: Its Origins, Its Transformations, and Its Prospects.* New York: Harcourt, Brace & World, 1961.

National Association of Home Builders. *Impact Fee Handbook.* Washington, D.C.: Home Builder Press, 1997.

Nicholas, James C., et al. *A Practitioner's Guide to Development Impact Fees.* Chicago: Planners Press, 1991.

Oldenberg, Ray. *The Great Good Place.* New York: Paragon House, 1989.

O'Neill, David. *The Smart Growth Tool Kit.* Washington, D.C.: ULI–the Urban Land Institute, 2000.

Oregon Transportation and Growth Management Program. *Commercial and Mixed-Use Development Code Handbook.* Salem, Oregon: Author, 2001.

Parks, David C. *Environmental Management for Real Estate Professionals.* Chicago: National Association of Realtors®, Institute of Real Estate Management, 1992.

Peiser, Richard B., and Anne B. Frej. *Professional Real Estate Development: The ULI Guide to the Business.* Second Edition. Washington, D.C.: ULI–the Urban Land Institute, 2003.

Porter, Douglas R., Susan B. Brecht, Lee E. Cory, Randy A. Faigin, Mel Gamzon, and Stephen L. Taber. *Housing for Seniors: Developing Successful Projects.* Washington, D.C.: ULI–the Urban Land Institute, 1995.

Procos, Dimitri. *Mixed Land Use: From Revival to Innovation.* Stroudsburg, Pennsylvania: Dowden, Hutchinson & Ross, 1976.

Rovig, Steven R., and Timothy R Osborn. *Drafting Real Estate Documents That Work. Part I—Condominiums, Master-Planned Communities and Mixed Use.* Seattle: Washington State Bar Association, 2001.

Salvesen, David. *Wetlands: Mitigating and Regulating Development Impacts.* Second Edition. Washington, D.C.: ULI–the Urban Land Institute, 1994.

Schmitz, Adrienne, et al. *Multifamily Housing Development Handbook.* Washington, D.C.: ULI–the Urban Land Institute, 2000.

Schmitz, Adrienne, et al. *The New Shape of Suburbia: Trends in Residential Development.* Washington, D.C.: ULI–the Urban Land Institute, 2003.

Schmitz, Adrienne, et al. *Real Estate Market Analysis.* Washington, D.C.: ULI–the Urban Land Institute, 2001.

Schneekloth, Lynda H., and Robert G. Shibley. *Placemaking: The Art and Practice of Building Communities.* New York: Wiley, 1995.

Schwanke, Dean, et al. *Mixed-Use Development Handbook.* Second Edition. Washington, D.C.: ULI–the Urban Land Institute, 2003.

Schwanke, Dean, et al. *Resort Development Handbook.* Washington, D.C.: ULI–the Urban Land Institute, 1997.

Simons, Robert A. *Turning Brownfields into Greenbacks: Developing and Financing Environmentally Contaminated Urban Real Estate.* Washington, D.C.: ULI–the Urban Land Institute, 1997.

Sitte, Camillo. *City Planning According to Artistic Principles.* New York: Random House, 1889. Reprinted 1965.

Suchman, Diane R. *Developing Infill Housing in Inner-City Neighborhoods: Opportunities and Strategies.* Washington, D.C.: ULI–the Urban Land Institute, 1997.

Suchman, Diane R. *Developing Successful Infill Housing.* Washington, D.C.: ULI–the Urban Land Institute, 2002.

Unwin, Raymond. *Town Planning in Practice: An Introduction to the Art of Designing Cities and Suburbs.* New York: Princeton Architectural Press, 1909. Reprinted 1994.

Warner, Sam Bass, Jr. *The Urban Wilderness: A History of the American City.* New York: Harper & Row, 1972.

Wright, Gwendolyn. *Building the Dream: A Social History of Housing in America.* New York: Pantheon Books, 1981.

Periodicals and Web Sites

Architectural Record
www.archrecord.construction.com

Architecture
www.architecturemag.com

Builder
www.BuilderOnline.com

Building, Design & Construction
www.bdcmag.com

Buildings
www.buildings.com

Development
www.naiop.org

Development Case Studies (ULI)
www.casestudies.uli.org

Estates Gazette
www.estatesgazette.com

Europroperty
www.europroperty.com

Information Packet: *Place Making and Town Center Development*
www.uli.org

Journal of the American Planning Association
www.planning.org

Metropolis
www.metropolismag.com

Multifamily Trends
www.urbanland.uli.org

National Real Estate Investor
www.nreionline.com

New Urban News
www.newurbannews.com

PAS Memo
www.planning.org

Planning
www.planning.org

Practical Real Estate Lawyer
www.ali-aba.org

Professional Builder
www.housingzone.com

Residential Architect
www.residentialarchitect.com

Urban Land
www.urbanland.uli.org

Zoning News
www.planning.org

Organizations

American Institute of Architects
1735 New York Avenue, N.W.
Washington, DC 20006
202-626-7300
http://www.aiaonline.org

American Planning Association
122 South Michigan Avenue, Suite 1600
Chicago, IL 60603
312-431-9100
www.planning.org

Congress for the New Urbanism
140 South Dearborn Street, Suite 310
Chicago, Illinois 60603
312-551-7300
www.cnu.org

Fannie Mae Foundation
400 Wisconsin Avenue, N.W.
North Tower, Suite One
Washington, DC 20016-2804
202-274-8000
www.fanniemaefoundation.org

Freddie Mac Foundation
8250 Jones Branch Drive
McLean, VA 22102
703-918-8888
www.freddiemac.com

Funders' Network for Smart Growth and Livable Communities
www.fundersnetwork.org

International Network for Traditional Building, Architecture
    and Urbanism
London, UK
44 20 7613 8520
www.intbau.org

Livable Places
634 South Spring Street, Suite 727
Los Angeles, CA
213-622-5980
www.livableplaces.com

Local Government Commission
Center for Livable Communities
Sacramento, CA
916-448-1198
www.lgc.org

National Apartment Association
201 North Union Street, Suite 200
Alexandria, VA 22314
703-518-6141
http://www.naahg.org

National Association of Home Builders
1201 Fifteenth Street, N.W.
Washington, DC 20005-2800
202-822-0434
www.nahb.com

National Association of Real Estate Investment Trusts
1875 I Street, N.W.
Washington, DC 20006
202-739-9400
www.nareit.com

National Association of Realtors®
700 Eleventh Street, N.W.
Washington, DC 20001
202-383-1014
www.nar.realtor.com

National Charrette Institute
Portland, OR
503-233-8486
www.charretteinstitute.org

National Multi Housing Council
1850 M Street, N.W., Suite 540
Washington, DC 20036-5803
202-974-2300
http://www.nmhc.org

National Town Builders Association
3320 N Street, NW
Washington, D.C. 20007
202-333-1902
www.ntba.net

National Trust for Historic Preservation
1785 Massachusetts Avenue, N.W.
Washington, DC 20036
202.588.6000
www.nationaltrust.org

Resource for Urban Design Information
Headington, Oxford, UK
44 0-1865 483602
www.rudi.net

Smart Growth Network
c/o International City/County Management Association
777 North Capitol Street, N.E., Suite 500
Washington, DC 20002
202-962-3623
www.smartgrowth.org

ULI–the Urban Land Institute
1025 Thomas Jefferson Street, N.W., Suite 500 West
Washington, DC 20007-2501
202-624-7000
www.uli.org

Index

Note : Italic page numbers refer to figures, photos, and illustrations. Bold page numbers refer to feature boxes and case studies.